THE OXFORD GUIDE TO

UNITED STATES
SUPREME COURT
DECISIONS

Second Edition

THE OXFORD GUIDE TO
UNITED STATES SUPREME COURT DECISIONS
Second Edition

EDITED BY

Kermit L. Hall
James W. Ely Jr.

OXFORD
UNIVERSITY PRESS
2009

OXFORD
UNIVERSITY PRESS

Oxford New York
Athens Auckland Bangkok Bogotá
Buenos Aires Calcutta Cape Town Chennai Dar es Salaam
Delhi Florence Hong Kong Istanbul Karachi
Kuala Lumpur Madrid Melbourne
Mexico City Mumbai Nairobi Paris São Paulo Shanghai Singapore
Taipei Tokyo Toronto Warsaw

and associated companies in
Berlin Ibadan

Copyright © by Oxford University Press 2009

First published by Oxford University Press, Inc.,
198 Madison Avenue, New York, New York 10016

Oxford is a registered trademark of Oxford University Press

Library of Congress Cataloging-in-Publication Data

The Oxford guide to United States Supreme Court decisions / edited by
   Kermit L. Hall, James W. Ely Jr.—2nd ed.
     p. cm.
   Rev. ed. of: The Oxford guide to United States Supreme Court decisions /
edited by Kermit L. Hall. 1999.
   Includes index.
   ISBN 978-0-19-537939-6 (alk. paper)
1. Constitutional law—United States—Encyclopedias. 2. Constitutional law—United States—Digests.
I. Hall, Kermit. II. Ely, James W., 1938-
   KF4548.5.O97 2009
   342.73002643—dc22

                                                                        2008023763

Printed in the United States of America
on acid-free paper

Contents

Introduction

This is a book dealing with the fodder of constitutional history—the cases and decisions of the Supreme Court of the United States, perhaps the leading judicial tribunal in the world today. The *Guide* analyzes on an individual basis the 440 most important cases in the Court's history. The analysis not only sheds light on the evolution of constitutional law but also maps the nation's underlying social, cultural, and political dynamics, a map traced in the actions of litigants and the justices who responded to them. Today, for example, we take the federal income tax for granted, but in the 1895 case of *Pollock* v. *Farmers' Loan & Trust* the high court declared such a tax unconstitutional. Only the adoption in 1913 of the Sixteenth Amendment altered the work of the justices. Today, we are caught in a furious struggle over the social and constitutional wisdom of affirmative action for historically underrepresented groups, such as African-Americans, but in 1857 the justices, in *Dred Scott* v. *Sandford,* upheld the legality of slavery while pronouncing that no person of African origin could ever be a citizen of the United States. And the list could go on and on. America's history has been, in effect, the history of the Supreme Court writ in its decisions, decisions that have often begun as small disputes among common people that eventually became enduring moments in our constitutional history.

These cases remind us that the Court is a formal, legal institution with an often extraordinary human face. The justices interact with one another based on the broadly defined constitutional requirement to decide cases and controversies, but they do so guided by customs, traditions, and practices forged over more than two centuries and personalities that often clashed as much as they blended with one another.

Historically, the chief justice, although technically the first among equals, often played a decisive role in shaping the Court's decision-making dynamics. Some chief justices have done a superb job of leading their colleagues. John Marshall's tenure on the bench from 1803 until his death in 1835 was perhaps the most important phase in the history of the Court. Marshall combined the authority of his office as chief justice with his considerable powers of persuasion. He convinced his colleagues, for example, to end the practice of seriatim opinions and substitute in their place an "opinion of the Court," a practice that brought unity to the Court and greater prestige to the Constitution that it interpreted. More than a century and a quarter later, Chief Justice Earl Warren provided similarly strong leadership in uniting colleagues in *Brown* v. *Board of Education* (1954) to strike down the historical practice of racial segregation in public education and thereby opened a new chapter in the history of equality in America. For that talent, Warren earned the title "Superchief."

The most successful of the chief justices have combined a talent to forge constitutional consensus while maintaining the social cohesion of the Court. That is no small task in an institution staffed by justices selected in part because of their records of individual accomplishment. The fact that they serve not at the whim of the chief justice but during good behavior makes the task of leadership even more daunting.

Personal dynamics help to shape the Court, and as a result, the decision-making process is one of the complex, closely studied, and still mysterious features of American government. Individual justices can differ over what the law means, how the Constitution is to be interpreted, and the power of the Court to decide any particular matter. That they bring different experiences to understanding these matters only adds to the rich brew that culminates in a Supreme Court opinion. The results are sometimes anything but unanimous. When the Court is badly fractured, with many concurring and dissenting opinions, the result is often a plurality opinion. In these circumstances, a majority of the justices agree on a result but they do not agree on the reasoning to support it. Lower courts and lawyers seeking to advise their clients in these circumstances confront not the law's majesty but its uncertainty. Moreover, a divided Court tends to drain public respect, since such differences tend to reinforce the modern view that the justices do not so much find the law as, in the end, make it. If justices trained in the law cannot agree on its meaning, then it seems unlikely that a public untutored in its ways will find much reason to vest confidence in their divided decisions.

The justices decide only a small fraction of all of the cases raised in the state or federal courts during any year. Less than one-tenth of a percent of all such cases ever get before the Court, let alone the justices. At the same time, the caseload or docket of the Court has grown phenomenally. In its first decade (1791–1800), the Court had little business and few cases, only 100 or so. The docket, however, steadily grew in the late nineteenth century and continued to do so in the twentieth. Whereas in 1920 there were only 565 cases on the docket, that number rose to more than 1,300 by 1950, more than 2,300 by 1960, and more than 6,000 by 1990. Yet the actual number of cases decided by the Court has shrunk significantly between 1990 and the present. Today, the Court decides approximately 75 cases per session, about half of what it did at the beginning of the decade. This reduction in the number of decided cases reflects the strong leadership of Chief Justice William H. Rehnquist, who, much like John Marshall, has insisted that it is more important what the Court decides as opposed to how many times it decides.

These changes also reflect the growing power of the Court over its own docket. Through the past two centuries Congress has steadily increased the discretionary power of the justices to decide what cases will come before them. In the nineteenth century the Court labored under a far greater load of cases that it was required to hear. The modern Supreme Court, however, has virtually complete discretion over which and what kinds of cases it grants review and decides by written opinions. The expansion of the Court's discretionary jurisdiction enables it not only to manage its caseload but to set its substantive agenda as well. As a result, the Court is no longer primarily concerned with resolving disputes per se or even with correcting the errors of lower courts. Instead, it addresses issues of national importance involving primarily constitutional and statutory interpretation. The vast majority of the cases it hears come on a writ of certiorari.

Change has also occurred in the way the justices decide the cases they do hear. In the past, after their discussion of a case in conference, the justices voted in reverse order of seniority; that is, the most junior first, after their discussion, which is held in descending order of seniority. Today they often dispense with a formal vote. After the discussion, the chief, if in the majority, typically assigns the case to one of the justices to write a formal opinion for the Court. The opinion writer then circulates a draft opinion for agreement and comment. The justices may respond with concurring opinions or dissents, hoping along the way to persuade the main author of the opinion to change the opinion. The process is something like a negotiation in which a major opinion may go through several drafts as the justices exchange views about wording in order to reach a position for the Court as a whole.

The Court is at once the most transparent and the least accessible branch of the government. No other institution is asked to explain itself through written opinions. Yet the actual process of decision making remains remote. The justices meet in secret conference, usually twice a week between October and June, to discuss the cases before them, to deliberate cases currently on the Court's docket, and to transact other miscellaneous business. A few of the justices have kept notes about these conferences that have subsequently been published, but there are no formal records of these meetings. The material that has been made available suggests considerable variation in the tenor of these meetings depending on the attitude and style of the presiding chief justice, the personalities of the associate justices, and the complexity and emotional content of the cases under discussion. While the conference remains a critical stage in the modern Court's decision-making process, the limited opportunity for extended discussion of cases has made the give-and-take of the postconference interaction of the justices increasingly important. New technology, such as photocopying and computer networking, along with a cadre of law clerks to support each of the justices, have further increased the significance of the period after the conference in reaching a position for the Court. The deliberations begun in the conference typically continue in a variety of informal ways until the Court announces its opinion, often many months later.

Over more than two centuries the form of Supreme Court opinions has changed greatly. In the first half of the nineteenth century, the Court followed what might be called a "grand style," characterized in the writings of Chief Justice Marshall and Justice Joseph Story. These justices tended to speak as the "mouthpieces of divinity," as oracles sending down pronouncements in often polished, spartan opinions. By the time of the Civil War, however, the "formal style" had become typical of high court opinions that stressed precedent and logic at the same time that they became long, turgid, often obscure, increasingly filled with legal jargon, full of legal citations, and as a result less readable. Justice Oliver Wendell Holmes, Jr., in the first third of the twentieth century was the rare exception to this style. Since the 1930s the so-called "legal realist" style has emerged, one typified by an appeal to socioeconomic and other nonlegal materials. The formal style still persists, however, with the justices busy crafting a layered set of "tests" and "prongs" and "standards" in their opinions. At the same time, the justices have become increasingly contentious, issuing more and more dissents and concurrences and producing still more plurality opinions.

The Court's opinions are contained in reports. The initial volumes of Supreme Court reports were purely commercial ventures, and the reporter received no government compensation. Alexander Dallas, of Philadelphia, was the first to publish a collection of high court opinions in 1790–91, and he was followed during the next eighty years by William Cranch, Henry Wheaton, Richard Peters, Benjamin Howard, Jeremiah Black, and John Wallace, all of whom added their names to select reports. Congress did not officially establish the office of reporter until 1816 and provided an annual salary of $1,000 a year later. The salary supplemented whatever the reporter made by the sale of the volumes he edited.

In 1874 Congress finally appropriated funds ($25,000) for the purpose of officially reporting the decisions of the Court. Thereafter, the opinions of the Court were compiled in *United States Reports*, which were extended back to the first volume of the private reports, with "1 *Dallas*" becoming the first volume of the series. Since 1921 the government has also taken on the responsibility of having the volumes published through the Government Printing Office rather than a private printer. Today, of course, the reports of the Supreme Court are widely available in a variety of unofficial media, including electronic ones.

How to Use the Guide

The *Guide* is organized alphabetically, with cross-references to other cases. Each case included as an entry opens with standard information. After the name of the case, readers will find the official *United States Reports* citation—for example, the case of *Kent* v. *Dulles* can be found at 357 U.S. 116, meaning that the case appeared in volume 357 of *United States Reports* and that it begins on page 116. The year the case was decided follows in parentheses. The article opening goes on to provide the date or dates argued (in *Kent* it was 10 April 1958) and decided (16 June 1958); the justices' vote (5 to 4); who wrote for the Court (Justice Douglas); who, if anyone, joined with a concurring opinion; and who dissented (Justices Clark, Burton, Harlan, and Whittaker). The end of each entry also lists the name of its author.

The only exception to the use of *United States Reports* occurs when cases recently decided were available at the time of publication only through the unofficial *Supreme Court Reports* or *U.S. Law Week*. There are, of course, citations to courts other than the Supreme Court in the body of many of the entries. The decisions of lower federal courts are cited in *Federal Cases*, for reports in the district and circuit courts up to 1880; the *Federal Supplement*, for district cases since 1880 and circuit cases from 1880 to 1932; and the *Federal Reporter*, for circuit court and U.S. Court of Appeals decisions since 1932. When citing state cases, I have relied on the official reports, which are issued by the courts themselves as the authoritative text of their decisions, rather than the widely used but unofficial reports of the West Publishing Company (National Reporter System) and Lawyers Co-operative Publishing Company (*American Law Reports*). Some states, of course, have ceased issuing their own reports and have instead adopted the National Reporter System as their official reporter.

Entries in the *Guide* are arranged in alphabetical order on a letter-by-letter rather than a word-by-word basis. Hyphens and spaces between words are ignored, but punctuation marks such as commas and semicolons are taken into account. In most instances, the arrangement is straightforward. The entry "Cohens v. Virginia" precedes "E. C. Knight v. United States"; however, "Cohens v. Virginia" also precedes "Cohen v. California," since the letter "s" in "Cohens" comes alphabetically before the "v" in "Cohen v." In addition, entries on cases in which the United States is involved as a plaintiff are listed under the name of the other party. For example, the case *United States* v. *Robel* is found as the entry "Robel, United States v." The same holds true for ex parte cases, such as "Siebold, Ex parte."

A case index is included at the end of this volume. It covers more than just the cases listed as entries; it encompasses all of the cases mentioned anywhere in the *Guide*. Hence, even if a case is not covered as an entry, it may well appear somewhere in the volume, and the case index is the best way to determine if it does.

The *Guide* also has a topical index that directs readers to concepts, persons, places, and institutions mentioned in the text of the entries. For example, a user interested in learning about all of the references made to "religion" in these cases can turn to the index.

The volume also contains two appendices. The first is the Constitution of the United States of America. The second includes a table indicating the succession of justices, the number of days that particular seats on the Court have been left vacant, the presidents who appointed the justices, the Senate votes (when the votes were taken) to confirm or reject nominees, and the length of service of each justice. Where appropriate these lists also include persons who were nominated for a position on the Court but who, for a variety of reasons, never served.

Finally, the *Guide* contains a glossary of terms designed to help the reader understand the sometimes arcane character of the Court and constitutional law.

Acknowledgments

It is with great sadness that I must note the passing of my good friend Kermit L. Hall. Kermit and I worked together on numerous projects over many years. He was the guiding spirit behind both editions of *The Oxford Companion to the Supreme Court of the United States* as well as *The Oxford Guide to United States Supreme Court Decisions*. Kermit's erudite scholarship and sage judgment will be sorely missed.

The second edition of the *Guide* is derived from the earlier work of Kermit (as editor-in-chief), the associate editors (James W. Ely Jr., Joel B. Grossman, and William M. Wiecek), and the many colleagues who contributed to the first and second editions of *The Oxford Companion to the Supreme Court of the United States*. It has been updated to include more than fifty cases from 1992 through 2008. The tables in Appendix Two have been revised to take account of changes in the membership of the Supreme Court, and a list of recommended books for further reading has also been added.

May 2008   James W. Ely Jr.

Directory of Contributors

Shirley S. Abrahamson
Chief Justice, Wisconsin Supreme Court

Dean Alfange, Jr.
Professor of Political Science, Emeritus,
University of Massachusetts, Amherst
(deceased)

Francis A. Allen
Edson R. Sunderland Professor of Law,
Emeritus, University of Michigan Law
School

Gordon E. Baker
Professor of Political Science, University of
California, Santa Barbara
(deceased)

Thomas E. Baker
Professor of Law, Florida International
University

Gordon Morris Bakken
Professor of History, California State
University, Fullerton

Howard Ball
Professor of Political Science, Emeritus,
University of Vermont.

Lawrence Baum
Professor of Political Science, The Ohio State
University

Maurice Baxter
Professor of History, Emeritus, University
of Indiana
(deceased)

Michal R. Belknap
Professor of Law, California Western School
of Law; Earl Warren Professor of Law and
Adjunct Professor of History, University of
California, San Diego

Herman Belz
Professor of American Constitutional History, Emeritus, University of Maryland, College Park

Michael Les Benedict
Professor of History, Emeritus, The Ohio
State University

Loren P. Beth
Professor of Political Science, Emeritus,
University of Georgia

David J. Bodenhamer
Professor of Legal History and Executive
Director of Polis Research Center, Indiana
University-Purdue University at Indiana-
polis

Edgar Bodenheimer
Professor of Law, Emeritus, University of
California, Davis
(deceased)

Daan Braveman
President of Nazareth College

Lisa Schultz Bressman
Professor of Law, Vanderbilt University

R. Randall Bridwell
Professor of Law, Charleston School of Law

Jon W. Bruce
Professor of Law, Vanderbilt University

Augustus M. Burns III
Associate Professor of History, University of
Florida
(deceased)

David L. Callies
Benjamin A. Kudo Professor of Law,
William S. Richardson School of Law, Uni-
versity of Hawai'i

Mark W. Cannon
McLean, Virginia

Bradley C. Canon
Professor of Political Science, University of
Kentucky

Lief H. Carter
Professor of Political Science and McHugh
Distinguished Professor of American Insti-
tutions and Leadership, Colorado College

Bill F. Chamberlin
Joseph L. Brechner Eminent Scholar in
Mass Communication and Director of
Marion Brechner Citizens Access Project,

University of Florida; Affiliate Professor, University of Florida College of Law

Peter J. Coleman
Professor of History, Emeritus, University of Illinois at Chicago
(deceased)

Richard C. Cortner
Professor of Political Science, Emeritus, University of Arizona

Robert J. Cottrol
Professor of Law, History, and Sociology, Harold Paul Green Research Professor of Law, George Washington University

Barbara H. Craig
Professor of Government, Wesleyan University

Charles G. Curtis, Jr.
Shareholder, Heller Ehrman LLP; Adjunct Professor, Marquette University Law School

George Dargo
Professor of Law, New England School of Law

Thomas Y. Davies
Elvin E. Overton Distinguished Professor of Law and National Alumni Association Distinguished Service Professor of Law, University of Tennessee, Knoxville

Brannon P. Denning
Professor of Law, Cumberland School of Law, Samford University

Donald A. Downs
Professor of Law and Political Science, University of Wisconsin, Madison

Mary L. Dudziak
Judge Edward J. and Ruey L. Guirado Professor of Law, History, and Political Science, University of Southern California

Gerald T. Dunne
Professor of Law, Emeritus, St. Louis University
(deceased)

Steven J. Eagle
Professor of Law, George Mason University

Walter Ehrlich
Professor of History and Education, Emeritus, University of Missouri-St. Louis
(deceased)

Theodore Eisenberg
Henry Allen Mark Professor of Law, Adjunct Professor of Statistical Sciences, Cornell Law School

Ward E. Y. Elliott
Burnet C. Wohlford Professor of American Political Institutions, Claremont McKenna College

Richard E. Ellis
Professor of History, State University of New York at Buffalo

James W. Ely, Jr.
Milton R. Underwood Professor of Law and Professor of History, Vanderbilt University

Leon D. Epstein
Hilldale Professor of Political Science, Emeritus, University of Wisconsin, Madison
(deceased)

Nancy S. Erickson
Senior Attorney, Legal Services for New York City, Brooklyn Branch

Malcolm M. Feeley
Claire Sanders Clements Dean's Chair Professor of Law, University of California, Berkeley

David Fellman
Professor of Political Science, Emeritus, University of Wisconsin, Madison
(deceased)

Paul Finkelman
President William McKinley Distinguished Professor of Law and Public Policy and Senior Fellow, Government Law Center, Albany Law School

Peter G. Fish
Professor of Law and Political Science, Duke University

Tony Freyer
University Research Professor of History and Law, University of Alabama

Eric T. Freyfogle
Max L. Rowe Professor of Law, University of Illinois at Urbana-Champaign

Tim Gallimore
Columbia, Missouri

Richard A. Gambitta
Director of Institute for Law and Public Affairs and Associate Professor of Political Science, University of Texas at San Antonio

Patrick M. Garry
Associate Professor of Law, University of South Dakota School of Law

Sheldon Goldman
Professor of Political Science, University of Massachusetts, Amherst

Leslie Friedman Goldstein
Professor of Political Science, University of Delaware

Stephen E. Gottlieb
Jay and Ruth Caplan Distinguished Professor of Law, Albany Law School, Union University

Kent Greenawalt
University Professor, Columbia University Law School

Joel B. Grossman
Professor of Political Science, John Hopkins University

Kermit L. Hall
President, State University of New York at Albany
(deceased)

Richard F. Hamm
Professor and Chair, Department of History, State University of New York at Albany

Christine B. Harrington
Professor of Politics, New York University

Beth M. Henschen
Adjunct Lecturer, Political Science, Eastern Michigan University

Gail Heriot
Professor of Law, University of San Diego

Herbert Hill
Professor of Emeritus of Afro-American Studies and Industrial Relations, University of Wisconsin, Madison
(deceased)

Charles F. Hobson
Editor, Papers of John Marshall, Institute of Early American History and Culture, College of William and Mary

Timothy S. Huebner
Associate Professor of History, Rhodes College

Dennis J. Hutchinson
Senior Lecturer in Law and William Rainey Harper Professor in the College, Master of the New Collegiate Division, and Associate Dean of the College, University of Chicago Law School

Harold M. Hyman
William P. Hobby Professor of History, Emeritus, and Director of the Center for the History of Leadership Institutions, Rice University

Stanley Ingber
Professor of Law, Department of Law, Politi-cal Science, and Criminal Justice Administration, John Jay College of Criminal Justice

Robert M. Ireland
Professor of American Constitutional and Legal History, University of Kentucky

Carol E. Jenson
Professor of History, University of Wisconsin, La Crosse

Herbert A. Johnson
Ernest F. Hollings Professor of Constitutional Law, Emeritus, University of South Carolina

John W. Johnson
Professor of History, University of Northern Iowa

James E. Jones, Jr.
Nathan P. Feinsinger Professor of Labor Law, Emeritus, University of Wisconsin, Madison

Craig Joyce
Andrews Kurth Professor of Law, Co-director of Institute for Intellectual Property & Information Law, University of Houston

Ronald C. Kahn
James Monroe Professor of Politics, Oberlin College

Yale Kamisar
Clarence Darrow Distinguished University Professor of Law, Emeritus, University of Michigan Law School, Ann Arbor

Susan L. Kay
Clinical Professor of Law, Associate Dean for Clinical Affairs, Vanderbilt University

Paul Kens
Professor of Political Science, Texas State University, San Marcos

Ken I. Kersch
Association Professor of Political Science, History, and Law, and Director of the Clough Center for the Study of Constitutional Democracy, Boston College

Douglas W. Kmiec
Professor of Constitutional Law and Caruso Family Chair in Constitutional Law, Pepperdine University School of Law

Joseph F. Kobylka
Professor of Political Science, Southern Methodist University

Donald P. Kommers
Joseph and Elizabeth Robbie Professor of Political Science and Professor of Law, University of Notre Dame

Alfred S. Konefsky
Distinguished Professor of Law, State University of New York at Buffalo

Milton R. Konvitz
Professor of Law and Industrial Labor Relations, Emeritus, Cornell University (deceased)

J. Morgan Kousser
Professor of History and Social Science, California Institute of Technology

Michael I. Krauss,
Professor of Law, George Mason University

Samuel Krislov
Professor of Political Science and Law, University of Minnesota Law School

Stanley I. Kutler
Professor of Law, Emeritus, University of Wisconsin Law School

David E. Kyvig
Distinguished Research Professor of History, Northern Illinois University

Wayne R. LaFave
David C. Baum Professor of Law and Center for Advanced Study Professor, Emeritus, University of Illinois at Urbana-Champaign

William Lasser
Professor of Political Science, Clemson University

Susan E. Lawrence
Associate Professor of Political Science, Rutgers University

William E. Leuchtenburg
William Rand Kenan Jr. Professor of History, Emeritus, University of North Carolina at Chapel Hill

Nelson Lund
Patrick Henry Professor of Constitutional Law and the Second Amendment, George Mason University

Thomas C. Mackey
Associate Professor of American History and Adjunct Professor of Law, University of Louisville

Harold G. Maier
David Daniels Allen Distinguished Professor of Law, Emeritus, Vanderbilt University

Diane C. Maleson
Professor of Law, Temple University

John Anthony Maltese
Albert Berry Saye Professor of Political Science, University of Georgia

Albert R. Matheny
Professor of Political Science, University of Florida

Lynn Mather
Professor of Law and Political Science, The Baldy Center for Law and Social Policy, University at Buffalo Law School

James May
Professor of Law, American University

Michael W. McCann
Gordon Hirabayashi Professor for the Advancement of Citizenship, Department of Political Science, University of Washington

Thomas R. McCoy
Professor of Law, Emeritus, Vanderbilt University

G. Roger McDonald
Lecturer in Government, John Jay College of Criminal Justice, City University of New York

Philip L. Merkel
Professor of Law, Western State University

Keith C. Miller
Ellis and Nelle Levitt Professor of Law, Drake University

Elizabeth B. Monroe
Associate Professor of History, Indiana University-Indianapolis

Ralph James Mooney
Wallace L. and Ellen A. Kaapcke Professor of Business Law, University of Oregon

Paul L. Murphy
Regents' Professor of American History, University of Minnesota, Twin Cities (deceased)

R. Kent Newmyer
Professor of Law and History, Emeritus, University of Connecticut

Michael A. Newton
Professor of the Practice of Law, Vanderbilt University

Donald G. Nieman
Professor of History and Dean of College of Arts and Sciences, Bowling Green State University

Jill Norgren
Professor of Government, Emeritus, John Jay College of Criminal Justice, City University of New York

Karen O'Connor
Jonathan N. Helfat Distinguished Professor, School of Public Affairs, American University

Timothy J. O'Neill
Professor of Political Science, Southwestern University

John V. Orth
William Rand Kenan Jr. Professor of Law, University of North Carolina at Chapel Hill

Ellen Frankel Paul
Deputy Director of the Social Philosophy and Social Center and Professor of Political Science, Bowling Green State University

J. W. Peltason
President, Emeritus, University of California

Leo Pfeffer
Attorney, Central Valley, New York
(deceased)

Richard Polenberg
Marie Underhill Noll Professor of History, Cornell University

Robert Post
David Boies Professor of Law, Yale Law School

H. Jefferson Powell
Frederic Cleaveland Professor of Law and Divinity, Duke University

Walter F. Pratt, Jr.
Dean and Educational Foundation Distinguished Professor of Law, University of South Carolina School of Law

C. Herman Pritchett
Professor of Political Science, Emeritus, University of California, Santa Barbara
(deceased)

Steven Puro
Professor of Political Science and Public Policy, St. Louis University

Michael L. Radelet
Professor and Chair Department of Sociology, University of Colorado at Bolder

Fred D. Ragan
Professor of History, Emeritus, East Carolina University

Inez Smith Reid
Judge for the District of Columbia Court of Appeals

Eric W. Rise
Associate Professor, Department of Sociology and Criminal Justice, University of Delaware

Donald M. Roper
Associate Professor of History, Emeritus, State University of New York, College at New Paltz

Gerald N. Rosenberg
Associate Professor of Political Science and Lecturer in Law, University of Chicago

Norman L. Rosenberg
DeWitt Wallace Professor of History, Macalester College

Lucy E. Salyer
Associate Professor of History, University of New Hampshire

Thomas O. Sargentich
Professor of Law, American University
(deceased)

Frederick Schauer
Frank Stanton Professor of the First Amendment, John F. Kennedy School of Government, Harvard University

John E. Semonche
Professor of American Constitutional and Legal History, University of North Carolina at Chapel Hill

Charles H. Sheldon
Claudius O. and Mary W. Johnson Distinguished Professor of Political Science, Washington State University
(deceased)

Suzanne Sherry
Herman O. Loewenstein Professor of Law, Vanderbilt University

Stephen A. Siegel
Professor of Law, DePaul University

Elliot E. Slotnick
Professor of Political Science, The Ohio State University

Rodney A. Smolla
Dean and Roy L. Steinheimer, Jr. Professor of Law, Washington and Lee University School of Law

Aviam Soifer
Dean, William S. Richardson School of Law, University of Hawai'i

Rayman L. Solomon
Dean and Professor of Law, Rutgers University School of Law-Camden

Harold J. Spaeth
Research Professor of Law, Professor of Political Science, Emeritus, Michigan State University

Peter W. Sperlich
Professor of Political Science, Emeritus, University of California-Berkeley

Robert J. Steamer
Professor of Political Science, Emeritus, University of Massachusetts, Boston

Barbara C. Steidle
Assistant Provost for Undergraduate Education and Assessment Services, and Associate Professor of History, Emeritus, Michigan State University

William B. Stoebuck
Professor of Law, Emeritus, University of Washington

Geoffrey R. Stone
Edward H. Levi Distinguished Service Professor of Law, University of Chicago

Rennard Strickland
Distinguished Professor of Law, Emeritus, University of Oregon

Susette M. Talarico
Albert Berry Saye Professor of American Government and Constitutional Law, Josiah Meigs Distinguished Teaching Professor, and Director of Criminal Justice Studies Program, University of Georgia

Mark V. Tushnet
William Nelson Cromwell Professor of Law, Harvard University

Melvin I. Urofsky
Professor of History and Public Policy, Emeritus, Virginia Commonwealth University

Sandra F. VanBurkleo
Associate Professor of History, Wayne State University

John R. Vile
Professor and Chair, Department of Political Science, Middle Tennessee State University

Stephen L. Wasby
Professor of Political Science, Emeritus, State University of New York at Albany

William M. Wiecek
Chester Adgate Congdon Professor of Public Law and Legislation, Syracuse University College of Law, and Professor of History, Maxwell School, Syracuse University

Robert A. Williams, Jr.
E. Thomas Sullivan Professor of Law and American Indian Studies, Director of the Indigenous Peoples Law and Policy Program, James E. Rogers College of Law, University of Arizona

Stephen C. Wood
Professor of Communication and Film Studies, University of Rhode Island

John R. Wunder
Professor of History and Journalism, University of Nebraska-Lincoln

Tinsley E. Yarbrough
Distinguished Professor of Political Science, Emeritus, East Carolina University

Mark G. Yudof
President, University of California, Former Chancellor of University of Texas System and Charles Alan Wright Chair in Federal Courts, University of Texas at Austin

THE OXFORD GUIDE TO

UNITED STATES SUPREME COURT DECISIONS

Second Edition

A

Abington School District v. Schempp, 374 U.S. 203 (1963), argued 27–28 Feb. 1963, decided 17 June 1963 by vote of 8 to 1; Clark for the Court, Brennan, Douglas, and Goldberg concurring, Stewart in dissent. *Schempp* was essentially a rerun of the Court's decision the previous term in **Engel* v. *Vitale* (1962). In the earlier case the Court identified a constitutional violation and struck the offending legislation; in *Schempp* it reasserted its logic and result as if to say, "We meant what we said." *Schempp* repeats both the *Engel* holding—the Establishment Clause forbids public schools from sponsoring religious practices akin to prayer—and its coalition of justices. This time, however, Justice Tom C. Clark (Presbyterian) wrote for the majority and the Court's religious diversity—Arthur Goldberg (Jewish) and William Brennan (Catholic)—was made manifest in separate concurring opinions.

Schempp came in the wake of a hostile response to *Engel*, which raged throughout the summer of 1962 and into the Court's next term. Representative L. Mendell Rivers accused the Court of "legislating—they never adjudicate—with one eye on the Kremlin and the other on the NAACP." Cardinal Spellman said it had struck "at the very heart of the Godly tradition in which America's children have for so long been raised." Representative Frank Becker called *Engel* "the most tragic [ruling] in the history of the United States," and offered an

amendment to reverse this (and, later, the *Schempp*) decision. According to the Gallup Poll, 76 percent of Americans supported this approach. All told, 150 such amendments were offered by 111 members of Congress, with Becker's coming to a vote but losing in the House of Representatives.

The *Schempp* decision actually decided two cases: itself and *Murray* v. *Curlett* (1963). The former was brought by the Schempps—a non-Jewish family sought out by the ACLU, which argued the case—who objected to a Pennsylvania law requiring that ten verses of the Bible be read at the opening of each public school day. The latter was brought by Madalyn Murray and her son William, professed atheists, who attacked a Baltimore statute providing for the "reading, without comment, of a chapter in the Holy Bible and/or the use of the Lord's Prayer" in opening exercises in city schools. Both of these cases saw the same type of amicus curiae group participation as in *Engel*, with separationists opposing the prayers and accommodationists supporting them.

Justice Clark's majority opinion was light on history and long on the importance of religion in American life. Its conclusion, however, was the same as that tendered the year before: the Constitution forbids state establishment of religion, prayer is religion, and thus prayer in public schools is constitutionally impermissible. For the first time, a "test" for Establishment Clause questions was formally articulated by the Court. To pass constitutional muster, legislation must have "a secular legislative purpose and a primary effect that neither advances nor inhibits religion" (p. 222). The fact that the religious material here was not, like that in *Engel*, composed by the state, was constitutionally inconsequential; the "wall of separation" was real and was to be kept high.

The concurring opinions were unexceptional, save for the religious affiliations of the justices who wrote them and their somewhat self-consciously apologetic tone; it was as if they sought to reassure the nation that the Court's posture was not antireligious. Most noteworthy was Brennan's seventy-four page opus reviewing the history of the First Amendment—and judicial and legislative glosses on it—which concluded that government may neither foster nor promote religion.

Justice Potter Stewart's dissent reasserted themes he initially voiced in *Engel*. Charging the majority with hostility (not neutrality) to religion, he would have upheld the practices as a legitimate accommodation. In addition, Stewart noted that the separationist doctrine enunciated by the Court in the two prayer cases posed a difficult interpretive conundrum: if states sought to protect free exercise rights (say, by paying military chaplains to minister to the needs of troops in battle zones) they could run afoul of the Establishment Clause by pursuing policies that were primarily (if not solely) religious in purpose. He contended that his approach, stressing the pre-eminence of free exercise values, would avoid this dilemma.

Joseph Kobylka

Ableman v. Booth; United States v. Booth, 21 How. (62 U.S.) 506 (1859), argued 19 Jan. 1859, decided 7 Mar. 1859 by vote of 9 to 0; Taney for the Court. In the spring of 1854, Benjamin S. Garland, a slaveowner from Missouri, went to Wisconsin seeking to recapture a runaway slave. Joshua Glover had escaped two years earlier and found work in a mill outside Racine. The slaveowner invoked the Fugitive Slave Act of 1850 and filed a complaint before the United States commissioner in Milwaukee, who promptly issued a warrant for Glover's arrest. A deputy marshal, with the assistance of the slaveowner, forcibly entered Glover's cabin, knocked him down, and carried him off bound and handcuffed to the Milwaukee jail.

A boisterous public meeting condemned the capture, resolved "the slave catching law of 1850 disgraceful and . . . repealed," and dispatched one hundred men to Milwaukee to secure Glover's release. In the meantime, Sherman M. Booth, an abolitionist and editor of an antislavery newspaper, obtained a writ of habeas corpus for Glover from a local county court judge. The federal marshal and the county sheriff refused to produce the prisoner on the theory that he was properly in federal custody and could not be released through a state court habeas proceeding. However, a crowd broke into the jail and rescued Glover, who was never recaptured. Soon thereafter, Booth and others were indicted and convicted for violating federal law by aiding and abetting the rescue.

This was the dramatic start of a long jurisdictional confrontation between state and federal authority. Federal prosecution of Booth produced repeated defiance by Wisconsin judges of federal authority, even that of the United States Supreme Court. At one point, the judges of the Wisconsin Supreme Court, in an attempt to forestall federal review, ordered their clerk to make no return to the writ of error issued by the United States Supreme Court and to enter no order in the case. Judges and legislators battled over state habeas corpus jurisdiction versus federal judicial authority.

The conflict culminated with Chief Justice Roger B. Taney's unanimous opinion in the companion cases of *Ableman v. Booth* and *United States v. Booth* (1859), though his decision did not end the struggle. Taney condemned the Wisconsin Supreme Court's stance, arguing it "would subvert the very foundations of this Government" (p. 525). His opinion echoed the broad nationalism of famous decisions of John Marshall's era, such as **McCulloch v. Maryland* (1819). It is ironic that *Ableman v. Booth*'s assertion of sweeping national power issued from the pen of a chief justice known for his strong states' rights views. Moreover, Taney's opinion in dictum expressed the unanimous view that the 1850 Fugitive Slave Act was "in all its provisions, fully authorized by the Constitution of the United States" (p. 526). When Booth was subsequently reindicted in a federal court in 1860, the Wisconsin Supreme Court still split evenly over whether Booth might be entitled to a writ of habeas corpus despite the mandate of the United States Supreme Court.

The Wisconsin legislature condemned Taney's decision as "despotism" and called for "positive defiance" by the states. Only the Civil War settled the issue.

Perhaps because of its connection to slavery and to Taney, widely reviled for his *Dred *Scott* opinion two years earlier, *Ableman* v. *Booth* is seldom invoked as precedent. *Ableman* v. *Booth* clearly established the lack of state judicial authority to issue writs of habeas corpus to remove someone from federal custody, yet the question was relitigated after the Civil War. *Tarble's Case* (1872) reached the same result and has become the standard citation for the supremacy of federal jurisdiction. Actually though, until *Ableman* v. *Booth* the law was not clear. A leading treatise on habeas corpus published in 1858 supported the position of the Wisconsin Supreme Court.

Many people considered *Ableman* v. *Booth* a frightening extension of *Dred Scott*. There were other contemporaneous conflicts over the authority of federal judges in the context of slavery, but antislavery forces saw *Ableman* v. *Booth* as the end of hope for constitutional argument against the Slave Power. The strong constitutional resistance expressed by the Wisconsin judges and the repeated calls by legislators and citizens of Wisconsin for forceful opposition provided a paradoxical mirror image of secessionist arguments advanced simultaneously in the South.

□ Robert M. Cover, *Justice Accused: Antislavery and the Judicial Process* (1975).

Aviam Soifer

Abrams v. Johnson, 521 U.S. 74 (1997), argued 9 Dec. 1996, decided 19 June 1997 by vote of 5 to 4; Kennedy for the Court, Breyer in dissent. Following the 1990 census, the Supreme Court was asked repeatedly to assess the constitutionality of so-called majority-minority legislative districts in the South. These efforts produced a mixed bag of constitutional results, with the justices placing important limitations on the use of race to gerrymander districts that would produce a majority of African-American voters. The states had taken these actions in an effort to comply with the Voting Rights Act of 1965 and its subsequent amendments.

The 1990 census revealed that population growth in Georgia entitled the state to one additional congressional district. The legislature the following year redrew its district lines and created not one but two majority African-American districts, adding the second in response to demands by the United States Department of Justice (DOJ). The DOJ, however, acting under the authority of the Voting Rights Act, refused to approve even this plan and placed additional pressure on the legislature to create a third majority African-American district, a demand to which the legislature acceded in 1992. White voters in one of these new districts, the Eleventh, immediately filed suit claiming that the new plan was racial gerrymandering in violation of the Equal Protection Clause of the Fourteenth Amendment. The Supreme Court in *Miller* v. *Johnson* (1995) agreed and threw the plan out as unconstitutional because it relied on race as a driving factor.

The federal district court in Georgia overseeing the case then waited for the legislature to act, but the legislators deadlocked and the court was left to perform the task of drawing new district lines. The Supreme Court's precedents provided that when judges redistrict they should give special attention to the policies followed by the legislature. Given the fact that the legislature had created two African-American districts in 1991, it followed that the district court would be expected to approve the same number.

After holding hearings the district court created only one African-American district. The judge argued that in order to establish a second majority-minority district he would have to use race as a predominant factor, a practice that the Rehnquist Court had clearly rejected. The Department of Justice and African-American voters led by Lucious Abrams filed suit claiming that the district court should have retained at least the two African-American districts agreed upon by the legislature in 1991.

The Supreme Court in a relatively brief opinion upheld the actions of the district court and sidestepped without overturning its previous precedents. Justice Anthony Kennedy's opinion found that the original 1991 plan, although drafted by the legislature, was itself illegitimate because it resulted from steady Department of Justice pressure to use race. Therefore, the district court was not required to defer to the legislature's decision. Kennedy also rejected arguments by the plaintiffs that the failure to create a second African-American district was a violation of the Voting Rights Act. To make his point, Kennedy observed that the

1996 victories of Representatives Cynthia A. McKinney and Sanford D. Bishop, Jr., both incumbent African-American Democrats who won reelection in new white districts, argued against DOJ's approach. White voters, it turned out, would select African-American candidates.

Justice Stephen Breyer's dissent argued that Kennedy and the majority gave too much attention to race and, as a result, drew the Court into the political thicket of legislative reapportionment. In these matters, Breyer insisted, the justices should follow their precedents and defer to state legislators. The decision by the Georgia legislature in 1991 to create two African-American districts was a response to a host of pressures, not just to the Department of Justice.

The Court's decision had two important consequences. First, it meant that Georgia did not have to redistrict until after the census in the year 2000. Second, it reaffirmed the position of a narrow majority of the justices that race can be a factor in redistricting but that it cannot be the predominant factor.

Kermit L. Hall

Abrams v. United States, 250 U.S. 616 (1919), argued 21 Oct. 1919, decided 10 Nov. 1919 by vote of 7 to 2; Clarke for the Court, Holmes in dissent. On 23 August 1918, Jacob Abrams, a Russian immigrant and an anarchist, was arrested in New York City along with several of his comrades, among them Molly Steimer, Hyman Lachowsky, and Samuel Lipman. They had written, printed, and distributed two leaflets, one in English and one in Yiddish, which condemned President Woodrow Wilson for sending American troops to fight in Soviet Russia. The Yiddish leaflet also called for a general strike to protest against the government's policy of intervention. Abrams and the others were indicted under the Sedition Act of 16 May 1918, which made it a crime to "willfully utter, print, write, or publish any disloyal, profane, scurrilous, or abusive language" about the United States' form of government, or to "willfully urge, incite, or advocate any curtailment of production" of things "necessary or essential to the prosecution of the war . . . with intent by such curtailment to cripple or hinder the United States in the prosecution of the war." Tried in October 1918, before federal district court judge Henry DeLamar Clayton, Jr., they were found guilty and sentenced to 15- to 20-year prison terms.

In March 1919, while Abrams and the others were out on bail, the Supreme Court upheld the convictions of antiwar socialists under the 1917 Espionage Act (*Schenck* v. *U.S.*) and under the 1918 Sedition Act (*Debs* v. *U.S.*). Both decisions were unanimous, and both were written by Oliver Wendell Holmes, who reasoned in *Schenck* that "[t]he question in every case is whether the words used are used in such circumstances and are of such a nature as to create a clear and present danger that they will bring about the substantive evils that Congress has a right to prevent" (p. 52).

Justice John H. Clarke's majority decision in *Abrams* closely followed Holmes's reasoning. The leaflets created a clear and present danger, Clarke said, because they had been distributed "at the supreme crisis of the war" and amounted to "an attempt to defeat the war plans of the Government" (p. 623). Moreover, he continued, even if the anarchists' primary purpose and intent had been to aid the Russian Revolution, the general strike they advocated would have necessarily hampered prosecution of the war with Germany.

But by the time the Court ruled in *Abrams*, Holmes had modified his view. Disturbed by the repression resulting from antiradical hysteria and influenced by the views of several friends and acquaintances—including Harvard Law School professor Zechariah Chafee, federal district judge Learned Hand, and political theorist Harold J. Laski—Holmes edged toward a more libertarian interpretation of the clear and present danger standard. Consequently, his dissent in the *Abrams* case, joined by Louis D. Brandeis, refined the standard in crucial ways.

Congress, Holmes now declared, "constitutionally may punish speech that produces or is intended to produce a clear and imminent danger that will bring about forthwith certain substantive evils that the United States constitutionally may seek to prevent" (p. 627). Holmes denied that "the surreptitious publishing of a silly leaflet by an unknown man" (p. 628) created such a danger, and he denied, too, the existence of the requisite intent, since Abrams' "only object" was to stop American intervention in Russia. Holmes reasoned that the First Amendment protected the expression of all opinions "unless they so imminently threaten immediate interference with the lawful and pressing purposes of the law that an immediate check is required to save the country" (p. 630).

The Supreme Court would wrestle with reformulations of the clear and present danger standard for fifty years, until, in *Brandenburg* v. *Ohio* (1969), it substituted a direct incitement test. What endures in Holmes's *Abrams* dissent is his eloquent discussion of the connection between freedom of speech, the search for truth, and the value of experimentation: "when men have realized that time has upset many fighting faiths, they may come to believe even more than they believe in the very foundations of their own conduct that the ultimate good desired is better reached by free trade in ideas—that the best test of truth is the power of the thought to get itself accepted in the competition of the market, and that truth is the only ground upon which their wishes safely can be carried out. That at any rate is the theory of our Constitution. It is an experiment, as all life is an experiment" (p. 630).

□ Richard Polenberg, *Fighting Faiths: The Abrams Case, the Supreme Court, and Free Speech* (1987).

Richard Polenberg

Adair v. United States, 208 U.S. 161 (1908), argued 29–30 Oct. 1907, decided 27 Jan. 1908 by vote of 7 to 2; Harlan for the Court, McKenna and Holmes in dissent. The Erdman Act of 1898 was enacted to prevent disruption of interstate commerce by labor disputes. It protected union members by prohibiting yellow dog contracts and the discharge or blacklisting of employees for union activity. An employer who discharged an employee for union membership challenged the constitutionality of the statute. Writing for the majority, Justice John Marshall Harlan posited equal bargaining power between employer and employee. He held the law to be an unreasonable invasion of personal liberty and property rights guaranteed by the due process clause of the Fifth Amendment. Relying on Fourteenth Amendment precedents, Harlan grafted the substantive conception of due process and freedom of contract onto the Fifth Amendment. He also found the act to be outside the scope of congressional commerce power. Ignoring the statute's legislative history, he asserted there was "no legal or logical connection" between union membership and interstate commerce (p. 178).

Justice Joseph McKenna in dissent called for judicial realism, whereas Justice Oliver Wendell Holmes echoed the position of restraint he had espoused in *Lochner* v. *New York* (1905): the legislature was the proper arbiter of public policy and could reasonably limit freedom of contract.

Conservatives extolled *Adair* for condemning "class legislation," while Roscoe Pound thought it epitomized "mechanical jurisprudence," the use of "technicalities and conceptualizations" to defeat the ends of justice. The precedent supported invalidation of state laws providing similar protections for unions (*Coppage* v. *Kansas*, 1915) until the New Deal era revolutionized labor-management relations.

Barbara C. Steidle

Adamson v. California, 332 U.S 46 (1947), argued 15–16 Jan. 1947, decided 23 June 1947 by vote of 5 to 4; Reed for the Court, Frankfurter concurring, Black, Douglas, Murphy, and Rutledge in dissent. *Adamson* reflected the intense debate over whether the Fourteenth Amendment's Due Process Clause incorporates specific provisions of the Bill of Rights, thus making them applicable to state criminal proceedings. The question was whether the prosecution's calling the jury's attention to the defendant's refusal to testify violated the Fifth Amendment's ban on self-incrimination. The majority reiterated the holding of *Palko* v. *Connecticut* (1937) that the Fourteenth Amendment "does not draw all the rights of the federal Bill of Rights under its protection," but incorporates only those that are so fundamental that they are "implicit in the concept of ordered liberty" (p. 54). It upheld the conviction because the prosecutor's comments did not result in an "unfair trial."

Justice Hugo Black argued in dissent that the due process clause should be read to guarantee that "no state could deprive its citizens of the privileges and protections of the Bill of Rights" and therefore argued that the Fourteenth Amendment incorporates "the full protection of the Fifth Amendment's provision against compelling evidence from an accused to convict him of a crime" (p. 75). The Court has never adopted Black's "total incorporation" approach. It has, however, incorporated nearly all the individual components of the Bill of Rights under a doctrine called "selective incorporation." Thus, in *Griffin* v. *California* (1965) the Court held that the Fourteenth Amendment does not permit state prosecutors to call the jury's attention to a defendant's failure to testify.

Thomas Y. Davies

Adarand Constructors, Inc. v. Peña, 515 U.S. 200 (1995), argued 17 Jan. 1995, decided 12 June by vote of 5 to 4; O'Connor for the Court, Scalia, Kennedy, Thomas concurring, Stevens, Ginsburg, and Souter in dissent. During the 1960s and 1970s state and federal governments undertook a host of what came to be known as affirmative action programs. The goal of such programs was to make it easier for minorities to overcome past discrimination based on segregation. The Supreme Court in *Fullilove* v. *Klutznick* (1989) sustained a 1977 law that provided a 10 percent "set aside" for minority business enterprises. The 1977 act was the first federal statute since the Freedman's Bureau Act of 1866 to contain an explicitly race-conscious classification. The Court's decision had a substantial impact, leading to the passage of a host of federal legislation. At the same time, the Court refused to extend the same authority to local and state governments to build such programs, and in the same year they decided *Fullilove*, the justices struck down a Richmond, Virginia, program that set aside 30 percent of construction funds for minority contractors. In *Richmond* v. *J. A. Croson Co.*, the justices concluded that such local programs deserved the most rigorous judicial scrutiny, called strict scrutiny, when race was involved. A year later, the high court decided the case of *Metro Broadcasting, Inc.* v. *FCC*, in which a bare majority of the Court, headed by Justice William J. Brennan, Jr., upheld a federal program to increase black ownership of broadcast licenses. Among other things, the Court confirmed that federal set-aside programs were not required to be tested under the strict scrutiny standard applied to local and state governments. In essence, the federal government had a special dispensation when it came to making color-conscious preferences.

The impact of the federal set-aside programs was pervasive and substantial. In 1994, for example, about $10 billion was at play. Among such programs spawned in the wake of *Fullilove* was one involving the Small Business Administration and the Department of Transportation. It provided financial incentives to government contractors that gave at least 10 percent of their business to minority subcontractors. Randy

Pech was the white owner of Adarand Constructors, Inc., of Colorado Springs, Colorado. Adarand made the low bid on a guardrail project in the San Juan National Forest, but the subcontract went instead to a Hispanic-owned company. Pech then brought suit against the Department of Transportation and its head, Federico Peña, claiming that the subcontracting policy violated constitutional guarantees of equal protection and due process. A federal district court and a court of appeals rebuffed these claims on the grounds that the federal government could invoke race-based affirmative action programs that were not subject to strict scrutiny.

The justices, however, reversed course and remanded the case back to the lower court for additional review. In doing so, the somewhat fragmented majority decided that strict scrutiny should be applied to race-conscious affirmative action programs. Justice Sandra Day O'Connor, writing for the majority, placed federal set-aside programs on the same constitutional plane with local and state efforts. That meant, according to O'Connor, that all government classification by race "should be subjected to detailed judicial inquiry to ensure that the personal right to equal protection of the laws has not been infringed" (p. 227). To be constitutional, measures based on racial classifications had to be narrowly tailored and had to further a compelling government interest. Justice Antonin Scalia went even further than O'Connor, noting his belief that the program could never withstand strict scrutiny. "In the eyes of the government," Scalia wrote, "we are just one race here. It is American" (p. 239). Justice Clarence Thomas, in another concurring opinion, described such programs as patronizing and paternalistic measures that prevented blacks from competing on terms that could prove their real worth.

The dissenters, led by Justice John Paul Stevens, insisted that the nation's unhappy history of race relations required the federal government to take remedial action. Justice Ruth Bader Ginsburg's dissent took specific exception to Scalia and Thomas by arguing that a carefully designed affirmative action program could work well within the confines of the Equal Protection Clause of the Fourteenth Amendment. In any case, Ginsburg insisted, the responsibility for crafting such plans rested with legislative bodies, and she chided the majority, which usually paid homage to the primacy of Congress, for failing to do so in this instance.

The Court's action did explicitly overrule *Metro Broadcasting*, but they did not overturn the Small Business Administration program. The case went back to the lower courts to determine whether the program violated the very demanding strict scrutiny test. Still, the message from the Court about affirmative action was that for any program to have a chance of passing constitutional muster it had to be narrowly tailored and it had to apply to individuals who were victims of past discrimination rather than simply helping any and all minorities.

Kermit L. Hall

Adkins v. Children's Hospital, 261 U.S. 525 (1923), argued 14 Mar. 1923, decided 9 Apr. 1923 by vote of 5 to 3; Sutherland for the Court, Taft and Holmes in dissent, Brandeis not participating. Reflecting widespread popular acceptance of laissez-faire economics, the Supreme Court in the 1890s fashioned the liberty of contract doctrine, which affirmed the constitutional right of private parties to enter contractual arrangements. This doctrine curtailed the power of government to interfere with contractual freedom through regulatory legislation. The landmark *Adkins* decision exemplified the Court's commitment to laissez-faire principles and the liberty of contract.

At issue in *Adkins* was a 1918 federal law establishing a minimum wage for women in the District of Columbia. The announced purpose of the act was to protect the health and morals of women from detrimental living conditions caused by inadequate wages. Felix Frankfurter, a future Supreme Court justice, appeared as counsel in support of the legislation. He sought to justify the measure as a valid exercise of the police power to ameliorate the handicaps experienced by women in the marketplace. Children's Hospital, on the other hand, contended that the statute was a price-fixing law that unconstitutionally interfered with the liberty of contract for employment.

Justice George Sutherland, speaking for the majority, invalidated the minimum wage law as a violation of the liberty of contract guaranteed by the due process clause of the Fifth Amendment. Although Sutherland recognized that the terms of contracts could be regulated in certain situations, he stressed that "freedom of contract is . . . the general rule and restraint the exception"

(p. 546). Distinguishing wage laws from measures limiting the hours of labor, he reasoned that the minimum wage law arbitrarily cast upon employers a welfare function that belonged to society at large. In view of the Nineteenth Amendment and changes in the legal position of women, Sutherland further maintained that women could not be subjected to greater restrictions on their liberty of contract than men. He argued that the minimum wage law disregarded the "moral requirement implicit in every contract of employment" that the value of labor and wages should be equivalent (p. 558). In short, wages must be ascertained by the operation of the free market.

In a forceful dissent, Chief Justice William Howard Taft asserted that lawmakers could limit the freedom of contract under the police power to regulate the maximum hours or minimum wages of women. He cautioned that the justices should not strike down regulatory statutes simply because they deem particular economic policies to be unwise. Justice Oliver Wendell Holmes questioned the constitutional basis of the liberty of contract doctrine. Noting that "pretty much all law consists in forbidding men to do some things that they want to do," Holmes pointed out that the Court had sustained many laws that limited contractual freedom (p. 568). He argued that legislators might reasonably conclude that fixing minimum wages for female employees would improve their health and morals.

The *Adkins* decision was a striking expression of laissez-faire constitutionalism. It demonstrated the Court's conviction that wage and price determinations were at the heart of the free market economy and must be secured against unwarranted legislative interference. During the 1920s and early 1930s the Supreme Court frequently cited *Adkins* for a broad interpretation of the liberty of contract doctrine. In particular, the justices invoked *Adkins* to overturn several state minimum wage laws.

As a consequence of the Great Depression and the political triumph of the New Deal, the Supreme Court in 1937 abandoned laissez-faire constitutionalism and permitted both federal and state governments to play a major role in directing economic life. The Court's new outlook was revealed in **West Coast Hotel* v. *Parrish* (1937), in which the justices narrowly upheld a Washington minimum wage law for women and minors and overruled *Adkins*. The decision in *West*

Coast Hotel marked the effective end of the liberty of contract doctrine as a constitutional norm.

□ Joel Francis Paschal, *Mr. Justice Sutherland: A Man Against the State* (1951).

James W. Ely, Jr.

Agostini v. Felton, 521 U.S. 203 (1997), argued 15 Apr. 1997, decided 23 June 1997 by vote of 5 to 4; O'Connor for the Court, Souter and Ginsburg in dissent.

Few issues have proved more vexing for the modern Supreme Court than the relationship between church and state. In 1985 the Court had reached something of a high-water mark in its efforts to drive a clear constitutional wedge between the two. By a 5-to-4 majority the justices in *Aguilar v. Felton* and its companion case of *School District of Grand Rapids* v. *Ball* (1985) gave a new interpretation to Title I of the Elementary and Secondary Education Action of 1965. Title I provided federal funds to public schools for remedial reading and math instruction to children from poor families without regard to the school they attended. Under this law public school teachers entered parochial schools to teach, often doing so on a voluntary basis. The Supreme Court in *Aguilar,* however, decided that the presence of public school teachers in parochial schools amounted to an unconstitutional entanglement of church and state in violation of the Establishment Clause of the First Amendment. In New York City, where both *Aguilar* and *Agostini* originated, public officials responded by spending more than $100 million in federal education funds to provide Title I services by, among other actions, leasing vans that were then parked on public streets just outside the religious schools. These mobile classrooms served more than twenty thousand students a year and required parochial school students and public school teachers to leave their classrooms and meet on seemingly neutral ground.

A majority of the justices themselves had invited the litigation that resulted in the *Agostini* decision. In *Kiryas Joel Board of Education* v. *Grumet* (1994), the justices indicated that they would welcome an appeal that would result in a reconsideration of *Aguilar* and, perhaps, its overruling. A year later the School Board of the City of New York responded to this invitation by taking the unusual step of filing a motion in Federal

District Court in Brooklyn under Rule 60(b) of the Federal Rules of Civil Procedure. That particular rule permitted a party to seek a motion to lift a court order when circumstances had so changed that the effect of the original order had become inequitable. Both the federal district court and the United States Court of Appeals for the Second Circuit refused to grant the motion because they said only the Supreme Court could reverse its own precedents. The justices accepted the case but they refused to apply Rule 60(b) to their decision, recognizing that if they did so, they would invite a flood of appeals from parties who had concluded that the justices were ready to abandon a precedent.

Justice Sandra Day O'Connor's opinion instead insisted that the Court had already over-ruled *Aguilar.* Citing two cases, *Witters* v. *Washington* (1986) and *Zobrest* v. *Catalina Foothills School District* (1993), a narrow majority repudiated several of the major presumptions applied in *Aguilar.* First, the Court disavowed the view that all government aid directed to the educational function of religious schools is unconstitutional. Public money could be made available to all students for secular purposes without violating the Establishment Clause. Second, it was entirely possible for on-premise programs conducted by public school teachers to be free of any religious connection. Third, O'Connor found that school boards were competent to erect administrative guidelines that would ensure that teachers performed in a neutral fashion without resorting to excessive monitoring and hence an entanglement of church and state. Finally, according to O'Connor, there was no reason to believe that the parents of secular school students would conclude that the presence of public school teachers in sectarian classrooms meant that the New York City Board of Education had placed its stamp of approval on religious education.

The dissenters, led by Justice David Souter, accused the majority of playing fast and loose with earlier rulings. According to Souter the previous decisions cited by the majority were limited rulings; the Court had not overturned *Aguilar.* Moreover, Souter continued, the Court's new ruling would authorize direct state aid to religious institutions and invite massive violations of the First Amendment's Establishment Clause.

The decision may have produced more smoke than light. As Justice O'Connor asserted, the law in question had never provided public funds to religious schools, and the overall effect was to help needy students suffering from academic deficiencies. Both proponents and opponents of various school voucher programs, which permit parents to pay parochial school tuition with public funds, placed their own conflicting meanings on the decision. Yet O'Connor's narrowly crafted opinion seemed an uncertain predictor of what the justices might do in a future case that raised the constitutional fate of vouchers directly.

Kermit L. Hall

Akron v. Akron Center for Reproductive Health, Inc., 462 U.S. 416 (1983), argued 30 Nov. 1982, decided 15 June 1983 by vote of 6 to 3; Powell for the Court, O'Connor, with White and Rehnquist, in dissent. The Court invalidated a number of restrictions imposed by the city of Akron, Ohio, on abortion: a ban on performing second-trimester abortions in clinics rather than hospitals, a requirement that physicians provide detailed information about abortions to women before they signed consent forms, and a twenty-four-hour waiting period between giving consent and having an abortion. The Court said that the hospital requirement increased the cost of abortions without a significant increase in the woman's safety, that the information specified by the ordinance was designed to persuade the woman not to have an abortion rather than to inform her about the procedure, and that the waiting period increased costs by requiring two trips and was unnecessarily inflexible.

Justice Sandra Day O'Connor wrote her first major abortion opinion in this case. She criticized the trimester approach adopted in *Roe* v. *Wade* as rigid and likely to come under strain as medical technology pushed the time of viability back into the second trimester or even earlier. She proposed that regulations of abortion be permitted unless they placed an "undue burden" on a woman's decision. For her, neither the hospitalization nor the waiting period did so, because abortions were available in local hospitals and the waiting period was "a small cost to impose to ensure that the woman's decision is well-considered in light of its certain and irreparable consequences on fetal life" (p. 474). With O'Connor in the majority, the justices also invoked the "undue burden" principle in *Planned Parenthood of Southeastern Pennsylvania* v. *Casey* (1992) while

sustaining a Pennsylvania law that had many of the same features of the Akron ordinance. The justices refused, however, to renounce their decision in *Roe*.

Mark V. Tushnet

Albemarle Paper Co. v. Moody, 422 U.S. 405 (1975), argued 14 Apr. 1975, decided 25 June 1975 by vote of 7 to 1; Stewart for the Court, Marshall, Rehnquist, and Blackmun concurring, Burger dissenting in part, Powell not participating. This case and *United Papermakers and Paperworkers* v. *Moody* were decided in the same opinion and dealt with two important issues under Title VII of the Civil Rights Act of 1964: (1) the standards a district court should use in deciding back pay awards to employees who suffered monetary loss because of racial discrimination; and (2) the requirements placed upon an employer to establish that preemployment tests that have a discriminatory effect are sufficiently "job related" to survive a legal challenge.

The plaintiffs in *Moody* consisted of present and former African-American employees of Albemarle Paper Company's mill in Roanoke Rapids, North Carolina. They charged that the company's seniority system perpetuated the overt segregation that existed in the plant's departmental job assignment system prior to 2 July 1965 (the effective date of Title VII), and they sought injunctive and back pay relief.

The Court found that tests used by the company were not sufficiently job related to be valid under Title VII and held that the trial court should have enjoined the use of the tests and awarded back pay. In deciding the issue of back pay awards, the Court ruled that such awards should follow closely upon a finding of discrimination and that ordering back pay was an appropriate incentive to employers to comply with Title VII. It concluded that the certainty of the remedy would best effectuate the statute. In all essential aspects this holding continues to provide a major form of relief under Title VII.

Herbert Hill

Albertson v. Subversive Activities Control Board, 382 U.S. 70 (1965), argued 18 Oct. 1965, decided 15 Nov. 1965 by vote of 8 to 0; Brennan for the Court, White not participating. The Internal Security Act, passed over President Truman's veto in 1950 and generally known as the McCarran Act, sought to expose the Communist party in the United States by the device of compulsory registration. The statute ordered communist organizations to register with the attorney general; the Subversive Activities Control Board (SACB) was created to administer the registration process. Registered organizations were required to disclose the names of their officers and the source of their funds. Members of registered organizations were subject to various sanctions, including denial of passports and the right to work in defense plants. The Supreme Court upheld the registration requirements in *Communist Party v. Subversive Activities Control Board (1961) but postponed any decision on the constitutionality of the sanctions until they were actually enforced.

As anticipated, the Communist party refused to register. The attorney general then asked the SACB to order individual party members to register. Albertson and others refused, claiming that registration, with resulting penalties, amounted to self-incrimination in violation of the Fifth Amendment. The Supreme Court unanimously agreed. While the statute purportedly granted immunity from prosecution for the act of registration, the Court held that registration could in fact be used as evidence in criminal prosecutions, or to supply investigatory leads.

The SACB was no more successful in other cases. The ban on defense plant employment was struck down in United States v. *Robel (1967). With this record of futility, the Nixon Administration allowed the SACB to die in 1973.

C. Herman Pritchett

Allegheny County v. ACLU Greater Pittsburgh Chapter, 492 U.S. 573 (1989), argued 22 Feb. 1989, decided 3 July 1989 by votes of 5 to 4 (to strike) and 6 to 3 (to uphold), Blackmun announced the judgment, O'Connor concurring in part, Brennan and Stevens concurring in part and dissenting in part, Kennedy concurring in judgment in part and dissenting in part. The Supreme Court's policy of the early 1980s favoring religious accommodation was manifest in *Lynch v. Donnelly (1984). There, against a challenge brought by the American Civil Liberties Union, it upheld a publicly sponsored Christmas display by a 5-to-4 vote. Applying the three-part "test" enunciated in *Lemon v. Kurtzman (1971), the Court held that in the context of a larger display—which

included a Santa, reindeers, and talking wishing wells—a creche had a secular purpose, did not have a primary effect advancing or inhibiting religion, and did not excessively entangle church and state. In Allegheny, the Court refused to extend Lynch to approve a seasonal display that focused predominantly on religious symbols.

Justice Harry Blackmun announced the judgment of the Court in an opinion joined only by Justice Sandra Day O'Connor. He held that the context contemplated by Lynch was the display itself, not that of the general holiday season. Thus, a creche—unadorned by other, more secular objects—could not constitutionally be placed in the public display of a country courthouse. A menorah, however, could occupy a similar setting, so long as it was in a context—surrounded by secular symbols—that emphasized the diversity of the holiday. Brennan, Marshall, and Stevens would have struck both displays; Rehnquist, White, Scalia, and Kennedy would have up-held them.

Joseph F. Kobylka

Allgeyer v. Louisiana, 165 U.S. 578 (1897), submitted 6 Jan. 1897, decided 1 Mar. 1897 by vote of 9 to o; Peckham for the Court. In Allgeyer v. Louisiana the Supreme Court for the first time ruled a state law unconstitutional for depriving a person of the right to make contracts. The case arose in Louisiana, which like other states prohibited businesses from operating within its jurisdiction unless they met certain conditions. To enforce this policy, Louisiana made it illegal for Louisianans to enter into certain insurance contracts by mail with companies operating outside the state. Allgeyer & Co. was prosecuted for entering into such an insurance contract with a New York company.

The Court had earlier held that insurance was not interstate commerce and so could not rule the Louisiana law unconstitutional for invading national jurisdiction. Instead, the Court held that the contract was effected in New York and lawful under New York. The Court then held that the Due Process Clause of the Fourteenth Amendment guaranteed the right to enter into lawful contracts.

Allgeyer v. Louisiana became the key case establishing the doctrine of "liberty of contract." Although the opinion itself only declared that the right to make lawful contracts was a liberty protected by the Due Process Clause, the courts developed the principle that freedom of contract was the rule and restraint the exception, the reasonability of which states had to justify. Employers regularly cited this principle to challenge legislation regulating terms of employment—setting maximum working hours or minimum wages, for example. Until the mid-1930s such challenges often were successful.

Michael Les Benedict

American Communications Association v. Douds, 339 U.S. 382 (1950), argued 10–11 Oct. 1949, decided 8 May 1950 by vote of 5 to 1; Vinson for the Court, Frankfurter concurring in part, Jackson concurring and dissenting, Black in dissent; Douglas, Clark, and Minton not participating. This case involved the constitutionality of cold war-era anticommunist legislation. The Supreme Court upheld section 9(h) of the Taft-Hartley Act (1947), which required officers of labor unions to sign affidavits indicating that they were not Communist party members or supporters and did not believe in unlawful overthrow of the U.S. government. Unions whose officers did not sign affidavits were unable to seek relief before the National Labor Relations Board for unfair labor practices.

The Court did not rest its judgment on a threat to national security, but on a threat to interstate commerce. The majority found that the statute fell within the broad scope of Congress's commerce power because the Communist party could reasonably be expected to engage in political strikes that were disruptive of the national economy. The Court recognized that the statute had a chilling effect on political rights protected by the First Amendment. Nevertheless, it ruled that the First Amendment was not violated because that statute protected the public from harmful conduct—political strikes— not harmful ideas. The Court then applied the clear and present danger test as a simple balancing test and concluded that Congress's interest in protecting the nation from political strikes outweighed the burden the act placed on the rights of union members.

Although *Douds* has not been specifically overturned, it is dubious authority. The statute replacing section 9(h) was struck down by the court in *United States* v. *Brown* (1965).

Mary L. Dudziak

American Insurance Company v. Canter, 1 Pet. (26 U.S.) 511 (1828), argued 8, 10, 11 Mar. 1828, decided 15 Mar. 1828 by vote of 7 to 0; Marshall for the Court. Questions of federalism were among the most difficult confronting the early Supreme Court. One of them was the appropriate division of admiralty and maritime jurisdiction between federal superior courts for the Florida territory and certain lesser courts that Congress had authorized the territory itself to establish. The *American Insurance Company* case involved an appeal by a libellant in admiralty from a salvage award by a local court in the Florida territory. The larger questions presented by the case included the power of Congress to acquire and govern territories and the source of that power; the division of jurisdiction between federal and local courts; the scope of the admiralty and maritime jurisdiction conferred by Article III; and the sources of law in the territories.

For a unanimous Court, Chief Justice John Marshall affirmed the award by the local court, explaining that when Congress had granted federal superior courts in the territory partial Article III jurisdiction, it had not conferred on them the full measure of federal judicial power. The Constitution extended such power to, *inter alia*, cases arising under the federal Constitution, laws, or treaties; and admiralty and maritime cases. Thus admiralty suits were not among those arising under the "laws and constitution of the United States" but were instead "as old as navigation itself; and the law admiralty and maritimes, as it has existed for ages, is applied by our courts to the cases as they arise" (p. 544). Marshall also stated that Congress derived plenary power to acquire and govern territories from the territories clause of Article IV, a position ignored by Chief Justice Roger B. Taney in the *Dred *Scott Case (1857).

Ralph James Mooney

American Library Association., Inc., United States v., 539 U. S. 194 (2003). Argued 5 March 2003, decided 23 June 2003 by vote of 6 to 3; Rehnquist for the Court, Kennedy and Breyer concurring, Stevens, Souter, and Ginsburg dissenting.

Congress enacted the Children's Internet Protection Act (CIPA) to prevent minors from using public libraries' Internet terminals to access obscene images. CIPA stipulated that public libraries could not receive federal assistance to provide Internet access unless they installed in their terminals software to block websites that purveyed such images.

Under the doctrine that Congress may not induce recipients of federal assistance to perform unconstitutional acts, Chief Justice William Rehnquist argued that public libraries' mission is to provide materials of the greatest benefit to the community; that Internet access in public libraries is not a protected public forum; that adult patrons can easily obtain access to an unblocked terminal by asking a librarian; and that the government is entitled to define the limits of the programs it establishes. From these premises, Rehnquist concluded that CIPA did not induce public libraries to perform unconstitutional acts.

Justice John Paul Stevens dissented on the ground that CIPA impermissibly conditioned receipt of government funding on the restriction of First Amendment rights because CIPA denied the libraries any discretion in judging the merits of the blocked websites.

Justice David Souter, with Ginsburg joining, dissented on the ground that blocking an adult's access to material harmful to minors is constitutionally impermissible content-based restriction on the communication of material in the library's control. He argued that strict scrutiny ought to have been applied, and that CIPA would fail this test because it was not narrowly enough tailored to achieve the government's compelling interest in protecting minors from accessing obscene images without infringing the fundamental rights of adult library patrons. In Justice Souter's view, CIPA's terms did *not* ensure that an adult library patron could obtain an unblocked terminal by simply asking.

T. J. Donahue

The Amistad, 40 U.S. 518 (1841), argued 22–24 February 1841, decided 9 March 1841 by vote of 7 to 1; Story for the Court, Baldwin in dissent. *The Amistad,* known formally as *United States v. The Libellants and Claimants of the Schooner Amistad, her Tackle, Apparel and Furniture, together with her Cargo, and the Africans mentioned in the Several Libels and Claims,* was one of the most significant cases involving slavery to come before the Supreme Court.

On 28 June 1839, the schooner *Amistad* left Havana for Puerto Principe, a Cuban coastal town. Its crew consisted of five whites, a mulatto cook, and a black cabin boy along with a cargo of wine, gold, silk, saddles, and fifty-three slaves, forty-nine adults and four children. The slaves had been recently imported from Africa in violation of Spanish law. On the fourth night at sea, the slaves freed themselves and mutinied, killing the captain and the mulatto cook. Two of the crew escaped overboard. The two owners of the slaves, Jose Ruiz and Pedro Montes, both citizens of Spain, barely escaped being murdered, apparently because the African mutineers realized that they needed them in order to sail the ship. Over the next six weeks the slaves commanded Montes to sail back to their homeland, present-day Sierra Leone. Instead, Montes guided the ship on a zig-zag course to the eastern shore of Long Island. There, on 26 August 1839, the ship and its cargo were discovered, first by two sea captains shooting birds, and then by the U.S. Coast Guard brig *Washington.* Both the sea captains and the crew of the *Washington* laid claim to the cargo under the law of salvage. The *Washington* seized the *Amistad* and its cargo, including the slaves, and took them to New London, Connecticut.

Over the next two years the slaves and their ostensible owners became engulfed in a major *cause celebre* that energized the fledgling anti-slavery movement and intensified the conflict over slavery. A small but energetic group of abolitionists, headed by Lewis Tappan, organized the "Amistad Committee" to seek funds and legal support for the captured Africans. The administration of President Martin Van Buren, on the other hand, insisted that the slaves and the cargo should be turned over to their Spanish owners under the provisions of a treaty with Spain of 1795. That agreement provided that property of one country taken possession of in the territorial waters of another country had to be returned to their owners. The Van Buren administration urged the federal court in Connecticut to comply with the request of the Spanish government that the "slaves" be extradited to Spain to stand trial for murder and mutiny and that the cargo be returned to its owners. Failing that action, the United States wanted the Africans tried as criminals in the United States.

In the lower federal courts, Roger S. Baldwin, a future governor of Connecticut, argued on behalf of the Africans. Baldwin insisted that the alleged mutiny had occurred in international waters and therefore the United States had no jurisdiction to punish the Africans. Baldwin also argued that the United States should not act as a slave-catcher for foreign slave-holders, especially since Spanish law explicitly disavowed the African slave trade. Justice Smith Thompson, who presided over the case as part of his circuit-riding duties, found in favor of the Africans. Thompson, however, refused to decide the question of whether they were slaves and, as such, the property of Ruiz and Montes. Instead, he ordered a civil trial to determine their status.

The civil trial began in New Haven on 8 January 1840. President Van Buren, in anticipating the outcome, ordered a naval warship to stand by in the harbor to whisk the Africans back to Havana before they could file an appeal. The court, however, found for the Africans. Baldwin filled the courtroom with horrific stories of the Middle Passage and abuse of the Africans by the Spanish. District Judge Andrew T. Judson responded by finding that the Africans had been born free, that they were kidnapped from their homeland of Africa, and that they should be returned there. The Van Buren administration immediately appealed, but Justice Thompson, on circuit, upheld Judson's ruling, modifying it only to provide that the decision about returning to Africa was entirely the choice of the Africans. The United States government had no obligation to pay their way back home, a clearly gratuitous holding since the Africans were essentially destitute.

The Van Buren administration appealed again, this time to the Supreme Court. Such an appeal made sense, because five of the nine justices were southerners who either owned or had owned slaves. Van Buren also believed that maintaining strong relations with Spain depended on complying fully with the 1795 treaty.

Fearing the high court might overturn the victories won below, Tappan persuaded Congressman and former President John Quincy Adams, then 74, to join with Baldwin in arguing the case before the high court. Adams launched a blistering attack against the actions of President Van Buren and the entire notion that the chief executive had a duty to return slaves based on the 1795 treaty. Adams also ridiculed southern intellectuals for their defense of slavery, invoked the Bible in support of the proposition that public officials had a duty to provide for human freedom, and insisted that the Declaration of Independence, with its claim that all men are created equal, settled the matter of how to dispose of the Africans.

Justice Joseph Story wrote for the majority. (During the time between the oral arguments and the decision by the Court, Justice Phillip P. Barbour died.) Story leaned heavily on the narrow legal reasoning of Roger Baldwin rather than Adams's extraordinarily powerful yet bitterly sarcastic arguments. Story found that the Africans had been kidnapped; they were "property rescued from pirates" (p. 132). Given this reality, Story concluded that even under the laws of Spain the slaves were due their freedom. The United States government had no responsibility to return them either to the Spanish government or to Ruiz and Montes. Story insisted that the 1795 treaty, when it addressed the issue of returning "merchandize," meant goods, not human beings. For slaves to be returned as property under international law, the treaty governing them had to specify explicitly that "property" meant slaves. The 1795 treaty did not. According to Story, the condition of being property could not be implied to human beings. Story also affirmed Thompson's finding that the Africans were free to stay in or leave the United States, but the government had no obligation to pay for their travel back to Sierra Leone. Justice Henry Baldwin of Pennsylvania casted a lone, unwritten dissent.

The Amistad Committee eventually raised sufficient funds to pay for the return voyage of the Africans, who left in November 1841. Only one African, Sarah, ever returned to America. She attended Oberlin College. For the next two decades the Spanish government pressed the United States for compensation, but John Quincy Adams led the opposition against that effort until his death in 1847. With the election of President Abraham Lincoln in 1860, Spain's efforts ended and the debate over slavery passed from the courtroom to the battlefield.

Kermit L. Hall

Apodaca v. Oregon, 406 U.S. 404 (1972), argued 1 Mar. 1971, reargued 10 Jan. 1972, decided 22 May 1972 by vote of 5 to 4; White for the plurality, Blackmun concurring, Powell concurring in the judgment, Douglas, Brennan, Stewart, and Marshall in dissent. Until 1970 it was assumed that juries consisted of twelve members and that unanimous votes were required. *Williams v. Florida* (1970), however, permitted state juries of fewer than twelve members. *Apodaca,* a companion case to *Johnson* v. *Louisiana* (1972), held that the Sixth Amendment jury trial guarantee, applied to the states by the Fourteenth Amendment, does not require a unanimous jury verdict in noncapital state criminal cases.

The plurality was unable to decide whether Congress, when it passed the Sixth Amendment in 1789, had intended to freeze the size of the jury at twelve. On balance it decided that the right to trial by jury was primarily designed to protect against corrupt or over-zealous prosecutors or judges and therefore "perceive[d] no difference between juries required to act unanimously and those permitted to convict or acquit by votes of 10–2 or 11–1" (p. 411). *Johnson* permitted conviction by a 9-to-3 vote.

Justice Lewis Powell, whose concurrence provided the controlling vote, believed that the Sixth Amendment did require unanimity but that the Fourteenth Amendment did not apply all elements of the Sixth Amendment to the states: the states could employ nonunanimous juries, but the federal courts could not. The dissenters argued that a nonunanimous verdict in either state or federal courts was inconsistent with the constitutional requirement that a criminal jury's decision be "beyond a reasonable doubt." Thus, while separate majorities held that the Sixth Amendment required unanimous jury verdicts and that the Fourteenth Amendment incorporated the Sixth in its entirety, the net result was that the states may employ nonunanimous juries. *Apodaca* and *Johnson* still govern, but few states have adopted the jury nonunanimity rule in criminal cases. The Court subsequently raised doubts about the statistied assumptions on which *Apodaca* was based in *Ballew* v. *Georgia* (1978).

Stephen E. Gottlieb

Aptheker v. Secretary of State, 378 U.S. 500 (1964), argued 21 Apr. 1964, decided 22 June 1964 by vote of 6 to 3; Goldberg for the Court, Clark, Harlan, and White in dissent. The Passport Act of 1926 authorized the secretary of state to grant passports, required for foreign travel, to American citizens. Under pressure of the Cold War following World War II, the State Department adopted a policy of refusing passports to American communists or persons whose travel abroad would prejudice the interests of the United States. This policy generated widespread controversy, and many persons were denied passports who asserted they were not communists. In *Kent* v. *Dulles* (1958) the Supreme Court ruled that the

right of American citizens to travel across national frontiers was a part of the "liberty" protected by the Fifth Amendment, and that the secretary of state was not authorized by the Passport Act to promulgate regulations denying passports.

Another statute was available, however. The Internal Security Act of 1950 required all "communist-action" organizations to register with the attorney general and denied passports to members of such organizations. The registration provisions were upheld by the Supreme Court in *Communist Party* v. *Subversive Activities Control Board* (1961). But the State Department's effort to resume passport denials under this authorization was rejected in *Aptheker* v. *Secretary of State* (1964), involving two leading members of the American Communist party. Justice Arthur Goldberg recognized that the right to travel was not absolute but held that the language of the Internal Security Act was too broad, taking no account of individual communists' degree of activity in the organization or the purposes of their travel. However, restrictions on travel to particular countries or specific areas were subsequently upheld in *Zemel* v. *Rusk* (1965).

C. Herman Pritchett

Argersinger v. Hamlin, 407 U.S. 25 (1972), argued 6 Dec. 1971, reargued 28 Feb. 1972, decided 12 June 1972 by vote of 9 to 0; Douglas for the Court; Brennan, Stewart, Burger, Powell, and Rehnquist concurring.

Argersinger was charged with carrying a concealed weapon, an offense punishable by imprisonment up to six months, a thousand-dollar fine, or both. Indigent, he was tried without counsel by a judge, found guilty, and sentenced to ninety days in jail. Argersinger then filed a habeas corpus action in the Florida Supreme Court alleging that he was deprived of his Sixth Amendment right to counsel. The Florida court rejected his claim.

The U.S. Supreme Court reversed. It extended *Gideon* v. *Wainwright* (1963), holding that "absent a knowing and intelligent waiver, no person may be imprisoned for any offense, whether classified as petty, misdemeanor, or felony, unless he was represented by [appointed or retained] counsel at his trial" (p. 37). In concurrence, Justice Lewis F. Powell expressed concern that the majority's decision would substantially burden the already congested criminal justice system and would allow those fined rather than imprisoned to present equal protection challenges.

Seven years later in *Scott* v. *Illinois* (1979), the Court clarified its *Argersinger* decision, holding that defendants charged with offenses where imprisonment is authorized but not actually imposed do not have a Sixth Amendment right to counsel. The Court also noted that despite concerns when *Argersinger* was decided, the decision had proved "reasonably workable" (p. 373).

Susan E. Lawrence

Arizona v. Fulminante, 499 U.S. 279 (1991), argued 10 Oct. 1990, decided 26 Mar. 1991 by vote of 5 to 4; Rehnquist and White for the Court, White, Blackmun, Marshall, and Stevens in dissent on various parts of the opinion. This case produced one of the most fractured divisions among the justices in the history of the Court. Chief Justice William Rehnquist wrote the opinion for the Court, but he did so only on certain aspects of the case, while Justice Byron R. White wrote for a majority in two other important areas.

The case began in 1982 with the abuse and murder near Mesa, Arizona, of an eleven-year-old girl, the stepdaughter of Oreste Fulminante. Fulminante was considered a prime suspect, but there was insufficient evidence to bring a charge. Shortly thereafter he was arrested in New Jersey for gun possession and placed in a federal prison in New York. While incarcerated there, word spread among the convicts that Fulminante had murdered the young girl. As a result, the other prisoners directed a program of intimidation and harassment at him, making the slightly built prisoner fear for his life. Fulminante befriended one of the inmates, who offered to extend protection to him, but only if he told him the truth about the murder. The other inmate, unknown to Fulminante, was also an informant for the Federal Bureau of Investigation. Not only did Fulminante confess to the informant about the crime but he said the same things to the informant's wife when released from prison. As a result, he was convicted in Arizona and sentenced to death.

Fulminante appealed the conviction to the Arizona Supreme Court, arguing that his confession had been coerced and then improperly admitted. Counsel for Fulminante cited the Supreme Court's decision in *Chapman* v. *California* (1967) to claim that three forms of governmental misconduct—coerced confessions, absence of counsel, and a biased judge—had been sufficient to automatically invalidate a conviction and trigger a new trial. None of these practices could be considered "harmless error," a category of government action that, while not approved of, was, according to *Chapman*, not sufficient to overturn a conviction. The "harmless error" analysis meant that some kinds of actions, such as improper jury instructions or the exclusion of certain testimony, could be overlooked if other evidence would have produced the same result at trial.

Before the high court the case produced the unusual outcome of two opinions. One block of justices, led by Justice Byron R. White, agreed with the Arizona Supreme Court that Fulminante deserved a new trial free from any reference to the confession that he gave the FBI informant and his wife. At the same time, however, Chief Justice William H. Rehnquist produced another majority that held that while Fulminante deserved a new trial, coerced confessions were not automatically excluded from harmless error analysis. In this instance, Justice Anthony Kennedy joined the chief justice and deserted Justices Thurgood Marshall, Harry Blackmun, and John Paul Stevens. Justice David Souter, newly appointed to the Court by President George Bush, sided with the chief justice. Souter, of course, had replaced Justice William J. Brennan, Jr., who had been one of the steadfast supporters of the Court's position that coerced confessions could never fall under harmless error analysis.

Thus the new conservative majority on the Rehnquist Court overturned many decades of precedent requiring appeals judges to dismiss any case that included a coerced confession. In its place the Court substituted a new standard. If it could be shown that other evidence, obtained independently of the confession, was also introduced at trial and was adequate to sustain a verdict of guilty, the conviction should hold no matter the nature of the confession. According to Rehnquist, this new standard meant that the use of a tainted confession must be harmless beyond a reasonable doubt. The introduction of a coerced confession was appropriate because such a confession was simply a trial error that could be quantitatively assessed in the context of other evidence presented. White, however, countered that the Court had dislodged one of the fundamental tenets of the criminal justice system. The decision, according to its critics, encouraged law enforcement officials to break the rules and retreat from a long-held position that coerced confessions were almost in a class by themselves as a form of governmental misconduct. "Ours is an accusatorial and not an inquisitorial system," they proclaimed (p. 293). In practice, however, the impact of the Court's decision has been relatively slight, and appellate courts have continued to reverse convictions based mainly on coerced confessions. What the longer term impact of *Fulminante* will be remains to be seen.

Kermit L. Hall

Arlington Heights v. Metropolitan Housing Development Corp., 429 U.S. 252 (1977), argued 13 Oct. 1976, decided 11 Jan. 1977 by vote of 7 to 1; Powell for the Court, Marshall and Brennan concurring in part and dissenting in part, White in dissent; Stevens not participating. The case originated in an attempt by the Metropolitan Housing Development Corp. (MHDC), a nonprofit developer, to build racially integrated low- and moderate-income housing in the Chicago suburb of Arlington Heights. The village Board of Trustees denied MHDC's rezoning petition, thus preventing it from building. MHDC then brought suit in federal district court alleging that the denial was racially discriminatory in violation of both the Fourteenth Amendment of the U.S. Constitution and federal law. The district court upheld the village's decision but was reversed by the U.S. Court of Appeals for the Seventh Circuit.

In the Supreme Court the crucial issue was the standard for proving racial discrimination under the Fourteenth Amendment; the decision focused on the difference between a racially disproportionate impact and racially discriminatory intent. The Court, following *Washington v. Davis* (1976), rejected a showing only of racially disproportionate impact. It held that proof of racially discriminatory intent or purpose was necessary to make out a constitutional violation. Examining the historical background of the zoning decision, the sequence of events leading up to it, and the official minutes, the Court held that the original plaintiffs had failed to prove that racial discrimination was a motivating factor in the village's decision. The court of appeals' decision was reversed and remanded for consideration of the statutory claim.

The decision has been criticized for giving insufficient direction as to what counts as proof of discriminatory purpose and for maintaining high barriers for overcoming housing discrimination, both locally and nationally. When the case was argued, only 27 (.04 percent) of the village's 64,000 residents were African-American. The village estimates that in 1989 that number had risen only to approximately 300 (.4 percent) of its more than 75,000 residents.

Gerald N. Rosenberg

Armstrong, United States v., 517 U.S. 456, 116 S.Ct. 1480, 134 L.Ed.2d 687, argued 26 Feb. 1996, decided 13 May 1996 by a vote of 8 to 1 Chief Justice Rehnquist delivered the opinion of the Court, Justices Souter and Ginsburg filed concurring opinions, Justice Breyer filed an opinion concurring in part and concurring in the judgment, and Justice Stevens filed a dissenting opinion. Armstrong, an African-American from Los Angeles, California, challenged his federal indictment for conspiracy to distribute "crack" cocaine on the ground that he was selected for prosecution because of his race, in violation of the equal protection component of the Due Process Clause of the Fifth Amendment. The majority held that he was not entitled to discovery because he failed to show that the government declined to prosecute similarly situated suspects of other races. Although defendant presented some evidence that every crack cocaine case prosecuted in Los Angeles concerned a black defendant, and that federal drug sentencing laws have a discriminatory effect, he failed to identify individuals who were not black and who could have been prosecuted but were not. The Court rejected the Ninth Circuit's presumption that "people of *all* races commit *all* types of crimes."

Justice John Paul Stevens, in a dissent since championed by many scholars, was the sole justice to review the political and social context of the defendants' claim. First, he noted that the Anti-Drug Abuse Act of 1986 treats one gram of crack cocaine as the equivalent of 100 grams of powder cocaine for sentencing purposes, leading to sentences for crack offenders that average three to eight times longer than sentences for comparable powder defendants. He further documents that while 55 percent of persons who have used crack are white, they represent only 4 percent of federal offenders convicted of trafficking in crack, leading to an average sentence for blacks of over 40 percent longer than for whites. He argued that this troubling racial pattern of enforcement, coupled with the United States' legacy of slavery, should permit the discovery order.

The Court reiterated the extraordinarily high showing a defendant must make in order to obtain discovery on a selective prosecution claim in *United States* v. *Bass* (2002). There, the Court, in a per curiam opinion, reversed a discovery order issued by the Sixth Circuit in favor of a black defendant who argued that nationwide statistics demonstrated that the United States charges blacks with death-eligible offenses more than twice as often as it charges whites. Raw statistics regarding overall charges, the Court said, say nothing about charges brought against "similarly situated defendants."

Susan R. Klein

Ashwander v. Tennessee Valley Authority, 297 U.S. 288 (1936), argued 19–20 Dec. 1935, decided 17 Feb. 1936 by vote of 8 to 1; Hughes for the Court, Brandeis concurring, McReynolds in dissent. Claiming that the Tennessee Valley Authority Act was unconstitutional, minority shareholders of a utility company sought to annul their board's agreement to purchase electricity from the T.V.A. The Court upheld the act and found Congress had authority to construct dams for national defense and improve interstate commerce. The sale of electricity—a byproduct—was authorized by Article IV, section 3 of the Constitution, granting the federal government power to sell property it lawfully acquires.

Justice Louis Brandeis believed the constitutional question should never have been addressed because the case involved a simple internal dispute among shareholders. He maintained that the Court should avoid making decisions on the constitutionality of legislation, and the case is remembered for his list of guidelines—the "Ashwander rules": (1) The Court will not determine the constitutionality of legislation in nonadversary proceedings; (2) it will not anticipate a question of constitutional law; (3) it will not formulate a rule of constitutional law broader than needed; (4) it will not rule on constitutionality if there is another ground for deciding the case; (5) it will not determine a statute's validity unless the person

complaining has been injured by it; (6) it will not invalidate a statute at the instance of persons who have taken advantage of its benefits; and (7) the Court will always ascertain whether any reasonable interpretation of a statute will allow it to avoid the constitutional issue.

Paul Kens

Atkins v. Virginia, 536 U.S. 304 (2002), argued 20 Feb. 2002, decided 20 June 2002 by vote of 6 to 3; Stevens for the Court, O'Connor, Kennedy, Souter, Ginsburg, and Breyer concurring, Rehnquist, Scalia, and Thomas in dissent. The issue before the Court was whether the execution of mentally retarded criminals is "cruel and unusual punishment" prohibited by the Eighth Amendment. Directly overturning *Penry* v. *Lynaugh* (1989), the Court held that such executions violate the Constitution. Relying primarily on the number of state legislatures that had enacted statutes prohibiting the execution of mentally retarded criminals and the consistent direction of such legislation since the Court's decision in *Penry*, the Court decided that the execution of mentally retarded criminals violated contemporary standards of decency. In addition to violating evolving standards of decency, the Court found that the execution of mentally retarded criminals constituted excessive punishment because it does not advance the deterrent and retributive purposes of the death penalty. The Court also determined that such executions increase the risk that death will be imposed in spite of factors that may call for a less severe penalty. In dissent, Justice Antonin Scalia accused the Court of basing its opinion on the personal views of its members rather than on a proper interpretation of the Eighth Amendment or an accurate assessment of current social attitudes. In a separate dissent, Chief Justice William Rehnquist took the Court to task for consulting foreign laws, the views of professional and religious organizations, and opinion polls, in its determination of what is a publicly acceptable punishment. Opponents of capital punishment have interpreted *Atkins* as signaling a decline in the Court's support for the death penalty, but others have contended that the Court merely acted to reduce the likelihood of bad convictions so as to assure the future of the death penalty in the United States.

Jennifer L. Culbert

Austin v. United States, 509 U.S. 602 (1993), argued 20 Apr. 1993, decided 28 June 1993 by vote of 9 to 0; Blackmun for the Court, Scalia and Kennedy concurring. The use of civil forfeiture to seize the property of individuals involved in the illicit drug trade was one of law enforcement's most potent weapons. Between 1985 and 1993, for example, governments at all levels had taken more than $3 billion in cash and property. Although tied to criminal activity, such as the possession of illegal drugs, forfeiture is a civil claim essentially brought against an individual's property rather than against the individual engaged in wrongdoing. Under such circumstances, many of the due process safeguards extended to either the suspect or convicted criminal do not apply.

Forfeitures stirred widespread unfavorable press and media attention, with much of it focused on innocent owners of property who had lost it to the government. There was also concern about whether the punishment fitted the crime, notably in cases in which smalltime drug users and sellers lost houses and other valuable property out of all proportion to the crimes they had committed. Embedded in these actions, moreover, was the question of whether the Eighth Amendment's prohibition against excessive fines and cruel and unusual punishment applied to the civil forfeitures in drug cases and not just to criminal proceedings. Proponents of an active forfeiture policy argued that the Eighth Amendment applied only against criminal actions and that, in any case, civil forfeitures were "remedial" rather than punitive measures. By the early 1990s an unusual coalition of critics of civil forfeitures had developed, with conservative Republican representative Henry Hyde, of Illinois, and liberal Democrat John Conyers, of Detroit, joining with the American Civil Liberties Union to demand limits on the powers of government to seize property.

Austin emerged as a pivotal case in the development of forfeiture law. Richard Lyle Austin was a convicted cocaine dealer from Garretson, South Dakota. Austin in 1990 pleaded guilty in state court to one count of possessing cocaine with intent to distribute. Shortly thereafter the United States government filed an action against Austin's property, notably his mobile home, worth about $3,000, and his auto body shop, worth about $33,000. Austin claimed that the forfeiture was excessive given the nature of his crime, and he asserted the Eighth Amendment's protection against excessive fines. The federal district court in South Dakota and the United States Court of Appeals for the Eighth Circuit sustained the government's action, but in the case of the latter it did so in remarkably guarded language. The government had claimed that it could seize any property regardless of an individual's past criminal record or the scope of the crime committed. "We are troubled by the Government's view," the Circuit Court responded, "that any property, whether it be a hobo's hovel or the Empire State Building, can be seized by the government because the owner . . . engaged in a single drug transaction" (964 F. 2d 818[1992]). This extraordinary level of skepticism by the appeals court almost certainly explains why the Supreme Court decided, over the strong opposition of the Department of Justice, to hear *Austin.*

Justice Harry Blackmun's historically rooted opinion sharply limited the federal government's power to seize homes and businesses used in illegal drug trafficking. Blackmun concluded that the Eighth Amendment did apply to property forfeited in civil proceedings and was not limited to criminal cases. The test to determine whether the amendment applied, Blackmun concluded, was whether the forfeiture amounted to a monetary punishment. He rejected the government's position that forfeiture was merely a remedy and not a punishment. The exact scope of that test, however, was the business of the lower courts and not of the Supreme Court. Hence the justices in *Austin* declined to provide specific guidance about whether or not innocence should be considered and what guidelines would be appropriate to determine whether the Eighth Amendment had been violated. In a concurring opinion, Justice Antonin Scalia insisted that the measure of a forfeiture's excessiveness should be the relationship between the seized property and the offense. Justice Anthony M. Kennedy also concurred, raising doubts about the soundness of Blackmun's historical analysis of the Eighth Amendment. In the same term, the justices, this time in a six-member plurality opinion, decided *United States v. Parcel of Land* (1993), holding that title to property acquired from the proceeds of crime does not automatically belong to the government.

Austin was an important constitutional milestone in the growing although hardly complete limitation by the Court on the power of government to seize property. The justices continued to accept the constitutionality of the practice and the wisdom of the policy under-pinning forfeiture, as their opinion in *Bennis* v. *Michigan* (1996) made clear. Still, Blackmun's opinion in *Austin* was the first significant hedge on one of the government's toughest yet most controversial weapons in the war on drugs.

Kermit L. Hall

B

Bailey v. Drexel Furniture Co., 259 U.S. 20 (1922), argued 7–8 Mar. 1922, decided 15 May 1922 by vote of 8 to 1; Taft for the Court, Clarke, without opinion, in dissent. Immediately following the unexpected invalidation of the first federal child labor law in 1918, Congress sought another way to protect dependent and exploited children in the workplace. With the two houses again virtually unanimous, the Child Labor Tax law was enacted (1919), its justification resting upon contemporary precedents, notably Chief Justice Edward D. White's opinion in *McCray* v. *United States* (1904), which sustained the imposition of confiscatory excises to end the production of offending articles.

While White lived, the Court did not render a decision in the first child labor tax case, *Atherton* v. *Johnston* (1922), but, following his death, the new chief justice, William Howard Taft, massed the bench in *Bailey* to invalidate the Child Labor Tax. His opinion sought to distinguish *McCray* and the other cases in which the Court had legitimated using the taxing power for regulatory purposes. The constitutionally sanctioned regulatory measures, he asserted, had involved "only . . . incidental restraint and regulation," while the stigmatized statute imposed a penalty whose "prohibitory and regulatory effect" was palpable (pp. 36–37). As in *Hammer* v. *Dagenhart* (1918), the Court found in *Bailey* that Congress had exceeded its authority and invaded the states' internal affairs.

Although Taft's distinction lacked merit, the lone dissenter, Justice John H. Clarke, failed to challenge it. With the coming of the New Deal, this distinction began to erode, but Congress relied primarily thereafter upon the commerce power to protect the social and economic welfare of the country.

Stephen B. Wood

Baker v. Carr, 369 U.S. 186 (1962), argued 19–20 Apr. 1961, set for reargument 1 May 1961, reargued 9 Oct. 1961, decided 26 Mar. 1962 by vote of 6 to 2; Brennan for the Court, Stewart and Clark concurring, Frankfurter and Harlan in dissent, Whittaker not participating. After serving for fifteen years on the Supreme Court, Chief Justice Earl Warren, himself the author of the Court's opinion in the celebrated school desegregation case, *Brown* v. *Board of Education* (1954), called *Baker* v. *Carr* "the most vital decision" during his service on the Court, and the apportionment revolution it inaugurated as the most important achievement of his Court. *Baker* v. *Carr* did not establish the "one-person, one vote principle"—that was first announced in *Gray* v. *Sanders* (1963) and was confirmed with respect to congressional and legislative districts in *Wesberry* v. *Sanders* (1964) and *Reynolds* v. *Sims* (1964). But *Baker* v. *Carr* opened the federal courts to urban interests that had been unable to force state legislators to reapportion state legislatures or to redistrict congressional seats to reflect the urbanization of the United States, or to secure any redress of their grievances either from Congress or their respective state courts.

Warren might have exaggerated the importance of the case, but it clearly inaugurated a decade of lawsuits, at the end of which the political map of the nation had been redrawn. Some have termed this a revolution in redistributing political power, although there is continuing controversy as to whether the realignment of legislative districts that clearly did transfer legislative votes from the rural to the urban and suburban populations has had significant policy consequences.

Baker v. *Carr* was initiated in Tennessee in 1959 when a number of plaintiffs from Memphis, Nashville, and Knoxville brought an action before the federal district court in Nashville against Joseph Cordell Carr, the Tennessee secretary of state, and George McCanless, the attorney general. The Tennessee Constitution required the General Assembly to apportion the members of the General Assembly among the state's ninety-five countries after each decennial census. But the last time it had done so was in 1901, and even then it had failed to give city voters a fair share of seats. The Tennessee courts had been equally unsympathetic and declined to intervene.

The *Baker* plaintiffs, pointing out that the federal courts were the only forum that offered any promise of relief, asked for a declaratory judgment that the Tennessee apportionment act was unconstitutional and an injunction to prevent state officers from conducting any more elections under it. The three-judge district court, following established precedent, dismissed the complaint on the grounds that the relief requested and the legal wrongs alleged were not within the scope of judicial power conferred on federal courts by Article III of the Constitution and the federal statutes implementing that article. Furthermore, said the district court, even if the Courts had jurisdiction, the questions presented to it were nonjusticiable, that is, they were "political questions" unsuited for judicial inquiry and adjustment.

On direct appeal to the Supreme Court, amicus briefs were filed by various urban-based groups, and most importantly, by Solicitor General Archibald Cox in behalf of the recently inaugurated Kennedy administration. As Justice Tom Clark pointed out in his concurring opinion, *Baker* v. *Carr* was one of the "most carefully considered" Supreme Court decisions of modern times. The Court heard three hours of oral argument on 19 and 20 April 1961, three times more than it gives to most cases, and then held the case for another three hours of argument at the opening of the 1961 term. And as Justice Clark commented, *Baker* was considered "over and over again by us in Conference and individually" (p. 258).

The Court announced its decision on 26 March 1962 in five opinions taking up 163 pages. The opinions were unusually sharp-toned for their day. Justice Clark, for example, characterized Justice Felix Frankfurter's 64-page dissent as "bursting with words that go through so much and conclude with so little."

Justice William Brennan, speaking for the Court, carefully avoided explicit discussion of the merits of the case. There was little doubt that the majority felt that Tennessee had acted unconstitutionally, but it limited its holding to questions of jurisdiction, standing, and justiciability. Justice Brennan distinguished between the two grounds relied upon by the district court—jurisdiction and nonjusticiability—pointing out that in instances of nonjusticiability, consideration of the cause is not wholly and immediately foreclosed; rather, the Court's inquiry necessarily proceeds to the point of deciding whether the duty asserted can be judicially identified and its breach judicially determined, and whether protection for the right can be judicially molded. Where jurisdiction is lacking, however, the case goes no further.

Justice Brennan quickly concluded that the subject matter was within the jurisdiction of federal courts, and that the plaintiffs had a sufficient interest in the weight of their votes to have standing. More difficult to decide was whether the question presented was justiciable. In revisiting the doctrine of political questions, first announced by Chief Justice Roger B. Taney in *Luther* v. *Borden* (1849), Justice Brennan asserted that political questions chiefly relate to separation of powers issues (which raise questions about relations among coequal branches of the national government) and thus call for judicial deference. In contrast, federalism questions (which raise issues about the consistency of a state's action with the federal Constitution) do not call for such judicial deference. "Prominent on the surface of any case held to involve a political question," he wrote, "is found a textually demonstrable constitutional commitment of the issue to a coordinate political department; or a lack of judicially discoverable and manageable standards for resolving it; or the impossibility of deciding without an initial policy determination of a kind clearly for nonjudicial discretion; or the impossibility of a court's undertaking independent resolution without expressing lack of respect due coordinate branches of government; or an unusual need for unquestioning adherence to a political decision already made; or the potentiality of embarrassment from multifarious pronouncements by various departments on one question" (p. 217). He also distinguished between questions such as those presented by *Luther* v. *Borden*, arising under the Guarantee Clause of Article IV, where "judicially manageable standards are lacking," and those arising under the Equal Protection Clause, where standards are "well developed and familiar" (p. 226).

Perhaps the most difficult obstacle for the majority was the one precedent of *Colegrove* v. *Green* (1946). In *Colegrove* the Court had refused to force the Illinois legislature to correct the inequities in the state's congressional apportionment that had given Illinois both the largest and smallest congressional districts in the United States, one nine times the size of the other. *Colegrove* was a 3 to 3 to 1 decision (Justice Robert Jackson had been absent as the U.S. prosecutor at the Nuremberg War Crimes Tribunal, and no one had as yet been appointed to replace the recently deceased Chief Justice Harlan F. Stone). Justice Frankfurter, speaking for the Court, but with the concurrence of only two other justices, coined the phrase "political thicket," which has come to be the recognized shorthand warning against federal courts intervening in political questions where they allegedly have neither commission nor competence to decide. Justice Brennan, however, dismissed Justice Frankfurter's opinion as "the minority opinion," arguing that four of the seven sitting judges in *Colegrove* had found no constitutional obstacles to federal courts reviewing the constitutionality of legislative apportionments.

Although in *Baker* the Court limited its holding to jurisdictional matters, it did not restrict its holding to situations such as in Tennessee where the legislature had failed to comply with its own constitution. Justice Brennan made it clear that any legislature that failed to reapportion its districts

in such a fashion as to reflect in some way population equality was in jeopardy of violating the Equal Protection Clause. His opinion thus called into question the constitutionality of legislative apportionment in practically every state in the Union. "We conclude," wrote Justice Brennan, "that the complainant's allegations of denial of equal protection present a justiciable constitutional cause of action upon which appellants are entitled to a trial and a decision" (p. 237).

Justices William O. Douglas, Tom Clark, and Potter Stewart, while joining the opinion of the Court, wrote separate concurrences. To Justice Douglas the issues were uncomplicated: it was a voting rights case and voting rights have long been within the protection of federal courts. Justice Clark took issue with Justice Harlan's dissenting opinion, which contended that the Court's decision would mean that the Equal Protection Clause required "mathematical equality among voters." (In this, Justice Clark was a poor prophet, for that is what before too long became the controlling standard.) Rather, Justice Clark concluded that all that had to be decided was that Tennessee's apportionment is a "crazy quilt without rational basis" (p. 254). Unless the federal courts provided relief, he claimed, there could be no remedy for what he believed to be a patent violation of the Equal Protection Clause.

Justice Stewart wrote to emphasize that the Court had decided only three things and no more: that federal courts possessed jurisdiction of the subject matter, that the appellants had standing to challenge the Tennessee apportionment statutes, and that reapportionment was a justiciable issue.

Justice Frankfurter, in the last opinion he would write before retiring from the Court, was obviously distressed by the short shrift given to his *Colegrove* opinion and by what he alleged to be the Court's "massive repudiation of the experience of our whole past in asserting destructively novel judicial power demands" (p. 251). He reiterated his *Colegrove* view that the federal courts should not intervene in the "essentially political conflict of forces by which the relation between population and representation has time out of mind been and now is determined" (p. 267). He predicted that the injection of the courts into this clash of political forces in political settlements could undermine their authority. As in *Colegrove*, Frank-furter told those aggrieved by the Tennessee legislature that the remedy "must come through an aroused popular conscience that sears the conscience of the people's representatives" (p. 270). The Court, he contended, was being asked to "choose among competing bases of representation—ultimately, really, among competing theories of political philosophy" (p. 300) and that was not an appropriate issue for judges. He pointed out that representation according to population is not, in our history or Constitution, enshrined as the only standard or the standard by reference to which the reasonableness of apportionment plans may be judged.

Justice John M. Harlan, in his dissenting opinion, went to the merits. He contended that even if federal courts had jurisdiction—which he did not think to be the case—there is no federal constitutional requirement that state legislatures must be structured so as to reflect equally the voice of every voter. There is nothing in the federal Constitution, said Justice Harlan, to prevent Tennessee, if it so wishes, from giving rural voters more electoral weight than urban ones. Moreover, he warned that "the majority has wholly failed to reckon with what the future may hold in store" when federal courts try to determine what is and what is not a constitutional apportioning policy (p. 339).

In an extended appendix, Justice Harlan set out to prove the inadequacy of arithmetical formulas as measures of the "irrational rationality" of Tennessee's apportionment. The disparity in electoral strength among the various counties in Tennessee, he argued, may be accounted for by various economic, political, and geographic considerations. It is a constitutionally permissible decision to preserve the electoral strength of the rural interests, notwithstanding shifts in population.

It did not take long for other states to go through the door opened by *Baker* v. *Carr*. In one year, thirty-six states had become involved in reapportionment lawsuits. During the next several years the Court rounded out the reapportionment revolution. Justices Harlan and Frankfurter proved to be inaccurate prophets about the difficulties that the courts would have in finding appropriate judicial standards. The judges quickly retreated from the "rationality test"—that apportionment plans were to be evaluated in terms of whether or not they had any rational basis—to what many think to be a simplistic but nonetheless more manageable

standard of mathematical strict equality—one person, one vote. Within a short time the Court had concluded that no factors—not geographical districts, nor a desire to keep governmental units intact, nor a federal compromise in which one chamber would represent population and the other governmental units such as countries—but strictly equal population districts would pass constitutional muster. The Court, in a series of cases, moved from a requirement of "substantial equality among districts" to "precise mathematical equality" to a distinction between congressional districts where strict equality is required, and state legislative districts where some tolerance is allowed to permit consideration of other appropriate factors.

□ Jack W. Peltason, *Federal Courts in the Political Process* (1955). Jack W. Peltason, *Fifty-Eight Lonely Men: Southern Federal Judges and School Desegregation* (1971). Jack W. Peltason, *Understanding the Constitution*, 12th ed. (1991).

J. W. Peltason

Ballard v. United States, 329 U.S. 187 (1946), argued 5 Oct. 1946, decided 9 Dec. 1946 by vote of 5 to 4; Douglas for the Court, Jackson concurring in the result; Frankfurter, Vinson, Jackson, and Burton in dissent. Edna W. Ballard appealed her conviction for fraudulent use of the mails by challenging the practice of the federal courts in California of systematically excluding women from juries. The charges stemmed from her leadership of the "I Am" movement, whose teachings included the claims that she, her son, and her husband were spiritually in touch with Saint Germain and that the Ballards had performed hundreds of miracle cures.

Federal law then required that federal court juries had to have the same qualifications as those of the highest state court of law. California law did make women eligible for jury duty, but as a matter of systematic state practice, the California state courts did not summon women to serve. Federal courts in California followed the state practice.

The Supreme Court reversed Ballard's conviction, reasoning that the totality of federal statutes on the subject of juries reflected a design to make them fair cross sections of the community and truly representative of it. Since California law made women eligible jurors, they were part of the "community" from which federal juries must draw a cross section. All-male federal juries in such states were inconsistent with the congressional scheme. Although the case technically turned on how best to interpret the statutory mandate of Congress, the reasoning about the desirability of having a fair cross section of the community for jury service was later used in *Taylor v. Louisiana* (1975) to explain the meaning of the Sixth Amendment phrase "trial by jury." The justices in *J. E. B. v. Alabama Ex Rel. T. B.* (1994) went even further and held that the Fourteenth Amendment's guarantee of equal protection of the laws barred the exclusion of potential jurors on the basis of their race.

Leslie Friedman Goldstein

Ballew v. Georgia, 435 U.S. 223 (1978), argued 1 Nov. 1977, decided 21 Mar. 1978 by vote of 9 to 0; Blackmun for the Court, Stevens, White, and Powell concurring. Pursuant to state law, Ballew was tried and convicted of a misdemeanor by a jury of five persons. He had filed a pretrial motion to impanel a jury of twelve (or at least six), arguing that a five-person jury would deprive him of his Sixth and Fourteenth Amendment rights to trial by jury. Ballew was sentenced to one year imprisonment and a fine of two thousand dollars. The Georgia courts rejected Ballew's appeal but the Supreme Court ruled in his favor.

Ballew is the Court's most recent ruling on the proper size of state criminal juries. The Anglo-American trial jury for centuries had been a body of twelve, deciding unanimously. However, *Williams v. Florida* (1970) had caused considerable uncertainty regarding this matter. *Williams* held that a state criminal jury of six was permissible but did not indicate what the smallest constitutionally adequate jury might be. *Colegrove v. Battin* (1973) increased the uncertainty by authorizing six-person federal civil juries. And the Court compounded the problem by approving nonunanimous majority verdicts for state criminal juries in *Johnson v. Louisiana* (1972) and *Apodaca v. Oregon* (1972). *Ballew* answered this question by establishing six as the minimum.

Justice Blackmun's opinion reviewed the many empirical studies, inspired by *Williams*, on the effects of six-person juries and then held that a criminal jury of five was unable to fulfill the constitutional purposes and functions of a jury. While this holding was consistent with the evidence, it did not

fairly regard it. Though Justice Blackmun declared that the studies cited had raised "significant questions about the wisdom and constitutionality of a reduction below six" (p. 232), none, in fact, was an investigation of five-person juries. Rather, what these studies had shown was that six- and twelve-person juries were not functionally equivalent. The functional equivalence of six- and twelve-person juries was the foundation and chief claim of *Williams*. If the Court had truly relied on them, it would have been obligated to overturn *Williams* instead of reaffirming it.

As a result of *Ballew* and the other cases herein cited, juries with as few as six members may now be employed in federal civil cases and in both civil and criminal cases in state courts.

Peter W. Sperlich

Bank of Augusta v. Earle, 38 U.S. 519 (1839), argued 30 Jan.-1 Feb. 1839, decided 9 Mar. 1839 by vote of 8 to 1; Taney for the Court, Baldwin concurring, McKinley in dissent. This case marked the first time the Supreme Court ruled on the powers of a state over a corporation chartered in another state. Three banks chartered outside of Alabama bought bills of exchange in that state and sued the makers of the bills when the makers refused to pay the bills on the grounds that foreign banks were not authorized to do business in Alabama.

The banks argued that a foreign corporation had a constitutional right to do business in any state and that an adverse ruling would invalidate millions of dollars of financial transactions, causing the current depression to worsen. The makers of the bills contended that a state could exclude a foreign corporation from doing business within its boundaries and that Alabama had done so.

The Supreme Court adopted a middle ground, holding that a state could exclude a foreign corporation from doing business or could impose reasonable conditions on that business, but that the exclusion or conditions must be clearly stated. Since Alabama had not expressly prohibited foreign banks from dealing in bills of exchange, the Court ruled for the banks and thereby avoided the financial disorder that had been predicated for a contrary holding. The principles of the case continue to be good law, although the Supreme Court has ruled that a state may not, through its regulation of foreign corporations, impose an undue burden on interstate commerce.

Robert M. Ireland

Bank of the United States v. Deveaux, 5 Cranch (9 U.S.) 61 (1809), argued 10–11 Feb. 1809, decided 15 Mar. 1809 by vote of 6 to 0; Marshall for the Court, Livingston not participating. The Constitution gives federal courts jurisdiction over cases between citizens of different states (this is known as diversity jurisdiction). *Deveaux* involved the issue of whether a corporation can sue or be sued in a federal court under diversity jurisdiction and, if so, how the citizenship of the corporation is to be determined for diversity purposes. The Bank of the United States sued Deveaux, a Georgia tax collector, in federal court to recover property he had seized when the bank refused to pay a Georgia tax. Deveaux argued that the federal court had no jurisdiction because the bank as a corporation was not a citizen for purposes of diversity of citizenship jurisdiction and, in the alternative, that if the bank was a citizen, there was no diversity since some of its shareholders resided in Georgia. The Court held that a corporation was a "citizen" for purposes of diversity jurisdiction but that there was no diversity in this case because the citizenship of the corporation was to be determined by the citizenship of its shareholders, some of whom resided in the same state as the defendant. Later, Marshall and other members of the Court reportedly expressed regret over the decision because it severely limited the right of corporations to sue or be sued in federal court and thereby diminished federal judicial power. But *Deveaux* remained valid until it was overruled in **Louisville Railroad Co. v. Letson* (1844), which held that the citizenship of a corporation for diversity purposes was that of the state that chartered it.

Robert M. Ireland

Barenblatt v. United States, 360 U.S. 109 (1959), argued 18 Nov. 1958, decided 8 June 1959 by vote of 5 to 4; Harlan for the Court, Black, joined by Warren and Douglas, in dissent, Brennan also dissenting. This decision signaled a retreat from **Watkins v. United States* (1957), which had placed limits on the ability of congressional committees to inquire into political beliefs and associations. *Watkins* and similar decisions provoked concerted efforts in Congress to curb the Court's authority, which, although

unsuccessful, nevertheless persuaded a majority to be more circumspect for a time in protecting the rights of alleged subversives. *Barenblatt* upheld the conviction for contempt of Congress of a witness who had refused to testify before the House Committee on Un-American Activities about his beliefs and his membership in a communist club at the University of Michigan.

The Court dismissed Barenblatt's First Amendment claim through a "balancing of interests." It defined the government's interest as national self-preservation despite the fact that the only evidence concerning the club was that its members held abstract intellectual discussions. At the same time, it treated the First Amendment interest as essentially irrelevant. The Court also found that the House committee had made clear the pertinency of its questions, contrary to *Watkins*, where the Court held that pertinency had not been made clear, even though the committee's explanation had been essentially the same in both cases. Although *Barenblatt* has never been explicitly overruled, the Court has since displayed far less reluctance to reverse convictions of uncooperative witnesses before such committees on constitutional grounds.

□ Dean Alfange, Jr., "Congressional Investigations and the Fickle Court," *University of Cincinnati Law Review* 30 (Spring 1961): 113–171.

Dean Alfange, Jr.

Barnes v. Glen Theatre, Inc., 501 U.S. 560 (1991), argued 8 Jan. 1991, decided 21 June 1991 by vote of 5 to 4; Rehnquist for the Court, White, joined by Marshall, Blackmun, and Stevens, in dissent. In this case the Supreme Court upheld an Indiana statute that prohibited the knowing or intentional appearance in public in a condition of nudity; as applied in this case it required female dancers to wear "pasties" and a "G-string" when performing. Respondents were two South Bend establishments that provided totally nude dancing as entertainment. In *Schad* v. *Borough of Mount Ephraim* (1981), the Court had ruled that barroom-type nude dancing, which was expressive conduct, merited some First Amendment protection. But the ordinance in *Schad* covered all live entertainment, making it both more content-specific than Indiana's statute and overbroad by being applicable to other forms of protected expression. Indiana's statute prohibited all forms of public nudity, not simply live entertainment.

The Court treated Indiana's law as a "time, place, and manner" measure that regulated the incidental effects of speech. Such regulation is valid if it satisfies a four-part test developed in *United States* v. **O'Brien* (1968): if it is "within the constitutional power of the government; if it furthers an important or substantial governmental interest; if the governmental interest is unrelated to the suppression of free expression; and if the incidental restriction on alleged First Amendment freedoms is no greater than is essential to the furtherance of that interest" (pp. 376–377).

Justice William Rehnquist concluded that the Indiana law met this test. Most importantly and controversially, he maintained that the measure was "unrelated to the suppression of free expression" because "the perceived evil that Indiana seeks to address is not erotic dancing, but public nudity" (pp. 2461, 2463). The breadth of Indiana's statute saved it in this regard.

Justice Byron White's dissent was directed primarily to this key contention. Because the dancers' nudity is itself an important expressive component of their dance, "it cannot be said that the statutory prohibition is unrelated to expressive conduct" (p. 2474).

Donald A. Downs

Barron v. Baltimore, 7 Pet. (32 U.S.) 243 (1833), argued 11 Feb. 1833, decided 16 Feb. 1833 by vote of 7 to 0; Marshall for the Court. A wharf owner sued the city of Baltimore for economic loss occasioned by the city's diversion of streams, which lowered the water level around his wharves. He claimed that the city took his property without just compensation in violation of the Fifth Amendment. This presented the question of whether the Fifth Amendment restrained the states. After surveying the history of the Bill of Rights, Chief Justice John Marshall concluded that the first ten amendments restrained only the federal government, thus requiring Americans to look to state constitutions for protection of their civil and political liberties. The opinion marked a retreat from Marshall's earlier nationalism, one impelled by the changing composition of the Court and the growth of states' rights sentiment. The Court reaffirmed the holding of *Barron* in *Permoli* v. *New Orleans* (1845).

With the ratification of the Fourteenth Amendment in 1868, the application of the Bill of Rights to the states again became an issue. In **Hurtado* v. *California* (1884), the Court held that the Fourteenth Amendment was a limit on state power. Not until the twentieth century incorporation cases, beginning with **Gitlow* v. *New York* (1925) did *Barron* lose its authoritative status. Today almost all of the guarantees of the Bill of Rights have been incorporated as restraints on the states.

David J. Bodenhamer

Bates v. State Bar of Arizona, 433 U.S. 350 (1977), argued 18 Jan. 1977, decided 27 June 1977 by vote of 5 to 4; Blackmun for the Court; Burger, Powell, and Rehnquist in dissent. In *Bates* the Supreme Court struck down state legal ethics codes that prohibited lawyers from advertising. Two young lawyers, John Bates and Van O'Steen, sought to create a test case by placing a newspaper advertisement indicating that they offered "legal services at very reasonable fees" and listing some of the fees they charged. The Board of Governors of the State Bar recommended that the two lawyers be suspended. The Arizona Supreme Court upheld the decision but reduced the punishment to censure.

In the U.S. Supreme Court the attorneys attacked the Arizona rule on two grounds: that it violated the Sherman Antitrust Act by creating a restraint of trade, and that it violated the First Amendment by restraining the right of free speech. The Supreme Court rejected the antitrust claim, but held that their First Amendment rights of speech, together with the right of the public consumers of legal services to receive their message, outweighed any adverse effects on professionalism that advertising might have. The Court subsequently limited the First Amendment right in *Ohralik* v. *Ohio State Bar Association* (1978), where it sanctioned a policy of totally barring in-person solicitation of clients.

Bates opened up the practice of law to greater competition and made possible the growth of legal clinics that provide routine legal needs of the middle and lower middle class. One empirical study in Arizona found that, after *Bates*, the average cost of these legal services declined. The case, along with **Goldfarb* v. *Virginia State Bar* (1975), which prohibited bar sponsored fee schedules, signaled the end to total self-regulation of the bar, which the leadership of the American legal profession has decried.

Rayman L. Solomon

Batson v. Kentucky, 476 U.S. 79 (1986), argued 12 Dec. 1985, decided 30 Apr. 1986 by vote of 7 to 2; Powell for the Court, White, Marshall, O'Connor, and Stevens (with Brennan) concurring, Burger and Rehnquist in dissent. Batson, a black man, was tried for second-degree burglary and the receipt of stolen goods. The judge conducted the voir dire examination of the potential jurors, excused some of them for cause, and then permitted prosecution and defense to exercise their peremptory challenges—six and nine respectively. The prosecutor's exercise of the peremptories removed all four black persons on the panel. Batson moved for a discharge of the jury, asserting that the removal of all of the black panelists violated his Sixth and Fourteenth Amendment rights to a jury drawn from a cross section of the community as well as his Fourteenth Amendment right to the equal protection of the laws. The trial judge denied the motion and Batson was convicted on both counts. The Supreme Court of Kentucky denied Batson's appeal and affirmed the verdict. The U.S. Supreme Court reversed.

Ruling in favor of Batson, the Court placed substantial limits on the prosecutor's use of peremptory challenges. Overruling *Swain* v. *Alabama* (1965) in part, the Court applied the equal protection principle to the exercise of peremptory challenges. For all practical purposes, it thereby transformed peremptory challenges into challenges for cause, even if the holding refers to a lesser (but undefined) standard to sustain a disputed peremptory challenge than would be required to support a challenge for cause. The *Batson* Court's claim that it did not "undermine the contribution the [peremptory] challenge generally makes to the administrations of justice" (pp. 98–99) is entirely unconvincing.

The thrust of *Batson* is not toward color-blind but color-conscious law, applying a racial test to the prosecutor's use of peremptory challenges. The ultimate effect of *Batson* may even be the de facto introduction of racial quotas for trial juries since the racially disproportionate use of peremptories now may be attacked as constitutionally improper. Given the lack of standards for a successful rebuttal, the only safe use of peremptories will be racially proportionate to venire and or community makeup.

The Court failed to distinguish between the selection of the jury venire (where *representativeness* is the chief concern) and the selection of the jury (where *impartiality* must be the primary consideration). The Court also failed to distinguish between general and particular jury fitness. A person's general fitness to be a juror (to be included in the venire) is, indeed, not a matter of race. A person's suitability to serve on a particular jury, however, may well be related to race. It is not difficult to imagine a crime that so offends a particular social group that it must be feared that all of its members lack the impartiality of the proper juror. When exercising peremptory challenges, attorneys must be able to act upon this fear. To hold otherwise is to forfeit at least the *appearance* of jury impartiality. Given that the *facts* of jury impartiality cannot be known with certainty, the appearance of impartiality becomes a matter of extraordinary importance. All this the Court did not recognize (p. 97).

The use of peremptory challenges typically brings into conflict the goals of jury impartiality and jury representativeness. Until *Batson*, this conflict was resolved in favor of impartiality, that is, the Court agreed that the essential nature of a peremptory challenge was found in its exercise without explanation, judicial inquiry, or control by the court. *Batson* overturned *Swain* but pretended otherwise by taking the position that jury selection can meet both goals. Only Justice Thurgood Marshall freely admitted that he regarded representativeness as more important than impartiality, and that this reevaluation, in fact, pointed toward the abolition of the traditional peremptory challenge.

Batson was limited in three ways. It applied only to the prosecution, only to criminal trials, and only to challenges in which the excluded juror was of the same race as the defendant. In *Edmonson* v. *Leesville Concrete* (1991), however, the Court held that a private litigant in a civil case could not exclude prospective jurors because of their race. The majority concluded that there was sufficient interaction between a court and the jury selection process to satisfy the "state action" requirement. While this decision did not explicitly also extend the *Batson* principle to either private defense lawyers or public defenders in criminal cases, the logic of *Edmonson* makes this result foreseeable if not inevitable. In *Powers* v. *Ohio* (1991), the Court held that white defendants are entitled to new trials if convicted by juries from which blacks had been improperly excluded because of their race.

The Supreme Court has vigorously expanded the *Batson* principle. In *Georgia v. McCollum* (1992) Justice Harry Blackmun's majority opinion made it unconstitutional for prosecutors and defense counsel to discriminate in using peremptory challenges based on race in civil cases. Two years later, in *J. E. B* v. *Alabama Ex Rel. T.B.* (1994) the Court went even further in holding that the Equal Protection Clause of the Fourteenth Amendment required that potential jurors could not be excluded on the basis of gender.

Peter W. Sperlich

Belle Terre v. Boraas, 416 U.S. 1 (1974), argued 19–20 Feb. 1974, decided 1 Apr. 1974 by vote of 7 to 2; Douglas for the Court, Brennan and Marshall in dissent. Appellees owned a house in the small Long Island village of Belle Terre, New York. They leased it to six unrelated college students and were subsequently cited for violating a zoning ordinance that limited occupancy in one-family dwellings to traditional family units or to groups of not more than two unrelated people. Excluded from the ordinance were lodging, boarding, fraternity, and multiple-dwelling houses.

The owners of the house plus three of the tenants brought suit challenging the ordinance. Among their claims was the contention that the ordinance violated their constitutional right of privacy. The Court rejected that argument and upheld the ordinance, saying that it bore a rational relationship to a permissible state objective. "A quiet place where yards are wide, people few, and motor vehicles restricted are legitimate guidelines in a land-use project addressed to family needs," Justice William O. Douglas wrote. "The police power is not confined to elimination of filth, stench, and unhealthy places" (p. 9).

Justice Thurgood Marshall dissented on the grounds that the ordinance unnecessarily burdened appellees' First Amendment freedom of association and their constitutional right to privacy. Marshall argued that because of that infringement of fundamental rights, a mere rational basis test was not enough to sustain the ordinance. Rather, he argued that the ordinance could "withstand constitutional scrutiny only upon a clear showing that the burden imposed is necessary to protect a compelling and substantial governmental interest" (p. 18).

John Anthony Maltese

Bennis v. Michigan, 516 U.S. 442 (1996), argued 29 Nov. 1995, decided 4 Mar. 1996 by vote of 5 to 4; Rehnquist for the Court, Stevens, Souter, Breyer, and Kennedy in dissent. State and federal governments had enacted a wide range of forfeiture statutes designed to help combat narcotics and other pervasive offenses. Such statutes were potent weapons and moneymakers for states and the federal government. Some of these statutes, as was true with the 1925 Michigan antinuisance law, often had as much of an impact on an innocent owner as they did on the guilty parties. The Michigan statute explicitly provided that an owner need not have known or consented to illegal use of the property. In these cases of forfeiture, landlords, plane and boat lessors, mortgagees and lienholders, and various co-owners could claim that illegally used property, which had become subject to forfeiture, occurred entirely without their knowledge or participation. The *Bennis* case drew the problem in the starkest possible terms.

Tina Bennis, of Detroit, Michigan, co-owned with her husband, John, a 1977 Pontiac that he used, once, to engage in oral sex with a prostitute in the front seat. He was convicted and the trial court ordered the car seized. The court refused to recognize the interest of Tina Bennis in the car, although the evidence was indisputable that she had no knowledge that her husband was engaged in sexual relations with a prostitute and that she had provided most of the funds to buy the car through baby-sitting and odd jobs. Although an intermediate appeals court overturned the decision, the Michigan Supreme Court sustained the trial court's action, noting that Michigan, unlike some other states, had not provided an "innocent-owner" defense and, therefore, no federal constitutional safeguard had been broken. Tina Bennis then appealed to the United States Supreme Court.

Bennis's attorney argued that confiscation of the car constituted a violation of her due process rights under the Fourteenth Amendment and the takings clause of the Fifth Amendment. Mrs. Bennis, her counsel insisted, could not prevent an illegal act of which she had no knowledge and that, in any case, the government should be allowed to take property of a joint owner only when it was clear that person was at least negligent in allowing it to be used unlawfully. Counsel for the state of Michigan, however, concluded that the state had an interest in protecting the safety, health, and morals of its citizens and that the owner of an automobile used for prostitution was strictly liable for that use and could not argue ignorance of the activity conducted in it. Bennis, the state of Michigan declared before the high court, had not taken "all reasonable steps" to prevent her husband's crime.

A sharply divided Supreme Court found in favor of the state of Michigan and the forfeiture. Chief Justice William Rehnquist cited a long line of cases that held that an owner's interest in property may be forfeited by reason of the use to which it was put even though the owner did not know that it was to be put to such use. According to Rehnquist, accepting the notion that ignorance was a basis for Bennis to retain ownership would lead to a host of schemes where one owner would keep the other in ignorance in the hope that, should the activity be discovered, the property would not be lost. Moreover, since the state confiscated the automobile through a proper set of proceedings, Bennis could not make a claim either that she had been denied due process or that she deserved compensation for her one-half of the car. The government, Rehnquist concluded, was not required to compensate an owner for property that it lawfully acquired. If the residents of Michigan did not like the law, then they should alter it through the legislative process. As for Tina Bennis, she assumed all of the risks associated with marrying John in the first place. If there was a remedy for Tina, it was for John to pay back to her the one-half interest (about $300) lost when the car was forfeited.

Justice John Paul Stevens entered a dissent that reminded the majority that for centuries prostitution had taken place, often in settings far more glamorous than the seat of an automobile. According to Stevens, the notion that this practice could be halted through the punishment of innocent third parties made no sense. While Stevens agreed with Rehnquist that there was a long line of precedents on which to ground property forfeiture, he went on to note that past practice and magnitude had to be balanced. "While our historical cases establish the propriety of seizing a freighter when its entire cargo consists of smuggled goods, none of them would justify the confiscation of an ocean liner just because one of its passengers sinned while on board" (p. 478). In this instance, Stevens noted, the record made

clear that the principal use of the car was not to provide a regular site for the husband to carry out forbidden trysts. "An isolated misuse of a stationary vehicle," Stevens concluded, "should not justify the forfeiture of an innocent owner's property on the theory that it constituted an instrumentality of the crime" (p. 478).

The *Bennis* decision reflected the Rehnquist Court's disposition to defer to state legislative authority in fighting crime by sustaining a harsh economic penalty for criminal conduct. While most of the provisions of federal law usually exempt innocent owners, a ruling in favor of Bennis could have set greater protections for all state and federal seizures. What the Court's ruling did, however, was to endorse those jurisdictions, such as Michigan, that did not take account of the interests of innocent owners and that refused to pass forfeiture statutes that shifted the burden of proof to the government to establish the guilt of the owner whose property was seized.

Kermit L. Hall

Benton v. Maryland, 395 U.S. 784 (1969), argued 12 Dec. 1968, reargued 24 Mar. 1969, decided 23 June 1969 by vote of 7 to 2; Marshall for the Court, Harlan and Stewart in dissent. The issue in *Benton* was whether the Due Process Clause of the Fourteenth Amendment prohibits a state from subjecting a person to double jeopardy. The Court had confronted that precise issue thirty years earlier in *Palko* v. *Connecticut* (1937), where it ruled that the double jeopardy standard of the Fifth Amendment did not apply to the states. Rejecting the doctrine of incorporation, *Palko* applied the principle that the Fourteenth Amendment's Due Process Clause incorporates only those rights that are "implicit in the concept of ordered liberty" (p. 324).

In *Benton* the Court overruled *Palko* in part, holding that the double jeopardy prohibition applies to the states through the Fourteenth Amendment. Most significantly, the Court rejected the *Palko* notion that states can deny rights to criminal defendants so long as the denial is not shocking to a universal sense of justice. Instead, the Court ruled that states must extend those guarantees in the Bill of Rights that are fundamental to the American scheme of justice.

With respect to the guarantee against double jeopardy, the Court observed that its origins can be traced to English common law, which was adopted in our country's jurisprudence. Every state has some form of the prohibition in its constitution or common law. Accordingly, the guarantee against double jeopardy is clearly among those rights that are deeply ingrained in the American system and thus made applicable to the states through the Fourteenth Amendment.

Daan Braveman

Berman v. Parker, 348 U.S. 26 (1954), argued 19 Oct. 1954, decided 22 Nov. 1954 by vote of 9 to 0; Douglas for the Court. A Washington, D.C., urban renewal statute allowed the city to condemn land and sell it to private developers, who would redevelop it according to the renewal plan. The plan included not only slum eradication but also beautification projects. A landowner challenged the statute, mainly on the ground that, under the Takings Clause of the Fifth Amendment, the condemnation was not "for public use." The owner argued unsuccessfully that there was no public use because the land was to be sold to a private developer and for the purpose of beautification. The Supreme Court upheld the statute.

The decision is important in two ways. First, it established that aesthetics are a legitimate public purpose for which government may regulate and condemn land. This principle has encouraged increased governmental intervention to achieve aesthetic and environmental goals. Second, *Berman* made clear that the phrase "public use" in the Takings Clause did not mean that land condemned had to remain in government ownership or be used physically by the public. The Court seemed to hold that eminent domain might be used to advance any goal that government could pursue under any of its powers. Subsequent decisions have confirmed this broad understanding of Berman. Thus, under the Takings Clause, "public use" means only public purpose.

William B. Stoebuck

Betts v. Brady, 316 U.S. 455 (1942), argued 13–14 Apr. 1942, decided 1 June 1942 by vote of 6 to 3; Roberts for the Court, Black in dissent. After indictment for robbery, Betts asked the trial court to appoint an attorney to assist in his defense. The trial judge refused; Betts represented himself and was convicted. While incarcerated, Betts filed habeas corpus petitions. Lower courts rejected these petitions, and Betts

filed a certiorari petition with the U.S. Supreme Court.

At issue before the Court was Betts's claim that the trial court's refusal to extend the right to counsel to noncapital felonies constituted a violation of the Sixth Amendment provision as incorporated by the Fourteenth Amendment. In his opinion for the Court, Justice Owen J. Roberts rejected Betts's claim, concluding that most states did not require appointment of counsel for fair trials and that the circumstances of his case did not suggest that such assistance was necessary. The Court distinguished Betts's situation from that of an earlier Court decision, *Powell* v. *Alabama* (1932), where young African-American defendants were charged with a capital offense and where the Court concluded that appointed counsel was essential for a fair trial.

Justice Hugo Black was joined in dissent by Justices William O. Douglas and Frank Murphy. Black emphasized that Betts's petition would have been granted had he been a defendant in federal criminal proceedings, that the petitioner was entitled to the procedural protection provided by the federal Constitution, and that the right to counsel was fundamental to criminal due process.

Betts v. *Brady* was ultimately overruled by *Gideon* v. *Wainwright* (1963), where the minority position in *Betts* was unanimously adopted by the Court.

Susette M. Talarico

Bigelow v. Virginia, 421 U.S. 809 (1975), argued 18 Dec. 1974, decided 16 June 1975 by vote of 7 to 2; Blackmun for the Court, Rehnquist, joined by White, in dissent. In February 1971 the *Virginia Weekly* of Charlottesville published an advertisement for the Women's Pavilion, a New York City for-profit organization that assisted women in obtaining abortions. The *Weekly*'s editor, Jeffrey C. Bigelow, was prosecuted for violating a Virginia statute that made it a misdemeanor to publish or "encourage or prompt the procuring of abortion." Bigelow argued that the statute was unconstitutionally overbroad and a violation of his free press rights under the First Amendment. But the Virginia courts declared the statute a proper consumer protection measure, and, relying on U.S. Supreme Court precedent, held that Bigelow lacked standing to raise the overbreadth issue because the "commercial" nature of the advertisement rendered it unprotected by the First Amendment.

In 1942 the Supreme Court had held that "commercial speech" was unprotected because it was more like an economic inducement than the exposition of ideas (*Valentine* v. *Chrestenson*). But the expansion of First Amendment freedoms in the intervening decades, and the fact that the Supreme Court had recently made abortion a constitutionally protected right (**Roe* v. *Wade*, 1973), compelled Justice Harry Blackmun (the author of *Roe*) and the Court to reconsider the commercial speech doctrine. The Court thus ruled that the *Weekly*'s advertisement merited First Amendment protection because it conveyed truthful information about a matter of significant public interest.

Bigelow set the stage for the Court's decision the next year formally to give some constitutional protection to commercial speech (*Virginia State Board of Pharmacy* v. *Virginia Citizens Consumer Council*, 1976). Today commercial speech is considered a "quasi-protected" category of expression. The justices reaffirmed this principle in **44 Liquormart, Inc.* v. *Rhode Island* (1996) when they struck down a state ban on the truthful, nonmisleading advertising of the price of alcoholic beverages.

Donald A. Downs

BMW of North America, Inc. v. Ira Gore, Jr., 517 U.S. 559 (1996), argued 11 Oct. 1995, decided 20 May 1996 by vote of 5 to 4; Stevens for the Court, Breyer concurring, Scalia, Thomas, Ginsburg, and Rehnquist in dissent. One of the sharpest areas of controversy in American law concerns the duties owed by product manufacturers to consumers. For people injured by a defective product or negligent behavior by a producer, a big court award is often the best hope for compensation. Such awards, however, can also have devastating consequences for a business, especially when it must pay punitive damages. These are damages paid to punish a business for past conduct and to prevent similar conduct in the future. They stand apart from compensatory damages, which are designed to compensate an individual for an actual loss. Since the early 1980s state legislatures had wrestled with the question of how to reform the tort system generally and the role of punitive damages in particular. It was in this context that *BMW* reached the Supreme Court.

The case involved a Birmingham, Alabama, oncologist, Dr. Ira Gore, Jr. He had paid $40,750 for a black BMW 535si only to discover nine months later that his supposedly "new" car had been damaged in transit and then repainted by BMW. The company had never disclosed to Gore that the car had been repainted, a practice common in the automobile business and one regulated in many states by a provision that only if the repair amounted to more than 3 percent of the value of the car did the company have a duty to disclose. The cost of the paint job was $601. Gore, however, claimed that BMW had breached its contract with him and committed a fraud in the process. A trial court agreed and awarded Gore $4,000 in compensatory damages and $4 million in punitive damages. The jury set the punitive damage figure based on evidence that BMW had sold nearly 1,000 such refinished cars in the United States. The Alabama Supreme Court heard the case on appeal, upheld the verdict, but cut the punitive damage award in half, to $2 million.

A divided United States Supreme Court found in favor of BMW. The company had argued before the justices that the Due Process Clause of the Fourteenth Amendment rendered such punitive damage awards unconstitutional as "grossly excessive" in relation to the state of Alabama's legitimate interests in punishing unlawful conduct and preventing a repetition of it. Justice John Paul Stevens, writing for the majority, agreed. Stevens and the majority were reacting to skyrocketing punitive damage awards and the windfalls they brought to plaintiffs who had not suffered serious injury. Stevens cited not only the Due Process Clause but also what he termed elementary notions of fairness that formed the fabric of the Constitution in siding with the company. Stevens also concluded that it was inappropriate for the Alabama courts to take account of conduct by BMW elsewhere in the country as a basis upon which to calculate punitive damages. Hence, Alabama courts could consider only the economic interests of Alabama consumers in making decisions about damages. Stevens also observed that the three most important indicators of the appropriateness of a punitive damage award were not met. In this instance, BMW's conduct was not reprehensible, the punitive damages and compensatory damages were entirely out of balance, and there was a huge gap between how BMW would have been punished for comparable conduct under criminal law. Stevens, however, refused to draw a bright line designating the point at which such damages became excessive, and he remanded the case back to Alabama. In essence, the Court had set a standard not unlike that associated with obscenity: they knew it when they saw it.

The dissenters, led by Justices Antonin Scalia and Ruth Bader Ginsburg, insisted that the majority's decision undermined the historic role of the states in dealing with punitive damages. Such decisions, they concluded, were better left to state legislatures than to the Supreme Court. As important, Scalia concluded that the Court's opinion actually offered no guidance to legislatures about what would be constitutionally acceptable and, therefore, threatened to throw the entire tort reform effort into chaos.

BMW was in some ways a victory for business, since it placed some judicial limits on punitive damage awards as a constitutional matter. Yet the decision hardly did away with punitive damages. The decision did spur efforts in Congress to pass tort reform legislation, especially in the area of consumer products and punitive damages. President Bill Clinton, however, ended up vetoing a proposed statute that would have allowed punitive damages only if there was "clear and convincing evidence" that a defendant had been guilty of "conscious, flagrant indifference" to the rights or safety of others. Clinton, urged on by trial lawyers' organizations, did so in the belief that the legitimate problems of ordinary people should not be sacrificed to get rid of frivolous lawsuits. In the states, the tort reform effort continued to grind away, although *BMW* now hangs over it in a not altogether informative way.

Kermit L. Hall

Boerne v. Flores, 521 U.S. 507 (1997), argued 19 Feb. 1997, decided 25 June 1997 by a vote of 6 to 3; opinion delivered by Kennedy; concurring opinions by Scalia and Stevens; dissenting opinions by Breyer, O'Connor, and Souter. In 1993, Congress passed the Religious Freedom and Restoration Act (RFRA), which expressly forbade control of religious uses of land by local governments. The intent of the act was to restore strict scrutiny of local land use controls affecting religious uses under the doctrine of *Sherbert v. Verner* (1963) after the U.S. Supreme Court's decision in *Employment Div., Dept. of Human Resources v. Smith* (1990). That same year, the City of Boerne, Texas, turned down a

request for an addition to the Spanish Mission style St. Peter the Apostle Roman Catholic Church, a designated landmark in the City's historic district. The addition would have replaced nearly 80 percent of the church, so the city council found that such expansion would impermissibly alter the exterior of the structure. P. F. Flores, archbishop of San Antonio, Texas, challenged that denial on the ground that RFRA exempted St. Peters from landmark designation.

In *City of Boerne v. Flores*, the Supreme Court held the statute unconstitutional on the ground that Congress exceeded its authority. While Congress relied on the Fourteenth Amendment to the U.S. Constitution in imposing RFRA's requirements on the states, the Court held that RFRA is not a proper exercise of Congress's section 5 powers to enforce the life, liberty, or property guarantees in that amendment because it contradicts vital principles necessary to maintain the separation of powers and the federal-state balance. The Court held that RFRA attempted a substantive change in constitutional protections rather than a response to prevent state unconstitutional behavior. As such, RFRA is a considerable congressional intrusion into the states' traditional prerogatives and general authority to regulate under the police powers.

Congress responded by passing the Religious Land Use and Institutionalized Persons Act (RLUIPA) in 2000, which specifically lists rezoning on its list of forbidden land use controls affecting religious properties. The result has been a fresh series of challenges. Several commentators expect RLUIPA to share the same fate as its unconstitutional predecessor or that courts will restrict its applicability, and the relatively few recent federal circuit court of appeals decisions appear to support this position. For example, *Civil Liberties for Urban Believers v. Chicago*, 342 F.3d 752 (7th Cir. 2003) confirmed a district court finding that placing churches on an "equal footing" with nonreligious assembly uses satisfied any RLUIPA requirements for local government, even if churches had to expend money to find suitable locations within city limits.

A random survey of federal district court opinions are more generally supportive of RLUIPA. Concluding that RLUIPA is a constitutional exercise of Congressional power under the Commerce Clause and the Fourteenth Amendment and did not violate the First or Tenth Amendments, the second circuit upheld the application of the act to overturn local government denial of an application for additions to a church school on substantial burden to religious freedom grounds.

David L. Callies

Bolling v. Sharpe, 347 U.S. 497 (1954), argued 10–11 Dec. 1952, reargued 8–9 Dec. 1953, decided 17 May 1954 by vote of 9 to 0; Warren for the Court. Chief Justice Earl Warren held that the Due Process Clause of the Fifth Amendment implicitly forbade most racial discrimination by the federal government just as the Equal Protection Clause of the Fourteenth Amendment restricts states. Having just held in *Brown* v. *Board of Education* (1954) that states could not segregate public schools on the basis of race, Warren wrote that "to impose a lesser duty" in the District of Columbia—where the Fifth Amendment covered congressional action—would be "unthinkable" (p. 500) but many scholars accused Warren of begging the question.

Dennis J. Hutchinson

Bowers v. Hardwick, 478 U.S. 186 (1986), argued 31 Mar. 1986, decided 30 June 1986 by vote of 5 to 4; White for the Court, Blackmun and Stevens in dissent. In this case, the Supreme Court refused to extend the constitutional right of privacy to protect acts of consensual homosexual sodomy performed in the privacy of one's own home. The narrow majority led by Justice Byron White differentiated this case from earlier right-to-privacy decisions, saying that those decisions were limited to circumstances involving "family, marriage, or procreation"—things that bore "no connection" to homosexual activity (p. 191). Indeed, White claimed that the right to privacy was limited to the reach of those previous cases. He further claimed that the proposition that "any kind of private sexual conduct between consenting adults is constitutionally insulated from state proscription is unsupportable" (p. 191). To argue that the right to engage in such conduct is a fundamental right" 'deeply rooted in this Nation's history and tradition' or 'implicit in the concept of ordered liberty' is, at best, facetious," White wrote (p. 194). He pointed out that until 1961 all fifty states had outlawed sodomy and that twenty-four states and the District of Columbia continued to do so in 1986. He then rejected Hardwick's claim that such laws lack a rational basis.

White also differentiated the *Hardwick* case from *Stanley* v. *Georgia* (1969), arguing that *Stanley* should be understood as a First Amendment case that was not relevant to the issues raised in *Hardwick*. Although *Stanley* protected individuals from prosecution for possessing and reading obscene materials in the privacy of their homes, White stressed that it did not offer blanket protection to otherwise illegal conduct simply because it occurs in the home.

The present case evolved out of the arrest of Michael Hardwick, a gay Atlanta bartender, for performing oral sex with another man in his own bedroom. They were discovered by a police officer who had come to serve a warrant on Hardwick for not paying a fine for drinking in public. The officer was given permission to enter the house by another tenant who did not know whether Hardwick was at home. Under Georgia law, sodomy (defined as "any sexual act involving the sex organs of one person and the mouth or anus of another") was a felony that could bring up to twenty years in prison.

Although the district attorney did not prosecute, he did not drop the charge. Hardwick then brought a civil suit challenging the law's constitutionality in federal court. The defendant was Georgia's attorney general, Michael J. Bowers. The district court granted Bowers' motion to dismiss, but a divided panel of the Court of Appeals for the Eleventh Circuit reversed on the grounds that the Georgia statute violated Hardwick's fundamental rights. The Supreme Court then granted Bowers's petition for certiorari. Since the only claim before the Court dealt with homosexual sodomy, it expressed no opinion about the constitutionality of the Georgia statute as applied to acts of heterosexual sodomy.

Justice Lewis Powell was the crucial swing vote in the case. It appears that at conference he tentatively agreed to provide the fifth vote for striking down the Georgia statute, but then later changed his mind. Powell felt that a prison sentence for sodomy would create a serious Eighth Amendment issue that could be used to strike down the statute, but Hardwick had not been prosecuted. Thus, Powell was unable to apply the Eighth Amendment issue to this case, and he was apparently uncomfortable with using the right of privacy to strike down the statute. In October 1990, Powell told law students at New York University that he had "probably made a mistake" in ultimately voting the way he did. Nonetheless, he maintained that *Hardwick* was "a frivolous case" since no one had been prosecuted.

Had Powell not changed his vote, Justice Harry Blackmun would have written the majority opinion. Instead, White wrote the majority opinion, Powell added a carefully worded concurrence that pointed out the Court's inability to address the Eighth Amendment issue, and Blackmun wrote a harsh dissent. When the decision was handed down, both White and Blackmun took the unusual step of reading detailed portions of their opinions from the bench.

Blackmun strongly criticized the majority opinion, saying that the case was no more about a "fundamental right to engage in homosexual sodomy" than *Stanley* v. *Georgia* was about a fundamental right to watch obscene movies. Rather, he concluded, "this case is about 'the most comprehensive of rights and the right most valued by civilized men,' namely, 'the right to be let alone'" (p. 199). Blackmun also took issue with the majority's refusal to consider whether the Georgia statute ran afoul of the Eighth or Ninth Amendments or the Equal Protection Clause of the Fourteenth Amendment. "The Court's cramped reading of the issue before it makes for a short opinion," Blackmun concluded, "but it does little to make for a persuasive one" (pp. 202–203).

John Anthony Maltese

Bowsher v. Synar, 478 U.S. 714 (1986), argued 23 Apr. 1986, decided 7 July 1986 by vote of 7 to 2; Burger for the Court, Stevens, joined by Marshall, concurring, White and Blackmun in dissent. In this decision, the Supreme Court struck down a key provision of the Balanced Budget and Emergency Deficit Control Act of 1985. The statute provided that there should be progressive annual cuts in the federal budget deficit. The contested provision stated that the cuts would be specified by the comptroller general if Congress could not agree on them.

The constitutional challenge rested on the fact that the comptroller general is regarded as a legislative branch officer who is removable only by joint resolution of both houses of Congress. The majority concluded that the specification of budget cuts was an executive function and that to vest such a function in a legislative branch officer violated the principle of separation of powers.

Justice John Paul Stevens, concurring in the judgment, concluded that the comptroller general's function should be seen as legislative in nature. He reasoned that a legislative action could not be taken by a single legislative officer but instead must be adopted by both houses of Congress and presented to the president for approval or veto (see *Immigration and Naturalization Service v. Chadha,* 1983).

The majority concluded that a "legislative action" consists of the adoption of general legal standards, whereas an "executive action" consists of acting pursuant to statute. This sequential definition of the separation of powers is formalistic and, as Justice Stevens's concurrence shows, subject to different interpretations. Nonetheless, *Bowsher* reinforces the idea that the separation of powers should be given some bright-line meaning despite the difficulties of doing so in an era of complex government.

Thomas O. Sargentich

Boy Scouts of America v. Dale, 530 U.S. 640 (2000), argued 26 Apr. 2000, decided 28 June 2000 by vote of 5 to 4, Rehnquist for the Court, Stevens and Souter in dissent.

In 1990, Boy Scouts of America (BSA) revoked the membership of Assistant Scoutmaster and Eagle Scout James Dale, charging that Dale failed to meet BSA's standards, which "forbid membership to homosexuals." Dale, assisted by Lambda Legal, filed suit in the New Jersey courts.

In *Roberts* v. *United States Jaycees* (1984) and *Rotary International* v. *Rotary Club of Duarte* (1987), the Supreme Court has recognized a "right to associate for the purpose of engaging in those activities protected by the First Amendment . . . as an indispensable means of preserving other individual liberties" (*Roberts* p. 618). This freedom of expressive association implied the right to be able to control political, religious, or cultural messages attributed to a group.

In this manner, freedom of association may come into tension with the goal of nondiscrimination. Freedom of expressive association case law attempts to balance these competing claims—the right of a group to control its message versus the right of individual or potential group members to be treated without prejudice. The Court's precedents hold that compelling state interests, unrelated to the suppression of ideas, may justify some infringement upon freedom of association, provided the state does so by the least restrictive means.

In *Dale*, the Court held, 5 to 4, that the forced inclusion of homosexuals as BSA members would significantly alter Boy Scouts' message, impairing its First Amendment right of "protected association." The majority accepted BSA's assertion that it is a private association that "teaches that homosexual conduct is not morally straight." Relying on *Hurley* v. *Irish-American GLB Group* (1995), BSA could not to be compelled to send a message it did not want to send. The Court also noted that expansive definitions of the term "public accommodation" in state statutes increasingly threaten First Amendment values.

Justice John Paul Stevens asserted in dissent that Dale's mere membership could not be construed as BSA's own speech, unless one concludes that "homosexuals are simply so different from the rest of society that their presence alone . . . should be singled out for special First Amendment treatment" (p. 696).

Boy Scouts is also about the progress and status of the gay civil rights movement. The Court had held in *Bowers* v. *Hardwick* (1986) that the right of privacy should not be extended to acts of adult consensual homosexual sodomy performed at home, a position it overturned in *Lawrence* v. *Texas* (2004). The Court in *Lawrence* appeared to be responding to, or sharing, the public's growing sentiments of limited tolerance.

Erin Ackerman

Boyd v. United States, 116 U.S. 616 (1886), argued 11, 14 Dec. 1885, decided 1 Feb. 1886 by vote of 9 to 0; Bradley for the Court, Miller concurring. *Boyd* was the first decision of the Supreme Court to give extensive consideration to the relationship between the Fourth and Fifth Amendments. Although later opinions have restricted its expansive interpretation of the two amendments, *Boyd* remains a landmark in the development of protections for the right to privacy.

The case concerned an allegation that E. A. Boyd & Sons had imported plate glass without paying the duty required by the 1874 customs act. As authorized by the act, the United States attorney obtained a court order that the Boyds produce their invoices for the glass. The case was a civil proceeding, involving no criminal charges. The Boyds contended that the compulsory production of records violated their rights under the Fourth Amendment prohibiting

unreasonable searches and seizures and the Fifth Amendment protecting freedom from compulsory self-incrimination.

The entire Court upheld the Boyds' arguments, with the exception of two justices who declined to accept the Fourth Amendment argument. Justice Joseph P. Bradley, writing for the Court, relied on over two centuries of English and American legal history to support his conclusion that the two amendments protected the privacies of individual life from governmental intrusion. He rejected arguments that the amendments applied only in criminal proceedings and when there had been a physical invasion of property. Accordingly, he concluded that a section of the customs statute was unconstitutional because it authorized the compulsory production of records. Bradley also anticipated the exclusionary rule by holding that the admission of the invoices into evidence was unconstitutional.

Walter F. Pratt, Jr.

Bradwell v. Illinois, 16 Wall. (83 U.S.) 130 (1873), argued 18 Jan. 1873, decided 15 Apr. 1873 by vote of 8 to 1; Miller for the Court, Bradley, Field, and Swayne concurring, Chase in dissent. Myra Bradwell (1831– 1894), who had studied law with her attorney husband, James B. Bradwell, founded and published the *Chicago Legal News*, the leading midwestern legal publication. An Illinois statute provided that any adult "person," of good character and having the requisite training, was eligible for admission to the bar. The Illinois Supreme Court denied her admission, however, because she was a woman. Bradwell then sought a writ of error from the U.S. Supreme Court, claiming that her right to practice law was one of the privileges protected by the Fourteenth Amendment.

The Court's majority upheld the action of the Illinois court on the grounds that the Privileges and Immunities Clause of the Fourteenth Amendment, having been given its first (and extremely restrictive) interpretation only the day before in the *Slaughterhouse Cases* (1873), did not embrace the right to practice a profession. *Bradwell* v. *Illinois* thus confirmed the narrow view of the clause that has characterized the Court's approach to it ever since. But the decision is best remembered for dicta in Justice Joseph P. Bradley's concurrence. He stated: "The paramount destiny and mission of woman are to fulfill the noble and benign offices of wife and mother. This is the law of the Creator" (p. 141). It was not until almost one hundred years later that the Court began to use the Fourteenth Amendment to overturn sex discriminatory state laws, and then it used the "equal protection" clause of that amendment rather than the "privileges and immunities" clause (*Reed v. Reed, 1971).

Nancy S. Erickson

Brandenburg v. Ohio, 395 U.S. 444 (1969), argued 27 Feb. 1969, decided 9 June 1969 by unanimous vote; per curiam decision. *Brandenburg v. Ohio* was decided in the context of the significant expansion of First Amendment freedoms in the 1960s. It was the final step in the Supreme Court's tortuous fifty-year development of a constitutional test for speech that advocates illegal action.

Clarence Brandenburg was convicted of violating an Ohio criminal syndicalism statute for advocating racial strife during a televised Ku Klux Klan rally. The statute was identical to one previously upheld by the Supreme Court in *Whitney v. California* (1927). The Court fashioned a test that was significantly more protective of dangerous speech than the previous "clear and present danger" test employed in previous cases. *Whitney* was overturned.

In its various incarnations, the old clear and present danger test had permitted the punishment of speech if it had a "tendency" to encourage or cause lawlessness (*Schenck v. U.S.*, 1919), or if the speech was part of a broader dangerous political movement, like the Communist party (*Dennis v. U.S.*, 1951). The *Brandenburg* test, however, allowed government to punish the advocacy of illegal action only if "such advocacy is directed to inciting or producing imminent lawless action and is likely to incite or produce such action" (p. 447).

By requiring an actual empirical finding of imminent harm, this test protects the advocacy of lawlessness except in unusual instances. But government may still punish speech that is demonstrably dangerous. The test is also distinctly more objective than the old danger test. *Brandenburg* is the lynchpin of the modern doctrine of free speech, which seeks to give special protection to politically relevant speech and to distinguish speech from action.

Donald A. Downs

Branzburg v. Hayes; In re Pappas; United States v. Caldwell, 408 U.S. 665 (1972),
argued 22–23 Feb. 1972, decided 29 June 1972 by vote of 5 to 4; White for the Court, Stewart, Brennan, Marshall, and Douglas in dissent. Social unrest during the early 1970s prompted an increased grand jury interest in information collected by investigative reporters who often claimed First Amendment privilege to protect the confidentiality of sources.

Paul Branzburg of the *Louisville Courier-Journal* moved to quash a Kentucky grand jury subpoena that sought additional information about his story on the manufacture of hashish. Television journalist Paul Pappas refused to answer a Massachusetts grand jury's questions about his coverage of the Black Panthers. A Northern District of California federal grand jury held *New York Times* reporter Earl Caldwell in contempt for refusing to appear to answer questions about the Black Panthers. A Ninth Circuit Court of Appeals later reversed the ruling.

The U.S. Supreme Court, in a sharply divided vote, decided against a special First Amendment privilege for the press. Justice Byron White relied on common law and case law to hold that a reporter's responsibility to a grand jury did not differ from any other citizen. The grand jury, he said, was entitled to "everyman's evidence" (p. 688). White concluded that only legislatures could establish additional protection for reporters' testimonial privilege.

Justice Potter Stewart, dissenting for himself, William Brennan, and Thurgood Marshall, argued that protecting the confidentiality of sources was essential to newsgathering. He thus would have required the showing of a compelling interest before a grand jury could obtain privileged information from reporters. Justice William O. Douglas also dissented vigorously and emphasized the importance of the public's access to information.

The *Branzburg* case prompted spirited discussion and a movement for shield laws to protect the press. A number of states added statutes or modified those in place, but shield proponents were unable to persuade Congress to pass a national privilege protection law. Nearly twenty years later in *Cohen v. Cowles Media* (1991), White again wrote for a majority of five to deny a claim of a special press privilege. The Court held that the First Amendment does not protect a newspaper from litigation if an editor, asserting the public's right to information, breaks a reporter's promise of confidentiality to a source.

Carol E. Jensen

Brecht v. Abrahamson, 507 U.S. 619 (1993), argued 1 Dec. 1992, decided 21 Apr. 1993 by vote of 5 to 4; Rehnquist for the Court, Souter, White, Blackmun, and O'Connor in dissent.

In the early 1990s the Supreme Court struggled over the scope of the habeas corpus authority of the federal courts to hear and scrutinize state court criminal justice rulings. That struggle was part of a larger societal debate about how to deal with rising crime rates. Law enforcement officials, for their part, insisted that the federal courts had too willingly accepted habeas corpus petitions and in so doing failed to foster an appropriate sense of finality and of timely punishment. Defendants' rights advocates countered that by restricting access to habeas corpus protections in the federal courts, innocent persons would be wrongly convicted and prisoners denied a constitutional means of redress.

Brecht raised these concerns in a case involving Todd A. Brecht, who had been convicted in a Wisconsin court for shooting his brother-in-law to death. The prosecutor made known to the jury that Brecht had refused to say anything else to authorities after being read his Miranda rights, which include a provision advising him that he had a right to remain silent. The Supreme Court had ruled in *Stone* v. *Powell* (1976) that a jury should not be told of a defendant's refusal to talk. Brecht sought a writ of habeas corpus on the grounds that the trial judge had erred in permitting the trial to go forward.

Chief Justice William H. Rehnquist, who sought to limit the scope of habeas corpus, succeeded in forging a majority to do just that. The general standard for error by the prosecution in a trial requires a conviction to be overturned unless the error was "harmless beyond a reasonable doubt." Rehnquist added teeth to this requirement by finding that a state ruling should not be disturbed unless the violation "had a substantial and injurious effect or influence in determining the jury's verdict" (p. 627). He said federal habeas corpus review should be reserved for the most outrageous cases in which clear evidence proved that a prisoner had been harmed by prejudice in the trial. If a defendant's guilt was not actually in doubt, the federal courts should not overturn a state verdict. In this case, Rehnquist decided, the error was harmless and the guilt of Brecht beyond doubt.

The *Brecht* decision further narrowed the grounds for appeal through a habeas corpus proceeding. At the same time, however, the justices left open a narrow window of appeal in the case of *Withrow* v. *Williams* (1993), decided at the same time as *Brecht*. The dissenters in *Brecht*, led by Justice David Souter, decided that federal courts should remain open to appeals from state prisoners challenging their convictions on the grounds that they were interrogated by the police without being told of their right to remain silent. In *Withrow*, of course, the prisoner had not been advised of his rights; in *Brecht* he had. Still, the two decisions underscored the close division and continuing tension in the Court over the habeas corpus issue.

Kermit L. Hall

Breediove v. Suttles, 302 U.S. 277 (1937), argued 16–17 Nov. 1937, decided 6 Dec. 1937 by vote of 9 to 0; Butler for the Court. This case involved a challenge to the Georgia poll tax by a white male citizen who claimed that it denied his right to equal protection of the laws under the Fourteenth Amendment and his Nineteenth Amendment right not to be discriminated against in voting on account of sex. The law required a tax of one dollar per year before registering to vote but exempted persons under 21 and over 60, blind persons, and females who did not register to vote. The Supreme Court unanimously upheld the law and rejected the claim. Observing that the Equal Protection Clause does not require absolute equality, Justice Pierce Butler asserted that it was reasonable to limit the poll tax in the manner of the statute. He explained that it would be impossible to make the tax universal because many people were too poor to pay. He said further that women were naturally entitled to special considerations that permitted the state to discriminate in their favor. The Nineteenth Amendment challenge failed because it would have made the amendment in effect a limitation on the state taxing power.

Herman Belz

Briscoe v. Bank of the Commonwealth of Kentucky, 11 Pet. (36 U.S.) 257 (1837), argued 28 Jan., 1 Feb. 1837, decided 11 Feb. 1837 by vote of 6 to 1; McLean for the Court, Story in dissent. With the death of

John Marshall in 1835, the Supreme Court's orientation shifted away from his nationalist outlook. *Briscoe* v. *Bank of Kentucky* manifested this change in the field of banking and currency in the first full term of the court's new chief justice, Roger B. Taney. Article I, section 10 of the Constitution prohibited states from using "bills of credit," but the precise meaning of a "bill of credit" remained unclear. In *Craig* v. *Missouri* (1830) the Marshall Court had held, by a vote of 4 to 3, that state interest-bearing loan certificates were invalid under the constitutional prohibition. However, in the *Briscoe* case, the Court upheld the issuance of circulating notes by a state-chartered bank even when the Bank's stock, funds, and profits belonged to the state, and where the officers and directors were appointed by the state legislature. The Court narrowly defined a "bill of credit" as a note issued by the state, on the faith of the state, and designed to circulate as money. Since the notes in question were redeemable by the bank and not by the state itself, they were not "bills of credit" for constitutional purposes. By validating the constitutionality of state bank notes, the Supreme Court completed the financial revolution triggered by President Andrew Jackson's refusal to recharter the Second Bank of the United States and opened the door to greater state control of banking and currency in the antebellum period.

George Dargo

Bronson v. Kinzie, 42 U.S. 311 (1843), submitted without oral argument, decided 23 Feb. 1843 by vote of 6 to 1; Taney for the Court, McLean in dissent, Story and McKinley not participating. *Bronson* exemplified the Supreme Court's determination to protect private contracts from infringement by state legislation. At issue were two 1841 Illinois statutes that limited mortgage foreclosure sales and gave mortgagors expanded rights to redeem foreclosed property. These measures were retroactive, applying to mortgages made before the acts were passed. Prior to passage of the statutes, John H. Kinzie had mortgaged his property to Arthur Bronson. Bronson sought to foreclose the mortgage free of the legislative restrictions.

Chief Justice Roger B. Taney held that this legislative attempt to modify the terms of the existing mortgage was an unconstitutional impairment of the obligation of contract. Taney agreed that a state could alter the remedies available to enforce past as well as future contracts. He nonetheless emphasized that such changes could not materially impair the rights of creditors. In broad language Taney extolled the virtue of the Contract Clause: "It was undoubtedly adopted as a part of the Constitution for a great and useful purpose. It was to maintain the integrity of contracts, and to secure their faithful execution throughout this Union" (p. 318). In dissent, Justice John McLean argued that the statutes simply modified the remedy for the enforcement of contracts.

The Court long adhered to the *Bronson* rule, invalidating state laws that interfered with contractual rights in the guise of regulating remedies. The decision was effectively superseded, however, by *Home Building and Loan Association* v. *Blaisdell* (1934), in which the justices ruled that contracts were subject to the reasonable exercise of state police power.

James W. Ely, Jr.

Brown v. Board of Education, 347 U.S. 483 (1954), argued 9 Dec. 1952, reargued 8 Dec. 1953, decided 17 May 1954 by vote of 9 to 0; Warren for the Court (*Brown I*); 349 U.S. 294 (1955), reargued, on the question of relief, 11–14 April 1954, decided 31 May 1955 by vote of 9 to 0; Warren for the Court (*Brown II*). With a brisk, nontechnical and unexpectedly unanimous opinion running only ten pages, Chief Justice Earl Warren ignited a legal and social revolution in race relations and constitutionalism. "*Brown* was the beginning," Alexander M. Bickel later wrote—the beginning not only of substantive changes in the American social structure but also in the nature and expectations of how the Supreme Court interpreted the Constitution.

Background. The decisions—on the merits (*Brown I*) and on relief (*Brown II*)—culminated a litigation campaign by the National Association for the Advancement of Colored People (NAACP) and its legal arm, the Legal Defense and Education Fund, Inc., that began twenty years earlier. Beginning in the mid-1930s, the NAACP brought suits first at the state and then at the federal level challenging, on constitutional grounds, the legal regime of "Jim Crow"—state-imposed racial segregation in public accommodations and in education. The goal was to abolish Jim Crow and to spur substantive improvement in public education for African-Americans. The primary obstacle facing the NAACP was *Plessy* v. *Ferguson* (1896), in which the Supreme Court had held 7 to 1 that state-imposed racial segregation in public facilities was not "unreasonable" and therefore did not violate the Equal Protection Clause of the Fourteenth Amendment.

The initial steps in the strategy did not confront *Plessy* frontally but sought to undermine it. When the Supreme Court invalidated Missouri's out-of-state tuition program for African-American law students in 1938 (*Missouri ex rel. Gaines* v. *Canada*), everyone knew that the legal superstructure of Jim Crow was vulnerable. Successive decisions by the Court, largely involving cases brought by the NAACP, continued the erosion of Jim Crow in public transportation and in education.

The biggest break occurred in 1948, when the United States attorney general, for the first time, signed an amicus curiae brief in a race case (*Shelley* v. *Kraemer*), which signaled the federal government's symbolic support for the NAACP strategy. The Court held radically restrictive covenants unconstitutional in that case, but the watershed did not come until two years later in 1950, when the Court invalidated segregation in graduate schools (*McLaurin* v. *Oklahoma State Board of Regents*) and in law schools (*Sweatt* v. *Painter*). The Court's opinions in both cases noted the inequality of facilities created by Jim Crow, but disapproved, for the first time, the "intangible" but genuine harms of racial segregation—such as inability of blacks to associate with white colleagues and the consequent limitation to their education. Unbeknownst outside the Court, many of the justices concluded privately in 1950 that *McLaurin* and *Sweatt* sealed the fate of Jim Crow and of *Plessy* itself.

The stumbling block in the *Brown* litigation, which affected more than a dozen states and the District of Columbia, and their millions of school children, and which was in progress when the 1950 cases were decided, was the scope of relief. When *Brown* was first argued in 1952, the Court internally was divided not so much on the merits but on how, and at what pace, to order relief. The Court remained at loggerheads over the issue during the summer of 1953 when fate intervened. Chief Justice Fred Vinson, who wrote *Sweatt* and *McLaurin* but hesitated to require massive desegregation, died suddenly. His replacement, Earl Warren,

responded to the situation by convincing his colleagues to decide the merits in one opinion and to defer the question of relief to a second opinion following reargument. At the time, Warren's greatest achievement was thought to be massing a Court unanimous in both vote and opinion; to do so, he had to convince at least two justices, Robert H. Jackson (concurrence) and Stanley F. Reed (dissent), to suppress opinions that they were then preparing. The Court's ultimate unanimity was publicly applauded and was said to buttress the wisdom of the result.

Opinions. Warren later revealed in his memoirs that he wrote *Brown I* in a short, nonaccusatory, and nontechnical style so that it could be understood by laymen and even be reprinted widely in the public press. The opinion elided all of the hard questions: the evidence of the historical understanding of the Equal Protection Clause—upon which the parties had been directed to focus their reargument—was deemed "inconclusive"; *Plessy's* claim that segregation caused no harm was refuted by modern social science data (including highly controversial works cited in Footnote 11); and *Plessy* itself was disingenuously circumscribed ("In the field of public education, separate but equal has no place" [p. 494]). Warren tried to show that the Court had incrementally chipped away at *Plessy* in the preceding cases and, in a larger sense, that the logic of *Plessy* had self-destructed over time, as African-Americans became more successful in various fields, and as education became more central to American life. Indeed, *Brown* self-consciously avoided questioning the entire structure of Jim Crow in all of its applications but focused exclusively on segregated education and on its harm to those separated because of their race.

If *Brown I* contained moral clarity without explicit doctrinal foundation, *Brown II*—rendered one year later—lacked both. The NAACP urged desegregation to proceed immediately, or at least within firm deadlines. The states claimed both were impracticable. The Court, fearful of hostility and even violence if the NAACP views were adopted, embraced a view close to that of the states—but with insistence that progress begin soon. Nonetheless, the opinion equivocated on every line and essentially returned the problem to the courts where the cases began for appropriate desegregative relief—with, in the phrase that soon was condemned for its invitation to recalcitrance, "all deliberate speed." A Court admirably unanimous on the merits in 1954 became ambiguously, indeed emptily, unanimous on the key issue of relief in 1955.

Brown II imposed substantial costs on all concerned. The burden of producing multi-million-student desegregation plans was placed on the plaintiffs and the NAACP, who were undermanned, thinly financed, and targets of hostility. The justices had privately hoped that the Department of Justice, which had participated in all of the *Brown* arguments, would energetically support the plaintiffs, but President Eisenhower chronically avoided the issue and promised no more than "to obey the law of the land." School districts were caught in a political whipsaw between a handful of reform-minded residents who wished to make desegregation work and the vast majority who resisted change and saw the issue as fuel for their own devices. Southern congressional leaders and regional governors were especially outspoken in their defiance of the decisions.

The Court itself suffered symbolically to some extent. If *Brown I* was a clarion call, *Brown II*'s ambivalence implicitly diminished the moral imperative of the first decision. As organized resistance, especially in Congress, and less organized resistance at the grass roots, mounted, the Court retreated and did not hear another case involving segregation for more than three years after *Brown II*. Then, in *Cooper* v. *Aaron* (1958), the Court's opinion on the Little Rock, Arkansas, school crisis of 1957–1958, spoke more to the importance of the Court's own power than to the substantive issue of *equal protection of the laws.

Aftermath. Between *Brown II* and *Cooper* v. *Aaron*, the Court refused to hear further cases involving segregation and the scope of *Brown* but issued a series of controversial per curiam decisions based solely on requests for review of lower court decisions. The Court invalidated segregated state parks, beaches and bath houses, golf courses, and even public transportation. The final decision (*Gayle* v. *Browder*, 1956) was tinged with irony, because it effectively overruled *Plessy*—a step the Court found unnecessary to take in *Brown* and that the per curiam order did not even admit was in issue. The reasonless per curiam orders prompted many legal scholars to warn that the Court was acting more out of conviction than principle and urged the justices to

explain their actions, both to refute southern charges of willfulness and to provide guidance for future cases involving racial issues in nonsegregation situations. *Bolling* v. *Sharpe* (1954), the companion case to *Brown* from the District of Columbia, provided the rudimentary doctrinal apparatus to meet the need, but the Court eschewed the opportunity.

Because *Brown II* provided so little guidance, either as to relief or as to the precise doctrinal foundation of *Brown I*, the Court put itself in the position of reexplaining, and effectively remaking, the basic principle in every successive segregation case. After reaffirming *Brown* against gubernatorial resistance in 1958 at Little Rock, the Court turned a doctrinal and substantive corner with *Green* v. *County School Board of New Kent County* in 1968 when it held that compliance with *Brown II* required not simply abolition of state-imposed segregative practices but the effective desegregation of formerly segregated schools. After *Green*, busing for racial balance was inevitable, which the Court confirmed in *Swann* v. *Charlotte-Mecklenburg County Board of Education* (1971).

On one level, *Brown* was remarkably ineffectual. By 1964, a decade after the first decision, less than 2 percent of formerly segregated school districts had experienced any desegregation. As *Brown* was applied outside the original jurisdictions where segregation was imposed or permitted by law, local resistance became even more fierce and sustained. Yet *Brown* was a potent catalyst for ambitious social change, both in Congress, where the aspirations of *Brown* helped prompt the Civil Rights Act of 1964 and the Voting Rights Act of 1965, among others, and in the federal courts themselves, where the decision's bold moral hopes and impatience with formal doctrinal obstacles encouraged a generation of lawyers and activists to improve society under the rubric of constitutional exegesis. Inspired by *Brown*, lawyers and judges breathed new life into not only the Equal Protection Clause of the Fourteenth Amendment but also its Due Process Clause (in both its procedural and its more controversial substantive senses). The Court itself was emboldened in part by the experience of *Brown* to expand federal protection for state defendants in criminal proceedings and to strengthen the protection of the First Amendment to critics of first state and then of the federal government during the decade following *Brown*. For example, the constitutional doctrine of "freedom of association," which was created by the Court in *NAACP* v. *Alabama* (1958), was directly related to school desegregation: state officials tried to compel the publication of the organization's membership lists in part to discourage support for desegregating schools.

Earl Warren's opinion for the Court in *Brown I* made the decision seem inevitable, and today, as Warren said in the companion case, a contrary result seems unthinkable. Yet the outcome was the product of a lengthy process that involved more than the NAACP and critical maneuvers inside the Court during the 1953 term. In many respects, the seeds for *Brown* were sown in the early 1930s, when the justices were presented with case after case in which black criminal defendants in the South were victimized by police, judges, and all-white juries. The stark reality of Jim Crow, and its routine brutality, impelled the Court to begin the process of dismantling Jim Crow piecemeal well before the NAACP strategy hit full stride during World War II. The courage of African-American servicemen during the war, and President Harry Truman's willingness to make civil rights a national issue in 1948—with a presidential commission and at the Democratic Convention as well as in *Shelley* v. *Kraemer*—provided the important symbolic presence of national support that helped to steel the Court's will to move from protection of African-American individuals to African-Americans as a class, and, inevitably, as a social movement. Whatever the consequences borne out by the case law, *Brown* remains a potent symbol of the aspiration for the Constitution and the values it enshrines.

□ Alexander M. Bickel, *The Least Dangerous Branch* (1962). Charles L. Black, Jr., "The Lawfulness of the Segregation Decisions," *Yale Law Journal* 69 (1960): 421–430. Dennis J. Hutchinson, "Unanimity and Desegregation," *Georgetown Law Journal* 68 (1979): 1–96. Richard Kluger, *Simple Justice* (1975). Philip B. Kurland, "*Brown* v. *Board of Education* Was the Beginning," *Washington University Law Quarterly* (1979): 309–405. Gerald Rosenberg, *The Hollow Hope* (1990). Mark Tushnet, *The NAACP's Legal Strategy Against Segregated Education, 1925–1950* (1987).

Dennis J. Hutchinson

Brown v. Maryland, 12 Wheat. (25 U.S.) 419 (1827), argued 28 Feb. and 1 Mar. 1827, decided 12 Mar. 1827 by vote of 6 to 1; Marshall for the Court, Thompson in dissent. In *Brown* v. *Maryland*, importers of foreign goods challenged a state law that required all persons who sold such goods to purchase a license. They alleged that it violated the ban on import taxes in Article 1, section 10 of the Constitution, as well as interfered with federal authority over interstate and foreign commerce. Chief Justice John Marshall sustained both contentions. He formulated the "original package" doctrine, which held that the taxing power of a state does not extend to imports from abroad so long as they remain in the original package. Only after the goods became mixed with the general property in the state could the state treat them as it did all domestic goods for sale. Marshall held a license tax on the importer to be indistinguishable from a tax on the import itself. Roger B. Taney, who succeeded Marshall as chief justice, had argued the case as counsel for the state of Maryland, but he later wrote that he believed the case had been correctly decided.

Marshall hinted that the *Brown* decision applied to domestic imports from a sister state, but in *Woodruff* v. *Parham* (1869) the Court held that the original package rule did not apply to goods moving in interstate commerce. In 1976 the Court further diluted the *Brown* doctrine when in *Michelin Tire Corporation* v. *Wages* it decided that a state might assess a value-based property tax upon a foreign import stored in a warehouse awaiting sale. To exempt a foreign import from a uniform state property tax, declared the Court, would accord it preferential treatment.

Robert J. Steamer

Brown v. Mississippi, 297 U.S. 278 (1936), argued 10 Jan. 1936, decided 17 Feb. 1936 by vote of 9 to 0; Hughes for the Court. In *Brown* v. *Mississippi*, the Supreme Court reversed the convictions of three African-American Mississippi tenant farmers for the murder of a white planter. At the trial, the prosecution's principal evidence was the defendants' confessions to police officers. During the trial, however, prosecution witnesses freely admitted that the defendants confessed only after being subjected to brutal whippings by the officers. The confessions were nevertheless admitted into evidence; the defendants were convicted by a jury and sentenced to be hanged; and the convictions were affirmed by the Mississippi Supreme Court on appeal.

Aided by financial contributions from the National Association for the Advancement of Colored People and the Commission on Interracial Cooperation, ex-Mississippi governor Earl Leroy Brewer appealed the convictions to the U.S. Supreme Court, which the Court unanimously reversed under the Due Process Clause of the Fourteenth Amendment. Although reaffirming the fact that the Self-Incrimination Clause of the Fifth Amendment did not apply to the states, Chief Justice Charles Evans Hughes nevertheless held that a criminal conviction based upon confessions elicited by physical brutality violated the fundamental right to a fair trial mandated by the Due Process Clause. *Brown* began a line of cases involving the methods by which confessions were elicited from criminal defendants that culminated with *Miranda v. Arizona* (1966).

Richard C. Cortner

Browning-Ferris Industries v. Kelco Disposal, Inc., 492 U.S. 257 (1989), argued 18 Apr. 1989, decided 26 June 1989 by vote of 7 to 2; Blackmun for the Court, O'Connor and Stevens dissenting in part. In *Browning-Ferris Industries*, the Court considered whether the Excessive Fines Clause of the Eighth Amendment applies to punitive damage awards in civil cases between private parties. The issue arose in a case involving the waste disposal business in Burlington, Vermont. Plaintiffs sued Browning-Ferris Industries (BFI) alleging that the company had attempted to drive them out of that business. The jury found for the plaintiffs and judgment was entered for more than $150,000 in treble compensatory damages and $6 million in punitive damages. On appeal to the Supreme Court, BFI argued that the punitive damages award was excessive and violated the Eighth Amendment, which reads: "Excessive bail shall not be required, nor excessive fines imposed, nor cruel and unusual punishments imposed."

The Court held that the Eighth Amendment does not apply to awards of punitive damages in cases between private parties. Although the Eighth Amendment received little debate in the First Congress, the word "fine" was understood to mean a payment to a sovereign. The "undisputed purpose and history" of that amendment confirm the conclusion that it places no limits on the amount of punitive damages that can be awarded to private parties. Rather, the amendment restricts the government's power to punish and deter individuals.

The Court left open two related issues. First, it did not decide whether the Excessive Fines Clause applies in civil cases brought by the government. Second, because the question was not properly presented, the Court did not decide whether the Due Process Clause limits a court's power to award punitive damages. However, in *BMW of North America v. Virginia* (1996) the justices for the first time held a punitive damage award was excessive under the Due Process Clause of the Fourteenth Amendment. The punitive damage award in this case was $2 million; the actual damage award for the precipitating injury was $4,000.

Daan Braveman

Buchanan v. Warley, 245 U.S. 60 (1917), argued 10–11 Apr. 1916, decided 5 Nov. 1917 by vote of 9 to 0; Day for the Court. In this case the Supreme Court considered the constitutionality of a Louisville, Kentucky, ordinance that required residential segregation by race. Enacted in 1914, the law prohibited blacks and whites from living in houses on blocks where the majority of houses was occupied by persons of the other race. In a case designed to test a type of legislation then appearing in several upper south states, a contract for the sale of property was arranged between a white seller and a black purchaser. In a unanimous decision the Supreme Court declared the law unconstitutional.

Justice William R. Day said the Civil Rights Act of 1866 and the Fourteenth Amendment secured the right of blacks to acquire property without state legislation discriminating against them solely because of color. More generally, the Court asked whether a white man could be denied the right to dispose of his property to a purchaser solely because the purchaser was black. Although acknowledging that race hostility was a problem that the law to some extent was bound to recognize, Justice Day stated that its solution "cannot be promoted by depriving citizens of their constitutional rights and privileges" (p. 81). Day concluded that the law violated the rights of both whites and blacks to dispose of their property and directly violated the Fourteenth Amendment prohibition of interference with property rights, except by due process of law. The Court distinguished *Plessy* v. *Ferguson* (1896) and *Berea College* v. *Kentucky* (1908) as approving reasonable regulations of Fourteenth Amendment rights under the separate but equal rule. This decision placed limits on the movement to segregate blacks and showed that protection of property rights could have the effect of securing civil rights.

Herman Belz

Buck v. Bell, 274 U.S. 200 (1927), argued 22 Apr. 1927, decided 2 May 1927 by vote of 8 to 1; Holmes for the Court, Butler in dissent without opinion. Gifted with the ability to express himself in tersely developed phrases, Justice Oliver Wendell Holmes provided some of his most quoted expressions in *Buck* v. *Bell* (1927). Upholding in an 8-to-1 opinion a Virginia law that provided for sterilization, Holmes not only continued a long held disposition to allow states the full sweep of their police powers but also laced his opinion with the prejudices shared by a nation.

The case had its beginnings in the Progressive Era with Albert Priddy, superintendent of the State Colony for Epileptics and Feeble-Minded at Lynchburg, Virginia. Enthusiastically endorsing the drive for race improvement through eugenical sterilization, Priddy practiced sterilization with the encouragement of the colony's board of directors. Since the legislation did not clearly sanction sterilization, a court in 1918 warned Priddy of his personal liability and he discontinued the operation.

State budget problems coincided with Priddy's efforts to get unequivocal legislation. With Aubrey Strode representing Priddy and the eugenical community, the 1924 assembly enacted a statute that provided for release, after sterilization, of individuals who otherwise might require permanent institutionalization. The law outlined procedures to be followed, including approval of the institution's board, appointment of a guardian, a hearing, and appeals to the courts.

Carrie Buck became caught in the web of events in 1924. A victim of rape, Carrie became pregnant. The family with which the eighteen-year-old lived had her committed to the colony, once the revised Binet-Simon I.Q. test revealed her mental age as nine. Her mother, Emma, who had been found to have a mental age of less than eight years, was also confined in the colony. After the birth of her daughter, Vivian, on 28 March 1924, Priddy recommended that Carrie be sterilized because she was feebleminded and a "moral delinquent." Concluding that Vivian inherited the same condition from her mother who had in turn inherited it from her mother, Priddy had a perfect test case. The colony board accepted his recommendation and retained attorneys, Strode to represent the colony and Irving Whitehead, former member of the colony's board and friend of Strode, to represent Carrie.

The trial in the county circuit court took place on 18 November 1924. Strode presented eight witnesses and an expert's disposition to prove Carrie's feeblemindedness. Describing the Buck family as part of the "shiftless, ignorant, and worthless class of anti-social whites" in the South, the court heard that Vivian, the third generation, was "not quite normal."

Whitehead called no witness to dispute either the "experts" or the allegations made about Carrie and her family. He could have challenged the charge of Carrie's illegitimacy and emphasized her church attendance and rather average school record. Whitehead failed in his defense because he intended to fail. The end he sought appears to have been the same as that sought by Priddy and Strode.

Now named *Buck* v. *Bell*, because John H. Bell had replaced Priddy at the colony, Whitehead in 1925 appealed the case to the United States Supreme Court. Strode's brief argued that due process had been afforded and that state police powers allowed its officers to protect and decide for persons such as Carrie Buck. Whitehead countered that the law discriminated against those confined to institutions and that a state could not surgically deprive persons of their "full bodily integrity." If allowed to do so, he warned, new classes, even "races" might be brought within the scope of the law and the "worst forms of tyranny practiced" in a "reign of doctors . . . inaugurated in the name of science."

Holmes rejected the argument for equal protection in his May 1927 opinion, noting that the law "indicates a policy, applies it to all within the lines and seeks to bring [others] within the lines . . . so fast as its means allow" (p. 208). Accepting eugenical arguments, he felt procedural guarantees had been "scrupulously" followed. Holmes contended that if the nation could call upon its "best citizens" for their lives during war it could demand a "lesser" sacrifice of those who "sap the strength" of society (p. 207). Prevention of procreation by degenerates would benefit society because "[t]hree generations of imbeciles are enough" (p. 207).

After the Court's ruling, Carrie was sterilized in October 1927. Numerous states passed similar laws and Nazi Germany gave the fullest sweep to the movement. This case provides a strong argument for careful scrutiny, especially at the local level, of ideas grounded upon popular notions of science.

□ Paul A. Lombardo, "Three Generations, No Imbeciles: New Light on *Buck* v. *Bell*," *New York Law Review* 60 (April 1985): 30–62.
Fred D. Ragan

Buckley v. Valeo, 424 U.S. 1 (1976), argued 16 Nov. 1975, decided 30 Jan. 1976 by varying votes on specific questions; opinion was unsigned, Burger, Blackmun, Rehnquist, White, and Marshall all dissented in part, Stevens not participating. Rarely has the Court recast congressional legislation in so many substantial particulars as it did in this case in ruling on the several provisions of the Federal Election Campaign Act (FECA) of 1971, as amended in 1974, and on relevant provisions of the Revenue Act of 1971, as amended in 1974. As the per curiam opinion indicates, different majorities of the eight participating justices decided the various challenges raised by candidates and others seeking to prevent the new campaign legislation from taking effect in the 1976 election.

The Court invalidated a provision of the law that permitted Congress to choose a majority of voting members of the Federal Election Commission (FEC) created to administer and enforce the FECA. Holding that this arrangement violated the Appointments Clause that empowered only the president to nominate such officers, the Court effectively told Congress to rewrite this portion of the FECA (which it promptly did) in order to maintain the FEC's considerable powers. The powers themselves were upheld, as were the FECA's detailed disclosure and reporting requirements.

More complicated were the Court's holdings on the First Amendment challenges to FECA restrictions of contributions and expenditures in federal elections. It upheld the several contribution limits (for example, the thousand-dollar maximum that each individual can contribute to a congressional or presidential candidate in each election campaign) on the ground that they are appropriate legislative weapons against improper influence stemming from the dependence of candidates on large contributions. On the other hand, expenditure limits were invalidated as substantial and direct restrictions on political expression in violation of the First Amendment. The Court thus erased Congress's attempt to fix not only overall limits on a candidate's expenditures, but also the limits on how much others could spend relative to a candidate (apart from direct contributions to the candidate) and the limits on how much candidates could spend from their own or their family's funds.

Invalidation of the last of these limits illustrates the nature of the Court's distinction between contributions and expenditures. Using millions of one's own dollars in a campaign, though effectively substituting for large contributions from others, does not corrupt or even seem to corrupt the candidate. Nevertheless, unwealthy opponents might well regard the Court-granted freedom of a rich candidate to spend millions from family wealth as an especially unfair advantage because they could not now, under the law, so readily compensate by finding a few very large contributors. A larger and more significant legal loophole was created by the Court's invalidation of the provision for limiting how much individuals and groups could spend to help candidates. These expenditures need only be "independent" of the candidate and the candidate's campaign committee in order to be unlimited as contributions to candidates are not.

In contrast to its mixed response to Congress's regulations of private campaign finance, the Court fully upheld the new provisions for public funding of presidential campaigns. These provisions include income tax check-off funds for parties to conduct presidential nominating conventions, for presidential primary candidates (on a matching basis), and for presidential general election candidates (on a virtually full-funding basis). Such funding, the Court held, is within Congress's power to spend under the General Welfare Clause, and it does not violate either the First Amendment or the Fifth Amendment's Due Process Clause. The latter issue arose because the arrangement for distributing funds was more likely to help major parties and their candidates than minor parties, new parties, or independents. But the Court interpreted the law as allowing sufficient opportunity for minor parties and their candidates to qualify for public funds, even though at lower levels.

One last element of judicial law-making should be noted. In upholding public funding, the Court also ruled that it is constitutionally valid to require, as Congress had done, that a presidential candidate must agree to an expenditure ceiling as a condition for receiving such funding. A ceiling thus voluntarily accepted does not fall under the Court's general prohibition of expenditure ceilings. Accordingly, if Congress or state legislatures should want to fix expenditure ceilings for candidates for other offices, the constitutional means to do so is to provide public funds along with the ceilings. But the Court made clear, in *Federal Election Commission* v. *National Conservative Political Action Committee* (1985), that such ceilings cannot be applied to those spending independently to help a publicly funded candidate.

Leon D. Epstein

Budd v. New York, 143 U.S. 517 (1892), argued 17–18 Nov. 1891, decided 29 Feb. 1892 by vote of 6 to 3; Blatchford for the Court, Brewer, Field, and Brown in dissent. *Budd* v. *New York* was an appeal from a decision of the New York Court of Appeals, *People* v. *Budd* (1889), which had upheld the constitutionality of a New York statute regulating rates charged by grain elevators, the same issue that had been resolved in *Munn* v. *Illinois* (1877). Conservative critics of *Munn* urged its repudiation in light of the doctrine of substantive due process that had grown ever more potent since 1877 and that had recently triumphed in Justice Samuel Blatchford's majority opinion in *Chicago, Milwaukee & St. Paul Railway Co.* v. *Minnesota* (1890).

But in *Budd* Justice Blatchford reaffirmed *Munn*, upholding the legitimacy of regulating grain elevators as businesses affected with a public interest. Rate regulation of such enterprises did not deny their owners due process of law in violation of the Fourteenth Amendment. Because regulation was confined to the territorial jurisdiction of New York, Blatchford found no violation of the Commerce Clause of Article I, section 8, either.

All this was too much for Justice David J. Brewer, dissenting. Brewer denounced the basic doctrine of *Munn* as "radically unsound" (p. 548) and trumpeted his clarion of laissezfaire constitutionalism. "The paternal theory of government is to me odious," Brewer wrote (p. 551). Though never explicitly overruled, *Munn* and *Budd* suffered an erosion of their authority through the New Deal.

William M. Wiecek

Bunting v. Oregon, 243 U.S. 426 (1917), argued 18 Apr. 1916, reargued 12 June 1916, reargued 19 Jan. 1917, decided 9 Apr. 1917 by vote of 5 to 3; McKenna for the Court, White, Van Devanter, and McReynolds in dissent, Brandeis recused. A 1913 Oregon law established a ten-hour day for all workers, men as well as women, in mills, factories, and manufacturing establishments, and required time-and-a-half pay for overtime. Bunting, a foreman in a mill, required an employee to work thirteen hours but did not pay the overtime and was convicted of violating the law. The National Consumers' League secured the services of Louis Brandeis to defend the law, but before the case came up for argument, he was appointed to the Court. Felix Frankfurter took over the case and submitted a massive "Brandeis brief" laden with facts showing that long hours were detrimental to workers' health.

The Court was badly split on this issue, primarily because some of the justices saw the overtime requirement as a wage regulation, the first step toward statutorily established minimum rates; the case had to be reargued twice. Finally a bare majority agreed that the time-and-a-half provision did not constitute a wage regulation but a penalty designed to discourage overtime work.

In his opinion, Justice Joseph McKenna indicated that the Court need not pass on the wisdom of the act but should accept the judgment of the Oregon legislature that a ten-hour maximum was necessary or useful for preserving the health of employees. The fact that the law did not apply to all workers, but only to those in certain industries, did not constitute discrimination that violated the Due Process Clause. Three members of the Court dissented without opinion.

Melvin I. Urofsky

Burlington Industries, Inc. v. Ellerth, 118 S.Ct. 2257 (1998); **Faragher v. City of Boca Raton,**

118 S.Ct. 2275 (1998); *Burlington* argued 22 April 1998, *Faragher* argued 25 March 1998, both decided 26 June 1998 by vote of 7 to 2; Kennedy for the Court in *Burlington*; Souter for the Court in *Faragher*, Thomas and Scalia dissenting in both.

Although these two cases were filed and argued separately, they both involved Title VII of the Civil Rights Act of 1964, they both were decided on the same day, they both engendered the same voting pattern among the justices, they both shared important language, and they both substantially clarified the law of sexual harassment in the workplace. The effect of the two decisions was to make some lawsuits against employers easier to win while rewarding companies with effective anti-harassment policies by limiting their legal exposure. The Court decided the cases at a particularly crucial time. The law of sexual harassment in the workplace had become substantially confused since the justices first addressed the issue in *Meritor Savings Bank v. Vinson* (1986). The sexual harassment suit by Paula Corbin Jones against President William Jefferson Clinton also served to heighten press interest in both cases.

In *Burlington* the justices faced the issue of so-called quid pro quo harassment. Kimberly Ellerth quit her job after 15 months as a sales-person in one of Burlington's many divisions. She insisted that her supervisor, Tom Slowik, had subjected her to constant harassment and demanded that she provide sexual favors in return for job advancement. Ellerth rebuffed all of these overtures, yet there was not tangible evidence that she had suffered retaliation. Moreover, she never informed Burlington Industries of the harassment, although the company's policies encouraged employees to do so. Moreover, she was promoted once.

The facts in *Faragher* were different. Beth Ann Faragher resigned her position as a lifeguard for the City of Boca Raton, Florida, after many years of service. Once she resigned, she claimed that her immediate supervisors, Bill Terry and David Silverman, had created a sexually hostile environment at work by repeatedly subjecting her and other female lifeguards to uninvited and offensive touching and by making lewd, offensive remarks about them. Unlike *Burlington*, the *Faragher* case raised the issue of what constituted a hostile work environment for women.

The high court's decisions in both cases drew sustained initial support from groups ranging from women's rights advocates to business organizations. Justice Anthony M. Kennedy's opinion in *Burlington* held that an employee who resists a supervisor's advances need not have suffered a tangible job detriment, such as dismissal or loss of a promotion, to be able to pursue a lawsuit against the company. At the same time, Kennedy also explained that such a suit cannot succeed if the company in question has an anti-harassment policy which an employee fails to use. In order for the company to be held liable under this new ruling it had to have been directly involved in the act of harassment, knew that such activity was going on, and failed to develop a set of aggressive policies to deal with harassment. Under these circumstances, the Court held that Ellerth should have the opportunity at trial to prove her case and that the company should have the opportunity to defend itself by showing it had a strong anti-harassment policy that the complaining employee had ignored.

Justice David Souter in *Faragher* claimed the same majority in awarding a judgment to the lifeguard against the City of Boca Raton. Souter found that employers are responsible for preventing and extinguishing harassment in the workplace. They are liable for even those harassing acts of supervisory employees that violate clear policies and of which top management has no knowledge.

Both decisions contained an identical pagelong set of rules to be applied in sexual harassment cases in the workplace. First, employers are responsible for harassment engaged in by their supervisory employees. Second, when a quid pro quo condition can be demonstrated (i.e., a discharge or demotion), the employer is absolutely liable. And third, where there is no tangible action, an employer can defend itself by showing that it took reasonable care to prevent and correct harassing behavior and that the complaining employee had failed to take advantage of preventive or corrective opportunities provided by the company.

Justices Clarence Thomas and Antonin Scalia dissented on two counts. First, they claimed that in both cases the Court was legislating rather than interpreting the law. Second, they intended that employers should face liability only for their own actions rather than for the actions of management and supervisors.

Taken together these two decisions reframed the law of sexual harassment in the workplace. In a third case, *Oncale* v. *Sundowner Offshore Services* (1998), the justices unanimously held that federal law against workplace harassment applies to people of the same sex. The issue before the courts is the conduct of the individuals involved, not their sex or the presence or absence of sexual desire.

Kermit L. Hall

Burton v. Wilmington Parking Authority, 365 U.S. 715 (1961), argued 21, 23 Feb. 1961, decided 17 Apr. 1961 by vote of 6 to 3; Clark for the Court; Harlan, Frankfurter, and Whittaker in dissent. In this case the Court addressed the vexing if not logically inscrutable problem, judged pivotal to the success of the civil rights movement at the time, of defining the meaning of state action under the Fourteenth Amendment. The city built a public parking garage within which it leased space to a restaurant. A Delaware statute provided that a restaurant was not obliged to serve persons whose reception would be offensive to the major part of its customers. An African-American who was refused service claimed discrimination in violation of the Fourteenth Amendment. The Supreme Court held, 6 to 3, that a sufficient degree of state action was present to constitute a denial of the equal protection of the laws. Justice Tom C. Clark for the majority emphasized that the state owned and operated the building in which the incident occurred and hence had a responsibility to prevent it. The state's inaction under the circumstances made it a party to the discrimination, rendering it unlawful. The decision did little to clarify the state action problem. Justice Clark limited the scope and precedential value of the decision in stating that "to fashion and apply a precise formula for recognition of state responsibility under the Equal Protection Clause is an 'impossible task,'" and in observing: "Only by sifting facts and weighing circumstances can the nonobvious involvement of the State in private conduct be attributed its true significance" (p. 722). The dissenters urged that the case be remanded to the state court for clarification of its decision upholding the restaurant in relation to the state law under which the restaurant acted.

Herman Belz

Bush v. Gore, 531 U.S. 98 (2000). The accusation of partisan decision making on the U.S. Supreme Court was never more intense than in the wake of the decision in Bush v.

Gore, when five conservative justices relied on innovative readings of the Constitution in order to resolve the 2000 presidential election dispute in favor of the more conservative candidate.

The outcome of the election between Vice President Al Gore (Democrat) and Texas Governor George W. Bush (Republican) came down to an unbelievably close vote in Florida. Trailing by just a few hundred votes, the Gore campaign requested hand recounts of ballots in four Democratic counties, arguing that manual inspections might lead to the discovery of legal votes that were inadvertently uncounted by the vote-tabulating machines. The strategy of the Bush campaign was to mobilize all political resources and sympathetic office holders to block all efforts at hand recounts.

Bush v. *Gore* arose at the end of the recount saga, after the Florida supreme court ruled that state law required a statewide manual recount of all ballots in which a machine failed to register a vote for president. Less than twenty-four hours later, the five most conservative justices on the U.S. Supreme Court issued an emergency injunction halting this recount, with Justice Scalia explaining that the review of these ballots threatened "irreparable harm to [Bush], and to the country, by casting a cloud upon what he claims to be the legitimacy of his election." The four dissenters, led by Justice Stevens, responded that "counting every legally cast vote cannot constitute irreparable harm."

Oral arguments were held two days later, and late the following day, on 12 December, the same five justices ruled that no more recounting could take place. They noted that the Florida supreme court did not articulate a more specific standard for determining a legitimate vote than the statutory standard of "clear intent of the voter," and this made it possible that identical ballots would be treated differently in different parts of the state. This, they said, violated the equal protection clause of the Fourteenth Amendment. They did not explain what this innovative interpretation might mean more generally for vote counting in American elections, or even how it applied to the original vote totals in Florida, where balloting and counting practices varied widely from county to county. Instead, the majority said simply, "our consideration is limited to the present circumstances, for the problem of equal protection in election processes generally presents many complexities."

While under different circumstances it might have been possible to remand the case back to the Florida supreme court so that it might create a more explicit counting standard, the majority announced that it was their belief that Florida intended to resolve all disputes by 12 December so that the state would benefit from a federal law that ensured the state's electoral college votes would not be challenged in the Congress. Because their decision was handed down on the evening of 12 December, the majority invoked this deadline in support of their conclusion that there was no time left to count votes in Florida.

Three members of the majority—Chief Justice Rehnquist and Justices Scalia and Thomas—added a concurring opinion in which they argued that the state's election statutes did not support the remedy of a statewide recount under these circumstances, and thus the Florida supreme court's decision violated Article II of the U.S. Constitution, which gives to the state *legislature* the exclusive authority to determine the manner by which presidential electors will be chosen.

Each of the four dissenters wrote separately to argue that the U.S. Supreme Court had no business interfering in this presidential election dispute. Two of the dissenters, Justices Breyer and Souter, expressed some sympathy for the equal protection argument, but they stressed that these issues were more properly addressed by the state and (if necessary) the Congress. They argued it would have been best to remand the case to the Florida supreme court as the institution authorized to determine whether Florida should continue counting under a more explicit recount standard. Justices Stevens and Ginsburg emphasized that the Florida supreme court's interpretation of the state statute was completely defensible and that the majority's opinion was inconsistent with the previously expressed views of those justices on equal protection and federalism. The practical effect of this decision was to declare Bush the president elect. Gore conceded the election the following day. While the majority insisted that its intervention was an "unsought responsibility," the most frequently cited language in the *Bush* v. *Gore* opinions belonged to Justice Stevens, who lamented that the actual loser of this presidential election was "the Nation's confidence in the judge as an impartial guardian of the rule of law."

Howard Gillman

Bush v. Vera et al., 517 U.S. 952 (1996), argued 5 Dec. 1995, decided 13 June 1996 by vote of 5 to 4; O'Connor for the Court, Kennedy and Thomas concurring, Stevens and Souter dissenting. In the 1993 case of *Shaw* v. *Reno*, the Supreme Court had struck down a North Carolina plan that relied on race to redistrict congressional districts. A bitterly divided Court had concluded that if the state used race to undertake such redistricting, the plan had to withstand the demanding test of strict scrutiny under the Equal Protection Clause of the Fourteenth Amendment. In *Bush* the Court returned to the same issue, doing so at the same time it decided another case, *Shaw* v. *Hunt*, which involved North Carolina once again. In both instances the justices struck down redistricting measures, although they were hardly of one mind about either the reasons for or the wisdom of doing so.

Of the two cases, that from Texas presented the greater challenge. Unlike the facts in *Shaw* v. *Hunt*, those in *Bush* were not nearly as extreme. The Texas legislature had redrawn three congressional districts in keeping with the census returns of 1990 and the requirements of the Voting Rights Act of 1965 and its amendments. Two of these districts were majority black and one majority Hispanic. The newly redrawn legislative districts were more compact and regularly sized than in North Carolina, and the black defendants insisted that, while race had been an issue, it was secondary to more traditional concerns, such as making sure that incumbents won reelection and that ongoing partisan politics were satisfied. The net effect of the redrawn districts was to consolidate black and Hispanic voters, which had traditionally been Democratic, and to give Republicans even greater opportunities in the remaining districts where, in many instances, the numbers of nonwhite voters were reduced. Thus Republican governor George Bush joined hands with black and Hispanic voters to support the redistricting legislation. The plaintiffs in the case were voters, one of them Al Vera, who were neither white nor Hispanic. They insisted that their votes had been marginalized as a result of the redrawn boundaries and that the legislature had actually violated the Voting Rights Act and the Equal Protection Clause of the Fourteenth Amendment.

There was no majority opinion; instead, the Court spoke in a splintered voice. Justice Sandra Day O'Connor's plurality opinion was joined by Chief Justice William H. Rehnquist and Justice Anthony M. Kennedy. Justices Antonin Scalia and Clarence Thomas agreed that the redistricting plan was an unconstitutional violation of the Equal Protection Clause, but they refused to add their names to O'Connor's opinion because it seemed to accept the proposition that under certain circumstances race could be constitutionally used to draw district voting lines. O'Connor found that in Texas race had not been the only factor used in creating the new districts but that the others (partisan politics and the needs of incumbents) had been subordinated to race. To make her point, O'Connor noted that the Texas legislature had examined race on a block-by-block basis while taking account of other data at the precinct level. Such an approach, according to O'Connor, gave a clear message that race had been used as a proxy for political gerrymandering. Political identity, the justice concluded, should not be predominantly racial.

The dissenters argued that the Court had set itself on an unrealistic and unworkable path when it decided *Shaw* v. *Reno* originally and that it should recognize as much. As important, the dissenters believed that in this instance the states should enjoy greater latitude than the Court had granted them to remedy the problem of underrepresentation of minorities in Congress and to meet the requirements of the Voting Rights Act. According to Justice John Paul Stevens, there was no workable constitutional principle that could discern whether the message conveyed was a distressing endorsement of racial separatism or a call to integrate the political process.

Justice O'Connor herself contributed to the unsettled nature of the constitutional issues by taking the unusual step of writing a concurring opinion to go along with her opinion for the Court. In effect, O'Connor was concurring with herself. In the concurring opinion she agreed with the dissenters that compliance with the Voting Rights Act could itself be a sufficiently compelling state interest to justify the creation of a compact, majority black district. The four other justices in the plurality, however, refused to decide that question.

Kermit L. Hall

Butchers' Benevolent Association of New Orleans v. Crescent City Livestock Landing and Slaughterhouse Co. See SLAUGHTER-HOUSE CASES.

Butler, United States v., 297 U.S. 1 (1936), argued 9–10 Dec. 1935, decided 6 Jan. 1936, by vote of 6 to 3; Roberts for the Court, Stone, Brandeis, and Cardozo in dissent. The Agricultural Adjustment Act of 1933 represented a major New Deal effort to ameliorate the depression in agriculture and raise farm prices by limiting production. Farmers who agreed to reduce crop acreage received benefit payments, the funds coming from a tax levied on the first processor of the commodities involved. Butler, a processor, refused to pay the tax. The circuit court of appeals upheld Butler, and the government appealed.

By a vote of 6 to 3 in *United States* v. *Butler* (1936) the Supreme Court declared the tax unconstitutional. Justice Owen J. Roberts's opinion for the majority, characterized by Leonard Levy as "monumentally inept," undertook a preliminary explanation of the Court's limited role in deciding constitutional questions. The judicial duty was simply "to lay the Article of the Constitution which is invoked beside the statute which is challenged and to decide whether the latter squares with the former" (p. 62). This simplistic explanation of the process of constitutional interpretation has been generally considered unrealistic.

Roberts did, however, settle a long-standing dispute concerning the taxing power of Congress. Article I, section 8, authorizes Congress to levy taxes "to pay the debts and provide for the common defense and general welfare of the United States. . . ." James Madison contended that "general welfare" purposes were limited to authorizations elsewhere in the Constitution, whereas Alexander Hamilton held that this language amounted to an independent power to tax and spend, provided only that the "general welfare" was served. Accepting Hamilton's view, Roberts determined that the processing taxes were justified under the General Welfare Clause.

Robert's support for the spending power was irrelevant, however, for he immediately transferred the argument to an entirely new issue. Whether the spending was for national rather than local welfare was of no consequence, because the statutory plan to regulate and control agricultural production invaded the reserved powers of the states and so was invalid under the Tenth Amendment.

Justices Harlan F. Stone, Louis D. Brandeis, and Benjamin N. Cardozo dissented. In a scathing rebuttal Stone called Roberts's ruling "a tortured construction of the Constitution" (p. 87). But the most widely noted language in Stone's dissent was his warning against judicial arrogance: "Courts are not the only agency of government that must be assumed to have capacity to govern. . . . [T]he only check upon our own exercise of power is our own sense of self-restraint" (p. 79). These words were widely read as a rebuke to the Court's conservatives who had been declaring New Deal statutes unconstitutional.

As a threat to other New Deal programs, the Roberts opinion was soon a dead letter. The tax provisions of the Social Security Act were upheld in *Steward Machine Co. v. Davis (1937), and the agricultural program struck down in Butler was reenacted by Congress under the commerce power and upheld in *Mulford v. Smith (1939) and *Wickard v. Filburn (1942).

In retrospect, the principal positive contribution of the Butler majority is the principle, as restated by Chief Justice Warren E. Burger in *Fullilove v. Klutznick (1980), that the power to provide for the general welfare "is an independent grant of legislative authority, distinct from other broad congressional powers" (p. 247). Otherwise, the opinion by Roberts is valueless. Justice Felix Frankfurter in International Association of Machinists v. Street (1961) spoke of "the severely criticized, indeed rather discredited case of United States v. Butler" (p. 807). The most enduring feature of the decision is Stone's dissent; his plea for judicial self-restraint has been invoked on many subsequent occasions by Court minorities, both liberal and conservative. In *Shapiro v. Thompson (1969) Justice John M. Harlan cited the Butler fiasco in warning his colleagues that cases come to the Court with "an extremely heavy presumption of validity" (p. 675).

C. Herman Pritchett

Butz v. Economou, 438 U.S. 478 (1978), argued 7 Nov. 1977, decided 29 June 1978 by vote of 5 to 4; White for the Court, Rehnquist for the minority, which concurred in part and dissented in part. After successfully aborting a complaint against him filed by the secretary of agriculture and subordinates, Economou, a commodities dealer, sued these officials for $32 million claiming they had proceeded against him because he was a critic of department policies. The government sought to quash the suit, claiming absolute immunity was conferred in accordance with Spalding v. Vilas (1896) and Barr v. Matteo (1959). The court of appeals reversed the district court's dismissal.

Justice White's careful opinion denied absolute immunity and somewhat disingenuously asserted that neither Spalding nor Barr granted such immunity where a claim of violation of a constitutional right was involved. Spalding had found a common-law exemption of high federal officials from "suits where they were carrying out duties imposed . . . by law" even if allegations of personal animosity were involved (p. 495). The plurality opinion in Barr v. Matteo was similarly sweeping, involving a press release by a government official containing substantial errors. But White noted these cases dealt with the scope of the officials' authority, not the harm of an alleged unconstitutional action.

Conceding the value to decision-making of all immunity from litigation, White argued that immunity is such a departure from the rule of law that it must be carefully measured. Judges and prosecutors and others in the executive branch in judgelike positions needed the immunity. Other executive officials were entitled only to the "qualified good-faith immunity" that previous decisions had extended to state officials. Immunity exists for mere error, so long as the official acted without malice or knowledge of illegality and reasonably could have believed the actions lawful and constitutional. But where the official knew, or should have known, of an unconstitutional deprivation of rights, immunity should be controlled.

Rehnquist's minority opinion suggests the majority standards exposed officials excessively to frivolous suits since ingenious lawyers would have no difficulty in recasting claims in constitutional terms. In Harlow v. Fitzgerald (1982) the Court rejected a claim by President Richard Nixon's aides of absolute immunity, but modified the Economou standard by eliminating the subjective test that required a hearing of evidence as to the decision maker's attitudes, conduct, and such. The remaining test—that the official has immunity unless no reasonable decision maker could deem the action lawful—facilitates summary judgment on frivolous complaints.

Samuel Krislov

C

Calder v. Bull, 3 Dall. (3 U.S.) 386 (1798), argued 8 and 13 Feb. 1798, decided 8 Aug. 1798 by vote of 4 to 0; seriatim opinions by Chase, Paterson, Iredell, and Cushing, Ellsworth and Wilson not participating. *Calder* v. *Bull* was one of the Supreme Court's first decisions involving constitutional limitations on governmental power. The Connecticut legislature enacted a resolution granting a new hearing in a probate trial. The Calders, disappointed heirs, challenged this action as a violation of the ban in Article I, section 10, on ex post facto laws. Justices William Paterson, James Iredell, and William Cushing accepted the legislature's action because before Independence the legislature had functioned as the state's highest appellate court and was thus merely continuing to act in that capacity (Connecticut had not yet adopted a new constitution).

Assuming that the legislature's resolution was a "law" within the meaning of the Ex Post Facto Clause, Justices Samuel Chase, Paterson, and Iredell agreed that the clause was addressed only to laws imposing retroactive punishment (by creating criminal sanctions for actions that were legal when carried out or increasing the punishment set for a particular offense and applied retrospectively) and thus was inapplicable in civil disputes. Chase and Paterson, in addition, rested their rejection of the Calders' argument on the grounds of textual interpretation. Citing such sources as Blackstone,

The Federalist, and the constitutions of other states, they concluded that the expression "ex post facto" was a technical legal term that, long before the Revolution, had come to apply only to laws imposing or increasing criminal punishment, and the Constitution's makers must have "understood and used the words in their known and appropriate signification" (p. 397). Both justices buttressed this reading of the clause by noting its close proximity to provisions such as the impairment of Contracts Clause that would be redundant if "ex post facto" were extended to cover civil legislation.

Alone among the justices, Chase raised and then rejected another possible ground for invalidating the Connecticut resolution: its incompatibility with "the very nature of our free Republican governments" (p. 388). In a long and rambling paragraph Chase denied "the omnipotence of a state Legislature" even in the absence of express constitutional limits on its power. Using language reminiscent of Locke, Chase insisted that "the great first principles of the social compact" determined what actions of a legislature could be regarded as "a rightful exercise of legislative authority" (pp. 387–388). He went on to list a number of actions that could not be deemed legitimate regardless of the absence of any express constitutional prohibition; among them were ex post facto laws in the technical, criminal sense and "a law that takes property from A and gives it to B" (p. 388). Chase avoided applying these fundamental principles in *Calder* v. *Bull* itself, if indeed he even meant to suggest that judges were entitled to enforce them against the legislature, on the ground that whatever rights the losing heirs might have had to the property had not yet vested when the legislature acted and thus were still subject to interference by law.

Iredell appears to have interpreted Chase's opinion to assert a power in courts to pronounce a statute "void, merely because it is, in [the judges'] judgment, contrary to the principles of natural justice" (p. 399). Observing that persons of intelligence and good will disagree about the dictates of natural justice, Iredell denied that judicial invalidation of a statute on such a basis could express anything but a difference of opinion, and he expressly limited the exercise of judicial review to the enforcement of express limitations on legislative power.

The subsequent career of *Calder* v. *Bull* has been controversial. Early nineteenth-century critics attacked its limitation of the Ex Post Facto Clause to criminal statutes. Justice William Johnson appended a long note to the report of an 1829 case, *Satterlee* v. *Mathewson*, arguing with considerable force that *Calder's* actual holding rested on the characterization of the Connecticut legislature's action as judicial rather than legislative in nature, and criticizing the *Calder* justices' use of legal authority. In the modern era, the case has been the subject of widely varying interpretations. Some scholars maintain that *Calder* is direct evidence of an "original understanding" that courts would enforce unwritten fundamental-law limitations on governmental power, while others insist that the case reflected the transition from the Revolutionary era's political rhetoric of social compact and natural rights to the text-bound interpretivism of the later Marshall Court. Whatever they may have meant originally by their remarks, Chase's invocation of constitutional principles transcending the constitutional text and Iredell's insistence on the textual nature of judicial review continue to play a role in the debate over the legitimacy of the Supreme Court's jurisprudence.

□ Suzanna Sherry, "The Founders' Unwritten Constitution," *University of Chicago Law Review* 54 (1987): 1127–1177.

H. Jefferson Powell

California, United States v., 332 U.S. 19 (1947), argued 13–14 Mar. 1947, decided 23 June 1947 by vote of 6 to 2; Black for the Court, Reed and Frankfurter in dissent, Jackson not participating. The United States sued California to determine whether the federal or the state governments owned or had paramount rights in and power over the submerged lands lying between the low-water mark and the three-mile limit. At stake were huge royalties and rights from gas and oil deposits. Until this time the federal government had not claimed ownership, nor had it denied it, but had left control over the submerged coastal lands to the states.

The Court held that the federal government had full power and dominion over the submerged lands, and Justice Hugo Black rejected the states' claims that the thirteen colonies had separately acquired ownership of the three-mile strip at the time they achieved independence. The federal government had always had dominion over coastal waters, even if it chose not to exercise that power or if it had delegated it to the states.

Justice Felix Frankfurter took the states' claims of historic ownership more seriously and argued that no evidence existed to show that the Constitution or the states ratifying it had intended the federal government to have dominion, which implies ownership, of the coastal strip.

Several years later Congress reversed the rulings in this and two other offshore oil cases by quit-claiming the coastal strips to the states in the Submerged Lands Act (1953).

Melvin I. Urofsky

California v. Acevedo, 500 U.S. 565 (1991), argued 8 Jan. 1991, decided 30 May 1991 by vote of 6 to 3; Blackmun for the Court, Scalia concurring, Stevens in dissent. Until the 1991 *Acevedo* case was decided, two different rules governed the search of closed containers found in a motor vehicle. In *United States* v. *Ross* (1982), the Court held that if the police had probable cause to search an entire vehicle for contraband and came upon a closed container in the course of the automobile search, they could open the container without first obtaining a warrant. On the other hand, in *Arkansas* v. *Sanders* (1979) the justices had held that if probable cause focused exclusively on a particular closed container whose presence in a vehicle was purely fortuitous, the police had to obtain a search warrant before opening it.

In *Acevedo* the Court eliminated the warrant requirement for closed containers set forth in the *Sanders* case and adopted "one clear-cut rule" for all searches of closed containers found in an automobile. There is no difference, the Court concluded, whether the search of a vehicle coincidentally turns up a container, or the search of a container coincidentally turns up in a vehicle.

A number of commentators predicted that the reasoning of *Acevedo* would apply (or be extended) to closed containers outside vehicles. Indeed, in *Acevedo* Justice Antonin Scalia concurred in the result on the ground that the validity of the search of a closed container anywhere, so long as it occurs outside a home, should not depend upon whether the police could have obtained a warrant.

Yale Kamisar

Callins v. Collins, 510 U.S. 1141 (1994), decided 22 Feb. 1994 to deny a writ of certiorari, Scalia concurring, Blackmun in dissent. The justices denied without opinion a writ of certiorari to hear the appeal of Bruce Edwin Callins, a murderer awaiting execution in Texas for the 1980 killing of a man during a robbery. The Court's action was another indication of the hardening line the justices took on capital punishment and criminal justice generally, but for Justice Harry Blackmun it was too much to accept. Blackmun took the unusual step of issuing a dissent without a written opinion from the Court. He announced that he was unequivocally turning against the death penalty because he no longer believed that the procedural safeguards erected in the 1970s were working. Blackmun had voted with the majority in *Gregg* v. *Georgia* (1976) that had restored the death penalty. His dissent in *Callins* made clear that he believed he had made a mistake in that case and that he would not make another one. Justice Antonin Scalia's dissent mocked both Blackmun's passion and his constitutional logic. Callins was shortly put to death by lethal injection.

Kermit L. Hall

C & A Carbone, Inc. v. Clarkstown, 511 U.S. 383 (1994), argued 7 Dec. 1993, decided 16 May 1994 by vote of 6 to 3; Kennedy for the Court, O'Connor concurring, Souter in dissent, joined by Rehnquist and Blackmun.

This case dealt with the ability of state and local governments to regulate the disposal of solid and hazardous wastes through so-called flow control ordinances. Such measures require that persons handling these materials bring them to one specified facility, usually owned or under contract with a local government, where they are sorted and baled before being shipped off for permanent disposal. These measures became particularly popular in the 1980s as local governments, such as that in Clarkstown, New York, sought to provide a steady stream of wastes that would, in turn, ensure a fixed base of revenue by which to finance ambitious waste-to-energy facilities. Similar measures were also invoked by local governments to make sure that they had sufficient revenue to fund garbage transfer stations. The flow control measures placed pressure on garbage haulers and on landfill operators, who had the advantage under the old system of a cheap but often environmentally questionable place to dump wastes.

City authorities in Clarkstown adopted their flow control measure as a way to finance a new transfer station. The station was constructed and operated by a private contractor for a period of five years, at which time the town promised to buy it for one dollar. The town made the operation profitable by guaranteeing a minimum waste flow of 120,000 tons per year for which the contractor charged haulers an $81 per ton fee. A key feature of the Clarkstown ordinance required that all nonrecyclable residue from any private operations had to be brought to the city-supported transfer station.

C & A Carbone, Inc. operated a business that received solid waste and sorted it prior to disposal. Much of the solid waste that they received, however, came from outside the jurisdiction of Clarkstown, but city officials insisted that the materials coming from the Carbone plant fell under the flow control restrictions, which meant the company had to pay the fee before hauling waste for disposal outside the town. Such a regulation, the company insisted, hampered them in competing with other companies not subject to the ordinance. Carbone, in fact, knowingly violated the ordinance, a fact that became clear when one of its trucks dumped a load of unrecyclable solid waste following a traffic accident. The lower federal courts upheld the constitutionality of the city ordinance, but the Supreme Court overturned it as a violation of the Commerce Clause of the Constitution.

Justice Anthony Kennedy returned to a 1978 decision in striking down the law. In *Philadelphia* v. *New Jersey*, the Court held that solid waste was a subject of interstate commerce. Justice Kennedy brushed aside Clarks-town's argument that the wastes involved were entirely from within the area and found instead that the ordinance had a direct economic effect beyond the town's boundaries. By hoarding its garbage, Kennedy went on, the town had discriminated against interstate commerce in favor of local business, an action that was permitted only when the locality could demonstrate that no other measures were available to it.

The Court's decision was a victory for garbage haulers and, perhaps even more important, for regional landfills, which could offer cheaper fees to haulers for dumping wastes that would have otherwise been under stricter solid waste management. At the same time, the decision will likely drive up the costs to taxpayers in those areas that wish to use solid waste plants to produce energy and to manage closely garbage and hazardous materials.

Kermit L. Hall

Cantwell v. Connecticut, 310 U.S. 296 (1940), argued 29 Mar. 1940, decided 30 May 1940, by vote of 9 to 0; Roberts for the Court. In *Lovell* v. *City of Griffin* (1938), the Supreme Court sustained the free speech rights of Jehovah's Witnesses without discussing the claim of free exercise of religion. In *Cantwell* v. *Connecticut*, however, the Court relied on that clause to uphold the Witnesses' practices.

Cantwell dealt with a Witness who went from door to door asking the resident if he or she would like to hear a record or accept a pamphlet. Both materials included an attack on the Catholic religion—and this in an overwhelmingly Catholic neighborhood. The Jehovah's Witness was convicted for failing to obtain the required approval by the secretary of public welfare.

The Court adjudged the conviction invalid, expressing what would become a universal rule of law. A state may regulate the times, the places, and the manner of soliciting contributions and holding meetings on its streets, but cannot forbid them altogether. The First Amendment provided for both a freedom to believe and to act.

Leo Pfeffer

Carroll v. United States, 267 U.S. 132 (1925), argued 4 Dec. 1923, rescheduled 28 Jan. 1924, reargued 14 Mar. 1924, decided 2 Mar. 1925 by vote of 6 to 2; Taft for the Court, McReynolds and Sutherland in dissent. George Carroll and John Kiro were convicted of transporting liquor in an automobile in violation of the Volstead Act (National Prohibition). Federal officers acknowledged that they were not following Carroll and Kiro at the time of arrest but that when they saw them, they suspected that they were carrying prohibited liquor and decided to give chase. The Supreme Court considered the constitutionality of the car search that yielded the evidence and specifically reviewed Carroll and Kiro's claim that since there was no basis to search the car, the resulting evidence should have been excluded from trial.

The Court rejected their claim and recognized the car search exception to the warrant requirement for the first time. Detailing the legislative history of the National Prohibition Act, Chief Justice William H. Taft concluded for the majority that Congress intended to distinguish the need for a search warrant in private dwellings from searches conducted in automobiles or other moving vehicles. Furthermore, Taft emphasized that such a distinction was consistent with Fourth Amendment guarantees and other Supreme Court decisions and argued that "the right to search and the validity of the seizure are not dependent on the right to arrest" (p. 158).

Justice James McReynolds was joined in dissent by Justice George Sutherland. He argued that there was insufficient cause to stop the vehicle without a warrant, that the mere suspicion that existed was ill founded, and that the Volstead Act did not authorize arrest or seizure on simple suspicion. McReynolds noted that without explicit statutory authorization, the common-law tradition that distinguished between arrest without warrant in the case of felonies and misdemeanors should apply. He concluded, then, that the "validity of the seizure under consideration depends on the legality of the arrest," and supported Carroll's contention that his Fourth (and Fifth) Amendment rights had been violated (p. 169).

The Court has continued the position first articulated in *Carroll* that although the privacy interests in an automobile have constitutional protection, its mobility justifies less sweeping protection and therefore exemption from more customary warrant requirements. Later Court decisions have not extended this exception to any or all movable containers (e.g., *United States* v. *Chadwick,* 1977), although the Court has continued to apply less stringent protection for automobiles than stationary objects.

Susette M. Talarico

Carlton, United States v., 512 U.S. 26 (1994), argued 28 Feb. 1994, decided 13 June 1994 by vote of 9 to 0; Blackmun for the Court, O'Connor and Scalia (with Thomas) concurring. The United States sued the executor of an estate for tax liability imposed by dint of a retroactive amendment to the federal estate tax. While ex post facto laws are prohibited by Article I, section 10, of the U.S. Constitution, *Calder* v. *Bull* (1798) held the ban applicable only to the retroactive punishment of actions that were legal when carried out, or to the retrospective increase of punishment for past misconduct. In *Carlton,* the Court considered the extent to which retroactivity would be permitted in civil tax legislation.

A provision of the estate tax adopted in October 1986 granted a considerable deduction for the sale of stock in an employer corporation to an employee stock ownership plan (ESOP). In December 1986, Carlton purchased shares in a corporation on behalf of the estate, sold the stock to the company's ESOP, and consequently claimed a large tax deduction. In December 1987, the tax provision was modified so that the deceased must have owned the stock "immediately before death." Applying the amendment retrospectively, the Internal Revenue Service disallowed the deduction and imposed additional estate tax liability.

Justice Harry Blackmun, writing for the Court, found that Congress intended the original deduction to create an incentive for employee ownership of corporations and had not contemplated that executors would procure tax deductions by buying corporate shares and reselling them to ESOPs. Thus, the intent of the amendment was to correct a "mistake" in the original legislation that would resulted in significant and anticipated revenue losses through "essentially sham transactions" (p. 32). Blackmun concluded that the retroactive amendment comported with due process because its purpose was "neither illegitimate nor arbitrary" and because it "acted promptly and established only a modest period of retroactivity" (p. 32).

Justice Blackmun also emphasized that limited retroactivity was customary and practically necessary in producing tax legislation, and that Carlton's reliance on the original statute "is insufficient to establish a constitutional violation. Tax legislation is not a promise, and a taxpayer has no vested right in the Internal Revenue Code" (p. 33).

Carlton is broadly consistent with the Court's earlier pronouncement in a tax case that the applicability of the Due Process Clause depends upon whether "retroactive application is so harsh and oppressive as to transgress the constitutional limitation" (*Welch* v. *Henry,* 1938) (p. 147). It also is consistent with cases upholding retroactive legislation adopted to undo perceived overreaching, such as the opportunistic departure of firms from industry plans during the drafting of new regulations (*Pension Benefit Guaranty Corporation* v. *R. A. Gray & Co.,* 1984). On the other hand, the Court has found retroactive liability unconstitutional if it imposes severe and unanticipated burdens on a limited group (*Eastern Enterprises* v. *Apfel,* 1998). Reflecting this tension, Justice O'Connor's concurrence in *Carlton* stressed that "[t]he governmental interest in revising the tax laws must at some point give way to the taxpayer's interest in finality and repose" (pp. 37–38).

Steven J. Eagle

Carter v. Carter Coal Co., 298 U.S. 238 (1936), argued 11, 12 Mar. 1936, decided 18 Mar. 1936 by vote of 5 to 4; Sutherland for the Court, Cardozo, Brandeis, and Stone in dissent, Hughes dissenting in part. The *Carter* case arose in the vortex of controversy surrounding President Franklin D. Roosevelt's New Deal efforts to curb the disastrous effects of the Depression. The critical issue before the Court involved competing visions of federalism and the appropriate allocation of power between state and federal government. Much New Deal legislation was premised on the belief that the commerce power granted Congress extensive authority to regulate labor relations, commercial activities, agriculture, and the like. The idea was diametrically opposed to the vision of the commerce power embraced by a majority of the Supreme Court. The *Carter* decision was viewed by many as yet another example of Court intransigence that led ultimately to Roosevelt's unsuccessful court-packing plan.

The Bituminous Coal Conservation Act of 1935 sought to stem overproduction and ruinous competition. Wages were so appalling in the coal industry that labor unrest and strikes, sometimes accompanied by violence, had become endemic. The act created local boards to set minimum prices for coal and also provided for collective bargaining to achieve acceptable wage and hour agreements. Congress based its authority for the law squarely on its ability to regulate interstate commerce.

Justice George Sutherland's majority opinion brushed aside the bare recitation of the direct effect of coal mining on the economy. He drew what was for him a critical distinction. Although Congress's motives might be laudable, the Commerce Clause and the Tenth Amendment worked in tandem to define the appropriate spheres of state and federal governments. Since the powers of Congress are rigidly enumerated in the Constitution, it cannot cede its powers to others. Sutherland acknowledged that such a system was cumbersome, but he argued that the benefits of preserving the boundaries between states and the federal government were central to the integrity of the constitutional system. Congress, in short, had overstepped its constitutional limits. In a sentence reminiscent of a seduction he said, "Every journey to a forbidden end begins with the first step; and the danger of such a step by the government in the direction of taking over the powers of the states is that the end of the journey may find the states so despoiled of their powers, or—what may amount to the same thing— so relieved of the responsibilities which possession of the powers necessarily enjoins, as to reduce them to little more than geographical subdivisions of the national domain" (p. 866). Sutherland also drew on the distinction between items of production and things in commerce. Congress may regulate once goods enter into commerce or when there is a direct effect on commerce. Since he found no direct effect on commerce and since the coal was still in the production phase, only the states could constitutionally regulate coal mining.

Justice Benjamin Cardozo in dissent had a more pragmatic view of the situation. In response to the majority's direct/indirect test he said that "a great principle of constitutional law is not susceptible of comprehensive statement in an adjective" (p. 327).

Carter represents the twilight of the Tenth Amendment and states' rights. One year later, in *National Labor Relations Board* v. *Jones & Laughlin Steel Corp.* (1937), the Court adopted Cardozo's minority position. The Commerce Clause became the basis for a massive restructuring of the federal-state relationship. By the early 1990s, however, the Supreme Court had signaled its unhappiness with what it considered to be the extraordinary uses by Congress of the commerce power. Hence, in *United States* v. *Lopez* (1995), the justices by a 5-to-4 majority struck down a federal law based on the commerce power that made it illegal to possess a firearm within one thousand feet of a public or private school.

Diane C. Maleson

Champion v. Ames, 188 U.S. 321 (1903), argued 15–16 Dec. 1902, decided 23 Feb. 1903 by vote of 5 to 4; Harlan for the Court, Fuller in dissent. Known as the *Lottery Case, Champion* v. *Ames* raised crucial questions regarding the extent of congressional power over interstate commerce and the existence of a federal equivalent of the state police power. These issues were central to the Progressives' attempts to make federal authority commensurate with the nation's emerging needs.

Champion challenged the constitutionality of an 1895 statute designed to suppress lottery traffic in interstate commerce under which he had been indicted. The majority focused on two major issues: whether lottery tickets were subjects of commerce and the scope of the interstate commerce power. Justice John Marshall Harlan ruled the tickets were items of real value, whose carriage across state lines was indeed interstate commerce. Defining the commerce power in extensive terms that recognized congressional authority to prohibit certain transportation and to meet expanding needs, he held the lottery act constitutional.

The minority opinion differed on definitions and the scope of power. It equated lottery tickets with contracts and negotiable instruments, which were not considered objects of traffic; denied that the tickets were intrinsically injurious; and maintained that federal exercise of the police power violated the Tenth Amendment. Despite Harlan's guarded language, both proponents and opponents viewed the decision as establishing a de facto federal police power, and national protective legislation increased rapidly. However, the focus on the injuriousness of the product provided a measure of flexibility that permitted the Court to retrench as progressivism waned.

Barbara C. Steidle

Chaplinsky v. New Hampshire, 315 U.S. 568 (1942), argued 5 Feb. 1942, decided 9 Mar. 1942 by vote of 9 to 0; Murphy for the Court. While distributing religious pamphlets for Jehovah's Witnesses, Chaplinsky attracted a hostile crowd. When a city marshal intervened, Chaplinsky denounced him as a "racketeer" and a "Fascist" and called other officials "agents of Fascists." The Court upheld Chaplinsky's conviction for violating a state law against offensive and derisive speech or name-calling in public.

Justice Frank Murphy advanced a "two-tier theory" of the First Amendment. Certain "well-defined and narrowly limited" categories of speech fall outside the bounds of constitutional protection. Thus, "the lewd and obscene, the profane, the libelous," and (in this case) insulting or "fighting" words neither contributed to the expression of ideas nor possessed any "social value" in the search for truth (pp. 571–572).

This two-tier approach retains importance for those who believe that carefully crafted controls over certain categories of speech (such as pornography, commercial advertising, or abusive epithets) do not violate First Amendment guarantees. Although the Court continues to cite *Chaplinsky's* position on "fighting words" approvingly, subsequent cases have largely eroded its initial, broad formulation; libelous publications and even verbal challenges to police officers have come to enjoy some constitutional protection. *Chaplinsky* remains the last case in which the Court explicitly upheld a conviction only for "fighting words" directed at public officials.

Norman L. Rosenberg

Charles River Bridge v. Warren Bridge, 11 Pet. (36 U.S.) 420 (1837), argued 7–11 Mar. 1831, reargued 19–26 Jan. 1837, decided 12 Feb. 1837 by vote of 4 to 3; Taney for the Court, McLean, Story, and Thompson in dissent. To provide the public better access from Charlestown to Boston, the Massachusetts legislature in 1785 incorporated the Proprietors of the Charles River Bridge to build a bridge connecting Boston to its northern hinterland via Charlestown and authorized the proprietors to collect tolls on the bridge. In 1828 the legislature authorized Charlestown merchants to build the new Warren Bridge and to collect tolls for its use until they had been reimbursed, when their bridge would revert to the state and become free.

The Charles River Bridge proprietors sought an injunction to halt construction of the new bridge, asserting that the Warren Bridge charter violated both the Massachusetts constitutional guarantee of "life, liberty and property" and the Contracts Clause of the U.S. Constitution, which prevented state impairment of contracts. After the Supreme Judicial Court of Massachusetts affirmed denial of the injunction the Charles River Bridge proprietors sought a writ of error from the U.S. Supreme Court. In 1831 the Court heard arguments, but the justices' divergent views on the protection of vested property rights, as well as illnesses and vacancies on the bench, delayed decision. In 1837 the case was reargued before a court dominated by Democratic appointees.

Daniel Webster and Warren Dutton, appearing for the Charles River Bridge, relied on Contracts Clause and vested-rights arguments. According to them the Warren Bridge charter violated the state's contract obligation to the Charles River Bridge proprietors by effectively destroying their exclusive property in tolls, which was the essence of the original grant.

John Davis and Simon Greenleaf for the Warren Bridge proprietors argued that the Charles River Bridge had not been granted an exclusive right to the line of travel. When the Charles River Bridge proprietors accepted an extension of their charter, they acknowledged the state's ability to make competing grants. The grant to the Warren Bridge was within the legislature's authority.

Chief Justice Roger B. Taney's majority opinion and Justice Joseph Story's dissent presented contrasting views of legal principles, government responsibility, and economic progress—views that reflected their different political affiliations. They disagreed on matters of judicial interpretation of charters, the powers of the states, and the relative importance of the rights of the community and the rights of the individual.

Taney, one of Andrew Jackson's recent Democratic appointees, held that the legislature, representing the sovereign power of the people, had granted the privilege to build a bridge and collect tolls to the Charles River Bridge proprietors. Taney reasoned that the legislative grants should be construed narrowly to protect the public interest. Narrow construction disposed of any implied exclusive rights to the line of travel; the legislature's later authorization of a competing grant did not destroy the proprietors' property in tolls. While Taney declared that the "rights of private property must be sacredly guarded" (p. 548), he asserted that "the object and end of all government is to promote the happiness and prosperity of the community . . .; and it can never be assumed, that the government intended to diminish its power of accomplishing the end for which it was created" (p. 547).

Justice Story insisted in dissent that the Charles River Bridge charter was a form of contract granted for valuable consideration. The proprietors had offered to build the bridge to further the public good and the legislature had conferred the right to collect tolls. Where valuable consideration was received, courts should construe public contracts in favor of the grantee. Story's broad construction of the bridge charter inferred an exclusive grant to collect tolls along the line of travel. "If the government means to invite its citizens to enlarge the public comforts and conveniences, . . . there must be some pledge that the property will be safe; . . . and that success will not be the signal of a general combination to overthrow its rights, and to take away its profits" (p. 608).

The decision of the majority recognized that demand for improved technologies would lead to their rapid adoption. It warned that older corporations would "awaken from their sleep" (p. 552) and called upon the courts to protect vested property rights. Fearing this threat to the millions of dollars ventured in new enterprises, Taney fashioned his opinion to justify creative destruction of old property in order that new ventures might prosper.

□ Stanley I. Kutler, *Privilege and Creative Destruction: The Charles River Bridge Case* (1971).

Elizabeth B. Monroe

Cherokee Cases, collective name of two companion cases of the 1830s: *Cherokee Nation* v. *Georgia*, 5 Pet. (30 U.S.) 1 (1831), argued 5 Mar. 1831, decided 18 Mar. 1831 by vote of 4 to 2; Marshall for the Court, Johnson and Baldwin concurring, Thompson in dissent; and *Worcester* v. *Georgia*, 6 Pet. (31 U.S.) 515 (1832), argued 20 Feb. 1832, decided 3 Mar. 1832 by vote of 5 to 1; Marshall for the Court, Baldwin in dissent. The *Cherokee Cases* evolved out of attempts by Georgia to assert jurisdiction over Cherokee lands within the state that were protected by treaty. In *Cherokee Nation* v. *Georgia*, Chief Justice John Marshall held that the Supreme Court had no jurisdiction to hear a Cherokee request to enjoin Georgia's effort. He defined Cherokees as a "domestic, dependent nation," rather than a sovereign nation for Article III purposes, and as being wards of the federal government (p. 2).

The Court modified *Cherokee Nation* one year later in *Worcester* v. *Georgia*. A Congregational missionary had been convicted of failure to have a license Georgia required to live in Cherokee country. The Court held the Georgia laws void because they violated treaties, the contract and commerce clauses of the Constitution, and the sovereign authority of the Cherokee nation. Georgia refused to acknowledge the proceeding.

Marshall no longer considered the *Cherokee Nation* case controlling, although he did not overrule it. Instead he emphasized the concept of "nation," as opposed to "domestic" or "dependent." He held that Indian nations were a distinct people with the right to retain independent political communities. President Andrew Jackson, however, refused to enforce the Court's ruling and supported the removal of the Cherokees to Indian Territory. Many Cherokees perished during their exodus, known since as the "Trail of Tears."

John R. Wunder

Chicago, Burlington & Quincy Railroad Company v. Chicago, 166 U.S. 226 (1897), argued 6, 9 Nov. 1896, decided 1 Mar. 1897 by vote of 7 to 1; Harlan for the Court, Brewer in dissent, Fuller not participating.

In this case the Court unanimously held that the Fourteenth Amendment's Due Process Clause compelled the states to award just compensation when it took private property for public use. (Justice Brewer concurred on this point while dissenting from other parts of the judgment.) The case, which came to the Court as an appeal from a ruling of the Illinois Supreme Court upholding a jury award of one dollar when a street was opened across a railroad track, was among the earliest instances in which the Court applied the due process concept to protect substantive property rights. It was an important step in the Court's development of due process limits on state control of economic liberties. Yet *Chicago B. & Q.R.R. v. Chicago* remains good law despite its relation to the doctrine of laissez-faire constitutionalism. In contemporary constitutional law, the case stands as an early example of the doctrine that the Fourteenth Amendment's Due Process Clause incorporates the specific guarantees of the Bill of Rights.

In a dissenting opinion, Justice David J. Brewer agreed that the Due Process Clause required the states to pay compensation when private property was taken, but argued that the jury verdict provided only nominal, rather than just, compensation to the railroad.

Stephen A. Siegel

Chicago, Milwaukee & St. Paul Railway Co. v. Minnesota, 134 U.S. 418, argued 13, 14 Jan. 1890, decided 24 Mar. 1890 by vote of 6 to 3; Blatchford for the Court, Miller concurring, Bradley, Gray, and Lamar in dissent. When the Court in *Munn* v. *Illinois* (1877) upheld legislative power to control railroad rates, it also ruled that governmentally set rates were not subject to judicial review. This ruling was an application of the traditional principle that the Court determined the Constitution's allocation of power among branches of government but did not supervise the discretionary exercise of those powers. Yet in *Chicago, M. & St. P. Ry.* v. *Minnesota*, the Court voided legislation that did not permit judicial review of rates set by the state's Railroad and Warehouse Commission. This was the first case in which the Court adopted a modern approach to the constitutional arrangements of the regulatory state. Implicit in the Court's ambiguous opinion was the fundamental tenet of contemporary administrative law: due process requires judicial review of administrative agency procedures and decisions to determine their fidelity to constitutional norms. In particular, the Court asserted the power to judge the reasonableness of utility rates. With this decision, the Court began to review not only whether a particular branch of government had authority to act but also the reasonableness of the procedures through which officials act and the reasonableness of the decisions themselves.

Stephen A. Siegel

Chimel v. California, 395 U.S. 752 (1969), argued 27 Mar. 1969, decided 23 June 1969 by vote of 6 to 2 (with one vacancy); Stewart for the Court, Harlan concurring, White and Black in dissent. If the police have lawfully arrested a person for some criminal offense, how extensive a warrantless search may they make incident to that arrest? The Supreme Court answered this question in many different ways over a span of about sixty years. These responses ranged all the way from search of the person of the arrestee only to search of the person and the entire premises where the arrest was made. *Chimel* adopted a position between these extremes and has become the Court's major statement on the limits of a warrantless search pursuant to a lawful arrest.

To appreciate *Chimel*, it is important to understand the prior state of the law announced in *Harris* v. *United States* (1947) and *United States* v. *Rabinowitz* (1950). The *Harris-Rabinowitz* rule had these characteristics: (1) the scope of a permissible search was not limited to the person or areas the arrestee might reach to destroy evidence or obtain a weapon and thus appeared, to cover the entire premises where the arrest was made; (2) it was never made clear whether such a warrantless search was permissible only if there was probable cause evidence of the crime would be found on the premises; and (3) the search was limited in its intensity and length by the items being sought.

Chimel involved a warrantless search of the defendant's home, incident to his arrest there, for the fruits of a burglary. The Court, in overruling *Harris* and *Rabinowitz*, first stated that the person of an arrestee may be searched so as to deprive him of weapons by which he could resist arrest or escape and also to prevent his concealment or destruction of evidence. The Court then continued: "And the area into which an arrestee might reach in order to grab a weapon or evidentiary items must, of course, be governed by a like rule. A gun on a table or in a drawer in front of one who is arrested can be as dangerous to the arresting officer as one concealed in the clothing of the person arrested. There is ample justification, therefore, for a search of the arrestee's person and the area 'within his immediate control'—construing that phrase to mean the area from within which he might gain possession of a weapon or destructible evidence" (p. 763).

The *Chimel* dissenters offered this rationale for retaining the *Harris-Rabinowitz* rule: (1) warrantless arrests are generally upheld without regard to whether there was time to get a warrant; (2) this is so because there is very often a risk of flight making acquisition of a warrant impracticable; (3) police thus will often arrest without either an arrest or search warrant, and the arrest itself creates "exigent circumstances," as if police then leave to get a warrant "there must almost always be a strong possibility that confederates of the arrested man will in the meantime remove the items for which the police have probable cause to search" (p. 774); (4) thus, if after arrest the police have "probable cause to believe that seizable items are on the premises" (p. 773), they should be permitted to make an emergency search without a search warrant.

Empirical data, however, indicate that in a substantial number of cases arrests are not made under circumstances requiring immediate action to prevent escape. The "exigent circumstances" referred to by the *Chimel* dissenters often will have been unnecessarily created by the police themselves by not having a search warrant in hand at the time of the arrest. This is evident from the facts of *Chimel*. The burglary for which the defendant was arrested occurred a month earlier; the police knew he had not fled in the interim but continued to reside and work in the area; the police obviously felt there was no emergency because they obtained an arrest warrant and delayed serving it for several days; and no explanation was offered as to why the police could not have obtained a search warrant at the same time.

☐ David E. Aaronson and Rangeley Wallace, "A Reconsideration of the Fourth Amendment's Doctrine of Search Incident to Arrest," *Georgetown Law Journal* 64 (1975): 53–84.

Wayne R. LaFave

Chinese Exclusion Cases, a series of disputes settled by the Supreme Court during the 1880s and 1890s: *Chew Heong* v. *United States*, 112 U.S. 536 (1884), argued 30 Oct. 1884, decided 8 Dec. 1884 by vote of 7 to 2, Harlan for the Court, Field and Bradley in dissent; *United States* v. *Jung Ah Lung*, 124 U.S. 621 (1888), argued 9 Jan. 1888, decided 13 Feb. 1888 by vote of 6 to 3, Blatchford for the Court, Harlan in dissent; *Chae Chan Ping* v. *United States* (also recorded as *The Chinese Exclusion Case*), 130 U.S. 581 (1889), argued 28 Mar. 1889, decided 13 May 1889 by vote of 9 to 0, Field for the Court; and *Fong Yue Ting* v. *United States, Wong Quan* v. *United States*, and *Lee Joe* v. *United States*, 149 U.S. 698 (1893), argued 10 May 1893, decided

15 May 1893 by vote of 6 to 3, Gray for the Court, Brewer, Field, and Fuller in dissent. These decisions refined congressional legislation designed to prevent Chinese immigration.

In 1882 Congress passed the first of a series of Chinese Exclusion Acts prohibiting Chinese laborers and miners from entering the United States. An 1884 amendment required all Chinese laborers who lived in the United States before 1882 and who left the country with plans to return to have a reentry certificate. Six years later, the Scott Act (1888) became law. This statute prohibited Chinese laborers abroad or who planned future travels from returning. Over twenty thousand Chinese were stranded. The Scott Act did allow merchants and teachers to return if they had proper papers. This loophole began the "paper names" industry whereby Chinese created new identities to return.

Congress passed a second exclusionary act, known as the Geary Act (1892). This law continued the ban on Chinese laborers and added the denial of bail to Chinese in habeas corpus proceedings and the requirement for all Chinese to have identification certificates or face deportation. The McCreary Act (1893) further defined laborers to include merchants, laundry owners, miners, and fishers. Finally, the Chinese Exclusion Act of 1902 permanently closed the door on all Chinese immigration.

The government of China, Chinese living in the United States, and Chinese-Americans challenged the constitutionality of these anti-Chinese laws. The first case to reach the Supreme Court was *Chew Heong* v. *United States* (1884). In this case a Chinese laborer who resided in the United States in 1880 but left in 1881 was denied reentry in 1884 because he did not have a certificate. In a habeas corpus proceeding, he was denied a writ by Justice Stephen Field; on appeal Justice John Harlan led a divided Court in a reversal of Field's decision. Harlan determined that Chew Heong had befallen a statutory glitch, leaving before the 1882 act and returning after the 1884 amendments. Field and Justice Joseph Bradley dissented.

In 1888 the Court decided *United States* v. *Jung Ah Lung*. The defendant, a Chinese laborer, had been an American resident before 1882, and he had left to return to China in 1883 with a reentry certificate. When Jung tried to return in 1885, he did not have his certificate and was denied reentry. He sued for a writ of habeas corpus, which was issued. Once again a divided Court, this time led by Justice Samuel Blatchford, upheld the challenge of the Chinese to the enforcement of the Exclusion Act of 1882 as amended in 1884. The government argued that Chinese challenges through writs of habeas corpus were not allowed. Had the Court accepted this argument, Chinese rights would have been seriously curtailed. Once again Justice Field dissented, but he was gaining followers, including Justice Harlan.

After *Jung Ah Lung*, Congress passed the Scott Act, and the Supreme Court was quickly asked its interpretation in *Chae Chan Ping v. United States* (1889). Under the Scott Act, reentry certificates were abolished. Instead, an outright prohibition of reentry was established. Chae, a San Francisco Chinese laborer, left the United States to visit China before the Scott Act was passed but after the 1884 amendment. Although he had a reentry certificate, he was prevented from reentry and denied a writ of habeas corpus. The Supreme Court in an opinion written by Justice Field unanimously found the Scott Act constitutional.

The final Chinese attempt to challenge the Exclusion Acts came in 1893. In 1892 Congress renewed the Exclusion Act of 1882 for another ten years, and it added a new requirement that all Chinese laborers had to have certificates of residence or face deportation. Three Chinese were subsequently found guilty of not having residence papers, and they appealed. In the 1893 cases the Court completed the closing of the door to Chinese immigration and the restriction of basic freedoms to Chinese-Americans by holding that Congress had the power retroactively to require Chinese to have residential certificates and allowing those without certificates to be deported.

After initially offering narrow holdings to protect Chinese reentry to the United States, the Supreme Court eventually succumbed to the anti-Chinese hysteria of the era and ratified far-reaching restrictions on basic rights for Chinese under American law.

□ Milton R. Konvitz, *The Asian and the Asiatic in American Law* (1946).

John R. Wunder

Chisholm v. Georgia, 2 Dall. (2 U.S.) 419 (1793), argued 5 Feb. 1793, decided 18 Feb. 1793 by vote of 4 to 1; seriatim opinions by Jay, Cushing, Wilson, and Blair, Iredell in dissent. The first great case decided by the Court, *Chisholm* presented a conflict between federal jurisdiction and state sovereignty. The plaintiff, a citizen of South Carolina and the executor of a South Carolina merchant, sued the state of Georgia for the value of clothing supplied by the merchant during the Revolutionary War. Georgia refused to appear, claiming immunity from the suit as a sovereign and independent state. The Constitution (Article III, sec. 2) extended federal judicial power to controversies between "a State and Citizens of another State." The Court entered a default judgment against Georgia. The opinions of James Wilson and John Jay were ringing declarations of the nationalist view that sovereignty resided in the people of the United States "for the purposes of Union" and that as to those purposes Georgia was "not a sovereign state" (p. 457). *Chisholm* roused old Antifederalist fears of "consolidation" while raising the prospect of creditors flocking to the federal courts. The immediate consequence of the decision was action by Congress ultimately leading to the Eleventh Amendment (1798), which took away jurisdiction in suits commenced against a state by citizens of another state or of a foreign state. This was the first instance in which a Supreme Court decision has been superseded by constitutional amendment.

Charles F. Hobson

Chisom v. Roemer, 501 U.S. 380 (1991), argued 12 Apr. 1991, decided 20 June 1991 by vote of 6 to 3; Stevens for the Court, Scalia, joined by Rehnquist and Kennedy, in dissent, Kennedy in dissent. **Houston Lawyers' Association v. Attorney General of Texas**, 111 S.Ct. 2376 (1991), argued 22 Apr. 1991, decided 20 June 1991 by vote of 6 to 3; Stevens for the Court, Scalia, joined by Rehnquist and Kennedy, in dissent. The 1982 amendments to the Voting Rights Act of 1965 amended section 2 to make clear that practices that result in the denial or abridgement of voting rights, even if not the product of discriminatory intent, are unlawful. The amendments extended section 2's protection beyond the Fifteenth Amendment that, under *Mobile* v. *Bolden* (1980), proscribes only intentional discrimination in voting. *Chisom* holds that section 2's "results test" applies to state judicial elections.

For purposes of electing two of Louisiana's seven Supreme Court justices, Orleans

Parish, in which black voters constituted a majority, was combined into a multimember district with three parishes in which white voters constituted a majority. The five other justices were elected in single-member districts. Black Orleans Parish voters alleged that the multimember district denied their voting rights, but the question arose whether section 2 applies to judicial elections. The Supreme Court noted that section 2, prior to its amendment in 1982, was regarded as applying to judicial elections, and that *Clark v. Roemer* (1991) had held that section 5 of the Voting Rights Act, which requires certain states to submit for approval changes in voting procedures with federal authorities, applies to judicial elections. The Court held that the use of the word "representatives" in section 2 did not reflect Congress's desire to limit section 2 to legislators and executive officials. *Houston Lawyers' Association* held that section 2 applies to the election of trial judges.

Theodore Eisenberg

City of Boerne, Texas v. Flores, 117 S.Ct. 2157 (1997), argued 19 Feb. 1997, decided 25 June 1997 by vote of 6 to 3; Kennedy for the Court, O'Connor, Souter, and Breyer in dissent. The city of Boerne, Texas, had refused to allow a Catholic church to enlarge its building in a neighborhood zoned for historic preservation. The church then sued the city, claiming that under the Religious Restoration Act of 1993 it was interfering with the practice of a religious institution.

Congress passed the act in response to a 1990 Supreme Court decision, *Employment Division v. Smith*, which held that members of a Native American church who used peyote in their rituals were not exempt from Oregon's narcotics laws. The Religious Freedom Restoration Act had broad support in Congress, garnering a unanimous vote in the House of Representatives and all but three votes in the Senate. Congress invoked section 5 of the Fourteenth Amendment in passing the new law, which provided that Congress had the power to enforce, by appropriate legislation, the amendment's guarantees of due process and equal protection of the laws. While a ruling of the Supreme Court can be overturned only by a constitutional amendment, supporters of the Religious Freedom Restoration Act insisted that they were not confronting the justices but merely legislating a new standard of review for laws affecting religion. A fed-

eral district judge in San Antonio declared the law unconstitutional on the grounds that Congress has usurped the federal judiciary's exclusive authority to interpret the meaning of the Constitution, but the United States Court of Appeals for the Fifth Circuit reversed that decision and upheld the statute. The act was also unpopular in the states, and some sixteen states filed friends of the court briefs that recounted, among other things, that prisoners were making often fanciful religious claims under the law.

The question before the Supreme Court was whether Congress was appropriately enforcing the Fourteenth Amendment by passing the act or instead going beyond its authority and giving a substantive meaning to the amendment. Justice Kennedy for the majority held that Congress had exceeded its authority because it was determining what amounted to a constitutional violation, a task left under the Constitution exclusively to the federal courts. According to Kennedy, the Religious Freedom Restoration Act was not a remedial action or preventative measure but an attempt at forming a substantive change in constitutional interpretation. In perhaps its most significant constitutional finding, the majority ruled that there had to be some congruence or proportionality between the means adopted by Congress and the end to be achieved in enforcing the Fourteenth Amendment. Through its actions, Kennedy concluded, Congress had placed a burden on the states that made it difficult, if not impossible, for them to exercise their traditional authority to regulate the health and welfare of their citizens.

The dissenters, led by Justice Sandra Day O'Connor, agreed with the standard the majority applied to congressional action under the Fourteenth Amendment, but they disagreed about the basis that the majority had relied on. O'Connor believed that the proper course of action was to overturn the *Smith* decision rather than declare the Religious Freedom Restoration Act unconstitutional.

City of Boerne was the third case in three years in which the Court had struck down major congressional acts that limited the power of the states. In **Seminole Tribe of Florida v. Florida* (1996) it invalidated part of the Indian Gaming Regulatory Act, and in *United States v. *Lopez* (1995) it ruled that a federal gun control law exceeded the power of Congress to regulate interstate commerce. As a result, the decision in *City of Boerne* was not so much about church and state relations, although it had important consequences for them, but instead about the limits placed on Congress's expansive interpretation of its own powers. The justices made clear that they would not tolerate the other branches of government trespassing on their role of determining conclusively what the Constitution means.

Kermit L. Hall

City of Monterey v. Del Monte Dunes at Monterey, Ltd., 526 U.S. 687 (1999), argued 7 Oct. 1998, decided 24 May 1999 by vote of 5 to 4. Kennedy announced the judgment of the Court and delivered the opinion for a unanimous Court with respect to four of the five parts of the decision; Souter, joined by O'Connor, Ginsburg, and Breyer, dissented in part.

Del Monte Dunes brought suit under 42 U.S.C. section 1983 after receiving five formal decisions by the city denying Del Monte the right to develop a 37.6 acre parcel located in the city of Monterey, California, and imposing more rigorous requirements on the proposed development. A section 1983 action allows a party to seek damages when deprived of a federal right. Del Monte Dunes alleged the city deprived it of due process of the law and equal protection of the law, and effected a regulatory taking of their property without paying just compensation.

The federal district court found for the city on Del Monte's due process claim and, over the city's objection, permitted the jury to ascertain liability under Del Monte's taking claim. It instructed the jury to find for Del Monte if it "found either that Del Monte Dunes had been denied all economically viable use of its property" or that the city's rejection of Del Monte's development proposals "did not substantially advance a legitimate public purpose" (p. 700). The jury found for Del Monte in the amount of $1.45 million and the Ninth Circuit Court of Appeals affirmed.

This was the first takings case in which the Court upheld the award of monetary damages for a regulatory taking. Significantly, the Court held that the question of liability on a regulatory takings claim was properly submitted to a jury in a section 1983 action. The case also reminds governmental officials that there must be a good faith effort

to deal with property owners. The Court left uncertain, however, the relationship of substantive due process to the law of regulatory takings.

Randy T. Simmons

Civil Rights Cases, 109 U.S. 3 (1883), submitted on the briefs 7 November 1882, argued 29 March 1883, decided 15 October 1883 by vote of 8 to 1; Bradley for the Court, Harlan in dissent. Few decisions better illustrate the Supreme Court's early inclination to interpret narrowly the Civil War Amendments than the *Civil Rights Cases*. There the Court declared unconstitutional provisions of the Civil Rights Act of 1875 that prohibited racial discrimination in inns, public conveyances, and places of public amusement. The decision curtailed federal efforts to protect African-Americans from private discrimination and cast constitutional doubts on Congress's ability to legislate in the area of civil rights, doubts that were not completely resolved until enactment of the Civil Rights Act of 1964.

The *Civil Rights Cases* presented two conflicting views of the Thirteenth and Fourteenth Amendments. The conservative view saw the amendments in narrow terms: the Thirteenth Amendment simply abolished slavery; the Fourteenth granted the freed people citizenship and a measure of relief from state discrimination. The more radical view believed the amendments helped secure to the freed people and others all rights of free people in Anglo-American legal culture. Moreover, the amendments gave the national government authority to protect citizens against both state and private deprivations of rights.

Justice Joseph P. Bradley's majority opinion rejected the more radical interpretation of the new amendments. He held that the Fourteenth Amendment only prohibited state abridgement of individual rights. In Bradley's view the 1875 Civil Rights Act was an impermissible attempt by Congress to create a municipal code regulating the private conduct of individuals in the area of racial discrimination. He asserted in dicta that even private interference with such rights as voting, jury service, or appearing as witnesses in state court were not within the province of Congress to control. An individual faced with such interference had to look to state government for relief. Bradley also rejected the contention that the Thirteenth Amendment allowed Congress to pass the 1875 legislation, declaring that denial of access to public accommodations did not constitute a badge or incident of slavery. In his view such a broad construction of the Thirteenth Amendment would make the freed person "the special favorite of the laws."

In his dissent, Southerner and former slaveholder Justice John Marshall Harlan rejected the majority's narrow construction of the Civil War Amendments. Asserting that the decision rested on grounds that were "narrow and artificial," Harlan argued that the Thirteenth Amendment gave Congress broad powers to legislate to insure the rights of freed people (p. 26). He contended that the freedom conferred by the Thirteenth Amendment went beyond the simple absence of bondage. It encompassed freedom from the incidents of slavery, including all "badges of slavery" (p. 35).

Along with the decision in the *Slaughterhouse Cases (1873), which effectively stripped the Fourteenth Amendment's Privileges or Immunities Clause of significant meaning, and U.S. v. Cruikshank (1876), which upheld congressional efforts to protect blacks and others against private deprivations of constitutional rights, the Civil Rights Cases fashioned a Fourteenth Amendment jurisprudence considerably less protective of individual rights than many of its framers had envisioned. The extent to which the Court's narrow reading of Fourteenth Amendment protections helped usher in and foster the era of extensive segregation in southern and other states is open to debate. But the Supreme Court's decision in the Civil Rights Cases largely mandated the withdrawal of the federal government from civil rights enforcement. That withdrawal would not be reversed until after World War II.

In 1964 Congress again passed legislation prohibiting discrimination in public accommodations. Ironically, the Bradley opinion, which expressly did not rule on whether or not the Constitution's Commerce Clause provided a basis for congressional legislation in this area, played a role in the drafting of the 1964 statute. The 1964 act's public accommodations provision was based on the Commerce Clause.

□ Eugene Gressman, "The Unhappy History of Civil Rights Legislation," Michigan Law Review 50 (1952): 1323–1358.

Robert J. Cottrol

Clark Distilling Co. v. Western Maryland Railway Co., 242 U.S. 311 (1917), argued 10–11 May 1915, ordered for reargument 1 Nov. 1915, reargued 8–9 Nov. 1916, decided 8 Jan. 1917 by vote of 7 to 2; White for the Court, Holmes and Van Devanter in dissent. Responding to Anti-Saloon League complaints that it was impossible to enforce state prohibition laws in the face of a flood of interstate liquor shipments, Congress in February 1913 enacted the Webb-Kenyon Act forbidding the shipment of intoxicating liquor into a state in violation of its laws. President William H. Taft vetoed the act as unconstitutional, on the basis of a series of Court rulings that the Commerce Clause required common carriers to accept interstate shipments of liquor as not subject to state law until after received by the consignee. Congress immediately overrode Taft's veto, and shortly West Virginia obtained an injunction against the Western Maryland Railway and the Adams Express Companies to prevent them from carrying liquor into West Virginia in violation of its law against manufacture, sale, or possession of intoxicating liquors. The Clark Distilling Company sued Western and Adams to compel the carriers to accept shipments of liquor that had been ordered for personal use, which was not explicitly forbidden, and deliver them in West Virginia.

Anti-Saloon League general counsel Wayne Wheeler defended the Webb-Kenyon law before the Supreme Court because the Justice Department declined to do so. The Court held that while the unquestionable power of the government to regulate interstate commerce in intoxicating liquors did not have to be fully or uniformly exercised, it did extend to prohibiting interstate commerce in violation of state law. This validation of the Webb-Kenyon Law bolstered temperance forces on the eve of the 1917 congressional battle over adoption of the Eighteenth Amendment.

David E. Kyvig

Classic, United States v., 313 U.S. 299 (1941), argued 7 Apr. 1941, decided 26 May 1941 by vote of 5 to 3; Stone for the Court, Douglas in dissent. Two Supreme Court decisions before World War II allowed white Democrats in the one-party South to disfranchise black citizens by denying them primary ballots. Newberry v. United States (1921) concluded that Congress lacked power under Article I, section 4 of the Constitution to regulate party primaries. *Grovey* v. *Townsend* (1935) held that a state party convention's exclusion of African-Americans from primary participation constituted private rather than state action and, therefore, the Fourteenth and Fifteenth Amendments did not apply.

The newly created Civil Rights Section of the Justice Department brought this successful test case establishing federal authority to redress corruption and discrimination in the state electoral process. The government charged the Louisiana election commissioners with willfully altering and falsely counting congressional primary election ballots in violation of federal civil rights statutes.

The Supreme Court overruled *Newberry* to hold that Congress's power under Article I, section 4 to regulate "elections" includes the power to regulate primaries when state law makes the primary an integral part of the procedure for choosing candidates for federal office. The Court also reasoned that Article I, section 2 guarantees citizens the right to vote in congressional primaries and to have their votes properly counted; moreover, this right is protected against interference by individual as well as state action. While *Grovey* was not mentioned, the reasoning in *Classic* undercut the rationale of that decision to make inevitable its overruling in *Smith* v. *Allwright* (1944), which held that primary elections for either federal or state office were subject to the Constitution.

Thomas E. Baker

Clinton v. City of New York, 118 S.Ct. 2091 (1998), argued 27 April 1998, decided 25 June 1998 by vote of 6 to 3; Stevens for the Court, Scalia, O'Connor, and Breyer concurring and dissenting in part or whole.

Since the late nineteenth century, presidents have sought the power to eliminate selectively provisions from legislation presented to them by Congress. The Constitution in Article I, however, requires that the chief executive must either accept or reject any measure in full rather than rejecting particular pieces. Republican President Ronald Reagan in the 1980s had urged such power as a way of fostering a balanced budget by curbing the spending of a Democratic Congress. The line-item veto emerged in the 1990s as one of the important clauses in the Republicans' so-called "Contract With America," and the Republican-controlled Congress in 1996 finally passed the Line Item Veto Act. That measure allowed the President to cancel individual items of federal spending and tax breaks.

Although the act passed with solid majorities in both houses, its opponents acted aggressively to overturn it. Led by Democratic Senator Robert Byrd of West Virginia, six members of Congress brought suit in federal court challenging the act's constitutionality. The Supreme Court, in *Raines* v. *Byrd* (1997) rebuffed this effort and sustained the Clinton administration. The justices found that the lawmakers bringing the suit lacked standing to challenge the statute, because they were not personally affected by it. President Clinton continued to invoke his powers, ultimately rewriting 11 laws and eliminating 82 provisions, including money for New York City hospitals and a tax break for Idaho potato growers. These two groups sued and this time the Court accepted the cases for full hearing.

The Clinton administration, through Solicitor General Seth P. Waxman, conceded that a true line-item veto would be unconstitutional, but the measure at hand was not one. Instead, Waxman insisted, the law was constitutional because the president first signed the measure in question and then selectively eliminated portions of it as an exercise of the authority that Congress had delegated to him. As long as Congress had not identified a particular provision as exempt from the veto, then the president retained the prerogative to eliminate it.

A majority of the Supreme Court, however, rejected this logic. Speaking for the majority, Justice John Paul Stevens insisted that the statute violated the presentment clause of the Constitution in Article I. The president lacked constitutional authority to modify the text of legislation presented to him; he had either to accept or reject it in toto. The dissenters, led by Justice Antonin Scalia, insisted that the measure was a proper constitutional experiment. Scalia reasoned that there was no meaningful difference between the president canceling a particular provision of a law and refusing to spend money that Congress had appropriated. The Court avoided dealing with the explosive issue of the delegation of congressional powers to executive branch agencies, a practice that has become commonplace in the modern administrative state.

Although members of Congress supportive of the line-item veto have proffered other schemes, there seems little likelihood that any of them will stand the test of high court scrutiny. If a true line-item veto is to be added to the president's powers, as it already exists among the governors of 40 states, then it will almost certainly have to come through a constitutional amendment.

Kermit L. Hall

Clinton v. Jones, 520 U.S. 681 (1997), argued 13 Jan. 1997, decided 27 May 1997 by vote of 9 to 0; Stevens for the Court. The case involved the question of whether President Bill Clinton could delay proceedings in a sexual harassment suit brought by Paula Corbin Jones, an employee of the state of Arkansas while Clinton was governor. Jones had complained that in 1991 Governor Clinton had requested that she come to his hotel room in Little Rock, where he allegedly displayed his private parts to her. Her suit, which sought $700,000 in damages, claimed that Mr. Clinton used the powers of his office to violate her civil rights. President Clinton's attorneys argued that the case should not be heard until after his term as president had ended, since the suit would disrupt the performance of his duties as chief executive. The high court, moreover, in *Nixon* v. *Fitzgerald* (1982), had held that a president has absolute immunity from civil lawsuits over actions taken in his official capacity.

Justice John Paul Stevens's sober opinion dismissed the *Fitzgerald* precedent since the conduct in question was unofficial rather than official. Stevens concluded, moreover, that Ms. Jones had a right to an orderly disposition of her case. While the Court recognized that great respect was due to the office of the president, that office did not confer any special privilege on the chief executive to be free from civil proceedings. Stevens noted that the decision by Federal District Judge Susan Weber Wright, of Arkansas, to delay the trial in 1994 was an abuse of judicial discretion that took no account of Paula Jones's interests in proceeding with the case. The unanimous Court also rejected Clinton's argument that the unique responsibilities of the president and the concept of separation of powers limited the federal courts from interfering with the executive branch.

Only three other presidents have been the subject of civil lawsuits involving incidents before they took office. Suits against Theodore Roosevelt and Harry Truman were dismissed; John F. Kennedy settled a suit involving a car accident during his 1960 campaign.

Kermit L. Hall

Cohen v. California, 403 U.S. 15 (1971), argued 22 Feb. 1971, decided 7 June 1971 by vote of 5 to 4; Harlan for the Court, Blackmun in dissent, joined by Burger and Black, and White in part. In April 1968 Paul Robert Cohen wore a jacket bearing the words "Fuck the Draft" in a Los Angeles courthouse. He was arrested and subsequently convicted for violating a California statute prohibiting any person from "disturb[ing] the peace . . . by offensive conduct." The Supreme Court had to decide whether Cohen's speech was punishable because it fit one of the "exceptions" to free speech protected by the First Amendment.

The Court conceded that Cohen's expletive was "vulgar," but it concluded that his speech was nonetheless protected by the First Amendment. It was neither an "incitement" to illegal action nor "obscenity." Nor did it constitute "fighting words" (personally abusive epithets), for it had not been directed at a person who was likely to retaliate or at someone who could not avoid the message. Therefore, the conviction could be justified only by the state's desire to preserve the cleanliness of discourse in the public sphere. The Court refused to permit state such a broad power, holding that no objective distinctions can be made between vulgar and nonvulgar political speech, and that the emotive aspects of speech are often as important as the purely cognitive. "It is . . .often true," Justice Harlan wrote, "that one man's vulgarity is another's lyric . . . words [which] are often chosen as much for their emotive as their cognitive force" (pp. 25–26).

By expanding the constitutional foundation for protecting provocative and potentially offensive speech, *Cohen* has become a landmark decision.

Donald A. Downs

Cohen v. Cowles Media Co., 501 U.S. 663 (1991), argued 27 Mar. 1991, decided 24 June 1991 by vote of 5 to 4; White for the Court, Blackmun and Souter in dissent. During the 1982 Minnesota gubernatorial race, Dan Cohen, a campaign adviser to the Republican candidate, leaked damaging information about the Democratic candidate to reporters from the Minneapolis and St. Paul newspapers after they promised not to identify him as their source. Editors at the two papers, over the objection of the reporters, broke the promise of confidentiality and identified Cohen. Cohen was fired from his job, and he sued the papers for fraudulent misrepresentation and breach of contract.

A trial court awarded Cohen $200,000 in compensatory damages and $500,000 in punitive damages. The Minnesota Court of Appeals said Cohen failed to establish a fraud claim and reversed the punitive damages award. It upheld the finding of breach of contract and the compensatory damages award. But the Minnesota Supreme Court reversed the compensatory damages award, holding that enforcement of confidentiality under contract law would violate the newspapers' rights because identifying Cohen amounted to an editorial decision protected under the First Amendment.

The Supreme Court reversed, holding that the First Amendment does not forbid the general application of Minnesota's contract law to the press even if it has incidental effects on news gathering and reporting. Justice Byron White wrote that the newspapers' First Amendment claim was "constitutionally insignificant" and that contract law "requires those who make certain kinds of promises to keep them" (p. 2519). The Court directed the Minnesota Supreme Court to reconsider whether Cohen's claim could be upheld under an oral contract doctrine or if Minnesota's Constitution could be interpreted to shield the press from Cohen's claim.

Justices Harry Blackmun and David Souter dissented, saying the First Amendment prohibits the use of generally applicable laws to burden societal interest in truthful political speech without a compelling state interest. Souter argued separately that laws of general applicability "may restrict First Amendment rights just as effectively as those directed specifically at speech itself" (p. 2522).

The decision could be significant. Anonymous sources may dry up. In addition, shield law protection for reporters may be diminished because of the Court's position that confidentiality promises are a matter of contract law and not a First Amendment immunity to gather and report the news.

Tim Gallimore

Cohens v. Virginia, 6 Wheat. (19 U.S.) 264 (1821), argued 13 Feb. 1821, decided 3 Mar. 1821 by vote of 6 to 0; Marshall for the Court.

Philip and Mendes Cohen sold lottery tickets in Virginia under the authority of an act of Congress for the District of Columbia. The Cohens appealed their conviction for violating the state statute, which had banned such lotteries. Virginia asserted that the Eleventh Amendment precluded the Supreme Court from hearing the case and that section 25 of the Judiciary Act of 1789 did not apply.

The *Cohens* case reflected the effort by several states, including Virginia, to challenge John Marshall's opinion in *McCulloch* v. *Maryland* (1819). Marshall seized on *Cohens*, which some historians believed was contrived, to reemphasize federal judicial power. He asserted that the Constitution made the Union supreme and that the federal judiciary was the ultimate constitutional arbiter. While the states could interpret their own laws, any federal question must ultimately be resolved, as section 25 provided, only by the federal courts. The Eleventh Amendment did not prevent federal courts from deciding properly a legitimate federal question, even where a state was the appellee.

Marshall avoided Virginia noncompliance by holding that the lottery statute applied only in the District of Columbia, but Virginia states' rights advocates nonetheless blasted his judicial nationalism.

Kermit L. Hall

Coker v. Georgia, 433 U.S. 584 (1977), argued 28 Mar. 1977, decided 29 June 1977 by vote of 7 to 2; White for the plurality, Brennan and Marshall concurring, Powell concurring in part and dissenting in part, Burger and Rehnquist in dissent. While serving sentences for murder, rape, kidnapping, and aggravated assault, Coker escaped from a Georgia prison and, while committing an armed robbery, raped a woman. He was convicted of these crimes and received the death sentence for rape. The jury, under Georgia's bifurcated trial procedure and following the statutory guidelines approved in *Gregg* v. *Georgia* (1976), found that two aggravating circumstances existed: the petitioner had prior capital felony convictions and the rape was committed in the course of committing another capital felony, armed robbery. The Georgia Supreme Court reviewed the sentence for comparability and affirmed it. The U.S. Supreme Court reversed.

Justice Byron White's plurality opinion held that the Eighth Amendment's proscription of cruel and unusual punishments prohibited punishments that are grossly disproportionate to the crime. Such penalties are a purposeless and needless imposition of pain and suffering. White noted that Georgia was the only state to impose the death penalty for rape of an adult woman and that Georgia juries themselves rarely called for the death penalty in rape cases. White repeatedly emphasized that the death penalty, the deliberate taking of a human life, was proportional only to the crime of first degree murder. Justice Lewis Powell concurred only to the extent that the crime was not committed with excessive brutality and that the victim did not sustain serious or lasting injury.

The result highlights the tensions inherent in *Gregg* and *Woodson* v. *North Carolina* (1976). If civilized standards require highly individualized sentencing, then the very reasons for rejecting mandatory sentencing should validate jury findings in some cases that certain persons with long histories of criminal behavior deserve the death sentence. Coker's record did not contradict such a finding in his case.

Lief H. Carter

Colegrove v. Green, 328 U.S. 549 (1946), argued 7–8 Mar. 1946, decided 10 June 1946 by vote of 4 to 3; Frankfurter for the Court, Black in dissent, Jackson not participating (Stone's death left one vacancy). Qualified voters challenged the apportionment of congressional districts in Illinois as lacking appropriate compactness and equality. A three-judge district court dismissed the case and Justices Felix Frankfurter, Stanley Reed, and Harold Burton affirmed that action. These justices branded apportionment a political question and reasoned that invalidation of Illinois districts might, in requiring statewide elections, create an evil greater than that remedied. Such party contests should be resolved by the state legislature subject to congressional supervision. Justice Wiley B. Rutledge concurred in the result, convinced that the short time between a judicial judgment and the impending election made an equitable remedy difficult. Justice Hugo Black, joined by William Douglas and Frank Murphy, believed the failure to reapportion the Illinois districts since 1901 denied the equal protection of the laws and of the guarantee in Article I of the right to vote for congressional representatives.

Weakened by the close division of the justices and by the continuing inaction of state legislatures, the Court declared in *Baker* v. *Carr* (1962) that apportionment issues were cognizable under the Fourteenth Amendment's Equal Protection Clause. This action set the stage for later decisions requiring approximate equality of electoral districts.

John R. Vile

Coleman v. Miller, 307 U.S. 433 (1939), argued 10 Oct. 1938, reargued 17–18 Apr. 1939, decided 5 June 1939 by vote of 7 to 2; Hughes for the Court, Butler and McReynolds in dissent. The Court faced three issues: (1) could the lieutenant-governor of Kansas break a tie in the state senate in favor of the proposed Child Labor Amendment; (2) could the state ratify an amendment it had previously rejected; and (3) could a state ratify an amendment thirteen years after Congress proposed it with no time limit? The court was "equally divided" (p. 447) on the first issue and thus left standing the Kansas Supreme Court's judgment sanctioning the lieutenant governor's participation. Citing congressional promulgation of the Fourteenth Amendment, the Court held that the latter two issues were political questions for Congress to decide. Concurring Justices Hugo Black, Owen Roberts, Felix Frankfurter, and William Douglas wanted to entrust all amending issues to Congress. The dissenters, citing *Dillon* v. *Gloss* (1921), argued that Kansas's ratification was untimely. Addressing similar issues in the companion case, *Chandler* v. *Wise*, the majority dismissed an action against Kentucky's governor, declaring his certification of the state's ratification conclusive.

Coleman muddied the amending process and introduced the ambiguous precedent of the Fourteenth Amendment. Subsequent decisions concerning political questions could limit *Coleman's* reach. Thus, in *Idaho* v. *Freeman* (1981), a U.S. district court sanctioned a state's rescission of ratification of the proposed Equal Rights Amendment after Congress extended the amendment's original seven-year deadline.

John R. Vile

Collector v. Day, 11 Wall. (78 U.S.) 113 (1871), argued 3 Feb. 1871, decided 3 Apr. 1871 by vote of 8 to 1; Nelson for the Court, Bradley in dissent. *Collector* v. *Day* was one in a line of cases involving intergovernmental tax immunities, and, as such, traced its origins to the latter part of Chief Justice John Marshall's opinion in *McCulloch* v. *Maryland*

(1819), which held that a state could not tax an instrumentality of the federal government. Following this reasoning, the Court had held in *Dobbins* v. *Erie County* (1842) that a state could not tax the income of a federal officer. *Collector* v. *Day* was the reciprocal of *Dobbins*, holding that the federal government could not tax the income of a state judge. Justice Samuel Nelson relied on the Tenth Amendment and on doctrines of dual sovereignty to hold that the state and federal governments were independent of each other and that the states retained all aspects of sovereignty not delegated to the federal government. Consequently, he reasoned, the federal government could not tax essential instrumentalities of the states. The *Day* doctrine was weakened by the Court's decision in *Helvering* v. *Gerhardt* (1938) and finally explicitly overruled in *Graves* v. *O'Keefe* (1939).

William M. Wiecek

Columbus Board of Education v. Penick, 443 U.S. 449 (1979), argued 24 Apr. 1979, decided 2 July 1979 by vote of 7 to 2; White for the Court, Burger and Stewart concurring, Powell and Rehnquist in dissent. Notwithstanding the intervening decisions of *Milliken* v. *Bradley* (1974) and *Pasadena City Board of Education* v. *Spangler* (1976), which cast doubt on the Court's continuing desire to uphold large urban school desegregation plans, the Court reaffirmed the basic principles of *Swann* v. *Charlotte-Mecklenburg* (1971) and *Keyes* v. *Denver School District No. 1* (1973). It reiterated that proof of purposeful segregation in a substantial portion of an urban school district created a strong presumption that the school board had practiced systemwide segregative intent and had tolerated systemwide segregative effects—or both—thus warranting wholesale district-wide relief. Contrary evidence of the board's objectives was viewed with skepticism. Even where current racial imbalance in the schools could be shown to have been caused by innocent behavior on the part of the board, as long as the system was infected with segregative intent when *Brown* v. *Board of Education* (1954) was decided, the school board remained liable to dismantle the dual system if it had not taken substantial steps since then to do so.

Justice Lewis Powell reiterated the view he expressed in *Keyes* that the de facto/ de jure distinction made no sense. Justice William Rehnquist filed a lengthy dissent

complaining of the Court's unwarranted intrusion into local education policy making and, in effect, of the Court's entire post—*Green* v. *County School Board of New Kent County* (1968) case law. In *Missouri* v. *Jenkins* (1995) Rehnquist carried a 5-to-4 majority in holding that the lower federal courts in Missouri had improperly ordered the state to help pay for a showcase desegregation plan for Kansas City schools.

Dennis J. Hutchinson

Communist Party v. Subversive Activities Control Board, 367 U.S. 1 (1961), argued 11–12 Oct. 1960, decided 5 June 1961 by vote of 5 to 4; Frankfurter for the Court, Warren, Black, Douglas, and Brennan in dissent. The Internal Security Act, passed over President Truman's veto in 1950 and generally known as the McCarran Act, sought to expose the Communist party in the United States by the devices of compulsory registration. The statute ordered communist organizations to register with the attorney general; the Subversive Activities Control Board (SACB) was created to administer the registration process. Registered organizations were required to disclose the names of their officers and the source of their funds. Members of registered organizations were subject to various sanctions, including denial of passports and the right to work in defense plants.

The SACB promptly identified the American Communist party as a "communist action organization" and ordered it to register, which the officers of the party refused to do. After eleven years of litigation, including one remand by the Supreme Court to the board because of the possibility that the record was tainted by perjured testimony, the Court finally upheld the registration provisions of the act in *Communist Party* v. *SACB* (1961). But it postponed any decision on the constitutionality of the statutory sanctions until they were actually enforced.

When passports were subsequently denied to party members, this action was held to be an unconstitutional violation of the right to travel in *Aptheker* v. *Secretary of State* (1964). In *Albertson* v. *SACB* (1965) the Court ruled that compulsory registration of party members violated the Fifth Amendment. *United States* v. *Robel* (1967) voided the ban on party members working in defense plants. Other provisions of the McCarran Act remained in effect and were the subject of much controversy, but the SACB was allowed to die in 1973 by failure to appropriate funds.

C. Herman Pritchett

Cooley v. Board of Wardens of the Port of Philadelphia, 12 How. (53 U.S.) 299 (1852), argued 9–11 Feb. 1852, decided 2 Mar. 1852 by vote of 6 to 2; Curtis for the Court, Daniel concurring, McLean and Wayne in dissent, McKinley absent. A Pennsylvania statute provided that any vessel entering or leaving the port of Philadelphia was required to pay one-half the usual pilotage fee if its master chose not to employ a local pilot. The fee went into a fund for the relief of infirm pilots and pilots' widows and orphans. The fee affected interstate and international commerce flowing into Philadelphia and was challenged as an interference with Congress's power to regulate such commerce.

The Taney Court had previously been unable to resolve Commerce Clause issues presented in *New York v. Miln* (1837), the *License Cases* (1847), and the *Passenger Cases* (1849) because of complications posed by issues of slavery and federalism that lay under the surface of all Commerce Clause cases of the era. The Court had either evaded such questions or, in trying to resolve them, had splintered confusingly. In *Cooley*, the Court was finally able to achieve a coherent resolution of a Commerce Clause issue. Justice Benjamin R. Curtis defined the question in terms of the subject matter of regulation rather than the nature of the commerce power, with some subjects being national in scope and others, like pilotage laws, local. Though this formula failed to enlist the support of states'-rights enthusiasts such as Justice Peter V. Daniel and nationalists such as Justices John McLean and James M. Wayne, its pragmatism has proved enduring. *Cooley* ranks with *Gibbons* v. *Ogden* (1824) as one of the most important Commerce Clause cases of the nineteenth century.

Donald M. Roper

Cooper v. Aaron, 358 U.S. 1 (1958), argued 28 Aug. and 11 Sept. 1958, decided 12 Sept. 1958 by vote of 9 to 0; Warren for the Court. In *Brown* v. *Board of Education* (1954) the Court decided unanimously to invalidate racial segregation in the public schools and discard the separate but equal doctrine articulated in *Plessy* v. *Ferguson* (1896). In holding that in the field of public education "separate" could never be "equal," the Court gave new meaning to the Equal Protection Clause of the Fourteenth Amendment. Yet the ambiguous enforcement standard formulated in *Brown II* (1955) encouraged unanticipated defiance throughout the South.

In accordance with the first *Brown* decision, the city of Little Rock, Arkansas, school board established a plan for desegregation starting in September 1957 at Central High School. The day before desegregation was to begin, Governor Orval Faubus, claiming that public disturbances were imminent, ordered the Arkansas National Guard to prevent the entrance of nine black students. For three weeks, Faubus, President Dwight Eisenhower, the Little Rock school board, the city's black community, the NAACP, rabid segregationists, and the local federal district court were embroiled in intractable confrontation. After the federal district court found the governor's assertions concerning impending disorder groundless, Faubus withdrew the guard, but when the "Little Rock nine" entered Central a few rabble-rousers galvanized the crowd outside, forcing the students' withdrawal. The next day President Eisenhower dispatched combat-ready paratroopers, who enforced the federal court's original desegregation order.

At the end of the school year, in order to end the tension, Little Rock school officials asked for and received from the federal district court a two-and-a-half year delay in implementing desegregation. The NAACP appealed the case, *Cooper* v. *Aaron*, to the Supreme Court.

The *Cooper* case was the first significant legal test of the enforcement of *Brown*. The issues were: whether a good faith postponement of a desegregation program due to anticipated racial unrest would violate the constitutional rights of black students, and whether the governor and legislature of a state were bound by decisions of the U.S. Supreme Court. In an unprecedented action all nine members of the Court signed the opinion. They held, first, that even postponing plans for desegregation in good faith and the interest of preserving public peace would violate black students' rights under the Equal Protection Clause. Thus no delay was allowed. Second, governors and state legislatures were bound under the Supremacy Clause of the Constitution to uphold decisions of the Supreme Court just as they were bound by oath to uphold the Constitution itself. "No state legislative, executive, or judicial officer," the Court said, "can War against the Constitution without violating his undertaking to support it" (p. 18). No governor has the right to annul judgments of the federal courts.

The *Cooper* decision, however, initially fostered rather than discouraged southern resistance. Even during the dramatic dispatch of paratroopers, Eisenhower did not defend the *Brown* decision, which he personally opposed, creating the distinct impression that he would implement desegregation only under extreme circumstances. Yet neither the American public nor the Court knew the complete truth. In the September trial of Faubus involving his use of the national guard to prevent desegregation, the Justice Department declined to introduce evidence that demonstrated conclusively that prior to and during the crisis the Justice Department, school officials, a federal judge, and Faubus himself engaged in surreptitious contacts to negotiate an end to the confrontation in a manner that ultimately proved to be politically advantageous to the governor. The Justice Department even attempted, clandestinely and unsuccessfully, to persuade the NAACP to withdraw its suit on behalf of the nine black students.

Thus, notwithstanding the strong language of the *Cooper* decision, the federal judiciary faced massive southern resistance virtually alone until the sit-in cases and Martin Luther King, Jr.'s nonviolent civil rights movement, coupled with the support of Presidents Kennedy and Johnson, stimulated passage of the Civil Rights Act of 1964. That act endorsed *Brown* by name, and authorized the attorney general to intervene directly in school desegregation suits. Most important, Title VI, which cut off federal funds to institutions practicing racial discrimination, was used by the Department of Health, Education, and Welfare to compel compliance by threatening to withhold federal school funds.

Tony Freyer

Corrigan v. Buckley, 271 U.S. 323 (1926), argued 8 Jan. 1926, decided 24 May 1926 by vote of 9 to 0; Sanford for the Court. This case involved a restrictive covenant formed by white property owners in the District of Columbia in 1921 to prevent the sale of property to black citizens. Subsequently a white owner made a contract to sell her property to a black person, provoking a suit to enforce the covenant and stop the sale. Federal courts in the District of Columbia upheld enforcement of the covenant. In a unanimous decision, the Supreme Court in effect affirmed this outcome by dismissing the suit for lack of jurisdiction. Justice Edward T. Sanford disposed of the constitutional argument raised against the covenant by noting that the Fifth Amendment limited the federal government, not individuals; the Thirteenth Amendment, in matters other than personal liberty, did not protect the individual rights of blacks; and the Fourteenth Amendment referred to state action, not the conduct of private individuals. The Court observed that while the Civil Rights Act of 1866 conferred on all persons and citizens the legal capacity to make contracts and acquire property, it did not prohibit or invalidate contracts between private individuals concerning the control or disposition of their own property. Justice Sanford furthermore denied, without elaboration, that judicial enforcement of the restrictive covenant was tantamount to government action depriving persons of liberty and property without due process of law. Sanford's statement was regarded in the next two decades as having settled the question whether judicial enforcement of racial covenants was state action under the Fourteenth Amendment. The decision temporarily closed the door to racial integration in housing that had been pried open in *Buchanan* v. *Warley* (1917). In *Shelley* v. *Kraemer* (1948) the Court held such covenants valid between the parties to the agreement, but judicially unenforceable as a form of state action prohibited by the Equal Protection Clause of the Fourteenth Amendment.

Herman Belz

Counselman v. Hitchcock, 142 U.S. 547 (1892), argued 9–10 Dec. 1891, decided 11 Jan. 1892 by vote of 9 to 0; Blatchford for the Court. In *Counselman*, the Court considered the constitutionality of a federal statute granting a witness immunity from a criminal prosecution based on evidence obtained from the witness in a judicial proceeding. Notwithstanding this statute, Charles Counselman, claiming the Fifth Amendment privilege against self-incrimination, refused to answer certain questions before a federal grand jury. Confined for contempt of court, Counselman sought a writ of habeas corpus. The Court upheld his refusal to testify. It held that the privilege against self-incrimination could be exercised not only by an accused person in a criminal case but also by a witness in any investigation, including grand jury proceedings. It also ruled that the federal immunity statute did not compel the appellant to testify because its scope of protection was not as broad as that afforded by the privilege against self-incrimination. The statute prevented the direct use of appellant's testimony in any federal proceeding but did not prohibit the use of his testimony to search for other evidence to be used against him.

There was broad language in *Counselman* that a valid immunity statute must afford a person compelled to testify absolute protection from prosecution for any offense to which the testimony relates. In *Kastigar v. United States* (1972), however, the Court held that an immunity statute need not safeguard a person compelled to testify against a prosecution based on evidence obtained independently of the compelled testimony.

Edgar Bodenheimer

Cox v. New Hampshire, 312 U.S. 569 (1941), argued 7 Mar. 1941, decided 31 Mar. 1941 by vote of 9 to 0; Hughes for the Court. Beginning in the late 1930s the Jehovah's Witnesses, complaining that a variety of police laws denied them religious freedom, set out to test such legislation. Initially successful, the sect received a mild judicial rebuff in *Cox v. New Hampshire*. A Manchester city ordinance required every parade or procession upon a public street to obtain a license and pay a fee. A group of Jehovah's Witnesses marched single file through the streets carrying placards to advertise a meeting without the license or fee. They were arrested. Cox, their leader, argued that the defendants did not have a parade. They also claimed that the ordinance was invalid under the Fourteenth Amendment for depriving them of their freedom to worship, freedom of speech and press, and freedom of assembly. The ordinance, they contended, vested unreasonable, arbitrary power in the licensing authority and was vague and indefinite.

A unanimous Supreme Court upheld the measure as a reasonable police regulation designed to promote the safe and orderly use of the streets. The Court made clear that it was treating the license requirement as

a traffic regulation and that the conviction was not for conveying information or holding a meeting.

The loss was a temporary setback to the Witnesses' program. *Cox* initiated a long line of cases establishing the right of government to make reasonable regulations concerning the time, place, and manner of speech, so long as those regulations were not used to prevent speech or to favor some speakers over others.

Paul L. Murphy

Coyle v. Smith, 221 U.S. 559 (1911), argued 5–6 Apr. 1911, decided 29 May 1911 by vote of 7 to 2; Lurton for the Court, McKenna and Holmes in dissent without opinion. In an enabling act providing for the admission of Oklahoma to statehood, Congress stipulated that Guthrie would be the temporary capital until 1913. Accepting this provision, Oklahoma was admitted into the Union on an equal footing with the original states in 1907. Three years later, the Oklahoma legislature provided for the removal of the capital to Oklahoma City. When a suit challenging the action was instituted, the Oklahoma courts upheld the act of the state legislature.

The question was whether Congress, in its acknowledged discretion to admit new states, could impose conditions that would bind the state after its admission. Drawing upon a tradition stretching back to the Northwest Ordinance of 1787, the majority found the restrictions that Congress placed on Oklahoma invalid and upheld the state's right to locate its capital where it chose. Congressional discretion to admit a state was not subject to judicial review, but once the national legislature had acted the new states were entitled to all the governmental powers that the older ones enjoyed. Although the majority justices could find no constitutional language imposing such a check on congressional power, they did not hesitate to read the unwritten tradition of state equality into the Constitution itself.

John E. Semonche

Craig v. Boren, 429 U.S. 190 (1976), argued 5 Oct. 1976, decided 20 Dec. 1976 by vote of 7 to 2; Brennan for the Court, Blackmun, Powell, Stevens, and Stewart (as to result) concurring, Burger and Rehnquist in dissent. The Court announced for the first time that sex-based classifications were subjected to stricter scrutiny under the Equal Protection

Clause of the Fourteenth Amendment than was provided by the rational basis or "ordinary scrutiny" test. As stated by Justice William J. Brennan, the constitutional standard that would have to be met for a statute classifying by gender is that it "must serve important governmental objectives and must be substantially related to those objectives" (p. 197). This standard appeared to be somewhat less rigorous than the strict scrutiny test applied to "suspect" classifications such as race. Brennan claimed that (although the Court had never before mentioned it) this was the test that had applied to gender discrimination ever since *Reed v. Reed* (1971). (The period 1971–1976 coincided with a nearly successful effort at the congressional and state level to add an Equal Rights Amendment to the Constitution.)

The Oklahoma law at issue in *Craig* allowed females aged 18–20 to purchase beer of 3.2% alcohol. Males could not purchase beer until age 21. The law was challenged by two underage men, Mark Walker and Curtis Craig, joined by a female beer vendor, Carolyn Whitener. By the time the case was argued at the Supreme Court, both men had turned 21, so the woman's standing proved decisive.

Oklahoma defended the statute as a prophylactic against drunk driving, offering statistics showing that arrests of males 18–20 out-numbered those of females of similar age by a factor of ten for "drunk" driving (2 percent vs. .18 percent), by a factor of eighteen for "driving under the influence," and by a factor of ten for public drunkenness.

Brennan ruled for the Court that, while enhancing traffic safety did demonstrate an important government interest, the statistical evidence offered by Oklahoma did not meet the other half of the test: the gender line drawn by the state did not "substantially" further the government's goal. Also, explaining that the Twenty-first Amendment did not alter otherwise applicable equal protection standards, he rejected the state's argument that the extra legislative power secured by that amendment should cause this statute to be sustained.

Justice Harry Blackmun concurred in the result and in all of the opinion except the discussion of the Twenty-first Amendment. Justice Lewis Powell concurred but stated that he would have preferred a rule that said gender classifications must bear a "fair and substantial relation" to the object of legislation. Justice John Paul Stevens concurred

but suggested that rather than three differing degrees of equal protection scrutiny the Court should apply the rule that states must govern impartially. For him the requirement of impartiality entailed measuring the importance of the government interest, the degree to which any classification furthers that interest, and the degree of obnoxiousness of the classification. While this law did further traffic safety somewhat, and while that was an important goal, he felt that the offensiveness of a gender-based law outweighed these two considerations here.

Justice Potter Stewart argued that the rationality test employed in *Reed v. Reed* still was the appropriate test for gender discrimination, but that this statute did not satisfy even that minimum standard and thus was unconstitutional.

Justice William Rehnquist dissented, objecting both to the introduction of a new level of scrutiny and to its application to male plaintiffs, since males were not in need of special solicitude from the Court. He argued that rationality was the correct test and that the statistical evidence easily satisfied that standard. Chief Justice Warren Burger expressed general agreement with Rehnquist's dissent but argued that the Court should not have taken the case, because, he said, it should never have extended standing to Ms. Whitener, a mere saloon-keeper.

Leslie Friedman Goldstein

Craig v. Missouri, 4 Pet. (29 U.S.) 410 (1830), argued 2–3 Mar. 1830, decided 12 Mar. 1830 by vote of 4 to 3; Marshall for the Court, Johnson, Thompson, and McLean dissenting. *Craig* demonstrated the transitional character of the late Marshall Court. The question presented was whether a Missouri statute authorizing loan certificates issued by the state violated Article I, section 10's ban on bills of credit. Arguing for Missouri, Senator Thomas Hart Benton, a leading critic of judicial nationalism, urged the Court to uphold the statute as a legitimate exercise of state sovereignty. He also argued that section 25 of the Judiciary Act of 1789, under which the case came up to the Supreme Court, was unconstitutional, an argument that strengthened those in Congress working for its repeal.

Speaking for a bare majority, Chief Justice John Marshall struck down the statute, grounding his reading of the constitutional prohibition of state paper money in the history of the Confederation. He also reaffirmed the Court's jurisdiction under section 25, contending as he had done in *Cohens v. Virginia* (1821) that the justices had no discretion in taking jurisdiction. Justices William Johnson, Smith Thompson, and John McLean dissented, finding enough latitude in the wording of the statute to exempt it from the operation of the constitutional bar.

Just seven years later, the dissenters won the day in *Briscoe* v. *Bank of Kentucky* (1837), when the Court, now under Chief Justice Roger B. Taney, upheld a variant currency scheme, by which a state bank's notes served as a circulating medium.

R. Kent Newmyer

Crosby v. National Foreign Trade Council, 530 U.S. 363, argued 22 March 2000, decided 19 June 2000 by vote of 9 to 0; Souter for the Court, Scalia and Thomas, concurring in the judgment. *Crosby* held that federal law preempted a Massachusetts law prohibiting companies doing business with Burma from contracting with the state. Massachusetts enacted its law to protest Burma's human rights record. Three months later, Congress imposed its own sanctions. Congress also delegated authority to the president to impose further sanctions or lift sanctions, as warranted, and instructed the president to pursue a multilateral strategy to democratize Burma.

The Supreme Court concluded that Massachusetts' law stood as an obstacle to the goals of the federal statute, and was preempted, despite the latter's lack of an express preemption clause. Specifically, the Court found that the Massachusetts act's rigidity conflicted with the flexibility to impose or lift sanctions that Congress granted the president. In addition, the state law applied to parties and activities that Congress exempted, undermining the limited nature of congressional sanctions. Finally, the Massachusetts law hindered the pursuit of a multilateral strategy to democratize Burma by penalizing countries whose aid was needed for that effort. The Court rejected arguments that the lack of express preemption implicitly authorized the state law.

By deciding *Crosby* on narrow preemption grounds, the Court avoided important questions concerning the constitutional limits on state action affecting foreign affairs or foreign commerce. The willingness to find

preemption absent clear statutory language, and the refusal to presume (as it has in other cases) that a clear statement from Congress is required to preempt states' exercise of their police powers implies that the Court is sympathetic to claims of federal priority in foreign affairs.

Brannon P. Denning

Crow Dog, Ex Parte, 109 U.S. 557 (1883), argued 20 Nov. 1883, decided 17 Dec. 1883 by vote of 9 to 0; Matthews for the court. Crow Dog, a Brule Sioux, was tried, convicted, and sentenced to death for the murder of another Sioux, who was known as Spotted Tail, in a Dakota territorial court. He sought release on a writ of habeas corpus, arguing that tribal and not federal law should apply because territorial courts lacked jurisdiction over crimes committed by one Indian against another in Indian country.

Sioux tribal law required that Crow Dog, as punishment for murder, must support Spotted Tail's dependent relatives but did not subject him to execution. Crow Dog contended that he was not subject to the criminal laws of either Dakota Territory or the United States. The United States maintained that federal criminal jurisdiction over Indian country was acquired under the Sioux Treaty of 1868 interpreted in connection with general federal Indian statutes.

The Supreme Court held that the Dakota territorial court was without jurisdiction. Crow Dog was governed in his relationship with other reservation Indians solely by the tribal laws of the Brule Sioux and was responsible only to the tribal law enforcement authorities. The Court regarded exclusive tribal jurisdiction over tribal members as a surviving attribute of tribal sovereignty despite treaty language that appeared to subject the Sioux to the laws of the United States.

The *Crow Dog* decision did not deny the power of Congress to legislate over Indian affairs or to curtail the scope of Indian self-government. But the Court declared that Congress had not done so in any clear fashion and thus found no congressional intent to limit Indian self-government. The Court stated that the tribes retained their right of "self-government [and] the maintenance of order and peace among their own members" (p. 568). Unless this power is limited by explicit legislation or surrendered by the tribe, Indian tribes retain exclusive judicial jurisdictions over reservation Indian affairs.

Thus today most tribes operate their own tribal court systems. Except to the extent mandated by the Indian Civil Rights Act (1968), the structure and procedure of such courts is determined by the tribes themselves.

The decision in *Crow Dog* prompted action by nineteenth-century reformers who wanted Indians to be absorbed into the mainstream of American life. One goal of the assimilationists was to have the same laws applied to Indians as applied to all other citizens and to outlaw the Indians' own "heathenish" laws and customs. The fact that Crow Dog could not be executed for murder shocked them and their congressional supporters. Congress appended to the Appropriation Act of 3 March 1885, an Indian section known as "The Major Crimes Act" specifying seven crimes over which the federal courts were authorized to exercise jurisdiction. Thus, within two years, in reaction against *Crow Dog,* Congress enacted new legislation making it a federal crime for one Indian to murder another within Indian country. Today, there are fourteen enumerated offenses under the amended Indian Major Crimes Act.

Despite legislation aimed at reversing its specific outcome, *Crow Dog* remains a major precedent in Native American affairs. *Crow Dog* affirms that treaties and statutes are interpreted in favor of retained tribal self-government and property rights. Doubts and ambiguities in treaties and statutes are to be resolved in Indians' favor and federal Indian laws are interpreted liberally toward carrying out their protective purposes. *Crow Dog* established that federal protection of tribal self-government has never depended on any particular tribal social structure or political organization.

Crow Dog articulated the fundamental constitutional principle that federal laws do not preempt tribal authority unless Congress's intent to do so is clear. Congressional intent to include tribes within the scope of laws applying generally to persons, groups, corporations, or associations must be firmly established because of Indian tribes' unique status. The broad concepts of tribal self-government articulated in *Crow Dog* continue as a basic constitutional guide in modern Indian law.

Rennard J. Strickland

Cruikshank, United States v., 92 U.S. 542 (1876), argued 30–31 Mar. and 30 Apr. 1875, decided 27 Mar. 1876 by vote of 9 to 0; Waite for the Court, Clifford concurring. The *Cruikshank* case arose after an armed white force in Reconstruction Louisiana killed more than one hundred black men over a disputed gubernatorial election. Three white men involved in the 1873 Colfax Massacre were found guilty of violating section 6 of the Enforcement Act of 1870, which forbade conspiracies to deny the constitutional rights of any citizen. The convicted defendants appealed on the grounds that the indictments were faulty.

The case came before a Supreme Court that had evinced a growing concern about congressional efforts to broaden federal power. Emphasizing the distinctions between the rights of federal and state citizens, the Court found the indictments deficient because they did not allege the denial of federal rights. The right to assemble and to bear arms in the First and Second Amendments, respectively, protected citizens only from congressional interference. The right to due process and equal protection in the Fourteenth Amendment limited actions by states, not those by individuals. Finally, interference with the right to vote was not an actionable offense because the indictment did not allege that the defendants' actions were motivated by the victims' race.

The Court concluded that punishment for the offenses committed in the Colfax Massacre lay with the state. Unfortunately, the likelihood that southern states would prosecute such offenses was small. The *Cruikshank* opinion encouraged violence in the Reconstruction South and is one of several Supreme Court decisions that marked the nation's retreat from Reconstruction.

Lucy E. Salyer

Cruzan v. Director, Missouri Department of Health, 497 U.S. 261 (1990), argued 6 Dec. 1989, decided 25 June 1990 by vote of 5 to 4; Rehnquist for the Court, Brennan, joined by Marshall, Blackmun, and Stevens, in dissent. In June 1990, the U.S. Supreme Court issued its first pronouncement concerning the constitutional interests of dying medical patients. The case dealt with the fate of Nancy Cruzan, a woman mired in a permanently unconscious state in the wake of an automobile accident in which she sustained severe brain injuries. Her parents sought judicial authorization to act on their daughter's behalf to end the artificial nutrition maintaining Nancy's existence. Nancy had previously made informal oral declarations indicating she would not have wished to be maintained in a permanently vegetative state. The Missouri Supreme Court had ruled, however, that there was inadequate evidence to establish the now-incompetent patient's preferences. In the absence of "clear and convincing" evidence of the patient's will, the Missouri court refused to permit a guardian's determination to withdraw life-preserving medical treatment. The parents appealed to the U.S. Supreme Court, contending that Nancy's constitutional right to reject unwanted medical treatment had been violated.

By a 5-to-4 margin, the Supreme Court rejected this challenge. Chief Justice William Rehnquist's majority opinion ruled both that a state may confine terminal decisions on behalf of incompetent patients to instances when the patient has previously expressed such a preference and that the state may demand clear evidence of the patient's wishes. These precautions were reasonable, the majority declared, in order to safeguard against potential abuses. Missouri could legitimately be concerned about subjective, "quality of life" decisions being made on behalf of incompetent patients. The Court was dubious that family members—in the absence of clear prior expressions—would make precisely the decision the patient would want.

While the Supreme Court rejected the constitutional challenge, the *Cruzan* decision contains much encouragement for the advancement of patient rights to shape medical intervention in natural dying processes. The majority was willing to assume that a competent patient has a constitutionally based liberty right to reject life-preserving medical treatment. Moreover, the Court did not draw any distinction between artificial nutrition and other forms of medical technology. Likewise, no distinction was drawn between a patient facing unavoidable, imminent death and one whose life might be preserved for years. Finally, the Court appears to have endorsed giving full recognition to a patient's prior expressions even after the patient has lost competence. This increases the incentive for people to make advance directives governing their medical handling in the event of later incompetence.

The *Cruzan* decision does nothing to disrupt the policies regarding incompetent medical patients that prevail in most states. Most states allow guardians to make medical decisions—including rejection of

life-preserving intervention—on behalf of incompetent patients even without clear prior expressions. Some states authorize a "substituted judgment" standard, which allows consideration of informal patient declarations as well as other indices of the patient's preferences. Some states allow guardians to secure withdrawal of life-preserving care where such a decision promotes the "best interests" of the patient. A "best interests" determination includes consideration of a patient's previous informal declarations. *Cruzan* makes clear that nothing in the Constitution prevents states from continuing to use such standards.

More recently, the justices have made clear that there is no constitutional right to die. A unanimous Court in *Vacco* v. *Quill* (1997) and *Washington* v. *Glucksberg* (1997) held that while a person can refuse treatment that may result in death, that same person has no constitutional right to an assisted suicide brought on, for example, by administering life-ending drugs.

Norman L. Cantor

Cumming v. Richmond County Board of Education, 175 U.S. 528 (1899), argued 30 Oct. 1899, decided 18 Dec. 1899 by vote of 9 to 0; Harlan for the Court. Three years after its decision in **Plessy* v. *Ferguson,* the Supreme Court refused to enforce the "equal" part of the "separate but equal" doctrine. *Cumming,* the Court's first decision on racial discrimination in schools, has never been explicitly overruled, nor has anyone ever satisfactorily explained why the Court, and especially the erstwhile racial egalitarian Justice John Marshall Harlan, concluded that *Cumming* did not present a "case of clear and unmistakable disregard of rights" (p. 545).

Pressured by black voters and facing an explicit "separate but equal" state law, the school board of Augusta, Georgia, in 1879 established the first public high school for African-Americans in the state. Ware High School thrived until 1897, when reportedly at the suggestion of a black private school principal, the school board closed it, claiming that the money was needed for black primary education. Black parents sued.

Because the state law was so clear, local Judge Enoch Callaway did not reach the constitutional issue. Callaway's injunction was overturned by Georgia Supreme Court Justice Thomas J. Simmons, who hardly bothered to say why. On further appeal, former Reconstruction Congressman and Senator George F. Edmunds argued that if a school board supported high schools for whites, the Equal Protection Clause of the Fourteenth Amendment at least required it to offer blacks a high school.

Citing no lower court decisions, most of which went against him, Justice Harlan announced that plaintiffs had to prove that the board's decision had been motivated solely by a "hostility to the colored population because of their race" (pp. 544–545), a nearly impossible standard. Fortunately, most judges in subsequent cases ignored the opinion.

J. Morgan Kousser

Cummings v. Missouri, 71 U.S. 277 (1867), argued 15, 16, 19, and 20 Mar. 1866, decided 14 Jan. 1867 by vote of 5 to 4; Field for the Court, Miller in dissent. **Ex parte Garland,** 71 U.S. 333, argued 13–15 Mar. 1866, decided 14 Jan. 1867 by vote of 5 to 4; Field for the Court, Miller in dissent. These cases challenged the constitutionality of retrospective loyalty oaths established during the Civil War. *Cummings* involved a Missouri regulation requiring persons in various occupations to swear that they had not aided or sympathized with the rebellion; *Garland* concerned a federal statute compelling attorneys who practiced in federal courts to swear that they had not supported the Confederacy.

Writing for 5-to-4 majorities in both cases, Justice Stephen J. Field noted that although the laws did not impose fines or imprisonment, they were punitive measures because they prevented former rebels from practicing their occupations. Therefore, he held that they violated the Constitution's ban on bills of attainder and ex post facto laws. They were bills of attainder, Field explained, because they subjected a designated class to punishment without a trial; they were ex post facto laws because they imposed punishment for acts that had not been criminal when committed or inflicted additional punishment for acts that had been. Speaking for the four Republicans on the Court, Justice Samuel Miller denied that the measures inflicted punishment and therefore that they were bills of attainder or ex post facto laws. They were, he contended, regulations to assure that practitioners in various professions possessed the qualifications—including the moral character—essential to serve the public.

The Court has never repudiated these decisions, and in *U.S. v. Brown* (1965) it invoked them to strike down a federal law excluding former communists from serving as officers of labor unions.

Donald G. Nieman

Curtiss-Wright Export Corp., United States v., 299 U.S. 304 (1936), argued 19–20 Nov. 1936, decided 21 Dec. 1936 by vote of 7 to 1; Sutherland for the Court, McReynolds in dissent, Stone not participating. The powers of the federal government in foreign affairs are derived principally from inferences based on the history and structure of the Constitution, rather than from specific constitutional language. In *Curtiss-Wright*, the Supreme Court relied on just such inferences to conclude not only that the foreign affairs power vested in the national government as a whole, but that the president of the United States had "plenary" powers in the foreign affairs field not dependent upon congressional delegation.

Congress, acting by joint resolution, had authorized the president to place an embargo on arms shipments to countries at war in the Chaco region of South America. Acting pursuant to the resolution, President Franklin Roosevelt proclaimed such an embargo. When Curtiss-Wright Export Corp. was indicted for violating the embargo, it defended itself on the grounds that the embargo and the proclamation were void because Congress had improperly delegated legislative power to the executive branch by leaving what was essentially a legislative determination to the president's "unfettered discretion."

The Court ruled that the joint resolution and the president's actions were not based on unconstitutional delegation of nonenumerated powers because of "fundamental differences" in national power with respect to internal and to external affairs. Key language from the Court's dictum explaining this conclusion has become a basis for broad executive branch claims to inherent presidential power in foreign affairs.

Justice George Sutherland argued that the powers of sovereignty in foreign affairs did not depend upon express grants in the Constitution. The foreign affairs power had been transmitted immediately from Great Britain to the united colonies as an essential element of nationhood upon the success of the Revolution. Although many scholars have refuted Justice Sutherland's "springing sovereignty" analysis on historical grounds, there is general agreement that the foreign affairs power resides exclusively in the national government.

A more controversial question is raised by the presumptive identity between national power and executive power over foreign affairs that the Court's language and holding suggest. The opinion concluded that if sovereign power resided in the federal government, the power to deal with foreign nations must reside in the executive branch. Consequently, no allocation of specific powers, other than the general conferral of executive power in Article II of the Constitution, was necessary to empower the president to act in foreign affairs matters.

Despite the controversy surrounding it, the *Curtiss-Wright* decision is one of the Supreme Court's most influential. Most cases involving executive branch-legislative branch conflicts involve political questions that the courts refuse to adjudicate. Therefore, the sweeping language of *Curtiss-Wright* is regularly cited to support executive branch claims of power to act without congressional authorization in foreign affairs, especially when there is no judicial intervention to interpret the meaning of that text.

The Court's characterization of the president's power as "plenary" has been cited as legal sanction for executive branch initiatives in foreign affairs that often result in Congress being faced with a *fait accompli*. The *Curtiss-Wright* opinion has been cited to support the president's power to enter into executive agreements with foreign nations, claims of executive privilege in national security and other matters, as well as much of the executive branch activity during the Vietnam War. *Curtiss-Wright* was also cited to attack the constitutionality of the 1973 War Powers Act, requiring the president under certain conditions to withdraw combat troops committed abroad if not authorized by Congress.

The Court has not recognized the full scope of executive power suggested by Justice Sutherland's sweeping language. Congressional authorization may be necessary to legitimize many executive acts. In *Regan v. Wald* (1984), for example, the Supreme Court cited *Curtiss-Wright* in upholding the constitutionality of the president's regulations restricting travel to Cuba expressly on the ground that they had been authorized by Congress. On the other hand, in *Federal Energy Administration* v. *Algonquin SNG, Inc.* (1976), the Court validated presidential restrictions on oil imports based on very broad congressional language delegating apparently unlimited regulatory authority to the executive branch.

Harold G. Maier

D

Dames & Moore v. Regan, 453 U.S. 654 (1981), argued 24 June 1981, decided 2 July 1981 by vote of 9 to 0; Rehnquist for the Court, Stevens concurring in part, Powell concurring in part and dissenting in part. This decision upheld certain actions taken by President Jimmy Carter in January 1981 to settle the controversy resulting from the seizure of American personnel as hostages at the American Embassy in Tehran, Iran, in 1979. To secure the hostages' release, the United States agreed with Iran to terminate legal proceedings in U.S. courts involving claims by U.S. nationals against Iran, to nullify attachments against Iranian property entered by U.S. courts to secure any judgments against Iran, and to transfer such claims from U.S. courts to a newly created arbitration tribunal. These agreements were implemented by executive orders.

The Court upheld these presidential actions against challenges that they were unauthorized by law. The Court concluded that the International Emergency Economic Powers Act (IEEPA) authorized the president to nullify the attachments and to transfer Iranian assets. It also approved the suspension of claims filed in U.S. courts even though no specific statutory provision authorized that step. In so doing the Court relied on inferences drawn from related legislation, a history of congressional acquiescence in execu-

tive claims settlement practices, and past decisions recognizing broad executive authority.

This decision has been criticized for applying a too-undemanding standard to the question of presidential power, in particular by relying on inferences from statutes that do not directly deal with certain subjects at hand and, especially, on legislative acquiescence in executive activity. On any view, this decision is an important recognition of broad presidential power in foreign relations.

Thomas O. Sargentich

Danbury Hatters' Case. See LOEWE V. LAWLOR.

Darby Lumber Co., United States v., 312 U.S. 100 (1941), argued 19–20 Dec. 1940, decided 3 Feb. 1941 by vote of 9 to 0; Stone for the Court. The Fair Labor Standards Act (often called the Wages and Hours Act), adopted in 1938, was the last major piece of New Deal legislation. The statute provided for the setting of minimum wages and maximum hours for all employees in industries whose products were shipped in interstate commerce and made violation of the wages and hours standards unlawful. The act applied to all employees "engaged in commerce or in the production of goods for commerce."

The Constitution authorizes Congress "to regulate commerce . . . among the several states." In the classic case of *Gibbons* v. *Ogden* (1824) the Supreme Court gave a broad reading to the federal commerce power, and regulation of commerce has been a major congressional concern. Around the beginning of the twentieth century Congress began to explore use of the Commerce Clause as a kind of national police power. An act forbidding the interstate transportation of lottery tickets was upheld in *Champion* v. *Ames* (1903). The Pure Food and Drug Act of 1906 prohibited the introduction of impure food and drugs into the states by interstate commerce. The Mann Act (1910), forbidding the transportation of women in interstate commerce for the purpose of prostitution and debauchery, was upheld in *Hoke* v. *United States* (1913).

This technique of closing the channels of commerce to achieve social welfare purposes was then utilized by Congress in the federal Child Labor Act of 1916. The statute prohibited transportation in interstate commerce for products of commercial operations where children under fourteen years of age had been employed and where certain dangerous conditions had prevailed. The Supreme Court called a halt to such use of the commerce power in the famous case of *Hammer* v. *Dagenhart* (1918), where a bare majority held the Child Labor Act unconstitutional as an infringement on powers reserved to the states under the Tenth Amendment. The Court's argument was based on the concept of dual federalism—that powers delegated to the national government by the Constitution are nevertheless limited by the reserved powers of the states. In a noteworthy dissent to the *Hammer* decision, Justice Oliver Wendell Holmes rejected this view, arguing that use of a power specifically conferred on Congress by the Constitution "is not made any less constitutional because of the indirect effects that it may have" (p. 277).

When the Fair Labor Standards Act came before the Supreme Court in *United States* v. *Darby*, it was upheld unanimously. Because Congress in adopting the act had exercised its undoubted power over the movement of goods across state lines, there would have been little need for discussion of the constitutional issue except for the decision in *Hammer* v. *Dagenhart*. Justice Harlan F. Stone, writing for the Court, had to dispose of that roadblock. Invoking "the powerful and now classic dissent of Mr. Justice Holmes," Stone wrote, "The conclusion is inescapable that *Hammer* v. *Dagenhart* was a departure from the principles which have prevailed in the interpretation of the Commerce Clause both before and since the decision and that such vitality, as a precedent, as it then had has long since been exhausted. It should be and now is overruled" (pp. 115–116).

While the constitutionality of the Wages and Hours Act was ratified by *Darby*, problems with respect to the coverage of the act remained, for the statute had failed to invoke the total power of Congress over commerce. Rather, it was made applicable to employees engaged "in commerce" or "in the production of goods for commerce." Consequently there was much confusion as to whether specific employees were covered by the act. A noteworthy controversy arose over the applicability of the federal statute to state employees. In *Maryland* v. *Wirtz* (1968) the Court rejected a contention that enforcing the act's standards against state employees violated state sovereignty. But eight years later the Court accepted that contention. In *National League of Cities* v. *Usery* (1976) the Court by vote of 5 to 4 overruled *Wirtz*, rehabilitated *Hammer* v. *Dagenhart*, and held that federal wage and hour standards for state and municipal employees were unconstitutional. In turn, *Usery* was reversed nine years later in *Garcia* v. *San Antonio Metropolitan Transit Authority* (1985).

C. Herman Pritchett

Dartmouth College v. Woodward, 4 Wheat. (17 U.S.) 518 (1819), argued 10–12 Mar. 1818, decided 2 Feb. 1819 by vote of 5 to 1; Marshall for the Court, Washington and Story concurring separately, Duvall in dissent without opinion. In 1816, New Hampshire's newly elected Jeffersonian-Republican governor, William Plumer, and the Republican-dominated legislature determined to transform Dartmouth College by ousting what they regarded as a self-perpetuating Federalist hierarchy among the college's trustees and replacing it with trustees appointed through the political process. They therefore enacted statutes that revised the royal charter of 1769 that created the college, changing the institution to a "University," altering the procedures of internal control, and imposing external, public restraints on the governance of the school. The college's extant trustees determined to contest the constitutionality of this action.

When the case reached the United States Supreme Court for argument in 1818, the college's lawyers, led by Daniel Webster, directed their arguments to the meaning and impact of the Contract Clause of the Constitution (Article I, section 10), contending that the New Hampshire legislature, in amending the original charter of the college, had passed a law "impairing the Obligation of Contracts." Webster argued that in effect the state legislature had "take[n] away from one . . . rights, property, and franchises, and give[n] them to another" (p. 558). He asserted that the Contract Clause should be interposed as a constitutional barrier to state activity of this kind.

Chief Justice John Marshall responded in his characteristically facile manner. Though the Court had previously decided Contract Clause cases, Marshall, for the first time, extended the protection of the Contract Clause to a corporate charter. Since the college insisted that it was entitled to constitutional protection from the legislative acts, Marshall had to analyze the relationship between the Contract Clause and the legal status of the college. He found that the college charter was a contract and that the college under the charter was a private and not a public corporation. This last point was important because the New Hampshire state courts had construed the college to be a public, and not a private entity, and therefore subject to the state's regulatory power. If the college were held to be private, the state could not interfere with its vested rights, particularly its property rights of acquisition, management, or control, because the Contract Clause, according to Marshall, was directed at acts affecting private property. The Contract Clause prevented the state from impairing the obligations of the original contract between the college and the state (as successor to the colonial government under the original royal grant). When a charter or an act of incorporation is found to be a contract between a state and a private party, it is protected from legislative interference. Only Justice Joseph Story's concurring opinion modified the sweep of Marshall's statements, suggesting that legislatures could retain certain prerogatives by including "reservation" clauses in corporate charters that allowed legislatures to alter or amend the charter.

By construing the Contract Clause as a means of protecting corporate charters from state interventions, Marshall derived a significant constitutional limitation on state authority. As a result, various forms of private economic and social activity would enjoy security from state regulatory policy. Marshall thus encouraged, through constitutional sanction, the emergence of the relatively unregulated private, autonomous economic actor as the major participant in a liberal political economy that served the commonwealth by promoting enlightened self-interest.

□ G. Edward White, *History of the Supreme Court of the United States*, vols. 3–4, *The Marshall Court and Cultural Change, 1815–35* (1988).

Alfred S. Konefsky

Daubert v. Merrell Dow, 509 U.S. 579 (1993), argued 30 Mar. 1993, decided 28 June 1993 by vote of 9 to o; Blackmun for the Court, Rehnquist and Stevens concurring and dissenting in part.

The advance of science raised troubling new questions for courts about the admissibility of testimony by expert witnesses in complex cases involving environmental and medical liability. In this case, Merrell Dow Pharmaceuticals had manufactured and distributed the drug Bendectin to help pregnant women deal with morning sickness. Doctors had prescribed the drug to more than 30 million women between 1956 and 1983, when the company voluntarily withdrew it from the market. The drug was widely viewed as being the cause of deformities in newly born children, and hundreds of lawsuits had been filed against Merrell Dow. Jason Daubert and Eric Schuller were born with badly deformed limbs, and their parents sued the drug company, claiming that Bendectin was the cause.

All of the parents faced a significant hurdle in bringing their cases against Merrell Dow. The Court in *Frye v. United States* (1923) had held that in order for scientific testimony to be admissible as evidence it had to be generally accepted by scientists. This rule, which meant that most scientific testimony had to be based on data published in journals and subjected to peer review, was designed to protect jurors from so-called junk science that could mislead them. The same rule, however, meant that cutting-edge scientific advances were often barred from the courtroom. Moreover, both state and federal judges found themselves increasingly pressed to weigh the credibility of expert witnesses in the mushrooming areas of consumer liability and environmental hazards. A federal trial court had invoked the *Frye* rule in refusing to admit scientific testimony on behalf of the boys' families that purported to link Bendectin with the children's deformities. The district court ruled for Merrell Dow and the Court of Appeals for the Ninth Circuit affirmed that decision.

The Supreme Court, however, reversed the court of appeals and ordered the case back to trial. Justice Harry Blackmun, writing for the Court, revised the rule in *Frye* and held that pertinent evidence based on scientifically valid principles could be used as long as it was relevant and reliable. Blackmun also found, with Justices Rehnquist and Stevens dissenting in part, that the adoption of the Federal Rules of Evidence in 1975 had effectively usurped the *Frye* precedent when it broadened the basis for admitting scientific, technical, and specialized knowledge into a trial. Blackmun said that while publication and peer review may help a judge determine the relevance of expert testimony, it should not be a prerequisite for admission. Blackmun did recognize that by abandoning the *Frye* precedent the Court was potentially creating a free-for-all of expert witnesses that might confuse both jurors and judges, but he also insisted that vigorous cross-examination, the common sense of jurors, and careful jury instructions would solve these problems.

Daubert opened the courtroom door to more and different kinds of expert scientific testimony. It meant that federal judges had greater discretion over what testimony they would allow at trial, and it encouraged lawyers to bring to the courts new kinds of techniques, such as DNA fingerprinting.

Kermit L. Hall

Davis v. Bandemer, 478 U.S. 109 (1986), argued 7 Oct. 1985, decided 30 June 1986: for justiciability by vote of 6 to 3, White for the Court, O'Connor, Burger, and Rehnquist in dissent; against merits by vote of 7 to 2, White for the Court, Powell and Stevens in dissent. Two central issues were posed in this case, in which Democrats contended that Indiana state legislative district lines were drawn by Republicans for partisan advantage: (1) is political gerrymandering justiciable? and, if so, (2) did the districting in Indiana violate the Constitution's Equal Protection Clause? In a complex division, the Court answered yes (6–3) to the first question and no (7–2) to the second. The plurality opinion, upholding both outcomes, was written by Justice

Byron White for himself, William Brennan, Thurgood Marshall, and Harry Blackmun. Lewis Powell and John Paul Stevens would have upheld a district court decision that responded positively to both questions. The three remaining justices, Sandra Day O'Connor, Warren Burger, and William Rehnquist, would have reversed the lower court's judgment invalidating the Indiana districting on the ground that political gerrymandering claims were nonjusticiable.

The plurality opinion concluded that political gerrymandering is subject to judicial scrutiny, but only where there is "continued frustration of the will of a majority of the voters or a denial to a minority of voters of a fair chance to influence the political process" (p. 133). The opinion found no evidence that Indiana's 1981 redistricting consigned the opposition party to seemingly perpetual minority status throughout the decade regardless of voting trends.

Davis v. *Bandemer* drew widespread attention. Ironically, amicus curiae briefs were filed by the Republican National Committee supporting Indiana's Democrats and by California's Democratic congressional delegation in support of the Republican redistricting—in both instances reflecting concerns outside Indiana. Some legislative and congressional redistrictings after the 1990 census were expected to trigger appeals to the Supreme Court to apply the 1986 ruling's guidelines.

Gordon E. Baker

Davis v. Beason, 133 U.S. 333 (1890), argued 9–10 Dec. 1889, decided 3 Feb. 1890 by vote of 9 to 0; Field for the Court. *Davis* v. *Beason* interpreted free exercise of religion narrowly and inconsistently. Idaho had enacted a territorial statute denying the vote to those who advocated or practiced plural marriage or belonged to an organization that did. Samuel B. Davis and a number of nonpolygamous Mormons, after trying unsuccessfully to vote in the 1888 election, sued. The Idaho court treated their disfranchisement solely as a political question. On appeal, the U.S. Supreme Court upheld the statute as within the territorial powers of the legislature to set voter qualifications. The justices held that religion was a matter of belief, which was constitutionally protected but that conduct was outside the purview of the First Amendment. The Court then defined polygamy as conduct rather than religious belief. Using the Idaho statute as a soapbox for a diatribe on polygamy, Justice Stephen J. Field concluded that "crime is not the less odious because sanctioned by what any particular sect may designate as religion" (p. 345). The preservation of a monogamous family unit was more important to American society than religious liberty for believers in polygamy. "Religion" was defined solely as having reference to one's view of relations with the creator and to the obligations they imposed.

Paul L. Murphy

Debs, In re, 158 U.S. 564 (1895), argued 25–26 Mar. 1895, decided 27 May 1895 by vote of 9 to 0; Brewer for the Court. By refusing to grant a writ of habeas corpus to Eugene Debs, president of the American Railway Union, the Supreme Court sanctioned the use of injunctions against striking labor unions. During the depression of the 1890s, the Pullman company, while still paying dividends, reduced its workers' pay literally to the starvation level. The laborers went on strike and were soon adopted by the newly formed American Railway Union. The union pursued a strategy of boycotting railroads using Pullman cars. Members refused to handle trains with the cars; if dismissed by the road, then all the company's union members would strike. This plan was a direct challenge to the General Managers Association, a group of twenty-six Chicago railroads. Claiming that their contracts required them to use Pullman cars, they provoked strikes throughout the Midwest and nation by firing trainmen who refused to handle Pullman cars. Contending that the strikers were interfering with interstate commerce and the mails, the association urged federal intervention. Attorney General Richard Olney, fearing the violence of a large strike, came to the association's aid. While wanting to send in the army, Olney settled initially for lesser measures. He created more than five thousand special deputies to preserve order, prepared a case of criminal conspiracy against the union leaders, and sought an injunction in federal circuit court that would prohibit interference with the railroads' businesses. Not surprisingly, these actions and the activities of strikebreakers provoked rioting. To suppress violence, blown out of proportion by an alarmist press, the government sent in troops.

The federal circuit court, reasoning that the strike was a combination in restraint of interstate commerce, granted a sweeping injunction. The decree applied to the leaders of the union, all those who combined with them, and any persons whomsoever. It commanded such individuals to cease hindering the railroads, including by means of persuading employees, from carrying the mails and engaging in interstate commerce. Within a week of his arrest for criminal conspiracy, Debs and his fellow officers were again arrested for contempt of court for violating this injunction. While they were in jail the strike folded and the new union crumpled. Though the criminal trial collapsed, the contempt of court charge netted Debs six months' imprisonment. He sought release by writ of habeas corpus to the Supreme Court, arguing that he was tried for a criminal act in a court of equity and thus denied his constitutional right of trial by jury.

Justice David J. Brewer, speaking for a unanimous Supreme Court, rejected Debs's plea. Refusing to rest the decision on the narrow ground of a conspiracy in restraint of trade, he based the ruling on broad principles. Brewer asserted that the government of the United States, though a government of enumerated powers, had full attributes of sovereignty, within those powers. It could forcibly remove any obstructions to commerce or the mails, either by military power or through an appeal to the federal courts' equity power. He labeled the union's action to be a public nuisance, which like a private nuisance was subject to equity jurisdiction. That Debs's acts violated the criminal law did not bar equitable relief. The actions also threatened the property rights of the railroads, which were protected under equity jurisdiction. Therefore, no matter what occurred on the criminal side of the law, the equity side could also be utilized. To preserve their authority in such equity proceedings courts needed the power to punish through contempt. Thus, Brewer rejected the argument that Debs had been denied a jury trial. Brewer touted the use of federal tribunals as a better method than armed force in settling labor troubles; it met the potential mob violence not with force but with the rule of law. For the next thirty years, corporations faced with labor troubles turned to the Federal courts; the Pullman injunction proved the model for many others. Not until the New Deal era did such labor injunctions fade away.

Richard F. Hamm

Dejonge v. Oregon, 299 U.S. 353 (1937), argued 9 Dec. 1936, decided 4 Jan. 1937 by vote of 8 to 0; Hughes for the Court, Stone not participating. The Court overturned the conviction of Dirk DeJonge, who had been prosecuted under Oregon's criminal syndicalism law for helping to conduct a meeting in Portland organized by the Communist party to protest police shootings of striking longshoremen and raids on workers' homes and halls. Despite the party affiliations of DeJonge and the other organizers, no more than 15 percent of those at the meeting were communists. One lecturer discussed the Young Communist League, and DeJonge tried to sell some party publications, but no one advocated criminal syndicalism or unlawful conduct, and the meeting was completely orderly. The principal evidence against DeJonge was party literature found elsewhere that tended to establish that the Communist party promoted criminal syndicalism. The Oregon Supreme Court held that a person could be convicted under the statute for doing nothing more than participating in a wholly innocent meeting called by the party. In reversing the Oregon court's decision, Chief Justice Charles Evans Hughes declared, "[P]eaceable assembly for lawful discussion cannot be made a crime" (p. 365). The Oregon criminal syndicalism law had deprived Dejonge of the rights to free speech and peaceable assembly guaranteed by the Due Process Clause of the Fourteenth Amendment.

Michal R. Belknap

DeLima v. Bidwell. See INSULAR CASES.

Dennis v. United States, 341 U.S. 494 (1951), argued 4 Dec. 1950, decided 4 June 1951 by vote of 6 to 2; Vinson for the Court, Black and Douglas in dissent, Clark not participating. In *Dennis* the Supreme Court affirmed the convictions of eleven Communist party leaders for violation of the Smith Act. In the process the Court significantly modified the so-called clear and present danger test.

The section of the statute at issue in *Dennis* made it a crime to teach or advocate the violent overthrow of any government in the United States, to set up an organization to engage in such teaching or advocacy, or to conspire to teach, advocate, or organize the violent overthrow of any government in the United States. Although the Smith Act was designed to combat the Communist party, because that organization was closely tied to the Soviet Union and because the United States and the U.S.S.R. were allies during World War II, the government refrained from using the new law against communists for several years. In the late 1940s, however, Soviet-American relations deteriorated. President Harry Truman, a Democrat, sought to rally public support for an anti-Soviet foreign policy by characterizing this conflict as a struggle between communism and freedom, and Republicans responded by castigating him for ignoring the threat posed by domestic communism. Under intense political pressure to prove that the Truman administration was not soft on communism, Justice Department lawyers obtained indictments on 20 July 1948 charging the members of the Communist party's national board with violation of the Smith Act's conspiracy provisions.

A 1949 trial before federal district judge Harold Medina, conducted amid mounting anticommunist hysteria, ended with the conviction of all eleven defendants. This tumultuous, nine-month-long proceeding featured judicial bias, which manifested itself in questionable rulings on the admission and exclusion of evidence, as well as the employment of dubious tactics by both the prosecution and the defense. The convicted communists appealed their convictions to the Second Circuit Court of Appeals, but it unanimously affirmed them. Judge Learned Hand's opinion rebuffed defense attacks on the impartiality of the judge and jury, on the prosecution's use of informant witnesses, and on Medina's conduct of the trial. It also rejected the communists' contention that the Smith Act was unconstitutional.

The Supreme Court granted certiorari only on that issue. Hence, the justices did not have before them a complete record of what had gone on at the trial and did not realize how unimpressive the prosecution's evidence had been. Even if he had known these things, Chief Justice Fred Vinson, who seldom displayed much sympathy for civil liberties claims, probably would have voted to affirm. He believed the government had to protect itself from communists and that it dared not wait until their preparations for its overthrow had reached the point of rebellion. The clear and present danger test precluded punishing speech unless it posed an immediate threat of a serious substantive evil. Consequently, Vinson employed a modified version of that principle (now known as the "grave and probable danger" rule), which Judge Hand had developed. "In each case," Virson wrote, courts "must ask whether the gravity of the 'evil' discounted by its improbability, justifies such invasion of free speech as is necessary to avoid the danger" (p. 510). This rule afforded far less protection to freedom of expression than had the clear and present danger test.

Only three other justices endorsed Vinson's opinion. Unable to accept what the chief justice had done to the clear and present danger test, Robert Jackson insisted that it was inapplicable to conspiracies, such as communism, but that the convictions could be sustained because the defendants were guilty of conspiring to overthrow the government. Felix Frankfurter also concurred, suppressing his distaste for the Smith Act because of his commitment to the principle of judicial self-restraint. Both Hugo Black and William O. Douglas filed vigorous dissents.

The Justice Department interpreted *Dennis* as authorization for an all-out attack on the Communist party. The Court's subsequent ruling in *Yates* v. *United States* (1957) thwarted this assault, but *Yates* neither held the Smith Act unconstitutional nor overruled the 1951 decision. Although *Dennis* is inconsistent with more recent rulings, the Supreme Court has never repudiated its grave and probable danger rule.

□ Michal R. Belknap, *Cold War Political justice: The Smith Act, the Communist Party and American Civil Liberties* (1977).

Michal R. Belknap

Dillon v. Gloss, 256 U.S. 368 (1921), argued 22 Mar. 1921, decided 16 May 1921 by vote of 9 to 0; Van Devanter for the Court. This case involved a conviction for transporting intoxicating liquors in violation of the Volstead Act. Dillon raised two issues. First, he challenged the provision requiring ratification of the Eighteenth Amendment within seven years. Second, he argued that the law under which he was charged was not effective until one year after the Eighteenth Amendment was proclaimed by the secretary of state (and hence after his arrest) rather than one year after its ratification. On the first issue, Justice Willis Van Devanter decided that Congress could set a reasonable deadline so that ratification was "sufficiently contemporaneous . . . to reflect the will of the people in all sections at relatively the same time period" (p. 375). On the second

issue, the Court ruled that the amendment's date of consummation, not its proclamation, was controlling.

The Eighteenth Amendment was the first to specify a deadline within its text. When the Equal Rights Amendment was proposed, the deadline was placed in an accompanying authorizing resolution that, in a debated move, Congress later extended. Deadlines within the texts of amendments are presumably self-enforcing. Without distinguishing internal from external deadlines, *Dillon* v. *Gloss* ruled that ratifications must be contemporaneous and left to the judgment of Congress. **Coleman* v. *Miller* (1939) reinforced and widened *Dillon* in declaring that the ratification issue was a political question for congressional resolution.

John R. Vile

District of Columbia v. Heller, 128 S. Ct. 2783 (2008), argued 18 Mar. 2008, decided 26 June 2008 by vote of 5 to 4; Scalia for the Court; Stevens, joined by Ginsburg, Breyer, and Souter, in dissent; Breyer, joined by Stevens, Ginsburg, and Souter, also in dissent. The District of Columbia's gun control statute, the strictest in the nation, prohibited most residents from possessing handguns and required that all firearms be mechanically disabled at all times. Heller, the one plaintiff in this test case with standing to sue, carried a pistol while on duty as a security guard, but he was forbidden to keep a handgun in his home for self-protection.

The D.C. gun control regulations were struck down, marking the first time in history that the federal courts had invalidated a statute under the Second Amendment. This was also the first Supreme Court opinion to address the fundamental interpretive question of whether the Second Amendment protects an individual right to have weapons for private purposes such as self-defense, or only a right to keep and bear arms in connection with service in a governmentally regulated military organization. The Court adopted the individual-rights interpretation, based on a very lengthy analysis of the original meaning of the constitutional text. Deploying a competing set of textual and legislative history arguments, Justice John Paul Stevens dissented, arguing for the military-service interpretation, which would have left the government free to disarm the entire civilian population.

The Court invalidated D.C.'s safe-storage rule because the constitutional right would be empty if it did not include at least a right to render a weapon operable for immediate self-defense in the home. The handgun ban was struck down because handguns are the most popular weapon chosen by Americans for self-defense. Justice Stephen G. Breyer's dissent insisted that D.C.'s strict gun control laws should be upheld—even assuming that there is some constitutional right to have weapons for self-defense because courts should defer to the superior expertise of legislators in balancing the public's interest in preventing violence against the individual's interest in self-protection. The majority opinion responded that this balancing of interests had already been performed by the Constitution itself.

Technically, this was a narrow decision. It applies only to federal laws, and the Court has not yet decided whether the Second Amendment applies to state laws under the modern doctrine of Fourteenth Amendment incorporation. The holding in the case, moreover, covers only the kind of extreme and unusual restrictions adopted in the D.C. statute. Scalia's opinion, however, also contains legally gratuitous endorsements of several common forms of gun control. A great deal of new litigation will be triggered by this case, some of which will test how far the Court is willing to go in preventing government from obstructing or restricting the constitutional right to keep and bear arms for self defense that *Heller* has recognized.

Nelson Lund

Dobbins v. Erie County, 16 Pet. (41 U.S.) 435 (1842), argued 14 Feb. 1842, decided 4 Mar. 1842 by vote of 9 to 0; Wayne for the Court. In *Dobbins*, the captain of a United States revenue cutter stationed in Pennsylvania challenged the validity of that state's taxation on the income derived from his office. The United States Supreme Court, reviewing a decision by the Pennsylvania Supreme Court upholding the validity of the tax, unanimously reversed, holding that "the unconstitutionality of such taxation by a state as that now before us may be safely put—though it is not the only ground—upon its interference with the constitutional means which have been legislated by the government of the United States to carry into effect its powers to lay and collect taxes, duties, imposts, etc., and to regulate commerce" (p. 449). *Dobbins's* classic formulation of the principle that the state governments cannot lay a tax upon the constitutional means

employed by the federal government to execute its constitutional powers was implicitly overruled by the Supreme Court's 1939 decision in *Graves* v. *New York*.

Dobbins was an important case in a line of nineteenth-century Supreme Court precedents, beginning with Chief Justice John Marshall's opinion in *McCulloch* v. *Maryland* (1819), interpreting the doctrine of intergovernmental immunities broadly. This doctrine holds that the federal and state governments possess some degree of reciprocal immunity from each other's taxing and regulatory powers. It has been sharply curtailed in its scope since the mid-1930s by the Court. *Dobbins* thus is no longer good law.

Robert A. Williams

Dodge v. Woolsey, 18 How. (59 U.S.) 331 (1856), argued 6 Feb. 1856, decided 8 Apr. 1856 by vote of 6 to 3; Wayne for the Court, Campbell, Catron, and Daniel in dissent. In 1845 the Ohio legislature enacted a general banking act, which authorized any bank chartered thereunder to pay the state 6 percent of its annual profits in lieu of any taxes imposed by the state. In 1851 Ohio adopted a new state constitution that in effect repealed the tax immunity in the statute of 1845. In 1853 the legislature increased the tax on banks beyond that allowed in the statute of 1845. John W. Woolsey, a citizen of Connecticut and a shareholder of a Cleveland bank, sought an injunction from a federal circuit court to prevent George C. Dodge, Cuyahoga County, Ohio, treasurer, from collecting the tax on the bank, claiming the tax unconstitutionally impaired the obligation of a contract. The "contract" was the relationship between the state and any corporation chartered under the 1845 act.

The Supreme Court upheld the injunction on the ground that the tax provision in the 1845 statute constituted a contractual obligation of the state, which it had impaired by the constitution of 1851 and the statute of 1853. Justice John A. Campbell wrote a dissenting opinion in which he denounced the arrogance of corporations and argued that the Supreme Court was unconstitutionally encroaching upon the rights of a sovereign state. Subsequent decisions of the Court, while attempting to distinguish *Woolsey*, severely confined the holding in that case by ruling that for a tax exemption to be valid it would have to be contained in a specific corporate charter and not in a general statute.

Robert M. Ireland

Dolan v. City of Tigard, 512 U.S. 374 (1994), argued 23 Mar. 1994, decided 24 June 1994 by vote of 5 to 4; Rehnquist for the Court, Stevens and Souter dissenting. As the political and ideological agenda of the high court has shifted to the right in the past decade, so too has its interest in the rights of landowners. In the 1987 case of *Nollan v. California Coastal Commission,* the justices held that municipalities had to show some relationship between the conditions they set to issue a building permit and the projected impact of a proposed development. In *Nollan* the issue did not arise directly, but it did in *Dolan,* and the results were beneficial for property owners.

Florence Dolan owned an electrical and plumbing supply store in the central business district of Tigard, Oregon, a suburb of Portland. Business was good; Dolan proposed to double the size of her store on land that she already owned and to pave over what was a gravel parking lot. The Tigard city planning commission agreed to the expansion, but with two requirements. First, she must give the city property lying within the Fanno Creek flood plain for the purpose of improving drainage and minimizing flooding that might result from rain running off the impervious asphalt rather than percolating through the gravel. Second, the commission required that she give the city an additional strip of land adjacent to the flood plain for use as a pedestrian and bicycle path to relieve congestion in the central business district created by the store's expansion.

Dolan objected to both requirements. She concluded that the proposed changes were unrelated to her store expansion and that, as a result, they constituted an uncompensated taking of property under the Fifth Amendment. The Land Use Appeals Board, a trial court, and the Oregon Supreme Court all found in favor of the city.

The United States Supreme Court's decision reflected a powerful division among the justices over the nature and scope of land-use planning. The justices did not disturb the underlying concept of zoning and the right of municipalities to regulate land use, but they did substantially alter the terms of the relationship between landowners and government when land-use questions arose.

Chief Justice William Rehnquist, writing for the majority, invoked the Fifth Amendment, noting that its Takings Clause was "as much a part of the Bill of Rights as the First Amendment or Fourth Amendment," and should not "be relegated to the status of poor relation" (p. 392). According to Rehnquist, a city could not require a public easement as a condition of permission to build or expand unless it was prepared to show what he termed a "rough proportionality" between the requirement and the particular harm posed by the development (p. 391). While the majority agreed that the city was properly within its power to worry about flooding on Fanno Creek and the impact of additional traffic on the central business district, it had not shown with sufficient precision what the consequences were.

In making such decisions, then, Rehnquist imposed a second test, the demonstration of a necessary connection—a reasonable relationship—between what was proposed as a land-use requirement and the impact of the development project. In this instance, Rehnquist said, the burden belonged not on the landowner but on the government to demonstrate that relationship. The chief justice took particular aim at the requirement by the city that the pedestrian and bike path be "public," since such a requirement meant not only that Dolan lost the use of her property but that she could not regulate individuals who came onto it. Such actions, the majority concluded, amounted to a taking of private property that was not properly compensated as required by the Fifth Amendment. Effectively, the majority decided, as it had earlier in *Nollan,* that government had to prove that any condition imposed on development must "substantially advance" a legitimate government objective. Local governments, moreover, in making that case, had to frame it on an individualized rather than a general basis.

The dissenters, led by Justices John Paul Stevens and David H. Souter, preferred to leave the burden on the developer to prove that the actions of the government were unwarranted. Otherwise, the motives of the city in attempting to regulate development and land use would always be cast in doubt. Both Stevens and Souter noted that the majority's opinion was a striking departure from the Court's previous jurisprudence, which had granted broad authority to local governments to regulate land use. Stevens also insisted that the Court had failed to take account of the benefits that Ms. Dolan would have enjoyed as a result of the dedication of part of her land, not the least of which were the elimination of tort liability on the now public land and the fact that she would no longer have to maintain and pay taxes on it.

Dolan drew in stark terms the difficulties encountered in trying to weigh the benefits of averting the problems of urban life—floods, traffic congestion, and such—with the private interest in commercial development. The Court's actions placed new burdens on local governments and, at the same time, almost certainly meant that governments would ask developers for more costly information and require consultants to interpret it. There is every reason to believe that the costs for everyone in the development process will rise and that local governments will turn to general zoning restrictions rather than site-specific requirements to regulate land use, since such zoning measures have legislative force and are less susceptible to challenge than are the quasi-judicial proceedings of a regulatory body, such as a planning commission.

Kermit L. Hall

Dombrowski v. Pfister, 380 U.S. 499 (1965), argued 25 Jan. 1965, decided 26 Apr. 1965 by vote of 5 to 2; Brennan for the Court, Harlan, joined by Clark, in dissent, Black and Stewart not participating. Dombrowski, an officer of the Southern Conference Educational Fund, sought an injunction against the governor of Louisiana, law enforcement officers, and the chairman of the state's Legislative Joint Committee on Un-American Activities for prosecuting or threatening to prosecute his organization under several state subversion statutes. Dombrowski alleged that the statutes violated the First Amendment and that he and his civil rights colleagues were subjected to continuous harassment, including arrests without intent to prosecute and seizures of necessary internal documents.

A three-judge federal court dismissed the complaint, holding that Dombrowski had not demonstrated the required irreparable injury and that this was a case for invocation of the "abstention doctrine" to permit the state courts to interpret the statutes consistent with the federal Constitution.

The Supreme Court reversed. Justice William Brennan's opinion held that the statutes clearly violated the First Amendment. Further, he argued that the continuous threats of prosecution, seizure of records, and harassment sufficiently chilled free expression to justify federal court intervention.

Injunctive relief in these circumstances was clearly appropriate as an exception to the general rule against federal court intervention in state criminal prosecutions. In dissent, Justice John Harlan argued that permitting federal court intervention, even under these circumstances, was a significant and unwarranted departure from the principle of comity and a threat to the integrity of the federal system.

Dombrowski, seen by civil rights lawyers as a loophole in the traditional principle of nonintervention, unleashed a torrent of lawsuits seeking federal court protection against state prosecutions. The loophole, however, proved only temporary; the Supreme Court closed it substantially in **Younger* v. *Harris* (1971).

Charles H. Sheldon

Downes v. Bidwell. See INSULAR CASES.

Dred Scott Case. See SCOTT V. SANDFORD.

Duncan v. Kahanamoku, 327 U.S. 304 (1946), argued 7 Dec. 1945, decided 25 Feb. 1946 by vote of 6 to 2; Black for the Court, Murphy and Stone concurring, Burton and Frankfurter in dissent, Jackson absent. The *Duncan* case is often associated with the Japanese exclusion cases (**Hirabayashi* v. *United States,* 1943; **Korematsu* v. *United States,* 1944; and *Ex parte Endo,* 1944) because it involved wartime curtailment of fundamental civil liberties under the aegis of military authority.

After the attack on Pearl Harbor by Japanese naval forces on 7 December 1941, Hawaii's territorial governor, Joseph B. Poindexter, acting under the authority of the territorial Organic Act of 1900, suspended the writ of habeas corpus, placed Hawaii under martial law, and relinquished civilian gubernatorial and judicial authority to U.S. Army General Walter C. Short. On the next day, General Short created military tribunals that had power to try civilians for offenses against federal or territorial law and for violation of orders of the military government he had established. He closed all civil courts. This regime of military authority was terminated in October 1944.

In an appeal by two civilians tried by military tribunals, Justice Hugo Black, in a cautiously circumscribed opinion, held that the Organic Act's authorization of martial law did not include the power to supplant civilian courts with military tribunals. Black drew extensively on English and American history to support civilian supremacy over the military. But he carefully avoided constitutional issues raised by the creation of military government, confining himself to statutory construction.

William M. Wiecek

Duncan v. Louisiana, 391 U.S. 145 (1968), argued 17 Jan. 1968, decided 20 May 1968 by vote of 7 to 2; White for the Court, Black, Douglas, and Fortas concurring, Harlan, joined by Stewart, in dissent. Duncan was convicted of misdemeanor battery without benefit of a jury and sentenced to sixty days in jail and a fine of $150. The crime was punishable by a maximum of two years in prison and a $300 fine. Duncan was denied a jury trial because the Louisiana Constitution required juries only in capital cases or where imprisonment at hard labor could be imposed. His appeal to the United States Supreme Court claimed a Sixth Amendment right to a jury trial, although the Court had not yet incorporated that portion of the Bill of Rights into the Fourteenth Amendment.

According to the majority, the test for selective incorporation was whether the right under consideration was "fundamental." In earlier cases a right qualified as fundamental only if a civilized system could not be imagined without it. However, under the new and prevailing test, if history indicated that a procedural right found in the Bill of Rights was an integral part of the "Anglo-American regime of ordered liberty," it was deemed fundamental.

Justice Byron White's opinion argued that the right to trial by jury had enjoyed such an uninterrupted history and, consequently, was to be incorporated "bag and baggage" into the due process clause of the Fourteenth Amendment and thus applied to the states. Duncan's conviction was reversed. The Court also denied Louisiana's claim that this was a petty offense that did not require a jury trial. The majority admitted that some minor offenses may not require a jury trial but left these petty offenses undefined. Justice Hugo Black, joined by William Douglas, concurred, arguing again the correctness of his total incorporation dissent in *Adamson* v. *California* (1947). Justice Abe Fortas concurred but expressed grave doubts about imposing the federal model onto the

states. Justice John Harlan, joined by Potter Stewart, dissented because he feared a further loss of state prerogatives.

Charles H. Sheldon

Duplex Printing Co. v. Deering, 254 U.S. 443 (1921), argued 22 Jan. 1920, decided 3 Jan. 1921 by vote of 6 to 3; Pitney for the Court, Brandeis, Holmes, and Clarke in dissent. In response to growing public pressure to control the unprecedented concentrations of economic power that developed after the Civil War, Congress enacted the Sherman Antitrust Act (1890). It proscribed "unlawful restraints and monopolies" in interstate commerce as well as conspiracies to erect them. Soon thereafter federal judges began to employ the measure to combat efforts to unionize workers and to deny labor its traditional self-help weapons. To counteract this "government by injunction," Congress included in the Clayton Act (1914) provisions that sought to preclude application of antitrust legislation against organized labor.

The Supreme Court reached the issue in *Deering,* a six-judge majority holding that the Clayton Act did not insulate labor unions engaged in illegal activities, such as the conduct of a secondary boycott. Justice Mahlon Pitney asserted that the machinist union's coercive action constituted an unlawful conspiracy to "obstruct and destroy" (p. 460) the interstate trade of complainant, a company with which they were not "proximately or substantially concerned" (p. 472). Writing for the three dissenters, Justice Louis D. Brandeis charged the majority with ignoring law and reality: the injunction imposed by the Court deprived labor of forms of a collective action Congress had tried "expressly" to legalize (p. 486).

For more than a decade, the majority's narrow interpretation of the nation's antitrust legislation sanctioned judicial application of injunctions against workers seeking to organize to advance their interests. With the dramatic transformation of opinion brought about by the Great Depression, Congress included in the Norris-LaGuardia Act (1932) provisions to exempt organized labor from antitrust injunctions, and the Supreme Court legitimated this fundamental New Deal legislation.

Stephen B. Wood

E

Eastern Enterprises v. Apfel, 524 U.S. 498 (1994), argued 4 March 1994, decided 25 June 1994 by vote of 5 to 4; O'Connor for the plurality; Kennedy, concurring in the judgment and dissenting in part; Stevens and Breyer in dissent. *Eastern Enterprises* considered whether a statute imposing a retroactive exaction of money on a former employer to shore up a coal industry retirement and health fund was unconstitutional, and whether the law should be analyzed under the Fifth Amendment's Takings Clause or Due Process Clause. The plurality found the statute unconstitutional under the Takings Clause. The dissent deemed it constitutional under the Due Process Clause. Justice Anthony Kennedy, the swing vote, found the statute unconstitutional, but joined the dissent in using due process analysis.

Justice Sandra Day O'Connor observed that the Coal Industry Retiree Health Benefit Act was an understandable solution to a significant funding problem, but added: "When, however, that solution singles out certain employers to bear a burden that is substantial in amount, based on the employers' conduct far in the past, and unrelated to any commitment that the employers made or to any injury they caused, the governmental action implicates fundamental principles of fairness underlying the Takings Clause" (p. 537). Justice John Paul Stevens's dissent, on the other hand, emphasized that the legislation was reasonable and could

have been anticipated in light of "an implicit understanding on both sides of the bargaining table that the operators would provide the miners with lifetime health benefits" (p. 551).

Justice Kennedy agreed with the plurality that the act was "arbitrary," but asserted that, since its constitutionality "appears to turn on the legitimacy of Congress' judgment rather than on the availability of compensation . . . the more appropriate constitutional analysis arises under general due process principles" (p. 545). He maintained that the Court's prior Takings Clause cases had involved alleged government arrogation of specific property interests, not the imposition of a general obligation to make payments (pp. 542–545).

Steven J. Eagle

E. C. Knight Co., United States v., 156 U.S. 1 (1895), argued 24 Oct. 1894, decided 21 Jan. 1895 by vote of 8 to 1; Fuller for the Court, Harlan in dissent. In early 1892, the American Sugar Refining Company, the corporate successor to the Sugar Trust, acquired all of the stock of its leading competitors. The company thereby secured control of almost all sugar refining in the United States, and the federal government soon filed a civil challenge under the newly enacted Sherman Antitrust Act of 1890.

In its first decision interpreting the act, the Supreme Court affirmed the lower court's dismissal of the government's suit. Chief Justice Melville W. Fuller declared that the key question was whether a monopoly of manufacturing could be suppressed under the Sherman Act. He stressed the power of each state to protect the lives, health, property, and morals of its citizens, and noted that this power encompassed the regulation of practical monopolies within the state's borders. In Fuller's view, while the Constitution granted Congress exclusive authority to regulate activities that constituted commerce among the several states, activities not belonging to interstate or foreign commerce fell exclusively within the jurisdiction of state police power.

The Court conceded that the ability to control the manufacture of an article involved simultaneous control over the article's subsequent disposition in interstate commerce and further agreed that combinations to control manufacturing might tend to restrain interstate trade. The Court declared, however, that this was an insufficient basis for congressional regulation because these were not direct but merely indirect or incidental effects on interstate commerce. The Court insisted upon a sharp distinction between manufacturing and commerce and stated that a producer's intention to distribute its products in other states subsequent to their manufacture provided no basis for the exercise of congressional Commerce Clause power. If indirect effects on interstate commerce could justify a federal challenge to the sale of manufacturing stock and the acquisition of refineries, the Court declared, Congress would have sweeping power to regulate the details of not only manufacturing but of "every branch of human industry" (p. 14) whenever ultimate interstate distribution was contemplated. The states simultaneously would be denied any police power authority over these matters within their own borders. The Court declared that Congress had framed the Sherman Act in the light of these "well-settled principles" (p. 16) and that the government's suit therefore exceeded the scope of the act.

Justice John Marshall Harlan dissented. He believed that the Sherman Act constitutionally could reach combinations like the one challenged in this case. Harlan declared that such dominating combinations had the object and ability to control not only manufacturing but also the price at which manufactured goods were sold in interstate commerce and therefore should be deemed to affect interstate commerce directly. Accordingly, he believed, Congress could seek to remove such combinations because they constituted unreasonable restraints of interstate trade. In Harlan's view, if Congress was not empowered to deal with such threatening interstate combinations, Americans would be left unprotected because individual states would not have sufficient power to control them effectively.

Scholars have differed concerning the origins and impact of the Court's decision. Some scholars, for example, see the decision as largely the product of a politically conservative Court majority fearful of extensions of federal government power. In recent years, an increasingly prominent alternative view has been that the majority genuinely sought to preserve substantial state regulatory authority over the in-state operations of corporations in the ultimately unrealized expectation that the states would use those powers effectively to block monopolistic combinations.

Some maintain that the Court's decision helped pave the way for the great merger waves that began in the late 1890s, which dramatically increased the levels of economic concentration in the United States. Yet the Court strongly supported the application of the Sherman Act in a series of other major cases soon after the *Knight* case was decided. Doctrinally, the Court's limited conception of the scope of federal commerce authority, and particularly its direct-indirect effects test, retained validity until the late 1930s, when it was finally rejected by the Court in favor of a much more expansive view of federal power.

□ Charles W. McCurdy, "The *Knight* Sugar Decision of 1895 and the Modernization of American Corporation Law, 1869–1903," *Business History Review* 53 (1979): 304–342.

James May

Edelman v. Jordan, 415 U.S. 651 (1974), argued 12 Dec. 1973, decided 25 Mar. 1974 by vote of 5 to 4; Rehnquist for the Court, Douglas, Brennan, and Marshall (joined by Blackmun) in dissent. As interpreted by the Supreme Court, the Eleventh Amendment generally prohibits suits against a state in the federal courts, without its consent, by citizens of that state or of other states. *Edelman* v. *Jordan* concerns the scope of exceptions to that prohibition.

John Jordan filed a class-action lawsuit against several Illinois state and county officials (in effect, against the state), arguing that they were administering federal aid under aged, blind, or disabled programs in violation of the Fourteenth Amendment and of federal regulations by initiating payments later than was required by federal law. A federal district court found the state rules to violate federal regulations and ordered retroactive payments to individuals whose rights had been violated.

On appeal, the state officials argued that ordering retroactive payments was barred by the Eleventh Amendment. The court of appeals ruled against them, but the Supreme Court reversed its decision. The Court held that participation by Illinois in the federal program did not constitute a waiver of its Eleventh Amendment immunity to suits. It also held that a 1908 decision, *Ex parte Young*, which allowed suits against states to obtain injunctions affecting their future policies, did not extend to suits for retroactive payments by a state. The dissenters attacked both these holdings.

The impact of *Edelman* has been limited by more recent decisions that allow Congress to overcome the immunity of states from lawsuits through its powers to enforce the Fourteenth Amendment (*Fitzpatrick* v. *Bitzer*, 1976) and to regulate commerce (*Pennsylvania* v. *Union Gas Co.*, 1989). Because of the breadth of those powers, these decisions significantly narrow state immunity.

Lawrence Baum

Edmonson v. Leesville Concrete Co., 500 U.S. 614 (1991), argued 15 Jan. 1991, decided 3 June 1991 by vote of 6 to 3; Kennedy for the Court, O'Connor, Rehnquist, and Scalia in dissent.

Extending its decision in **Batson* v. *Kentucky* (1986), the Court held that potential jurors could not be peremptorily excluded from a federal jury on the basis of race in civil as well as criminal trials. Such exclusion, the Court held, violates the excluded juror's Fifth Amendment rights. An opposing litigant has third-party standing to raise the excluded juror's rights in the opposing litigant's behalf. The equal protection component of the Fifth Amendment applies even though the exclusion is effectuated by a private attorney or private party and not by the state itself. "If a government confers on a private body the power to choose the government's employees or officials,"

Justice Anthony Kennedy held, "the private body will be bound by the constitutional mandate of race-neutrality" (p. 2085).

The dissenters, led by Justice Sandra Day O'Connor, argued that "[n]ot everything that happens in a courtroom is state action," and that the peremptory exclusion of civil jurors "is fundamentally a matter of private choice" not covered by the Fifth and Fourteenth Amendments (p. 2089).

A year later, however, the Court in **Georgia* v. *McCollum* (1992) extended the principle from *Batson* that neither the prosecutor nor defense counsel can challenge jurors on the basis of race in civil cases.

William Lasser

Edwards v. California, 314 U.S. 160 (1941), argued 28 Apr. 1941, reargued 21 Oct. 1941, decided 24 Nov. 1941 by vote of 9 to 0; Byrnes for the Court, Douglas and Jackson concurring. The Supreme Court has long recognized a constitutional right to travel, even though the source of the right remains obscure. The Court upheld this right, even though further obscuring its source, in *Edwards* v. *California*.

In *Edwards*, the Court relied on the Commerce Clause of Article I, section 8 to invalidate a California statute, popularly known as the "Okie Law." The statute prohibited a person from bringing any nonresident indigent person into California. The Court held that the transportation of persons constituted commerce within the meaning of the clause. The Court suggested in dicta that it would not accept stereotypical judgments about the poor as justification for laws discriminating against them. Justice Robert H. Jackson, concurring, urged the Court to hold that interstate travel is a privilege of U.S. citizenship and that the statute violated the Privileges and Immunities Clause of the Fourteenth Amendment. Jackson argued that a person's property status should not be used by a state to qualify one's rights as a citizen of the United States.

The legacy of *Edwards* is twofold. First, it strengthened the constitutional right of travel. Second, it foreshadowed later court decisions that voided statutes discriminating against the poor.

Patrick M. Garry

Edwards v. South Carolina, 372 U.S. 229 (1963), argued 13 Dec. 1962, decided 25 Feb. 1963 by vote of 8 to 1; Stewart for the Court, Clark in dissent. *Edwards* was a "time, place, and manner" case in which the Supreme Court, reversing the convictions of civil rights demonstrators, established the principle that the Due Process Clause of the Fourteenth Amendment, which incorporates the provisions of the First Amendment, does not permit a state to make criminal the peaceful expression of unpopular views.

Approximately two hundred African-American high school and college students walked in groups of fifteen from a church in Columbia, South Carolina, to the grounds of the state capitol, an area normally open to the public. Their purpose in visiting this traditional public forum was to protest discrimination against blacks and to seek repeal of the laws that produced unequal treatment. Three dozen law enforcement officers were on the capitol grounds when the demonstrators arrived. They informed the students of their right to be peacefully present there. For the better part of an hour, the demonstrators walked through the grounds in an orderly fashion carrying placards expressing their pride in being black and their opposition to segregation. During this time, a crowd of two hundred to three hundred curious, but nonhostile, onlookers gathered at the periphery of the capitol grounds. Police protection at all times was adequate to meet any foreseeable possibility of disorder.

Nonetheless, the police informed the students that they would be arrested if they did not disperse within fifteen minutes. The students commenced to sing "The Star-Spangled Banner" and other patriotic and religious songs. When fifteen minutes expired, the students were arrested and their conviction for common law breach of the peace was upheld by the South Carolina Supreme Court.

Harold J. Spaeth

Eichman, United States v., 496 U.S. 310 (1990), argued 14 May 1990, decided 11 June 1990 by vote of 5 to 4; Brennan for the Court, Rehnquist, White, Stevens, and O'Connor in dissent. United States v. Eichman involved two consolidated appeals by the United States in cases in which appellees had been prosecuted for publicly burning American flags in violation of the 1989 Flag Protection Act. This law prohibited the knowing mutilation, defacement, physical defilement, burning of, or trampling on any American flag. Two U.S. district courts ruled the act unconstitutional, based on the Supreme Court's ruling in *Texas v. Johnson* (1989).

Johnson had declared unconstitutional a Texas statute that prohibited knowing desecration of venerated objects in a manner that "the actor knows will seriously offend one or more persons" (p. 400). Texas had applied the statute to a person who had burned an American flag during a protest at the Republican national convention in Dallas in 1984. Indeed, Congress passed the Flag Protection Act in order to give the Supreme Court an opportunity to reconsider its Johnson ruling.

In Johnson, Justice William Brennan found Texas's statute invalid because Texas's interest in preserving the flag as a symbol of nationhood was integrally related to the state's disagreement with the message conveyed. The law became operative "only when a person's treatment of the flag communicates some message" (pp. 12–13). This basis for state action violated the central First Amendment tenet that political speech may not be abridged simply because of its content, however controversial. Texas's law went beyond a mere "time, place, and manner" regulation, which is directed at only the "incidental effects" of expressive conduct, such as excessive noise or unsafe conduct, rather than the message, per se. Accordingly, the Supreme Court applied the strictest standard of review to the law, rather than the more deferential standard that governs restrictions relating only to incidental effects. (U.S. v. *O'Brien, 1968).

In Eichman, however, the government contended that the Flag Protection Act was not directed at offensive expressive conduct, but rather at all forms of flag mistreatment. The law did not single out "offensive" forms of mistreatment, as had Texas's law. Thus, the United States maintained that the act should not be subject to the most exacting constitutional scrutiny.

The Supreme Court disagreed: "Although the Flag Protection Act contains no explicit content-based limitation on the scope of prohibited conduct, it is nevertheless clear that the Government's asserted interest is 'related to the suppression of free expression'" (p. 2408). Justice Brennan intimated that a majority of the Court would construe virtually any law directed at forms of flag desecration as constitutionally suspect, for such laws are inescapably linked to government's disapproval of the message conveyed.

In dissent, Justice John Paul Stevens maintained that the Flag Protection Act and similar laws are consistent with the First Amendment. First, they leave protestors with ample alternative means of conveying their ideas, so the impact on free speech is minimal. Second, they are more neutral concerning the specific content of speech than the majority alleged. "The flag uniquely symbolizes the ideas of liberty, equality, and tolerance . . . the message thereby transmitted [by the flag] does not take a stand upon our disagreements, except to say that those disagreements are best regarded as competing interpretations of shared ideals" (p. 2411).

Eichman reaffirmed the Court's commitment to protecting extremely provocative expression.

Donald A. Downs

Eisenstadt v. Baird, 405 U.S. 438 (1972), argued 17–18 Nov. 1971, decided 22 Mar. 1972 by vote of 6 to 1; Brennan for the Court, Burger in dissent, Powell and Rehnquist not participating. This case expanded the right of privacy articulated in **Griswold* v. *Connecticut* (1965). *Griswold* had invalidated a Connecticut law banning the use of contraceptives by married couples. *Eisenstadt* held that a Massachusetts ban on the distribution of contraceptives to unmarried individuals was equally unper-missible. "If the right of privacy means anything," Justice William Brennan wrote, "it is the right of the *individual*, married or single, to be free from unwarranted governmental intrusion into matters so fundamentally affecting a person as the decision whether to bear or beget a child" (p. 453).

Massachusetts law made it a felony for anyone to distribute contraceptives to unmarried persons. The law allowed contraceptives to be distributed only to married couples and only by registered doctors and pharmacists. The Court held that the distinction between married and unmarried persons violated the Equal Protection Clause of the Fourteenth Amendment and that the statute was not a legitimate health measure since it was both discriminatory and overbroad and since other laws already regulated the distribution of unsafe drugs.

At issue was William Baird's conviction for giving away Emko Vaginal Foam to a woman after a lecture on birth control and overpopulation at Boston University. Baird was not an authorized distributor of contraceptives. Justice Byron White concurred, arguing that a legitimate health interest would have been raised if Baird had not distributed a form of contraception requiring a prescription. Chief Justice Warren Burger dissented, saying that a legitimate health interest already existed.

John Anthony Maltese

Elfbrandt v. Russell, 384 U.S. 11 (1966), argued 24 Feb. 1966, decided 18 Apr. 1966 by vote of 5 to 4; Douglas for the Court, White, Clark, Harlan, and Stewart in dissent. The issue in this case was the constitutionality of a loyalty oath for Arizona state employees. A legislative gloss interpreting the oath made it a violation knowingly to be a member of the Communist party or any other organization having as its purpose violent overthrow of the state government. A violation would subject the employee to discharge and to prosecution for perjury. A school teacher contended that she did not understand the gloss since the statute provided no opportunity for a hearing. The state supreme court upheld the statute. On certiorari, the U.S. Supreme Court remanded the case for consideration in light of *Baggett* v. *Bullitt* (1964). Again the state supreme court upheld the statute, and certiorari was again granted.

The legislative gloss, the Court said, could be interpreted to condemn a member of an organization that had both legal and illegal purposes even though that person did not subscribe to the illegal purposes. This, the Court concluded, interfered with the freedom of association guaranteed by the First and Fourteenth Amendments. Persons who do not share an organization's unlawful purposes and do not participate in its unlawful activities pose no threat as citizens or as public employees. Previously, in *Wieman* v. *Updegraff* (1952) and *Garner* v. *Board of Public Works* (1951), the Court had held that loyalty oath statutes may punish only employees who know of the unlawful purpose of the organization; in *Elfbrandt* the Court added that the employee must have a specific intent to further this purpose.

Milton R. Konvitz

Elrod v. Burns, 427 U.S. 347 (1976), argued 19 Apr. 1976, decided 28 June 1976 by vote of 5 to 3; Brennan for the Court, Stewart and Blackmun concurring, Burger, Powell, and Rehnquist in dissent, Stevens not participating. Five members of the Court, in two separate opinions, imposed a First Amendment barrier to time-honored party patronage practices. In Cook County, Illinois, a newly elected Democratic sheriff sought to discharge non-civil service employees who were Republican appointees of a previous Republican sheriff. The Supreme Court affirmed a court of appeals judgment for injunctive relief. Although unprotected by civil service laws, the employees were not in policy-making positions, were assumed to be performing their duties satisfactorily, and were being discharged solely because they were Republicans occupying positions now meant for Democrats. Dismissals in these circumstances, the Court declared, severely restrict political belief and association as protected by the First Amendment. More controversially, it also held that such restrictions are not outweighed by any contribution of patronage to the democratic process. Government could serve asserted vital purposes by less restrictive means than patronage dismissals.

Justice William Brennan's plurality opinion seemed to challenge the patronage system so broadly as to raise doubts about even the validity of government hiring of party supporters. Unwilling to join that broad a challenge, Justices Potter Stewart and Harry Blackmun concurred only with reference to the unconstitutionality of discharging non-confidential, nonpolicy-making employees. In dissent, Justice Lewis Powell wrote an especially strong defense of patronage. It contributed sufficiently, Powell said, so that the state's interest in preserving it is greater than the burden on First Amendment rights.

In *Branti* v. *Finkel* (1980), *Elrod* was extended to protect Republican assistant public defenders from dismissal by a new Democratic public defender. Ten years later, the Court invoked the principles of *Elrod* and *Branti* to invalidate patronage practices in promotions, transfers, recalls from layoffs, and hiring in its decision in **Rutan* v. *Republican Party of Illinois* (1990).

Leon D. Epstein

Enemy Combatant Cases, collective name for a cluster of cases arising from the detention of alleged enemy terrorists following the attacks of 11 September 2001 that destroyed the World Trade Center Towers: (1) *Rasul* v. *Bush,* 542 U.S. 466 (2004), argued 20 Apr. 2004, decided 28 June 2004 by vote of 6 to 3; Stevens for the Court; Kennedy concurring; Scalia, joined by Rehnquist and Thomas, dissenting; (2) *Hamdi* v. *Rumsfeld,* 542

U.S. 507 (2004) argued 28 Apr. 2004, decided 28 June 2004 by vote of 6 to 3; O'Connor for the Court; Souter, joined by Ginsburg, concurring in part and dissenting in part; Scalia, joined by Stevens, dissenting; Thomas dissenting; (3) *Hamdan* v. *Rumsfeld,* 548 U.S. 557 (2006), argued 28 Mar. 2006, decided 29 June 2006 by vote of 5 to 3; Stevens for the Court; Breyer, joined by Kennedy, Souter, and Ginsburg, concurring; Kennedy, joined in part by Souter, Ginsburg, and Breyer, concurring; Scalia, joined by Thomas and Alito, dissenting; Thomas, joined by Scalia and Alito in part, dissenting; Alito, joined in part by Scalia and Thomas; Roberts not participating; (4) *Boumediene* v. *Bush,* 553 U.S. ___, 128 s.Ct. 2229 (2008), decided 12 June 2008 by vote of 5 to 4, Kennedy for the Court; Souter, joined by Ginsburg and Breyer, concurring, Scalia, joined by Roberts, Alito, and Thomas, dissenting; Roberts, joined by Scalia, Alito, and Thomas, dissenting. On 20 September 2001, President George W. Bush, addressing a Joint Session of Congress, declared, "we are a country awakened to danger and called to defend freedom. . . . Whether we bring our enemies to justice, or bring justice to our enemies, justice will be done." Congress then passed a joint resolution authorizing the president to use "all necessary and appropriate force against those nations, organizations, or persons" responsible for the terrorist attacks on the United States.

The president issued an executive order on 16 November 2001 authorizing a trial by military commission for "any individual who is not a United States citizen" and had been a member of al Qaeda, assisted with acts of international terrorism, or knowingly harbored international terrorists. Following the paradigm of a nation at war, the military opened a hastily prepared facility on the U.S. Naval Base at Guantanamo Bay, Cuba, and prisoners began to arrive there from battlefields in Afghanistan in January 2002. President Bush decided that the detainees at Guantanamo would be characterized as "unlawful enemy combatants" who could be prosecuted by military commission under the laws and customs of war, and that they did not qualify for the status of "prisoner of war" under the relevant rules of the 1949 Geneva Conventions. President Bush also relied on the laws and customs of warfare as the international legal authority to detain the captured individuals, while citing his executive privilege during wartime as the basis of domestic legal authority to continue that detention until the conclusion of hostilities. There was no public discussion of when, or even if, that indeterminate threshold could be met in the case of a nonstate terrorist group acting across international boundaries.

These actions ignited a storm of domestic and international criticism and led to four defining cases of the Bush presidency. The United Nations Security Council and the European Parliament accepted that the attacks on American soil implicated an inherent right of sovereign self defense against the nonstate, transnational terrorist network, although the Administration determination of a state of war created many anomalies in the legal regime regulating armed conflicts. The Geneva Conventions were drafted to apply to combatants acting under the authority of sovereign nations. The detainee cases arose from complex intersections of human rights norms, the scope of unreviewable executive discretion claimed by the U.S. commander-in-chief during a time of national crisis, the acceptable balance of powers between the executive and legislative branches, and the degree of judicial deference due to the treaty determinations made by the executive, particularly in interpreting the Geneva Conventions during a time of conflict against an unconventional enemy.

In *Rasul* v. *Bush* (2004), Justice John Paul Stevens wrote for the majority in extending the application of the federal habeas corpus statute to the detainees incarcerated at the Guantanamo Bay Naval Base. By the express terms of its agreements with Cuba, the United States exercises "complete jurisdiction and control" over the naval base. The *Rasul* majority issued a narrowly reasoned opinion extrapolating the federal habeas statute to petitions raised by detainees at Guantanamo, who challenged the basis of their detention even though they were being held outside the geographic boundaries of any federal district. Within several months, virtually every Guantanamo Bay detainee filed a habeas corpus action in the U.S. District Court for the District of Columbia, seeking release from custody.

On the same day *Rasul* was issued, Justice Sandra Day O'Connor wrote for a plurality of the court in *Hamdi* v. *Rumsfeld* (2004). Hamdi was a natural-born American citizen seized on an Afghanistan battlefield holding an assault rifle. The Guantanamo detainees

were held not on the basis of pending criminal charges, but in order to prevent their return to hostilities. The *Hamdi* decision invalidated the executive claim of unfettered discretion in determining the appropriate status for detainees in U.S. custody. The *Hamdi* plurality held that the military could not detain a U.S. citizen without conducting a minimal hearing to decide if that person could be lawfully held as a combatant. Many of the Guantanamo detainees alleged that they were tourists or that they were captured doing relief work or missionary training. They claimed, therefore, that they were entitled to release because they fell outside the purview of the laws of war. Although *Hamdi* applied to American citizens, the United States swiftly established an administrative procedure whereby all Guantanamo Bay detainees could challenge the military's determination that they had engaged in hostilities against the United States. The procedures permitted detainees to go before a Combatant Status Review Tribunal (CSRT), be informed of the factual basis for detention, submit evidence in an effort to demonstrate noncombatant status, and obtain the assistance of a translator and a "Personal Representative" in presenting their case.

Congress responded to the flood of post-*Rasul* habeas filings by adopting the Detainee Treatment Act of 2005 (DTA). This act provided that "no court, justice, or judge shall have jurisdiction" over habeas petitions filed by Guantanamo Bay detainees. It also provided that "exclusive jurisdiction to determine the validity of any final decision of [CSRT proceedings] that an alien is properly detained as an enemy combatant" resides in the U.S. Court of Appeals for the District of Columbia Circuit.

In *Hamdan* v. *Rumsfeld* (2006), a badly splintered court held that Congress did not intend to deprive the federal courts of jurisdiction over pending habeas petitions when it enacted the Detainee Treatment Act. The plurality opinion held that although Congress authorized the president to create military commissions in Article 21 of the Uniform Code of Military Justice (UCMJ), the president's executive order violated the UCMJ. By failing to comply with the legislative limitations on military commissions, President Bush exceeded his executive authority in acting unilaterally. Moreover, Justice Stevens wrote a plurality opinion that found that the commissions themselves violated Common Article 3 of the Geneva Conventions. Common Article 3 sets forth a minimum set of rules governing non-international armed conflicts, in particular the right to trial before "a regularly constituted court, affording all the judicial guarantees which are recognized as indispensable by civilized peoples."

In response to the *Hamdan* decision, Congress expressly empowered the president to establish military commissions by enacting the Military Commissions Act of 2006 (MCA). The MCA recognized the statutory category of "unlawful enemy combatant" and mandated that "[n]o court, justice, or judge shall have jurisdiction to hear or consider an application for a writ of habeas corpus filed by or on behalf of an alien detained by the United States who has been determined by the United States to have been properly detained as an enemy combatant or is awaiting such determination." In *Boumediene* v. *Bush* (2008), a deeply divided Court ruled that the detainees held at Guantanamo Bay enjoy a constitutionally protected right to file habeas petitions in federal courts, and that Congress improperly abrogated this right in the MCA. The majority conclusion that the CSRT process and the statutory appeals process provided an "inadequate" substitute for the constitutionally grounded right to file a habeas corpus petition provoked strong dissents.

Until the *Boumediene* decision, the Enemy Combatant cases signified the essence of a Court striving to balance the constitutional allocation of powers between coordinate branches. while at the same time rendering narrowly construed opinions designed to preserve presidential flexibility during conflict. Though it prescribed no pathway to the future and gave no guidance to federal judges for its implementation, in *Boumediene* the Court strove instead to protect individual liberties against the power of the coordinate branches of government, even when these branches act in concert.

Michael A. Newton

Engel v. Vitale, 370 U.S. 421 (1962), argued 3 Apr. 1962, decided 25 June 1962 by vote of 7 to 1; Black for the Court, Douglas concurring, Stewart in dissent, White not participating. The Supreme Court did not work from a blank slate when it first faced the constitutionality of governmentally sponsored prayers in public schools. In **Everson* v. *Board of Education of Ewing Township*

(1947), **Illinois ex rel. McCollum* v. *Board of Education* (1948), and **Zorach* v. *Clauson* (1952), it had held the Establishment Clause of the First Amendment to require a "wall of separation" between church and state. The height of this "wall," however, was unclear. *Everson* and *Zorach* allowed public accommodation of religious practices, but *McCollum* struck them down. Additionally, during this period the Court declined to hear *Doremus* v. *Board of Education* (1952)—a case squarely raising the constitutionality of Bible reading in public schools. Nine years later, in **Engel* v. *Vitale* (1962), it took up a similar question.

Not only was the Court's slate cluttered with legal precedents, but it also contained the badge of modern constitutional litigation: substantial interest group presence. Pushing the strong separationist line it had drawn since *Everson*, the American Civil Liberties Union joined the parents of ten public school students in a suit claiming that a state-authored prayer—"Almighty God, we acknowledge our dependence upon Thee, and we beg Thy blessings upon us, our parents, our teachers and our Country"—was an unconstitutional establishment of religion. Supporting the ACLU position were amicus curiae briefs filed by the American Ethical Union, the American Jewish Committee (joined by the Anti-Defamation League of B'nai B'rith), and the Synagogue Council of America (joined by the National Community Relations Advisory Council).

Essentially, the separationist argument boiled down to this: any state support given to religion, either direct or indirect, violates the Constitution. In support of this contention, these litigants offered legal precedents and a history of the religion clauses that drew heavily from the writings of Thomas Jefferson (the "wall" metaphor was initially his) and James Madison. Particular emphasis was placed on the latter's "Memorial and Remonstrance against Religious Assessments."

Although they had the numerical edge, separationist groups were not the only organized litigators involved in *Engel*. Sharing oral argument with counsel for the school board was Porter R. Chandler, an attorney frequently called "the Cardinal's lawyer" because of his close association with the Archdiocese of New York. Chandler appended himself to the case by intervening on behalf of parents and children in the school district. Appearing as amicus curiae in support of the prayer were the Board of Regents of the State of New York and twenty state attorneys general. Essentially, they contended that the prayer, because it created no Establishment Clause problems, facilitated free exercise values, was not coercive, and involved no expenditure of public monies.

The majority opinion of Justice Hugo Black sided with separationist interests. He held that use of public schools to encourage prayer was "a practice wholly inconsistent with the Establishment Clause" (p. 424). Drawing solely on British and American history to support this judgment, Black cited no precedent to reach this conclusion. Seemingly as an after-thought, he commented that the Constitution did not require that all religious values be purged from public life, but merely that schools could not sponsor them.

Justice Potter Stewart tendered the sole dissent, charging the majority with misconstruing the meaning of the First Amendment's religious clauses. His reading of them led him to two conclusions: government cannot coerce one's religious beliefs— the Free Exercise Clause was preeminent, and the Establishment Clause simply forbids governmental establishment of an official church. Though unpersuasive to others on the Court at this time, the second line of argument was to be given new life by Justice William Rehnquist in his *Wallace* v. *Jaffree* (1985) dissent.

Moreover, in *Rosenberger* v. *University of Virginia* (1995) the justices held that the University of Virginia had to provide a financial subsidy to a student religious publication on the same basis as other student publications.

Joseph F. Kobylka

Erie Railroad Co. v. Tompkins, 304 U.S. 64 (1938), argued 31 Jan. 1938, decided 25 Apr. 1938 by vote of 8 to 0; Brandeis for the Court; Butler, McReynolds, and Reed concurring; Cardozo not participating. The Judiciary Act of 1789 provided that "the laws of the several states . . . shall be regarded as rules of decision in trials at common law" in federal courts (sec. 34). This provision, which in modern times is known as the Rules of Decision Act, requires federal courts to follow state substantive law in cases where the federal courts have jurisdiction because the parties are citizens of different states, but does not define the sources of state law.

In *Swift* v. *Tyson* (1842), Justice Joseph Story construed the phrase "laws of the several states" to include statutes and the law of real property but to exclude "contracts and other instruments of a commercial nature," which federal courts could construe in the light shed by the "general principles and doctrines of commercial jurisprudence" (p. 19). Story thus called into being a general federal common law in the field of commercial law. His words transformed what had merely been an ambiguity into an enigma.

Standing alone, *Swift* would not have severely distorted the federal system. But after the Civil War, the notion of a general federal common law underwent a seemingly limitless expansion beyond the commercial law ambit of *Swift*, extending to municipal bonds, civil procedure, corporations, torts, real property, and workers' compensation. At the same time, the power of the federal courts was expanding exponentially, and federal courts were using doctrines of substantive due process and liberty of contract to annul federal and state economic regulation. Conservatives extolled these substantive developments and the concomitant expansion of federal courts' diversity jurisdiction as vital to the protection of eastern investors' interests in the southern and western states, while progressives denounced the resort to federal courts by large corporations seeking to avoid state regulatory policies. A particularly notorious example of this occurred in the *Black & White Taxicab* case of 1928, where federal courts invoked a *Swift*-derived "general law" to enable a corporation to avoid state antitrust legislation. Disturbed by such use of federal judicial power, progressives determined to eradicate *Swift*.

Their opportunity came in *Erie*, which over-ruled *Swift*. Writing for the Court, Justice Louis D. Brandeis declared that "there is no federal general common law" (p. 78). He found *Swift* to be inconsistent with the intentions of the legislators who drafted the Rules of Decision Act. In an action unique in the history of the Court, Brandeis held one of its decisions, *Swift*, unconstitutional, presumably as an intrusion on rights reserved to the states by the Tenth Amendment.

Erie did not eliminate the notion of a federal common law, however. On the same day that he handed down his *Erie* opinion, Brandeis also acknowledged the existence of specialized bodies of federal common law. Nor did *Erie* resolve the enigma of

Swift. Since 1938, the Court has attempted without much success to articulate guidelines that would achieve "the twin aims of the *Erie* rule: discouragement of forum-shopping and avoidance of inequitable administration of the laws" (*Hanna* v. *Plummer*, 1963, p. 468). Justice William J. Brennan suggested an approach that balances state and federal policy interests (*Byrd* v. *Blue Ridge Rural Electric Co-operative, Inc.*, 1958), while Chief Justice Earl Warren in *Hanna* sought to protect the Federal Rules of Civil Procedure from being overridden by state law through use of an analytical algorithm that traces the rules' validity to their statutory source, the Rules Enabling Act of 1934, and thence to the Constitution itself. The debate engendered by *Swift* and *Erie* will persist as the Court continues to define the contours of judicial federalism in the United States.

□ John H. Ely, "The Irrepressible Myth of Erie," *Harvard Law Review* 87 (1974): 693–740.

William M. Wiecek

Escobedo v. Illinois, 378 U.S. 438 (1964), argued 29 Apr. 1964, decided 22 June 1964 by vote of 5 to 4; Goldberg for the Court, Harlan, Stewart, White, and Clark in dissent. When Danny Escobedo, a murder suspect, was taken to the police station and put in an interrogation room, he repeatedly asked to speak to the lawyer he had retained. Escobedo's lawyer soon arrived at the station house and repeatedly asked to see his client. Despite the persistent efforts of both Escobedo and his lawyer, the police prevented them from meeting. The police also failed to advise Escobedo of his right to remain silent. In response to accusations that he had fired the fatal shot, Escobedo made some incriminating remarks and then confessed to the crime.

Even though Escobedo had been interrogated before adversary proceedings had commenced against him (compare *Massiah* v. *United States*, 1964), the Supreme Court threw out his confession. Because of the accordion-like quality of Justice Arthur Goldberg's opinion for the narrow majority, a great deal of confusion resulted. At some places the opinion seemed to say that a person's right to counsel is triggered once he becomes the "prime suspect" or once the investigation shifts from the "investigatory" to the "accusatory" stage and begins to

"focus" on him. (Because this reading of the opinion threatened to cripple police interrogation, it alarmed many members of the bench and bar). At other places, however, the opinion seems to limit the case's holding to the specific facts preceding Escobedo's confession.

Two years later *Escobedo* was shoved offstage by the equally controversial case of *Miranda* v. *Arizona* (1966). *Miranda* shifted from a "prime suspect," or "focal point," test to a "custodial interrogation" standard, moving from *Escobedo's* right-to-counsel rationale to one grounded primarily in the privilege against self-incrimination. Thus, although *Miranda* maintained the momentum in favor of suspects' rights generated by *Escobedo*, it largely displaced that case's rationale.

Yale Kamisar

Euclid v. Ambler Realty Co., 272 U.S. 365 (1926), argued 27 Jan. 1926, reargued 12 Oct. 1926, decided 22 Nov. 1926 by vote of 6 to 3; Sutherland for the Court, Van Devanter, McReynolds, and Butler in dissent. During the first quarter of the twentieth century, many municipalities, including Euclid, Ohio, enacted comprehensive zoning schemes. These zoning ordinances were challenged on various constitutional grounds, and state courts disagreed as to their constitutionality. The zoning ordinance enacted by the Euclid village council is noteworthy because litigation over its validity reached the Supreme Court. In *Euclid* v. *Ambler Realty Co.*, the justices concluded that zoning was a constitutional exercise of the police power, thereby laying the foundation for virtually universal implementation of this form of land use regulation.

In 1922, Euclid was a community of fewer than ten thousand citizens located in the Cleveland metropolitan area and in the path of urban expansion. The village council adopted a comprehensive zoning ordinance dividing the town into use districts, area districts, and height districts. These districts or zones overlapped, so that development of each parcel of land in the community was restricted as to use, area, and height. The use limitations, the controversial feature of the ordinance, were cumulative in nature. With a few minor exceptions, single-family dwellings were the only structures permitted in the most restrictive use zone (U-1). Progressively more intensive uses were permitted in five other use zones (U-2 through U-6), with virtually all types of residential, commercial, and manufacturing use permitted in the least restrictive zone (U-6).

Ambler Realty Co. owned a large, unimproved tract of land in Euclid. It apparently was holding this sixty-eight-acre parcel for investment, planning to sell it for industrial development. A considerable portion of the property was zoned U-6 and thus could be used for industrial purposes. However, the rest of the property was zoned U-2 or U-3, thereby being significantly restricted and substantially reduced in value.

Ambler Realty Co. filed suit in federal district court challenging the validity of the Euclid zoning ordinance on due process, equal protection, and taking grounds. The court ruled in favor of the landowner, finding that its property had been taken without just compensation, and granted an injunction prohibiting the village from enforcing the ordinance.

The Supreme Court reversed the lower court's decision, sustaining the constitutionality of zoning as a means of regulating private land use. The Court initially noted that zoning could only be justified as an exercise of the police power to promote the public welfare. Drawing an analogy to nuisance law, the Court concluded that a zoning arrangement must be viewed in a given context. The Court focused on the prohibitory aspects of the Euclid ordinance, particularly the exclusion of commercial enterprises and apartment buildings from certain residential zones, and found a rational relationship between these restrictions and the health, safety, and general welfare of the citizens of the municipality. It noted a number of factors that established this nexus, including the minimization of traffic hazards and the reduction of noise. The Court stressed that it was upholding the zoning ordinance in its "general scope." It, however, recognized the possibility that an ordinance might be unconstitutional as applied to a specific parcel.

The *Euclid* decision established the legal foundation for zoning. Over time, local governments throughout the country employed this system of land use control with, of course, numerous variations. Nevertheless, as anticipated in *Euclid*, landowners soon attacked zoning ordinances as they applied to particular parcels. One such case reached the Supreme Court shortly after *Euclid*. In *Nectow* v. *City of Cambridge* (1928), the Court

ruled in favor of the landowner, holding that application of the zoning ordinance to the parcel greatly reduced the land's value without enhancing the public welfare.

Having established the constitutionality of comprehensive zoning and demonstrated that a zoning ordinance valid in its general terms might be unconstitutional in application, the Supreme Court essentially withdrew from the zoning scene, leaving subsequent battles to be fought primarily in state courts. Since 1970, however, the Court has reentered the picture and rendered numerous decisions regarding various land use regulation techniques. For example, the Court in *Dolan* v. *City of Tigard* (1994) placed new limits on the ability of government to require developers to set aside part of their land for environmental or other public uses. Nonetheless, the Court has shown no inclination to reconsider its landmark decision in *Euclid*.

□ Daniel R. Mandelker, *Land Use Law*, 2d ed. (1988, supp., 1991).

Jon W. Bruce

Evans v. Abney, 396 U.S. 435 (1970), argued 12–13 Nov. 1969, decided 29 Jan. 1970, by vote of 6 to 2; Black for the Court, Douglas and Brennan in dissent, Marshall not participating. *Evans* is one of a series of Supreme Court decisions that have considered racially discriminatory land-use covenants and other, privately created, racial land-use limits. *Evans* dealt with a public park in Macon, Georgia, which was open only to white residents in accordance with restrictions placed on the park by the donor of the property in 1911. In *Evans* v. *Newton* (1966), the Court decided that the city could not operate this all-white park without violating the Equal Protection Clause. Upon remand, Georgia courts decided that, in light of the clearly expressed discriminatory intent of the donor, the only suitable way to carry out the donor's wish was to return the property to his heirs.

In *Evans* v. *Abney* the Court upheld this action even though the effect was to close the park to blacks. Georgia courts reached their decision by relying on racially neutral, well-settled principles for the interpretation of wills. In accord with these interpretive principles, the donor's intent was best carried out, not by eliminating the racial restrictions, but by ending the park. The effect of the action, the Court noted, was not racially discriminatory because both whites and blacks lost access to the park land.

In reaching this conclusion the Court distinguished the case from its landmark ruling, *Shelley* v. *Kraemer* (1948), in which the Court announced that a state court violated the Equal Protection Clause when it enforced a privately created racial land-use covenant.

Eric T. Freyfogle

Everson v. Board of Education of Ewing Township, 330 U.S. 1 (1947), argued 20 Nov. 1946, decided 10 Feb. 1947 by vote of 5 to 4; Black for the Court, Jackson, Frankfurter, Rutledge, and Burton in dissent. *Everson* involved a New Jersey statute that authorized boards of education to reimburse parents, including those whose children went to Catholic parochial schools, for the cost of bus transportation to and from school. To Arch Everson, a local resident and taxpayer, this practice violated the Establishment Clause.

At first reading it would seem that all the Court's members agreed with Everson. Justice Hugo Black, speaking for the Court, concluded that with the period of early settlers, the American people believed that individual religious liberty could be best achieved by a government that was stripped of all power to tax, to support, or otherwise to assist any or all religions. In 1785–1786 Thomas Jefferson and James Madison led a successful fight against a tax to support Virginia's established church. A major part of the fight was the latter's great "Memorial and Remonstrance." In it Madison argued that a true religion did not need the support of law; that no person, either believer or nonbeliever, should be taxed to support a religious institution of any kind; that the best interest of a society required that the minds of men always be wholly free; and that cruel persecutions were the inevitable result of government-established religions. The "Memorial" led to the rejection of the tax measure and to the enactment of Jefferson's famous Virginia Bill for Religious Liberty.

At this point it would seem that Justice Black had made an incontrovertible case for a judgment of unconstitutionality. But for him, and four others, the net result was just the opposite. We must not, he said, strike down New Jersey's statute because it reaches the verge of its power or deprives its citizens of benefits because of their religion. The First Amendment requires the state to be neutral in its relation with groups of religious and non-believers, it does not require the state to be their adversary. State power is no more to be used to handicap than to favor religions. The state contributes no money to the parochial schools. It does not support them. Its legislation, as applied, does no more than provide a general program to help parents get their children, regardless of their religion, safely and expeditiously to and from accredited schools. New Jersey has not in the slightest breached a wall between church and state. Its statute is therefore constitutional.

While a minority of the Court—Justices Wiley Rutledge, Felix Frankfurter, Robert H. Jackson, and Harold Burton—agreed with the basic premise expressed by Justice Black, they disagreed with the idea that it was not to be applied in *Everson*.

Everson remains good law. More importantly, however, the case held that the religion clauses of the First Amendment are made applicable to the states by the Fourteenth Amendment, and it set out a standard by which the religion clauses were to be interpreted. The heart and soul of the *Everson* opinion, which has been and still is invoked in full or part, is that neither the state or federal government can set up a religion.

Leo Pfeffer

F

Fairfax's Devisee v. Hunter's Lessee, 7 Cranch (11 U.S.) 603 (1813), argued 27–28 Feb. 1812, decided 15 Mar. 1813 by vote of 3 to 1; Story for the plurality, Johnson dissenting, Marshall, Washington, and Todd absent. *Fairfax's Devisee* was the prelude to the great constitutional confrontation between Virginia jurists and the United States Supreme Court that culminated in *Martin* v. *Hunter's Lessee* (1816). It implicated the politically sensitive questions of state wartime confiscation of Loyalist property, state obligations under the unpopular Jay Treaty of 1794, and the authority of the Supreme Court over decisions of state supreme courts under section 25 of the Judiciary Act of 1789. The Virginia Supreme Court of Appeals upheld title to property on the Northern Neck derived from state confiscation. On a writ of error, Justice Joseph Story, writing for himself and only two other justices, virtually voided the state confiscation act and upheld the claim derived from a Loyalist's title. On remand, the Virginia Supreme Court of Appeals refused to honor the mandate of the Supreme Court; it held section 25 unconstitutional; and Judge Spencer Roane denounced the "centripetal" tendencies of power to accumulate in the federal government. This set the stage for *Martin* v. *Hunter's Lessee*.

William M. Wiecek

Fay v. Noia, 372 U.S. 391 (1963), argued 7–8 Jan. 1963, decided by vote of 6 to 3; Brennan for the Court, Harlan, Clark, and Stewart in dissent. The relationship between the national government and the states is the central problem of American federalism. This is illustrated in examining how the state and federal courts interact with respect to the administration of criminal justice. The availability of federal habeas corpus to persons who have been convicted of crime in state courts is such an issue.

Since the enactment of the Judiciary Act of 1789, all federal courts have been authorized to grant writs of habeas corpus to federal prisoners. Not until the adoption of the Judiciary Act of 1867, however, was federal habeas corpus made available to state as well as federal prisoners in all cases where a violation of a federal right was alleged.

Fay v. *Noia* is a notable example of the expansion of the rights of state prisoners through a federal habeas corpus proceeding. Noia had been convicted in a New York court of a felony murder. The question arose whether he could gain federal habeas corpus relief after he was denied state post-conviction relief because the time had lapsed for a review by a state appellate court. The bone of contention was the admissibility of a confession that in the case of two confederates had been held to have been coerced. As construed by the Supreme Court, the Due Process Clause of the Fourteenth Amendment prohibits the use in any state court of coerced confessions.

The U.S. District Court for the Southern District of New York denied Noia relief, holding that under the federal habeas corpus statute a state prisoner could be granted the writ only if the applicant had exhausted the remedies available in the state courts. The federal court of appeals reversed the district court, holding that "exceptional circumstances" were present that excused compliance with the state rule relating to appeals. This court held that a state remedy was no longer available to Noia at the time the federal habeas proceeding was commenced; the state had conceded that Noia's confession had been coerced, relying entirely on his failure to take a timely appeal from his original conviction to a state appellate court.

The Supreme Court agreed with the court of appeals. The Court majority refused to apply the rule that state procedural defaults constitute an adequate and independent state ground for barring a direct review by the Supreme Court of the original conviction. It held that the rule relating to direct review should not be extended to limit the power granted to federal courts by the federal habeas corpus statute. In other words, because of the crucial importance of the writ of habeas corpus, Noia's failure to make a timely appeal in the state courts was not an intelligent and understanding waiver of his right to seek federal relief.

Justice William Brennan asserted that there is no higher duty than to maintain unimpaired the right to seek the writ, whose "root principle is that in a civilized society, government must always be accountable to the judiciary for a man's imprisonment . . ." (p. 402).

There was another important procedural issue in this case. A long line of court decisions and a federal statute had established the proposition that after a state prisoner has been convicted in a state trial court, before seeking a federal writ, he must first exhaust all available state remedies. Normally, a prisoner had to exhaust appeals to state appellate courts, which usually meant review by the state supreme court. The U.S. Supreme Court in *Darr* v. *Burford* (1950) held that state remedies were not exhausted until a defendant had also attempted to secure a review of the highest state court action in the U.S. Supreme Court by means of the writ of certiorari. The Court, of course, denies more than 90 percent of the applications for certiorari and almost never gives reasons for doing so. In *Fay* v. *Noia*, the Court

abandoned the position it had taken in *Darr*, holding that a petition to the Supreme Court for certiorari is not a "state remedy." The justices condemned the *Darr* rule as unduly burdensome, since most petitions for certiorari clogged the Court's calendar and needlessly consumed time. More recently the Court has moved aggressively in *Sandin* v. *Conner* (1995), *Brecht* v. *Abrahamson* (1993), and *Herrera* v. *Collins* (1993) to limit the scope of habeas corpus, effectively reducing access by persons who have been convicted of a crime in state courts and in so doing extending the power of the states in matters of criminal justice.

□ David Fellman. *The Defendant's Rights Today* (1976), chap. 5.

David Fellman

Federal Election Commission v. Wisconsin Right to Life, Inc., 127 S. Ct. 2652 (2007), argued 25 Apr. 2007, decided 25 June 2007 by vote of 5 to 4; Roberts for the Court, joined in Parts I and II by Scalia, Kennedy, Thomas, and Alito; Roberts, joined by Alito, delivered an opinion in Parts III and IV; Alito filed a concurring opinion; Scalia, joined by Kennedy and Thomas, concurred in part and concurred in the judgment; Souter, joined by Stevens, Ginsburg, and Breyer, dissented. In *McConnell* v. *Federal Election Commission* (2003), the Supreme Court upheld the essential features of the Bipartisan Campaign Reform Act of 2002 (BCRA, or "McCain-Feingold," after its two major sponsors). This ruling included the approval, against a First Amendment facial challenge, of major new restrictions on campaign advertising. BCRA's Section 203 made it a federal crime for a corporation, union, or nonprofit advocacy group to engage in "electioneering communication" that refers to a candidate for federal office within sixty days of a general election or thirty days of a primary.

Wisconsin Right to Life (WRTL) raised an "as-applied" challenge to BCRA's restrictions on its ads during the thirty-day blackout period before the 2004 Wisconsin primary. The ads urged listeners to contact Wisconsin's senators to oppose a filibuster and allow a vote on President George W. Bush's judicial nominees. Senator Russ Feingold was running for reelection, and the mention of his name in the ads would therefore trigger a BCRA violation. Asserting a First Amendment right to run these ads, WRTL sued the Federal Election Commission (FEC). The Court ruled in support of WRTL's First Amendment claim. As in previous campaign reform cases, dating back to *Buckley* v. *Valeo* (1976), the usual fractured opinions prevailed in this case.

Because of these divided opinions, Chief Justice John Roberts was only able to deliver an opinion of the Court stating that the issue was not moot, and three justices parted company with him on the reasons for the ruling that Section 203 was unconstitutional as applied to WRTL's "issue ads." Roberts attempted to carve out room for First Amendment protection for these ads, while Justice Antonin Scalia argued in a concurrence that *McConnell* should have been directly overruled because no test could avoid vagueness that chills speech and also conform to *McConnell*. The chief justice, Scalia contended, in effect had overruled *McConnell*. Justice David H. Souter, in dissent, argued that WRTL's ads fell within the prohibited category articulated in *McConnell*: express advocacy or "the functional equivalent of express advocacy."

Roberts, in the section of his opinion that garnered the approval only of Justice Samuel A. Alito, Jr., articulated an objective test for as-applied challenges to Section 203 that would "give the benefit of the doubt to speech, not censorship" (p. 2674), while not reconsidering *McConnell*. Under the test that he proposed, "a court should find that an ad is the functional equivalent of express advocacy only if the ad is susceptible of no reasonable interpretation other than as an appeal to vote for or against a specific candidate" (p. 2667). Roberts found WRTL's ads "plainly not the equivalent of express advocacy," thus falling outside of BCRA's regulatory reach.

Thus, contrary to the belief of BCRA supporters that issue ads are little more than a subterfuge to circumvent prohibitions on corporate and union contributions to political campaigns, a deeply divided Court somewhat narrowed the reach of BCRA by deciding that the First Amendment at least protects ads that, like WRTL's, mention candidates by name but avoid stating their positions or indicating that they are running in an election. Some supporters of BCRA tried to minimize the impact of the decision, while others went to the opposite extreme and viewed it as an opening salvo in the evisceration of BCRA's restrictions on electioneering ads. Campaign-finance-

reform skeptics and supporters of the First Amendment, in contrast, saw the decision as a hopeful sign that the Court was inching away from deference to Congress when it comes to restricting political speech. From this perspective, the Court was taking a step back, however hesitant and inconclusive, from *McConnell's* willingness to curb speech during the height of the campaign season.

Ellen Frankel Paul

Federal Maritime Commission v. South Carolina State Ports Authority, 535 U.S. 743 (2002), argued 25 Feb. 2002, decided 28 May 2002 by vote of 5 to 4; Thomas for the Court, Stevens, Souter, Breyer, and Ginsburg in dissent.

A federal statute prohibits marine terminal operators from discriminating against terminal users. The Federal Maritime Commission is authorized to enforce the law. A company claimed that the South Carolina State Ports Authority had discriminatorily refused berthing space to a cruise ship, and brought an adjudicative complaint before the commission. The commission rejected the Port Authority's claim that state sovereign immunity extends to proceedings before federal administrative agencies. The Supreme Court held that state sovereign immunity bars a federal agency from adjudicating a private party's complaint against a nonconsenting state.

The text of the Eleventh Amendment restricts only the "judicial Power" of the United States, while federal administrative agencies exercise executive power. But the majority opinion candidly acknowledges that the Court's previous decisions have rendered the amendment's text essentially irrelevant. The Court currently takes state sovereign immunity to be a background structural principle that applies to federal-law claims brought by private parties against their own states or other states, in either state court or federal court. Given those textually ungrounded decisions, the further extension of state immunity to administrative proceedings was a predictable step.

The most impressive objection to the Court's decision is not textual, but structural. State immunity does not extend to suits against states brought by the United States, rather than a private party; in such cases, the Court had previously reasoned, the suit against an unconsenting state requires an exercise of political responsibility by elected officials. The same is true of proceedings before federal administrative agencies, whose officers are appointed by the president, and who are subject to congressional oversight.

Adrian Vermeule

Feiner v. New York, 340 U.S. 315 (1951), argued 17 Oct. 1950, decided 15 Jan. 1951 by vote of 6 to 3; Vinson for the Court, Frank-furter concurring, Black, Douglas, and Minton in dissent. On the evening of 8 March 1949 college student Irving Feiner stood atop a wooden box on a street corner in Syracuse, New York, and harangued a mixed-race crowd of seventy-five to eighty people. Feiner excoriated President Harry Truman, the American Legion, and local officials, and he urged blacks to take up arms and fight for equal rights. The crowd became unruly, some of its members supporting Feiner and some opposing him. One man threatened violence. A policeman asked Feiner three times to get down off the box. When he refused, the officer arrested him for violation of a New York statute that made it a crime to use offensive, threatening, abusive, or insulting language with intent to provoke a breach of the peace. Feiner contended that his arrest and conviction violated his First Amendment right to freedom of expression, but the Supreme Court disagreed. Chief Justice Fred Vinson took the position that because the arrest was necessary to preserve order in the face of a clear and present danger to public safety, it was constitutional. In a strong dissent Justice Hugo Black argued that Feiner was being sent to the penitentiary because the views he had expressed on matters of public interest were unpopular. *Feiner* v. *New York* exemplifies the conservative, pro-government position generally taken by the Vinson Court in free speech cases.

Michael R. Belknap

Feist Publications, Inc. v. Rural Telephone Service Company, Inc., 499 U.S. 340 (1991), argued 9 Jan. 1991, decided 27 Mar. 1991 by vote of 9 to 0; O'Connor for the Court, Blackmun concurring. Rural published a local white-pages telephone directory. Feist resorted Rural's listings and included them in a regional directory overlapping Rural's service area. Rural claimed copyright infringement. The Supreme Court held Rural's copyright invalid.

Feist's importance lies in its reaffirmation of copyright's historic character as the law

of authorship and its rejection of the latter-day heresy that copyright also protects works, or portions of works, which are the product not of authorship but of "industrious collection" (or "sweat of the brow"). In short, "copyright rewards originality, not effort" (p. 1297).

In so deciding, the Court relied on the Copyright Clause of the Constitution, which authorizes Congress to grant exclusive rights in creative works only to their "Authors," and the Court's own precedents, including *Harper & Row* v. *Nation Enterprises* (1985), which reinforced prior rulings that no one can claim authorship in facts or other nonoriginal matter. In addition, the Court found that the current Copyright Act limits protection in compilations like Rural's directory to the compiler's originality in selecting or arranging preexisting data or other materials.

Feist's impact upon claims of copyright protection in so-called low authorship works beyond directories—from certain computer databases to page numbers in law reports and statutory compilations—may be great. Whether Congress can legislate noncopyright protection in these instances, for example, via the Commerce Clause, remains to be seen. But by jealously guarding the public domain against appropriation by would-be copyright owners of matter that they have not authored, *Feist* at least assures more careful consideration of such claims by Congress and the courts.

Craig Joyce

First English Evangelical Lutheran Church of Glendale v. County of Los Angeles, 482 U.S. 304 (1987), argued 14 Jan. 1987, decided 9 June 1987 by vote of 6 to 3; Rehnquist for the Court, Stevens in dissent. *First Lutheran* is the Supreme Court's landmark pronouncement that a land-use regulation can amount to a taking of property, with compensation therefore due the owner, even if the regulation is withdrawn upon a successful judicial challenge. The First English Evangelical Church owned buildings that were destroyed by a flood. After the flood a new county ordinance prohibited all construction in a flood plain area that included the church's land. California courts decided that the church could seek compensatory damages for the alleged taking only if (1) the ordinance was first declared an unlawful taking, and (2) the county then chose not to rescind the ordinance. The Court, in effect, reversed the second component of this state court ruling. The justices announced that invalidation and withdrawal of an excessive ordinance are not adequate remedies; the local government must, in addition, pay compensation for the excessive interferences with property rights that occur prior to the date that the offending ordinance is withdrawn.

Although the Court announced that compensation is due for temporary takings, it did not explain when in the land-use regulatory process a taking occurs. Nor did the Court intimate how damages might be calculated. The Court did suggest that no taking occurs "in the case of normal delays in obtaining building permits, changes in zoning ordinances, variances, and the like" (p. 321). Justice John Paul Stevens in dissent argued that the ruling would unduly inhibit local land-use regulatory processes because regulators, facing uncertain liability, might refrain from legitimate land-use planning. After the case was remanded, lower courts decided that the flood plain ordinance did not effect a taking.

Eric T. Freyfogle

First National Bank of Boston v. Bellotti, 435 U.S. 765 (1978), argued 9 Nov. 1977, decided 26 Apr. 1978 by vote of 5 to 4; Powell for the Court, Burger concurring, White, Brennan, Marshall, and Rehnquist in dissent. Reversing the highest court of Massachusetts, a bare majority of the Supreme Court held unconstitutional the portion of a state statute that banned corporations from spending to influence the outcome of a ballot referendum concerning a graduated income tax. Such corporate expenditure is protected by the First Amendment no less than anyone else's expenditure in the exercise of the right to free speech. The Court thus added another constitutional barrier to the major obstacles already erected by *Buckley* v. *Valeo* (1976) against legislative efforts to restrict campaign expenditures.

Banks and other corporations, like individuals, are free to spend their funds to advocate or oppose public policies submitted for voter consideration. They could still, however, be constitutionally prohibited, as they are by federal and many state laws, from contributing money to candidates for elective office. And, it turned out, corporations could also be prohibited from spending on behalf of a candidate independently of a candidate's campaign (*Austin* v. *Michigan Chamber of Commerce,* 1990).

In *Bellotti,* the Court appears to follow its distinction in *Buckley* between campaign expenditures and campaign contributions to candidates. Expenditures are entitled to a constitutional protection not afforded to contributions that might be thought, when large, to corrupt elected officials. *Bellotti* is significant in extending the protection of expenditures to outlays of corporate funds. Justices Byron White and William Rehnquist, in vigorous dissenting opinions, separately dispute this result, contending that states should have the power to determine the potential harm of corporate campaign expenditures.

Leon D. Epstein

Flast v. Cohen, 392 U.S. 83 (1968), argued 12 Mar. 1968, decided 10 June 1968 by vote of 8 to 1; Warren for the Court, Douglas, Stewart, and Fortas concurring separately, Harlan in dissent. A group of taxpayers sued to enjoin the allegedly unconstitutional expenditure of federal funds for the teaching of secular subjects in parochial schools. A federal court decided that they lacked standing to sue as taxpayers under *Frothingham* v. *Mellon* (1923), but the Supreme Court reversed and held that, under certain limited circumstances, taxpayers could sue in federal courts to challenge federal expenditures.

Chief Justice Earl Warren's opinion rejected the contention that *Frothingham* articulated a constitutional requirement that absolutely barred taxpayer suits. Rather, he said, *Frothingham* was more deeply rooted in policy considerations that permitted greater discretion to federal judges to entertain such suits. Taxpayer suits would be permitted if the petitioner was a proper and appropriate party to invoke federal judicial power. Standing to sue would be measured by a two-part test: first, a taxpayer could challenge the constitutionality only of the exercise of congressional power under the Taxing and Spending Clause of Article I, section 8. It would not be enough merely to challenge "incidental" expenditures under Congress's enumerated powers; second, the taxpayer must show that the challenged enactment is prohibited by a specific constitutional limitation on Congress's taxing and spending power and not merely by a general limitation on its powers, such as the Tenth Amendment.

Flast satisfied both requirements. She challenged an expenditure under the Taxing and Spending Clause alleging it violated the establishment and free exercise clauses of the First Amendment. Frothingham would have met the firxt nexus, but not the second. She had challenged the Maternity Act of 1921, which was enacted under the Taxing and Spending Clause; but she claimed only that it violated Congress's general legislative powers, the Due Process Clause of the Fifth Amendment, and the Tenth Amendment. Thus in *Flast* the Court was able to distinguish *Frothingham* without overruling it.

Justice William O. Douglas, urging the widest latitude for "private attorneys general" to sue (and thus broad taxpayer access to the courts), argued that *Frothingham* was incompatible with the spirit if not the holding in *Flast*, and should be overruled. In dissent, Justice John M. Harlan conceded that *Frothingham* was too rigid and should be modified but contended that *Flast* went too far and would open the courts to abuse that strained the judicial function.

Flast was central to the Warren Court's liberal activist philosophy of increasing public access to federal courts and making them more receptive to public law litigation. But it remained unclear how far the decision went in removing traditional barriers to such litigation. Warren formally declined to speculate on whether "the Constitution contains other specific limitations" on the taxing and spending power (p. 105). But *Flast* was widely seen as an invitation to litigants to seek redress of their constitutional grievances in the federal courts without having to demonstrate the traditional personal injury or harm. A flood of taxpayer lawsuits, many challenging the legality of the war in Vietnam, followed.

In *United States* v. **Richardson* (1974), and *Valley Forge Christian College* v. **Americans United for Separation of Church and State* (1982), the more conservative Burger Court closed the door again to taxpayer suits, at least for cases that did not meet *Flast's* specific test. Speaking in the latter case, Justice William H. Rehnquist firmly rejected the *Flast* philosophy: "Implicit [in *Flast*] is the philosophy that the business of the federal courts is correcting constitutional errors, and that 'cases and controversies' [required by Article III] are at best merely convenient vehicles for doing so and at worst nuisances that may be dispensed with . . . This

philosophy has no place in our constitutional scheme" (p. 489).

Joel B. Grossman

Fletcher v. Peck, 6 Cranch (10 U.S.) 87 (1810), argued 15 Feb. 1810, decided 16 March 1810 by vote of 4 to 1; Marshall for the Court, Johnson dissenting in part; Cushing and Chase not participating. In *Fletcher* v. *Peck* the Supreme Court employed the Contracts Clause of the Constitution as an instrument of judicial nationalization. In 1974, after notorious bribery involving virtually every member of the Georgia legislature, two U.S. senators, and many state and federal judges (including Justice James Wilson of the Supreme Court), the Georgia legislature authorized the sale of thirty-five million acres in the Yazoo area (present-day Alabama and Mississippi) to four land companies for 1.5 cents per acre. Corrupted legislators were defeated at the polls and in 1796, the legislature rescinded the Yazoo grant, invalidating all property rights derived from it. In the meantime, however, purchasers under the 1794 statute sold off millions of acres. One of the purchasers under this later sale, Robert Fletcher, brought what amounted to a collusive suit against his seller, John Peck, for breach of warranty of title, the ultimate objective being to invalidate the legislative rescission.

Fletcher v. *Peck* presented Chief Justice John Marshall with a dilemma. He had to uphold the original legislative grant, corrupted by bribery, in order to reassure investors who took land under state grants, while voiding the later, untainted statute. He therefore proceeded cautiously. The only question before the Court, Marshall said, was title; to remedy political corruption, citizens should resort to the polls, not to the courts. Having sidestepped the corruption issue, Marshall deftly took up the constitutional issues. Could legislatures deprive bona fide investors of the lands they had acquired under the corrupt grant? Each buyer, said Marshall, had procured "a title good at law, he is innocent, whatever may be the guilt of others, and equity will not subject him to the penalties attached to that guilt. All titles would be insecure, and the intercourse between man and man would be very seriously obstructed, if this principle be overturned" (pp. 133–134).

Marshall held the rescinding act an unconstitutional abridgment of the obligation of lawful contracts under the Contract

Clause. Equally important, he tied the rights protected by that clause to the natural law doctrine of vested rights: when an agreement was "in its nature a contract, when absolute rights have vested under that contract, a repeal of the law cannot divest those rights" (p. 134). He concluded that "either by principles which are common to our free institutions, or by the particular provisions of the constitution of the United States" (p. 139), a state legislature could not enact legislation that impaired contracts or disturbed land titles supposedly acquired in good faith.

Fletcher v. *Peck* provoked public outcry, particularly from proponents of states' rights who accused the Court of pandering to speculators and of imposing a doctrinal strait-jacket on frontier legislatures. Marshall's opinion did in fact support land speculators and protected the titles of some unscrupulous investors as well as bona fide purchasers of western lands. But Marshall considered contractual rights and obligations essential to the American experiment in self-rule. Thus, *Fletcher*'s legacy was complex: it was a bench-mark in Marshall's campaign to protect the law of property and contracts from legislative interference, an early statement about the need to separate politics from law, and an example of judicial receptivity to the needs of investors in an age of capital scarcity. At the same time, it reflected the Court's commitment to the security of contracts and property rights as protected under the Constitution.

□ C. Peter Magrath, *Yazoo: Law and Politics in the New Republic* (1966).

Sandra F. VanBurkleo

Fletcher v. Rhode Island See LICENSE CASES.

Florida v. Bostick, 501 U.S. 429 (1991), argued 26 Feb. 1991, decided 20 June 1991 by vote of 6 to 3; O'Connor for the Court, Marshall in dissent. What constitutes a "seizure" within the meaning of the Fourth Amendment? Police practices need not be "reasonable"—indeed, are not regulated by the Fourth Amendment at all—unless they are considered "searches" or "seizures." In this case, which involved a growing anti-drug police tactic known as "working the buses" (randomly approaching a bus passenger and asking him for identification and to grant permission to search his luggage),

the Court took a narrow view of what constitutes a "seizure."

Police boarded an interstate bus on which Bostick was a passenger, asked for his identification, and questioned him. Bostick later claimed that an illegal "seizure" had occurred because a reasonable person in those circumstances would not have felt free to leave; moreover, he had done nothing to arouse suspicion. Bostick contended the illegal seizure tainted and invalidated his subsequent "consent" to search his luggage (a search that turned up cocaine).

The Florida Supreme Court agreed. It excluded the cocaine and banned the use of bus-boarding tactics. But the U.S. Supreme Court held that the state court had committed error when it adopted a flat rule prohibiting the police from boarding buses and approaching passengers at random as a means of drug interdiction.

The Court noted that Bostick's movement was restricted by a factor independent of police conduct—by his being a passenger on a bus. (If he had left the bus, Bostick would have risked being stranded and losing whatever luggage he had locked away in the luggage compartment.) Under such circumstances, the Court pointed out, the appropriate inquiry is not whether a reasonable person would feel free to leave but whether he or she would feel free to "terminate the encounter" or to "ignore the police presence" (p. 2387). Although the Court remanded the case to the state court for further findings on this issue, it broadly hinted that Bostick had not been "seized" within the meaning of the Fourth Amendment.

Yale Kamisar

Fordice, United States v., 505 U.S. 717 (1992), argued 13 Nov. 1991, decided 26 June 1992 by unanimous vote; White for the Court, O'Connor and Thomas concurring, Scalia concurring in the judgment in part and dissenting in part.

The Supreme Court changed the face of public education with its decision in *Brown* v. *Board of Education* (1954) and its progeny. *Brown I* held that separate schools for different races were not equal and *Brown II* (1955) declared that public schools had an affirmative obligation to dismantle their de jure segregated system. While desegregation made slow but progressive strides at the elementary and secondary levels, the concept of "separate but equal" persisted at the university level. Mississippi's public university system was established in 1848 and the system remained exclusively for white students until 1871, when it opened a separate school to educate African-Americans. By the 1950s Mississippi had established five universities for white students and three universities for African-American students.

By the mid-1980s Mississippi's university system remained largely segregated. The university system claimed to have replaced its previous discriminatory practices with good-faith, race-neutral policies and procedures. Yet there was less then 1 percent of African-American students enrolled at Mississippi's historically white universities. A class action suit, filed against the governor of Mississippi and various other state agencies and officers, reached the Supreme Court. The justices ruled that the mere adoption of race-neutral policies did not satisfy the state's obligation to dismantle its prior dual system Analyzing the admission standards, program duplication, and operations of all eight public universities, the Court found that policies traceable to prior segregation continued to foster discriminatory effects.

The majority of the Court emphasized that the burden of proof was on the state to show that it had dismantled its prior segregated system. Justice Antonin Scalia, however, filed a dissenting opinion expressing his disagreement with placing theburden of proof standard on the state in the context of higher education.

Anna Lisa Garcia

Frank v. Mangum, 237 U.S. 309 (1915), argued 25–26 Feb. 1915, decided 19 Apr. 1915 by vote of 7 to 2; Pitney for the Court, Holmes in dissent. In one of the most sensational murder cases of the era, Leo Frank, one of the owners of the National Pencil Factory in Atlanta, was accused of killing a thirteen-year-old female employee. In a clear miscarriage of justice, Frank was convicted and sentenced to death. An atmosphere of violence surrounding the courtroom had led the trial judge to ask that the defendant and his counsel not be present when the verdict was returned. As the jurors were being polled, their voices were drowned out by the cheers of the crowd outside.

After the failure of numerous motions and state appeals, Frank's lawyers sought a writ of habeas corpus in the federal district court; its denial brought the case to the Supreme Court. Counsel argued that mob intimidation had deprived Frank of due process of

law. Justice Mahlon Pitney, for the majority, saw any trial impropriety cleansed by the Georgia appellate process, but Justice Oliver Wendell Holmes, in dissent, condemned the trial and the intimidation of the jury.

Although the Court during this time period liberally used the Due Process Clause of the Fourteenth Amendment to supervise state action concerning property, it hesitated in finding a similar federal supervisory power over state criminal proceedings. Such reluctance would dissipate as early as *Moore v. Dempsey* (1923), but this was much too late to save Leo Frank, who was lynched after Georgia's courageous governor had commuted the sentence to life imprisonment.

John E. Semonche

Freeman v. Pitts, 503 U.S. 467 (1992), argued 7 October 1991, decided 31 March 1992 by vote of 8 to 0; Rehnquist for the Court, Scalia concurring, Souter concurring, Blackmun concurring in an opinion joined by Stevens and O'Connor, Thomas not participating. This case continued the line of cases following *Brown* v. *Board of Educ. (II)* (1955) governing court oversight of constitutionally mandated desegregation of public schools. *Green* v. *Board of New Kent County* (1968) elaborated the parameters of court analysis of whether a formerly de jure segregated school district has effectively desegregated, that is, achieved "unitary status," and hence may be relieved of further obligations under a court-ordered remedial action plan. In *Freeman*, the Supreme Court considered whether a district court may relinquish supervision of a school district's efforts partially, declaring unitary status as to some aspects of a system's operations while withholding that finding as to other aspects. The DeKalb County School District had moved for final dismissal of pending desegregation litigation in light of its remedial efforts. The district court found that the district had become unitary with regard to four "*Green* factors"—student assignments, transportation, physical facilities, and extracurricular activities—but had not satisfactorily acted as to two important factors over which the district had virtually complete control: faculty assignments and resource allocation. Reversing the decision of the court of appeals, the justices agreed that a court may, where justified, order incremental or partial withdrawal of judicial supervision and control as to the areas of compliance, and retain supervision as to the areas of noncompliance.

Although *Freeman* sanctioned district courts' consideration of whether black students continue to receive a poorer quality of education than whites—a factor not named by *Green*—the decision underscored the Court's growing commitment to the restoration of school systems to state and local authorities, a trend that has continued in subsequent desegregation litigation (for example, *Belk* v. *Charlotte-Mecklenburg Bd. of Educ.*, 2001; *Missouri* v. *Jenkins*, 1995).

Rhonda V. Magee Andrews

Frontiero v. Richardson, 411 U.S. 677 (1973), argued 17 Jan. 1973, decided 14 May 1973 by vote of 8 to 1; Brennan for plurality, Powell, Burger, Blackmun, and Stewart concurring; Rehnquist in dissent. This case presented a constitutional challenge to a federal law that awarded a salary supplement in the form of an extra housing allowance and extra medical benefits to every married male in the "uniformed services" of the United States. A married female in the military, however, received the supplement only if she could prove she paid more than half of her husband's living costs. The suit was brought by Sharron Frontiero, an Air Force lieutenant who paid slightly under half of her husband's living costs. Her challenge relied on the equal protection concept implied in the Fifth Amendment Due Process Clause.

Frontiero's lawyers argued that while there might be some reason for the differential treatment, that should not be enough to sustain the statute because gender discrimination, like race discrimination, should be viewed as constitutionally "suspect" and upheld only if the government proves "compelling" justification. This argument had been tried two years earlier in *Reed* v. *Reed* (1971) but the Court's opinion had ignored it, relying instead on the rational basis test to strike down the statute. In *Frontiero* the justices exhumed and dissected *Reed*.

Justice William Brennan's opinion for the plurality of four argued that the *Reed* result made no sense under the rational basis test. The statute in that case had preferred males to females as estate administrators; there was some reason for this, since males in 1971 were more conversant than females with the world of business. Brennan insisted that *Reed's* result implied that gender classifications are, like race, suspect and therefore demand strict scrutiny, which requires proof that the classification is "

necessary for attaining a compelling government interest." They argued that this test is appropriate for four reasons: (1) sex like race is an "immutable" accident of birth, which is generally irrelevant to the purpose of a statute; (2) like race it has long been the basis of invidious discrimination in the United States; (3) like race it is a highly visible trait; and (4) Congress, by proposing the Equal Rights Amendment (E.R.A.) and sending it to the states for ratification, had endorsed the idea that sex classifications are "inherently invidious" (p. 687) or "suspect" (p. 688). Respect for a "co-equal branch of government" thus counseled treating sex as a suspect classification.

Justice Lewis Powell agreed that the classification was unconstitutional, but argued to the contrary that respect for other branches of government and for the constitutional amending process counseled delay in making gender a suspect classification, for that change was precisely the point of the E.R.A. (At the time of this decision, thirty states of the required thirty-eight had ratified the E.R.A., and six years remained of the initial seven-year ratification period.) Powell reminded the Court that *Reed* had struck down the sex discrimination in question without invoking strict scrutiny and insisted that the *Reed* standard would "abundantly" support Frontiero's challenge as well. Stewart's lone concurrence avoided all these issues and was simply a one-sentence statement that the law challenged here worked an "invidious discrimination" and was thus unconstitutional on the authority of *Reed*.

Justice William Rehnquist's dissent simply cited as its foundation the reasoning of the district court judge, whose opinion had employed the rational basis test and had argued that the savings accrued in not requiring married servicemen to document actual financial dependency of their wives, when more than a million cases were involved and when only a small fraction was likely to be ineligible for the benefit, amply satisfied the test. Judge Rives mentioned in a footnote that *Reed*, too, had employed the rational basis test.

Thus, although the Court upheld Frontiero's claim and invalidated the law by an 8-to-1 vote, there was no majority for establishing sex as a suspect classification. That issue was not explicitly addressed again by the Supreme Court until *Craig* v. *Boren* (1976), in which the justices adopted a test somewhere between strict scrutiny and the rational basis test, known variously as "heightened" or "intermediate" scrutiny.

Leslie Friedman Goldstein

Frothingham v. Mellon, 262 U.S. 447 (1923), argued together with **Massachusetts v. Mellon,** 3–4 May 1923, decided 4 June 1923 by a vote of 9 to o; Sutherland for the Court. Frothingham and the state of Massachusetts brought suit against the U.S. secretary of treasury to invalidate the Federal Maternity Act of 1921. Under this statute the federal government would contribute funds to the states for the purpose of "promoting the welfare and hygiene of maternity and infancy." Participating states were required to comply with federal regulations and match federal appropriations.

Massachusetts claimed the federal plan usurped authority reserved to the states by the Tenth Amendment. Frothingham argued that the use of federal appropriations to carry out the plan resulted in a taking of her property without due process of law. The Court did not address either of these substantive complaints but rejected the cases for want of jurisdiction. Frothingham's case depended upon whether she had the required standing to challenge this statute in court. Her only claim to that status was that she was a federal taxpayer. Reasoning that her interest in any federal appropriations act was remote, the Court ruled that she did not have standing. To obtain standing, it ruled, a taxpayer must not only present a claim that the statute is invalid but also must show that some immediate personal injury was sustained. Here there was no case or controversy. This rule against taxpayer standing remained until it was modified in* Flast v. Cohen (1968).

Paul Kens

Fullilove v. Klutznick, 448 U.S. 448 (1980), argued 27 Nov. 1979, decided 2 July 1980 by vote of 6 to 3; Burger for the Court, Marshall, Brennan, and Blackmun concurring, Stewart, Rehnquist, and Stevens in dissent. In the Public Works Employment Act of 1977, Congress provided for a 10 percent "set aside" for minority business enterprises (MBEs). This was the first federal statute containing an explicitly race conscious classification since the Freedman's Bureau Act of 1866.

The MBE provision was challenged by a group of nonminority contractors, which

argued that the provision violated the "equal protection component" of the Fifth Amendment's Due Process Clause recognized in *Bolling v. Sharpe* (1954). A federal district court dismissed the suit and the Court of Appeals for the Second Circuit affirmed the lower court's action.

Six justices of the Supreme Court voted to uphold the set-asides, although they differed sharply in their reasoning. One plurality (Burger, Powell, and White) deferred to the unique status accorded congressional judgments on racial issues by Article I's spending and commerce clauses and the Fourteenth Amendment's Enforcement Clause (section 5). Congress need not "act in a wholly 'color-blind' fashion" (p. 482), and the set-aside were a "reasonably necessary means of furthering the compelling governmental interest in redressing the discrimination that affects minority contractors" (p. 515). Chief Justice Warren Burger's opinion accepted the government's contention that Congress had acted with due deliberation and knowledge even though there had been no specific legislative hearings or deliberations on the set-aside. The 1977 act did not appear out of nowhere; Congress had been struggling with the plight of MBEs for years, and its members were familiar with the discriminatory practices of the construction industry. The evidentiary and justiciability restraints that hobble judicial action do not apply to Congress. It may act to eradicate social evils where a court must wait for a case challenging constitutional or statutory violations. Furthermore this was not an inflexible quota; it was temporary in duration, limited in coverage, and selective in enforcement.

A second plurality (Marshall, Brennan, and Blackmun) relied on the rationale developed by Brennan in *Regents of the University of California v. Bakke* (1978). Since the set-asides did not elevate any individual or group to a status of racial superiority, the stringent test of equal protection applied to invidious racial distinctions was inapposite. However, the risk that even so well-intentioned a program might impose unfair burdens on innocent third parties necessitated judicial scrutiny more demanding than the traditional equal protection test. The set-aside provision, in the opinion's judgment, withstood this heightened scrutiny.

The three dissenters were not persuaded. For Potter Stewart and William Rehnquist, the MBE set-asides were a return to the discredited *Plessy v. Ferguson* (1896) rule of preferences "based on lineage"—of a "government of privileges based on birth" (p. 531). Government endorsement of racial classifications, even when these classifications are drawn to advance salutary rather than invidious objectives, perpetuates the socially divisive belief that race should count. Rather than celebrating the plenary powers granted to Congress, Stewart and Rehnquist argued that if "a law is unconstitutional, it is no less unconstitutional just because it is a product of the Congress of the United States." In their opinion, only courts of equity acting in proceedings that identify specific victims and victimizers possess the "dispassionate objectivity" and "flexibility" necessary to "mold a race conscious remedy" consistent with the Constitution's command of strict race neutrality (p. 527).

John Paul Stevens's dissent emphasized the absence of hearings on the MBE provision or any legislative findings of discriminatory practices. He questioned whether the program would distribute compensation "in an even handed way" (p. 539) and not, as is often the case, to the least disadvantaged members of the group. And he questioned whether non black minority groups, which in his judgment lacked the discriminatory history of blacks that warranted special treatment, could or should qualify for special treatment.

Fullilove's impact was substantial. The ruling encouraged minority set-aside programs at the national level (e.g., the Highway Improvement Act of 1982 and the International Security and Development Assistance Authorizations Act of 1983) and at the state and local levels. The state and local versions, however, have not weathered judicial scrutiny. In *Richmond* v. *J.A. Croson Co.* (1989), the Court held that the special dispensation for color-conscious preferences accorded Congress did not extend to other governmental entities. Six years later, in *Adarand Constructors, Inc.* v. *Peña* (1995) the justices struck an even harder blow at affirmative action by holding that federal affirmative action programs, like state affirmative action programs, had to meet a test of "strict scrutiny" in order to be constitutional.

□ Drew S. Days III, "Fullilove," *Yale Law Journal* 96 (January 1987): 453–485.

Timothy J. O'Neill

Furman v. Georgia, 408 U.S. 238 (1972), argued 17 Jan. 1972, decided 29 June 1972

per curiam by vote of 5 to 4; Stewart, White, Douglas, Brennan, and Marshall each concurred separately; Burger, Blackmun, Powell, and Rehnquist dissented jointly and separately. The Supreme Court, for the first time, struck down the death penalty under the cruel and unusual punishment clause of the Eighth Amendment. A jury in Georgia had convicted Furman for murder, and juries in Georgia and Texas had convicted two other petitioners for rape. All three juries imposed the death penalty without any specific guides or limits on their discretion. The Supreme Court in *McGautha* v. *California* (1971) had previously held that such guidelines were unnecessary. All three petitioners were African-American. Three justices for the majority found that jury discretion produced a random pattern among those receiving the death penalty and that this randomness was cruel and unusual. Two justices found capital punishment a per se violation of the Constitution.

More specifically, Justice William O. Douglas concluded that death was disproportionately applied to the poor and socially disadvantaged; he virtually equated the Eighth Amendment with equal protection values. Justice Potter Stewart argued that the failure of the legislature to call for a mandatory death sentence, coupled with the infrequent imposition and execution of death sentences, in practice made the penalty cruel and unusual in the same way that being struck by lightning is cruel and unusual. White insisted that the infrequency of execution prevented the penalty from serving as an effective deterrent and from consistently meeting social needs for retribution. For White the penalty's social irrationality made it cruel and unusual.

Justices William Brennan and Thurgood Marshall both concluded that the death penalty was per se cruel and unusual. Brennan found the punishment degrading to human dignity, arbitrarily severe, and unnecessary. Marshall attacked the penalty most directly, finding it excessive, unnecessary, and offensive to contemporary values.

The dissenters argued that the courts should not challenge legislative judgments about the desirability and effectiveness of punishments. They also pointed to opinion polls showing general public support for the penalty.

Furman halted all executions in those thirty-nine states that sanctioned the death penalty. More than six hundred people waited on death row at the time. *Furman* also seemed to create three Eighth Amendment options: mandatory death sentences for crimes carefully defined by statute, development of guidelines to standardize jury discretion, and outright abolition. Of these, outright abolition was least likely, since a majority of the justices acknowledged the validity of the retributive motive in punishment and only two condemned the penalty per se. But, like life and death themselves, the course of the law has taken unforseen turns.

In *Gregg* v. *Georgia* (1976), the Court embraced a form of guided jury discretion, although the guidelines do not systematically reduce randomness. Juries sitting in the penalty phases of capital trials as prescribed by *Gregg* consider unique aggravating and mitigating circumstances in each case. This trend has effectively overruled *Furman*'s holding because juries, even when they operate under statutory guidelines, consider unique circumstances. This process inevitably perpetuates inconsistencies in sentencing, but the Court no longer finds these inconsistencies constitutionally unacceptable.

Lief H. Carter

44 Liquormart/Peoples Super Liquor Stores v. Rhode Island, 517 U.S. 484 (1996), argued 1 Nov. 1995, decided 13 May 1996 by vote of 9 to 0; Stevens for the Court, Kennedy, Souter, Ginsburg, Thomas, Scalia, O'Connor, Breyer, and Rehnquist concurring in different parts. The *44 Liquormart* case was the most important free speech case of the 1995–96 term, but it was also limited in its impact, since it dealt with advertising as speech rather than the more contested areas of political and religious expression.

The case resulted from a 1956 Rhode Island law, similar to ones in ten other states, that banned liquor prices in newspapers and other advertising media, even to the exclusion of using the word "sale." The ban also extended to media in other adjoining states that published or broadcast into Rhode Island. Such measures had assumed increasing importance by the early 1990s, as the Clinton administration and various consumer groups attempted to restrict the use of cigarettes, fatty foods, and the abuse of alcohol.

Historically, commercial speech received less protection than did, for example, political expression. In 1976 the justices held in *Virginia State Board of Pharmacy* v. *Virginia Citizens Consumer Council* that a

free-enterprise economy depended on the free flow of information and that truthful, nonmisleading advertising was entitled to First Amendment protection. The Court reiterated its position in *Central Hudson Gas* v. *Public Service Commission of New York* (1980), where the justices established a four-part test that stressed the accuracy and lawfulness of the advertising. At the same time, such speech has never enjoyed the same high degree of protection granted political and artistic expression.

The uncertain constitutional status of commercial speech became evident as the Rhode Island case moved through the lower federal courts. The federal district court in Rhode Island that originally heard the *44 Liquormart* case declared the Rhode Island statute unconstitutional, but the Court of Appeals for the First Circuit overturned that decision and found in favor of Rhode Island. The court of appeals noted especially that competitive price advertising would ultimately increase sales, and hence alcohol consumption, and that the Twenty-First Amendment (repealing Prohibition) gave the advertising ban an added presumption of validity.

Counsel for Rhode Island argued before the Supreme Court that forcing customers to enter the store to learn the price of liquor would indeed drive up the price and restrict consumption. The authority to limit advertising of prices was clearly within the police powers of the state, since, among other things, it would likely result in fewer drunk drivers on the road. In many ways, however, the economic analysis presented by Rhode Island was inconclusive.

Lawyers for the liquor sellers took a different tack by drawing on the *Central Hudson* precedent. They argued that since the state permitted the sale of liquor, it could not also argue that it was so dangerous that it could not be freely advertised.

The high court sided with the liquor store and struck down the ban. Justice John Paul Stevens's opinion held that "a state legislature does not have the broad discretion to suppress truthful, nonmisleading information for paternalistic purposes" (p. 531). Justices Anthony M. Kennedy, Clarence Thomas, and Ruth Bader Ginsburg joined in this reasoning, although each of them penned separate concurring opinions, all of which made the point that Rhode Island had failed to demonstrate that it had a substantial state interest in keeping the price of alcohol high and consumption low. Moreover, even though the Twenty-First Amendment had repealed Prohibition and gave the states the power to regulate alcohol, it did not follow that First Amendment free speech guarantees were ended. Justice Thomas, for his part, argued that commercial speech should be heavily protected and that government should never keep its citizens ignorant of the choices before them. Justice Antonin Scalia agreed that the law should be struck down, but he found different grounds. According to Scalia, neither the framers of the First or the Fourteenth Amendments had any concept of commercial speech. He urged the Court, therefore, to avoid further muddying the interpretive waters and merely affirm its existing precedents.

The other justices—Sandra Day O'Connor, William H. Rehnquist, Stephen G. Breyer, and David H. Souter—believed that while the ban should have been overturned, the grounds that the Court used should have been narrower. O'Connor noted that the states could use other means for promoting temperance, such as raising taxes and establishing minimum prices.

While the 44 Liquormart decision grabbed national attention, its impact was limited to price advertising, a special category of commercial speech. Both federal and state officials have continued successfully to keep alcohol and cigarette advertising away from children.

Kermit L. Hall

G

Garcia v. San Antonio Metropolitan Transit Authority, 469 U.S. 528 (1985), argued 19 Mar. 1984, reargued 1 Oct. 1984, decided 19 Feb. 1985 by vote of 5 to 4; Blackmun for the Court, joined by Brennan, White, Marshall, and Stevens; Powell in dissent, joined by Burger, Rehnquist, and O'Connor; Rehnquist filed a separate dissent; O'Connor filed a separate dissent, joined by Powell and Rehnquist.

Garcia reversed the Supreme Court's 1976 decision in *National League of Cities* v. *Usery*. That decision had restricted Congress's power to regulate the states "as states"; *Garcia* removed virtually all federalism-based constitutional limitations on congressional power under the Commerce Clause.

Garcia involved the application of the maximum hours and minimum wage provisions of the Fair Labor Standards Act to a city-owned and -operated public transportation system. Under the rule established in *National League of Cities*, as summarized by the Court in *Hodel* v. *Virginia Surface Mining and Reclamation Association* (1981), the economic activities of the states or of their political subdivisions could be regulated by Congress only if four tests were met. First, the statute at issue had to regulate the states "as States." Second, the statute must address "matters that are indisputably attribute[s] of state sovereignty"; third, such regulation must "directly impair" the states' ability to "structure integral operations in areas

of traditional governmental functions." Finally, "the nature of the federal interest" must be substantial enough to "justify state submission" (p. 264). Despite a number of attempts to clarify the meaning of these tests, no clear lines had been established at the time of *Garcia*.

On the surface, *Garcia* seemed to present the question of whether operating a municipal transportation system was a "traditional" or "essential" state function under the *National League of Cities* rule, and whether the federal regulation of such a system interfered with an attribute of state sovereignty. In previous cases, federal courts had held that licensing ambulance drivers, operating a municipal airport, and disposing of solid wastes were protected from federal regulation under *National League of Cities*, while regulating traffic on public roads, operating a mental health facility, and providing in-house domestic services for the aged and handicapped were not protected. Instead of making such a determination in *Garcia*, Justice Harry Blackmun gave up, and overruled *National League of Cities* altogether.

Blackmun's frustration with the Court's inability to arrive at meaningful and clear distinctions under the *National League of Cities* precedent is evident throughout his opinion. The distinctions drawn in prior cases, he declared, were "elusive at best"; such distinctions were "unworkable," "illusory," and not susceptible to "reasonably

115

objective" measurement. The emphasis on traditional governmental functions, moreover, was unfairly biased against state activities that were innovative or unorthodox.

Rejecting all such attempts, Blackmun held that the protection of the states' interests in the federal system was left not to the courts but to the other institutions of government, particularly Congress. "The structure of the Federal Government itself was relied on to insulate the interests of the States," he wrote (p. 551). "The Framers chose to rely on a federal system in which special restraints on federal power over the States inhered principally in the workings of the National Government itself, rather than in discrete limitations on the objects of federal authority" (p. 552). Specifically, Blackmun cited the representation of the states in the Senate, and noted the many federal laws that operated to the benefit of the states.

Four justices dissented. Among other arguments, the dissenters challenged Blackmun's assertion that the federal government adequately represents state interests. "Members of Congress are elected from the various States," wrote Justice Lewis Powell, "but once in office they are Members of the Federal Government" (pp. 564–565). The dissenters pointed out the significance of the Seventeenth Amendment, which provided for the direct election of Senators, and invoked *Marbury* v. *Madison* and the doctrine of judicial supremacy to counter the majority's conclusion that the Court should play no role in the supervision of congressional regulation of the states.

Most significantly, the dissenters indicated a hope that *Garcia* would itself be overruled some day. Justice William Rehnquist, in a brief but painful dissent, expressed confidence that the *National League of Cities* principle, now repudiated, "will . . . in time command the support of a majority of this Court" (p. 580). "The Court today surveys the battle scene of federalism and sounds a retreat," added O'Connor. "I share Justice Rehnquist's belief that this Court will in time again assume its constitutional responsibility" (pp. 580, 589) Since *Garcia* the Court has moved aggressively to reassert the prerogatives of the states. For example, in *United States* v. *Lopez* (1995) the justices struck down a federal law making it a crime knowingly to possess a firearm within one thousand feet of a public or private school because the statute did not flow from any enumerated power. In *City of Boerne, Texas* v. *Flores* (1997)

the Court reaffirmed its exclusive power to judge the constitutionality of basic rights, striking down the Religious Restoration Act of 1993. A majority of the justices found that Congress had exceeded its authority when it passed the law giving the practice of religion more protection than the Court itself had found to be constitutionally required. In doing so, the justices rejected Congress's expansive interpretation of its own powers and took an increasingly generous view of the role of the states in the federal system.

William Lasser

Gault, In re, 387 U.S. 1 (1967), argued 6 Dec. 1966, decided 15 May 1967 by vote of 8 to 1; Fortas for the Court, Black and White concurring, Harlan concurring in part and dissenting in part; Stewart in dissent. From the turn of the century until the 1960s, the assumptions of juvenile justice had drawn inspiration from the reform ideology of the Progressives. State intervention into the juvenile's life was justified as *parens patriae*, that is, a protective, paternal interest in the welfare of a wayward or otherwise distressed child. This approach led to a nationwide institutional distinction between the adversary process of adult criminal adjudication and the flexible and informal decision making created for juvenile proceedings. Separate legislative codes and correctional alternatives were established for juveniles whose behavior would have been considered criminal if they were adults.

The growing problem of juvenile misconduct and a popular perception that the juvenile justice system was failing both society and its clientele called into question the assumptions of that system and attracted the attention of both scholars and government officials. Following the Supreme Court's landmark rulings that brought unprecedented procedural reforms to federal and state criminal justice systems, it seemed inevitable that the justices would also place the nation's juvenile justice system under the scrutiny of constitutional due process.

The Court first signaled its interest in the area in *Kent* v. *United States* (1966), a 5-to-4 decision that rejected a cursory waiver of Kent's juvenile status so that he might be tried as an adult. The majority used the occasion to speculate that a juvenile—faced with incarceration in an informal juvenile proceeding, yet unprotected by the due process guarantees afforded adults under the Constitution—might encounter "the worst of both worlds" (p. 556). Developing this theme boldly a year later, Justice Abe Fortas's opinion in *Gault* attacked the entire juvenile justice system, with only Justice Potter Stewart disagreeing on the merits of the case.

At issue was the commitment of fifteen-year-old Gerald Gault to Arizona's State Industrial School until his majority (a maximum of six years), following his adjudication as a "delinquent child" for making an obscene phone call to a neighbor while on probation for another juvenile offense. Had Gault been tried as an adult, his maximum punishment would have been a fifty-dollar fine or two months' incarceration. What made Gault's case significant was that, despite the severity of his punishment, Arizona law afforded him virtually no "due process" at all—no offical notice of his precipitous hearings (he was committed within a week of the offense), no notification that counsel could be present at the hearings, no opportunity to confront or cross-examine the woman who complained about the phone call, and no protection against self-incrimination. His questionable admission about taking part in the phone call became the primary basis for the commitment.

Fortas took the opportunity to question broadly the wisdom of *parens patriae* as the guiding principle of juvenile adjudication. He then tailored a careful holding that extended many (but not all) of the rights of adult criminal defendants, under the Due Process Clause of the Fourteenth Amendment, to those juveniles subject to a deprivation of liberty upon adjudication of delinquency. Included were adequate and timely notice of charges and hearings, notice of the right to counsel at adjudication, the right to confront and cross-examine witnesses, and the protection against self-incrimination. Justice Fortas argued that the extension of these protections would not interfere fundamentally with the distinctive informality and flexibility of juvenile adjudication.

The majority opinion was controversial both on the Court and off. Justices Hugo Black and John M. Harlan used the case as an occasion to continue their ongoing debate about the proper interpretation of "due process" as it applied to the states—a debate that grew more heated in a subsequent juvenile justice case, *In re *Winship* (1970). Justice Stewart dissented primarily on the ground that the majority's decision ran the risk of

making the juvenile process identical to the adult criminal process, thus recreating the problem that the Progressives had attacked at the turn of the century.

Gault and its practical consequences for juvenile justice (particularly the decision's emphasis on procedural compliance and its injection of defense counsel into the system) have produced considerable controversy, although the case remains the constitutional landmark for juvenile adjudication. Critics have attacked the decision as part of the larger "due process revolution" of the 1960s, charging that the Warren Court majority placed too much faith in the efficacy of procedural remedies to accomplish substantive reforms in criminal justice. Particularly with regard to *Gault*, critics complain that an overemphasis on due process, on the one hand, diverts attention from the larger substantive issue of the system's fundamental capacity to develop appropriate remedies for delinquent behavior and, on the other hand, adds to the case management woes of the already overburdened juvenile courts.

□ John R. Sutton, *Stubborn Children: Controlling Delinquency in the United States, 1640–1981* (1988). Stanton Wheeler and Leonard S. Cottrell, Jr., *Juvenile Delinquency: Its Prevention and Control* (1966). Albert R. Matheny

Geduldig v. Aiello, 417 U.S. 484 (1974), argued 26 Mar. 1974, decided 17 June 1974 by vote of 6 to 3; Stewart for the Court, Brennan in dissent. Pregnancy was the topic of two important Supreme Court decisions in its 1973 term. In January, *Cleveland Board of Education* v. *LaFleur* (1974) effectively ended mandatory maternity leaves. Anyone who thought that *LaFleur* signaled a new judicial sensitivity to women's rights was quickly disillusioned by *Geduldig*, decided in June.

Carolyn Aiello was one of three state employees who challenged California's disability benefits system. This plan, financed by salary deductions, excluded from coverage any hospitalization resulting from a normal pregnancy. The workers claimed that the denial of pregnancy benefits constituted sex discrimination and therefore violated the Equal Protection Clause of the Fourteenth Amendment.

The Supreme Court upheld the law, although it had already been amended to include pregnancy. Justice Potter Stewart pointed out that *LaFleur* had relied, not on equal protection, but on due process, and was therefore not a precedent to be followed. California's policy benefits, he said, bore the required rational relationship to the state's legitimate goal of reducing costs. And the law did not discriminate against women; instead, it merely distinguished between pregnant women and all other (i.e., non-pregnant) persons: "There is no risk from which men are protected and women are not" (pp. 496–497). Justice William Brennan disagreed, writing in his dissent that policy distinctions based on "physical characteristics inextricably linked to one sex" denied equal protection (p. 501). The Pregnancy Discrimination Act of 1978 enacted the dissenters' view by requiring equal treatment for pregnant employees.

Judith A. Baer

Geier v. American Honda Motor Co., 529 U.S. 861 (2000), argued 7 December 1999, decided 22 May 2000, by vote of 5 to 4; Breyer for the Court, Stevens in dissent. The doctrine of implied preemption dictates that federal law overrides state law when state law is in conflict with federal law, as when state law obstructs the accomplishment of the objectives of federal law. The Court determined in *Geier* that state tort claims against an auto manufacturer posed an obstacle to the achievement of the safety objectives of a federal statute and federal regulations. State-law tort actions were therefore preempted.

Plaintiff brought state tort claims against defendant American Honda Motor for injuries she received in a car crash allegedly because her Honda automobile lacked an airbag passive restraint device. The auto was manufactured when federal regulations did not require the installation of an airbag but instead allowed manufacturers a number of passive restraint options. The Court, in preempting the state tort claims, opined that a state tort damage award would effectively set a mandatory airbag standard that would obstruct the objective of the federal regulations, which was to achieve safety through a phasing-in of passive restraint devices.

The Court indicated that even if the federal statute contained a provision that expressly preempted some state law but failed to demonstrate congressional intent to preempt state tort law, ordinary preemption principles still applied to impliedly preempt state tort law in an appropriate

case, as when state law conflicted with or posed an obstacle to federal law. A court could even imply preemption when the federal statute contained a clause that appeared to save common-law claims from override. The decision put in question the survival of state tort claims in the face of numerous federal statutes that regulate safety, traditionally an area of state tort law concern.

Susan Raeker-Jordan

Gelpcke v. Dubuque, 1 Wall. (68 U.S.) 175 (1864), argued 15 Dec. 1863, decided 11 Jan. 1864 by vote of 8 to 1; Swayne for the Court, Miller in dissent, Taney not participating. The competition of northern cities before the Civil War for rail traffic resulted in imprudent bond issues, with consequent defaults and repudiations. Dubuque, Iowa, promoters issued bonds in amounts that exceeded the debt limit specified in the state constitution. A reform-minded state supreme court reversed earlier holdings sustaining the validity of the bonds. The bondholders appealed to the U.S. Supreme Court, arguing that federal courts, under *Swift* v. *Tyson* (1842), could construe state constitutions when state supreme court precedent was inconsistent. In *Leffingwell* v. *Warren* (1862), the Supreme Court had stated that it was obliged to follow the most recent state supreme court holdings construing state constitutions.

Yet in *Gelpcke* v. *Dubuque,* Justice Noah Swayne rejected the latest Iowa Supreme Court construction. Federal judges were not bound by state courts' oscillations, Swayne asserted. "We shall never immolate truth, justice, and the law, because a State tribunal has erected the altar and decreed the sacrifice," he wrote (pp. 206–207). Justice Samuel Freeman Miller (an Iowan) dissented, arguing that only state judges should have final authority to construe the state's constitution and laws.

Investors, law writers, and legal academics praised *Gelpcke*. Critics charged that it deepened animosities between federal judges and the elected state courts and that it throttled urban development. In its disdain for state judicial authority, *Gelpcke* was a precursor of substantive due process.

Harold M. Hyman

Genesee Chief v. Fitzhugh, 12 How. (53 U.S.) 443 (1852), argued 2, 5, 6 Jan. 1852, decided 20 Feb. 1852 by vote of 8 to 1; Taney for the Court, Daniel in dissent. In *Genesee*

Chief the Supreme Court expanded the scope of federal admiralty jurisdiction to encompass navigable fresh water lakes and rivers. The Supreme Court in an 1825 admiralty decision, *The Thomas Jefferson*, had adopted the traditional English rule restricting admiralty jurisdiction to tidal waters. Congress, however, desired to promote trade on interior waterways and enacted a statute in 1845 extending the jurisdiction of the federal courts to certain cases arising on the Great Lakes. The Supreme Court, in an opinion by Chief Justice Roger B. Taney, sustained the 1845 act and overruled its earlier decision. Taney emphasized that the English rule was unsuitable in the United States, with its network of navigable rivers and lakes. He concluded that admiralty jurisdiction depended upon "the navigable character of the water, and not upon the ebb and flow of the tide" (p. 457). In dissent, Justice Peter V. Daniel maintained that federal admiralty power was determined by the English practice at the time the Constitution was ratified.

The decision in *Genesee Chief* significantly encouraged commerce and navigation. By rejecting the tidal waters doctrine, the Supreme Court allowed Congress to regulate shipping on inland lakes and rivers by uniform admiralty principles. Moreover, the ruling exemplified the Court's willingness to accommodate legal doctrine to the emergence of new technology. The invention of the steamboat had revolutionized travel on inland waterways and rendered the tidal waters rule obsolete.

James W. Ely, Jr.

Geofroy v. Riggs, 133 U.S. 258 (1890), argued 23 Dec. 1889, decided 3 Feb. 1890, by vote of 9 to 0; Field for the Court. T. L. Riggs, a U.S. citizen, died intestate, leaving as heirs family members who included both American and French nationals. The French descendants claimed, as part of their inheritance, property located in Washington, D.C. But the American heirs argued that the local law of Maryland, which the Federal District had incorporated, prohibited the descent of real estate to aliens. The issue was: could French aliens inherit from a U.S. citizen land situated in a U.S. territorial jurisdiction such as the District of Columbia?

After losing in the lower federal court the aliens appealed to the Supreme Court. Their argument was that a provision of an 1853 treaty between the United States and France permitted the descent of real estate to French nationals in "all states" whose local law so permitted. In addition, though it made no specific reference to Frenchmen, another treaty of 1800 governing Washington, D.C., had displaced the property law incorporated from Maryland. The Americans countered, however, that the District of Columbia was not a "state" within the meaning of the 1853 treaty.

Justice Stephen Field's opinion held that for purposes of the treaty a "state" was any political entity with an established government, including Washington, D.C. Reasoning that the American litigants' interpretation of the treaty would result in discrimination against aliens and jeopardize reciprocity between the United States and France, the Court held that the French heirs could inherit property in the District of Columbia.

The decision expanded the right to transfer property and the rights of aliens primarily in Washington, D.C. But the precedent also applied if ambiguity existed in a particular state's law.

Tony Freyer

Georgia v. McCollum, 505 U.S. 42 (1992), argued 26 Feb. 1992, decided 18 June 1992 by vote of 7 to 2; Blackmun for the Court, Rehnquist and Thomas concurring, O'Connor and Scalia dissenting.

The Supreme Court in *Batson* v. *Kentucky* (1986) issued one of its most far-reaching criminal justice decisions. It held that the guarantee of equal protection of the laws in the Fourteenth Amendment meant that states could not eliminate prospective jurors based on race. State laws had typically allowed prosecutors to use so-called peremptory challenges, which permitted the exclusion of a juror without explanation. Before *Batson* prosecutors had used these challenges to shape juries sympathetic to the state's case. *Batson*, however, required that such challenges had to be exercised in a racially neutral way. The Court's holding, however, did not apply to defense counsel, since, for purpose of the Fourteenth Amendment's State Action Clause, such individuals were deemed to be private rather than public persons. The justices in *Georgia* v. *McCollum* addressed just this issue.

The case involved an appeal from a ruling by the Georgia Supreme Court involving three white owners of a dry-cleaning establishment in Albany, Georgia. The three had been indicted for assaulting two black customers.

In response, leaders of the black community called for a boycott of the dry-cleaning business. The state attorney general's office asked the trial judge to order the defense counsel not to use their peremptory challenges to exclude blacks from the jury. The Georgia Supreme Court heard this issue on appeal and declined to extend the *Batson* precedent to defense counsel. The state of Georgia then appealed to the U.S. Supreme Court.

Justice Harry Blackmun's opinion for the Court stretched the *Batson* principle to cover these new circumstances. Blackmun held that "the Constitution prohibits a criminal defendant from engaging in purposeful discrimination on the ground of race in the exercise of peremptory challenges" (p. 59). Moreover, Blackmun argued, it is "an affront to justice to argue that a fair trial includes the right to discriminate against a group of citizens based on their race" (p. 57). The Fourteenth Amendment requirement that state action be present in order to invoke the Equal Protection Clause was satisfied based on the argument that defense lawyers in criminal cases were essentially acting as agents of the state in helping to compose a governmental body, the jury.

The seven-vote majority, however, was weaker than the actual numbers suggest. Two of the votes, by Chief Justice William H. Rehnquist and Justice Clarence Thomas, were cast for the new rule only because the previous year, in *Edmonson v. Leesville* (1991), the Court had extended the *Batson* principle to civil trials, where both sides could be private parties. Moreover, many defense attorneys worried, as did the two dissenters in the case, that the new rule would actually make it more difficult for minority defendants to place on the jury persons who might be supportive of them based on race and ethnicity. Justice Sandra Day O'Connor complained that the new ruling would make mixed-race juries harder to attain.

Kermit L. Hall

Gertz v. Robert Welch, Inc., 418 U.S. 323 (1974), argued 14 Nov. 1973, decided 25 June 1974 by vote of 5 to 4; Powell for the Court, Blackmun concurring; Burger, Douglas, Brennan, and White in dissent. *Gertz v. Robert Welch, Inc.* arose in 1969 when *American Opinion* magazine, a publication of the John Birch Society, attacked Elmer Gertz, an attorney who was representing clients in a suit for civil damages against a policeman who had earlier been convicted of second-

degree murder. *American Opinion* falsely stated that Gertz had been responsible for framing the policemen in his murder trial, that Gertz had a criminal record, and that he was a "Leninist" and a "Communist-fronter." Gertz sued for defamation.

In 1964 the Supreme Court had held in *New York Times Co. v. Sullivan* that plaintiffs who were public officials could not recover damages for defamation unless they could demonstrate that the defamation had been published with "'actual malice'—that is, with knowledge that it was false or with reckless disregard of whether it was false or not" (pp. 279–280). In the aftermath of *New York Times* there was considerable uncertainty about the range of application of this revolutionary rule of actual malice. The Court's opinion in *Gertz* was to resolve this uncertainty by establishing a doctrinal structure that would remain stable for the next decade.

The Supreme Court held that the First Amendment required public figures and public officials to demonstrate actual malice but that all other libel plaintiffs, like Elmer Gertz, need only prove some degree of "fault." *Gertz* also held that the First Amendment prohibited the recovery of punitive or presumptive damages in the absence of actual malice, although it specifically held that mental anguish was a compensable form of "actual" damage.

An important weakness of *Gertz* is that it never explained why the Constitution should preempt common-law defamation doctrine as applied to all cases involving private plaintiffs. In 1985, in *Dun & Bradstreet, Inc. v. Greenmoss Builders*, the Court began to cut back the application of the *Gertz* rules so that they would only pertain to defamations which, although about private plaintiffs, were also about matters of "public concern."

Robert C. Post

Gibbons v. Ogden, 9 Wheat. (22 U.S.) 1 (1824), argued 4–9 Feb. 1824, decided 2 Mar. 1824 by vote of 6 to 0; Marshall for the Court, Johnson concurring. It was thirty-five years after ratification of the Constitution before the Supreme Court decided a case related to the clause empowering Congress to regulate interstate and foreign commerce (Article I, sec. 8). In *Gibbons v. Ogden* (1824), Chief Justice John Marshall delivered an opinion that was a classic statement of nationalism. Over the years, it became a source of extensive authority for Congress to address new problems in the regulation of the national economy. Judges and lawyers would analyze it to explain the distribution of powers between nation and states in the American federal system.

The case arose during the early days of the steamboat. In 1807, Robert Fulton, the most successful of the many inventors seeking a practical steam-propelled craft, ran his boat up the Hudson River at the speed prescribed by a New York law and thereby acquired a monopoly of steam navigation on the state's waters. Ambitious interlopers challenged this monopoly, which led to lively litigation. One line of cases involved Aaron Ogden, who held a state-required Fulton-Livingston license, and Thomas Gibbons, who held a federal coasting license and ran competing boats between New Jersey and Manhattan. The New York courts repeatedly upheld the monopoly against such competition (*Livingston* v. *Van Ingen,* 1812, and *Gibbons* v. *Ogden,* 1820). By 1824 the dispute reached the U.S. Supreme Court on appeal.

Daniel Webster made the principal argument for Gibbons. He set out the options for interpreting the Constitution in matters concerning state and national powers over interstate commerce: (1) exclusive national power; (2) fully concurrent state and national powers; (3) partially concurrent state power not reaching "higher branches" of that commerce; and (4) supremacy of a national statute over a contrary state statute. In arguing for the first of these, Webster construed commerce broadly and warned against a tangle of conflicting local policies. One of Ogden's counsel, Thomas Emmet, insisted that states had frequently legislated on many interstate matters and ought to have fully concurrent power over commerce between the states.

Marshall spoke for the entire Court, except William Johnson, who filed a concurring opinion. Marshall plainly preferred the exclusive option. He defined commerce expansively, far beyond mere exchange of goods, to include persons and new subjects such as the steamboat. Nevertheless, he held back from deciding the case on exclusivity grounds, probably because of the possible impact such a broad reading of federal power might have on slave-holding states, nervous as they were about federal authority. But Justice Johnson, a South Carolinian who was a fervent nationalist on this question, adopted that option. In the actual holding, Marshall construed Gibbons's

federal license to nullify the New York grant of monopoly. He saw a conflict of congressional and state statutes, thus selecting the narrowest strategy and postponing a more comprehensive ruling.

Lawyers and judges explored this question in several cases over the next quarter-century and finally arrived at a compromise formula that acknowledged a partially concurrent state power over interstate commerce. In **Cooley* v. *Board of Wardens* (1852), the Taney Court decided that some subjects of commerce required a uniform rule and national uniformity, while others permitted a degree of state action. However, *Cooley's* general formulation left many specifics unclear.

During its conservative periods, the Court expressed hostility to both national and state regulatory powers. For example, in the late nineteenth century, both state railroad regulation and national antitrust reform suffered from narrow and tortured readings of the Commerce Clause. This judicial negativism persisted until the 1930s, albeit with respectful citations to *Gibbons.* After the constitutional revolution that began in 1937, the Court read the steamboat case differently to permit almost unlimited federal power, whether for regulating the economy or, as in Marshall's time, for stimulating its growth. Entirely new uses for the commerce power, notably protection of civil rights, have emerged. At the same time, the Court has allowed a broad field for state legislation, no doubt much broader than Chief Justice Marshall would have favored.

□ Maurice G. Baxter, *The Steamboat Monopoly: Gibbons v. Ogden, 1824* (1972).

Maurice G. Baxter

Gideon v. Wainwright, 372 U.S. 335 (1963), argued 15 Jan. 1963, decided 18 Mar. 1963 by vote of 9 to 0; Black for the Court, Douglas, Clark, and Harlan concurring. Clarence Earl Gideon was charged with breaking and entering a poolroom with intent to commit a misdemeanor, a felony under Florida law. Being without funds, Gideon requested that counsel be appointed for him; the Florida trial court refused and Gideon conducted his own defense "about as well as could be expected from a layman" (p. 337). The jury returned a verdict of guilty. Gideon filed a habeas corpus petition in the Florida Supreme Court claiming that his federal constitutional rights had been abridged by the trial court's refusal to appoint counsel for him; the Florida Supreme Court denied relief and Gideon appealed *in forma pauperis* to the U.S. Supreme Court.

The Court appointed Abe Fortas, a prominent lawyer who later served as a justice, to argue Gideon's case and address whether **Betts* v. *Brady* (1942) should be overruled. *Betts* had held that, in state courts, the Fourteenth Amendment's Due Process Clause only required that appointed counsel be provided to indigents in special circumstances. However, the Court had not upheld a single denial of right to counsel under the *Betts* rule since its 1950 decision in *Quicksal* v. *Michigan*. The Court was looking for an opportunity to overrule *Betts,* and *Gideon* provided that opportunity.

A unanimous Court overruled *Betts* and held that the Sixth Amendment, as applied to the states by the Fourteenth Amendment, required that counsel be appointed to represent indigent defendants charged with serious offenses in state criminal trials. At his retrial, Gideon was represented by appointed counsel who uncovered new defense witnesses and discredited prosecution witnesses; a new jury acquitted Gideon.

In overruling *Betts,* Justice Hugo Black, for the majority, argued that the Court was "returning to . . . old precedents, sounder we believe than the new" (p. 334). In **Powell* v. *Alabama* (1932), the Court had held that when an indigent defendant is charged with a capital offense in a state court and is incapable of making his own defense, due process requires that counsel be appointed for him. It noted that "the right to be heard would be of little avail if it did not comprehend the right to be heard by counsel" (p. 68). In **Johnson* v. *Zerbst* (1938), the Court declared a right to appointed counsel in federal criminal cases. By 1942, thirty-five states required that counsel be appointed to represent indigents in serious non-capital as well as capital cases. Indeed, in *Gideon* twenty-two states filed an amicus curiae brief urging reversal of *Betts* and only three states, including Florida, argued that *Betts* should be upheld.

Gideon was widely interpreted as applying only to felony cases; but, in **Argersinger* v. *Hamlin* (1972), the Court extended the right to appointed counsel to misdemeanors when the defendant is sentenced to imprisonment. In another case decided the same day as *Gideon, Douglas* v. *California,* the Court held that the Equal Protection Clause

conferred a right to appointed counsel for first appeals of right. In subsequent years, *Gideon* spawned two lines of cases. One series of cases deals with the Sixth Amendment right to counsel and at what stages of the criminal justice process the defendant must be allowed the benefit of counsel. Another line of cases acknowledges that the right to counsel implies the right to effective counsel and attempts to develop standards for determining when that right had been denied.

Today, most large cities and some states have public defender offices that provide counsel to indigents in criminal cases. In other regions, trial court judges appoint private attorneys to represent indigent defendants. A 1984 Department of Justice survey reported that two-thirds of the nation's population is served by public defenders. Various studies have shown that a defendant's chance of being convicted is not significantly affected by whether he is represented by a public defender or private counsel, although defendants who proceed without counsel are significantly more likely to be convicted. *Gideon,* along with **Mapp* v. *Ohio* (1961), marked the beginning of the Court's "due process revolution," which resulted in the constitutionalization of state criminal procedure and a series of only partially successful attempts to convince the Court to extend due process guarantees to civil and quasi-legal proceedings.

□ Anthony Lewis, *Gideon's Trumpet* (1964).
Susan E. Lawrence

Gitlow v. New York, 268 U.S. 652 (1925), argued 12 Apr. 1923, reargued 23 Nov. 1923, decided 8 June 1925 by vote of 7 to 2; Sanford for the Court, Holmes and Brandeis in dissent. The landmark *Gitlow* case marks the beginning of the "incorporation" of the First Amendment as a limitation on the states. This process, which continued selectively over the next fifty years, resulted in major changes in the modern law of civil liberties, affording citizens a federal remedy if the states deprived them of their fundamental rights. Ironically, however, the Court rejected Gitlow's free speech claim. At the time the ruling's significance was largely doctrinal.

Benjamin Gitlow was a member of the left-wing section of the Socialist party. He was convicted for violating the New York Criminal Anarchy Law of 1902, which made it a crime to advocate the violent overthrow of the government. Specifically, he had been arrested during the 1920 Red Scare for writing, publishing, and distributing sixteen thousand copies of a pamphlet called *Left-wing Manifesto* that urged the establishment of socialism by strikes and "class action . . . in any form." He was also charged with being an "evil disposed and pernicious person," with a "wicked and turbulent disposition," who tried to "excite discontent and disaffection." At his trial, the famed attorney Clarence Darrow sought to frame the entire issue as one of freedom of speech on the grounds that the *Left-wing Manifesto* advocated nothing but urged abstract doctrine. The New York court, however, ruled that communists had to be held responsible for the potential danger of their abstract concepts and upheld the conviction.

The Supreme Court used the case as an occasion to examine the concept that the speech and press protections of the First Amendment should be extended to the states. Gitlow's brief, prepared by the brilliant ACLU lawyer Walter H. Pollak, argued persuasively that liberty of expression was a right to be protected against state abridgment. This, he contended, was established by the authoritative determination of the meaning of liberty as used in the Fourteenth Amendment and by implicit declarations with respect to the related right of free assembly. The Court was impressed. Justice Edward T. Sanford, speaking for the majority, agreed that "for present purposes, we may and do assume that freedom of speech and of the press . . . are among the fundamental personal rights and 'liberties' protected by the due process clause of the Fourteenth Amendment from impairment by the States" (p. 666). He nonetheless sustained the New York law and upheld Gitlow's conviction. "[A] state may punish utterances endangering the foundations of organized government and threatening its overthrow by unlawful means," Sanford wrote (p. 667). Gitlow's pamphlet, while not immediately inciting criminal action, could be viewed as a "revolutionary spark" that might at some later time burst into "sweeping and destructive conflagration" (p. 669).

Justice Oliver Wendell Holmes wrote a famous dissent in which Justice Louis D. Brandeis concurred. He disagreed with the majority's ruling that words separated from action could be punished. Holmes declared, "The only difference between the expression of an opinion and an incitement in the narrower sense is the speaker's enthusiasm for the result. Eloquence may set fire to reason. But whatever may be thought of the redundant discourse before us, it had no chance of starting a present conflagration" (p. 673). This view, which called for punishment of action, not expression, under the clear and present danger doctrine, was to be embraced by the Supreme Court in the 1960s.

The *Gitlow* decision launched "incorporation" of the First Amendment. It was not until *Stromberg* v. *California* (1931), however, that the Court actually ruled a state law unconstitutional on First Amendment free speech grounds.

Paul. L. Murphy

Goldberg v. Kelly, 397 U.S. 254 (1970), argued 13 Oct. 1969, decided 23 Mar. 1970 by vote of 6 to 3; Brennan for the Court; Black, Burger, Stewart in dissent. The procedure in New York City for the termination of welfare payments required seven-day notice and gave the welfare recipient the right to submit a written statement of protest. It did not, however, afford an evidentiary hearing before termination of benefits. The Court held that procedural due process under the Fourteenth Amendment required that welfare recipients be afforded an evidentiary hearing before termination of benefits.

The right to submit only a written statement, or affording a posttermination evidentiary hearing, did not meet requirements of due process. The pretermination hearing need not be, however, in the nature of a judicial or quasi-judicial trial. But the recipient must be afforded an opportunity to confront and cross-examine witnesses, to retain an attorney if so desired, and to present oral evidence to an impartial decision maker, whose conclusion must rest solely on legal rules and evidence adduced at the hearing.

While the state has an interest in conserving fiscal and administrative resources, this interest is outweighed by the interest of the recipient in uninterrupted receipt of public assistance, which is not mere charity but a means to promote the general welfare. The governmental interests that prompt the provision of welfare prompt as well its uninterrupted provision to those eligible to receive it. Welfare benefits, the Court said, "are a matter of statutory entitlement for persons qualified to receive them" (p. 262). The Court thus injected the concept of "entitlement" into the concept of property right protected by the Due Process Clause.

Milton R. Konvitz

Gold Clause Cases (1935), common collective name for three companion cases of the New Deal era: *Norman* v. *Baltimore & Ohio Railroad Co.,* 294 U.S. 240; *Nortz* v. *United States,* 294 U.S. 317; and *Perry* v. *United States,* 294 U.S. 330. All three argued 8–11 Jan. 1935, decided 18 Feb. 1935 by vote of 5 to 4; Hughes for the Court, McReynolds in dissent in each case. As part of the New Deal program to conserve gold reserves during the economic emergency of the Great Depression, Congress in 1933 abrogated the clauses in private and public contracts stipulating payment in gold. Consequently, such obligations could be paid in devalued currency. In these three cases, bondholders challenged this action as a breach of the obligation of contract and a deprivation of property without due process.

Speaking for the Court, Chief Justice Charles Evans Hughes sustained the power of Congress to regulate the monetary system. He ruled that the gold clauses in private contracts were merely provisions for payment in money. Further, Hughes concluded that Congress could override private contracts that conflicted with its constitutional authority over the monetary system. With respect to the gold clauses in government bonds, however, Hughes found that Congress had unconstitutionally impaired its own obligations. However, he determined that the bondholders could recover only nominal damages for breach of contract and thus could not sue in the Court of Claims. In a bitter dissenting opinion, Justice James C. McReynolds charged that the congressional action portended confiscation of property and financial chaos. He extemporaneously declared that "this is Nero at his worst."

Although the Supreme Court in effect permitted Congress to impair existing contracts, the *Gold Clause Cases* reaffirmed comprehensive congressional power over monetary policy. Moreover, as a practical matter, enforcement of the gold clauses would have had a deleterious impact on the depressed national economy.

James W. Ely, Jr.

Goldfarb v. Virginia State Bar, 421 U.S. 773 (1975), argued 25 Mar. 1975, decided 16 June 1975 by vote of 8 to 0; Burger for the Court, Powell not participating.

The Goldfarbs were unable to find a lawyer who would perform a real estate title examination for a fee less than that prescribed in a minimum fee schedule published by the Fair-fax County [Virginia] Bar Association and enforced by the Virginia State Bar. They alleged that the fee schedule constituted price fixing, in violation of section 1 of the Sherman Antitrust Act.

The Supreme Court found that the bar association's activities constituted a classic case of price fixing. The fee schedule established a rigid price floor; every lawyer contacted by the petitioners adhered to it; no lawyer would charge less. Moreover, ethics opinions issued by the Virginia bar threatened disciplinary action for regularly charging less than the suggested minimum fee. Since only attorneys licensed to practice in Virginia could legally examine a title, consumers had no alternative but to pay the prescribed fee.

The Court also held that because a substantial portion of the funds used for purchasing homes in Fairfax County came from outside Virginia, interstate commerce was sufficiently affected to bring this action under the Sherman Act. It rejected the contention that Congress never intended to include "learned professions" within the meaning of "trade or commerce" in section 1 of the Sherman Act. Moreover, the Court held that such anticompetitive activities were not exempt from the Sherman Act as "state action."

In holding that minimum fee schedules violate federal antitrust law, *Goldfarb* opened the door to price competition in legal services. Perhaps the greatest immediate impact of the Court's decision was the development of low-cost legal clinics that handle relatively routine matters such as wills and divorces.

Beth M. Henschen

Goldwater v. Carter, 444 U.S. 996 (1979), decided 13 Dec. 1979 by vote of 6 to 3 (certiorari granted, vacated, and remanded with directions to dismiss the complaint); Rehnquist, Burger, Stewart, Powell, Stevens, and Marshall concurring, Brennan, White and Blackmun in dissent. Senator Barry Goldwater and other members of Congress challenged President Jimmy Carter's termination of the Mutual Defense Treaty with Taiwan without consulting or securing the prior approval of the Senate. Article II, section 2, clause 2 of the Constitution states that the president has the power to make treaties, provided that two-thirds of the Senate concur. However, the Constitution does not address the question of how a treaty may be abrogated.

The Supreme Court summarily reversed a court of appeals decision holding that the president had authority to terminate a treaty without congressional approval. Justice William Rehnquist, in a concurring opinion joined by Chief Justice Warren Burger and Justices Potter Stewart and John Paul Stevens, argued that this was a nonjusticiable political question because it involved the "authority of the President in the conduct of our country's foreign relations . . . specifically a treaty commitment to use military force in the defense of a foreign government if attacked" (pp. 1002–1004). The Court was "asked to settle a dispute between coequal branches of government, each of which has resources available to protect and assert its interests, resources not available to private litigants outside the judicial forum" (p. 1004). Justice Lewis Powell concurred separately, arguing that the issue was not "ripe" for judicial decision since Congress had not yet confronted the president about the treaty.

In dissent, Justice William Brennan argued that the political question doctrine does not apply when the Court merely examines whether a particular branch has been "constitutionally designated as the repository of political decision-making power" (p. 1007). This was a constitutional law question, he said, that falls within the competency of the courts. Addressing the merits of the case, Brennan argued that since abrogation of the Taiwan Defense Treaty was related to the president's decision to recognize the government of mainland China, and since the president alone has the power to recognize foreign governments, he had the authority to abrogate the treaty.

Joel B. Grossman

Gomillion v. Lightfoot, 364 U.S. 339 (1960), argued 18–19 Oct. 1960, decided 14 Nov. 1960 by vote of 9 to 0; Frankfurter for the Court, Douglas and Whittaker concurring. Black voters charged that an Alabama law, changing the city boundaries of Tuskegee in such a way as to exclude all but four or five black voters without eliminating any white ones, was unconstitutional. A federal district court dismissed the complaint and

the Court of Appeals for the Fifth Circuit affirmed. The Supreme Court reversed unanimously.

That the Supreme Court would in 1960 strike down this obvious race-based denial of constitutional rights is not so unusual. What is interesting is that Justice Felix Frankfurter had to find a way to skirt his own *Colegrove* v. *Green* (1946) holding that questions relating to legislative apportionment are nonjusticiable "political questions" and thus outside the scope of federal judicial power. Frankfurter felt strongly that federal courts should not enter the reapportionment battlefield, but he was equally passionately against racial discrimination. To reconcile these two values, he keyed his *Gomillion* decision to Fifteenth Amendment rather than to Fourteenth Amendment grounds. "The appellants in *Colegrove*," he wrote, "complained only of a dilution of the strength of their votes as a result of legislative inaction over the course of many years. The petitioners here complain that affirmative legislative action deprives them of their votes . . . . When a legislature thus singles out a readily isolated segment of a racial minority for special discriminatory treatment, it violates the Fifteenth Amendment . . . . [A] part from all else, these considerations lift this controversy out of the so-called 'political' arena and into the conventional sphere of constitutional litigation" (pp. 346, 347).

Justices William O. Douglas and Charles Whittaker, concurring separately, would have struck down Alabama's action as a violation of the Fourteenth Amendment.

Gomillion's opening of federal courts to charges of racial gerrymandering reflected no softening in Frankfurter's views that courts should stay out of legislative apportionment issues, but it did encourage urban interests to keep pressing federal courts for relief. A few days after *Gomillion*, the Court noted probable jurisdiction in *Baker* v. *Carr* (1962), which did directly raise the justiciability of reapportionment cases.

J. W. Peltason

Gompers v. Buck's Stove & Range Co., 221 U.S. 418 (1911), argued 27 and 30 Jan. 1911, decided 15 May 1911 by vote of 9 to 0; Lamar for the Court. When workers struck the Buck's Stove Company, the American Federation of Labor organized a boycott of the company's products. The manufacturer secured an injunction against the boycott, from which the union planned an appeal.

Before it could do so the company sought a criminal contempt citation against Samuel Gompers and two other union leaders, claiming that they had violated the injunction by publishing the company's name on its "Unfair" and "We don't patronize" lists in *The American Federationist*. The defendants appealed the citation, claiming that what they printed in the paper was protected speech under the First Amendment, an argument the Court completely ignored. While he reversed the criminal contempt citation on a technicality, Justice Joseph Lamar's opinion made it clear that the Court sided with employers in their battles against labor. Lamar cited approvingly one case after another to demonstrate that the courts frowned on any action, including speech, that injured property rights.

Melvin I. Urofsky

Gonzales v. Carhart; Gonzales v. Planned Parenthood Federation of America, 127 S. Ct. 1610 (2007), argued 8 Nov. 2006, decided 18 Apr. 2007 by vote of 5 to 4; Kennedy for the Court; Thomas, joined by Scalia, concurring; Ginsburg, joined by Stevens, Souter, and Breyer, in dissent. In *Gonzales v. Carhart*, a skirmish in the legal war over the constitutional right to abortion—as announced by the Supreme Court in **Roe v. Wade* (1973) and reaffirmed in **Planned Parenthood of Southeastern Pennsylvania v. Casey* (1992)—a sharply divided Court upheld the constitutionality of the Partial-Birth Abortion Ban Act of 2003.

As part of their campaign to overturn *Roe*, anti-abortion activists fashioned a strategy targeting late-term abortions, with the aim of incrementally undermining the distinction implicitly drawn by abortion rights proponents between abortion and infanticide. This campaign resulted in the passage of laws prohibiting abortions using the process known as intact dilation and extraction (or "partial-birth" abortions) in approximately thirty states. In *Stenberg v. Carhart* (2000), however, the Court invalidated Nebraska's partial-birth abortion law on the grounds that it did not provide the constitutionally required exception for cases affecting a woman's health. The U.S. Congress then passed a national ban on this type of abortion three times. The first two were vetoed by President William Clinton, but the third ban—the statute at issue in *Gonzales v. Carhart*—was signed into law by President George W. Bush.

The 2003 act criminalized the intentional provision of second-trimester abortions via intact dilation and extraction, in which the doctor extracts the fetus intact (or largely intact). Writing for the majority, Justice Anthony M. Kennedy argued that the act was consistent with *Casey*'s central premise that the government has a legitimate interest in preserving fetal life, and that the state has the power to restrict abortion after viability if the law contains exceptions for pregnancies that endanger the woman's life and health. The Court relied on the fact that alternative methods of second-trimester abortions are available, that the act was specific about the class of abortions prohibited, that it provided for exceptions for abortions that threatened a woman's life, and that it was premised on factual findings by Congress that a "moral, medical, and ethical consensus exists that the practice of performing a partial-birth abortion . . . is a gruesome and inhumane procedure that is never medically necessary and should be prohibited" (p. 1624).

Writing for the dissenters, Justice Ruth Bader Ginsburg argued that the act did not accord appropriate solicitude for a woman's health, that it was premised on congressional findings of fact regarding the benefits and uses of the procedure that were either false or the subject of disagreement among medical experts. She asserted, moreover, that since it regulated only a method of abortion, the act's provisions were not rationally related to its stated purpose of protecting fetal life. Ginsburg forcefully argued her longstanding conviction that a women's "right to make an autonomous choice" regarding reproduction is indispensable to her status as a full American citizen (p. 1649).

Ken I. Kersch

Gonzales v. Raich, 545 U.S. 1 (2005), argued 29 Nov. 2004, decided 6 June 2005 by vote of 6 to 3; Stevens for the Court; Scalia concurring; O'Connor, joined by Rehnquist and Thomas, dissenting; Thomas dissenting. In 1996, California voters approved Proposition 215, which authorized the limited use of marijuana for medicinal purposes. Two physicians wrote prescriptions for their patients, believing marijuana was the only drug available that would provide effective treatment. However, the federal Controlled Substances Act (CSA) classifies marijuana as a Schedule I drug, making its possession and use a crime. Federal and state officials took steps to prevent the two patients from using the drug, and the patients sought injunctive and declaratory relief, raising a variety of constitutional issues. The question before the Supreme Court, however, was a narrow one: Did Congress have the authority, pursuant to the Commerce Clause, to bar the cultivation and use of marijuana otherwise authorized by state law?

The Court has held repeatedly—most recently in *United States* v. **Lopez* (1995) and *United States* v. *Morrison* (2000)—that Congress may use the commerce power to regulate three classes of activities: (1) channels of interstate commerce, (2) instrumentalities of and persons or things in commerce, and (3) activities that substantially affect commerce. *Raich* fell within the third category: federal control of purely local activities that, when aggregated, posed the specter of a "substantial effect" on interstate commerce.

This doctrine has proved controversial, especially given decisions made at the turn of the twentieth century celebrating state sovereignty and placing limits on federal authority. Both *Lopez* and *Morrison* stressed that the commerce power must be assessed in the light of residual state sovereignty and that there is no "general" federal police power. The California measure arguably comported with these understandings. As Justice Sandra Day O'Connor stressed in her *Raich* dissent, adherence to these principles seemed to suggest that the Court should both recognize the role of the states as "laboratories of democracy" and affirm their core authority to "protect the health, safety, and welfare of their citizens" (p. 42).

The majority disagreed, concluding that "Congress had a rational basis for believing that failure to regulate the intrastate manufacture and possession of marijuana would leaving a gaping hole in the CSA" (p. 22). For them, the question was not whether a specific, purely local, and quite possibly noneconomic activity has an actual, substantial impact on interstate commerce. Rather, it was "whether a 'rational basis' exists for so concluding" (p. 22)—a relatively forgiving standard that bars conflicting state actions, given the continuing force of the Court's preemption doctrines. *Raich* also preserves the substantial effects doctrine in the face of the argument that commerce is limited to trade or exchange among the states.

Mark R. Killenbeck

Good Faith Exception. See LEON, UNITED STATES V.

Good News Club, Inc. v. Milford Central School, 533 U.S. 98 (2001), argued 28 Feb. 2001, decided 11 June 2001 by vote of 6 to 3; Thomas for the Court, Scalia concurring, Breyer concurring in part, Stevens and Souter in dissent, joined by Ginsburg.

The school district in Milford, New York, enacted a "community use" policy, authorizing the after-school use by district residents of school buildings for, *inter alia,* "instruction in . . . education, learning or the arts," "social, civil and recreational meetings," and "other uses pertaining to the welfare of the community" (p. 102). The district refused to permit the Good News Club—a "private Christian organization"—to use school facilities for "a fun time of singing songs, hearing a Bible lesson, and memorizing scripture," on the ground that the proposed use was "the equivalent of religious worship," noting that the community-use policy prohibited use of school facilities "for religious purposes" (p. 103).

In *Good News,* the Court employed its viewpoint-neutrality and public-forum doctrines to resolve a dispute about the place of religious expression and activity on public property. Writing for the majority, Justice Clarence Thomas insisted that "speech discussing otherwise permissible subjects cannot be excluded from a limited public forum on the ground that the subject is discussed from a religious viewpoint" (p. 112). Having created a "limited public forum," the district could not regulate access to that forum in a "viewpoint-based" fashion. In the Court's view, the exclusion of the Good News Club, on the ground that its proposed activities were akin to religious instruction or worship, constituted viewpoint discrimination; that is, religious "uses pertaining to the welfare of the community" were excluded, *precisely because* they were religious.

Good News highlights a difficulty with the Court's treatment of religious-expression cases in Free Speech Clause terms: Are courts able to police the line between "speech from a religious viewpoint," on the one hand, and "religious worship," on the other? Justice John Paul Stevens conceded, in dissent, that the Court's free-speech doctrines protect "religious speech that is simply speech about a particular topic from a religious point of view" (p. 130), but nonetheless insisted that expression amounting to "religious worship" or "proselytization" must be treated differently, given the Establishment Clause.

Richard W. Garnett

Good, United States v., 510 U.S. 43 (1993), argued 6 Oct. 1993, decided 13 Dec. 1993 by vote of 5 to 4; Kennedy for the Court, Rehnquist, Thomas, Scalia, and O'Connor in dissent. The *Good* decision stemmed directly from the United States government's so-called war on drugs. Federal officials attempted to stem the drug trade by seizing the property of suspected drug dealers, declaring it forfeit to the United States, and then selling it at auction. Between 1984 and 1992 the Department of Justice seized a total of $1.9 billion in property, while seizures by the Drug Enforcement Administration doubled between 1986 and 1992, rising to $856 million in the latter year. For more than a century, such proceedings had been carried out under the guise of the Fourth Amendment's requirement that civil forfeitures be executed through arrest warrants based on probable cause that the goods were subject to seizure. There was no requirement that the individual whose goods were to be seized had a right to a hearing before they were taken.

Hawaii police officers in January 1985 executed a search warrant against the home of James Daniel Good. The search uncovered about eighty-nine pounds of marijuana, marijuana seeds, and related drug paraphernalia. Good eventually pleaded guilty, received a one-year jail sentence, and forfeited to the state of Hawaii about $3,000 in cash found on the premises.

Four and one-half years later federal officials won from a federal magistrate a warrant to seize Good's house and the four acres of ground on which it was situated. The government acted without ever informing Good; federal agents showed up and took possession of the home and grounds. Good charged that such an action took his property without due process of law, in contravention of the Due Process Clause of the Fifth Amendment, and that, in any case, the action by the government was invalid because it had not been timely, coming as it did four and one-half years after his conviction in a Hawaiian court. The Court of Appeals for the Ninth Circuit reversed the federal magistrate's action, holding that the government had failed to provide proper notice and a hearing for Good and that, while the action fell within the five-year period for seizure outlined in federal law, the government had failed to follow the required internal notifications and reporting requirements.

Justice Anthony M. Kennedy's opinion affirmed the due process ruling by the court of appeals but rejected the timeliness requirements. The majority distinguished between real and personal property, of which the former was immobile but the latter was subject to removal if not seized promptly. As Justice Kennedy put it, "real property cannot abscond" (p. 57). The justices also held that in the case of real property the simple issuance of a warrant by a magistrate was not sufficient due process, since these proceedings, at which the person whose property was to be seized was not present, created an unacceptable risk of error and afforded little or no protection to an innocent owner. When seizing real property, therefore, the federal government had to provide a hearing that would give suspects the opportunity to argue that it was not obtained through illegal means or that its value was much greater than the amount of illegally obtained profit. At the same time, the Court overturned the other part of the court of appeals ruling, holding that the government had only to file an action within the five-year period and that internal timing requirements could be completed later.

The *Good* opinion curbed the sweeping powers enjoyed by the federal government (and many states) in seizing the assets of suspected and convicted drug dealers. The Court acted in part because forfeiture law tended to victimize not only criminal wrongdoers but also legitimate banks, lending institutions, vendors of goods and services, and innocent purchasers and renters.

Nonetheless, the majority's opinion drew the wrath of Chief Justice William H. Rehnquist and Justices Antonin Scalia, Sandra Day O'Connor, and Clarence Thomas. They insisted that precedent had long since established that the federal government could, under the Fourth Amendment, seize property from a suspected drug dealer and make it susceptible to civil forfeiture based solely on the issuance of a properly executed warrant. In their view, the subsequent hearing dealing with the forfeiture was sufficient due process protection.

Kermit L. Hall

Graham v. Richardson, 403 U.S. 365 (1971), argued 22 Mar. 1971, decided 14 June 1971 by vote of 9 to 0; Blackmun for the Court, Harlan specially concurring. This Supreme Court case established the doctrine that alienage, like race, is a suspect classification under the Fourteenth Amendment. Aliens are such, said the Court, because they are a discrete and politically powerless minority. As a result, governmental classifications based on alienage are subject to strict scrutiny; to pass muster constitutionally, they must be closely related to a compelling governmental interest.

In this case, Arizona regulations conditioning the receipt of welfare benefits either on U.S. citizenship or residence within the United States for a specified number of years failed to meet this test and thereby violated the Equal Protection Clause. The states in question justified their regulations on the basis of their special public interest in favoring their own residents over aliens in the dispersal of limited public resources.

In voiding the state residency requirements, the Supreme Court provided an alternative basis for its decision: the Constitution grants the federal government authority to admit aliens and the conditions under which they may reside in the United States. State laws disabling aliens, as in *Graham,* may interfere with overriding federal policies and thereby violate the Supremacy Clause.

Decisions subsequent to *Graham*—such as *Foley* v. *Connelie* (1978) and *Ambach* v. *Norwick* (1979)—have intimated that federal classifications based on alienage may demand lesser scrutiny while those of the states will be scrutinized under the Supremacy, rather than the Equal Protection, Clause. The Court has also held that a denial of essential services such as Medicare would be scrutinized more carefully than barriers to other programs. But it did uphold the ineligibility of non-permanently resident aliens for the Medicare Supplemental Medical Insurance Program in *Mathews* v. *Diaz* (1976).

Harold J. Spaeth

Granger Cases. See CHICAGO, BURLINGTON & QUINCY RAILROAD CO. V. CHICAGO; MUNN V. ILLINOIS.

Granholm v. Heald, 544 U.S. 460 (2005), argued 7 Dec. 2004, decided 16 May 2005 by vote of 5 to 4; Kennedy for the Court, Stevens and Thomas in dissent. New York and Michigan prohibited out-of-state, but not in-state, alcohol producers from selling directly to in-state consumers. Producers argued that this violated the dormant Commerce Clause doctrine's ban on discrimination against out-of-state goods. The two states claimed their laws were authorized by the Twenty-first Amendment, which trumped the dormant Commerce Clause doctrine. The Court rejected this view and invalidated the laws.

The opinion began with a review of the Wilson and Webb-Kenyon acts, which were early congressional responses to the Court's reliance on the dormant commerce power to invalidate state liquor regulations. These acts authorized states to enforce their own liquor laws free from the strictures of the dormant Commerce Clause. Justice Anthony M. Kennedy concluded that both acts affirmed "the Court's line of . . . cases striking down state laws that discriminated against liquor produced out of state" (p. 483), even though they removed barriers to nondiscriminatory laws held to "directly regulate" interstate commerce. The Twenty-first Amendment, Kennedy noted, was not intended to "give States the authority to pass nonuniform laws in order to discriminate against out-of-state goods" (pp. 484–485).

The Court distinguished earlier cases that upheld laws similar to New York's and Michigan's. These laws, the Court noted, were passed immediately after the Twenty-first Amendment's ratification and did not involve the kind of discrimination present in the New York and Michigan laws at issue in *Granholm.* Moreover, the Court concluded, those early cases were inconsistent with more recent cases, such as *Bacchus Imports, Ltd.* v. *Dias* (1984), which "confirm[ed] that the Twenty-first Amendment . . . does not displace the rule that States may not give a discriminatory preference to their own producers" (p. 486).

The Court rejected arguments that the direct shipment ban enabled states to police underage drinking and ensure the orderly collection of state taxes. "The States produce little evidence," the Court wrote, "that the purchase of wine over the Internet by minors is a problem" (p. 490), citing a Federal Trade Commission report suggesting the opposite was true. Nor was the Court persuaded that discrimination was necessary to address tax collection concerns.

In the principal dissent, Justice Clarence Thomas criticized the majority for misapprehending the import of the Wilson and Webb-Kenyon acts and for disregarding earlier cases with nearly identical facts, in which the Court interpreted the amendment to permit discrimination. Thomas argued that "the Webb-Kenyon Act overturned not only [cases barring nondiscriminatory state regulations] but also [cases involving the] 'nondiscrimination' principle" (p. 503). Thomas further argued that the plain meaning of Section 2 of the Twenty-first Amendment permitted the laws struck down by the majority.

Bacchus Imports, he complained was "unpersuasive" and "swept aside the weighty authority of this Court's early Twenty-first Amendment case law" (p. 524), substituting instead a test that only regulations dealing with the amendment's "core concerns," such as temperance, fell within the scope of the amendment. Given the early Court decisions supporting even discriminatory state laws governing imports of alcoholic beverages into the states, Thomas would have upheld the challenged laws.

Brannon P. Denning

Graves v. New York ex rel. O'Keefe, 306 U.S. 466 (1939), argued 6 Mar. 1939, decided 27 Mar. 1939 by vote of 7 to 2; Stone for the Court, Hughes and Frankfurter concurring, Butler and McReynolds in dissent. Until this case, there had been an explicit immunity of state employees from federal taxation and federal employees from state taxes, going back to the 1871 decision in *Collector* v. *Day*. This immunity had been reinforced in the famous Income Tax Cases (see **Pollock* v. *Farmers' Loan & Trust*, 1895), in which the Court had held that a tax on income was a tax on the source of that income.

New York imposed an income tax on a New York resident employed by the Federal Home Owners Loan Corporation, who paid the tax and then appealed on the basis of intergovernmental tax immunity. The Court held that nothing in the Constitution required such an immunity, nor did any act of Congress specifically grant immunity to federal employees. The Court thus concluded that salaries of federal employees were subject to regular state taxes.

Justice Harlan Fiske Stone's opinion specifically overruled *Collector* v. *Day* and other cases supporting immunity as well as the doctrine that a tax on income constitutes a tax on the source of that income.

Later in the year Congress enacted the Public Salary Tax Act, specifically extending federal income taxes to state employees and also consenting to state taxes on the incomes of federal employees, although under the ruling in this case such consent was no longer necessary.

Melvin I. Urofsky

Gray v. Sanders, 372 U.S. 368 (1963), argued 17 Jan 1963, decided 18 Mar. 1963 by vote of 8 to 1; Douglas for the Court, Stewart and Clark concurring, Harlan in dissent. Concerned with inequality of voting power, *Gray* v. *Sanders* proved to be the jurisprudential stepping-stone between **Baker* v. *Carr* (1962) and the 1964 legislative reapportionment cases.

Gray involved a challenge to Georgia's system that decided primary elections for statewide and congressional offices by county units in a pattern severely weighted against urban areas. Candidates who won the popular vote could, and at times did, lose the election. The Georgia statute had survived several earlier appeals to the Supreme Court, but the decision in *Baker* v. *Carr* triggered a fresh one.

Invoking the Equal Protection Clause of the Fourteenth Amendment, the Supreme Court upheld a federal district court's invalidation of the Georgia county unit system but set aside as "inapposite" the lower tribunal's suggested alternative analogous to the national Electoral College.

The Supreme Court declared *Gray* v. *Sanders* to be a voting rights case without implications for legislative representation—a point stressed by concurring Justices Potter Stewart and Tom C. Clark. Yet Justice William O. Douglas, speaking for the Court, concluded on a broader note that was to be sounded in subsequent reapportionment cases: "The conception of political equality from the Declaration of Independence, to Lincoln's Gettysburg Address, to the Fifteenth, Seventeenth, and Nineteenth Amendments can mean only one thing—one person, one vote" (p. 381).

In dissent, Justice John M. Harlan found the record inadequate to prove invidious effects in a matter profoundly touching the barrier between federal judicial and state legislative authority. To Harlan, *Gray* seemed one more judicial step into the forbidden "political thicket."

Gordon E. Baker

Green v. Biddle, 8 Wheat. (21 U.S.) 1 (1823), argued 16 Feb. 1821, decided 5 Mar. 1821 by vote of 6 to 0; Story for the Court, Washington absent. Motion for rehearing 12 Mar. 1821, reargued 8–11 Mar. 1822; decided 27 Feb. 1823 by vote of 4 to 0; Washington for the Court, Johnson concurring, Livingston, Todd, and Marshall absent. The decisions in *Green* v. *Biddle* were the Court's most important effort after *Fletcher* v. *Peck* (1810) to expand the Contracts Clause to encompass public as well as private agreements—in this case, the Virginia-Kentucky compact of 1792.

The compact provided that the validity of Kentucky land titles was to be "determined by the laws now existing," that is, Virginia's. Kentucky, however, enacted a system of Occupying Claimant Laws, providing that actual settlers, if ejected by nonresident titleholders, could secure compensation for improvements and crops. Litigation testing the validity of Kentucky's 1792 and 1812 occupant laws went up to the Supreme Court on a certificate of division from the federal circuit court in a case brought against an occupant by John Green of Virginia. Justice Joseph Story delivered an opinion in 1821 holding the Occupying Claimant Laws unconstitutional as a violation of the Contracts Clause of Article I, section 10 and inconsistent with the Compacts Clause in the same section.

Story's opinion encountered a storm of political opposition led by Kentucky's two powerful senators, Henry Clay and Richard Johnson. In the face of this resistance, the Story opinion was "withdrawn," to be replaced by an 1823 opinion for three justices by Bushrod Washington, joined by William Johnson's concurring opinion. (Chief Justice John Marshall was absent, Brockholst Livingston mortally ill, and Thomas Todd "indisposed.") Washington's opinion held the Virginia-Kentucky compact to be a contract and as such inviolate under the Contracts Clause, but impaired by the Kentucky statutes. Kentucky again resisted vehemently and continued to enforce its land claims statutes, while the furor in Congress over the authority of the Supreme Court continued unabated.

Sandra F. VanBurkleo

Green v. County School Board of New Kent County, 391 U.S. 430 (1968), argued 3 Apr. 1968, decided 27 May 1968 by vote of 9 to 0; Brennan for the Court. Characterized by the Court simply as a case about the appropriate scope of a school desegregation remedy under **Brown* v. *Board of Education II* (1955), *Green* was a watershed in the definition—or redefinition—of the substantive right enshrined in *Brown I*.

Virginia was one of four states whose racially segregated school systems were constitutionally challenged in the litigation collectively styled by the name of the lead case, *Brown* v. *Board of Education I*. For a decade after *Brown II* Virginia disingenuously handled compliance with *Brown* on a statewide basis by a State Pupil Assignment Law, which substantially impeded desegregation. Under threat of losing federal monies in 1965, the law was scrapped and the New Kent County school board adopted a "freedom-of-choice plan," which essentially allowed students in the rural, residentially integrated district to choose which of two schools they wished to attend—the formerly all-black Watkins School or the formerly all-white New Kent School. After three years of the new plan, no whites had elected to attend Watkins and only 115 blacks attended New Kent; 85 percent of blacks in the system still attended Watkins. The plaintiff black school children argued that the "freedom-of-choice plan" in practice operated to perpetuate the racially dual school system formerly mandated by state law.

Writing for the Court, Justice William J. Brennan framed the decisive issue in the case as whether the "freedom-of-choice plan" complied with *Brown II*. In an opinion that purported to be carefully limited, Brennan noted that "[w]e do not hold that a 'freedom-of-choice' plan might of itself be held unconstitutional . . . but [only] that in desegregating a dual system a plan utilizing 'freedom of choice' is not an end in itself" (pp. 439–440). The appropriate end to the Court was a plan that "promise[d] realistically to convert promptly to a system without a 'white' school and a 'Negro' school, but just schools" (p. 442).

The Court's underlying rationale was that a variety of factors, not necessarily found as fact by the trial court in *Green* but identified in federal studies, made "freedom of choice" unlikely to work—fear of hostility or retaliation to those electing to change schools, undue influence by public officials and private parties, ancillary effects of poverty, and unequal facilities between schools. Because of such factors, the Court concluded that freedom of choice was likely to fail to accomplish what *Brown II* required, the disestablishment of a dual system.

Green is the most significant school case decided after *Brown II*. Under a narrow reading of both *Brown* opinions, formerly state-segregated school systems could discharge their constitutional obligations by removing legally imposed attendance assignments based on race. Indeed, for a brief period, the National Association for the Advancement of Colored People (NAACP), which had brought *Brown* and its precursors, urged its local affiliates after *Brown II* to request "freedom of choice plans."

In the face of southern "massive resistance" to desegregation, and later of white flight first to private schools and then simply away from areas populated by black families, the NAACP changed its strategy to press for the type of relief sought, and eventually approved, in *Green*. The thrust of *Brown* was thus recast as one directed at the effects of dual systems instead of at their basis. The consequence was that compliance with *Brown*, at least in formerly state-segregated (de jure) systems, could soon only be demonstrated by schools with racial composition reflecting the school-age population. As white flight accelerated, only busing could achieve *Green*'s objective. NAACP counsel conceded during oral argument in *Green* that the new remedy paradoxically required the states and the Court to sanction what *Brown* notionally condemned—racially based pupil assignments. On a less conspicuous level, *Green* also diverted the emphasis in school desegregation from equality of education opportunity to numerical congruity in school attendance.

Dennis J. Hutchinson

Gregg v. Georgia, 428 U.S. 153 (1976), argued 31 Mar. 1976, decided 2 July 1976 by vote of 7 to 2; Stewart announced the decision in an opinion joined by Powell and Stevens; White, Burger, Rehnquist, and Blackmun concurring; Brennan and Marshall in dissent. With two companion cases from Florida and Texas, the Supreme Court reaffirmed the constitutionality of the death penalty in the wake of *Furman* v. *Georgia* (1972). The justices in *Gregg* upheld statutes that guide judge and jury when imposing the death penalty. The Court rejected claims that capital punishment was unconstitutional per se but implied strongly that mandatory death penalty statutes would violate the Eighth Amendment's proscription of *cruel and unusual punishment. *Woodson* v. *North Carolina* (1976), decided the same day, specifically outlawed the mandatory death sentence.

Gregg had been convicted of two counts of armed robbery and two counts of murder. The Georgia death penalty statute provided guidelines for the jury to follow in the sentencing stage of a bifurcated trial. The statute required the jury to find beyond a reasonable doubt and to specify in writing that at least one of ten specified aggravating circumstances existed before it could impose the death penalty. The aggravating circumstances included whether the accused (1) created a great risk of death to more than one person in a public place; (2) acted as either the agent of or the principal for another in the commission of a murder; (3) had a prior conviction for a capital felony; (4) had escaped from custody; or (5) had killed a firefighter or a criminal justice system officer in the performance of that officer's duties. The Georgia Supreme Court had previously struck down as insufficiently clear and objective an aggravating circumstance in which the offender had "a substantial history of serious assaultive criminal convictions."

The Georgia statute also required consideration of such mitigating circumstances as the offender's youth, cooperation with the police, and emotional state at the time of the offense. And it provided mandatory review of death sentences by the Georgia Supreme Court to consider whether (1) the sentence was influenced by passion, prejudice, or any other arbitrary factor; (2) the evidence supported the finding of an aggravated circumstance; and (3) the penalty was excessive or disproportionate in relation to similar cases and defendants.

The trial judge in *Gregg* advised the jury that it could recommend the death sentence or life imprisonment for each count and that it was free to consider mitigating as well as aggravating circumstances. Specifically, he instructed the jury that it could not impose the death sentence unless it found beyond a reasonable doubt that the murders were committed in one or more of the three applicable aggravating circumstances, that is, during the commission of other capital crimes, for the purpose of receiving the victim's property, or that the crime was outrageously heinous. The jury found the first two of these aggravating circumstances and imposed the death penalty on all counts. The Georgia Supreme Court found that the sentences for murder did not result from prejudice or other arbitrary factors and that they were not excessive in relation to the crime. But it reversed the sentences for robbery on the ground that the death penalty was rarely imposed for armed robbery in Georgia.

For the Supreme Court, Justice Potter Stewart declared that the Eight Amendment incorporated a "basic concept of human dignity." He found the death penalty was not cruel and unusual per se. The Fifth and Fourteenth Amendments' due process clauses imply it. More important, the concept of dignity is consistent with the purposes of deterrence and of retribution. In light of evolving standards of decency, the penalty, according to Stewart, is constitutional when it is proportional to the severity of the crime (not arbitrary) and is not a wanton infliction of pain. Legislatures need not prove that the death penalty deters, nor need they select the least severe penalty possible. Legislative choices of penalties thus carry a heavy presumption of validity. Stewart also emphasized that constitutional acknowledgment and public acceptance of the death penalty strengthen its presumptive validity and that retribution is a valid legislative consideration.

The Georgia statute, according to Stewart, effectively prevents arbitrary and disproportionate death sentences (1) because the bifurcated procedure allows full exploration of the evidence relating to the penalty; (2) because the sentencing body must make specific factual findings to support the result; and (3) because state supreme court review insures comparability and proportionality among defendants who receive the death penalty. Stewart rejected the argument that prosecutorial discretion, plea bargaining, and executive clemency, which introduce elements of randomness that comparability studies will not detect, made the death penalty arbitrary and hence in violation of the Eighth Amendment. He also endorsed Georgia's requirement that the sentencing body consider a broad scope of evidence and argument before determining the sentence.

Justice Byron White, joined by Warren Burger and William Rehnquist, stated that Gregg had failed in his burden of showing that the Georgia Supreme Court had not in this case insured against discriminatory,

freakish, or wanton administration of the death penalty. Nor had he demonstrated that the Georgia Supreme Court could not adequately do so in any and all cases. White also insisted that rational considerations, for example, the strength of evidence and the likelihood that the jury would in fact impose the penalty, determine the prosecutor's discretionary decision whether to seek the death penalty. Therefore, limited prosecutorial discretion did not make the penalty unconstitutionally arbitrary.

Basic criticisms of the reasoning in *Gregg* focus on the plurality's failure to connect persuasively its initial claim that the Eighth Amendment embodies a basic concept of human dignity with its conclusion that sentences may consider a wide range of information in deciding whether to apply the penalty. If, in other words, human dignity stands as an independent moral criterion for deciding when a punishment is cruel and unusual, then the plurality should have read into the amendment the specific moral and factual conditions that aggravate and mitigate the case for capital punishment.

By failing to do so, the Supreme Court gave little guidance to legislatures attempting to draft a death penalty statute with respect to (1) the criteria for choosing aggravating and mitigating circumstances; (2) the breadth of discretion sentencing bodies should retain once the circumstances are known; and (3) how the sentencing body will in practice determine whether a given circumstance does or does not exist. Indeed, without settling such matters it is difficult to see how an appellate court on mandatory review can determine that the requirement for comparability has been met, except by resorting to gross statistical comparisons. Such comparisons would violate the Court's requirement that juries take account of mitigating circumstances. A mandatory death penalty applied in narrowly defined circumstances would apparently achieve proportionality more effectively, but *Woodson* v. *North Carolina* struck down mandatory sentences precisely because they would not permit considering mitigating circumstances.

It is equally difficult to square the autonomous human dignity standard with the plurality's endorsement of retribution and deterrence. Penological evidence does not support the proposition that the death penalty serves effectively as either a general or a specific deterrent, and retribution lies too close to vengeance to accept as an unquestioned component of human dignity. Yet the plurality made no serious attempt to defend deterrence or retribution on either rational or human-dignity grounds. Similarly, the obvious randomizing tendencies introduced by prosecutorial discretion, plea bargaining, and executive clemency cried out for a human-dignity defense, but the plurality dismissed this difficulty without serious discussion. In short, *Gregg* failed to specify conditions and procedures for restricting in practice the arbitrariness it condemned. Justices William Brennan and Thurgood Marshall noted these points in dissent.

□ Hugo Adam Bedau, ed., *The Death Penalty in America* (1982). Welsh S. White, *The Death Penalty in the Eighties: An Examination of the Modern System of Capital Punishment* (1987).
Lief H. Carter

Griffin v. California, 380 U.S. 609 (1965), argued 9 Mar. 1965, decided 28 Apr. 1965 by vote of 7 to 2; Douglas for the Court, Stewart and White in dissent. The Fifth Amendment's privilege against self-incrimination, which binds the federal government, applies equally to the states through the Due Process Clause of the Fourteenth Amendment. The issue in this case was whether a state violates this privilege when it allows prosecutors and judges to comment adversely on a defendant's failure to testify in a criminal proceeding. In holding that it does, the Supreme Court said that such a practice makes the defendant pay a price for refusing to speak. He pays a price for his silence because the comments of the prosecutor or judge invite jurors to disregard the presumption of innocence to which he is constitutionally entitled. Even an innocent or honest person may have many reasons— timidity is one of them—for not taking the witness stand in his own defense. Needless to say, however, the privilege protects the guilty as well.

Allowing judges or jurors to draw inferences of guilt from the silence of the accused, remarked the Court, is a remnant of the inquisitorial system of criminal justice. Because the American system is accusatorial, the Fifth and Fourteenth Amendments must be construed to forbid comment on the defendant's failure to testify by either the prosecutor or the court. There is of course no way of keeping a jury from drawing an adverse inference from silence even in the absence of such commentary. But as

the Court said, "[w]hat it may infer when the court solemnizes the silence of the accused into evidence against him is quite another [matter]" (p. 614). *Griffin* overruled *Adamson v. *California* (1947).
Donald P. Kommers

Griffin v. County School Board of Prince Edward County, 377 U.S. 218 (1964), argued 30 Mar. 1964, decided 25 May 1964 by vote of 9 to 0; Black for the Court, Clark and Harlan concurring. Instead of complying with the mandate of *Brown v. *Board of Education II* (1955) to eliminate racial assignments to public schools, the Prince Edward County, Virginia, Board of Education, pursuant to state law, closed its public schools and provided tuition grants and tax credits to private schools attended only by white children. Justice Hugo Black's opinion for the Court impatiently swept aside plausible procedural defenses of the policy and announced that "[t]he time for mere 'deliberate speed' has run out" (p. 234), that the district court was empowered to enjoin further use of grants and credits, that the court could superintend the board's taxing and appropriation powers, and even that it could order the public schools reopened. On the final point, Justices Tom Clark and John M. Harlan "disagree[d]" without explanation—marking the first time since well before *Brown* that even partially dissenting views had been expressed in the Court with respect to litigation involving segregation and the Fourteenth Amendment.

Of greater significance was the Court's unequivocal rejection of tactics designed to forestall compliance with *Brown II*. After *Griffin,* affected school districts appeared to choose between either desegregating their racially dual systems or acquiescing in white flight to private academies.
Dennis J. Hutchinson

Griggs v. Duke Power Co., 401 U.S. 424 (1971), argued 14 Dec. 1970, decided 8 Mar. 1971 by vote of 8 to 0; Burger for the Court, Brennan not participating. *Griggs* is recognized as the most significant case in the development of employment discrimination law under Title VII of the Civil Rights Act of 1964. It provided new definitions of job discrimination that had far-reaching consequences.

The district court found that prior to the effective date of Title VII, the company discriminated on the basis of race in the hiring and assigning of workers at its facility in Draper, North Carolina. The company's longstanding practice was to hire blacks into an all-black labor classification where the highest paying job paid less than the lowest paying job in the all-white departments. Job promotion was based upon racial lines of progression within segregated departments. On 2 July 1965, the date on which Title VII became effective, the company established a new policy of requiring applicants for jobs in the traditional white classifications, including those who wished to transfer from other departments, to score acceptable grades on two aptitude tests in addition to fulfilling the requirement of a high school education. The district court held that the earlier practices "were beyond the reach" of Title VII and that the new tests were not intentionally discriminatory.

The Supreme Court overruled and held in favor of the black plaintiffs. It noted the systematic nature of employment discrimination and that Title VII was intended to eliminate such patterns of discrimination; thus the act required the removal of all barriers perpetuating the benefits that white employees obtain at the expense of blacks. Ostensibly neutral practices are unlawful, according to the Court, if they operate to maintain the effects of past discrimination.

The Court held further that intent or discriminatory purpose is irrelevant; it is consequences that matter. Tests used for hiring and promotion must be job related and validated under Equal Employment Opportunity Commission guidelines.

Finally the Court held invalid practices, however neutral in intent, that caused a disparate impact upon a group protected by the act. The *Griggs* disparate impact concept was based on the Court's construction of section 702 (a) (2) of Title VII and has been successfully invoked in many contexts. Although Title VII law has continued to evolve and the burden of proof had shifted to plaintiffs, the basic holdings of *Griggs* remain valid.

In *Ward's Cove Packing Co. v. Atonio* (1989), the Court in a 5-to-4 decision revised the standards governing proof of discrimination in Title VII disparate impact cases. Under the standard established in *Griggs*, the burden was upon the employer to prove that any disparate impact caused by his practices was justified by business necessity. Under the standards required in *Ward's*

Cove, the burden of proof remains with the plaintiff at all times. In *Price Waterhouse v. Hopkins* (1989), the Court shifted the burden of proof, holding that a disparate treatment plaintiff must demonstrate by direct evidence that employment practices substantially depended on illegitimate criteria. The Civil Rights Act of 1991 altered the burden once again.

Herbert Hill

Griswold v. Connecticut, 381 U.S. 479 (1965), argued 29 Mar. 1965, decided 7 June 1965, by vote of 7 to 2; Douglas for the Court, Goldberg, Harlan, and White concurring, Black and Stewart in dissent. *Griswold* is a curious but important case in American constitutional history. It concerned an "uncommonly silly law" (as Justice Potter Stewart called it) that was technically difficult to challenge on constitutional grounds, as evidenced by the divergent positions of the justices concurring with the majority position. These opinions not only made *Griswold* one of the most significant decisions of the 1965 term but fueled controversies both about the general character of constitutional lawmaking and about specific rights that have continued decades later.

Evolution of the Dispute. A Connecticut statue of 1879 made it a crime for any person to use any drug, article, or instrument to prevent conception. This statute had been challenged twice before, in 1943 (*Tileston v. Ullman*), where the Supreme Court held that the plaintiff lacked standing, and in 1961 (*Poe v. Ullman*), where the Court determined that the controversy was not ripe because the plaintiff had not been prosecuted.

By 1965, however, the Court determined to resolve the constitutionality of the statute. Suit was initiated by two members of the Planned Parenthood League of Connecticut. Its executive director and medical director had been convicted of violating the statute by giving information, instruction, and medical advice to married persons regarding means of preventing conception. The conviction was affirmed by the Supreme Court of Errors of Connecticut.

On appeal, the United States Supreme Court reversed by a 7-to-2 margin. The majority determined that: (1) the appellants had standing to raise the constitutional rights of people with whom they had a professional relationship; and (2) the statute was invalid because it infringed on the constitutionally protected right to "privacy" of married persons.

Implied Rights: The New Substantive Due Process? The majority holding in *Griswold* to a large extent was positioned within post-1937 constitutional theory. It protected basic constitutional rights and applied them against the states in conventional fashion under the Fourteenth Amendment, and it mandated a stricter scrutiny for laws that interfere with "fundamental personal rights" than for those that regulate economic relations. The Court's more controversial step of applying this logic to fundamental rights—here, of privacy—not expressly enumerated in the Bill of Rights likewise was hardly unprecedented. The Court previously had affirmed the unwritten rights to teach one's child a foreign language (*Meyer v. Nebraska*, 1923), to send one's children to private schools (*Pierce v. Society of Sisters*, 1925), to procreate (*Skinner v. Oklahoma*, 1942), to resist certain invasions of the body (*Rochin v. California*, 1952), and to travel abroad (*Aptheker v. Secretary of State*, 1964). What made *Griswold* a landmark case was the Court's willingness to explicitly justify at length this practice of investing such unenumerated rights with full constitutional status.

It is on this point that the justices were most divided. Indeed, four different lines of justification in defense of unenumerated fundamental rights were outlined by supporters of the majority decision. Justice William O. Douglas, writing for five members of the Court, referred to rights that are implicit in, or peripheral to, other express guarantees in the Bill of Rights. In his famous words, "specific guarantees . . . have penumbras, formed by emanations from those guarantees that help give them life and substance" (p. 484). Just as the Court earlier had found that First Amendment rights to freedom of speech implied a peripheral "right to freedom of association," he reasoned, so do the First, Third, Fourth, Fifth, and Ninth Amendments imply "zones of privacy" that form the basis for the general privacy right affirmed in this case.

Justice Arthur Goldberg, joined by Chief Justice Earl Warren and Justice William Brennan, staked out a more expansive approach to justifying the right of privacy. Although he found merit in the penumbra and emanations argument of Douglas, Goldberg argued further that "liberty protects those personal rights that are funda-

mental, and is not confined to the specific terms of the Bill of Rights." The Fourteenth Amendment may not incorporate all of the first eight amendments, Goldberg acknowledged. However, the specific "language and history of the Ninth Amendment" provide strong support for judicial incorporation of additional rights "so rooted in the traditions and conscience of our people as to be ranked fundamental" in our constitutional legacy (p. 487).

Justices John M. Harlan and Byron White advanced positions that, by contrast, severed altogether the link between the Fourteenth Amendment and the Bill of Rights. Harlan rejected the incorporation doctrine as a historically groundless and ineffective check on judicial discretion, while reproaching the "letter or penumbra" logic of Douglas as overly restrictive of future rights development. Instead, he affirmed a commitment to due process and liberty that "stands . . . on its own bottom," constrained only by the forces of history and cultural values that bind the court. By this logic, the Connecticut statute violated basic values "implicit in the concept of ordered liberty" (p. 500). Justice White rooted his argument in a similarly expansive interpretation of Fourteenth Amendment due process guarantees but focused his attention on the terms of strict scrutiny by which the Court should balance fundamental rights of individuals with compelling state interests in such cases.

The dissents by Justices Hugo Black and Potter Stewart expressed the same disdain for the Connecticut statute as had the majority. However, both denied that the state law infringed upon any fundamental constitutional right. In their view, such a right—whether rooted in the "implied rights" theories of Douglas and Goldberg or in the "natural justice" positions of Harlan and White—lacked specific constitutional authorization and represented an arbitrary exercise of judicial power that threatened the American system of government. "Use of any such broad, unbounded judicial authority would make of this Court's members a day-to-day constitutional convention," argued Black. This would amount to a "great unconstitutional shift of power to the courts which . . . will be bad for the courts and worse for the country" (p. 520).

Scholarly debate has amplified these disagreements among members of the Court. In particular, many critics of the decision have elaborated Black's charge that the majority was simply offering a new and unwarranted version of the old "substantive *due process" doctrine. Why, critics asked, is it less dangerous for Supreme Court justices to impose their personal preferences on legislators and society in matters of personal rights than in matters of economic relations? If the old *Lochner* logic was wrong, why is this new form of "Lochnerizing" not wrong as well? Moreover, are judges any more qualified to determine one form of rights than another? And is the legitimacy of a "government of laws" no less undermined by unrestrained, arbitrary judicial policy-making in one sphere than in another?

Defenders of the majority have ranged even more widely in their arguments than did the justices. Some supporters have emphasized the decision's solid groundings in past judicial practice, theoretical logic, and constitutional text. Indeed, both Douglas and Goldberg explicitly declined the invitation to follow in the substantive due process tradition. "We do not sit as a super-legislature to determine the wisdom, need, and propriety of laws that touch economic problems, business affairs, or social conditions," wrote Douglas. The law in question, by contrast, "operates directly on an intimate relation of husband and wife" that long has received constitutional protection (p. 482).

Other supporters of the majority instead have affirmed Justices Harlan and White's unabashed rejection of formalist illusions about textual constraints upon judicial action. They argue that legal interpretation is always discretionary, and that textual constraints on judges are far less important than cultural and political forces. Moreover, many scholars have defended the Court's zealous defense of personal rights as both within its institutional capacities and functionally necessary to maintaining liberty in our modern corporate society. Such arguments were sufficiently compelling that all nine justices, including Stewart, by 1973 had accepted the Court's role in giving the Fourteenth Amendment's Due Process Clause a substantive content that exceeds the Bill of Rights, although considerable differences remained about how and when that authority should be exercised.

Privacy Rights: Subsequent Case Law and Theoretical Disputes. Controversies over the constitutional grounding of unenumerated rights have been paralleled by controversies over the range of prac-tices and relations that such rights protect. Indeed, the majority in *Griswold* was far more expansive about legal justifications for a right of privacy than about its theoretical content and reach. And while the Court recognized that commitments to privacy have deep roots in American society and its laws, that legacy has provided a vague guide for determining the substantive scope of privacy rights in modern social relations. Not surprisingly, questions regarding conceptual coherence have continued to surround the doctrine.

Critics query whether the logic of "privacy" extends to all social relations—including the sale of contraceptives to unmarried individuals (*Carey* v. *Population Services International*, 1977), relations among homosexuals (**Bowers* v. *Hardwick*, 1986), and women's choices regarding abortion (**Roe* v. *Wade*, 1973). For example, is it really privacy that is most infringed by regulations restricting the sale and distribution of contraceptives? Do regulations of sales concern privacy more than those on solicitation, which was treated primarily as a matter of free speech in *Bolger* v. *Youngs Drugs Product Corp.* (1983)?

Moreover, the privacy doctrine has been increasingly attacked from both ends of the political spectrum. On the one hand, the doctrine as applied to abortion since *Roe* has continued to provoke the outrage of conservatives over both the expansion of judicial authority and its resulting protections for allegedly immoral individual actions. Ironically, conservatives have rejected the privacy doctrine because it limits state intervention into the lives of citizens.

On the other hand, the privacy doctrine has been assailed from the political left for advancing a far too truncated and archaic liberal understanding of freedom. Critics on the left condemn the *Griswold* decision for limiting the privacy protection for contraception use to persons bound in conventional marriage relations. This shield for contraception use was extended a few years later to unmarried persons in **Eisenstadt* v. *Baird* (1972), but the Court's repeated denial of protection for homosexual relationships has revealed privacy limits as a challenge to traditional norms regarding sexuality (*Bowers*). Moreover, while the privacy logic has been useful to limit at least some unwanted state intervention in intimate sexual matters, it has also been employed to preclude a positive state role in educating citizens and providing funding essential for the exercise of rights to use birth control and receive an abortion. Some critics thus argue for the need to replace the privacy logic with a more affirmative conception of autonomy rights that is more consistent with the goals of equality and empowerment.

Legacy. The legacy of the privacy rights doctrine thus points to the perennial problem of Court efforts to deal with changing social needs, values, and interests through invocation of traditional norms long supportive of quite different relationships. The right of privacy affirmed in *Griswold* still stands, but clearly is jeopardized by increasingly restrictive Court rulings on protections for abortion, its most important doctrinal application.

□ Rhonda Copelon, "Beyond the Liberal Idea of Privacy: Toward A Positive Right of Autonomy," in *Judging the Constitution: Critical Essays on Judicial Lawmaking*, edited by Michael W. McCann and Gerald L. Houseman (1989), pp. 287–316. Allan Dionisopolous and Craig Ducat, eds., *The Right to Privacy: Essays and Cases* (1976). Louis Henken, "Privacy and Autonomy," *Columbia Law Review* 74 (1974): 1410–1433. "Symposium on the *Griswold* Case and the Right of Privacy," *Michigan Law Review* 64 (1965): 197–282.

Michael W. McCann

Grosjean v. American Press Co., 297 U.S. 233 (1936), argued 14 Jan. 1936, decided 10 Feb. 1936 by vote of 9 to 0; Sutherland for the Court. The Court unanimously invalidated a license tax on the business of selling advertising (in the amount of 2 percent of the gross receipts from such sales) imposed by Louisiana in 1934 on all newspapers with a circulation of more than twenty thousand copies per week. The tax was challenged as an abridgment of freedom of the press and as a violation of equal protection. It was noted by counsel that only thirteen of the 163 newspapers in the state had sufficient circulation to be required to pay it, and twelve of those thirteen were actively opposed to the Huey Long administration, at whose instigation the tax was enacted.

The Court considered only the free press challenge. It equated the license tax to the "taxes on knowledge" imposed on newspapers and advertising by Parliament in the eighteenth century, whose purpose was not to raise revenue but to reduce the circula-

tion of newspapers and thus limit public access to criticisms of the Crown. The obviously similar motivation of the Louisiana legislature was plainly crucial to the Court's conclusion here. The tax was held unconstitutional because it was hostile to the press. It applied only to "a selected group of newspapers" (p. 251) and was "a deliberate and calculated device in the guise of a tax to limit the circulation of information" pertaining to public affairs (p. 250).

The year after *Grosjean*, the Court made clear that newspapers are not exempt from nondiscriminatory general taxation. In *Giragi v. Moore* (1937), it dismissed without opinion a claim for such an exemption. The Court has since categorically declared that newspapers are subject to all forms of nondiscriminatory economic regulation, including taxation (*Minneapolis Star & Tribune Co. v. Minnesota Commissioner of Revenue,* 1983).

Dean Alfange, Jr.

Grove City College v. Bell, 465 U.S. 555 (1984), argued 29 Nov. 1983, decided 28 Feb. 1984 by vote of 6 to 3; White for the Court, Powell concurring in part and dissenting in part, Brennan, joined by Marshall and Stevens, concurring in part and dissenting in part. In this case the Court found that Title IX of the Education Amendments of 1972 prohibited gender discrimination in colleges and universities that receive federal funds. Grove City College's enrollment of students who received Basic Educational Opportunity Grants from the federal government was found sufficient to trigger Title IX, although the college, as a matter of principle, received no other federal funds. But the sanction of Title IX—the cutoff of federal funds—was limited to the discriminatory program and could not be applied to any other programs at the school. Thus, under the Court's ruling a university that discriminated against women could continue to receive federal funding so long as specific discriminatory programs did not.

Reaction to *Grove City* was immediate. Civil rights and women's groups were outraged by the decision. So too were many members of Congress who saw this case as a prime example of the weakening of the Reagan administration's civil rights commitment. *Grove City* originally had been filed by the Justice Department under the Carter Administration. It took the position that Grove City College was not in compliance with Title IX because all programs needed to comply in order for a school to have funding eligibility. However, when the case reached the Supreme Court the Reagan Administration Justice Department retreated from that position to one urging only a limited cutoff of funding.

In 1987, over the veto of President Ronald Reagan, Congress enacted the Civil Rights Restoration Act to overturn *Grove City*. The bill specified that Title IX applies to any college or university if any part of the institution receives federal assistance. Thus, all of the university's federal funds are now at risk even if there is proven discrimination in only one program.

Karen O'Connor

Groves v. Slaughter, 15 Pet. (40 U.S.) 449 (1841), argued 12, 13, 15-18 Feb. 1841 and decided 10 Mar. 1841 by vote of 5 to 2; Thompson delivered the judgment of the Court but wrote only for himself and Wayne; Taney, McLean, and Baldwin concurring only in the result; McKinley and Story in dissent; Catron was absent for illness and Barbour had just died. *Groves* v. *Slaughter* involved explosive problems arising out of the relationship among slavery, the interstate slave trade, federal commerce power, and state police power. Mississippi by 1832 constitutional amendments prohibited the introduction of slaves into the state for sale, but did not enact legislation enforcing the prohibition. A purchaser defaulted on notes given for imported slaves, and the seller contended that the state constitutional prohibition was void because of conflict with the federal commerce power.

Justice Smith Thompson's opinion avoided the constitutional issues by holding that the constitutional prohibition was not self-executing. But Justice John McLean insisted on delivering a concurring opinion filled with crypto-abolitionist dicta, which provoked Chief Justice Roger B. Taney and Justice Henry Baldwin to deliver counterconcurrences refuting McLean's points with proslavery dicta. Taney and Baldwin both insisted that state control over slavery and African-Americans was exclusive of all federal power. The inability of the Court to cohere on, or even to evade, constitutional questions implicated by interstate commerce and slavery was symptomatic of deep divisions among the justices, which in turn reflected the emerging sectional controversy over slavery in the country.

William M. Wiecek

Grovey v. Townsend, 295 U.S. 45 (1935), argued 11 Mar. 1935, decided 1 Apr. 1935 by vote of 9 to 0; Roberts for the Court. In 1923 Texas prohibited blacks from participating in the Democratic primaries in the state, but in *Nixon* v. *Herndon* (1927) the Supreme Court ruled this law violated the Equal Protection Clause of the Fourteenth Amendment. The Texas legislature then authorized the party's executive committee to prohibit blacks from voting in party primaries, but in *Nixon* v. *Condon* (1932) the Court ruled that this still constituted impermissible state action because the party executive committee was a creation of the legislature. Even before the Court decided the *Grovey* case, the Texas Democratic Party took steps to protect their whites-only primary system. In May 1932 a convention of Texas Democrats limited party membership to whites. R. R. Grovey, a black resident of Houston, sued the county clerk for refusing to give him a ballot for a Democratic primary election. Justice Owen Roberts ruled that the party convention's decision to exclude blacks from the Democratic primary was not state action because the party was a voluntary association of its members, who had acted in their private capacity to exclude blacks. Roberts reached this conclusion despite his acknowledgment that the state regulated primaries in a variety of ways, including a requirement that sealed ballot boxes be turned over to county clerks after each primary election. In the absence of state action, Roberts found that the white primary was constitutional when authorized by a party convention without any encouragement from the state legislature. This holding was later specifically reversed in *Smith* v. *Allwright* (1944).

Paul Finkelman

Grutter v. Bollinger, 123 S. Ct. 2325 (2003), argued 1 Apr. 2003, decided 23 June 2003, by vote of 5 to 4; O'Connor for the Court, joined by Stevens, Souter, Ginsburg, and Breyer, joined in part by Scalia and Thomas, Ginsburg concurring, joined by Breyer, Scalia concurring in part and dissenting in part, joined by Thomas, Thomas concurring in part and dissenting in part, joined by Scalia, Rehnquist dissenting, joined by Scalia, Kennedy and Thomas, Kennedy dissenting. **Gratz v. Bollinger,** 123 S. Ct. 2411 (2003), argued 1 Apr. 2003, decided 23 June 2003, by vote of 6 to 3; Rehnquist for the Court, joined by O'Connor, Scalia, Kennedy and Thomas, O'Connor concurring, joined in part by Breyer, Thomas concurring, Breyer concurring in the judgment, Stevens dissenting, joined by Souter, Souter dissenting, joined in part by Ginsburg, Ginsburg dissenting, joined by Souter and joined in part by Breyer.

In these two cases, the Supreme Court revisited for the first time since *Bakke* the question of whether, and in what manner, the Equal Protection Clause of the Fourteenth Amendment permits a public university to consider the race of applicants in its admissions decisions. In *Grutter*, the Court considered the admissions policy for the University of Michigan Law School; in *Gratz*, it considered the admissions policy for the University of Michigan's undergraduate program.

Both policies had as a goal the admission of a racially diverse student body and, to that end, took into consideration an applicant's race. The policies differed, however, in how they factored race into the admissions process. The law school's policy required that each applicant be individually evaluated based on his or her entire file (undergraduate grade point average, law school admissions test (LSAT) scores, a personal statement, letters of recommendation, and an essay describing the way in which the applicant would contribute to the life and diversity of the law school). It instructed admissions officials to ensure that applicants had the ability to "do well enough to graduate with no serious academic problems," but also to assess "the applicant's likely contribution to the intellectual and social life of the institution." One express aim of the policy was to "achieve that diversity which has the potential to enrich everyone's education and thus make a law school class stronger than the sum of its parts." Special attention was to be given to the inclusion of students from groups that have been historically discriminated against, such as African-Americans, Hispanics, and Native Americans, who without this commitment might not be represented in the student body in meaningful numbers. For those underrepresented groups, the stated goal was to enroll a "critical mass," in order to "ensure their ability to make unique contributions to the character of the Law School."

At the undergraduate level, the university sought to increase the number of underrepresented minorities through an admissions policy that assigned twenty points to every applicant from an underrepresented minor-

ity group, one-fifth of the one hundred points needed to guarantee admission and more than the points assigned to any other attribute.

In *Grutter*, applying strict scrutiny, the Court approved the law school's approach. First, it held that a state's interest in achieving a racially diverse student body is a compelling state interest because of the educational benefits that flow from diversity. It then held that the law school's admission's policy was narrowly tailored to achieve that end because, while giving some weight to the race of an applicant, it was not a quota and it guaranteed individualized consideration. As Justice Sandra Day O'Connor explained in her opinion for the Court: "The Law School engages in a highly individualized, holistic review of each applicant's file, giving serious consideration to all the ways an applicant might contribute to a diverse educational environment."

In *Gratz*, however, the Court reached the opposite conclusion. Bound by the holding in *Grutter* that diversity is a compelling state interest, the Court held that undergraduate admissions policy was not narrowly tailored to meet that end, because the automatic assignment of twenty points to each applicant from an underrepresented minority group did not provide for any individualized consideration. Rather, the undergraduate approach made the factor of race decisive for virtually every minimally qualified underrepresented minority applicant.

Only Justices O'Connor and Stephen Breyer agreed with the outcome in both cases. For both, the key difference in the policies was the fact that the undergraduate policy did not provide for a "meaningful individualized review of applicants." Four members of the Court, Chief Justice William Rehnquist and Justices Antonin Scalia, Clarence Thomas, and Anthony Kennedy, would have held both policies unconstitutional. Both Rehnquist and Kennedy argued that neither policy was narrowly tailored to achieve the end of racial diversity; the chief justice described the law school's policy as a "sham" to cover a scheme of racially proportionate admissions. Both Scalia and Thomas argued that the equal protection clause prohibits any consideration of race in admissions. In *Grutter*, Scalia described the claimed educational benefits of a diverse student body, "cross-racial understanding," "better preparation of students for an increasingly diverse workforce and society," and good "citizenship," as lessons of life not law. Thomas argued that the real interest at stake was not the incremental "educational benefit" that emanates from the "fabled critical mass of minority students," but rather the school's interest in maintaining a "prestige" law school whose normal admissions standards disproportionately exclude blacks and other minorities." Quoting Frederick Douglass, he deplored the negative stereotyping that he sees as an inevitable outcome of race preferences in admissions programs.

Two members of the Court, Justices John Paul Stevens and David Souter, would have dismissed *Gratz* for lack of a plaintiff with proper standing. Only Justice Ruth Bader Ginsburg would have held both policies constitutional, although Souter would have as well absent the standing issue. Ginsburg's dissent in *Gratz*, joined in part by Breyer, criticizes the majority for continuing to apply the same equal protection standard to all official race classifications, rather than distinguishing between policies of exclusion and policies of inclusion. Given the history of racism and its continued effects in this country, she maintained that race-consciousness (in the latter sense) may be constitutional if "benign," and if it does not "trammel unduly upon the opportunities of others or interfere too harshly with legitimate expectations of persons in once-preferred groups."

Although the Court's rulings in these cases upheld generally the use of race-conscious admissions policies in education, its opinion in *Grutter* states that "We expect that 25 years from now, the use of racial preferences will no longer be necessary to further the interest approved today." Scalia and Thomas agreed that there had to be a time limit, but not one so casually announced. Ginsburg, joined by Breyer, agreed that race-conscious admissions programs must have a "logical end point," but cautioned that the twenty-five-year goal could be only a "hope" and not "firmly forecast."

Alison E. Grossman

Guest, United States v., 383 U.S. 745 (1966), argued 9 Nov. 1965, decided 28 Mar. 1966 by vote of 9 to 0; Stewart for the Court, Clark concurring, Harlan and Brennan concurring and dissenting; **United States v. Price,** 383 U.S. 787 (1966), argued and decided on same dates as *Guest*, also by vote of 9 to 0;

Fortas for the Court. These cases arose from incidents of violence connected with the modern civil rights movement. *Guest* resulted from the Klan-style murder of Lemuel Penn, an African-American Washington, D.C., educator, in Georgia; *Price* stemmed from the murders of three civil rights workers in Neshoba County, Mississippi. In its rulings, the Court gave broad readings to two Reconstruction-era civil rights statutes—one forbidding conspiracies to interfere with rights "secured" by the Constitution and federal law, the other punishing violations, under color of law, of rights "secured or protected" by U.S. law. *Guest* came close, moreover, to rejecting the holding of the *Civil Rights Cases* (1883) that Congress's power to enforce the Fourteenth Amendment extended only to state, not private, action.

In overturning a federal district judge's dismissal of most counts of an indictment against eighteen defendants in *Price*, Justice Abe Fortas concluded that the first of these Reconstruction-era statues reached Fourteenth Amendment rights in addition to the privileges of national citizenship it had traditionally covered and further held that private citizens acting in concert with local police could be tried for violating the other statute's "under color of law" provisions. In *Guest*, Justice Potter Stewart reversed the dismissal of charges against six defendants, two of whom had already been acquitted in state court of Lemuel Penn's murder. Stewart upheld a count of the indictment charging an interference with interstate travel as a privilege of national citizenship. Since another count of the indictment charged false reports to police as part of the defendants' conspiracy to intimidate African-Americans in the equal utilization of public facilities, Stewart was also able to reinstate that count without challenging the precedent created in the *Civil Rights Cases*. In separate opinions, however, three justices agreed that Congress had authority to punish private interferences with Fourteenth Amendment rights.

Tinsley E. Yarbrough

Guinn v. United States, 238 U.S. 347 (1915), argued 17 Oct. 1913, decided 21 June 1915 by vote of 8 to 0: White for the Court, McReynolds recused. To convince poor and illiterate whites to support literacy and property qualifications for voting, southern Democrats in the late nineteenth and early twentieth centuries included escape clauses in their suffrage restriction laws. The least subtle of these was the grandfather clause, which allowed anyone to register to vote if he had been eligible in 1867, before the Fifteenth Amendment was ratified, or it he were a legal descendant of such a man. Some representatives of the southern upper class opposed this as too transparent an attempt to evade the Constitution, or because they wished to disfranchise the white, as well as the black, lower class.

Accordingly, restrictionists limited the time for qualifying under the grandfather clause in the five Old South states that adopted it, beginning with Louisiana in 1898. In September 1910, however, Oklahoma passed a literacy test with a permanent grandfather clause. Fearing political oblivion if his party lost its African-American support, Republican U.S. District Attorney John Emory brought criminal charges under the 1870 Ku Klux Klan Act against two election officials. The state's Democratic party provided the opposing counsel. Only after President William Howard Taft determined that he needed the votes of African-American delegates to win renomination at the Republican convention in 1912 did the Justice Department embrace this thoroughly political suit.

In *Williams v. Mississippi (1898), the Supreme Court had refused to throw out Mississippi's notoriously discriminatory voting barriers because the lawyer for the African-American plaintiffs, Cornelius J. Jones, had offered evidence only of the intent of the delegates to the Mississippi Constitutional Convention. Presented with evidence of effect as well as of intent by attorney Wilford H. Smith in *Giles v. Harris* (1903), the Court, through "liberal" Justice Oliver Wendell Holmes, declared the whole matter a "political question." Yet in *Guinn* and two companion cases, the Court received no evidence of either intent or effect, sidestepped precedent, and joined Louisiana-bred Chief Justice Edward D. White's opinion declaring the statute a prima facie violation of the Fifteenth Amendment.

There were two main reasons why the Court decided the case in this manner. First, *Guinn* had no practical effect. In all the ex-Confederate states, the grandfather clauses had already lapsed, and Oklahoma continued administrative discrimination without further legal challenge. Second, the grandfather clause was a symbolic embarrassment that even the president of the Louisiana Constitutional Convention of 1898 had termed "ridiculous." The decision in *Guinn* was neither inevitable nor particularly progressive.

J. Morgan Kousser

H

Hague v. Congress of Industrial Organizations, 307 U.S. 496 (1939), argued 27–28 Feb. 1939, decided 5 June 1939 by vote of 5 to 2; Roberts for the Court, Stone and Hughes concurring, McReynolds and Butler in dissent, Frankfurter and Douglas not participating. The problem of state attempts to control public meetings first came before the Supreme Court in *Hague* v. *CIO*. The case involved the constitutionality of a Jersey City municipal ordinance requiring permits from a "director of public safety" for the conduct of public meetings and for the distribution of printed material in streets, parks, and other public places. Mayor Frank "I am Law" Hague had used the ordinance particularly against labor union activities. With support from the American Civil Liberties Union an injunction was sought against Hague's systematic denial of First Amendment rights. The injunction ordered the city to stop evicting union organizers and to cease interfering with meetings and the distribution of literature.

Upholding the injunction in a plurality opinion, the Supreme Court found the ordinance unconstitutional but the justices disagreed in their reasoning. Justice Owen Roberts, for the Court, defined the streets and parks as public forums protected by the First Amendment as a part of the privileges, immunities, rights and liberties of citizens. Stone, concurring, felt that the ordinance violated the right of U.S. citizens peaceably to assemble as guaranteed by the Fourteenth Amendment's Due Process Clause.

The ruling was significant in opening public areas like streets and parks to free public discussion of ideas, no matter what the subject. Such use, the Court ruled, could be regulated, but not arbitrarily denied or abridged because the authorities did not favor the ideas being discussed. The ruling proved a boon to the labor movement, and was popular as the curtailment of the arbitrariness of local officials.

Paul L. Murphy

Hall v. Decuir, 95 U.S. 485 (1878), argued 17 Apr. 1877, decided 14 Jan. 1878 by vote of 9 to 0; Waite for the Court, Clifford concurring. In *Hall* v. *DeCuir*, the Court overturned a Louisiana Supreme Court decision that had awarded damages authorized by a Louisiana statute to Josephine DeCuir, a black woman, who had been refused admission to a steamship's stateroom reserved for whites during her voyage between New Orleans and Hermitage, Louisiana. The Court's opinion by Chief Justice Morrison R. Waite held that the statute burdened interstate commerce because the steamship also traveled between Louisiana and Mississippi. Waite held that the statute regulated interstate commerce, something within the exclusive province of Congress. In the absence of congressional action, states could not require carriers engaged in interstate commerce to offer integrated facilities even for trips that took place solely within state boundaries. Waite did not consider whether Congress might have intended, through inaction, to permit the states to control some aspects of interstate commerce incidentally in the exercise of their police power over intrastate activities, a power later acknowledged in the *Shreveport Rate Cases* (1914).

The concurring opinion by Justice Nathan Clifford demonstrated the Court's concern with preserving racial custom. It included a defense of what would later be termed the "separate but equal" doctrine.

The Court inconsistently held in *Louisville, New Orleans & Texas Railway* Co. v. *Mississippi* (1890), that a state statute requiring segregation in intrastate commerce did not run afoul of Congress's commerce power. It was not until after World War II that the Court recognized the illogic of these holdings and relied on the *Hall* precedent to void state legislation mandating intrastate segregation, because of its impact on interstate commerce.

Robert J. Cottrol

Hammer v. Dagenhart, 247 U.S. 251 (1918), argued 15–16 Apr. 1918, decided 3 June 1918 by vote of 5 to 4; Day for the Court, Holmes, McKenna, Brandeis, and Clarke in dissent. As the Progressive movement coalesced early in the twentieth century, Congress increasingly used the commerce power and taxing and spending power for police power purposes, enacting regulatory legislation to ameliorate social problems deemed national in character. Prominent among these problems was concern for children working outside their homes, who were dependent, often exploited, nearly always powerless to effect the conditions under which they labored. As it became increasingly apparent that state legislation could not effectively establish national regulatory standards, reformers turned to Congress, seeking federal legislation that would abolish child labor. In 1916, in what became recognized as the climax of the Progressive movement, substantial majorities in the House and the Senate enacted the Keating-Owen Child Labor Act, which utilized the commerce power to bar goods made by children from interstate commerce.

Because the Supreme Court had repeatedly legitimated national police power enactments, notably in such seemingly decisive holdings as *Champion* v. *Ames* (1903),

Hipolite Egg Company v. *United States* (1911), and *Hoke* v. *United States* (1913), it was widely expected that the Supreme Court would build upon this precedential foundation in its decision in *Hammer* v. *Dagenhart*. The earlier opinions seemed to establish the principle that Congress could use its power over commerce to prohibit interstate transportation as the national welfare dictated. Congress had authority, *Hoke* had declared, "to occupy, by legislation, the whole field of interstate commerce" (p. 320).

However, a five-justice majority on a bitterly divided bench rejected this constitutional justification and recurred to a line of reasoning thought to have been repudiated earlier in the century. Justice William Rufus Day's opinion rested upon the distinction between manufacture and commerce enunciated in *United States* v. *E. C. Knight Co.* (1895): the congressional "power is one to control the means by which commerce is carried on, which is directly the contrary of the assumed right to forbid commerce" (pp. 269–270). He condemned the Keating-Owen law as having reached an area of regulation wholly within the ambit of the states and exerting power not warranted in the Constitution. While conceding that child laborers needed protection, Day charged Congress with action destructive to federalism. "[T]he far-reaching result," if Congress was not stopped, he assented, was that "all freedom of commerce will be at an end . . . and thus our system of government be practically destroyed" (p. 276). This resort to the *grand peur* was characteristic of the doctrines of constitutional laissez faire to which the majority now returned.

Writing with uncharacteristic passion, Justice Oliver Wendell Holmes fashioned one of the most notable dissenting opinions in the Court's history. He excoriated the majority for intruding their personal judgments "upon questions of policy and morals" (p. 280). "I should have thought," Holmes wrote, "that if we were to introduce our own moral conceptions where, in my opinion, they do not belong, this was preeminently a case for upholding the exercise of all its powers by the United States" (p. 280). To Holmes, one analytical proposition was indisputable: the congressional prohibition applied only at the point where an offending state sought to transport its commercial products across its borders into national commerce. "Regulation means the prohibition of something" (p. 277), he argued, and he enumerated the line of constitutional development, stretching back to *Veazie Bank* v. *Fenno* (1869), in which the Court had lent sanction to national regulation of the kind embodied in the Keating-Owen law. "The power to regulate commerce and other constitutional powers could not be cut down or qualified," he asserted, as a consequence of their "indirect effects" (p. 278).

Holmes's revulsion at what he considered the majority's defiance of the democratic will mirrored the consternation evident throughout the country. Congress swiftly responded by enacting the second federal child labor law, using the taxing power to apply against manufacturers the same regulatory standards embodied in the Keating-Owen law. Even though the Court overturned this statute in *Bailey* v. *Drexel Furniture Co.* (1922), the minority was vindicated two decades later, following the Constitutional Revolution in 1937, when a unanimous bench in *United States* v. *Darby Lumber Co.* (1941) adopted and, indeed, went beyond the constitutional principles set forth in what Justice Harlan Fiske Stone characterized as Holmes's "powerful and now classic dissent" (p. 115).

□ Stephen B. Wood, *Constitutional Politics in the Progressive Era* (1968).

Stephen B. Wood

Harper v. Virginia State Board of Elections, 383 U.S. 663 (1966), argued 25–26 Jan. 1966, decided 24 Mar. 1966 by vote of 6 to 3; Douglas for the Court, Black and Harlan, joined by Stewart, in dissent. The Twenty-fourth Amendment (1964) to the U.S. Constitution banned poll taxes as a condition for voting in national elections. *Harper* challenged the $1.50 Virginia annual poll tax as a precondition for voting in state elections. A three-judge U.S. District Court followed *Bread-love* v. *Suttles* (1937) and dismissed the claim.

On appeal the Supreme Court overruled *Breedlove* in part and held that state requirements for fees or taxes that limit the right to vote are unconstitutional. Justice William O. Douglas, writing for the majority, argued that the political franchise is a fundamental right that cannot be denied because of lack of wealth, property, or economic status. Such standards constitute invidious discrimination that violates the Equal Protection Clause of the Fourteenth Amendment. He also suggested that lack of wealth—or

indigency—might be regarded as a suspect classification requiring strict scrutiny. *Harper* extends the *Reynolds* v. *Sims* (1964) principle that all voters must have an equal opportunity to participate in state elections.

The dissenters claimed that there was a rational basis for the Virginia poll tax and that states should have broad constitutional leeway under the Equal Protection Clause to establish voter qualifications. Both argued that property qualifications and poll taxes are part of the constitutional framework.

The impact of *Harper* was limited. Only three states used poll taxes (Alabama, Texas, and Mississippi) as a condition of voting at that time. And Douglas's suggestion that wealth be regarded as a suspect classification was rejected by *Dandridge* v. *Williams* (1970) and *San Antonio Independent School District* v. *Rodriguez* (1973).

Steven Puro

Harris v. Forklift Systems, Inc., 510 U.S. 17 (1993), argued 13 Oct. 1993, decided 9 Nov. 1993, by vote of 9 to 0; O'Connor for the Court, Scalia and Ginsburg concurring. Between 1991 and 1993 the number of sexual harassment claims filed around the country almost doubled to 12,500. The increase reflected the impact of the navy's Tailhook scandal, accusations against Senator Bob Packwood, and Anita Hill's charges against Clarence Thomas. It also, however, reflected the day-to-day reality of life in the American working place, where sexual innuendo and harassment were realities. Title VII of the Civil Rights Act of 1964 made it illegal for an employer to discriminate against an employee based on sex. The Supreme Court in *Meritor Savings Bank* v. *Vinton* (1986) held that Title VII gave individuals the right to be free from discriminatory intimidation and ridicule and that harassment included unwelcome sexual advances and requests for sexual favors. Such actions created a hostile work environment according to the Court. Yet *Meritor* also insisted that the best evidence of a hostile work environment was psychological damage done to the individual resulting in a failure to perform in the workplace. The Court in *Harris* fashioned new standards.

Teresa Harris in 1987 was a thirty-five year-old white woman who had worked for two years as rental manager at Forklift Systems, Inc. in Nashville, Tennessee. Two months before she quit in October of that year, she filed a complaint alleging that the company's president, Charles Hardy, had created a hostile work environment by, among other things, calling her a "dumbass woman" and asking her, and others, to retrieve coins from his front pants pocket. A federal district court in Tennessee had found that Harris was not protected by Title VII since the four-time divorced woman had not suffered any psychological injury on the job. The Court of Appeals for the Sixth Circuit affirmed this decision.

The Supreme Court, however, unanimously reversed the decision and remanded the case back to the lower court. Justice Sandra Day O'Connor's opinion made two important contributions to the constitutional law surrounding sexual harassment. First, O'Connor held that a person need not be damaged psychologically to demonstrate the presence of sexual harassment and a hostile work environment. The Court did not reject that standard but instead found that a person deserved the protection of federal law before she suffered a nervous breakdown. Moreover, O'Connor continued, it was not necessary for a plaintiff to show that her job performance had suffered as a result of the harassment. Instead, courts were expected to examine a whole constellation of conditions including the frequency of discriminatory conduct, the severity of such conduct, and whether it was physically threatening or humiliating. Hardy's counsel, for example, had argued that his client was merely joking and that other employees recognized his behavior as such. Indeed, Hardy asserted that Harris herself did not appear to mind. The Court rejected this premise.

Justices Antonin Scalia and Ruth Bader Ginsburg both concurred. The former insisted that the measure to be used in such cases was whether the harassment had the effect of altering the conditions of the working place in a discriminatory way; the latter suggested that sex discrimination be treated as seriously as discrimination based on race. *Harris* was important because it made it easier for women to allege harassment without, at the same time, damaging their own reputations by having to prove that they were either psychologically damaged or incompetent workers.

Kermit L. Hall

Harris v. McRae, 448 U.S. 297 (1980), argued 21 Apr. 1980, decided 30 June 1980 by vote of 5 to 4; Stewart for the Court, Brennan, joined by Marshall and Blackmun, and Stevens in dissent. *Harris* upheld the constitutionality of the Hyde Amendment, a law that barred the use of federal Medicaid funds for abortions except where the life of the mother would be endangered or in cases of rape or incest. The Court held that the right to choose abortion protected by *Roe* v. *Wade* (1973) did not require the government to subsidize that choice. According to the Court, *Roe* meant that the government could not put obstacles in the path of choice. The inability of poor women to purchase medical services, including abortions, without government assistance, said the Court, was not an obstacle the government had created. The dissenters argued that the government did burden the woman's choice of abortion as against childbirth by providing medical assistance when she chose the latter but not when she chose the former.

Critics of *Harris* argue that the only reason the government has for refusing to pay for abortions is that it believes that abortions are immoral, a belief that under *Roe* v. *Wade* may not be the basis for government action, and that the decision sanctions a two-class system of the availability of abortions. Defenders reply that abortion is not one of those situations, rare in our society, in which the government has the duty to alleviate the burdens, which are many, that result from the unequal distribution of wealth in a market-oriented economy.

Mark V. Tushnet

Harris v. New York, 401 U.S. 222 (1971), argued 17 Dec. 1970, decided 24 Feb. 1971 by vote of 5 to 4; Burger for the Court, Brennan, joined by Douglas and Marshall, in dissent, Black in dissent without opinion. Decided after Warren Burger and Harry Blackmun were appointed to the Supreme Court by President Richard Nixon, *Harris* was the first case to limit *Miranda* v. *Arizona* (1966). At his trial Harris testified in his own defense, denying that a bag sold to an undercover agent contained heroin. During police interrogation, however, which occurred without Harris being given the *Miranda* warnings, Harris had told a different story. To impeach his credibility, the prosecution cross-examined Harris about his answers during police questioning. On appeal, Harris's counsel argued that *Miranda* prohibited reference to those answers when it said: "[S]tatements merely intended to be exculpatory by the defendant are often used to impeach his testimony at trial. . . . These statements are incriminating in any meaningful sense of the word and may not be used without the full warnings and effective waiver . . . " (p. 477).

The Court limited the *Miranda* exclusion to evidence presented in the prosecution's case-in-chief and permitted use of answers given without warnings for impeachment purposes when defendants chose to testify. Burger wrote that while *Miranda* can be read as prohibiting the use of an uncounseled statement for any purpose, such a reading was unnecessary to its logic and thus not controlling. *Miranda*, he maintained, was not a license to use perjury with no risk of being confronted with prior inconsistent statements.

Bradley C. Canon

Hawaii Housing Authority v. Midkiff, 467 U.S. 229 (1984), argued 26 Mar. 1984, decided 30 May 1984 by vote of 8 to 0; O'Connor for the Court, Marshall not participating. *Midkiff* stands as the Supreme Court's most important explanation of the requirement that any governmental taking of private property must be for a "public use," as set forth in the Fifth Amendment. The case involved a challenge to a Hawaii statute that attempted to undercut a landowning oligopoly that had long tied up land titles in the state. The contested statute gave lessees of single family homes the right to invoke the government's power of eminent domain to purchase the property that they leased, even if the landowner objected. The challengers claimed that such a condemnation was not a taking for a public use because the property, once condemned by the state, was promptly turned over to the lessee.

In *Midkiff* the Court virtually eliminated public use as a limit on when governments can condemn property. A public use is present, the Court held, even when the property is immediately turned over to private hands and is never used by the public. The requirement is satisfied whenever the taking is rationally related to some conceivable public purpose; it is the purpose of the taking, not the use of the property, that is important. This meant, the Court said, that the condemnation power is equal in breadth to the police power. The Court also held that courts should defer to legislative determinations of whether a purpose is a public one unless the determination is without reasonable foundation.

Eric T. Freyfogle

Hayburn's Case, 2 Dall. (2 U.S.) 409 (1792). *Hayburn's Case* was an early and ambiguous precedent that raised issues of judicial review and justiciability. In 1792, Congress enacted legislation that required the United States Circuit Courts to hear disability pension claims by veterans of the War for Independence and to certify their findings to the secretary of war. Five of the then-six justices of the Supreme Court (Jay, Cushing, Wilson, Blair, and Iredell), sitting as judges of the three circuit courts, tendered opinions in the form of letters to President George Washington declining to serve in that capacity. All agreed that the statute imposed nonjudicial duties on the courts and thus violated the principle of separation of powers. All objected to the implied power of the secretary of war (an officer of the executive branch) to revise or to refuse to honor the courts' reports. Two of the letters objected to Congress's power to decline to make appropriations to support the courts' findings. Congress in the next session revised the claims procedure to obviate the constitutional difficulties. Despite its ambiguities Hayburn's case is regarded as an early assertion of the power of federal courts to hold statutes enacted by Congress unconstitutional and to refuse to enforce them. The case also anticipated problems of justiciability because of its concern for the finality of judicial determinations.

William M. Wiecek

Head Money Cases, 112 U.S. 580 (1885), argued 19–20 Nov. 1884, decided 8 Dec. 1885 by vote of 9 to 0; Miller for the Court. This case arose after Congress moved to assume greater control over immigration in the Immigration Act of 1882. Until that point, states had regulated the entry of immigrants. Though the states tended to be liberal in their admission of immigrants, concern about the potential financial burden of indigent immigrants prompted the biggest ports to impose head taxes or bonds upon ship captains to provide a fund for needy immigrants. In the *Passenger Cases* (1849) and *Henderson* v. *Mayor* (1876), the Supreme Court had struck down such regulations as an infringement on the federal commerce power. To alleviate the states' financial responsibility, Congress in the act of 1882 imposed a federal head tax of fifty cents per immigrant, which was given to the states for the support of immigrants in distress.

Shippers challenged the constitutionality of the federal head tax, principally on the grounds that it was not applied uniformly throughout the United States nor did it raise revenue for the common defense and general welfare of the country. The Supreme Court rejected such arguments, reiterating its earlier holdings that immigration was a form of foreign commerce over which Congress had plenary power. The head tax was a "mere incident of the regulation of commerce" (p. 595) not an exercise of the taxing power. The money collected was closely related to the government's legitimate interest in regulating immigration. The *Head Money Cases* helped to consolidate federal control over immigration and also helped to broaden congressional power to impose taxes in carrying out other constitutional powers.

Lucy E. Salyer

Heart of Atlanta Motel v. United States, 379 U.S. 241 (1964), argued 5 Oct. 1964, decided 14 Dec. 1964 by vote of 9 to 0; Clark for the Court, Black, Douglas, and Goldberg concurring. *Heart of Atlanta Motel* was the major constitutional test of the public accommodations provisions (Title II) of the Civil Rights Act of 1964 as well as an important reaffirmation of Congress's broad powers under the Commerce Clause. A motel owner in Atlanta, whose motel served mostly transient interstate travelers, refused to serve blacks as required by the act. He claimed that Congress had exceeded its Commerce Clause authority to regulate private businesses and also that the act was invalid under the Fifth Amendment's Due Process Clause and the Thirteenth Amendment.

A three-judge U.S. district court upheld Title II and permanently enjoined the motel from discriminating on account of race. The Supreme Court unanimously affirmed. Justice Tom Clark, citing *Gibbons* v. *Ogden* (1824) and a long line of cases upholding Congress's plenary power to regulate under the Commerce Clause, held that Congress could regulate both interstate commerce and intrastate activities that affected commerce as part of its "national police power" to legislate against moral wrongs.

Congress employed the Commerce Clause as primary authority for the act because the *Civil Rights Cases* (1883), as then interpreted, prohibited it from enforcing the Fourteenth Amendment against privately owned restaurants and hotels. Justices William O. Douglas and Arthur Goldberg, however, claimed that the statute could have been upheld under section 5 of the Fourteenth Amendment as well.

In *Katzenbach* v. *McClung* (1964), a companion case that tested the act's applicability to a small, essentially intrastate restaurant ("Ollie's Barbecue"), the Court found that even though the restaurant's customers were local, it purchased much of its food and supplies through interstate commerce and thus was also covered. Taken together the two cases provided a major impetus to congressional efforts to legislate on behalf of civil rights.

Steven Puro

Helvering v. Davis, 301 U.S. 619 (1937), argued 5 May 1937, decided 24 May 1937 by vote of 7 to 2; Cardozo for the Court, Butler and McReynolds in dissent. In this case the Court sustained the old-age benefits provisions of the Social Security Act of 1935. Writing for the majority, Justice Benjamin Cardozo adopted an expansive view of the federal taxing and spending power. He judged the old-age benefits provisions of the Social Security Act constitutional pursuant to Article I, section 8 of the Constitution.

In response to the claim that the Tenth Amendment prohibited Congress's use of the taxing and spending power to raise revenue for a purpose traditionally reserved to the states, Cardozo pointed out that the Social Security Act was born in response to a "nation-wide calamity" that was unsolvable without a concerted federal effort (p. 641). If some states funded programs and some did not, Cardozo speculated, indigents would flock to the funding states just as industry would flee those states to avoid the requisite new payroll taxes.

Only a few days before the Court handed down its decision in *Helvering,* Justice Willis Van Devanter announced his retirement. After waiting impatiently for more than four years, President Franklin Roosevelt finally had a Supreme Court nomination. This welcome prospect, coupled with the new voting stance of Justice Owen Roberts, meant that the president's much criticized court-packing plan was no longer necessary. As South Carolina Senator James F. Byrnes queried, "Why run for a train after you've caught it?"

John W. Johnson

Hepburn v. Griswold. See LEGAL TENDER CASES.

Herrera v. Collins, 506 U.S. 390 (1993), argued 7 Oct. 1992, decided 25 Jan. 1993 by vote of 6 to 3; Rehnquist for the Court, O'Connor, Kennedy, Scalia, Thomas, and White concurring in parts or in whole, Blackmun dissenting, joined by Stevens and Souter.

The case involved Leonel Torres Herrera, a death-row inmate in Texas, convicted of the 1981 murder of two state police officers. Herrera had an impoverished childhood, an abusive alcoholic father, and a history of post-traumatic stress disorder following service in Vietnam.

Several weeks before his execution, Herrera sought a writ of habeas corpus from the federal courts on the grounds that newly discovered evidence established his innocence. That evidence was a statement from his nephew, Raul Herrera, Jr., who claimed that his father, Leonel's brother, Raul Herrera, Sr., had told him in 1983 that he had killed the police officers. Raul Herrera, Sr., had died the following year. Leonel Herrera also presented statements from three other persons that supposedly corroborated this story. Texas law, however, provided that a motion for a new trial based on previously undiscovered evidence had to be presented within thirty days following conviction. The time had long since elapsed, therefore, under Texas law.

A federal district court judge in Texas, however, stayed Leonel's execution in order to allow state authorities to hear his claim of innocence. A three-judge panel of the United States Court of Appeals for the Fifth Circuit immediately lifted the stay, and Herrera then appealed to the Supreme Court with literally hours to go before his execution. In order to stay an execution, the rules of the Court require that five justices agree, and only four did. Yet those four justices were sufficient to permit the Court to hear the case on its merits. A Texas court then granted a stay of execution and the full Supreme Court heard Herrera's appeal many months later.

As was true with the vast majority of death penalty cases, the justices divided sharply. Chief Justice William H. Rehnquist rejected Herrera's argument that the thirty-day limit for a new trial violated the Due Process Clause of the Fourteenth Amendment. The states were free to set such limits, and fourteen states had in fact adopted the thirty-day rule. Only two states (New York and New Jersey), the Court noted, placed no time limits.

Rehnquist also concluded that the evidence presented by Herrera fell far short of the level of proof required to secure a new trial. The chief justice left open the possibility that what he called "truly persuasive" evidence might prompt the Court to order a new hearing in such cases, but the general rule stood that a state death-row inmate is not ordinarily entitled to a new hearing in federal court before being executed (p. 417). In the current circumstances, Rehnquist concluded, Herrera's best chance was to seek clemency from the governor, a process that historically had been used to prevent miscarriages of justice when the judicial process had been, as was true in this case, exhausted.

Justices Sandra Day O'Connor, Anthony M. Kennedy, and Byron R. White agreed with the chief justice's holding, but not with the reasoning he used to reach it. They made clear that the Constitution might still provide relief and that the Court could never permit the execution of an innocent person.

Justice Harry Blackmun took the unusual step of reading his opinion in open court, doing so shortly after former Justice Thurgood Marshall, long a critic of the death penalty, had died. Blackmun denounced the Court's holding as amounting to an action "perilously close to simple murder" (p. 446). Justices John Paul Stevens and David H. Souter signed all of Blackmun's eighteen-page dissent, although not the last paragraph, which contained the reference to "simple murder."

The Court had previously developed a line of cases that made it increasingly difficult for convicted persons to use a petition for a writ habeas corpus to raise a constitutional challenge to state convictions and executions. Its decision in *Herrera* furthered this process, leaving death-row inmates with diminished opportunities to assert that a constitutional right had been violated as grounds to prevent an execution. Herrera was subsequently executed by Texas officials, claiming his innocence to the end.

Kermit L. Hall

Hirabayashi v. United States, 320 U.S. 81 (1943), argued 10 and 11 May 1943, decided 21 June 1943 by vote of 9 to 0; Stone for the Court, Douglas and Murphy concurring in separate opinions with the result; Rutledge concurring in a separate opinion with the Court's opinion. At the beginning of World War II officials expressed concern about the presence of approximately 112,000 Japanese-Americans on the West Coast. At the urging of General John L. DeWitt of the Western Defense Command and numerous state and national officials, President Franklin D. Roosevelt on 19 February 1942 signed Executive Order no. 9066, empowering the secretary of war to create "military areas" from which civilians might be excluded. On 18 March Roosevelt established the War Relocation Authority for the purpose of interning all West Coast Japanese-Americans. Congress unanimously passed legislation implementing these executive orders.

General DeWitt subsequently imposed an 8:00 P.M. to 6:00 A.M. curfew for West Coast Japanese-Americans, prohibited Japanese-Americans from moving out of his defense command, and then prohibited Japanese-Americans from remaining within his command. They could neither leave their homes nor stay in them; instead they had to report to civilian control, or assembly, centers. From these centers the Japanese-Americans were evacuated to "relocation camps," where most remained until 1945.

Gordon Hirabayashi, an American-born citizen of Japanese ancestry and a senior at the University of Washington, intentionally violated the curfew and the order to report to a civilian control center. Hirabayashi believed if he obeyed the curfew and exclusion orders "he would be waiving his rights as an American citizen" (p. 81). Convicted on both counts, the court sentenced him to concurrent three-month sentences. On appeal the Supreme Court upheld the conviction for the curfew violation, and because of the concurrent sentences, refused to consider the constitutionality of the order to report to the assembly center.

Speaking for the Court, Chief Justice Harlan F. Stone argued that Congress and the president could constitutionally impose a curfew under the "power to wage war successfully" (p. 93). The big question, however, was whether Japanese-Americans, as a group, could be singled out for the curfew.

Stone noted that Japanese immigrants were ineligible for United States citizenship, that under Japanese law American-born children of Japanese immigrants were considered to be citizens of Japan and that "social, economic and political conditions" in the nation had "in large measure prevented their assimilation as an integral part of the white population" (p. 96). He pointed out that large numbers of Japanese-American children had been "sent to Japanese language schools" and that some of these schools were "generally believed to be sources of Japanese nationalistic propaganda . . ." (p. 97). There had, Stone observed "been relatively little social intercourse between them and the white population" (p. 98).

Stone felt "Congress and the Executive could reasonably have concluded that these conditions have encouraged the continued attachment of members of this group to Japan and Japanese institutions" and that "those charged with . . . the national defense" could "take into account" these factors in "determining the nature and extent of the danger of espionage and sabotage, in the event of an invasion or air raid attack" (pp. 98–99). The Court could not "reject as unfounded" the military and congressional judgment "that there were disloyal members of that population, whose number and strength could not be precisely and quickly ascertained" (p. 99).

Stone agreed that "racial discriminations are in most circumstances irrelevant" but argued that "in dealing with the perils of war, Congress and the Executive" could take "into account those facts which are relevant to measures for our national defense . . . which may in fact place citizens of one ancestry in a different category from others" (p. 100). In up-holding the curfew, Stone specifically declared that the Court was not considering whether more drastic measures would be permissible.

Although a unanimous decision, Justices William O. Douglas, Wiley Rutledge, and Frank Murphy qualified their support and sought to narrow the scope of the decision. Murphy's concurrence reads more like a dissent. He noted that this was "the first time" the court had ever "sustained a substantial restriction of the personal liberty of citizens of the United States based on the accident of race or ancestry." Murphy believed the internment bore "a melancholy resemblance to the treatment accorded to members of the Jewish race in Germany and in other parts of Europe" and went "to the very brink of constitutional power" (p. 111).

□ Roger Daniels, *Concentration Camps, North America* (1981). Roger Daniels, *The Decision to Relocate the Japanese-Americans* (1986). Peter Irons, *Justice At War* (1983).

Paul Finkelman

Hodgson v. Minnesota, 110 S.Ct. 2926 (1990), argued 29 Nov. 1989, decided 25 June 1990 by vote of 5 to 4 on one issue and 5 to 4 on another; Stevens announced judgment of Court on the first issue in an opinion joined by Brennan, Marshall, Blackmun, and O'Connor, from which Rehnquist, White, Scalia, and Kennedy dissented; O'Connor concurring in result on second issue with Rehnquist, White, Scalia, and Kennedy. *Hodgson,* the Court's first confrontation with the abortion issue after its decision in **Webster* v. *Reproductive Health Services* (1989), indicated that substantially greater restrictions on abortions were constitutionally permissible. The case involved a statute requiring minors seeking abortions to notify both parents; a minor who obtained a court's determination that she was mature or that an abortion without notice to the parents was in her best interests could have an abortion.

A majority of the Court held that the two-parent notification requirement was unconstitutional; it was not a reasonable method of assuring proper parental involvement in the abortion decision, given the large numbers of families in which the minor seeking abortion did not reside with both parents, often because the absent parent was physically abusive. The dissenters argued that a legislature could properly act with the majority of families in mind; in most families, notification of both parents would promote desirable consultation.

A different majority of the Court held that permitting minors to invoke a judicial "bypass" in lieu of parental notification was constitutional because it was "an expeditious and efficient means" to identify cases where notification of both parents would not be sound. The dissenters objected to requiring that minors disclose intimate personal details to a judge. Further, experience with the procedure showed that permission to obtain an abortion was almost never denied; however, obtaining permission burdened the minor's choice because of delays in scheduling hearings and difficulties in locating judges in rural areas who would make the necessary findings.

Hodgson was the first case in which Justice Sandra Day O'Connor voted to hold a restriction on the availability of abortions unconstitutional. In **Planned Parenthood of Southeastern Pennsylvania* v. *Casey* (1992), the justices held constitutional a Pennsylvania law that required a minor to inform one par-

ent of her plan to have an abortion. In this instance, Justice O'Connor voted with the majority to sustain not only the regulation but also the underlying precedent of *Roe.*

Mark V. Tushnet

Holden v. Hardy, 169 U.S. 366 (1898), argued 21 Oct. 1897, decided 28 Feb. 1898 by vote of 6 to 2; Brown for the Court, Brewer and Peckham in dissent, Field retired. To challenge his conviction for violating a Utah statute that prohibited employment of workers in mines for more than eight hours a day, Albert F. Holden initiated this habeas corpus proceeding against the sheriff, Harvey Hardy. Holden contended that the statute deprived him of freedom to contract with employees and violated three provisions of the Fourteenth Amendment: privileges or immunities, due process, and equal protection. The Supreme Court rejected these arguments, treating them as a single contention.

Justice Henry Billings Brown accepted the importance of freedom of contract. He emphasized, however, that the right was subject to limitation by a state's police power to protect the health, safety, or morals of its citizens. The Fourteenth Amendment, in his view, was not intended to inhibit severely the evolution of the states' exercise of powers to protect their citizens, because law was "to a certain extent a progressive science" (p. 385). Obscured by that sweeping pronouncement was Brown's pivotal conclusion that there was a reasonable basis in fact to support the legislature's judgment about the danger of mining. In spite of the opinion's recognition of state power, the real import of the decision lies in the implication that the Court would assess the reasonableness of any regulatory statute. The significance became apparent when the Court subsequently struck down a statute regulating the hours worked by bakers in **Lochner* v. *New York* (1905). Thus, in spite of its apparent support for state experimentation, *Holden* actually foreshadowed a period of active judicial supervision of economic legislation.

Walter F. Pratt, Jr.

Holder v. Hall, 512 U.S. 874 (1994), argued 4 Oct. 1993, decided 30 June 1994 by vote of 5 to 4; Kennedy announced the Court's judgment, writing for himself and Rehnquist and for O'Connor in part, O'Connor and Thomas concurring, Blackmun, Stevens,

Souter, and Ginsburg in dissent. Black voters of Georgia's Bleckley County brought suit challenging the county's single-member commission form of government as a violation of section 2 of the Voting Rights Act of 1965, which prohibits any "standard, practice, or procedure" that abridges voting rights on the basis of race. The plaintiffs argued that their voting rights were diluted because black voters had sufficient numbers to constitute a majority in one district if the commission consisted of five members elected from separate districts, as permitted by Georgia law. Under the existing system, with a single commissioner chosen by an at-large election, black voters were unable to elect their preferred candidate. The Court rejected the plaintiffs' claim, with the five members of the majority offering three different rationales for the judgment.

Justice Anthony Kennedy, joined by Chief Justice William H. Rehnquist and Justice Sandra Day O'Connor, found that the vote dilution challenge to the size of the commission under section 2 was unpersuasive because, under section 2, courts lack "a reasonable alternative practice" to use as a benchmark for evaluating the single-member structure (p. 880). Joined only by Rehnquist, Kennedy also rejected a rule that a practice covered by the preclearance requirement of section 5 of the act, which mandates federal approval of certain changes in voting practices, must also be covered by section 2. In her concurring opinion, Justice O'Connor disagreed. She read the texts of sections 2 and 5 to have "parallel scope" (p. 887) in determining coverage and therefore concluded, based on section 5 precedent, that the plaintiffs' claim implicated a "standard, practice, or procedure" under section 2 (p. 886). She nonetheless concurred in the judgment, based solely on the lack of a viable benchmark.

Holder is frequently noted for Justice Clarence Thomas's sweeping opinion, joined by Justice Antonin Scalia, concurring only in the judgment and calling for a major revision of the Court's voting rights jurisprudence. Thomas characterized the current interpretation of section 2 as "a disastrous misadventure in judicial policymaking" (p. 893) that has permitted courts to decide questions of political theory by favoring single-member districts that separate voters by race and thus heighten racial tensions. Turning to the text of section 2, he argued that the Court's precedents holding it applicable to vote dilu-

tion cases were erroneous; properly read, section 2 should protect only an individual voter's access to the ballot and not a minority group's right to influence election results.

The dissent took strong exception to the Thomas concurrence. Justice Harry A. Blackmun, writing for all four dissenters, insisted that both history and precedent support a broad reading of section 2 in order to implement its remedial purpose of eliminating racial discrimination from the election process. Blackmun also found no difficulty in identifying a five-member commission as a reasonable benchmark for measuring vote dilution. Justice John Paul Stevens's separate opinion for the same four justices rejected Thomas's narrow reading of section 2 as a "radical reinterpretation" that violated *stare decisis*.

Laura Krugman Ray

Holmes v. Jennison, 14 Pet. (39 U.S.) 540 (1840), argued 24–25 Jan. 1840, dismissed 4 Mar. 1840 by vote of 4 to 4; Taney for himself, Story, McLean, and Wayne; opinions in disagreement by Thompson, Baldwin, Barbour, and Catron; McKinley absent. Silas H. Jennison, governor of Vermont, ordered George Holmes, a resident of Quebec, arrested and sent back to Canada to be tried for murder even though the United States had no extradition treaty with Canada. The Vermont Supreme Court refused to issue a writ of habeas corpus. Dividing 4 to 4 over the question, the U.S. Supreme Court dismissed the case for want of jurisdiction.

Chief Justice Roger B. Taney affirmed the Court's jurisdiction as well as the exclusive power of the federal government to govern foreign relations. Because of that exclusive power, Taney reasoned, a state governor had no authority to surrender fugitives to a foreign country. Four justices disagreed, believing that the Court lacked jurisdiction over denial of habeas corpus by a state court. Justice Smith Thompson, however, implied in his opinion that Governor Jennison had no authority to order Holmes's surrender. Because five of the eight justices sitting on the case denied Jennison's authority, the Vermont Supreme Court ordered Holmes released even though the U.S. Supreme Court had refused, because of the tie vote, to take jurisdiction of the case. Taney's language in favor of the exclusive right of the federal government over foreign relations stands as the most notable and enduring feature of this case. Nationalists such as Joseph Story applauded Taney's reasoning, while states-rightists such as James Buchanan deplored it.

Robert M. Ireland

Home Building and Loan Association v. Blaisdell, 290 U.S. 398 (1934), argued 8 and 9 Nov. 1933, decided 8 June 1934 by vote of 5 to 4; Hughes for the Court, Sutherland, Butler, McReynolds, and Van Devanter in dissent. The Court's decision in *Home Building and Loan Association* v. *Blaisdell* was important not only because it upheld a critical state law passed during the Great Depression but also because it revealed the sharp divisions on the high court over the proper response to the economic crisis.

The legislation at issue was the 1933 Minnesota Mortgage Moratorium Law. The act authorized a Minnesota state court, when called upon by a beleaguered debtor, to consider exempting property from foreclosure "during the continuance of the emergency and in no event beyond May 1, 1935." The law was passed by a legislature especially mindful of the problems of farmers facing mortgage foreclosures.

This particular case arose as a result of the desire of Mr. and Mrs. John H. Blaisdell, who had received a mortgage on a house and lot from the Home Building and Loan Association, to avoid foreclosure and to extend their mortgage redemption period. A Minnesota district court sided with the Blaisdells on the condition that certainly monthly installments be paid in a timely fashion. The Supreme Court of Minnesota affirmed the ruling. The Loan Association appealed to the U.S. Supreme Court, maintaining that the Moratorium Law was in conflict with the Contracts Clause in Article I, section 10 of the Constitution and the due process and equal protection clauses of the Fourteenth Amendment. The Contract Clause argument proved especially crucial. The Loan Association maintained that the clause's language—"No State shall enter into any . . . Law impairing the Obligation of Contracts . . ."—prohibited Minnesota from altering the contractual relationship between the Blaisdells and the Loan Association.

Chief Justice Charles Evans Hughes and Justice Owen J. Roberts joined with the liberals and ruled the Moratorium Law constitutional by a vote of 5 to 4. Hughes wrote the majority opinion. He submit-

ted that "while emergency does not create power, emergency may furnish the occasion for the exercise of power" (p. 426). In what has been called the most important Contract Clause case since *Charles River Bridge* v. *Warren Bridge* (1837), Hughes stated that the Contract Clause was not absolute and that a state always possessed the authority to safeguard the vital interests of its citizens. Hughes found a "growing appreciation . . . of the necessity of finding ground between individual rights and public welfare." The chief justice concluded that the "question is no longer merely that of one party to a contract against another but of the use of reasonable means to safeguard the economic structure upon which the good of all depends" (p. 442).

For the four conservative dissenters, Justice George Sutherland argued that the Contract Clause should be interpreted literally. He refused to acknowledge that emergencies could justify state authorized modification of contracts. Sutherland predicted that if the Court allowed the Minnesota Moratorium Act to stand, it could well be the harbinger of greater invasions of the sanctity of contracts. And, if the Contract Clause was so interpreted, Sutherland lamented, all constitutional restrictions on legislative prerogative might collapse. Essentially, Sutherland threw down the constitutional gauntlet. Again and again over the next three years, the Four Horsemen would saddle up and ride out to attempt to thwart state and national attempts to come to terms with the hardships imposed by the Great Depression.

John W. Johnson

Honda Motor Co., Ltd. v. Oberg, 512 U.S. 415 (1994), argued 20 Apr. 1994, decided 24 June 1994; Stevens for the Court, Scalia concurring, Ginsberg and Rehnquist in dissent.

A 1910 amendment to the Oregon Constitution provided that, "no fact tried to a jury shall be otherwise re-examined . . . unless the court can affirmatively say there is no evidence to support the verdict." The Oregon courts held that contrary to the law in the federal courts and every other state, this provision prohibited any review of punitive damage awards for excessiveness. The question presented in *Oberg* is whether this provision violates the Fourteenth Amendment Due Process Clause. The Court concluded that it does.

The dissent argued that although the Court's opinions in *Pacific Mut. Life Ins. Co. v. Haslip* (1991) and *TXO Production Corp. v. Alliance Resources Corp.* (1993) did place constitutional outer limits on punitive damages, other Oregon procedures, which included proof by clear and convincing evidence and jury instructions that included specific substantive criteria, were sufficient to satisfy due process. However, the majority concluded that these procedures do not guard against excessive awards by juries that fail to follow the instructions and return "a lawless, biased, or arbitrary verdict" (p. 433).

As this quotation suggests, a key impetus behind the Supreme Court's punitive damage jurisprudence (see PUNITIVE DAMAGES) is a concern for runaway juries. The Court cites a study by Rustad (1992) that in over 10 percent of cases the judge found damages to be excessive. Since *Oberg*, the empirical literature on jury punitive damage awards supports the Supreme Court's concern that some juries have difficulty assessing punitive damages, but there are dissenting voices. *Oberg* is now one of several Supreme Court opinions establishing both substantive and procedural due process limitations on punitive damages. It was followed by *BMW of North America, Inc. v. Gore* (1996), *Cooper Industries, Inc. v. Leatherman Tool Group, Inc.*(2001), and *State Farm Mut. Auto. Ins. Co. v. Campbell* (2003).

Joseph Sanders

Houston, East and West Texas Railway Co. v. United States. See SHREVEPORT RATE CASES.

Hoyt v. Florida, 368 U.S. 57 (1961), argued 19 Oct. 1961, decided 12 Mar. 1961 by vote of 9 to 0; Harlan for the Court, Warren (with Black and Douglas) concurring. Gwendolyn Hoyt killed her husband with a baseball bat during a marital dispute over his adultery. She had offered to forgive and take him back, but his refusal provoked the homocide. She pleaded "temporary insanity" and was convicted of second-degree murder by an all-male jury.

Florida law provided that no female could serve on a jury unless she had specifically requested to be put on the jury list. Because men did not have to make these efforts, the law naturally produced a disproportionate number of male to female jurors, which resulted in many all-male juries. (Of ten thousand persons on her local jury list of eli-gibles, only ten were women.) Hoyt claimed that this statute denied her equal protection of the law because women jurors would have been more empathetic than men in assessing her defense of temporary insanity.

The majority rejected her claim on the grounds that Florida's exemption of women from jury duty was not arbitrary. Rather, it was a reasonable accommodation of community beliefs that women's social role was to serve family life in the home. The concurrence reasoned simply that Florida was making a good faith effort to let those women who wanted to do so serve on juries. Both groups ignored the implication of *Ballard* v. *U.S.* (1946) that women need to be included if juries are to represent a fair cross-section of the community. *Hoyt* was effectively overruled by *Taylor* v. *Louisiana* (1975).

Leslie Friedman Goldstein

Hudson & Goodwin, United States v. 7 Cranch (11 U.S.) 32 (1812), submitted without oral argument, decided 13 Feb. or 14 March 1812 by unknown vote. In this case the Supreme Court put an end to a decade-long dispute between Republicans and Federalists by denying the existence of a federal common law of crimes. That ruling remains good law today.

Barzillai Hudson and his codefendant George Goodwin were indicted in federal court in 1806 and 1807 for common-law seditious libel, for publishing a report that President Thomas Jefferson had conspired with Napoleon Bonaparte. Federal courts had for some time been upholding common-law convictions, but Republicans—who had won both the Congress and the presidency for the first time in 1800—had long insisted that federal courts had no constitutional power to create or enforce common-law crimes. The dispute over the common law of crimes had its roots in the most fundamental disagreement between Republicans and Federalists: Republicans generally denied that any branch of the federal government had any power not explicitly granted by the Constitution.

By 1812, when the *Hudson* case reached the Supreme Court, Republican appointees comprised a majority. The Court dismissed the indictments, holding that no federal court could exercise common law jurisdiction in criminal cases. The majority opinion, authored by Justice William Johnson, rested on the Republican principle that federal courts derive their powers solely from the Constitution and the Congress and have no residual jurisdiction. No dissents are recorded, but it is probable that Chief Justice John Marshall and Justices Bushrod Washington and Joseph Story dissented.

Suzanna Sherry

Hudson v. Michigan, 547 U.S. 586 (2006), argued 9 Jan. 2006, reargued 18 May 2006, decided 15 June 2006 by vote of 5 to 4; Scalia for the Court, joined by Roberts, Thomas, Alito, and Kennedy, in part; concurrence by Kennedy; dissent by Breyer, joined by Stevens, Souter, and Ginsburg. Following a search under warrant, Hudson was arrested for drug possession with intent to deliver. A Detroit police officer had knocked and announced the warrant but waited only three to five seconds before entering Hudson's residence, where he found a quantity of crack cocaine. Even though the prosecution admitted that the police officer's action violated the knock-and-announce requirement laid down by the Supreme Court in *Wilson* v. *Arkansas* (1995), Michigan appellate courts allowed the evidence under a state ruling that exclusion was not required when entry was made pursuant to a warrant, even without the proper knock-and-announce procedure.

In the majority opinion, Justice Antonin Scalia held that judges could not exclude evidence for a knock-and-announce violation only. He distinguished this case from evidence seized in a warrantless search, which requires suppression. The knock-and-announce rule was intended to protect police officers, private property, and the privacy and dignity of residents, not to prevent the government from seizing evidence appropriately described in a warrant. Applying a cost-benefit analysis common to Court decisions in this area since the 1980s, Scalia concluded that excluding evidence in these cases would "amount . . . to a get-out-of-jail-free card." (p 595).

Breyer, writing for the minority, argued that the Court had abandoned precedent dating to the thirteenth century, destroyed the legal incentive to comply with the Fourth Amendment's knock-and-announce requirement (which the Court had affirmed unanimously a decade earlier in *Wilson*), and undermined the exclusionary rule. The Court's decision in *Hudson* followed a general trend since the 1970s by treating the exclusionary rule as a judicial remedy

rather than a requirement under the Fourth Amendment.

David J. Bodenhamer

Hudson v. Palmer, 468 U.S. 517 (1984), argued 7 Dec. 1983, decided 3 July 1983 by vote of 5 to 4; Burger for the Court, O'Connor concurring, Stevens, joined by Brennan, Marshall, and Blackmun, concurring in part and dissenting in part. The Supreme Court held in this case that prison inmates do not have a right to privacy in their prison cells that would entitle them to Fourth Amendment protection against unreasonable searches. Palmer was an inmate at the Bland Correctional Center in Bland, Virginia. Hudson, an officer at the center, along with another corrections officer, conducted a "shakedown" search of Palmer's locker and cell. The officers found a ripped pillowcase in the trashcan and Palmer was charged with destroying state property. Palmer brought suit under section 1983 of the civil rights statutes (Title 42 of the U.S. Code) alleging that Hudson had conducted the search solely to harass him and further that Hudson had destroyed some of his noncontraband property in violation of the due process protections of the Fourteenth Amendment.

Chief Justice Warren Burger wrote for the majority that, under *Katz* v. *United States* (1967), there was no reasonable expectation of privacy in a prison cell; therefore the Fourth Amendment protection against unreasonable searches and siezures did not apply. The Court also dismissed Hudson's due process claim on the basis of *Parratt* v. *Taylor* (1981), which held that a state employee's negligent deprivation of an inmate's property does not violate the Due Process Clause if the state makes a meaningful postdeprivation remedy available.

Daryl R. Fair

Humphrey's Executor v. United States, 295 U.S. 602 (1935), argued 1 May 1935, decided 27 May 1935 by vote of 9 to o; Sutherland for the Court. In 1933, President Franklin D. Roosevelt removed a conservative member of the Federal Trade Commission, William E. Humphrey. Humphrey contested his removal in the U.S. Court of Claims, a suit carried on by the executor of his estate after his death.

In *Myers* v. *U.S.*, Chief Justice William Howard Taft had affirmed presidential removal of a postmaster and in obiter dictum stated that the president's removal power extended even to members of independent regulatory commissions. But in *Humphrey's Executor* Justice George Sutherland, speaking for a unanimous Court, held that a president may remove a commissioner only for cause and that an unqualified removal power violated the separation of powers. Sutherland distinguished *Myers* by asserting that a commissioner, unlike a postmaster, was not an executive officer but an official who acts quasi-legislatively and quasi-judicially.

Sutherland's opinion has been praised for liberating commissioners from fear of political reprisal but denounced for denying that a commissioner is a member of the executive branch, for hampering a president seeking to develop a coherent economic program, and for failing to acknowledge that Roosevelt had reason to believe he was acting in compliance with existing precedent. More angered by *Humphrey* because of its implication that he had willfully violated the Constitution than by the more important ruling in *Schechter Poultry Corp.* v. *U.S.* handed down that same day, Roosevelt was determined to seek ways to curb the Court, a course that led to his illfated court-packing plan of 1937. Unlike other decisions hostile to the New Deal, *Humphrey's Executor* has not been reversed, and its principle was expanded in *Wiener* v. *U.S.* (1958).

William E. Leuchtenburg

Hurley v. Irish-American Gay, Lesbian and Bisexual Group of Boston, 515 U.S. 557 (1995), argued 25 Apr. 1995, decided 19 June 1995 by a vote of 9 to 0; Souter for a unanimous Court.

At issue in *Hurley* was whether the sponsors of the Boston St. Patrick's Day parade could prohibit the display of banners identifying the marchers carrying them as Irish gay men, lesbians, and bisexuals.

The St. Patrick's Day parade is an annual tradition in South Boston, an enclave of middle- and working-class Irish-American families (pop. 38,000). Sponsored by the South Boston Allied War Veterans Council, a private nonprofit group, the parade also celebrates Evacuation Day, which commemorates the post–Revolutionary War departure of defeated British troops. In 1992, after gay rights organizations in New York City attempted to join the parade there, the Irish-American Gay, Lesbian and Bisexual

Group of Boston (GLIB) was founded to support the New York efforts and to join the St. Patrick's Day observances in Boston. Denied permission to march by Veterans Council group leader, John "Wacko" Hurley, GLIB contested its parade prohibition in Massachusetts state courts. Massachusetts law prohibits discrimination against homosexuals in employment, housing, and "any place of public accommodation, resort, or amusement." Massachusetts' Supreme Judicial Court (SJC) held that the parade was a public accommodation and thus the Veterans Council could not deny GLIB permission to march.

The SJC's ruling prompted Hurley to cancel the 1994 parade, arguing that this was his group's way of overruling the courts. In 1995 the parade was technically canceled, although a "protest march" against the court's ruling was held on 17 March. One month after the protest march, the case came before the United States Supreme Court for argument.

In a unanimous decision, the Court determined that to require the parade organizers to permit GLIB to march as a group with identifying banners violated the parade organizers' First Amendment right to free speech. Justice David Souter wrote that a parade is an instance of speech, a communicative event, and not a public accommodation to which a denial of access constituted an act of discrimination. The Court also noted that the parade organizers did not exclude homosexuals as such, not inquiring about the sexual orientation of marchers within approved parade units. Instead, the Veterans Council objected to GLIB as its own parade unit carrying its own banner. According to the Court, the exclusion of GLIB as a unit amounted to a speaker choosing his or her own message, which includes the "important manifestation of the principle of free speech . . . that one who chooses to speak may also decide 'what not to say.'" (p. 573) The Massachusetts courts' broad definition of the term public accommodation, therefore, infringed the right of free speech.

GLIB might have prevailed in this case had it been able to prove that the city was involved in running the parade. Souter noted that the city had run the parade until 1947 when it delegated the organizational responsibility to a private group. Although GLIB had attempted to make an argument that the parade was still linked to official city activities and thus the organizers' decision amounted to state action, this claim was rejected in the state courts.

Erin Ackerman

Hurtado v. California, 110 U.S. 516 (1884), argued 22–23 Jan. 1884, decided 3 Mar. 1884 by vote of 8 to 1; Matthews for the Court, Harlan in dissent. This case involved a provision in the constitution of California that authorized prosecutions for felonies by information, after examination by a magistrate, without indictment by a grand jury. The defendant, on the basis of information filed by district attorney, was tried for murder and sentenced to death. He argued on appeal that proceeding by information in capital cases violated the Due Process Clause of the Fourteenth Amendment asserting that this clause incorporated the Fifth Amendment requirement of grand jury indictment in federal capital cases, thus making it binding upon the states. The Supreme Court rejected the argument, holding that the Due Process Clause of the Fourteenth Amendment could not logically encompass the specific procedural guarantees of the Fifth Amendment.

The defendant also contended that due process signified those settled usages and modes of proceeding existing in the common and statute law of England before the settlement of the American colonies, unless unsuited to colonial conditions. He claimed that proceeding by information in capital cases was not authorized by English or colonial law. The Court disagreed, holding that other procedures may be consonant with due process. The test that the Court adopted was that any legal proceeding, whether sanctioned by age or newly devised, which preserved the fundamental principles of liberty and justice lying at the base of American political institutions, must be deemed to constitute due process. In the Court's opinion, the California procedure did not violate these principles.

Edgar Bodenheimer

Hustler Magazine v. Falwell, 485 U.S. 46 (1988), argued 2 Dec. 1987, decided 24 Feb. 1988 by vote of 8 to 0; Rehnquist for the Court, White concurring, Kennedy not participating. In a parody that appeared in *Hustler* magazine the prominent fundamentalist evangelist Reverend Jerry Falwell was depicted as a drunk in an incestuous sexual liaison with his mother in an outhouse.

A jury in the U.S. District Court for the Western District of Virginia found that the parody was not libelous, because no reasonable reader would have understood it as a factual assertion that Falwell had engaged in the described activity. Nevertheless, the jury awarded $200,000 in damages on a separate count of "intentional infliction of emotional distress," a cause of action that did not require that a false statement of fact be made.

The Supreme Court overturned the jury verdict and held that a public figure or official may not recover for intentional infliction of emotional distress arising from a publication unless the publication contains a false statement of fact that was made with actual malice (knowledge of falsity or reckless disregard for truth or falsity). That the material might be deemed outrageous and that it might have been intended to cause severe emotional distress were not enough to overcome the First Amendment. Vicious attacks on public figures, the Court noted, are part of the American tradition of satire and parody, a tradition of speech that would be hamstrung if public figures could sue them anytime the satirist caused distress.

Rodney A. Smolla

Hutchinson v. Proxmire, 443 U.S. 111 (1979), argued 17 Apr., 1979, decided 26 June 1979 by vote of 7 to 1 to 1; Burger for the Court, Stewart concurring in part and dissenting in part, Brennan in dissent. This case explored the scope of protection afforded members of Congress by the Constitution's Speech and Debate Clause (Art. 1, sec. 6). In addition, the Court revisited the question of who was a "public figure" when determining the standard of proof in *libel claims.

The case centered on the "Golden Fleece Award" bestowed by Senator William Proxmire on federal agencies he judged guilty of wasteful spending. An award was given to several agencies funding the research of Dr. Ronald Hutchinson, a psychologist developing an objective measure of aggression through experimentation on monkeys. Proxmire announced the award on the floor of the Senate, while noting it in a press release, his newsletter, media interviews, and other settings. Claiming "emotional anguish." Hutchinson sued Proxmire for defamation, asserting that his reputation had been damaged, his contractual relations interfered with, and his privacy invaded.

The Court narrowly viewed protected legislative acts under the Speech and Debate Clause. Immunity did not extend to newsletters, press releases, and activities not essential to the Senate's deliberations. Such activities did not fall under the Senate's informing function since they involved views and actions of one member and not collective chamber activity. Further, Hutchinson was not a "public figure," since he was thrust into the limelight by Proxmire's actions and did not personally seek it. Consequently, following *New York Times* v. *Sullivan* (1964), a lesser standard of proof than actual malice could prevail for Hutchinson. Justice William Brennan dissented from this narrow view of privileged legislative acts. A legislator's criticism of governmental expenditures, whatever its form, he argued, was protected by the Speech and Debate Clause.

Elliot E. Slotnick

Hylton v. United States, 3 Dall. (3 U.S.) 171 (1796), argued 23–25 Feb. 1796, decided 8 Mar. 1796 by vote of 3 to 0; seriatim opinions by Iredell, Paterson, and Chase.

In 1794, Congress levied a carriage tax on passenger vehicles. The U.S. government sued Daniel Hylton in the federal circuit court of Virginia for nonpayment of the required duty. Hylton claimed that the levy was a "direct tax" within the meaning of Article I,

section 8 of the Constitution, which prohibits Congress from levying direct taxes not apportioned according to the population of the several states. The controversy touched the sensitive question of the revenue-raising power of the new national government. The circuit court was divided on the question, but Hylton confessed to judgment (admitted liability) in order to test the constitutionality of the tax by an appeal to the Supreme Court. The three justices who heard the case—Samuel Chase, William Paterson, and James Iredell—unanimously agreed that the carriage levy was an indirect tax and, therefore, not proscribed by Article I. The Court's view on the tax issue remained the law until the *Income Tax Cases of 1895 (see *Pollock* v. *Farmers Loan & Trust Co.*). *Hylton* was also significant because it implicitly raised the issue of the Supreme Court's power of judicial review. While the members of the *Hylton* court never addressed that issue directly, the justices appeared to assume that they had the power to nullify unconstitutional acts of Congress. Justice Chase declared that if the Court did have such power, however, he would exercise it only "in a very clear case" (p. 175). Not until Chief Justice John Marshall's celebrated opinion in *Marbury* v. *Madison* (1803) did the Supreme Court finally explain its power of judicial review under the Constitution.

George Dargo

Illinois ex rel. McCollum v. Board of Education, 333 U.S. 203 (1948), argued 8 Dec. 1947, decided 8 Mar. 1948 by vote of 8 to 1; Black for the Court, Reed in dissent. *McCollum* v. *Board of Education* was one of the Supreme Court's early examinations of the part of the First Amendment that forbids establishment of religion. The Court decided that public schools could not allow religious teachers to offer religious instruction within school buildings. The tenor of the majority and concurring opinions was strictly separationist, suggesting a high wall between the state and religious activities.

The Illinois school board allowed students to receive religious instruction, Protestant, Catholic, or Jewish, for thirty or forty-five minutes in each school week. The instructors received no public funds but were subject to approval by the superintendent of schools. Students whose parents did not request religious instruction went elsewhere in the building; those enrolled for religious instruction were required to attend.

Justice Hugo Black, whose opinion for the Court in *Everson* v. *Board of Education* (1947) had applied the Establishment Clause against state agencies and endorsed broadly separationist guidelines, wrote for the Court again in *McCollum*. His opinion treated the school district's program as a plainly impermissible public aid to religion. A concurring opinion by Justice Felix Frankfurter, joined by four other justices, emphasized a historical trend against commingling sectarian and secular instruction in public schools and noted that almost two million students were in "released time" programs of one kind or another. Justice Reed's dissent argued that the Establishment Clause should be interpreted more narrowly to permit such incidental assistance to religion by the state. *McCollum*'s practical impact on "released time" programs was sharply circumscribed by the Court's next case on the subject, *Zorach* v. *Clauson* (1952).

Over the next three decades, however, the Court permitted more opportunities for states to provide aid to religion. In the landmark case of *Agostini* v. *Felton* (1997), the justices overturned their previous decision in *Aguilar* v. *Felton* (1985) and held that they would no longer presume that public employees will inculcate religion simply because they happen to be in a sectarian environment. Thus the decision in *Agostini* may well have created a more conducive environment for such programs as school vouchers.

Kent Greenawalt

Immigration and Naturalization Service v. Chadha, 462 U.S. 919 (1983), argued 22 Feb. 1982, reargued 7 Dec. 1982, decided 23 June 1983 by vote of 7 to 2; Burger for the Court, Powell concurring, White in dissent, Rehnquist in dissent. Born in Kenya of Indian parents and holding a British passport,

Jagdish Chadha had come to the United States to study in the mid-1960s. When his student visa expired, neither Great Britain nor Kenya would let him return so Chadha applied for permanent residency in the United States. After a lengthy hearing process his application to stay was approved by the Immigration and Naturalization Service (INS). Then, two years later the U.S. House of Representatives voted to "veto" the INS decision and Chadha faced deportation.

The legislative veto was a simple concept, originally "invented" by Congress in the 1930s as a way to retain some control over power delegated to the president to reorganize executive branch agencies. In the wake of the Vietnam War and the Watergate scandal, the legislative veto became especially attractive as a tool for controlling presidential excesses.

At the same time it became apparent that the legislative veto might be a means for exercising congressional control over administrative regulations. By the mid-1970s a tidal flood of regulations to implement all the environmental, consumer, and other social legislation that had passed over the previous decade was pouring out of Washington bureaucracies. Legislative vetoes offered members of Congress a way to respond to the complaints of powerful business and industrial interests subject to these regulations. Public interest groups that had fought long and hard to get legislation passed to accomplish their goals were faced with the prospect of losing regulation by regulation. Alan Morrison, chief litigator for consumer activist Ralph Nader, seized the opportunity to strike out at the legislative veto by taking over Chadha's case.

Department of Justice attorneys in both the Carter and Reagan administrations joined the case on behalf of the immigration service arguing with Morrison against the constitutionality of the legislative veto. Congress was forced to intervene to defend the constitutionality of its legislative veto. Chadha's small case had turned into a battle of Titans: Congress versus the president.

Chief Justice Warren Burger wrote the Court's opinion. The Constitution provides, Burger pointed out, "a single, finely wrought and exhaustively considered procedure" (p. 951) for exercise of the legislative power of the federal government. "Explicit and unambiguous provisions of the Constitution prescribe and define the respective functions of the Congress and of the Executive in the legislative process" (p. 945). Any actions taken by either house of Congress if "they contain matter which is properly to be regarded as legislative in character and effect" must conform with the constitutionally designed legislative process that includes bicameral passage and presentment to the president (p. 952). He then went on to spell out what the Court meant. "Legislative in character and effect" includes any action that has the "purpose and effect of altering the legal rights, duties, and relations of persons outside the legislative branch" (p. 952). Legislative vetoes represent efforts by one or both houses of Congress to subvert the "step-by-step, deliberate and deliberative process" (p. 959) for legislation set out in the Constitution and are thus unconstitutional.

In one fell swoop the Court in *Chadha* effectively overturned more congressional enactments than it had previously over its entire history. In Justice Lewis Powell's opinion the case should have been decided on far narrower grounds based on a balancing of the legislative veto's utility against its potential for intrusion into another branch's rightful domain. When Congress finds that a particular person does not satisfy the statutory criteria for permanent residence in this country, it has assumed, Powell argued, a judicial function, in violation of separation of powers. That, according to Powell, was the only issue raised by this case, and the only issue that should have been decided.

In a vehement dissent, Justice Byron White defended the legislative veto as "an important if not indispensable political invention that allows the president and Congress to resolve major constitutional policy differences, assures the accountability of independent regulatory agencies, and preserves Congress'[s] control over lawmaking" (p. 972). White's opinion attacked the rigidity of the majority's application of the constitutional lawmaking process as "irresponsible" in its failure to recognize the reality of the modern administrative state where much "law" is made outside the presentment clause process by unelected bureaucrats (p. 974).

It is too soon to tell whether *Chadha* foreshadows a Supreme Court intention to apply constitutional requirements strictly to police the struggle of power between the branches. *Bowsher* v. *Synar*, the 1986 challenge to the Gramm-Rudman-Hollings deficit reduction law, gives some evidence that the Court might be leaning in this direction, but two more recent decisions, *Morrison v. Olson*, the 1988 challenge to the special prosecutor law, and *Mistretta* v. *U.S.*, the 1989 challenge to the sentencing commission law, may presage a Court retreat from a strict reading of separation of powers requirements.

□ Barbara Hinkson Craig, *Chadha: The Story of an Epic Constitutional Struggle* (1988). Louis Fisher, "Judicial Misjudgments About the Lawmaking Process: The Legislative Veto Case," *Public Administration Review, Special Issue* (November 1985): 705–711.

Barbara Craig

Income Tax Case. See POLLOCK V. FARMERS' LOAN & TRUST CO.

Insular Cases. The *Insular Cases* are a group of some fourteen decisions of the period 1901–1904 that involve the application of the Constitution and Bill of Rights to overseas territories. The cases arose after the United States acquired island territories through the treaty ending the Spanish-American War (1898). The nation's determination to become a world power, as evidenced by the war and the acquisition of foreign territories, received overwhelming popular endorsement in the presidential election of 1900. The *Insular Cases* translated the political dispute into the vocabulary of the Constitution, with the Supreme Court eventually echoing the popular sentiment.

Two competing positions lay behind the arguments before the Court. One opinion, largely racially motivated, was that the people of the new territories were unfit to become citizens—a conclusion that foreclosed the possibility of statehood and relegated the people to permanent territorial status. The other view was the century-old tradition that all territory would eventually become states.

The *Insular Cases* presented three questions of constitutional law and statutory construction: (1) whether the national government had the power to acquire territories by treaty; (2) whether certain statutes applied to territories; and (3) whether the Bill of Rights applied automatically to any territory upon acquisition by the United States. In *De Lima* v. *Bidwell* (1901) the Court confirmed that the nation had the power to acquire territory, pointing for support to the long history of acquisitions.

The Court also considered whether duties could be imposed on goods shipped between Puerto Rico and the United States. For goods imported into the United States, the Court avoided the constitutional question by relying upon language in the Dingley Tariff Act (1897), which imposed tariffs on "all articles imported from foreign countries." In *De Lima*, Justice Henry Billings Brown wrote for the Court that Puerto Rico ceased to be "foreign" once ceded to the United States by treaty. Hence, the statute did not apply to Puerto Rico.

The Court could not, however, avoid the constitutional question for goods exported to Puerto Rico. So long as the United States military governed there, exports could be taxed under the war powers of Congress (*Dooley* v. *United States*, 1901). Once the special powers of the military ended, however, any imposition of tariffs seemed to violate the Constitution's requirement that duties be "uniform throughout the United States" (Art. I, sec. 8). In *Downes* v. *Bidwell* (1901) Brown reiterated that Puerto Rico was not "foreign"; but he reasoned that it was also not part of "the United States," a term that meant only the states themselves. Justice Edward D. White and three other justices concurred but rejected Brown's constitutional categories as being too restrictive of the nation's powers in world affairs. White concluded that constitutional limitations applied to a territory only after Congress had taken action to "incorporate" the territory into the United States. Chief Justice Melville W. Fuller rejected White's nebulous category between foreign and incorporated, reasoning that once a territory came under the nation's sovereign power, it became part of "the United States."

Later cases, involving the Bill of Rights, revealed a movement away from Brown's position to White's, which is still the prevailing view. Brown continued to find modest restrictions in the Constitution itself. For example, he held in *Hawaii* v. *Mankichi* (1903) that, in the absence of congressional action, only those rights that were "fundamental in their nature" would apply (p. 218). Justice White agreed with the conclusion that there was no requirement for indictment by a grand jury or a unanimous jury. But he again concluded that because Congress had not incorporated Hawaii into the United States, no part of the Bill of Rights applied.

A majority of the Court finally accepted the incorporation doctrine in *Dorr* v. *United States* (1904). Justice William R. Day noted that the natives of the Philippines were not fit for jury trials and that Congress need not accord them that right until it chose to incorporate the islands.

The cases present myriad justifications and tortured reasoning. Their clear import is that the justices wanted to allow the president and Congress the greatest possible freedom in world affairs. Many people thought that the opinions reflected the election results, since in the election of 1900 the voters had soundly rejected the Democrats' call to repudiate the acquisitions of overseas territories. But the cases show more than a politically savvy Court; they also anticipate the later debate over the application of the Bill of Rights to the states, when "incorporation" and "fundamental rights" would again be operative phrases. The Court's opinions therefore represent tentative, early arguments in what would become half a century of debate about the reach of the Bill of Rights.

□ James E. Kerr, *The Insular Cases: The Role of the Judiciary in American Expansionism* (1982).

Walter F. Pratt, Jr.

International Society for Krishna Consciousness, Inc. v. Lee, 505 U.S. 672 (1992), argued 25 Mar. 1992, decided 26 June 1992 by vote of 6 to 3; Rehnquist for the Court, Souter in dissent, joined by Blackmun and Stevens.

The First Amendment historically protected various kinds of "speech," including the charitable solicitation of money and the distribution of literature. The Hare Krishna movement, which requires that its members solicit money and distribute literature, had routinely turned to airports as one place to beg and proselytize simultaneously. Travelers making their way through the airports were likely to be confronted not just by Krishna groups but by a host of other individuals either seeking funds or pressing a spiritual agenda or both. The Port Authority of New York and New Jersey beginning in the 1970s attempted to ban these activities. The Krishnas, however, had been successful in defending themselves in every other federal jurisdiction save the federal Court of Appeals for the Second Circuit in Manhattan, whose judges had sustained the Port Authority's ban on begging but overturned another provision that prohibited the distribution of literature as a violation of the First Amendment.

The key issues before the Supreme Court involved the question of whether an airport could be construed as a public forum under the First Amendment. The Court's precedents in this area held that such a forum, like a park or a street corner, had greater protection from government interference than did a so-called nonpublic forum. If an area was designated a public forum, then government had to prove a compelling state interest in order to regulate speech there; if the area was a nonpublic forum, then government could regulate speech as long as its actions were reasonable.

Chief Justice William H. Rehnquist's opinion for the majority of the Court held that airports were not public forums. Airports were subject to special security requirements and their terminals were meant to serve travelers and employees, not the public at large. Therefore, the Port Authority had the power to make whatever reasonable regulations it thought necessary to avoid congestion and disruption to passengers seeking to board planes, claim luggage, or purchase tickets.

The dissenters, led by Justice David H. Souter, argued that an airport was undeniably a public facility and that solicitations could not be banned inside or outside of it. Souter argued that the airport lounge was the modern-day equivalent of a city park and that his colleagues should treat it as such.

At the same time, in an unsigned opinion, the justices did strike down by a 5-to-4 vote the Port Authority's ban on the distribution of literature. In this instance, Justice Sandra Day O'Connor agreed that airports were not public forums but that a ban on the distribution of literature failed to meet the minimal test of reasonableness. Chief Justice Rehnquist led the dissenters in asserting that O'Connor had made a distinction without a difference. There was no practical difference, Rehnquist argued, for a weary traveler whether a person was attempting to avoid a delay caused by someone soliciting money as opposed to someone foisting literature on him or her.

Kermit L. Hall

International Union v. Johnson Controls, Inc., 111 S.Ct. 1196 (1991), argued 10 Oct. 1990, decided 20 Mar. 1991 by vote of 9 to 0; Blackmun for the Court, White, joined by Rehnquist and Kennedy, concurring in part and concurring in the judgment, Scalia concurring in the judgment. In this landmark sex discrimination case, several unions and women employees brought a class action suit under Title VII of the Civil Rights Act of 1964, as amended by the Pregnancy Discrimination Act of 1978. The suit challenged the "fetal protection policy" of Johnson Controls, a battery-manufacturing company that, since 1982, had barred fertile women from high-paying jobs involving exposure to lead.

Reversing both the district court and the court of appeals, which had ruled in favor of the company, the Supreme Court held that the fetal protection policy was not facially neutral because it did not apply to males as well as females despite evidence that lead exposure also harms the male reproductive system. Since this was a policy of "disparate treatment," it could be justified under Title VII only as a bona fide occupational qualification (BFOQ). However, the Court held that since pregnant employees must be treated the same as other employees unless they differ in their ability to do the work, and since there was no showing here of such a disability, the BFOQ exception was not justifiable. The company's main concern was not with whether the female employees could do the job, but with whether lead exposure would harm their unconceived fetuses. However important this may be, the Court said, the health of a fetus is not essential to the business of battery manufacturing and thus cannot qualify as a BFOQ. The Court also rejected the company's claim that its policy was justified by a fear of tort liability. Justice Byron White, joined by Chief Justice William Rehnquist and Justice Anthony Kennedy, agreed that the Johnson Controls policy was discriminatory, but disagreed that the BFOQ defense was so narrow that it could never justify a sex-specific fetal protection policy.

Joel B. Grossman

J

Jackson v. Metropolitan Edison Co., 419 U.S. 345 (1974), argued 15 Oct. 1974, decided 23 Dec. 1974 by vote of 6 to 3; Rehnquist for the Court, Douglas, Brennan, and Marshall in dissent. In *Metropolitan Edison* the Supreme Court considered the issue of when private action is sufficiently public in nature that it becomes bound by constitutional provisions limiting governmental conduct. The case was brought by a resident of York, Pennsylvania, who claimed that Metropolitan Edison, a privately owned utility, violated her due process rights by terminating electric service without adequate notice and the chance for a hearing. The Supreme Court rejected the argument on the ground that the utility was a private entity and hence not bound by the Due Process Clause, which applies only to actions by the state.

The Court over the years has attempted unsuccessfully to develop a workable test to determine when private action is so public in nature, or so infused with public regulation and direction, that it amounts to state action within the meaning of the Due Process Clause. In *Metropolitan Edison* the plaintiff pointed to the partial monopoly granted by the state, the extensive state regulation, and the essential nature of utility operations as evidence of the state character of the utility's actions. The Court, however, deemed this evidence insufficient to label the utility's conduct as state action.

Metropolitan Edison remains good law on the state action issue, although it is one of many decisions that, taken together, provide confused guidance on the issue. The decision's practical effect for utilities has been altered by legislative enactments.

Eric T. Freyfogle

J.E.B. v. Alabama Ex Rel. T.B., 511 U.S. 127 (1994), argued 2 Nov. 1993, decided 19 Apr. 1994 by vote of 6 to 3, Blackmun for the Court, Kennedy and O'Connor concurring, and Rehnquist and Scalia in dissent. The high-profile criminal cases of William Kennedy Smith and Rodney King sharpened American interest in having a trial by a jury of one's peers, especially when issues arose over the gender and racial composition of juries. The Supreme Court in the landmark case of *Batson* v. *Kentucky* (1986) held that prosecutors were prohibited under the Equal Protection Clause of the Fourteenth Amendment from using peremptory challenges to excuse potential jurors solely on the basis of race. In *Edmonson* v. *Leesville Concrete Co.* (1991) the Court extended the *Batson* rule to civil trials. Until *J.E.B.*, however, the Court had never invoked the Equal Protection argument used in *Batson* to discern the legitimacy of gender-based peremptory challenges.

In 1991 Teresia Bible, the mother of Phillip Rhett Bowman Bible, brought a paternity action against James E. Bowman, Sr., in

Scottsboro, Alabama. (The town, of course, had been the site in the early 1930s of the infamous Scottsboro case in which seven African-American youths were convicted of the rape of two white women on a freight train and sentenced to death by an all-white jury.) In the paternity suit, the prosecutor for the state of Alabama used nine of his ten peremptory challenges to remove men from the panel, with the result that the jury was composed of twelve women. The prosecutor did so in the belief that women would be tougher on matters of paternity than would men, a view that the defense apparently subscribed to as well, since it used a similar number of peremptory challenges to remove female would-be jurors. When, however, the all-female jury convicted Bowman, his counsel immediately appealed, claiming that the Supreme Court's decision in *Batson* precluded the use of gender-based peremptory challenges. The Alabama court of appeals rejected this argument and sustained the trial court's verdict, including an order directing Bowman to pay child support.

The Court, however, speaking through Justice Harry A. Blackmun, overturned the verdict, doing so in blunt language that echoed for the issue of gender the kind of thinking the Court had invoked for the issue of race in *Batson*. "Virtually no support exists," Blackmun wrote, "for the conclusion that gender alone is an accurate predictor of [jurors'] attitudes" (p. 138). There was, Blackmun continued, no legitimate rationale for striking potential jurors based on "invidious, archaic and over broad stereotypes about the relative abilities of men and women" (p. 131). Blackmun concluded that "[w]e recognize that whether the trial is criminal or civil, potential jurors, as well as litigants have an equal protection right to jury selection procedures that are free from state-sponsored group stereotypes rooted in, and reflective of, historical prejudice" (p. 128). The Court did not reject the use of all peremptory challenges but said that in exercising this right gender could not be used as a proxy for bias. Justice Sandra Day O'Connor agreed but argued in her concurrence that the rule should apply only to the state, not to the defense. Justice Anthony M. Kennedy also concurred in the opinion, but he noted his belief that the Equal Protection Clause protected only individual and not group rights. A juror, in Kennedy's view, did not sit on a jury as the representative of

a racial or sexual group but only as an individual citizen.

Chief Justice William Rehnquist's dissent argued that the extension of *Batson* to gender discrimination was inappropriate and unwise. The use of race categories, Rehnquist concluded, was limited by "strict scrutiny," while gender categories were subjected only to "heightened scrutiny." In Rehnquist's view, race rather than gender was at the heart of the Fourteenth Amendment's commands and hence the use of gender in the exercise of peremptory challenges should be sustained. Justice Antonin Scalia authored an even sharper attack on the majority opinion, terming it nothing more than a politically correct holding divorced from the actual issues in the case and, in mocking terms, "an inspiring demonstration of how thoroughly up-to-date and right-thinking we justices are in matters pertaining to the sexes" (p. 156). Most important, Scalia concluded, the Court's decision threatened to eliminate peremptory challenges altogether.

While that outcome has yet to materialize, the reconciliation of peremptory challenges with the guarantees of the Equal Protection Clause of the Fourteenth Amendment remains an important piece of the high court's future business.

Kermit L. Hall

Johnson and Graham's Lessee v. McIntosh, 8 Wheat. (21 U.S.) 543 (1823), argued 17 Feb. 1823, decided 10 Mar. 1823 by vote of 7 to o; Marshall for the Court. This was the first Supreme Court case to define the legal relationship of Native Americans to the United States. It began in 1775 when the Piankeshaws ceded land in Illinois to a group of speculators, including William Johnson. However, Virginia in 1783 conveyed to the federal government its Illinois claims for the public domain.

In 1818 William McIntosh bought from the United States 11,560 acres of Illinois land that were part of Johnson's purchase. These same lands were claimed by Joshua Johnson and his son, Thomas J. Graham, and they brought an ejectment action against McIntosh. After losing in the lower courts, Johnson and Graham appealed.

The Supreme Court, in a unanimous decision written by Chief Justice John Marshall, found for McIntosh. Marshall held that the principle of discovery gave European nations an absolute right to New World lands. Once established, Native Americans had only a lesser right of occupancy that could be abolished. Marshall also found that the United States acquired title to Native American lands through Great Britain's conquest. He mistakenly declared that a conquered people's rights to property could not be applied to Native Americans because Indians were "fierce nomadic savages" (p. 590).

Thus, Indians could not transfer lands to individuals, such as William Johnson, or to nations other than the United States. Subsequent decisions of the Supreme Court eroded *McIntosh*, although this decision has yet to be specifically overruled.

John R. Wunder

Johnson v. Louisiana, 400 U.S. 356 (1972), argued 1 Mar. 1971, reargued 10 Jan. 1972, decided 22 May 1972 by vote of 5 to 4; White for the Court, Blackmun and Powell concurring, Douglas, Brennan, Marshall, and Stewart in dissent. The issues in *Johnson*, and its companion case *Apodaca* v. *Oregon* (1972), which had been left unresolved by *Duncan* v. *Louisiana* (1968), were whether the Fourteenth Amendment due process and equal protection clauses required states to observe jury unanimity in criminal cases, as is required in the federal courts. A jury had convicted Johnson of robbery by a 9-to-3 vote. Since Johnson's trial began before *Duncan* was decided, and that ruling had not been applied retroactively, its Sixth Amendment protections were not available.

Johnson contended that he had been denied due process because a non-unanimous verdict meant the reasonable-doubt standard of guilt had not been met. The fact that three jurors disagreed with the verdict indicated doubt, and the nine-person majority could not have voted conscientiously in favor of guilt beyond a reasonable doubt.

Justice Byron White responded that it was an unsupported assumption that the jury majority would not weigh carefully the arguments of dissenting jurors. Reasonable doubt was not ignored merely because three jurors disagreed. "[The] fact remains," wrote White, "that nine jurors—a substantial majority of the jury—were convinced by the evidence" (p. 362). The doubts of three jurors were simply not enough to impeach the jury's decision.

Because Louisiana required unanimity in twelve-person juries hearing capital cases and in five-person juries in other serious crimes, Johnson also argued that the less-then-unanimous verdict in his case was a denial of equal protection of the law. The Court, however, found nothing invidious in the varying jury classifications. Requiring the number of jurors who must be convinced beyond a reasonable doubt to increase with the seriousness of the crime and the severity of the punishment was a reasonable legislative judgment.

The several dissenters argued that the Sixth Amendment unanimity rule should be incorporated into the Fourteenth Amendment. Alternatively, they claimed that it was a fundamental due process right.

Charles H. Sheldon

Johnson v. Santa Clara County, 480 U.S. 616 (1987), argued 12 Nov. 1986, decided 25 Mar. 1987 by vote of 6 to 3; Brennan for the Court, O'Connor and Stevens concurring, White, Scalia, and Rehnquist in dissent. This was the first case in which the Court decided the legality of sex-based voluntary affirmative action under Title VII of the Civil Rights Act of 1964. In *United Steelworkers of America* v. *Weber* (1979), the Court had held that Title VII does not prohibit voluntary race-conscious affirmative action where it is necessary "to eliminate conspicuous racial imbalance in traditionally segregated job categories" (p. 209). In *Johnson*, the Court expanded this concept to include voluntary sex-conscious affirmative action where it is necessary to eliminate a "manifest imbalance that reflect[s] under-representation of women in 'traditionally segregated job categories'" (p. 631).

In 1978, the Santa Clara County (California) Transportation Agency adopted a temporary affirmative action plan designed to take into account the sex or race of qualified applicants with regard to promotion within traditionally segregated job classifications in which both women and members of racial minorities had been underrepresented. The agency acknowledged that although women constituted 36.4 percent of the area's labor market, they constituted only 22.4 percent of the agency's work force and were concentrated in classifications that traditionally employed women: women accounted for 76 percent of the agency's office and clerical employees but o percent of its skilled craft workers. The affirmative action program did not set aside a specific number of jobs for minority members and women but established annual goals as guidelines in hiring and promotion for a "statistically measurable yearly improvement" so as to attain, eventually, "a work force whose composition reflected the proportion of minorities and women in the labor force" (pp. 621–622).

In 1979, a vacancy for the job of road dispatcher was announced. Of the 238 positions in the skilled craft classifications, which included the road dispatcher's position, none had ever been held by a woman. The agency passed over Johnson, a male employee certified as eligible for promotion, and gave the job to Joyce, the female applicant, who was also certified as eligible but who had a slightly lower interview score. Both were rated as well qualified.

The Supreme Court affirmed the decision of the Court of Appeals for the Ninth Circuit and held that, pursuant to Title VII, the affirmative action plan was appropriate in permitting the agency to remedy the imbalance of men and women in skilled job classifications. The plan established flexible promotional goals, not rigid quotas, and while recognizing gender to be one of several factors to be considered, it required women to compete for promotion with other qualified applicants. The Court noted that because the plan authorized the agency to select any one of the qualified applicants, Johnson had no absolute entitlement to promotion. The Court concluded that the plan "unsettled no legitimate firmly rooted expectation on the part of the petitioner" (p. 638). The Court also found that the plan was a temporary measure designed to achieve a balanced work force, was not intended to maintain a permanent sexual or racial balance, and did not impose a complete ban on male employees' opportunities for advancement. It held that such a plan would further the statutory goal of Title VII by encouraging voluntary efforts to eliminate gender discrimination.

The majority limited its interpretation to Title VII prohibitions and did not clarify the relationship between statutory and constitutional standards. Justice Sandra Day O'Connor, writing separately, found the constitutional and statutory standards to be identical. In a vigorous dissent, Justice Antonin Scalia stated that the decision was an "enormous expansion" intended to alter social standards and not merely a decision to eliminate discrimination. He also argued that *Weber* should be overruled.

Johnson was the first case in which the Court held that voluntary affirmative action is permissible under Title VII to overcome the effects of societal discrimination. *Johnson* also established that the legality of voluntary affirmative action as approved in *Weber* applied to sex discrimination and to Title VII claims in public sector employment.

Herbert Hill

Johnson v. De Grandy, 512 U.S. 997 (1994), argued 4 Oct. 1993, decided 30 June 1994 by a vote of 7 to 2; Souter for the Court, O'Connor concurring, Kennedy concurring in part and concurring in the judgment, Thomas and Scalia in dissent.

One of the Supreme Court's first voting rights cases after *Shaw* v. *Reno* (1993), *De Grandy* involved a challenge by groups of Hispanic and African voters to Florida's redistricting of Dade County's (Miami) state legislative districts after the 1990 census. The plaintiffs argued that the redistricting plan violated section 2 of the Voting Rights Act of 1965 by diluting minority voting strength. Yet the plan yielded functional proportionality in Dade County by providing a proportion of majority-minority districts that roughly equaled the proportion of the minority voting-age population.

The plaintiffs specifically argued that more majority-minority districts could have been drawn had the legislature not lessened minority voting power by packing minority voters into districts in some instances and cracking minority voting strength by dividing cohesive minority populations among multiple districts in other instances. The federal district court found that Florida's failure to create as many majority-minority districts as possible necessarily yielded a section 2 violation. In response, the Supreme Court reiterated the totality-of-the-circumstances test, finding that the plaintiffs' evidence was insufficient to establish vote dilution in substantial measure because the plan provided rough proportionality for minority groups in the Dade County area. Justices Clarence Thomas and Antonin Scalia dissented on the grounds that an apportionment plan is not subject to section 2 challenge.

De Grandy reiterated that districting is more art than science and stressed that voting rights violations do not always flow from proof of certain background facts. Though the Court's analysis cut against the minority plaintiffs in *De Grandy*, its general thrust would later benefit minority voters in cases such as *Easley v. Cromartie* (2001).

Henry L. Chambers, Jr.

Johnson v. Zerbst, 304 U.S. 458 (1938), argued 4 Apr. 1938, decided 23 May 1938 by vote of 6 to 2; Black for the Court, Reed concurring, McReynolds and Butler in dissent, Cardozo not participating. Johnson was convicted in federal court of feloniously possessing, uttering, and passing counterfeit money. At the time of trial, he was indigent and unable to employ an attorney to represent him. While imprisoned, he filed for habeas corpus relief in a federal district court, arguing that he had been deprived of his Sixth Amendment right to counsel. The district court denied his claim and the court of appeals affirmed.

The Supreme Court held that under the Sixth Amendment, the federal courts have no jurisdiction to deprive an accused of his life or liberty unless he has the assistance of counsel or the trial court clearly determines, on the record, that he has intelligently and competently waived his right to counsel. In effect, the Court required that counsel be appointed for indigent defendants in all federal criminal cases. Six years earlier in *Powell v. Alabama* (1932), the Court had issued a more limited ruling applying to state courts, holding that the Fourteenth Amendment's Due Process Clause required that counsel be appointed in state courts when the defendant was charged with a capital offense and was incapable of making his own defense. The right to counsel in state courts was later expanded in *Gideon v. Wainwright* (1963) and *Argersinger v. Hamlin* (1972).

Susan E. Lawrence

Joint Anti-Fascist Refugee Committee v. McGrath, 341 U.S. 123 (1951), argued 11 Oct. 1950, decided 30 Apr. 1951 by vote of 5 to 3; Burton for the Court; Vinson, Reed, and Minton in dissent; Clark not participating. The Court handed down this surprising ruling at the height of cold war hysteria over domestic communism. It ruled on common law and constitutional grounds against the manner in which groups had been placed on the attorney general's list of subversive organizations. That list, created by President Harry S. Truman's Executive Order no. 9835 of 20 March 1948, included seventy-eight allegedly subversive organizations, falling into six categories. There was no requirement that the attorney general hold hearings before listing a group nor any provision for appeal from, or judicial review of, his decisions. Public officials and private citizens used the list extensively to

pillory, intimidate, and ostracize radicals and other dissidents. Three of the groups included on the list, the Joint Anti-Fascist Refugee Committee, the National Council of American-Soviet Friendship, and the International Workers Order, objected to being characterized as disloyal and filed suit seeking to have their names removed from the list. A federal district court dismissed their complaint; a divided court of appeals affirmed its ruling. The Supreme Court reversed, taking the position that listing the three organizations without affording them a hearing violated their constitutional rights. Because each member of the five-justice majority wrote this own opinion, the Court's decision lacked a coherent rationale.

Michal R. Belknap

Jones v. Alfred H. Mayer Co., 392 U.S. 409 (1968), argued 1–2 Apr. 1968, decided 17 June 1968 by vote of 7 to 2; Stewart for the Court, Harlan and White in dissent. This case established Congress's power under the Thirteenth Amendment to legislate against private racial discrimination. It thus limited the *Civil Rights Cases* (1883) holding that Congress lacked the power to reach private racial discrimination and became an important influence on the modern era of civil rights legislation.

Jones alleged that private defendants refused to sell him a home because he was black. He brought an action under a surviving remnant of the Civil Rights Act of 1866 (now Title 42, section 1982 of the U.S. Code) that grants all citizens the same right to purchase property. Section 1982 plainly invalidated nineteenth-century southern states' black codes limiting blacks' power to own or lease property. The question in *Jones* was whether the statute also reached private individual discriminatory acts. Justice Potter Stewart's opinion for the Court provided a questionable analysis of section 1982's text and legislative history and held that section 1982 reaches private behavior. Justice John M. Harlan's dissent noted that the Court's interpretation of section 1982 made that statute a broad fair housing law, announced by the Court only months after Congress enacted the Civil Rights Act of 1968, which contained a more detailed fair housing law.

Congress's power to enact laws prohibiting private racial discrimination under the Fourteenth Amendment is unclear, as suggested by the confusing array of opinions in *United States v. *Guest* (1966). *Jones* avoided addressing the Fourteenth Amendment power question by finding congressional power under the Thirteenth Amendment. It thus supplied a powerful new basis for federal race discrimination legislation. In the *Civil Rights Cases*, the Court had indicated that, under the Thirteenth Amendment, Congress may outlaw not only slavery itself but all badges or incidents of slavery as well. But it narrowly construed what those badges or incidents of slavery were and Congress's power to define them. It invalidated the Civil Rights Act of 1875, which prohibited discrimination in public accommodations, stating, "It would be running the slavery argument into the ground" (p. 24) to apply it to all private discriminatory acts in the area of public accommodations. In *Jones*, the Court more generously interpreted Congress's power to assess what social conditions might be badges or incidents of slavery and sustained applying section 1982 to private behavior.

Jones established the foundation for the later holding in *Runyon* v. *McCrary* (1976) that Title 42, section 1981 of the U.S. Code, a companion provision to section 1982, reaches private discrimination in contracts. Together, *Jones* and *Runyon* establish sections 1981 and 1982 as broad federal antidiscrimination provisions covering most contractual and property relationships. *Jones*'s questionable foundations reemerged in *Runyon*, when Justices White, Rehnquist, and Stevens voiced doubts about its correctness, and again thirteen years later in *Patterson* v. *McLean Credit Union* (1989). By the time *Patterson* arose, President Ronald Reagan's appointees to the Court had changed its receptivity to civil rights litigation. In *Patterson*, the Court took the unusual step of ordering the parties, on its own motion, to reargue the case and to address a question neither party had raised—whether *Runyon* had been correctly decided. Following reargument, the Court's *Patterson* opinion left *Runyon* technically intact. But *Patterson* severely limited *Runyon* and section 1981 by holding that it protects only the initial decision to contract and not post-contractual behavior. The limiting interpretation probably is as attributable to lingering discontent with *Jones* as it is to doubts about *Runyon* itself.

Whatever doubts members of the Court have had about *Jones* and *Runyon*, Congress has never modified *Jones*'s generous interpretation of section 1982 and *Runyon*'s

interpretation of section 1981. Congress's most important response to the Court was the Civil Rights Act of 1991, which overruled *Patterson* by interpreting section 1981 to include post-contractual behavior.

□ Charles Fairman, *History of the Supreme Court of the United States*, vol. 6, *Reconstruction and Reunion, 1864–88: Part One* (1971).
Theodore Eisenberg

Jones v. Flowers, 547 U.S. 220 (2006), argued 17 Jan 2006, decided Apr. 26, 2006 by a vote of 5 to 3; Roberts for the Court, Thomas in dissent, joined by Scalia and Kennedy, Alito not participating. A homeowner sued in state court for a determination that the notice provided by the state in connection with the sale of his land for unpaid taxes was insufficient to satisfy the constitutional requirements of due process under the Fourteenth Amendment. Reversing the state court, the Supreme Court ruled that due process does not require that a property owner receive actual notice before the government sells his or her property for tax delinquency. However, a reasonable effort must be made to apprise the interested parties of the pendency of the action and afford them an opportunity to present their objections. In this case, the state had merely published a notice in a newspaper after being alerted that notice by certified mail had not been unsuccessfully delivered.

The Court held that when notice of a tax sale via certified mailed is returned unclaimed, the state is required by due process to take additional reasonable steps to attempt to provide notice to a landowner before selling the property, if it is practicable to do so. It concluded that there were reasonable steps the state could have taken when the certified letter was returned. The Court suggested that the state could have: (1) sent the notice by regular mail so that a signature was not required, (2) posted the notice on the front door, or (3) addressed the notice letter to "Occupant." The failure to take additional steps rendered the state's efforts to provide notice insufficient to satisfy due process. The dissenters maintained the state's method of notice was reasonably calculated to reach the property owner, and that there was no due process violation.
David L. Callies

Jones v. Van Zandt, 5 How. (46 U.S.) 215 (1847), submitted on printed argument 1

Feb. 1847 and decided 5 Mar. 1847 by vote of 9 to 0; Woodbury for the Court. *Jones v. Van Zandt* presented abolitionists with their first opportunity to mount a direct legal challenge to the constitutionality of the Fugitive Slave Act of 1793. A conductor of the Underground Railroad was exposed to civil liability under the act for harboring a fugitive. Salmon P. Chase, then in private practice, contended in argument that the statute was unconstitutional because: (1) the federal government lacked power to support slavery; (2) slavery was incompatible with the Declaration of Independence and contrary to "natural right"; (3) the statute violated various provisions of the Bill of Rights, including the Due Process Clause of the Fifth Amendment; and (4) the Fugitive Slave Clause of Article IV, section 2 of the Constitution was merely an interstate compact giving no power of enforcement to Congress.

Justice Levi Woodbury for the Court spurned these arguments. He stated that the legitimacy of slavery was a political question for the states to resolve, and that the Fugitive Slave Clause was "one of [the] sacred compromises" of the Constitution (p.231). Whatever a judge's views of the morality or policy of slavery, Woodbury went on, he was bound to uphold the Constitution and statutes as he found them and could not refuse to enforce them because of their conflict with moral obligation. As Justice Joseph Story had before him in *Prigg* v. *Pennsylvania* (1842), Wood-bury upheld the constitutionality of the 1793 statute. *Jones* therefore was one in an unbroken line of proslavery decisions of the antebellum Court.

William M. Wiecek

K

Kagama, United States v., 118 U.S. 375 (1886), argued 2 Mar. 1886, decided 10 May 1886 by vote of 9 to o; Miller for the Court. *Kagama* applied the broad principles governing Indian relations that Chief Justice John Marshall had articulated in *Worcester* v. *Georgia* (1832) to the question of whether a federal criminal statute specifically applicable to Indians was constitutional. The Court upheld the statute and its application.

In *Ex parte *Crow Dog* (1883), the Court had held that tribal, not federal, law applied to criminal acts committed by an Indian in Indian country. In response, Congress enacted the "Major Crimes Act" as part of the Indian Appropriations Act of 1885, which extended the jurisdiction of federal courts to seven specified crimes, including murder and manslaughter committed by one Indian against another in Indian country. Applying *Worcester* in the *Kagama* case, the Court unanimously held that protection of Indians constituted a national obligation and thus sustained the power of Congress to legislate for Indians on reservations. In obiter dictum, Justice Samuel F. Miller added that state courts lacked jurisdiction over crimes committed by Indians on reservations because federal power preempted state authority. He added that the states had historically been the Indians' "deadliest enemies" (p. 384).

The *Kagama* Court relied on Marshall's analogy to the common-law guardian-ward relationship as a figure explaining federal authority over Indian affairs. But the federal-Indian relationship derives not from common law but from the Constitution's grant of power to the federal government over Indian relations. Although that power is broad, Indians may claim constitutional protection in their dealings with the federal government. Courts continue to affirm the *Worcester* principles of self government within tribal territory.

Rennard J. Strickland

Kansas v. Hendricks, 521 U.S. 346 (1997), argued 10 Dec. 1996, decided 23 June 1997 by vote of 5 to 4; Thomas for the Court, Kennedy in dissent. Kansas in 1994 passed the Sexually Violent Predator Act that required the indeterminate confinement in mental hospitals of persons deemed to be violent sex offenders suffering from a mental abnormality. The act established a mental abnormality as an inability to control sexual conduct to such an extent that the person became a menace to the health and safety of others.

Leroy Hendricks was an avowed pedophile with a forty-year history of molesting children. Only death, Hendricks had said, would end his practice of sexually abusing children. In 1984 he was convicted of taking indecent liberties with two thirteen-year-old boys. When his prison sentence for that crime ended, Kansas authorities sought to commit him under the act. Hendricks argued that such treatment was tantamount to being punished twice for the same crime and being subjected to an ex post facto law, both practices prohibited under the Due Process Clause of the Fourteenth Amendment. Kansas authorities, however, argued that placing Hendricks in a mental hospital was an involuntary civil rather than a criminal commitment. The Kansas Supreme Court sided with Hendricks, finding that in order for a person to be committed to a mental hospital he had to have a mental illness and not just a mental abnormality.

The United States Supreme Court reversed that decision by a vote of 5 to 4, a vote that suggests more division among the justices than actually existed. Both sides disagreed with the analysis of the Kansas Supreme Court and both turned instead directly to the arguments by Hendricks's counsel that the state court had ignored. Moreover, even the dissenters, led by Justice Stephen G. Breyer, went out of their way to offer guidance about how Kansas and other states could fashion laws that were constitutional. Justice Clarence Thomas, speaking for the Court's majority, made that effort unnecessary.

The majority relied on the Court's past decisions involving involuntary civil commitments to find that all the state had to do was establish an individual's dangerousness and mental incapacity, whether that incapacity resulted from mental illness or mental abnormality. Since Hendricks had readily admitted that the only way he would stop preying on children was to die, the Court found that the state of Kansas had grounds to commit him. The majority also rejected Hendricks's claim that he was being punished twice. Involuntary civil commitment to a mental hospital, Thomas concluded, was not punishment but a form of treatment. That there was no known cure for his condition did not mean that the self-admitted pedophile should be able to live outside a mental hospital. If anything, Justice Thomas argued, it meant that there was no more appropriate place for him. Thomas also noted that the state had erected a considerable degree of procedural protection, including the use of legal counsel to present evidence and cross-examine witnesses, that prevented inappropriate commitments.

The dissenters found the Kansas law unacceptable because it offered no treatment to Hendricks. As such, the decision to commit Hendricks could only be understood as a form of punishment. In order for the law in Kansas and similar measures in other states

to stand, there had to be a treatment component to go along with the incarceration of the individual.

Hendricks remains in custody until such time as the evidence establishes that he is no longer dangerous. As a constitutional matter, the high court has signaled its approval of protective, preventative incapacitation.

Kermit L. Hall

Kastigar v. United States, 406 U.S. 441 (1972), argued 11 Jan. 1972, decided 22 May 1972 by vote of 5 to 2; Powell for the Court, Douglas and Marshall in dissent, Brennan and Rehnquist not participating. In *Kastigar* the Court for the first time squarely confronted the question of whether witnesses can be compelled to testify before grand juries under a grant of use immunity. In 1970, Congress had substituted use for transactional immunity in the federal immunity statute. *Use immunity* prevents the government from using compelled testimony or any information derived from such testimony against the witness in a subsequent criminal prosecution. It is not as broad as transactional immunity, which prevents any prosecution of a witness for offenses related to the compelled testimony. *Kastigar* argued that the Fifth Amendment privilege against self-incrimination prohibits the compulsion of testimony under a grant of use immunity but instead requires transactional immunity at the very least.

In rejecting that argument, the Court first noted that the power to compel testimony in court or before a grand jury is firmly established and essential to the effective funcioning of government. That power, however, is not absolute but is limited by the Fifth Amendment privilege against self-incrimination. The Fifth Amendment protects a person from being forced to give testimony that could be used against him or her in a subsequent criminal prosecution. Use immunity, the Court concluded, is compatible with the Fifth Amendment because it ensures that the compelled testimony cannot lead to prosecution. In a subsequent prosecution, an affirmative duty is placed on the government to prove that evidence it seeks to use is derived from a source wholly independent of the compelled testimony. As a result, use immunity removes the danger that testimony will be used against the witness and, thus, does not violate the privilege against self-incrimination.

Daan Braveman

Katz v. United States, 389 U.S. 347 (1967), argued 17 Oct. 1967, decided 18 Dec. 1967 by vote of 7 to 1; Stewart for the Court, Harlan and White concurring, Black in dissent, Marshall not participating. *Katz* altered significantly the approach that courts must use in determining, under the Fourth Amendment, whether certain police conduct constitutes a "search" that is subject to the amendment's warrant and probable cause limitations. Illustrative of the pre-*Katz* approach is *Olmstead* v. *United States* (1928), where the Supreme Court held that it did not constitute a search for the authorities to place a tap on certain telephone wires and thereby eavesdrop on the defendant's telephone conversations. As the Court later put the matter in *Silverman* v. *United States* (1961), for there to be a Fourth Amendment search the police must have physically intruded into "a constitutionally protected area" (p. 682). *Katz* replaced the *Silverman* standard with a reasonable expectation of privacy test.

At his trial for transmitting wagering information by phone, the government introduced over Katz's objection evidence of his end of telephone conversations, overheard by federal agents who had attached an electronic listening/recording device to the exterior of a public phone booth habitually used by Katz. The lower court concluded there was no search because the wall of the booth had not been physically penetrated. The Supreme Court reversed, holding that "[t]he Government's activities in electronically listening to and recording the petitioner's words violated the privacy upon which he justifiably relied while using the telephone booth and thus constituted a 'search and seizure' within the meaning of the Fourth Amendment" (p. 512). This proposition was elaborated in Justice John M. Harlan's concurring opinion, later relied upon by lower courts and the Supreme Court itself in determining the meaning of *Katz*. Harlan stated that "there is a twofold requirement, first that a person have exhibited an actual (subjective) expectation of privacy and, second, that the expectation be one that society is prepared to recognize as 'reasonable'" (p. 516).

The first branch of the Harlan formulation should not be a part of any statement of what the Fourth Amendment protects. This is because the government could easily, either by edict or systematic practice, condition the expectations of the general public in such a way that there would be no hope of privacy. Harlan later appreciated this, stating in *United States* v. *White* (1971) that analysis under *Katz* must "transcend the search for subjective expectations" (p. 786). The Supreme Court has seldom addressed this point in more recent cases, though some of its statements are legitimate cause for concern. Illustrative is *California* v. *Ciraolo* (1986), holding that it is not a search to make an aerial observation of marijuana plants growing inside a fenced backyard, where it was intimated that defendant's ten-foot-high solid wood fence would not provide a subjective expectation of privacy because the plants could be seen by "a policeman perched on the top of a truck or a two-level bus" (p. 211). A person is unlikely therefore to get by the first *Katz* hurdle unless he or she has taken steps to ensure against all conceivable efforts at scrutiny.

As for the second prong of the Harlan elaboration, he stressed in *White* that "those more extensive intrusions that significantly jeopardize the sense of security which is the paramount concern of Fourth Amendment liberties" are searches (p. 1143). Unfortunately, the Supreme Court has not interpreted *Katz* this way, as is evident from two cases: *United States* v. *Miller* (1976), holding that a person has no justified expectation of privacy in a bank's records of his financial transactions because those documents "contain only information voluntarily conveyed to the banks and exposed to their employees in the ordinary course of business" (p. 442); and *Ciraolo*, holding that it is not a search for police to look down from an airplane into one's solidly fenced yard because "any member of the public flying over this airspace who glanced down could have seen everything that these officers observed" (pp. 213–214). In these and other cases the Court has failed to appreciate, as Justice Thurgood Marshall put it in his *Smith* v. *Maryland* (1979) dissent, that "privacy is not a discrete commodity, possessed absolutely or not at all" (p. 749).

Wayne R. LaFave, "The Forgotten Motto of Obsta Principiis in Fourth Amendment Jurisprudence," *Arizona Law Review* 28 (1986): 291–310.

Wayne R. LaFave

Katzenbach v. McClung, 379 U.S. 294 (1964), argued 5 Oct. 1964, decided 14 Dec. 1964 by vote of 9 to 0; Clark for the Court,

Black, Douglas, and Goldberg in separate concurrences. This decision is the Supreme Court's most expansive reading of the constitutional grant of power to Congress to regulate interstate commerce. The Court held that the Commerce Clause authorized Congress to regulate the racially discriminatory seating practices of Ollie's Barbecue, a small restaurant that purchased all of its food locally and served a local clientele. The discrimination was held to be subject to Congress's commerce power because some of the food that Ollie's purchased from its local supplier had originated out of state.

The Court stated that Congress need only demonstrate a "rational basis" for concluding that the local activity aggregated with other similar local activity would create a substantial economic effect on interstate commerce. The Court found that Congress could have rationally assumed that race discrimination by local restaurants would reduce the amount of food served in those restaurants and consequently reduce the amount of food purchased in interstate commerce by their suppliers. The Court suggested further that Congress could have reasonably concluded that race discrimination by local restaurants would deter individuals and industries from relocating through interstate commerce into areas where such practices prevailed.

The Court evidently accepted such an attenuated connection to interstate commerce, and thus assigned such pervasive legislative power to Congress under the Commerce Clause, because race discrimination demanded a national legislative solution. But nothing in the Court's opinion confines the Court's expansive reading of Congress's commerce power only to race discrimination cases. Thus, *Katzenbach* stands as authority for an apparently unlimited power in Congress to regulate any local activity if some aggregate economic impact on interstate commerce can be plausibly posited. In the Rehnquist Court, however, that assumption has been challenged. For example, in *United States* v. *Lopez* (1995), the justices held that the commerce power could not be used as the basis for Congress to pass laws making it a crime knowingly to possess a firearm within one thousand feet of a public or private school because the act did not flow from any enumerated power.

Thomas R. McCoy

Katzenbach v. Morgan, 384 U.S. 641 (1966), argued 18 Apr. 1966, decided 13 June 1966 by vote of 7 to 2; Brennan for the Court, Harlan and Stewart in dissent. A majority upheld a provision of the Voting Rights Act of 1965 stipulating that no person who had successfully completed the sixth grade in an accredited Puerto Rican school was to be denied the right to vote because of an inability to read or write English. The Court in 1959 had upheld state power to impose a fairly administered literacy test. Speaking for the *Morgan* majority, however, Justice William Brennan held that the earlier precedent was not the measure of congressional, as opposed to judicial, power to enforce the Fourteenth Amendment's equal protection guarantee. Congress, declared Brennan, need have only a rational basis for its laws; and Congress could reasonably have concluded that the challenged provision would help to eliminate discriminatory treatment in access to public services. Justice John M. Harlan charged in dissent, however, that the Court had already decided that a literacy test did not violate the Constitution and that, while Congress had broad discretion in choosing the means for enforcing the equal protection clause, its substantive scope, like that of other constitutional guarantees, was ultimately a question for the courts, not the legislature. If Congress could expand on the Court's interpretations of constitutional rights, Harlan concluded, it could also restrict the content of such guarantees.

Tinsley E. Yarbrough

Keeney v. Tamayo-Reyes, 504 U.S. 1 (1992), argued 15 Jan. 1992, decided 4 May 1992 by vote of 5 to 4; White for the Court, O'Connor in dissent, joined by Blackmun, Stevens, and Kennedy, and Kennedy in a separate dissent.

During the late 1980s and early 1990s the Supreme Court consistently narrowed the opportunities for state prisoners to bring constitutional challenges either to their convictions or sentences in federal courts through petitions of habeas corpus. *Keeney* marked an important milestone in that process, since it overturned a precedent favorable to petitioners from the Warren Court era. In *Townsend* v. *Swain* (1963), Chief Justice Earl Warren, writing for a 5 to 4 majority, held that a state prisoner could seek a writ of habeas corpus to secure a hearing in federal court if the material facts were not adequately developed at the state-court hearing. The majority made clear that the failure of defense counsel to represent a client adequately would not jeopardize a prisoner's eventual right to be heard in federal court. The only exception was a defendant that purposefully bypassed the state appeals system. One of the dissenters in that case was Justice Byron R. White, the same justice who wrote the majority opinion in *Keeney* overturning *Townsend*.

Keeney involved an Oregon inmate whose lawyer had failed to present evidence crucial to his appeal in state court. The critical fact in the case involved a poorly done Spanish translation of the plea agreement that the defendant signed, a translation so bad that he literally did not know what he was agreeing to. The Court of Appeals for the Ninth Circuit ordered a habeas corpus hearing, but the state of Oregon appealed.

Justice White found for the state of Oregon. He held that a new standard should be imposed, one that did away with the "deliberate bypass" rule of *Townsend* and replaced it with a requirement that a state inmate demonstrate "cause." Under existing high court rulings, moreover, attorney error was not a sufficient ground for asserting cause.

The dissenters argued that the petition should have been heard, since it was properly presented. Moreover, Justice Sandra Day O'Connor took the unusual step of advising lower federal court judges that there were ways to get around White's majority opinion and that they should use them. Nonetheless, the Court's actions constituted a further tightening of access to the federal courts through habeas corpus. Critics complained that doing so raised questions of constitutional fairness, since federal judges between 1976 and 1991 overturned more than 40 percent of all the death penalty cases they reviewed through habeas petitions.

Kermit L. Hall

Kelo v. City of New London, 545 U. S. 469 (2005), argued 22 Feb. 2005, decided 23 June 2005 by vote of 5 to 4; Stevens for the Court, Kennedy concurring, O'Connor and Thomas in dissent. The Fifth Amendment provides that "private property [shall not] be taken for public use, without just compensation." The acquisition of private property by eminent domain solely for private use would therefore be arbitrary and a violation of due process, and it would also run afoul of the public use requirement of the Fifth Amend-

ment. On the other hand, government may take private property for transfer to another private entity that would employ it for a public use, such as a regulated common carrier obligated to serve the general public.

In *Kelo*, Connecticut had declared New London a "distressed municipality." After the pharmaceutical manufacturer Pfizer Inc. announced that it would build a large research facility in the city, state and local officials hoped to use the facility as a catalyst for urban revitalization. Pursuant to an integrated development plan, a public agency condemned nearby non-blighted residential parcels for use in a project intended to create jobs, build tax revenue, and build momentum for the revitalization of the downtown area. Much of the land would be devoted to private shops, hotels, and offices complementing the Pfizer complex. By and large, these uses entailed no obligation to serve the general public.

Citing precedent, the Supreme Court concluded that "public use" should be interpreted broadly to encompass "public benefit," and it stressed deference to legislative judgments concerning the need for eminent domain. It declined to require the city to demonstrate that the takings were likely to achieve claimed economic benefit. The Court majority relied upon *Berman* v. *Parker* (1954) and *Hawaii Housing Authority* v. *Midkiff* (1984). In *Berman*, a blighted area was condemned pursuant to a District of Columbia redevelopment plan. The owner of a non-blighted department store objected to the condemnation of his building, but the Court unanimously upheld the condemnation, insisting that officials could determine that successful revitalization required comprehensive redevelopment. The Court declared that promoting community redevelopment through private enterprise was within the purview of the public use requirement.

Similarly, in *Midkiff*, the Court unanimously upheld a state statute intended to break up a land oligopoly by condemning the fee interests of a few large landowners for transfer to their many tenants with long-term ground leases. In that case, the Court held that public use was "coterminous" with government's police powers to protect the public health, safety, welfare, and morals.

In *Kelo*, the Court acknowledged that the ostensible public purposes justifying condemnation had, on occasion, been pretexts for private gain. It asserted, moreover, that courts would view "with a skeptical eye" (p. 487) one-to-one transfers of property that were not part of an integrated development plan. Justice Anthony Kennedy's concurrence also stressed the importance of comprehensive planning, while also noting the possibility that abuse might necessitate heightened judicial scrutiny in narrow categories of condemnation for economic development.

Dissenting, Justice Sandra Day O'Connor argued that the Court's reasoning—that "the incidental public benefits resulting from the subsequent ordinary use of private property render economic development takings 'for public use' " (p. 494)—conflates public and private use. She stressed that the Court's approval of condemnation in *Berman* was in the context of eliminating injurious conditions, and that the land oligopoly alleviated in *Midkiff* was "severe." According to O'Connor, the conflation of the police and takings power in *Berman*—as well as her own assertion in *Midkiff* that "[t]he 'public use' requirement is coterminous with the scope of a sovereign's police powers"—constituted "errant language" (p. 501). In an often-quoted passage, O'Connor declared that, under the broad view of eminent domain adopted by the majority, "nothing is to prevent the State from replacing any Motel 6 with a Ritz-Carlton, any home with a shopping mall, or any farm with a factory" (p. 503). Justice Thomas, in a separate dissent, urged the Court to return to the original and narrower meaning of the public use clause, warning that the harm inflicted by economic development takings would fall largely on poor communities.

Perhaps anticipating the public antipathy that *Kelo* would generate, the Court emphasized that the states were free to place more stringent restrictions on eminent domain. Slightly more than half have done so, with varying degrees of potential effectiveness. Many states now forbid takings for economic development, with an exception for the alleviation of "blight," though this term is often expansively defined.

The Court will almost certainly have to reconcile the deferential rational-basis review it accords state and local land use decisions with *Kelo*'s promise that courts will ferret out pretextual condemnations intended for private gain. This task will likely require the probing review of the actions of legislators

and officials that is the mark of heightened scrutiny.

Steven J. Eagle

Kendall v. United States ex rel. Stokes, 12 Pet. (37 U.S.) 524 (1838), argued 13, 19–24, 26–27 Feb. 1838, decided 12 Mar. 1838 by vote of 9 to 0; Thompson for the Court. The case originated when newly appointed postmaster general Amos Kendall refused to obey an order from the federal circuit for the District of Columbia that he honor a contract negotiated by his predecessor with the firm of Stockton and Stokes. Kendall, appointed by President Andrew Jackson to reform the Post Office, refused on the grounds that the contract was tainted with political favoritism, which it probably was. The matter was referred to Congress, which enacted a law requiring Kendall to follow the recommendations of the solicitor general of the treasury, Virgil Maxcy (who was a friend of the plaintiffs). Kendall refused again, arguing that the act of Congress was an unconstitutional infringement on the powers of the executive branch. This was the issue before the Supreme Court.

A unanimous decision, written by Justice Smith Thompson, went against Kendall holding that (1) not every officer in the executive branch was under the exclusive control of the president; (2) Congress could assign ministerial duties to such officers, and (3) such duties could be enforced by a writ of mandamus issuing from the federal circuit court. The case was significant because it resolved a conflict between the executive branch and Congress, while at the same time establishing a role for the courts in resolving such disputes. It clarified the mandamus-granting authority of federal circuit courts.

R. Kent Newmyer

Kent v. Dulles, 357 U.S. 116 (1958), argued 10 Apr. 1958, decided 16 June 1958 by vote of 5 to 4; Douglas for the Court, Clark, joined by Burton, Harlan, and Whittaker, in dissent. The State Department denied Rockwell Kent a passport pursuant to its 1948 policy of refusing to issue passports to communists and their supporters, or to those whose foreign travel would be contrary to the interests of the United States. Kent argued that this abridged his First Amendment rights and interfered with his right to travel. Justice William O. Douglas for the majority acknowledged that the right to travel was a liberty protected by the Due Process Clause of the Fifth Amendment. However, the majority ruled in favor of Kent on statutory grounds, holding that Congress had not given the secretary of state authority to withhold passports of citizens because of their beliefs or associations. The dissenters argued that the Immigration and Nationality Act of 1952 should be read as recognizing broad discretionary powers of the secretary of state in issuing passports.

The immediate decisional impact was that questions about Communist party membership were dropped from the passport application. Passports were promptly issued to Kent and others who had also contested the department on this matter. The broader legal impact was that the majority opinion recognized the right to travel abroad and dismantled barriers to its exercise. It is still good law.

The decision was criticized by some for not having fully addressed the First Amendment issues and for avoiding a ruling on constitutionality. However, a relatively narrow ruling was necessary to keep Justice Felix Frankfurter's crucial fifth vote for the majority.

Sheldon Goldman

Kentucky v. Dennison, 24 How. (65 U.S.) 66 (1861), argued 20 Feb. 1861, decided 14 Mar. 1861 by vote of 8 to 0; Taney for the Court. In 1859 Willis Lago, a free black from Ohio, helped a Kentucky slave named Charlotte escape to Ohio. Kentucky indicted Lago for theft and Governor Beriah Magoffin of Kentucky asked Ohio governor Salmon P. Chase to extradite Lago. Chase, an antislavery advocate, refused to comply, arguing that Lago had not committed a crime recognized by Ohio law. Magoffin waited until Chase left office in 1860 and renewed the requisition with the new Ohio governor, William Dennison, who also refused to comply. Magoffin then sought a writ of mandamus to force Dennison to act. Magoffin sued in the United States Supreme Court, under the court's original jurisdiction for cases between two states.

The case presented Chief Justice Roger B. Taney with a major dilemma. Taney was profoundly proslavery, deeply antagonistic toward the North, and desirous of settling all constitutional issues surrounding slavery in favor of the South. But with secession already in progress, Taney was loathe to rule that the Supreme Court or the federal government might have the power to force state governors to act. After chastising the Ohio governors for not cooperating with the criminal extradition clause of the Constitution, Taney ruled that the Court had no power to coerce a state to comply with its constitutional obligation. This decision remained good law until overturned by *Puerto Rico v. Branstad* (1987).

Paul Finkelman

Ker v. California, 374 U.S. 23 (1963), argued 11 Dec. 1962, decided 10 June 1963 by vote of 5 to 4; Clark for the Court, Harlan concurring in the result, Brennan dissenting in part joined by Warren, Douglas, and Goldberg. When the Court decided in *Mapp v. Ohio* (1961) to impose the exclusionary rule of the Fourth Amendment on the states through the Fourteenth Amendment, it was unclear to what extent federal standards of what constitutes unreasonable searches and seizures were applicable to the states. A case involving the marijuana dealings of George and Diane Ker resolved this issue. Reviewing their convictions, a consensus of eight justices agreed that the states were to be held to federal standards. The ninth justice, John M. Harlan, argued that states should be judged by a more flexible concept of fundamental fairness. The consensus, however, broke down in applying the principle to the facts of the case. A plurality of four justices found that the actions of the California authorities who had entered the Kers' apartment with a passkey and without a warrant and who seized marijuana used to convict them met federal standards of probable cause and reasonableness. Justice Harlan concurred only in affirming the convictions. The four justices in dissent argued that the arrests and subsequent seizure were illegal because in their view the unannounced entry into the apartment was unjustified.

Ker remains a very important component of the exclusionary rule. The doctrine that Fourth Amendment (i.e., federal) standards of reasonableness apply to the states through the Fourteenth Amendment is still controlling law. But the holding that an unannounced warrantless entry to a person's home is valid is inconsistent with subsequent Court rulings such as *Payton v. New York* (1980). However, in *Wilson v. Arkansas* (1995), the Rehnquist Court held that police are ordinarily required to knock and announce their presence before entering a house to execute a search warrant, but that there may be "reasonable" exceptions to the rule to account for a likelihood of violence or imminent destruction of evidence.

Sheldon Goldman

Keyes v. Denver School District No. 1, 413 U.S. 189 (1973), argued 12 Oct. 1972, decided 21 June 1973 by vote of 7 to 1; Brennan for the Court, Burger concurring in result without opinion, separate statement by Douglas, Powell concurring in judgment and dissenting in part, Rehnquist in dissent, White not participating. In the first nonsouthern school desegregation case to receive plenary consideration, the Supreme Court held that a school district that "racially or ethnically" segregated one part of a large urban district created an arguably rebuttable presumption that similar segregation throughout the district was not "adventitious" and implied that wholesale, districtwide relief under *Swann* v. *Charlotte-Mecklenburg* (1971) was not inappropriate (p. 208).

Although the opinion is tentative in tone and structured in terms of presumptions and future proceedings, *Keyes* was widely, and accurately, viewed as a green light for district-wide (if not necessarily interdistrict) desegregation of northern school districts. Justices William O. Douglas and Lewis Powell, in separate opinions, urged abandonment of the de jure/de facto distinction in school segregation cases, although Powell also suggested limits, and uniform guidelines, for *Swann*-type transportation decrees.

Justice William Rehnquist's dissent objected to the majority's use of evidentiary presumptions to extend *Green* v. *County School Board* (1968) to northern schools and argued further that *Brown* v. *Board of Education* (1954, 1955) required elimination of racial standards, not *Green's* achievement of an approved racial balance in public schools. The *Keyes* opinions ambiguously signaled *Green's* application to de facto segregation in the North but also indicated growing fissures within the Court over the issue. The Court's posture changed over time, and by 1995 Chief Justice Rehnquist had moved into the majority. In *Missouri* v. *Jenkins* (1995), a majority of the Court held that the lower federal courts in Missouri had improperly ordered the state to help pay for a showcase desegregation plan for Kansas City schools.

Dennis J. Hutchinson

Keyishian v. Board of Regents, 385 U.S. 589 (1967), argued 17 Nov. 1966, decided 23 Jan. 1967 by vote of 5 to 4; Brennan for the Court, Clark, Harlan, Stewart, and White in dissent. In this case the Court declared unconstitutional New York statutes and administrative rules designed to prevent employment of "subversive" teachers and professors in state educational institutions and to dismiss them if found guilty of "treasonable or seditious" acts. The Board of Regents of New York had prepared a list of subversive organizations, including the Communist party, membership in which was sufficient reason for a teacher's disqualification. Originally there was also an oath requirement, but this was rescinded by the regents.

The Court held that the proscription of "treasonable or seditious" conduct and of "advocacy" of violent overthrow was unconstitutional for vagueness: a teacher could not foretell whether statements about abstract doctrine were prohibited or whether only speech intended to incite action was grounds for dismissal. The complexity of the New York plan aggravated the vice of vagueness. The Court also held that the statutes were unconstitutional because they did not require that the teacher have specific intent to further the illegal aims of a proscribed organization and hence were overly broad. The decision's importance lay in its rejection of a state's power to make public employment conditional on surrendering constitutional rights that could not otherwise be abridged by direct state action as well as in its emphasis on academic freedom.

Milton R. Konvitz

Keystone Bituminous Coal Association v. De-Benedictis, 480 U.S. 470 (1987), argued 10 Nov. 1986, decided 9 Mar. 1987 by vote of 5 to 4; Stevens for the Court, Rehnquist in dissent. In *Keystone,* a divided Court upheld a Pennsylvania mining-subsidence statute against a claim that the statute effected a taking of private property without payment of just compensation. The challenged statute prohibited all underground mining that caused subsidence damage to surface structures, and it obligated mining companies to leave in place, for structural support, at least half of the coal that underlay a protected structure. The Court upheld the statute as a valid exercise of the state's police power, noting that the statute substantially advanced public interests in health, safety, and welfare and did not render the mining companies unable to mine at a profit.

In *Keystone* the Court continued its prior refusal to divide property parcels into components when determining whether the state had taken property. The Court denied that the small amount of coal left in place for surface support was a discrete property interest that the Pennsylvania statute had, in effect, taken without compensation.

Š*Keystone* is remarkable because the facts of the case were virtually identical to those of *Pennsylvania Coal Co.* v. *Mahon* (1922), a landmark of takings jurisprudence. In *Mahon* a state statute prohibited an owner from engaging in underground mining if the mining caused structural subsidence. The Court in *Mahon* struck down this statute as a taking because the statute served private interests and denied the mining company all economically viable use of the underlying coal. In *Keystone*, the Court appreciated the public nature of the harms caused by land subsidence; the Court viewed the new statute as one that furthered public interests, not private ones, and it saw land subsidence as a public nuisance.

Eric T. Freyfogle

Kidd v. Pearson, 128 U.S. 1 (1888), argued 4 Apr. 1888, decided 22 Oct. 1888 by vote of 8 to 0; Lamar for the Court, Woods deceased. An Iowa statute prohibited the manufacture of liquor for shipment outside the state. The measure was challenged as an unconstitutional regulation of interstate commerce by a state. The Supreme Court held that the statute did not interfere with federal commerce power and that it was a simple police power regulation, well within a state's authority. At least when liquor, a putatively noxious product, was the subject, *Kidd* demonstrated the willingness of the Court to uphold the police powers of the states.

The real significance of the case lay in its definition of "commerce." The Court drew a distinction between commerce and manufacturing, holding that commerce did not begin until manufacture was completed. But if congressional power under the Commerce Clause did not encompass production, federal regulations could not be constitutionally applied to manufacturing, agricultural, or extractive industries. The Court gradually deserted this holding over the years, broadening the permissible scope

of federal regulation and correspondingly narrowing state power.

On the exact point of state liquor laws, however, *Kidd* is not good law today. To the extent that Congress wishes to exercise its powers under the Commerce Clause, it may undercut or negate state liquor laws.

Loren P. Beth

Kilbourn v. Thompson, 103 U.S. 168 (1881), decided by a vote of 9 to 0; Miller for the Court. The House of Representatives in 1876 appointed a special committee to examine the dealings of a real estate partnership in Washington, D.C. Hallett Kilbourn was ordered by the committee to appear and testify. He refused to answer a question or produce records. The committee declared Kilbourn to be in contempt of Congress and ordered him committed to jail. He brought an action of false imprisonment against John Thompson, the sergeant-at-arms who had taken him into custody, and the members of the House committee.

The trial court held in favor of Thompson, but the Supreme Court reversed. The justices left open the question whether either house of Congress had power to punish for contempt, a question that was subsequently answered affirmatively. The Court invalidated the contempt order on the ground that it was rendered in pursuit of an unconstitutional objective. Congress may conduct investigations only for the purpose of gathering information relevant to contemplated future legislation. The proceedings at issue concerned debts owed by the real estate partnership to certain parties, including the United States. The Court viewed this as a judicial, not as a legislative, matter. Under these circumstances, the House exceeded its authority by investigating the private affairs of individuals. Consequently, it had no power to require Kilbourn to testify as a witness. Subsequently, however, the Supreme Court approved a broader investigative power, allowing Congress limited inquiry into private matters.

Edgar Bodenheimer

Kirkpatrick v. Preisler, 394 U.S. 526 (1969), argued 13 Jan. 1969, decided 7 April 1969 by vote of 6 to 3; Brennan for the Court, Fortas concurring, Harlan, Stewart, and White in dissent. In *Kirkpatrick* the Supreme Court affirmed a federal district court's rejection of Missouri's 1967 Congressional Redistricting

Act. In the companion case of *Wells* v. *Rockefeller* the Court reversed a decision sustaining the validity of New York's 1968 congressional redistricting statute.

Kirkpatrick significantly narrowed the range of permissible population deviations among districts permitted by the 1964 reapportionment. Moreover, it reflected a split within the Warren Court over the meaning, in *Wesberry* v. *Sanders* (1964), of the phrase "as nearly equal as practicable" (p. 21). Missouri's districts entailed 1960 population disparities ranging from 3.13 percent above to 2.83 percent below a statewide average. For the Court, Justice William Brennan insisted, "The 'as nearly as practicable' standard requires that the State make a good-faith effort to achieve precise mathematical equality. . . . Unless population variances among congressional districts are shown to have resulted despite such effort, the State must justify each variance, no matter how small" (pp. 530–531).

This standard drew strong criticism from four justices. Justice Abe Fortas concurred in the result but decried the majority's quest for an illusory mathematical precision based on inexact, obsolete census data. Separate dissents by Justices John M. Harlan and Byron White additionally faulted judicial intrusion into legislative common sense while minimizing traditional constraints of local boundaries on gerrymandering.

Although *Kirkpatrick* and *Wells* were both congressional redistricting cases, the Court's broad language left an impression that state legislative districting might be similarly restricted. That question was resolved in several 1973 cases that reiterated the more flexible phraseology of *Reynolds* v. *Sims* (1964) for state legislatures (*Mahan* v. *Howell*, 1973) while maintaining *Kirkpatrick's* narrower approach for congressional constituencies (*White* v. *Weiser*, 1973).

A decade later, New Jersey's congressional districting, with a total population variance range of less than 0.7 percent, was invalidated in *Karcher* v. *Daggett* (1983). Although that holding was based on the *Kirkpatrick* precedent, five members of the Court (four dissenters plus Justice John Paul Stevens, who concurred) questioned Brennan's quest for population precision, claiming that partisan gerrymandering was a greater threat to fair representation than were small population variances.

Gordon E. Baker

Klopfer v. North Carolina, 386 U.S. 213 (1967), argued 8 Dec. 1966, decided 13 Mar. 1967 by vote of 6 to 3; Warren for the Court, Harlan and Stewart in dissent. Under North Carolina's "nolle prosequi with leave" law, challenged in this case, a prosecutor could indefinitely suspend prosecution on an indictment without having to provide a reason to the court. Frustrated by a prosecutor who after his inability to obtain a conviction at a first trial decided to reinstitute charges but suspend prosecution indefinitely, Klopfer, the defendant, pressed for a trial or dismissal of charges. When neither was forthcoming, he attacked the law and the prosecutor's decision on the grounds that his Sixth Amendment guarantee of a speedy trial had been denied.

In accepting Klopfer's arguments and extending the Sixth Amendment speedy trial guarantee to the states under the same standards that apply to the federal government, the Supreme Court also gave its first significant interpretation of the Sixth Amendment's right to a speedy trial. It held that the right was "as fundamental as any of the rights secured by the Sixth Amendment" and traced it back to "the very foundation of our English law heritage" (p. 223). Furthermore, the Court ruled, although the accused was neither being held in custody nor subject to restrictions on his movement, nevertheless the "anxiety and concern accompanying public accusation," as well as the possibility of public scorn, was injury enough to violate his right to a speedy trial (p. 222). Despite its sweeping language, in subsequent cases, such as *Barker* v. *Wingo* (1972), the Court has employed a balancing test to interpret this right and in so doing has almost always held for the prosecution.

Malcolm M. Feeley

Knox v. Lee. See LEGAL TENDER CASES.

Koremratsu v. United States, 323 U.S. 214 (1944), argued 11 and 12 Oct. 1944, decided 18 Dec. 1944 by vote of 6 to 3; Black for the Court, Frankfurter concurring, Roberts, Murphy, and Jackson in dissent. Fred Korematsu, an American-born citizen of Japanese ancestry, grew up in the San Francisco Bay area. Rejected by the military for poor health, he obtained a defense industry job. In May 1942, when the Japanese internment began, Korematsu had a good job and a non-Japanese girl-friend. Rather than submit to incarceration, Korematsu moved to a nearby town, changed his name, had some facial surgery, and claimed to be Mexican-American. Korematsu ignored military orders prohibiting Japanese-Americans from either remaining on the California coast or moving from where they lived. As Justice Robert H. Jackson noted in dissent, Korematsu was "convicted of an act not commonly a crime. It consists merely of being present in the state whereof he is a citizen, near the place where he was born, and where all his life he has lived" (p. 243). Justice Owen J. Roberts, also dissenting, explained that Korematsu's only legal course of action was to enter a relocation center, which "was a euphemism for prison." Faced with the dilemma "that he dare not remain in his home, or voluntarily leave the area" and unwilling to be interned, Korematsu "did nothing" (p. 230). He was subsequently arrested, convicted, sentenced to five years in prison, paroled, and immediately interned at Topaz, Utah.

Korematsu is usually cited for Justice Hugo Black's assertion that "all legal restrictions which curtail the civil rights of a single racial group are immediately suspect" and should be given "the most rigid scrutiny" (p. 216). Significantly, this is the only case in which the Supreme Court has applied the "rigid scrutiny" test to a racial restriction and upheld the restrictive law.

As in *Hirabayashi* v. *U.S.* (1943), the Court majority never questioned the military's claim that Japanese-Americans threatened military security on the west coast. Justice Black fully accepted "the finding of the military authorities that it was impossible to bring about an immediate segregation of the disloyal from the loyal. . . . " Black argued that this "temporary exclusion of the entire group" was based on a military judgment (p. 219).

Ignoring the fact that nearly all Japanese-Americans were shipped to an internment camp after entering an assembly center, Black asserted that "Had the petitioner here left the prohibited area and gone to an assembly center we cannot say either as a matter of fact or law . . . [this] would have resulted in his detention in a relocation center" (p. 219). Since Korematsu was charged with remaining in a restricted area and failing to report to the assembly center, Black would not examine the constitutionality of the military forcing people into relocation camps. Black thought "It will be time enough to decide the serious constitutional issues which the petitioner seeks to raise when an assembly

or relocation order is applied or is certain to be applied to him . . . " (p. 220). In other words, Korematsu could litigate the constitutionality of the internment only after he had actually been incarcerated.

Black indignantly rejected the dissenters' claims that the internment was racist and that the "relocation centers" were "concentration camps." Black asserted that "Korematsu was not excluded from the Military Area because of hostility to him or his race. He *was* excluded because we are at war with the Japanese Empire, because the properly constituted military authorities feared an invasion of our West Coast" and because the military authorities believed the "military urgency" required "that all citizens of Japanese ancestry be segregated from the West Coast temporarily" (p. 223). Black never explained why segregating only people "of Japanese ancestry" was not racist.

In dissent Justices Roberts, Murphy, and Jackson distinguished the exclusion order and the order to report to an assembly center from the curfew approved in *Hirabayashi*. Roberts noted that "the two conflicting orders, one which commanded him to stay and the other which commanded him to go, were nothing but a cleverly devised trap to accomplish the real purpose of the military authority, which was to lock him up in a concentration camp" (p. 232).

Noting that the internment was justified "mainly upon questionable racial and sociological grounds not ordinarily within the realm of expert military judgment" (pp. 236–237), Justice Frank Murphy challenged Black's blind support for military expertise. Finding no evidence tying Japanese-Americans to sabotage or espionage, Murphy argued the internment was based on "the misinformation, half-truths and insinuations that for years have been directed against Japanese Americans by people with racial and economic prejudices—the same people who have been among the foremost advocates of the evacuation" (p. 239). Murphy believed the Japanese-Americans should have been treated "on an individual basis" through "investigations and hearings to separate the loyal from the disloyal, as was done in the case of persons of German and Italian ancestry" (p. 241). He noted that the first exclusion order was not issued until "nearly four months elapsed after Pearl Harbor" and that "the last of these 'subversive' persons was not actually removed until almost eleven months had elapsed" (p. 241).

Concluding such "leisure and deliberation" undermined the claim of military necessity, Murphy dissented "from this legalization of racism" (pp. 241–242).

Justice Jackson accepted that the military had the force to arrest citizens or that in the future this might happen again. He was not even willing to argue that "the courts should have attempted to interfere with the Army in carrying out its task" (p. 248). But he feared that "a judicial construction" that would "sustain this order is a far more subtle blow to liberty than the promulgation of the order itself." He argued that "once judicial opinion rationalizes such an order to show that it conforms to the Constitution, or rather rationalizes the Constitution to show that the Constitution sanctions such an order, the Court for all time has validated the principle of racial discrimination in criminal procedure and of transplanting American citizens." He believed the precedent then "lies about like a loaded weapon ready for the hand of any authority that can bring forward a plausible claim to an urgent need" (pp. 245–246). Jackson urged reversal in order to preserve the integrity of the constitutional system.

□ Roger Daniels, *Concentration Camps, North America* (1981). Roger Daniels, *The Decision to Relocate the Japanese-Americans (1986).* Peter Irons, *Justice At War* (1983).

Paul Finkelman

Kunz v. New York, 340 U.S. 290 (1951), argued 17 Oct. 1950, decided 15 Jan. 1951 by vote of 8 to 1; Vinson for the Court, Black and Frankfurter concurring in the result only, Jackson in dissent. *Kunz* helped establish that government restrictions on speech must be narrowly tailored so that they do not inappropriately limit expression protected by the First Amendment. In *Kunz,* the Court held that laws giving public officials broad discretion to restrain speech about religious issues in advance are an invalid prior restraint in violation of the First Amendment. The Court reversed the 1948 conviction of Baptist minister Carl J. Kunz for violating a New York City ordinance that prohibited religious services on public streets without a permit from the police commissioner. Although the ordinance specified no grounds for refusing permission to speak, Kunz was denied permits in 1947 and 1948 after he was accused of "scurrilous attacks" on Catholics and Jews under a previous permit. Kunz's conviction for violating the ordinance was upheld by the Appellate Part of the Court of Special Sessions and by the New York Court of Appeals. The Supreme Court said that New York's ordinance was too broad because it provided no standards that an administrator could use to determine who ought to receive permits to speak about religious issues. In dissent, Justice Robert Jackson said Kunz had used "fighting words" that were not protected by the First Amendment. He also criticized the Court for striking down the permit scheme when it had, in *Feiner v. New York* (1951), allowed local officials the discretion to arrest volatile speakers during their presentations.

Bill F. Chamberlin

L

Lanza, United States v., 260 U.S. 377 (1922), argued 23 Nov. 1922, decided 11 Dec. 1922 by vote of 9 to 0; Taft for the Court. Bootlegger Vito Lanza, convicted and fined in April 1920 for manufacturing, transporting, and possessing intoxicating liquor in violation of Washington state law, was subsequently charged with having violated the Volstead Act, the federal prohibition law, on the basis of the same evidence used in the state prosecution. A federal district court blocked the second prosecution as double jeopardy, and the U.S. Department of Justice appealed. In sustaining the second conviction of Lanza, a unanimous Supreme Court held that state and federal governments each had independent sovereignty to punish offenses against their peace and dignity. In respect to liquor control, states had original authority. While the Eighteenth Amendment established prohibition as national policy, its "concurrent power to enforce" clause preserved the right of each state to continue exercising an independent power as long as it was not inconsistent with federal statute. The Fifth Amendment only barred repeated proceedings by the federal government and did not apply to a situation of this sort. Since nearly every state either had a prohibition law prior to the adoption of the Eighteenth Amendment or had passed one immediately after ratification, the Lanza decision meant that prohibition violators could be indicted and punished twice for almost every offense.

While the Taft Court was clearly seeking, in this and other decisions, to buttress the new Eighteenth Amendment, the public perceived that traditional liberties were being restricted in the effort to enforce prohibition.

David E. Kyvig

Lassiter v. Northampton County Board of Elections, 360 U.S. 45 (1959), argued 18–19 May 1959, decided 8 June 1959 by vote of 9 to 0; Douglas for the Court. *Lassiter* is an important case in the history of the federal protection of voting rights. The Court rejected a black citizen's challenge to a state literacy test, finding that states have broad powers to determine the conditions of suffrage. The literacy test applied to voters of all races, and the Court would not draw the inference that it was being used to facilitate racial discrimination.

Lassiter had to be addressed in assessing the constitutionality of the Voting Rights Act of 1965. The act temporarily suspended literacy and other tests imposed as prerequisites to voting. In *South Carolina v. Katzenbach* (1966), the Court distinguished *Lassiter* on the ground that in most states covered by the 1965 act prerequisites to voting were instituted and administered in a discriminatory fashion for many years. In *Katzenbach v. Morgan* (1966), New York tested the 1965 act's effective prohibition of application of an English literacy requirement to persons

183

who completed the sixth grade in a non-English-speaking American school. The act thus gave voting privileges to many former residents of Puerto Rico who had migrated to New York.

If the Court had adhered to its approach in *Lassiter* it would have struck down the literacy requirement only if a court would conclude that the requirement discriminated against non-English-speakers. But the Court refused to ask the *Lassiter*-like question whether the judiciary would find the English literacy requirement unconstitutional. Section 5 of the Fourteenth Amendment required only that legislation be appropriate to enforce the Equal Protection Clause of the Fourteenth Amendment. It was Congress's decision to make. The challenged provision sought to secure for the New York Puerto Rican community nondiscriminatory treatment and was thus appropriate to enforce the Equal Protection Clause. Subsequent amendments to the Voting Rights Act prohibited all literacy tests as a prerequisite for voting.

Theodore Eisenberg

Lawrence v. Texas, 539 U.S. 558, argued 26 March 2003, decided 26 June 2003 by vote of 5-1-3; Kennedy for the Court, O'Connor concurring, Scalia authored the principal dissent, Thomas wrote a short separate dissent.

Striking down a Texas statute making it a crime for persons of the same sex to engage in intimate sexual conduct, the Court extended the federal right of privacy to same-sex partners and expressly overruled *Bowers v. Hardwick* (1986), which had rejected a federal due process challenge by homosexuals to state statutes that criminalized acts of sodomy between consenting adults in private.

The majority opinion refuted the historical claim asserted in *Bowers* of a long American tradition of prohibiting same-sex sexual relations and relied instead on the decriminalization of sodomy in other countries (such as the United Kingdom in 1967, as well as comparable action by the European Court of Human Rights in 1981) as evidence that Western views about homosexuality had changed. Justice Anthony Kennedy also noted that the reaffirmation of the right of privacy in *Planned Parenthood of Southeastern Pennsylvania v. Casey* (1992), and the decision in *Romer v. Evans* (1996), undermined the precedential strength of *Bowers*.

Justice Sandra Day O'Connor did not join the Court in overruling *Bowers*. Rather, her concurrence argued that Texas's ban on same-sex, but not opposite-sex, sodomy indicated nothing other than the state's moral disapproval of homosexuals and that laws premised merely on moral disapproval fail the test of minimum rationality required under the Equal Protection Clause of the Fourteenth Amendment.

Justice Antonin Scalia's dissent charged that "the court . . . has largely signed on to the so-called homosexual agenda," although insisting he has "nothing against homosexuals, or any other group, promoting their agenda through normal democratic means." Nonetheless, he lamented that "the court has taken sides in the culture war."

Justice Clarence Thomas's dissent said the Texas statute "is . . . uncommonly silly" and that he would vote to repeal it if a member of the Texas Legislature. However, finding no "general right of privacy" in the Constitution, he had no authority to invalidate the law as a judge.

State sodomy statutes are often a sign of general hostility toward homosexuals. Thus, their abolition in *Lawrence* may greatly expand the civil rights of gay people.

Daniel Pinello

Lee v. Weisman, 505 U.S. 577 (1992), argued 6 Nov. 1991, decided 24 June 1992 by vote of 5 to 4; Kennedy for the Court, Blackmun and Souter concurring, joined by Stevens and O'Connor, Scalia in dissent, joined by Rehnquist, White, and Thomas. *Lee v. Weisman* was the most important decision of the 1991–92 term involving the much vexed question of the role of religion in American life.

The case involved the practice by the Nathan Bishop Middle School of Providence, Rhode Island, of inviting members of the clergy to offer prayers at graduation ceremonies. In this instance, a student, Deborah Weisman, and her father, Daniel, who were Jewish, filed suit in 1989 after a rabbi offered an invocation and benediction at Bishop Middle School that Deborah attended. The rabbi's simple prayer had thanked God for the liberty that America enjoyed and asked for God's blessing on the teachers, students, and administrators of the school. The Weismans claimed that the school had essentially turned itself into a house of worship, and their position was supported by the American Civil Liberties Union.

The federal district court in Providence and the United States Court of Appeals for the First Circuit in Boston found the prayers unconstitutional. They did so based on the Supreme Court's ruling in *Lemon* v. *Kurtzman* (1971), in which the justices established a three-part test for deciding whether a government-sponsored religious event violated the Establishment Clause of the Constitution. That highly controversial test required that in order to pass constitutional muster, the practice had to have a secular purpose, could not primarily advance or inhibit religion, and had to avoid any excessive entanglements of government and religion. The administration of President George Bush had urged the Court to sustain the practice of the Providence schools and overturn *Lemon* and its test.

Justice Anthony M. Kennedy's opinion for the Court skirted *Lemon* and with it the need to establish a new standard of review. Prayer in the public schools was so obviously a violation of the Establishment Clause, Kennedy found, that *Weisman* could be decided without reexamining the Court's other church-state precedents. At the same time, Kennedy carefully stated that the decision to strike down the prayer activities in the Providence schools did not necessarily apply in cases that might involve adults. Kennedy also insisted that the First Amendment's Establishment Clause was just as important in the twentieth century as it was when written in the eighteenth century. If citizens are subjected, he wrote, "to state-sponsored religious exercises," the government itself fails in its "duty to guard and respect that sphere of inviolable conscience and belief which is the mark of a free people" (p. 592).

Justice Antonin Scalia authored a sarcastic, angry dissent. He scolded the *majority* for worrying about the mental state of adolescents who most likely simply ignored the prayer in any case. More important, Scalia wrote, was the accepted practice of using prayer to bring persons together voluntarily, a practice that the government and school boards should be able to promote.

Kermit L. Hall

Legal Tender Cases, collective name for three cases of the 1870s: *Hepburn* v. *Griswold*, 75 U.S. 603 (1870), argued 10 Dec. 1869, decided 7 Feb. 1870 by vote of 4 to 3, Chase for the Court, Miller in dissent; and *Knox* v. *Lee* and *Parker* v. *Davis*, 79 U.S. 457 (1871),

argued 23 Feb. and 18 Apr. 1871, decided 1 May 1871 by vote of 5 to 4, Strong for the Court, Chase, Clifford, and Field in dissent. The *Legal Tender Cases* stand for the proposition that the United States can compel creditors to receive its paper money in payment of debt. These cases also raised the issue of whether the Constitution is to be applied pursuant to the original understanding or judicially amended for unforeseen exigencies. The cases also illustrate that whenever a Supreme Court decision is at odds with the Constitution, the result may well be irreversible and beyond judicial overruling, legislative recall, or possibly formal constitutional amendment.

The legal tender controversy resulted from the decision of Secretary of Treasury (later Chief Justice) Salmon P. Chase to help finance the Civil War by issuing paper money not redeemable in species. Such money was popularly known as greenbacks. The bulk of subsequent monetary transactions—borrowing, lending, investment came to be conducted in paper currency rather than by gold coin, which also remained lawful money. To insure the acceptance of greenback dollars, it was proposed in Congress that they be made legal tender for debts and taxes. This meant that creditors were compelled to accept green-backs when offered or forfeit further interest on their debt, or possibly, the debt itself. Chase reluctantly went along, and Congress enacted the Legal Tender Act of 1862. Greenback dollars, however, rapidly depreciated in value.

Historically, legal tender had been the hallmark of an irredeemable, deteriorating paper money. The framers of the Constitution clearly intended to banish it from the American scene. Reflecting this view, Chief Justice John Marshall excoriated legal tender. In 1862, the legal tender statute was seen as a temporary, if unfortunate, expedient.

The doctrine of implied powers, derived from the war and borrowing authority, was repeatedly invoked in Congress to justify the legal tender quality of greenback dollars. The validity of the Legal Tender Act was challenged in *Hepburn* v. *Griswold*. Chief Justice Chase, with the support of three colleagues, reverted to his original reluctance and overturned the statute. Speaking for the Court, Chase found that the law was unconstitutional as applied to contracts made before its passage. He concluded that the act violated the Due Process Clause of the Fifth Amendment and impaired the obligation of contract contrary to the spirit of the Constitution.

Chase's judgment was flawed in two particulars. First was the sheer subjectivity of an appeal to an amorphous "spirit" of the Constitution, particularly when a substantial part of the Court, the Congress, and the presidency found that spirit quite compatible with what was done. Second, *Hepburn* was decided without a full bench. In 1863, the Court had been enlarged to ten, but sectional tension and reconstruction politics resulted in a fluctuating membership between seven (1866) and nine (1869). In consequence *Hepburn* was decided by a narrow 4-to-3 margin. The one existing vacancy was enlarged to two by the resignation of the venerable Justice Robert C. Grier between the decisional conference and the formal entry of judgment.

President Ulysses S. Grant promptly appointed two Republican stalwarts to bring the Court to its reconstituted strength of nine. The new tribunal almost immediately heard reargument on the constitutionality of legal tender. Grant's action aroused controversy, but it does not appear that he consciously packed the Court. The Legal Tender Act had become a party-line issue, and *Hepburn* had been foredoomed by the obvious reaction of debtors, fearful of having to repay in gold what had been borrowed in paper.

The stark fact of practical irreversibility was evident in the opening lines of Justice William Strong's opinion in *Knox* v. *Lee*. This case involved debts contracted after the passage of the Legal Tender Act. Such ex post facto obligations, noted Strong, constituted the greater part of the indebtedness of the country. He observed that the injustice of voiding retroactive application alone would be compounded by holding the act invalid across the board. Accordingly, the Court by vote of 5 to 4 overruled *Hepburn* and sustained the constitutionality of the Legal Tender Act. Although the Legal Tender Cases upheld broad congressional power over the currency, they impaired the Court's reputation for political independence and consistency.

Gerald T. Dunne

Lemon v. Kurtzman, 403 U.S. 602 (1971), argued 3 Mar. 1971, decided 28 June 1971 by vote of 7 to 0; Burger for the Court, Brennan and White concurring in part and dissenting in part, Marshall not participating. In this case, the Court considered the constitutionality of the Rhode Island Salary Supplement Act of 1969 and Pennsylvania's Non-Public Elementary and Secondary Education Act of 1968. Both laws allowed the state to support directly salaries of teachers of secular subjects in parochial and other nonpublic schools.

The issue was whether these laws violate the First Amendment religion clauses, which prohibit laws that "respect" the establishment of religion or limit its free exercise. In this case the Court established what has come to be known as the "Lemon Test," which Chief Justice Burger called "cumulative criteria developed by the Court over many years" (p. 642) to consider the constitutionality of statutes under the Establishment Clause. The Lemon test added a new "excessive entanglement" prong to the existing requirements that such laws be for a secular legislative purpose (*Abington School District* v. *Schempp*, 1963) and that their primary effect neither advance nor inhibit religion (*Board of Education* v. *Allen*, 1968).

The Court held that both statutes violated the excessive entanglement strand of the new test. The Court was particularly concerned that teachers in a parochial school setting, unlike the mere provision of secular books, may improperly involve faith and morals in the teaching of secular subjects; further, continuing surveillance by states to avoid this situation would nonetheless involve "excessive and enduring entanglement between state and church" (p. 619). Alluding to Thomas Jefferson's famous metaphor of a "wall of separation between church and state," which the Court had previously employed to define the meaning of the Establishment Clause, Burger observed that "far from being a wall," it is a "blurred, indistinct, and a variable barrier depending on all the circumstances of a particular relationship" (p. 614).

To ensure the separation of church and state, the state would have to undertake a comprehensive, discriminating, and continuing surveillance of religious schools, including state audits and on-school visits. The Court also found that these laws foster a broader, yet different type of entanglement—the potential for divisive politics among those who support and those who oppose state aid to religious education. Although the Court has viewed political division along religious lines as one of the principal evils that the First Amendment was designed to prevent, it chose not to make fear of political divisiveness a separate and fourth tier of the test.

Ronald Kahn

Leon, United States v., 468 U.S. 897 (1984), argued 17 Jan. 1984, decided 5 July 1984 by vote of 6 to 3; White for the Court, Blackmun concurring, Brennan, Marshall, and Stevens in dissent. In *Leon*, the Court heard arguments regarding whether it should create a broad exception to the Fourth Amendment's exclusionary rule for good-faith police mistakes. The Court did create an exception to the rule that allows evidence seized in almost all searches conducted pursuant to unconstitutional warrants to be used without restriction in criminal prosecutions. Notwithstanding that it is frequently labeled as "the good-faith exception," however, the *Leon* exception is actually more limited in scope, and based on a different rationale, than the broad exception that had been proposed.

The idea for a good-faith exception came from critics of the exclusionary rule, who asserted that many unconstitutional searches were made simply because the police made honest mistakes about confusing search rules. These critics also argued, applying the deterrence rationale for the exclusionary rule adopted in *United States* v. *Calandra* (1974), that suppressing evidence that was seized unconstitutionally because of honest police mistakes served no purpose because the police could not be deterred from future unconstitutional searches if they had acted by mistake. Thus, the critics proposed that unconstitutionally seized evidence should be admissible in criminal trials whenever the police had acted because of a good-faith, albeit mistaken, belief that the search was constitutional.

Defenders of the exclusionary rule opposed the proposed exception on the ground that unconstitutionally seized evidence should be suppressed as a matter of principle to enforce Fourth Amendment rights and to protect the integrity of the courts. They also expressed doubt that honest mistakes are a frequent cause of illegal searches and argued that there is no reason to think that suppression of evidence would be less likely to deter future police misconduct just because the police had made a mistake. Defenders of the rule also questioned whether courts could reliably distinguish between mistaken and willful unconstitutional searches and, as a result, voiced concern that any good-faith mistake exception would be so open-ended in practice that it would effectively end enforcement of Fourth Amendment search standards.

Although Justice Byron White's majority opinion is clearly influenced by the proposal for a broad good-faith exception, the *Leon* exception is more limited in both its scope and its rationale. With regard to its scope, the *Leon* exception is explicitly limited to searches for which the police have obtained a search warrant that is later ruled to be invalid. Most police searches are, however, conducted without search warrants. Thus, as a practical matter, it is doubtful that the *Leon* exception will affect evidence in many cases, especially because search warrants were rarely found to be invalid even prior to *Leon*.

With regard to *Leon's* rationale, White did not discuss police "good faith" generally but justified the exception on the narrow premise that the police should not be asked to second guess the validity of a judge's decision to issue a search warrant. He asserted that the exclusionary rule was only designed to reach police misconduct, not judicial errors; hence, he concluded that the rule should not apply to an invalid search warrant that is the fault of a judge rather than the police. Because of this narrow rationale, it is questionable whether *Leon* should be viewed as precedent for a broad good-faith exception that would apply to unconstitutional warrantless searches. Nevertheless, *Leon* is a significant development because it is the first decision to find a Fourth Amendment violation but nevertheless allow unrestricted use of unconstitutionally seized evidence in criminal proceedings, including the prosecution's case-in-chief at trial. At least implicitly, *Leon* appears to embrace the proposition that there need not be any recourse or remedy available to victims of Fourth Amendment violations.

Justice William J. Brennan's dissent, joined by Justice Thurgood Marshall, rejected the entire approach of the majority opinion. It argued that suppression of unconstitutionally seized evidence is constitutionally required without regard to its deterrent effect. Hence, the reason the violation occurred should be legally irrelevant.

Thomas Y. Davies

License Cases (*Thurlow* v. *Massachusetts; Fletcher* v. *Rhode Island; Peirce* v. *New*

Hampshire), 5 How. (46 U.S.) 504 (1847), argued 12, 14, 15, 20, 21 Jan. 1847, decided 6 Mar. 1847 by vote of 9 to 0; Taney, McLean, Catron, Daniel, Woodbury, and Grier delivered separate opinions. Establishing effective national authority to regulate interstate and foreign commerce was a primary reason for creating the Constitution of 1787. The Marshall Court asserted a broad national authority to regulate interstate commerce, though that power was limited by an extensive state police power. Local business interests secured state legislation protecting their enterprises at the expense of merchants residing in other states. Meanwhile, after 1830 the antislavery movement made the states' control of slavery the most explosive issue of the antebellum era.

The *License Cases* involved the legality of Massachusetts, Rhode Island, and New Hampshire statutes that taxed and otherwise regulated the sale of alcoholic beverages imported into those states. The statutes favored local retailers. The issue was whether the laws violated federal control of interstate commerce, or represented a lawful exercise of the state police power. The Court was unanimous in upholding the states' authority. Nine separate opinions written by six different justices revealed, however, that the slavery issue (raised by counsel in the Rhode Island case) prevented agreement on the reasons governing the result.

The decision shaped the Taney Court's formulation of a compromise policy known as the doctrine of selective exclusiveness, which influenced the application of the commerce power until national power superseded state authority as a result of the constitutional revolution of the New Deal era.

Tony Freyer

Lingle v. Chevron, U.S.A. Inc., 544 U.S. 528 (2005), argued 22 Feb. 2005, decided 23 May 2005 by vote of 9 to 0; O'Connor for the Court, Kennedy concurring. In *Agins* v. *City of Tiburon* (1980), the Court declared that government regulation of private property "effects a taking if [such regulation] does not substantially advance legitimate state interests." Although the Court quoted this formulation in subsequent cases, it did not decide a case based upon it. The issue was presented squarely for the first time in *Lingle*, and the Court repudiated its *Agins* formulation.

Chevron sold most of its products through independent dealers, who leased service stations from the corporation. The Hawaii legislature attempted to protect independent dealers and reduce retail gasoline prices by imposing ceilings on gasoline station rents. The lower federal courts determined that Hawaii's goals were legitimate, but they held that the rent-ceiling statute constituted a taking of property. The courts found that the statute would not substantially advance the state's goals, since rent ceilings could be offset by premiums the oil companies could charge for the transfer of station leases or by increases in wholesale gasoline prices.

The Supreme Court reversed, reasoning that the efficacy of a regulation had nothing to do with the magnitude or character of the burden that it placed on property owners, and that it was not germane to whether the burden "should be borne by the public as a whole" (*Armstrong* v. *United States* [1960]). On the other hand, the Court opined that ineffectiveness relates to whether a regulation is so arbitrary as to violate the Due Process Clause of the Fifth or Fourteenth Amendment. It therefore concluded that the due process inquiry "is logically prior to and distinct from the question whether a regulation effects a taking, for the Takings Clause presupposes that the government has acted in pursuit of a valid public purpose" (p. 543). Justice Anthony M. Kennedy's concurrence adumbrated the possibility that a regulation might be so arbitrary or irrational as to violate due process, and that the failure of a regulation to accomplish its stated goal was relevant in that determination.

In *Lingle*, the Court distinguished *Dolan v. City of Tigard* (1994) as using the "substantially advances" formulation in the "entirely distinct" context of ensuring that government exactions of property interests in connection with development applications advanced the same interests as those that could justify application denials.

The Court also used *Lingle* to restate takings jurisprudence, which it asserted was directed towards identifying "regulatory actions that are functionally equivalent to the classic taking in which government directly appropriates private property or ousts the owner from his domain." (p. 539). The Court described three inquiries as sharing this "common touchstone." The first two concerned physical takings, which impose a "unique burden" (*Loretto* v.

Teleprompter Manhattan CATV Corp. [1982]) and are the equivalent of a physical appropriation, which results in the total deprivation of beneficial use (*Lucas* v. *South Carolina Coastal Council* [1992]). The third inquiry, used for regulatory takings, involved an ad hoc, multifactor balancing test, stressing the economic impact of the regulation, its effect on the owner's investment-backed expectations, and the character of the regulation (*Penn Central Transportation Co.* v. *City of New York* [1978]).

Steven J. Eagle

Local 28 of Sheet Metal Workers International Association v. Equal Employment Opportunity Commission, 478 U.S. 421 (1986), argued 25 Feb. 1986, decided 2 July 1986 by vote of 6 to 3; Brennan for the Court, White, Rehnquist, and Burger in dissent. The Supreme Court affirmed lower court orders requiring a sheet metal workers local union in New York City to establish a minority membership goal of 29 percent to be achieved by a specified date, and to maintain a fund to increase nonwhite participation in apprenticeship training and union membership. Six members of the Court rejected the argument of the Solicitor General that federal courts have no power to order numerical goals for training and promotion as a remedy for employment discrimination. A majority of the Court also rejected the argument that relief could be awarded only to identified victims of discrimination and held that judges may order race-conscious affirmative action remedies in hiring, union membership and in other contexts to rectify "egregious" discrimination.

After years of futile action by state and municipal civil rights agencies, a federal district court had found the union guilty of violating Title VII of the Civil Rights Act of 1964 by discriminating against nonwhite workers in recruitment, selection, training and in admission to the union. The union was ordered to cease its discriminatory practices and to establish a nonwhite membership goal based on the percentage of nonwhites in the relevant labor pool. Twice the Court of Appeals affirmed with modifications and twice the district court found the union guilty of civil contempt for disobeying court orders.

In affirming these decisions, the Supreme Court held that affirmative action requirements were appropriate remedies for job discrimination under Title VII, and

within the context of such cases, this ruling remains intact.

Herbert Hill

Lochner v. New York, 198 U.S. 45 (1905), argued 23–24 Feb. 1905, decided 17 Apr. 1905 by vote of 5 to 4; Peckham for the Court, Harlan and Holmes in dissent. In 1905 the Supreme Court invalidated a New York regulation limiting the hours of labor in bakeries to ten per day or sixty per week. At the turn of the century it was not uncommon for journeymen bakers to work more than one hundred hours per week. In cities, bakeries were usually located in the cellar of a tenement house. The combination of long hours exposed to flour dust, plus the dampness and extremes of hot and cold in tenement cellars, was thought to have an ill effect on workers' health. Because this unsanitary environment affected both the product and the workers, the state in 1895 enacted legislation to regulate sanitary conditions as well as reform working conditions and reduce the hours of labor prevalent in the industry.

Proponents of shorter hours statutes had for decades been arguing that such legislation was needed to promote citizenship, improve family life, and protect health and safety. But mostly shorter hours laws were seen as a means to assure fairness for workers who were in no position to bargain for equitable conditions of employment. Opponents based their arguments on theories of social Darwinism and laissez-faire economics. To them such legislation represented unwarranted governmental intrusion into the marketplace.

Political conditions in late nineteenth-century New York did not favor laws regulating business and industry. State government was dominated by a business oriented Republican political machine headed by boss Thomas Collier Platt. Large cities were controlled by Democratic machines like Tammany Hall. Organized labor, the most likely proponent of such laws, represented only a small portion of the labor force. State regulation of the baking industry was made possible only when other reformers took an interest. Journalist Edward Marshall observed the squalor of New York City's cellar bakeries while serving on the Tenement House Committee of 1894. Beginning with an editorial in the *New York Press*, he led a crusade to clean up the industry and improve conditions of employment. Marshall was able to convince mainstream urban reformers that problems in the baking industry were linked to tenement reform and social reform generally. Meanwhile, Henry Weismann, an opportunistic leader of the Bakers' Union, seized the moment by getting his union behind the proposed law. Marshall's connection with urban mainstream reformers, however, provided the clout needed to push bakeshop regulation through the legislature. With their backing the Bakeshop Act unanimously passed both houses of the legislature and was signed by the governor on 2 May 1895.

The people hurt most by the new legislation were master bakers or "boss bakers." These were owners of the small shops that made up the bread baking industry. Most employed fewer than five workers and operated on a small margin of profit. Joseph Lochner owned this type of shop in Utica, New York. In 1902 he was fined fifty dollars for allowing an employee to work more than sixty hours in one week. Lochner appealed his conviction to the Appellate Division of the New York Supreme Court, where he lost by vote of 3 to 2. He then appealed to the New York Court of Appeals, where he lost again in a 4-to-3 ruling. Ironically, former labor leader Henry Weismann came to his aid. After a falling out with the Bakers' Union, Weismann had opened two bakeshops and become an active member of the Master Bakers' Association. He also studied law. With the help of attorney Frank Harvey Field, Weismann took Lochner's appeal to the Supreme Court of the United States.

Lochner claimed the Bakeshop Act violated the Fourteenth Amendment by depriving him of life, liberty, or property without due process of law. Due process was originally thought of only as a guarantee that laws would be enforced through correct judicial procedure, but the concept changed drastically in the late nineteenth century. Under a theory called "substantive due process" courts assumed the power to examine the content of legislation as well as the means by which it was enforced. In the late 1880s the doctrine was employed successfully to overrule state attempts at regulating railroads. But it carried the broader implication that the Court could invalidate any type of state economic or reform legislation determined to be in conflict with a right protected by the Constitution.

In Lochner's case, the right arguably infringed by New York's workday ceiling was "liberty of contract." This was not a right written into the Constitution. Rather, like substantive due process, it evolved through judicial interpretation of the Fourteenth Amendment. Justice Stephen Field, dissenting in the *Slaughterhouse Cases* (1873), first advanced the idea that the liberty protected by the Due Process Clause included "the right to pursue an ordinary trade or calling." With subsequent decisions expanding the idea, it became the means by which the judicial supervision envisioned by proponents of substantive due process could be applied to laws regulating the employer-employee relationship. Laws such as those requiring that wages be paid in cash rather than company scrip or setting standards for computing miners' pay were invalidated. By the 1880s this doctrine—liberty of contract—was being used by state courts to suggest that the Constitution protected a right to enter into any agreement free from unreasonable governmental interference. However, the United States Supreme Court had applied the theory only once, in *Allgeyer* v. *Louisiana* (1897).

Justice Rufus Peckham, who wrote *Allgeyer*, also wrote *Lochner*. He more firmly entrenched the doctrine of liberty of contract into constitutional law by ruling that New York's attempt to regulate hours of labor in bakeries "necessarily interfered with the right of contract between the employer and the employee." Peckham held that the liberty protected by the Fourteenth Amendment included the right to purchase and sell labor. Therefore, any statute interfering with it would be invalid "unless there are circumstances which exclude that right."

Liberty of contract was recognized, but it was not absolute. The protection it provided had to be balanced against the legitimate exercise of the state's power to govern. This authority was referred to as the police powers of the states. As originally understood, the phrase was used to simply distinguish the function of state governments from that of the federal government. In the late nineteenth century, however, it was transformed into an ill-defined limit on the power of states to govern within their own sphere of authority. When interpreted broadly as the duty to enhance the general welfare, police power could accommodate most any type of law. But Peckham had a narrow conception of police power in mind when he wrote the *Lochner* decision. For him only legislation designed to protect public morals, health, safety, or peace and good order represented a legitimate exercise of a state's police power.

In the *Lochner* case this became a question of whether the Bakeshop Act was necessary to protect the public health or health of bakers. In *Holden* v. *Hardy* (1898) the Court upheld an eight-hour day for workers in mines and smelters. There the danger was obvious. But the claim that baking was an unhealthy trade was not so graphic. Reformers maintained that long hours of labor in bakeshops created a likelihood that workers would develop respiratory ailments such as "consumption." Peckham rejected this idea out-right. Taking judicial notice of a "common understanding" that baking was never considered an unhealthy trade, he concluded that the Bakeshop Act was not a legitimate exercise of the police power and was therefore unconstitutional.

Dissenting, Justice John Marshall Harlan argued that the majority started its reasoning from the wrong presumption. Harlan believed that, when the validity of a statute was questioned on constitutional grounds, a presumption ought to exist in favor of the legislature's determination. In his words, legislative enactments should be enforced "unless they are plainly and palpably beyond all question in violation of the fundamental law of the Constitution" (p. 68). Harlan did not disagree that liberty of contract applied to this situation. Nor did he disagree that concern for worker health and safety would be the only legitimate justification for the Bakeshop Act. Harlan was simply more willing than Peckham and the majority to recognize that there was evidence supporting that claim. The very fact that there was room for debate should have laid to rest all arguments that the law was unconstitutional. The weighing of claims regarding health conditions in the industry was a matter of legislative discretion.

Taking a position similar to Harlan's, Justice Oliver Wendell Holmes maintained that a state law should be upheld unless a rational person would necessarily admit that it would infringe upon fundamental principles of American laws and traditions. But Holmes's famous dissent also criticized the majority's decision to expand liberty of contract and its narrow view of the police power. Recognizing that these doctrines reflected the theories of social Darwinism and laissez-faire economics, Holmes directly attacked the underlying premise of the decision. "A constitution is not intended to embody a particular economic theory," he wrote. "It is made for people of fundamentally differing views" (p. 74). For Holmes, the opinion was dangerous because it represented the unwarranted infusion into the Constitution of a new fundamental right.

Peckham claimed his opinion did not substitute the judgment of the Court for that of the legislature on the matter of health in the baking industry. But many observers thought this was exactly what he had done. The Bakeshop Act had passed the state legislature unanimously. One hundred and nineteen elected representatives had voted in favor of the workday ceiling. Even seven of the twelve appellate judges who had previously ruled on Lochner's case voted to uphold the law. Critics maintained that the Court had no special knowledge of the industry and that it was in no better position than the state legislature to determine if the trade was unhealthy. And, although it was not irrefutable that the baking trade was unhealthy, ample statistical support for that contention was included in the record before the Supreme Court.

The usurpation of legislative authority and glaring subjectivity of Peckham's ruling brought the case into the limelight. In 1910, President Theodore Roosevelt pointed at *Lochner* when denouncing the judiciary for erecting insurmountable obstacles in the path of needed social reform. Critics found it frustrating that the opinion of one appointed judge could reverse the reforms adopted by elected legislatures. For the next three decades, *Lochner* symbolized judicial misuse of power.

The specific outcome was not the most important thing about the *Lochner* case. It was a setback, but not a fatal blow to the shorter hours movement. By 1912 collective bargaining gave the union bakers of New York the ten-hour day. In *Muller* v. *Oregon* (1908) the Court upheld a work-day limit for women, and in *Bunting* v. *Oregon* (1917) it gave its blessing to a ten-hour ceiling for adult males as well as women and children working in most industries.

Of more lasting importance was the rationale adopted by the *Lochner* majority. It made the Court the overseer of all kinds of state regulatory legislation. Between 1905 and 1937, when the Court rejected this rationale in *West Coast Hotel* v. *Parrish* (1937), countless subsequent attempts to reform social and economic conditions were challenged on the precedent of *Lochner*. Many of these state regulations were upheld. But state statutes such as minimum wage laws, child labor laws, regulations of the banking, insurance, and transportation industries were vetoed by the Court. Enough reform statutes were invalidated that the history of constitutional law during that time is commonly called "the *Lochner* era."

The Court is said to have made the mistake in *Lochner* of becoming involved in formulating policy rather than interpreting the law. As Holmes pointed out, it also embraced one theory of the function of government at the expense of all others. Judicial construction alone had imbedded that theory into the fundamental law of the land. For these reasons the case still stands as a symbol of unrestrained judicial activism.

☐ Felix Frankfurter, "Hours of Labor and Realism in Constitutional Law," *Harvard Law Review* 23 (1916): 353. Paul Kens, *Judicial Power and Reform Politics: The Anatomy of Lochner v. New York* (1990). Bernard H. Siegan, "Rehabilitating Lochner," *San Diego Law Review* 22 (1985): 453. Cass R. Sunstein, "Lochner's Legacy," *Columbia Law Review* 87 (1987): 873.

Paul Kens

Loewe v. Lawlor, 208 U.S. 274 (1908), argued 4–5 Dec. 1907, decided 3 Feb. 1908 by vote of 9 to 0; Fuller for the Court. Popularly known as the Danbury Hatters' Case, *Loewe v. Lawlor* grew out of a unionization effort promoted by a secondary boycott sponsored by the American Federation of Labor, which had no direct interest in the dispute. Loewe, an employer, brought a treble-damage suit against individual members of the United Hatters of North America, including the resident union agent, Martin Lawlor. The union denied that it was a combination as defined by the Sherman Antitrust Act.

For a unanimous Supreme Court, Chief Justice Melville W. Fuller insisted that *every* combination in restraint of trade was illegal. Fuller stated that the Sherman Act required the Court to consider the union's actions as a whole, regardless of the intrastate character of particular actions. Fuller denied that Congress had intended to exempt unions from coverage by the act and maintained, therefore, that individual union members could be held liable for damages under section 7 of the act.

From a union perspective, *Loewe* provided a galling contrast to *United States* v. **E. C.*

Knight Co. (1895), which had exempted local activities of the nationwide Sugar Trust from the Sherman Act's prohibitions, while *Loewe* extended the act's coverage to comparable union actions. This made *Loewe* the most threatening of the Court's labor decisions, raising the specter of dissolution and damage suits against unions. Unions therefore moved into the political sphere, seeking statutory exemption from Congress. The Clayton Act of 1914 failed to provide explicit exemption, but relief ultimately came within the changed labor-management context in the late 1930s.

Barbara C. Steidle

Lone Wolf v. Hitchcock, 187 U.S. 553 (1903), argued 23 Oct. 1902, decided 5 Jan. 1903 by vote of 9 to 0; White for the Court. In *Lone Wolf*, the Supreme Court recognized a near-absolute plenary congressional power over Indian affairs, virtually exempt from judicial oversight. This decision marked a decisive shift from the doctrines of the **Cherokee Cases* (1831–1832), which emphasized inherent tribal sovereignty and land rights. *Lone Wolf* has permitted the United States to appropriate tribal lands and resources under the guise of fulfilling federal trust responsibilities.

The litigation in *Lone Wolf* sought to block congressional ratification of an agreement alloting tribal lands, on the grounds that the allotment violated the 1867 Treaty of Medicine Lodge by failing to obtain the required consent of three-fourths of adult male tribal members to land cessions. Justice Edward D. White rejected this claim, denying that the agreement violated property rights of tribal members or deprived them of due process of law. In conformity with the then-prevalent restrictive view of Indian tribal sovereignty, White held that Congress had plenary power over Indian property "by reason of its exercise of guardianship over their interests" (p. 565). He held this power to be political and not subject to judicial review. Under it, the United States could unilaterally abrogate provisions of treaties made with Indian nations, subject only to the requirement that actions of the United States toward its "wards" be guided by "perfect good faith" (p. 566).

Until recently, the *Lone Wolf* doctrine articulated an unreviewable congressional power and virtually standardless trust authority, which made it impossible for tribes to obtain judicial protection in disputes with the United States. Recent developments may suggest a narrower view of congressional power over Indian tribes as well as some constitutional limits on that power. In 1979 a federal judge called *Lone Wolf* "the Indian's *Dred Scott*." The most substantial limitation on congressional authority came in 1996, when the Court in *Seminole Tribe of Florida v. Florida* (1996) struck down as a violation of the Eleventh Amendment a complex statutory scheme enacted by Congress as part of the Indian Gaming Regulatory Act. Chief Justice William H. Rehnquist's opinion was a stunning victory for proponents of states' rights.

Jill Norgren

Lopez, United States v., 514 U.S. 549 (1995), argued 8 Nov. 1994, decided 26 Apr. 1995 by vote of 5 to 4; Rehnquist for the Court, Kennedy filing a concurring opinion, in which O'Connor joined, and Thomas filing a concurring opinion, Stevens, Souter, Breyer, and Ginsburg in dissent. Congress in 1990 enacted the Gun-Free School Zones Act, making it a federal offense to possess a firearm in a school zone. Congress relied on the authority of the Commerce Clause of the Constitution to justify passage of the legislation as a way of stemming the rising tide of gun-related incidents in public schools.

Alfonso Lopez, Jr., was in 1992 a senior at Edison High School in San Antonio, Texas. Acting on an anonymous tip, school authorities confronted Lopez and discovered that he was carrying a .38 caliber handgun and five bullets. A federal grand jury subsequently indicted Lopez, who then moved to have the indictment dismissed on grounds that the federal government had no authority to legislate control over the public schools. At a bench trial, the federal district court judge found Lopez guilty and sentenced him to six months' imprisonment and two years' supervised release. Lopez then appealed to the federal Court of Appeals for the Fifth Circuit, which reversed the conviction and held the Gun-Free School Zones Act unconstitutional as an invalid exercise by Congress of the commerce power.

The *Lopez* case posed the question of the extent to which Congress could exercise authority over street crime and, in so doing, intrude into constitutional space traditionally occupied by the states. Since the New Deal of the 1930s, the Supreme Court had accepted that Congress had broad authority to regulate virtually every aspect of

American life under the cover of the federal Commerce Clause. Moreover, the bombing of the federal office building in Oklahoma City, while it had occurred after passage of the Gun-Free School Zones Act, created a political environment where both the Clinton administration and Republican congressional leaders believed that the federal government had to combat domestic terrorist groups and the weapons that they used.

The case drew considerable attention from diverse interest groups. The National Education Association, for example, joined with the Clinton administration and various antigun groups to argue that schools had experienced difficulty in handling gun-related crimes. For the government, Solicitor General Drew S. Days argued that the law was different from other statutes dealing with firearms in that it targeted possession rather than sale. Yet Days also insisted that a close connection existed between violence in schools and the movement of guns in interstate commerce. The government insisted that guns were often used as part of the drug culture that was itself carried on through national commerce. The government also argued that in this instance Congress was merely trying to supplement state law rather than trying to supplant it, hence it did not have to demonstrate as strong a link between the movement of guns in interstate commerce and the establishment of gun-free schools zones as it might otherwise have had to do.

The National Rifle Association, the National Conference of State Legislatures, the Cato Institute, and trial lawyers and consumer groups fighting tort reform opposed the legislation. They insisted that while the goal of reducing school gun violence was laudable, Congress had failed to establish a rational relationship between banning guns and the mere possession of one. Since Congress could not make a link between firearms possession and interstate commerce, they insisted, there was no reason to regulate gun possession in schools in the first place. Such regulation, in any case, properly belonged at the state and local level, and it was simply beyond the power of Congress to regulate control over public schools. These same groups also worried that increasing federal authority over local crimes posed a threat to the states' sovereignty and to individual liberty.

A sharply divided Supreme Court affirmed the decision of the Fifth Circuit and struck down the law. Chief Justice William H. Rehnquist's majority opinion was one of the few times since the 1930s when the justices held a congressional action unconstitutional on the ground that it violated states' rights. Rehnquist held that the gun-free schools law far exceeded the bounds of the federal commerce power. Indeed, the chief justice found that given the theories advanced by the federal government in this case, "it is difficult to perceive any limitation on federal power, even in areas such as criminal law enforcement or education where States historically had been sovereign. Thus, if we were to accept the Government's arguments, we are hard-pressed to posit any activity by an individual that Congress is without power to regulate" (p. 564). To Rehnquist's opinion, Justice Clarence Thomas added a strongly worded concurrence that offered a conservative history of the commerce power that purported to show that the Court had permitted Congress to turn it into a "blank check" (p. 602).

The dissenters in the case insisted that Congress had historically had the power to do what it had done and that the buying, selling, and possessing of guns were deeply implicated in commercial activity. Justice Stephen Breyer argued in dissent that he could not understand why the majority would accept that Congress had the power to regulate the school environment by keeping it free from controlled substances, asbestos, and alcohol but not guns. The dissenters also charged that the decision threatened to return the justices to the era of substantive due process of law and the substitution of the views of the Court for those of elected public officials.

The *Lopez* decision underscored the significant changes wrought by Republican presidents Ronald Reagan and George Bush on the Court. The decision was widely viewed at the time as a stalking horse by the Court's conservative justices to attack a wide range of federal social policies. Perhaps most important, however, the decision affirmed the strong interest of the high court in supporting state sovereignty, a development that has become a hallmark of the Rehnquist court.

Kermit L. Hall

Lottery Case. See CHAMPION V. AMES.

Louisiana ex rel. Francis v. Resweber, 329 U.S. 459 (1947), argued 18 Nov. 1946, decided 13 Jan. 1947 by vote of 5 to 4; Reed for the Court, Burton in dissent. In November 1944, Andrew Thomas, a white St. Martinsville, Louisiana, druggist, was murdered, apparently by fifteen-year-old Willie Francis, who was black. With little help from his court appointed attorneys, Francis was quickly convicted and condemned to execution in the electric chair. But when Francis sat in it on 3 May 1946, it malfunctioned; the two-minute jolt of electricity failed to kill (or even disable) him. Reached by phone, the governor scheduled a new execution date for the next week.

But attorneys responding to the pleas of the inmate's father took the case to the Supreme Court. They argued that the attempt to execute Francis again would constitute double jeopardy, and, more importantly, cruel and unusual punishment under the Eighth Amendment. The justices refused to block a second execution attempt. The swing vote was cast in a concurring opinion by Justice Felix Frankfurter, usually a death penalty foe.

Petitions for rehearing and clemency were unsuccessful, and one year and six days after the original blunder, Willie Francis again sat in the electric chair. This time it worked.

Michael L. Radelet

Louisville, New Orleans & Texas Railway Co. v. Mississippi, 133 U.S. 587 (1890), argued 10 Jan. 1890, decided 3 Mar. 1890 by vote of 7 to 2; Brewer for the Court, Harlan in dissent. The Court upheld the constitutionality of a Mississippi statute that required railroads to provide "equal, but separate, accommodation for the white and colored races." The railroad argued that the statute was unconstitutional because its substantial effect on interstate commerce violated the Commerce Clause. Unlike arguments that would mature in the twentieth century, the case did not involve the Fourteenth Amendment.

The Mississippi statute, in its effect on interstate commerce, seemed identical to a Louisiana statute that had been declared unconstitutional in *Hall* v. *DeCuir* (1878). Both statutes used race as the criterion for determining treatment of passengers. The Louisiana statute mandated that all parts of vehicles be open to passengers, regardless of race; the Mississippi statute required separation by race, into "equal" facilities. In spite of the apparent similarities, the Court upheld the Mississippi statute.

The inconsistency between the two decisions evidences the Court's struggle to define federalism in the late nineteenth century. The Court had already so narrowed the scope of the Civil War Amendments that the national government had little role to play in protecting individual rights. Here, through interpretation of the Commerce Clause, the Court continued its efforts to preserve a major role for the states. Accordingly, Justice David J. Brewer accepted without question the Supreme Court of Mississippi's view that the statute applied only to intrastate commerce. The Court saw no significant burden on interstate commerce from the requirement that railroads add an additional car upon entering the state. Justice John Marshall Harlan dissented on the ground that the state statute was an unconstitutional regulation of interstate commerce.

Walter F. Pratt, Jr.

Louisville Railroad Co. v. Letson, 2 How. (43 U.S.) 497 (1844), argued 20 Feb. 1843, decided 7 Mar. 1844 by vote of 5 to 0; Wayne for the Court, Daniel, McKinley, and Taney not participating, Thompson had died. Letson, a New York resident, sued the Louisville Railroad Company, chartered by South Carolina, in federal circuit court under diversity of citizenship jurisdiction for breach of contract. The railroad argued that the federal circuit court had no jurisdiction because the U.S. Supreme Court had ruled, in *Bank of the United States* v. *Deveaux* (1809), that the citizenship of a corporation for purposes of diversity jurisdiction was that of its shareholders. The railroad maintained that there was no diversity since some of the its shareholders were citizens of New York.

On a writ of error from a decision upholding jurisdiction, the Court overturned *Deveaux* and held that for purposes of diversity jurisdiction a corporation is a citizen of the state that chartered it. Because a corporation would thus be a citizen of a single state rather than a citizen of all of the states in which its shareholders resided, *Letson* increased the opportunities of corporations to sue or be sued in federal court under diversity jurisdiction and enhanced federal judicial power. For the next two decades corporations resisted federal diversity jurisdiction as often as they favored it, but following the Civil War many of them found the federal courts more hospitable than state courts. In 1958 Congress somewhat limited the right of corporations to sue or be sued in federal court under diversity jurisdiction by providing that a corporation should be deemed a citizen of the state that incorporates it and of the state that is its principal place of business.

Robert M. Ireland

Lovell v. City of Griffin, 303 U.S. 444 (1938), argued 4 Feb. 1938, decided 28 Mar. 1938 by vote of 8 to 0; Hughes for the Court, Cardozo not participating. Although the Supreme Court suggested in *Gitlow* v. *New York* (1925) that the First Amendment's guarantee of free speech was applicable to the states through the Fourteenth Amendment, it was not until *Everson* v. *Board of Education* (1947) that it so held with respect to both the religious establishment and free exercise clauses. During the intermediate period the Court developed a technique it still occasionally uses of treating religion cases as if they were free speech cases. *Lovell* v. *Griffin* was an example of such treatment.

Alma Lovell, an adherent of the Jehovah's Witnesses, refused to abide by the city's ordinance that required the city manager's written permission for distribution or sale of circulars, magazines, pamphlets, or handbooks. She regarded herself as sent by "Jehovah to do His work," and that such an application would have been "an act of disobedience to His commandment."

The Court did not deal with the religious aspects of the case and did not even mention the Jehovah's Witnesses by name. Instead, it held the ordinance invalid as a violation of freedom of the press. The liberty of the press was not confined to newspapers and periodicals, the Court said; it necessarily embraced pamphlets and leaflets. Nor could the ordinance be saved because it related to distribution rather than publication; liberty of circulation was as essential as liberty of publication.

Leo Pfeffer

Lovett, United States v., 328 U.S. 303 (1946), argued 3 and 6 May 1946, decided 3 June 1946 by vote of 8 to 0; Black for the Court, Frankfurter, joined by Reed, concurring, Jackson not participating. The Bill of Attainder Clauses of Article I of the Constitution have been interpreted broadly to prohibit any legislative act, by Congress or a state legislature, that inflicts punishment on a designated individual without a judicial trial. Historically, the English experience and abuses after the Revolution made this device unpopular. Functionally, such special acts reflect the general mistrust of retroactive legislation and violate separation of powers.

The *Lovett* decision came during the cold war hysteria and McCarthy-era purges. Congress enacted a statute providing that no appropriated funds could be paid as salary to Lovett and two other named federal employees found to be disloyal. The Court ruled that this amounted to a bill of attainder.

The Court has struck down only three other statutes as forbidden bills of attainder: a state law that required clergy to take an oath that they had never aided the Confederacy; a congressional enactment that required a similar oath as a condition to practice law in federal courts; and a federal statute making it a crime for a member of the Communist party to serve as an officer of a labor union.

In his autobiography *All Our Years* (1948), Robert Morss Lovett claimed for the three "a place in history in spite of ourselves" and described the outcome as an occasion when "government triumphed over hate" (pp. 308–309). The decision stilled further congressional attempts to punish people by name in statutes.

Thomas E. Baker

Loving v. Virginia, 388 U.S. 1 (1967), argued 10 Apr. 1967, decided 12 June 1967 by vote of 9 to 0; Warren for the Court, Stewart concurring. In *Pace* v. *Alabama* (1883), the Court upheld an Alabama law that punished interracial fornication more severely than when the partners were of the same race. Since both partners were punished equally, it said, there was no violation of the Equal Protection Clause of the Fourteenth Amendment. This became known as the "equal discrimination" or "equal application" exception.

Later cases, such as *Shelley* v. *Kraemer* (1948), refused to apply it, however, and it was clearly inconsistent with the principle of racial nondiscrimination enunciated in *Brown* v. *Board of Education* (1954). But the Court was reluctant to address formally this very sensitive issue head on, recognizing that, coming on the heels of *Brown*, prohibiting laws against racial intermarriage would only further inflame southern resistance (*Naim* v. *Naim*, 1955). The doctrine was finally repudiated in the *Loving* case.

Loving, a white man who had married a black woman, challenged his conviction under the Virginia antimiscegenation law, which prohibited and punished racial intermarriage. Virginia was then one of sixteen southern states that had such laws. In the previous fifteen years, fourteen states had repealed laws outlawing interracial marriages. Chief Justice Earl Warren, for a unanimous Court, invalidated the law as an invidious racial classification prohibited by the Equal Protection Clause of the Fourteenth Amendment. Warren held that: "Under our Constitution, the freedom to marry, or not marry, a person of another race resides with the individual and cannot be infringed by the State" (p. 12).

Steven Puro

Lucas v. South Carolina Coastal Council, 505 U.S. 1003 (1992), argued 2 March 1992, decided 29 June 1992 by vote of 6 to 2; Scalia for the Court, Kennedy, concurring in the judgment, Blackmun and Stevens, dissenting. Souter filed a statement asserting certiorari improvidently granted. David H. Lucas bought two residential beachfront lots for $975,000 in 1986. Two years later, a new Beachfront Management Act (BMA) barred construction of any permanent habitable structures on the lots. A state trial court held that the lots were rendered "valueless" and had been "taken" by operation of the act. This finding was not disturbed when the South Carolina Supreme Court rejected the takings claim on grounds that it was bound to accept the legislature's determination that the BMA was designed to protect the state's beaches.

Justice Antonin Scalia reviewed Justice Oliver Wendell Holmes's exposition in *Pennsylvania Coal Co.* v. *Mahon* (1922) that a regulation would constitute a compensable taking when it went "too far," and also the Court's decision to apply this test through "essentially ad hoc, factual inquiries" in *Penn Central Transportation Co.* v. *City of New York* (1978). Scalia noted that the Court had eschewed ad hoc balancing of interests where there was a permanent physical invasion of land, as in *Loretto* v. *Teleprompter Manhattan CATV Corp.* (1982), or where the regulation denied all economically beneficial or productive use of land as in *Agins* v. *City of Tiburon* (1980).

Lucas deemed the *Agins* rule supported by the fact that "total deprivation of beneficial use is, from the landowner's point of view, the equivalent of a physical appropriation" (p. 1017). Regulations compelling that land be left in its natural state carry a "heightened risk that private property is being pressed into some form of public service under the guise of mitigating serious public harm" (p. 1018). In addition, the fact that any land regulation inevitably affects property values becomes less pressing in "the relatively rare situations where the government has deprived a landowner of all economically beneficial uses" (p. 1018). The opinion also noted that no compensation would be required if the regulations that deprives land of all economically beneficial use "inhere in . . . the restrictions that background principles of the State's law of property and nuisance already place upon land ownership" (p. 1029).

The left has criticized *Lucas* for countenancing conventional zoning while disabling ecoshed protection. The right has criticized *Lucas* for failing to define the "relevant parcel" taken, thus permitting government to take all value in a small area while asserting that the landowner has remaining value in other parts of the parcel.

The Court has stringently cabined *Lucas*, holding that it is not applicable where one house might be built on eighteen acres of land, in *Palazzolo* v. *Rhode Island* (2001), or where development is not barred permanently, but rather by an extended moratorium, in *Tahoe-Sierra Preservation Council, Inc.* v. *Tahoe Regional Planning Agency* (2002). Sweeping regulations increasingly are defended on the grounds that they embody longstanding "background principles" favoring the environment.

Steven J. Eagle

Luther v. Borden, 7 How. (48 U.S.) 1 (1849), argued 24–28 Jan. 1848, decided 3 Jan. 1849 by vote of 8 to 1; Taney for the Court, Woodbury concurring in part and dissenting in part. The Constitution provides that the federal government shall guarantee to each state a "Republican Form of Government" (Art. IV, sec. 4), but does not specify how much popular participation in state government is required to retain the republican character, nor does it identify which branch of the federal government, if any, is responsible for enforcing the guarantee. Until the 1840s, this imprecision was of no practical significance. In the federal system, each state was as republican as its enfranchised citizens wanted it to be in matters of suffrage

qualifications, apportionment, and tax burdens. But in 1842, the Dorr Rebellion implicated the Guarantee Clause as a remedy for disfranchised Rhode Islanders, whose state officials ignored reformist demands to democratize the ossified state constitution.

Though foremost among American states in the Industrial Revolution, Rhode Island suffered from an unusually backward constitutional order derived from the 1663 royal charter, which continued to serve as the state constitution. Severe disfranchisement of the urban population, composed largely of displaced Yankees and recent immigrants drawn to Rhode Island's cities to work in textile mills, was compounded by malapportionment that preserved dominant political power in rural districts. This produced a political anomaly in the period of Jacksonian democracy.

The so-called Dorr Rebellion was precipitated when suffrage reformers, despairing of remedies for disfranchisement and malapportionment from the extant state government, invoked the principles of the Declaration of Independence and attempted, in its words, to "alter or abolish" the oppressive government and "to institute [a] new government."

The reformers called an extralegal constitutional convention, drafted a new state constitution that substantially ameliorated disfranchisement and malapportionment, submitted the document for popular ratification, and held elections under it. A draft constitution submitted by the extant government failed of ratification, but the government refused to cede power, so for a few months in 1842, two opposing governments contended for legitimacy and possession of state offices.

The incumbent governor and legislators, covertly encouraged by President John Tyler's promise of federal military aid should violence occur, declared martial law. State judges convicted the reform governor, Thomas Wilson Dorr, of treason. The U.S. Supreme Court refused Dorr's 1845 appeal (*Ex parte Dorr*) for release on habeas corpus, because the federal writ did not reach state constitutions.

The Dorr supporter Martin Luther brought suit against a militiaman, Luther Borden, who had entered and searched Luther's home under authority of martial law. For Borden and the state, Daniel Webster denied that the Rhode Island situation justified invoking the Constitution's

Guarantee Clause. Luther's counsel claimed that the state's archaic constitutional arrangements prevented fair and peaceful redress of grievances through democratic procedures. Rhode Islanders had therefore exercised Americans' ultimate right inherent in popular sovereignty, that of replacing an oppressive government.

Luther v. *Borden* posed basic questions about the American constitutional order. Was the Supreme Court the appropriate institution to define the substantive content of republicanism? If frustrated in demands for orderly constitutional change, had Americans no alternatives to revolutionary violence? What was essential to a republican form of government?

The Supreme Court, speaking through Chief Justice Roger B. Taney, skirted these difficult questions. Taney articulated the "political questions" doctrine, which diverts responsibility for resolving certain constitutional issues to the legislative and executive branches of government. "The sovereignty in every States resides in the people," he concluded—with an empty concession as to how and whether they had exercised it in the Dorr cause—but "is a political question to be settled by the political power" (p. 47).

□ George M. Dennison, *The Dorr War: Republicanism on Trial, 1831–1861* (1976).
Harold M. Hyman

Lujan v. Defenders of Wildlife, 504 U.S. 555 (1992), argued 3 Dec. 1991, decided 12 June 1992 by a vote of 7 to 2; Scalia for the Court, Kennedy concurring in part joined by Souter, Stevens concurring in the judgment, Blackmun in dissent joined by O'Connor. In *Lujan,* which held that the environmental plaintiffs did not have standing to bring suit, Justice Antonin Scalia articulated his theory of standing as an element of the separation of powers. The Fish and Wildlife Service and National Marine Fisheries Service had rescinded a joint regulation that required federal agencies to coordinate with one of the services if the agency's actions in a foreign nation would affect endangered species. Arguing that the rescission violated the Endangered Species Act, the Defenders of Wildlife sued the agencies under the act's citizen suit provision, which authorizes "any person" to bring an action against any agency or person alleged to be in violation of the act.

Prior cases had established that standing derives from Article III's limitation that federal courts hear only "cases and controversies." One of the requirements for standing is that the plaintiff must demonstrate it is actually suffering or about to suffer injury. The Court held that "congressional conferral upon all persons of an abstract, self-contained, non-instrumental 'right' to have the Executive observe the procedures required by law" (p. 573) does not create a "right" the violation of which satisfies the injury-in-fact requirement of standing. Thus, the citizen suit provision did not suffice to create standing for the plaintiff. In explaining this conclusion, the Court's opinion indicated that the Constitution assigns the President the duty to "take care that the laws be faithfully executed." Were Congress by statute able to create a judicially enforceable right simply to make agencies follow the law, it would be usurping the President's constitutional duty and violating the separation of powers.

Lujan was one of a series of cases that interpreted the requirements of standing strictly and made it more difficult for plaintiffs to bring cases in federal courts. More recently, with the addition of Justices Stephen G. Breyer and Ruth Bader Ginsburg, in *Federal Election Comm'n* v. *Akins* (1998) and *Friends of the Earth* v. *Laidlaw* (2000), the Court applied the standing requirements more liberally.

William Funk

Lynch v. Donnelly, 465 U.S. 668 (1984), argued 4 Oct. 1983, decided 5 Mar. 1984 by vote of 5 to 4; Burger for the Court; O'Connor concurring; Blackmun, Brennan, Marshall, and Stevens in dissent. The city of Pawtucket, Rhode Island, owned and annually erected a Christmas display in its downtown shopping district. The display included, among other things, a Santa's house, a Christmas tree, cutout animal figures, colored lights, and a life-sized nativity scene. The plaintiffs, residents of Pawtucket, alleged that the presence of the nativity scene, or "crèche," in the display demonstrated official support for Christianity, violating the Establishment Clause.

By a five-justice majority, the Court denied the constitutional attack. It rejected the claim that the purpose or primary effect of the crèche's inclusion was to affiliate the city with the Christian beliefs associated with Christmas. Viewing the display within the context of the city's celebration of a national public holiday, the majority concluded that the crèche served the legitimate secular purpose of symbolically depicting

the historical origins of the Christmas holiday. In contrast, five years later, in *Allegheny County v. American Civil Liberties Union
(1989), the Court found the display of the
crèche in a public building, ungarnished
by other holiday decorations, to violate the
Establishment Clause.

Justice Sandra Day O'Connor, supply-
ing the crucial fifth vote, wrote a separate
concurrence rejecting traditional Establishment Clause analysis and substituting the
question whether government intends or is
perceived to endorse religion. This position,
introduced in Lynch, seemed to have gained
majority support in Allegheny County, at
least where the display of religious symbols
is at issue.

Lynch generally signified a reduction
in the separation of church and state, finding instead a constitutional mandate for
religious accommodation.

Stanley Ingber

M

Mahan v. Howell, 410 U.S. 315 (1973), argued 12 Dec. 1972, decided 21 Feb. 1973 by vote of 5 to 3; Rehnquist for the court, Brennan, Douglas, and Marshall in dissent, Powell not participating. This was the first of four cases in 1973 that clarified the permissible range of population equality in designing state legislative and congressional districts. *Mahan* involved a challenge to a 1971 Virginia statute apportioning the lower house of one hundred delegates into a combination of single-member, multi-member, and floater districts. A three-judge federal district court had found the plan unconstitutional because district population deviations ranged from plus 9.6 to minus 6.8 percent. Virginia defended these variances as resulting from a consistently applied state policy of following county and city boundaries, excepting only populous Fairfax County, which was divided into two five-member districts.

In reversing the lower court the Supreme Court repeatedly emphasized the reasoning in *Reynolds* v. *Sims* (1964), which had recognized greater population flexibility for state legislative than for congressional districts. The Court reaffirmed that some deviations from the equal population standard, when based on legitimate considerations of state policy, are constitutionally permissible. The Court concluded that the 16.4 percent total variance range in Virginia "may well approach tolerable limits" but did not exceed them.

Some four months later, the Court handed down the three remaining districting cases of the term, two involving state legislative districts in Connecticut (*Gaffney* v. *Cummings*) and Texas (*White* v. *Regester*). Total population variances were smaller (7.8 and 9.9 percent, respectively) than in Virginia, but not justified as in that state by consistently following local boundaries. The Court shifted the burden of proof to those challenging redistricting acts not exceeding such *de minimis* variances. In *White* v. *Weiser,* a unanimous Court upheld stringent population standards for congressional districts in Texas, following the precedent of *Kirkpatrick* v. *Preisler* (1969).

Gordon E. Baker

Mallory v. United States, 354 U.S. 449 (1957), argued 1 Apr. 1957, decided 24 June 1957 by vote of 9 to 0; Frankfurter for the Court. Although the power of the Supreme Court to overturn state convictions is limited to the enforcement of Fourteenth Amendment due process rights, the Court may formulate rules of evidence in the exercise of its "supervisory power" over the administration of federal criminal justice that go well beyond due process requirements. The best-known example is the McNabb-Mallory rule.

In *McNabb* v. *United States* (1943) the Court held, in the exercise of its supervisory power, that incriminating statements obtained from a suspect during his illegal detention (i.e., while held in violation of federal requirements that an arrestee be promptly brought before a committing magistrate) must be excluded in a federal trial whether or not the statements were made voluntarily. Although heavily criticized by law enforcement officials and members of Congress, the rule was reaffirmed in *Mallory* v. *United States* (1957). There, speaking for a unanimous Court, Justice Felix Frankfurter (author of the original *McNabb* opinion) emphasized that the police should have probable cause before they make an arrest and that it is not their function to arrest people "at large" and to question them later to determine whom they should charge. The decision provoked extreme outrage, particularly in Congress.

The *Mallory* rule offered an alternative to the "voluntariness" test for admitting confessions, but only in the federal courts. Nevertheless, many feared (and others hoped) that some day the Warren Court would impose the rule on the states as a matter of Fourteenth Amendment due process. The Supreme Court never did so. Instead it tackled the problem of confessions in a different way, increasingly resorting to the right to counsel and the privilege against self-incrimination. These efforts culminated in the famous case of *Miranda* v. *Arizona* (1966).

Because the McNabb-Mallory rule was not a constitutional doctrine but only an exercise of the Court's supervisory power, it was always subject to congressional revision or repeal. In 1968, after numerous attempts to do so, Congress finally passed legislation that crippled the rule.

Yale Kamisar

Malloy v. Hogan, 378 U.S. 1 (1964), argued 5 Mar. 1964, decided 15 June 1964 by vote of 5 to 4; Brennan for the Court, Harlan, Clark, Stewart, and White in dissent. Malloy pleaded guilty to taking part in an unlawful gambling operation. Connecticut's Superior Court sentenced him to a year in jail, but after ninety days his prison term was suspended and he was placed on probation for two years. While on probation he was called to testify in a state inquiry into gambling and other crimes. He refused to answer questions relating to his earlier arrest and conviction, citing his Fifth Amendment privilege against self-incrimination. Adjudged in contempt he was imprisoned until he was willing to answer. The Supreme

Court agreed to review the case after state courts had denied the defendant's application for a writ of habeas corpus on federal constitutional grounds.

The Fifth Amendment provides that "no person shall be compelled in any criminal case to be a witness against himself." The privilege was designed originally to protect the individual against the federal government. For decades the Supreme Court refused to impose it on the states. The Court had long adhered to the view that the Due Process Clause of the Fourteenth Amendment, which binds the states, requires only fundamental fairness—meaning the avoidance of cruel or arbitrary procedures—and that a state could try persons fairly and justly without according them a privilege sanctioned by little more than age and tradition.

Malloy's significance lies in the Court's sudden rejection of this older view; seven justices held that the states, through the Fourteenth Amendment, were indeed now bound by the Fifth Amendment's privilege against self-incrimination. *Malloy* thus effectively overruled *Twining* v. *New Jersey* (1908) and *Adamson* v. *California* (1947), cases seemingly reinforced as late as 1961 by *Cohen* v. *Hurley*. In these cases a prosecutor's comment on the failure of an accused to testify in a state proceeding was allowed to stand. The Court was unwilling to require the states to follow the harsh "no comment" rule it had derived from the Fifth Amendment privilege. But now, after *Malloy*, if a person invokes the privilege, all the Fifth Amendment standards that apply in a federal proceeding apply to the states.

This "incorporation" of the Self-Incrimination Clause of the Fifth Amendment into the Fourteenth was foreshadowed by the Court's increasing resolve to overturn state convictions based on confessions elicited by improper methods of influence. The time had come, the Court said, to recognize "that the American system of criminal prosecution is accusatorial, not inquisitorial, and that the Fifth Amendment privilege is its essential mainstay" (p. 7). The Court thus vindicated the right of a witness to remain silent. Unless a person freely chooses to testify, the entire burden of producing evidence to establish guilt shifts to the government.

Justices John M. Harlan and Tom Clark, dissenting, rejected the Court's decision to bind the states to the Fifth Amendment's self-incrimination clause. They would have adhered to the rationale of *Twining* and *Adamson* under which state practices were to be judged in terms of basic principles of justice implicit in the Fourteenth Amendment's Due Process Clause, apart from and independent of the specific—and historically determined—privileges and safeguards laid down in the Bill of Rights. In their view, the Due Process Clause is in its own right an exacting standard of justice whose meaning can and should be derived from accepted and evolving notions of decency in a civilized society. They argued that a discriminatory approach of this kind, which allows the states a good measure of flexibility in meeting the problems of local law enforcement, contributes "to the sound working of our federal system in the field of criminal law" (p. 27).

Justices Byron White and Potter Stewart concurred with the majority's view that the Fourteenth Amendment incorporated the privilege against self-incrimination. They dissented, however, because in their view the facts of the case did not warrant the application of the privilege. Given the inquiry's focus and the nature of the questions asked they felt that the defendant was in no danger of incriminating himself.

Donald P. Kommers

Mapp v. Ohio, 367 U.S. 643 (1961), argued 29 Mar. 1961, decided 19 June 1961, by vote of 5 to 3 to 1; Clark for the Court, Black and Douglas concurring, Harlan, Frankfurter, and Whittaker in dissent, Stewart writing separately. *Mapp* finalized the "incorporation" of Fourth Amendment protections into the Due Process Clause of the Fourteenth Amendment. It required state officers to comply with Fourth Amendment standards when making searches and also extended the Fourth Amendment exclusionary rule to prosecutions in state courts.

In *Wolf* v. *Colorado* (1949), the Court had unanimously expanded the protections afforded by the Due Process Clause of the Fourteenth Amendment by concluding that it did prohibit "arbitrary intrusion" by state police. The Court divided 5 to 4, however, on the exact scope of such protection. Four justices read the Fourteenth Amendment as incorporating all the protections of the Fourth Amendment, thus requiring state officials to comply with Fourth Amendment standards. Justice Felix Frankfurter's majority opinion did not, however, go that far. Although he wrote that due process includes

the "core of the Fourth Amendment," he declined to spell out the exact scope of due process protections applicable to searches (p. 27). He did conclude, however, that the Fourth Amendment exclusionary rule that had been created in *Weeks* v. *United States* (1914) need not be applied in state court proceedings. (The exclusionary rule vote was 6 to 3; Justice Hugo Black joined the majority because he did not think the Fourth Amendment required exclusion.)

Wolf's refusal to apply the exclusionary rule to the states was undermined eleven years later in *Elkins* v. *United States* (1960), in which a 5-to-4 majority concluded that the protections regarding searches afforded by the Due Process Clause were equivalent to those in the Fourth Amendment. (Justice Potter Stewart's majority opinion claimed *Wolf* had reached that conclusion; Frankfurter insisted in dissent that it had not.) Because *Elkins* was not a state prosecution itself, however, it did not provide a vehicle for overturning *Wolf's* refusal to apply the exclusionary rule to the state. The very next year, however, *Mapp* provided such an opportunity.

Seven police officers had broken into and searched Dolly Mapp's home in Cleveland, Ohio. The police claimed they had a warrant but never produced it. They said an informant had told them that a person wanted for a recent bombing was hiding in Mapp's home and also that gambling paraphenalia was being hidden there. In fact, the police found neither during an extensive search. Instead, they found several allegedly obscene books and pictures; Mapp was convicted of possession of obscene literature and imprisoned. In affirming her conviction, the Ohio Supreme Court concluded that, although the search had been "unlawful," *Wolf* nonetheless allowed the admission of the evidence.

In the Supreme Court, Mapp's attorney briefed and argued the case primarily on the obscenity issue. An amicus brief filed by the American Civil Liberties Union also argued, however, that the patently abusive search of Mapp's home by state officers also presented an opportunity to reconsider *Wolf*. Five justices seized that chance.

The voting in *Mapp*, however, was not a simple projection of the lineup a year earlier in *Elkins*. The opinion of the Court was written by Justice Tom Clark, who had dissented in *Elkins*. Clark had adopted the unusual posture of a provocateur with regard to

Wolf—voting in several pre-*Mapp* cases to press *Wolf* to its logical outcomes while hoping that (as he wrote in *Irvine* v. *California*, 1954) "strict adherence to the tenor of [*Wolf*] may produce needed converts for its extinction" (p. 139). On the other hand, Justice Stewart, who authored *Elkins* (and who later wrote that *Elkins* made it inevitable that the exclusionary rule would be applied to the states), refused to join the Court's opinion in *Mapp* because the exclusionary rule issue had not been properly briefed and argued. (During the oral argument, Mapp's attorney had stated that he was not asking the Court to overrule *Wolf*.)

As a result, the deciding vote in *Mapp* fell to Justice Black. Black was a staunch advocate of "incorporation," but his view of the exclusionary rule itself was highly idiosyncratic—in *Wolf* he alone had questioned whether the Fourth Amendment required the *Weeks* exclusionary rule; in *Mapp* he alone concluded that the rule was required only by the Fourth and Fifth Amendments in combination. As a result, the opinion of the Court represented the views of only a four-justice plurality regarding the basis for the exclusionary rule, but a five-justice majority for its application to the states. Thus, although the extension of the exclusionary rule clearly should have been expected to generate political controversy, the prevailing justices apparently paid scant attention to judicial statecraft in deciding the issue in *Mapp*.

Justice Clark offered both "principled" and pragmatic reasons for extending the *Weeks* rule to the states. Although at one point he called the rule a "deterrent safeguard," Clark's opinion largely paralleled the principled rationale offered for the rule in *Weeks*. He described the rule as being required by the Fourth Amendment and stressed that without the rule the Fourth Amendment would be reduced, in Justice Oliver Wendell Holmes's phrase, "to a form of words" (p. 648). Clark noted Justice (then Judge) Cardozo's complaint about the exclusionary rule that "the criminal is to go free because the constable has blundered." He answered, "The criminal goes free if he must, but it is the law that sets him free" (p. 659).

Clark also argued that the pragmatic policy considerations in *Wolf* had proved to be unsound. He noted that the states without exclusionary rules had not developed any effective alternative means of dealing with unreasonable police searches; in fact, several additional state supreme courts had adopted state exclusionary rules in the years since *Wolf*, including the especially influential decision of the California Supreme Court in *People* v. *Cahan* (1955).

The three *Mapp* dissenters (who all had dissented in *Elkins*) continued to reject the incorporation doctrine and, largely for that reason, also rejected the extension of the *Weeks* exclusionary rule to the "soverign judicial system[s]" of the states.

Thomas Y. Davies

Marbury v. Madison, 1 Cranch (5 U.S.) 137 (1803), argued 11 Feb. 1803, decided 24 Feb. 1803 by vote of 5 to 0; Marshall for the Court. *Marbury* was the first Supreme Court case to apply the emergent doctrine of judicial review to a congressional statute. William Marbury had been appointed a justice of the peace in the District of Columbia late in the administration of Federalist President John Adams. Along with a number of other Federalist partisans appointed to federal judgeships, Marbury fell within the group of "midnight judges" targeted for political attack by the incoming Republican administration of Thomas Jefferson. Marbury's signed and sealed commission remained undelivered when the new secretary of state, James Madison, took office. Madison refused to deliver the commission to Marbury, who then invoked the original jurisdiction of the United States Supreme Court, asking that the Court issue a writ of mandamus to Madison, ordering him to deliver the commission.

Congress altered the date of Supreme Court terms, thereby delaying hearing Marbury's case until February 1803. In the interval, the Federalist-sponsored Judiciary Act of 1801 was repealed and circuit judges appointed under its provisions were dismissed. *Stuart* v. *Laird* (1803), a challenge to the discharge of the circuit court judges, was argued on the date *Marbury* was decided. Justice William Paterson upheld the constitutionality of the dismissals. Newly elected Republican legislatures, at both the state and federal levels, were contemplating or bringing impeachment proceedings against Federalist judges. Republicans, including Jefferson himself, believed that, having lost at the polls, the Federalist party intended to frustrate Jeffersonian legislative programs through the power of the judiciary. This charged political atmosphere was aggravated by special circumstances present in Marbury's case. Chief Justice John Marshall had been appointed during the last months of the Adams administration and thus was virtually a "midnight judge" himself. (Ironically, Marshall was also the outgoing Federalist secretary of state who, probably because of an oversight, failed to deliver Marbury's commission.)

In his opinion for the Court, Marshall held that Marbury was entitled to his commission and that Madison had withheld it from him wrongfully. Mandamus was the appropriate remedy at common law, but the question presented was whether it was available under Article III's grant of original jurisdiction to the Supreme Court. To decide that question, Marshall was required to compare the text of Article III with section 13 of the Judiciary Act of 1789, by which Congress authorized the mandamus writ. Finding that the statute conflicted with the federal Constitution, Marshall considered it "the essence of judicial duty" (p. 178) to follow the Constitution. He concluded that "the particular phraseology of the Constitution of the United States confirms and strengthens the principle, supposed to be essential to all written constitutions, that a law repugnant to the constitution is void; and that *courts*, as well as other departments, are bound by that instrument" (p. 180).

Since affirming relief was denied, the decree in *Marbury* was self-executing, and notable as an example of self-restraint in the face of what Marshall described as an arbitrary denial of Marbury's property rights. The opinion also seemed to preach respect for those rights to Jefferson and his subordinates, and it provided the judiciary, both state and federal, with a potent weapon for protecting individual rights against the actions of legislative majorities. At the time, it was attacked in newspaper articles by Judge Spencer Roane of Virginia and Judge John Bannister Gibson of Pennsylvania in *Eakin* v. *Raub* (Pa., 1825). Critics contended then (as now) that the judiciary should not arrogate to itself the right to pass upon the validity of a legislative act. Such thinking, coupled with his personal animosity to Marshall, moved President Jefferson to encourage members of the House of Representatives to begin impeachment proceedings against Justice Samuel Chase during the summer of 1803.

Marbury was not the first case to enunciate the principle of judicial review. Precedents existed in the state courts and in the lower federal courts where judges had refrained from following a law they considered contrary to the provisions of the state or federal constitution. Marshall's was the first statement of the doctrine by the United States Supreme Court. Marshall delineated a comprehensive rationale for the practice of judicial review. He justified it by the concepts of limited government, the written constitution, and the rule of law. Colonial lawyers, most notably James Otis arguing the Writs of Assistance Case in Massachusetts (1761), had drawn upon Sir Edward Coke's statement in *Dr. Bonham's Case* (1610) that parliamentary statutes contrary to custom and right reason were invalid. In *The Federalist*, no. 78 (1788) Alexander Hamilton argued that limited government required that courts of justice be empowered to "declare all acts contrary to the manifest tenor of the Constitution void," and Marshall's opinion in *Marbury* reflected much of Hamilton's reasoning.

Marshall stressed the duty of judges to apply the law to cases before them. Carried to its logical conclusion, this meant that the life, liberty, and property of citizens depended upon the exercise of judicial review as a constitutional check on legislative discretion.

Marbury stands as the classic expression of judicial review in American constitutional law. It embodied what might be called "coordinate branch" judicial review. The more common form of judicial review in the federal system involves the statutes and judicial decisions of the states and the degree to which they conflict with the federal Constitution and thus violate the Supremacy Clause of Article VI. This subordination of state laws to the federal Constitution is what Professor Edward S. Corwin called the "linchpin of the Constitution," without which the federal union would falter.

Marshall's opinion conceded that the federal government has only the limited authority conferred upon it by the terms of the Constitution; all other political power and sovereignty is reserved either to the states or to the people by the Tenth Amendment. Thus concepts of limited government most vigorously circumscribed the powers of the federal government at least before the Civil War. In *Marbury*, Marshall was asked to expand the meaning of the Constitution to permit Congress to grant a mandamus power not expressly given under

Article III. But paradoxically, the authority to exercise judicial review was itself not conferred by any explicit constitutional provision or any act of Congress. The decision asserted one power even as it rejected the proffer of another.

The Court did not again exercise its power of "coordinate branch" judicial review until 1857 when it held the 1820 Missouri Compromise unconstitutional in the case of *Dred *Scott* v. Sandford*. After 1868, judicial review of state statutes and decisions has become more frequent in Supreme Court jurisprudence owing to the expanded functions of the federal government and the creation of American citizenship, with attendant rights under the Fourteenth Amendment. *Dred Scott* undermined a political compromise over slavery's expansion into the territories. It also dealt with the issue of federal jurisdiction—that is, whether diversity of citizenship conferred jurisdiction on the lower federal court over slavery's freedom suits. Chief Justice Roger B. Taney invoked a "higher law" than the Constitution in an effort to defend owners' property rights in slaves, just as antislavery publicists urged moral and natural law principles in support of federal power to abolish or restrict slavery. By 1900, the federal judiciary, led by the Supreme Court, evolved the principle of substantive due process to restrict state and federal legislative power to regulate economic enterprise. This required a broader concept of judicial review than had been provided in *Marbury*.

The Supreme Court's decision in *Cooper* v. Aaron* (1958) marked the high tide of expanded judicial review. Citing *Marbury*, the unanimous Court declared that "the federal judiciary is supreme in the exposition of the law of the Constitution, and that principle has ever since [*Marbury*] been . . . a permanent and indispensible feature of our constitutional system" (p. 18). *Cooper v. Aaron* slighted the fact that presidents have vetoed legislation on constitutional grounds (Andrew Jackson's veto of the Maysville Road bill in 1830 being one example), and that Chief Justice Marshall had always been careful to defer to the political branches—Congress and the president—when important matters of domestic and foreign policy were involved.

Although the significance of *Marbury* has been enlarged over time, the case remains one of the fundamental judicial opinions in American constitutional history. It correctly assessed the role of the judiciary in maintaining constitutional limitations on legislative action; it provided a rationale for subjecting statutes to constitutional examination; it commanded judges to abide by constitutional norms, and it recognized the limited jurisdiction of all federal courts.

□ Robert L. Clinton, *Marbury v. Madison and Judicial Review* (1989). Edward S. Corwin, *John Marshall and the Constitution: A Chronicle of the Supreme Court* (1921). Charles Grove Haines, *The American Doctrine of Judicial Supremacy*, 2nd ed. (1959). George L. Haskins and Herbert A. Johnson, *History of the Supreme Court of the United States*, vol. 2, *Foundations of Power: John Marshall*, 1801–15 (1981).

Herbert A. Johnson

Marshall v. Barlow's, Inc., 436 U.S. 307 (1978), argued 9 Jan. 1978, decided 23 May 1978 by vote of 5 to 3; White for the Court, Blackmun and Stevens in dissent joined by Rehnquist, Brennan not participating. This case involved the constitutionality of a provision in the Occupational Safety and Health Act (OSHA) that permitted inspectors to enter premises without a warrant to inspect for safety hazards and violation of OSHA regulations. The Court held that this provision violated the Fourth Amendment.

One issue was whether a warrant was required. The Court had previously held that no warrant was required to inspect either the premises of a liquor licensee or a licensed gun dealer's storeroom. Distinguishing these earlier cases because each concerned a closely regulated industry, the Court in *Barlow's* concluded that requiring warrants in the OSHA context would not "impose serious burdens on the inspection system or the courts" (p. 316).

As for the grounds to obtain an inspection warrant, *Barlow's* follows the rule in *Camara* v. Municipal Court* (1967) that traditional probable cause is unnecessary if the authorities can show that the contemplated inspection conforms to "reasonable legislative or administrative standards" (p. 538). Thus the Court in *Barlow's* concluded that a warrant "showing that a specific business has been chosen for an OSHA search on the basis of a general administrative plan for the enforcement of the Act derived from neutral sources" (p. 321) would suffice, for it would ensure against arbitrary selection of employers.

Wayne R. LaFave

Martin v. Hunter's Lessee, 1 Wheat. (14 U.S.) 304 (1816), argued 12 Mar. 1816, decided 20 Mar. 1816 by vote of 6 to 0; Story for the Court, Marshall not participating. This case involved the constitutionality of section 25 of the 1789 Judiciary Act, which empowered the Supreme Court to review the final judgments of the highest state courts where federal statutes or treaties were involved, or when a state statute or common law rule had been upheld, though challenged under the federal Constitution. Several states, most notably Virginia, condemned section 25 as an unconstitutional authorization for the federal judiciary to usurp state power. States' rights advocates believed that the Union rested on a compact among the states that granted the central government only limited and enumerated powers.

During the War for American Independence, Virginia enacted legislation confiscating Loyalists' property. Thomas Lord Fairfax, a Loyalist, subsequently devised his vast holdings in the Northern Neck to a British subject, but the property had passed into private hands because of the confiscatory statute. The Fairfax interests challenged the Virginia legislation as inconsistent with the state's obligations under the Treaty of Paris (1783) and Jay's Treaty (1794), which protected Loyalist holdings. In *Fairfax's Devisee* v. *Hunter's Lessee* (1813), Justice Joseph Story sustained the Fairfax interests. (Chief Justice John Marshall did not participate because of pecuniary interest and prior involvement as counsel.) Story's decision fueled already intense criticism of the Court. States' rights advocates, such as Spencer Roane and Thomas Ritchie, claimed that Story had reduced the states to mere administrative units lacking real sovereignty. The Virginia judiciary refused to enter judgment in favor of Fairfax, effectively denying the validity of section 25 of the 1789 Judiciary Act. The Virginia judges stated that they were under no obligation to obey the Supreme Court.

Virginia's intransigence brought the dispute back to the Supreme Court, this time as *Martin* v. *Hunter's Lessee*. Marshall again recused himself, although he played an important behind-the-scenes role. The Chief Justice framed the writ of error that brought the case to the Court and consulted extensively with Joseph Story, who again wrote the Court's opinion.

Story's opinion, the most important of his thirty-four years on the Court, rebuked Virginia for failing to comply with the Court's previous order. Story rejected the compact theory and Virginia's claim that it was equally sovereign with the United States. The American people, Story argued, had created the nation and lodged the national judicial power exclusively in the federal courts. Story sustained section 25 of the 1789 act and insisted that the power to interpret the Constitution had to rest with one ultimate source of authority, which was the United States Supreme Court. He also noted that the national government possessed certain implied powers, a position that Marshall adopted three years later in upholding the Bank of the United States in *McCulloch* v. *Maryland* (1819).

Story's opinion was a landmark in the history of federal judicial supremacy. More than even Marshall, Story upheld federal judicial supremacy over the states. Without Story's decision, the Supremacy Clause of the federal Constitution would have lost much of its salience, since the states would not have been bound to conform their laws to a national constitutional standard.

□ G. Edward White, *History of the Supreme Court of the United States,* vols. 3–4, *The Marshall Court and Cultural Change, 1815–35* (1988).

Kermit L. Hall

Martin v. Mott, 12 Wheat. (25 U.S.) 19 (1827), argued 17 Jan. 1827, decided 2 Feb. 1827 by vote of 7 to 0; Story for the Court.

During the War of 1812, President James Madison ordered some of the states to call out their militias because of the imminent danger of a British invasion. The president acted pursuant to the Enforcement Act of 1795, which Congress had enacted soon after the Whiskey Rebellion in western Pennsylvania in 1795. In compliance with the president's order, Governor Daniel Tompkins of New York ordered certain militia companies to assemble in New York City. Jacob Mott, a private in one of those companies, refused to obey the order. A court martial subsequently imposed a fine of ninety-six dollars for disobedience, which Mott refused to pay. Martin, the United States marshal, seized Mott's goods, whereupon Mott filed a civil suit to recover his property. The New York state courts gave judgment to Mott, and Martin appealed to the U.S. Supreme Court. In a landmark decision that defined the scope of the president's military power, the Supreme Court unanimously overturned the decisions of the states courts. Justice Joseph Story declared that since the president had acted pursuant to a valid exercise of Congress's power under Article I, section 8 (to call out the militia and to regulate its service), the president, as commander in chief, had the sole authority to determine whether the exigency that necessitated his use of statutory authority actually existed. *Martin* v. *Mott* was a major precedent supporting President Abraham Lincoln's decision to act decisively in the early days of the Civil War. The case gave substantive authority to the president as the commander in chief and was the earliest decision in a long line of cases broadly defining the executive power.

George Dargo

Martin v. Wilks, 490 U.S. 755 (1989), argued 18 Jan. 1989, decided 12 June 1989 by vote of 5 to 4; Rehnquist for the Court, Stevens, joined by Brennan, Marshall, and Blackmun, in dissent. A group of African-American firefighters alleged racial discrimination in hiring and promoting by Birmingham, Alabama, and a county personnel board. Before finally approving consent decrees providing for long-term and interim annual goals for the hiring and promotion of African-American firefighters, a federal district court ordered public notice of a hearing on the fairness of the decrees. The Birmingham Firefighters Association (BFA) appeared at the hearing, objected to the decrees, and sought to intervene. The Court denied their motions as untimely. Some other white firefighters, also members of the BFA, then brought a reverse discrimination action against the city and the personnel board. They argued that the consent decree made them victims of racial discrimination because they were being denied promotions in favor of less-qualified blacks.

The Supreme Court posed the issue as being a choice between whether the African-American plaintiffs should have joined all possibly affected parties before entry of the consent decree or whether possibly affected parties should have to seek to intervene in the lawsuit resulting in the consent decree. The Court held that the white firefighters, not having been parties to the original litigation, were not bound by the consent decree. The Court indicated that plaintiffs who seek to alter employment practices are best able to bear the burden of identifying those who might be adversely affected if plaintiffs prevail. Plaintiffs should join such

parties to their lawsuit. Such parties need not seek to intervene. The Civil Rights Act of 1991 limited the scope of *Martin* v. *Wilks* and made it marginally more difficult for third parties to attack hiring and promotion decisions based on employment discrimination consent decrees.

Theodore Eisenberg

Maryland v. Buie, 494 U.S. 325 (1990), argued 4 Dec. 1989, decided 28 Feb. 1990 by vote of 7 to 2; White for the Court, Stevens and Kennedy concurring, Brennan and Marshall in dissent. In *Buie* the Supreme Court considered the level of justification required by the Fourth Amendment before police, while effecting the arrest of a suspect in his home pursuant to an arrest warrant, can conduct a warrantless "protective sweep" of those premises to protect the safety of police officers or others. The Court adopted a two-pronged approach. First, police may always search closets and spaces immediately adjoining the place of arrest from which an attack could be launched. Second, a sweep of other places where a person may be found may be made only under circumstances that would warrant a reasonably prudent officer in believing that the area to be searched harbors an individual posing a danger to arresting officers and others. In **Wilson* v. *Arkansas* (1995) the justices affirmed this rule by holding that police are ordinarily required to know and announce their presence before entering a house to execute a search warrant, but that there may be "reasonable" exceptions to the rule to account for a likelihood of violence or imminent destruction of evidence.

Wayne R. LaFave

Maryland v. Craig, 497 U.S. 836 (1990), argued 18 Apr. 1990, decided 27 June 1990 by vote of 5 to 4; O'Connor for the Court, Scalia, joined by Brennan, Marshall, and Stevens, in dissent. Craig was convicted of child abuse after a trial where the victim testified by one-way closed circuit television, a procedure permitted by state law. The judge, jury, and defendant remained in the courtroom and the child was examined and cross-examined outside of the defendant's presence. On appeal the state court of appeals sided with Craig and questioned the constitutionality of the statute and challenged the procedures. On certiorari to the U.S. Supreme Court, Craig argued that the Sixth Amendment did not permit one-way closed circuit television testimony because it deprived her of an opportunity to confront her accuser.

For the Court, Justice Sandra Day O'Connor held that the Maryland statute did not violate the Sixth Amendment Confrontation Clause because its central purposes were realized in this novel procedure. These included efforts to insure the reliability of evidence, the opportunity to cross-examine witnesses, the taking of an oath, and observation of the witness's demeanor during testimony. Although O'Connor accepted the importance of face-to-face confrontation in criminal trials, she argued that it was not an indispensable element of criminal procedure, especially given the state's interest in protecting child witnesses from the trauma of direct confrontation with the accused. On this point O'Connor maintained that face-to-face confrontation was not an absolute right although the Court had held in Coy v. Iowa (1988) that "the Confrontation Clause guarantees the defendant a face-to-face meeting with witnesses appearing before the trier of fact" (p. 1016).

In dissent, Justice Antonin Scalia argued that the majority was conspicuously failing to sustain a categorical guarantee of the Constitution. He charged that the Court was ignoring explicit constitutional text and substituting "currently favored public policy" in its place (p. 3172). Conceding that society may well favor the use of one-way closed circuit televised testimony for child victims, and even implying that such a procedure may not necessarily be unfair, Scalia nonetheless stressed that it was not one that was permitted by the Constitution. Procedures that realize the intrinsic objectives of the Sixth Amendment's Confrontation Clause, he said, do not compensate for the failure to respect the Constitution's explicitly worded protection.

The controversy generated by the Craig decision will not quickly abate. In a companion case, Idaho v. Wright (1990), the Court ruled, also 5 to 4, that a physician's account of statements offered by an alleged child victim of sexual abuse was not reliable and therefore inadmissible unless such an account fell within a firmly rooted exception to the hearsay rule or was supported by a showing of "particularized guarantees of trustworthiness."

Susette M. Talarico

Massachusetts v. Mellon, 262 U.S. 447 (1923), argued 3 and 4 May 1923, decided 4 June 1923 by vote of 9 to 0; Sutherland for the Court. In 1921 Congress passed the Sheppard-Towner Act, which provided federal grants to promote state infant and maternity care programs. Congress had passed its first grant program, the Weeks Act, in 1911 to encourage state forest fire prevention programs, but there had been no constitutional challenge until Massachusetts attacked the Maternity Act in an original suit, charging that the law and its grants induced states to yield sovereign rights reserved to them and that the burden of taxation fell unequally on its citizens. The Court heard this case in conjunction with *Frothingham v. Mellon,* a taxpayer suit challenging the use of tax revenues for such programs.

Speaking for a unanimous Court, Justice George Sutherland held that the offer of grants did not force the states to do anything or to yield any rights, except if they voluntarily chose to participate in the program. Nor could he find any right of the states that had been threatened by the act that fell within judicial cognizance, and without some specific issue, the Court "is without authority to pass abstract opinions upon the constitutionality of acts of Congress" (p. 485). He found no burden other than that of taxation, which fell not on the states but on their inhabitants, who, as citizens of the United States, were properly subject to federal taxes. Perhaps most important, the Court held that a state could not, in its role of *parens patriae,* institute judicial proceedings to protect its citizens from operation of otherwise valid federal laws.

Melvin I. Urofsky

Massiah v. United States, 377 U.S. 201 (1964), argued 3 Mar. 1964, decided 18 May 1964 by vote of 6 to 3; Stewart for the Court, White in dissent. *Massiah* was decided at a time when the Warren Court's "revolution in American criminal procedure" was accelerating. According to *Massiah,* after the initiation of adversary judicial proceedings (by indictment, as in Massiah's case, or by information, preliminary hearing or arraignment), the Sixth Amendment guarantees a defendant the right to rely on counsel as the "medium" between himself and the government. Thus, once adversary proceedings have begun, the government cannot bypass the defendant's lawyer and deliberately elicit statements from the defendant himself.

The Burger Court revived and even expanded the *Massiah* doctrine in *Brewer* v. *Williams* (1977) and *United States* v. *Henry* (1980). As a result, the doctrine has become a more potent force than it had ever been during the Warren Court years.

After he had been indicted for federal narcotics violations, Winston Massiah retained a lawyer, pled not guilty, and was released on bail. Jesse Colson, a codefendant who had also pled not guilty and been released on bail, invited Massiah to discuss the pending case in Colson's car. Unknown to Massiah, his codefendant had become a government agent and had hidden a radio transmitter in his car. The Massiah-Colson conversation was broadcast to a nearby federal agent. As expected, Massiah made several incriminating statements.

The *Massiah* facts are a far cry from a typical confession case. *Massiah* was neither in "custody" nor subjected to "police interrogation" as that term is normally used. Indeed, Massiah thought he was simply talking to a friend and a partner in crime. Nevertheless, a 6-to-3 majority held that the defendant's statements could not be used against him at his trial. The decisive feature of the case was that after adversary proceedings had commenced against the defendant, and therefore at a time when he was entitled to a lawyer's help, the government had deliberately set out to elicit incriminating statements from him in the absence of counsel. This constituted a violation of the defendant's Sixth Amendment right to counsel.

The government argued that there was reason to think that Massiah was part of a large, well-organized drug ring and that therefore it was entirely proper for federal agents to continue their investigation of him and his alleged confederates even though he had already been indicted. The Supreme Court responded that, even though the police were justified in investigating other crimes when they obtained Massiah's statements, the defendant's own incriminating statements *pertaining to charges pending against him* could not be used at the trial of those charges. On the other hand, evidence pertaining to new crimes as to which the Sixth Amendment right to counsel had not attached at the time the evidence was obtained would be admissible even though other charges against the defendant were pending at the time. This approach was reaffirmed in *Maine* v. *Moulton* (1985).

Although overshadowed by, and often confused with *Miranda* v. *Arizona* (1966), the *Massiah* doctrine is a separate and distinct rule, and it supplements *Miranda* in important respects. *Miranda* is based on the privilege against compelled self-incrimination and the now-familiar *Miranda* warnings are required when a suspect is subjected to custodial police interrogation, which the Warren Court deemed inherently coercive. *Massiah* is based on the right to counsel. Its application turns not on the conditions surrounding police questioning, but on whether, at the time the government attempts to elicit incriminating statements from an individual, the criminal proceedings against that individual have reached the point at which the Sixth Amendment right to counsel attaches.

The difference between *Massiah* and *Miranda* is underscored by the "jail plant" situation, the case where a secret government agent is placed in the same cell with a person and instructed to induce him to implicate himself in the crime for which he has been incarcerated. *Miranda* does not apply, for the inherent coercion generated by custodial police interrogation is not present when a prisoner speaks freely to a person he believes to be a fellow inmate. Coercion is determined from the perspective of the suspect. Therefore, unless a person realizes he is dealing with a government agent, the government's efforts to elicit damaging admissions from him do not constitute "police interrogation" within the meaning of *Miranda*.

However, the *Massiah* doctrine would prohibit the government from using such tactics if adversary proceedings had already been initiated against the person, as the Court held in *United States* v. *Henry* (1980). But the secret government agent was not completely passive in that case; he stimulated conversations about the crime charged. The Court, however, has permitted the government to place a completely "passive listener" in a person's cell and use the statements acquired by such an agent even though adversary proceedings have commenced against the person. The line between "active" and "passive" agents—between eliciting incriminating statements and merely listening—is an exceedingly difficult one to draw.

□ Yale Kamisar, *Police Interrogation and Confessions* (1980) Welsh White, "Interrogation without Questions: *Rhode Island* v. *Innis* and

United States v. *Henry," Michigan Law Review* 78 (August 1980): 12k9–1251.

Yale Kamisar

Masson v. New Yorker Magazine, Inc., 501 U.S. 496 (1991), argued 14 Jan. 1991, decided 20 June 1991 by vote of 7 to 2; Kennedy for the Court, White, joined by Scalia, in partial dissent. In *Masson* the Supreme Court had to decide an unusual issue for the first time: the extent to which a journalist's "deliberate alteration" of an interviewee's words is protected by the First Amendment. Janet Malcolm had altered the words of a psychiatrist in an allegedly libelous manner. One of the six passages considered by the Court mistakenly quoted Dr. Jeffrey Masson describing himself as an "intellectual gigolo." The district court rendered summary judgment in favor of the *New Yorker* with respect to all of the contested alterations. The Court of Appeals for the Ninth Circuit affirmed, ruling in the *New Yorker's* favor by applying a "substantial truth" test to the alterations: they were protected by the First Amendment so long as they were "rational interpretations" of the actual statements. The Supreme Court reversed.

Under the prevailing First Amendment standards established in **New York Times* v. *Sullivan* (1964), libelous remarks about public figures are not actionable unless they are made with "knowledge of falsity" or "reckless disregard" of the truth (pp. 279–280). After acknowledging that alterations of quotations could harm reputation, Justice Anthony Kennedy rejected Masson's argument that any alteration other than grammatical or syntactical changes constitutes knowledge of falsity; such "technical distinctions" are "unworkable" (p. 2432). He also rejected the Court of Appeals' standard for encouraging journalistic irresponsibility.

Instead, the Court ruled that a deliberate alteration constituted knowledge of falsity if it "results in a material change in the meaning conveyed by the statement" (p. 2433). Applying this test, the majority held that most of the contested passages created issues of fact for the jury as to truth or falsity, and remanded the case.

In partial dissent, Justice Byron White agreed with the reversal, but argued that the majority's test permitted irresponsibility. Malcolm's alterations, in his judgment, amounted to falsehood "by any definition of the term" (p. 2437).

Donald A. Downs

Maxwell v. Dow, 176 U.S. 581 (1900), argued 4 Dec. 1899, decided 26 Feb. 1900 by vote of 8 to 1; Peckham for the Court, Harlan in dissent. Charles L. Maxwell challenged his conviction for robbery on two grounds: use of an information rather than indictment by a grand jury to initiate a prosecution; and trial before a jury of eight, not twelve. Both grounds, according to Maxwell, violated his privileges and immunities as protected by the Fifth and Fourteenth Amendments. He also argued that conviction by an eight-member jury violated the due process guaranteed by the Fourteenth Amendment.

Justice Rufus W. Peckham brusquely dismissed Maxwell's arguments and upheld the conviction, noting that the issues had been resolved in prior decisions. With that assertion, the Court continued to minimize the scope of the Privileges and Immunities Clause, a process begun in the **Slaughterhouse Cases* (1873). Any other approach, Peckham reasoned, relying on the pre-Civil War case of *Corfield* v. *Coryell* (Pa., 1823), would so "fetter and degrade the state governments by subjecting them to the control of Congress" as to violate "the structure and spirit of our institutions" (p. 590). Thus, in the Court's view, the states remained the primary protectors of most rights.

Justice John Marshall Harlan's dissent was a paean to the jury. He emphasized that at a minimum the Bill of Rights identified the privileges and immunities that the Fourteenth Amendment protected. Harlan therefore concluded that the states could not avoid the Sixth Amendment's guarantee of a trial by a jury of twelve members. He reached the same conclusion about due process, foreshadowing the Court's gradual incorporation of the Bill of Rights into the Fourteenth Amendment after World War II.

Walter F. Pratt, Jr.

McCardle, Ex parte, 74 U.S. 506 (1869), argued 2–4 and 9 Mar. 1868, decided 12 Apr. 1869 by vote of 8 to 0; Chase for the Court, Wayne had died. A product of the often-strained relations between the Supreme Court and Congress during Reconstruction, the *McCardle* case posed fundamental questions concerning Congress's ability to use its authority over the Court's appellate jurisdiction to curb judicial independence.

In late 1867, army officials responsible for administering Reconstruction in Mississippi arrested William McCardle, a Vicksburg editor, charging him with publishing libelous editorials that incited insurrection. Invoking the authority conferred by the Reconstruction Act (1867), they ordered McCardle tried by military commission. The editor challenged the government's action, asserting that *Ex parte *Milligan* (1866) precluded military trial of civilians when the civil courts were open and that the Reconstruction Act was therefore unconstitutional. Relying on the Habeas Corpus Act of 1867, which directed federal courts to issue writs of habeas corpus in cases involving persons who were confined in violation of their constitutional rights, he sought relief in the United States circuit court. When that tribunal rejected his argument, McCardle invoked a provision of the Habeas Corpus Act allowing the Supreme Court to hear appeals in habeas corpus, bringing the politically explosive question of the Reconstruction Act's constitutionality before the high court.

Republican leaders in Congress feared that the Court might strike down the act and destroy the party's Reconstruction program. Consequently, in March 1868, after the Court had heard arguments but before it had rendered a decision, Congress struck at the Court's jurisdiction by repealing the provision of the Habeas Corpus Act allowing appeals to the Supreme Court. Although Justices Robert C. Grier and Stephen J. Field wished to decide the case before Congress enacted the repeal, the majority rejected such a course. With the end of the Court's term approaching, the justices agreed to hold the case over until the next term.

When the Court issued its opinion, it bowed to Congress, dismissing the case for want of jurisdiction without passing judgment on the Reconstruction Act. Chief Justice Salmon P. Chase pointed out that the Constitution provided that the Court was to exercise its appellate jurisdiction "with such exceptions, and under such regulations as the Congress shall make." Because Congress possessed express authority to make exceptions to the Court's appellate jurisdiction, he continued, the 1868 repeal measure was constitutional, regardless of Congress's motive. Consequently, the Court had no jurisdiction to hear McCardle's appeal and must dismiss the case.

Although sometimes viewed as an example of the Reconstruction Court's supineness, *McCardle* actually suggests its resiliency. In concluding his opinion, Chase pointedly noted that while Congress had repealed the provision of the Habeas Corpus Act on which McCardle had relied, this did not affect the jurisdiction that the Court possessed under other statutes. This was a thinly veiled reference to the Judiciary Act of 1789, which authorized the Court to issue writs of habeas corpus to persons held under federal authority. Several months later, in *Ex parte Yerger* (1869), the Court agreed to hear a challenge to the Reconstruction Act brought under the 1789 statute by a Mississippi civilian who was charged with the murder of an army officer and held for trial by a military court. Although the Court again failed to reach the merits, its willingness to accept jurisdiction suggests that it had not been overawed.

McCardle has never been repudiated by the Court and has been read by some authorities to suggest unlimited congressional authority over the Court's jurisdiction. Indeed, some politicians have used it to support legislation prohibiting the Court from rendering unpopular decisions on controversial matters such as school prayer and busing. Others disagree, arguing that the case should not be read to permit Congress to use its authority to regulate the Court's jurisdiction to shield government policies from judicial review. They point out that in *McCardle*, because the avenue provided by the Judiciary Act remained open, the Court did not accept congressional action denying the federal courts authority to hear challenges to the Reconstruction Act. Moreover, they note that in *U.S. v. Klein* (1872), the Court limited Congress's authority, holding that it may not limit the Court's jurisdiction to control the results of a particular case.

□ Charles Fairman, *History of the Supreme Court of the United States*, vol. 6, *Reconstruction and Reunion, 1868–88. Part I* (1971).

Donald G. Nieman

McCleskey v. Kemp, 481 U.S. 279 (1987), argued 15 Oct. 1986, decided 22 Apr. 1987 by vote of 5 to 4; Powell for the Court, Brennan in dissent joined by Marshall, Blackmun, and Stevens; Blackmun in dissent joined by Marshall, Stevens, and Brennan; Stevens in dissent joined by Blackmun. Warren McCleskey, a black man, was convicted and sentenced to death for the 1978 murder of a white Atlanta police officer. On appeal, attorneys for the Legal Defense Fund argued that the Georgia death penalty statute was being implemented in a racially discriminatory fashion in violation of the Eighth and Fourteenth Amendments.

McCleskey's claim rested on a sophisticated study of Georgia death sentencing patterns conducted by Professor David Baldus. The study examined more than two thousand Georgia murders from the 1970s. Some 230 variables were analyzed for their ability to predict death sentencing. Other factors being equal, Baldus found the odds of a death sentence for those accused of killing whites were 4.3 times higher than the odds of a death sentence for those charged with killing blacks.

Justice Lewis Powell's majority opinion rejected McCleskey's claim. He suggested that the Baldus data should be presented to legislative bodies, rather than to the courts. To prevail under the Equal Protection Clause of the Fourteenth Amendment, McCleskey needed to prove that either the Georgia Legislature or the decision makers in his specific case acted with a discriminatory purpose. Nor could McCleskey prevail under the Cruel and Unusual Punishment Clause of the Eighth Amendment, Powell said, since the disparities in the treatment of homicide cases revealed in the Baldus study did not offend "evolving standards of decency."

The dissenting justices relied primarily on the Eighth Amendment, arguing that demonstration of a significant risk of discrimination, rather than definitive proof of its existence, is all that is needed to show a constitutional violation.

The Court rejected a second habeas corpus petition filed by McCleskey four years later in *McCleskey* v. *Zant* (1991).

Michael L. Radelet

McCleskey v. Zant, 111 S.Ct. 1454 (1991), argued 30 Oct. 1990, decided 16 Apr. 1991 by vote of 6 to 3; Kennedy for the Court, Marshall in dissent, joined by Blackmun and Stevens. Warren McCleskey's first challenge to his death sentence for murder was rejected by the Supreme Court in *McCleskey* v. *Kemp* (1987). Four years later he filed a second habeas corpus petition alleging that before his trial the state of Georgia had improperly induced him to make incriminating statements without the assistance of counsel. These statements (conversations with a fellow prisoner) were used against him at trial. The Court's decision, rejecting this claim, clarifies the standard for determining

"abuse of the writ" and substantially narrows the possibility of habeas corpus relief in death penalty cases.

Claims deliberately abandoned in earlier petitions for a writ and included in a subsequent petition clearly constitute abuse of the writ, as do those omitted through inexcusable neglect. To avoid this, in second and later petitions the defendant must show cause, that is, he must show that his failure to raise the claim earlier was impeded by factors beyond his control. He must also show that the errors of which he complains resulted in actual prejudice. The only exception to this "cause and prejudice" standard is when the presented claim reveals an error so fundamental that the conviction came despite the petitioner's factual innocence.

McCleskey supported his allegation of the state's involvement in eliciting his harmful statements only after his first petition for habeas corpus, but the Supreme Court held that the facts of the trial should have put him on notice that the claim should have been pursued immediately. Nor did McCleskey show that the alleged violation resulted in the conviction of an innocent defendant. Hence, relief was denied. McCleskey was executed on 25 September 1991.

Michael L. Radelet

McConnell v. Federal Election Commission, 540 U.S. 93 (2003), argued 8 Sept. 2003, decided 10 Dec. 2003 by vote of 5 to 4; Stevens and O'Connor for the Court, joined by Souter, Ginsberg, and Breyer (Titles I and II). Rehnquist for the Court (Titles III and IV), joined by in whole or part by O'Connor, Scalia, Kennedy, Souter, Stevens, Ginsberg, Breyer, and Thomas. Breyer for the Court (Title V), joined by Stevens, O'Connor, Souter, and Ginsberg. Scalia, Kennedy, Rehnquist, Thomas, Stevens, Ginsberg, and Breyer in dissent in various parts.

The 298-page opinion does not lend itself to easy summarization, but it did uphold two key provisions of the Bicameral Campaign Reform Act of 2002 (BCRA): the control of "soft money" and the regulation of "issue ads."

The historical evolution of national campaign finance law is well-known. Corporate contributions had been regulated since the 1900s; union contributions had been controlled since World War II. In *Buckley* v. *Valeo*, the Court reviewed the Federal Election Campaign Act Amendments of 1974, in particular their attempt to staunch the flow of money through political action committees (PACs). The justices upheld contribution limits, but struck down, on First Amendment grounds, limits on candidate and individual expenditures. The purpose of BCRA Title I was to take national parties out of the soft-money business. To rebut the appellant's First Amendment, federalism, and equal protection objections, the Court reasoned its way to two important conclusions: (1) contribution limits only marginally restrain free speech and association; and (2) not "strict scrutiny" but a less rigorous "closely drawn" standard would apply in reviewing BCRA's regulation of the electoral process. For the majority, congressional findings showing the influence of soft money on legislative calendaring, access to elected officials, and non-passage of social legislation met the "closely drawn" standard. These findings overcame Justice Anthony Kennedy's dissent that only quid pro quo corruption warranted regulation. BCRA (as qualified by the so-called Levin Amendments) could therefore also reach state committee activities regarding voter registration, voter identification, get-out-the-vote drives, and generic campaign efforts.

Title II of BCRA coined a new term, "electioneering communications," to respond to a statutory, not constitutional, interpretation in *Buckley* that had differentiated "express advocacy" (vote for Doe) from "issue ads" (Doe is soft on crime). The substance of a political communication, not its "magic words," was a proper legislative concern; the Court upheld dollar and timing limits on how electioneering communications could be made.

Titles III and IV (1) amended the Communications Act of 1934 to require broadcasters, forty-five days before a primary and sixty days before a general election, to sell qualified candidates "lowest unit charge" time for equivalent slots; (2) prescribed inflation index and periodic increases to contribution limit amounts; and (3) enacted "millionaire provisions" that allowed staggered contribution increases when triggered by an opponent's personal fund spending. Because the appellants claimed these provisions would impair their ability to run in future elections, these challenges were dismissed for lack of standing. To guard against perceived "corruption by conduit," BCRA section 318 prohibited contributions by minors. Because

the government provided "scant evidence" of any such abuse, this provision was invalidated on First Amendment grounds.

Title V amended the Communications Act to require broadcasters to keep publicly available certain political broadcast request records. The Court sustained these provisions because they were "virtually identical" to existing FCC recordkeeping regulations and any incremental burdens could be addressed by the FCC's rule-making and rule-enforcement authority.

The dissenters claimed that the majority erred in not applying a "strict scrutiny" standard and sustaining the First Amendment challenges. Justice Antonin Scalia addressed three "fallacies" that purportedly justified BCRA: (1) money is not speech (it is): (2) pooling money is not speech (it is by association); and (3) speech by corporations can be abridged (it cannot). Moreover, Congress had no reason to bemoan the vast amounts spent on elections. In the 2000 elections, a total of $2.4 billion was spent in hard and soft money. That figure paled in comparison with what America spent on movies ($7.8 billion) and cosmetics and perfume ($18.8 billion). Justice Scalia wrote, "If our democracy is drowning from this much spending, it cannot swim."

In concluding its Title I and II analysis, the Court conceded BCRA might not be the last word on national campaign election law.

George T. Anagnost

McCray v. United States, 195 U.S. 27 (1904), argued 2 Dec. 1903, decided 31 May 1904 by vote of 6 to 3; White for the Court, Fuller, Peckham, and Brown in dissent. In 1886, Congress passed legislation based on the taxing power to regulate the production of oleomargarine. Enacted to prevent product adulteration, the law also reflected industrial competition. McCray was fined fifty dollars for violating the law by purchasing for resale artificially colored oleo at the lower tax rate applied to the uncolored variety. The significant constitutional challenges claimed inappropriate use of the taxing power for regulation rather than for revenue; violation of the due process and taking of property clauses of the Fifth Amendment; and violation of states' rights to regulate business under the Tenth Amendment.

Justice Edward D. White argued vigorously against judicial interference with the powers of Congress, especially since an excise tax violated no expressed constitutional limitations on the taxing power. Nor did the Fifth and Tenth Amendments vitiate the original grant of the tax power. Due process was not violated when Congress categorized and taxed products to prevent fraud. Citing *McCulloch* v. *Maryland* (1819), White declined to hold the tax unconstitutional because of its potential negative impact on production of oleomargarine. Reserving the right to inquire into abuses, the Court sustained broad use of the taxing power for purposes beyond revenue raising.

McCray established the taxing power as an additional base for exercise of a federal police power. Constricted in the 1920s, the tax power was nevertheless reclaimed by the New Deal as a basis for general welfare legislation.

Barbara C. Steidle

McCreary County v. American Civil Liberties Union of Kentucky, 545 U.S. 844 (2005), argued 2 Mar. 2005, decided 27 June 2005 by vote of 5 to 4; Souter for the Court, O'Connor concurring, Scalia in dissent, joined by Rehnquist, Thomas, and Kennedy in part. Two Kentucky counties installed large framed copies of the Ten Commandments in their courthouses, accompanied by framed copies of other American historical documents. The American Civil Liberties Union (ACLU) challenged the displays under the Establishment Clause of the First Amendment. Originally, the displays included only framed copies of the Ten Commandments, which McCreary County hung in response to a legislative order, and which Pulaski Country hung in a ceremony that included statements of a religious nature, including some spoken by a pastor.

After the ACLU filed suit, the legislatures of both counties, in order to reflect the view that the Ten Commandments are the foundation for the laws of Kentucky, ordered new displays that included eight government documents with religious references. They also issued statements effectively endorsing the right to publicly acknowledge God. After the district court entered preliminary injunctions against the displays, the counties changed the displays to include additional government documents with religious references in an attempt to show that the Ten Commandments are a foundation of American law and government. The district court extended the injunctions to these displays as well.

Writing for the Supreme Court majority, Justice David H. Souter held that the displays violated the Establishment Clause. He evaluated them under the test from *Lemon* v. *Kurtzman* (1971), part of which asks whether governmental action has a secular legislative purpose. Souter refused to jettison purpose analysis or see it as requiring the Court to analyze the actual intent of the legislature. Asking instead whether an objective observer would perceive the displays as manifesting a predominantly religious purpose, he observed that the displays were part of the Judeo-Christian religious tradition and emphasized a religious message. Souter concluded that an objective observer would not be swayed by the later efforts to include other government documents. The counties did not disclaim the prior religious message, he noted, and the newest displays were too selective, leaving out many documents important to the foundation of American law but including those that validated the religious message of the Ten Commandments. Justice Sandra Day O'Connor concurred, stressing that the displays conveyed a message of religious endorsement. Justice Breyer joined the majority to invalidate the displays here, but voted with a different majority, comprised of the dissenters in this case, to uphold a Ten Commandments display in a case decided the same day, Van Orden v. Perry. He did not regard that display as having a similar history of religious endorsement.

Justice Antonin Scalia dissented, joined by Chief Justice William H. Rehnquist, Justice Clarence Thomas, and, in part, Justice Anthony M. Kennedy. Scalia rejected the notion that the Establishment Clause prohibits any public acknowledgment of God. He also contended that the displays were constitutional even under *Lemon*'s purpose prong, because: (1) no observers would find them noteworthy, and (2) the counties' earlier religious motivations were irrelevant.

Lisa Bressman

McCulloch v. Maryland, 4 Wheat. (17 U.S.) 316 (1819), argued 22 Feb.-3 Mar. 1819, decided 6 Mar. 1819 by vote of 7 to 0; Marshall for the Court. *McCulloch* was one of Chief Justice John Marshall's most important decisions, and among his most eloquent. It settled the meaning of the Necessary and Proper Clause of the United States Constitution and determined the distribution of powers between the federal government and the states. The specific issues involved were Congress's power to incorporate the Second Bank of the United States and the right of a state to tax an instrument of the federal government.

Background. The constitutionality of the power of Congress to charter a corporation had been the source of debate ever since Alexander Hamilton proposed the creation of the First Bank of the United States in 1791. James Madison in Congress and Thomas Jefferson in George Washington's cabinet opposed the measure as unauthorized by the Constitution. But Congress and Washington sided with Hamilton, who justified it by a loose construction of the Constitution, and Congress chartered the Bank for a twenty-year period. In 1811 a Jeffersonian-dominated Congress refused to renew the charter, primarily on constitutional grounds, and the First Bank quietly expired. However, following five years of inflation and economic chaos that coincided with the War of 1812, Congress, though still under Jeffersonian control, reversed itself and chartered the Second Bank of the United States in 1816. Despite this, many Jeffersonians continued to oppose the Bank. They viewed it as unconstitutional and denied its economic necessity. Several states, including Ohio, Kentucky, Pennsylvania, Maryland, North Carolina, and Georgia, adopted laws taxing its branches. An 1818 Maryland statute imposed a tax on all banks operating in the state "not chartered by the legislature." The Baltimore branch of the Bank, headed by its cashier, James McCulloch, refused to pay the tax. The Baltimore County Court upheld the state law. This judgment was quickly affirmed by the Court of Appeals of Maryland and was appealed to the United States Supreme Court, on a writ of error. The Supreme Court declared the Maryland tax unconstitutional and void.

Opinion of the Court. In rendering his opinion for the entire Supreme Court, Marshall first considered the question "has Congress power to incorporate a bank?" (p. 401). To answer this, he looked to the origins and nature of the federal union. The Constitution had been submitted to the people and ratified by specially elected conventions. As a consequence, "the government proceeds directly from the people; is 'ordained and established' in the name of the people" (p. 403). By asserting this, Marshall offered a nationalist alternative to the theory of the origins of the union propounded by Jeffersonians in the Kentucky and Virginia Resolutions of 1798–1799, which claimed that the federal government was a product of a compact of the states and had only specifically granted and limited power. "The government of the Union," Marshall argued in clear and strong terms, ". . . is, emphatically, and truly, a government of the people. In form and in substance it emanates from them. Its powers are granted by them, and are to be exercised directly on them, and for their benefit" (pp. 404–405).

Like Hamilton before him, Marshall resorted to a loose interpretation of the Constitution to justify Congress's authority to create the Second Bank of the United States. Marshall admitted that the federal government was one of enumerated powers and could only exercise those powers granted to it. But, he added, there could be no doubt "that the government of the Union, though limited in its powers, is supreme within its sphere of action" (p. 405). He observed that although the power to charter a corporation is not a specifically enumerated power, there is nothing in the Constitution that excludes it. This included the Tenth Amendment, which, unlike a predecessor provision in the Articles of Confederation, did not include the word "expressly" and therefore allowed "incidental or implied powers." Marshall further observed that the federal government was not established by a complex legal code, excessively detailed in a vain attempt to meet every exigency. Rather, the Constitution contained only a general outline of the federal government's structure and powers, in which only its most important objects were designated while the rest of its powers were to "be deduced from the nature of the objects themselves" (p. 407). He concluded, "we must never forget that it is a constitution we are expounding" (p. 407).

From these premises about the origins and nature of the Constitution, Marshall proceeded to justify the creation of the Bank of the United States. The Constitution had delegated certain specified powers to the federal government: to lay and collect taxes, to borrow money, to regulate commerce, to declare and conduct war, and to raise and support armies and navies. It was in the best interests of the nation, the chief justice observed, that Congress should have the means to exercise these delegated powers. In particular, the Bank was a convenient, useful, and essential instrument in the implementation of the nation's fiscal policies.

Since the Constitution had given Congress the power to "make all Laws which shall be necessary and proper for carrying into execution the forgoing Powers," the Bank of the United States was constitutional.

Marshall elaborated on the need for a loose and expansive interpretation of the powers of the federal government. He rejected the idea of a strict interpretation of the Constitution then espoused by states' rights Jeffersonians. Such a reading of the Constitution would make it unworkable. Marshall argued that the Necessary and Proper Clause had been included among the powers of Congress, not among its limitations, and was meant to enlarge, not reduce, the ability of Congress to execute its enumerated powers. Marshall declared:

Let the end be legitimate, let it be within the scope of the constitution, and all means which are appropriate, which are plainly adapted to that end, which are not prohibited, but consist with the letter and spirit of the constitution, are constitutional. (p. 421)

Marshall next addressed the issue "whether the state of Maryland may, without violating the Constitution," tax a branch of the Bank of the United States (p. 425). Since the Constitution and federal law were supreme under the Supremacy Clause of Article VI, they took precedence over the laws of the states. The state power to tax, important and vital as it was, is subordinate to the Constitution. A state cannot tax those subjects to which its sovereign powers do not extend. Marshall pointed out "that the power to tax involves the power to destroy" (p. 431). If a state had power to tax the bank, it could also tax other agencies of the federal government: the mail, the mint, patents, the customs houses, and the federal courts. In this manner the states could totally defeat "all the ends of government" determined by the people when they created the United States Constitution (p. 432). "This," Marshall observed, "was not intended by the American people. They did not design to make their government dependent on the states" (p. 432).

Impact and Reaction. The decision was controversial. Opponents of the Bank remained irreconcilable. They did not view the Bank primarily as an agency of the federal government. To them it was a profit-making corporation that performed a few government services. The Second Bank had been capitalized at $35 million. Eighty percent of its stock (on which substantial dividends were paid) was in private hands, and shareholders appointed four-fifths of the board of directors.

Critics of the decision also denounced Marshall's ringing endorsement of a broad interpretation of the power of the federal government. Most proponents of states' rights in Virginia had doubts about the bank's constitutionality, but in 1816 they had accepted the argument that it was needed to restore financial stability. Unlike the Bank's opponents in several other states, the advocates of local government in Virginia never tried to tax the Bank out of existence. They were troubled not that the court had upheld the constitutionality of the Bank, but that it had justified loose and expansive interpretation of the Constitution. Thomas Jefferson privately encouraged public opposition to the decision. John Taylor published an important book, *Construction Construed* (1820), denouncing the decision, and Virginia jurists Spencer Roane and William Brockenbrough wrote a series of essays for the *Richmond Enquirer* condemning the broad implications of the Court's ruling. Marshall personally responded to Roane in a series of anonymous newspaper articles upholding his own handiwork.

Critics of the decision also included James Madison, who as president of the United States (1809–1817) had signed the bill creating the Second Bank of the United States into law, and who generally supported most of the Supreme Court's nationalist rulings during the second decade of the nineteenth century. Despite this, he believed "that the occasion did not call for the general and abstract doctrine interwoven with the decision of the particular case." The real danger of Marshall's decision, Madison believed, was "the high sanction given to a latitude in expounding the Constitution which seems to break down the landmarks intended by a specification of the powers of Congress, and to substitute for a definite connection between means and ends, a legislative discretion as to the former to which no practical limit can be assigned." Among other things, the decision seemed to sanction a federal program of internal improvements. Such a program would have involved not only the building of roads, canals, and bridges, but also an assortment of educational, scientific, and literary institutions throughout the country. Both Jefferson and Madison favored such a program on policy grounds, but believed the jurisdictional problems raised by it were so complex and controversial that they could only be clarified through an amendment to the Constitution. In his *McCulloch* v. *Maryland* decision, Marshall aligned the U.S. Supreme Court with those aggressive nationalists like Henry Clay, John C. Calhoun, and John Quincy Adams, who argued that a constitutional amendment was not necessary since Congress already had power to enact such a program.

The Bank's victory in *McCulloch* v. *Maryland* turned out to be short-lived. In 1828 states' rights as a political movement triumphed with the election of Andrew Jackson to the presidency. Rejecting the binding quality of *McCulloch* v. *Maryland* and building on the lingering resentment that continued toward the Bank, Jackson in 1832 vetoed a bill to recharter it, on constitutional grounds. In a series of other vetoes, Jackson also effectively finished off any hope for a federal program of internal improvements. Despite this, Marshall's broad interpretation of the Necessary and Proper Clause as well as his view of the origins and nature of the federal union were ultimately to triumph on a more significant level. The Civil War brought an end to Jacksonian hegemony and discredited states' rights. The constitutional revolution that followed took the country in a strong nationalist direction. In the twentieth century *McCulloch* v. *Maryland* quickly became the virtually undisputed constitutional cornerstone for the federal government's broad involvement in the economy, for the New Deal and the Welfare State, and for various other social, scientific, and educational programs.

□ Gerald Gunther, ed., *John Marshall's Defense of McCulloch v. Maryland* (1969). Bray Hammond, *Banks and Politics in America from the Revolution to the Civil War* (1957). Harold J. Plous and Gordon E. Baker, "McCulloch v. Maryland: Right Principle, Wrong Case," *Stanford Law Review* 9 (1957):710–739. G. Edward White, *History of the Supreme Court of the United States*, vols. 3–4, *The Marshall Court and Cultural Change, 1815–35* (1988).

Richard E. Ellis

McKeiver v. Pennsylvania, 403 U.S. 528 (1971), argued 9–10 Dec. 1970, decided 21 June 1971 by vote of 6 to 3; Blackmun for the Court, White and Harlan concurring separately, Brennan concurring in part and dissenting in part, Douglas, Black, and Marshall in dissent. When the Supreme Court decided *In re *Gault* (1967) and applied criminal due process guarantees to state juvenile proceedings, the Sixth Amendment's right to trial by jury had not yet been "incorporated" into the Fourteenth Amendment. *Duncan* v. *Louisiana* (1968) accomplished that for adult criminal defendants but left open the question of whether juvenile defendants also had this right. *McKeiver*, actually several cases involving juvenile procedures in North Carolina and Pennsylvania, answered this question in the negative.

Justice Harry Blackmun, writing for a plurality of four justices, narrowly interpreted *Gault* and the previous term's *In re *Winship* (1970) as establishing only a standard of "fundamental fairness" to define due process in juvenile proceedings. Accordingly, the importance of the right to trial by jury in juvenile adjudications was to be balanced against its impact on the distinctively informal and flexible nature of juvenile justice. Blackmun then asserted that both *Gault* and *Winship* imposed due process guarantees primarily to improve the accuracy of fact finding in the juvenile process. An equally narrow interpretation of *Duncan* led Blackmun to conclude that the primary purpose of trial by jury is to prevent government oppression in adjudication, not to assure accurate fact finding. Thus, injection of the jury into juvenile adjudication would fundamentally disturb its character by making it more fully adversarial without necessarily enhancing its fact-finding accuracy. Blackmun's narrow reading of precedent, though frequently criticized, remains the prevailing interpretation. States are free to require juries in juvenile cases, but none has done so.

Albert R. Matheny

McLaurin v. Oklahoma State Regents for Higher Education, 339 U.S. 637 (1950), argued 3–4 Apr. 1950, decided 5 June 1950 by vote of 9 to 0. Vinson for the Court. *McLaurin* was a companion case to *Sweatt* v. *Painter* (1950), which defined the separate but equal standard in graduate education in such a way as to be unattainable. George W. McLaurin was an Oklahoma citizen and an African-American. Hoping to earn a doctorate in education, he applied for admission to graduate study at Oklahoma's all-white university at Norman. Initially denied admission on the basis of race, McLaurin was ordered admitted by a federal district court. But because Oklahoma law required that graduate instruction must be "upon a segregated basis," McLaurin found himself enshrouded in the segregationist equivalent of a plastic bubble: in class, he sat in a separate row "reserved for Negroes"; in the library he studied at a separate desk; in the cafeteria he ate at a separate table. McLaurin sought relief from these measures by returning to the district court, and eventually appealing to the Supreme Court. The case was argued and decided simultaneously with the *Sweatt* case in which applicant Heman Sweatt was seeking admission to the University of Texas's all-white law school.

In a brief and blunt ruling, Chief Justice Fred Vinson ordered an end to McLaurin's separate treatment. Such practices, Vinson observed, denied McLaurin "his personal and present rights to the equal protection of the laws" (p. 642) as required by the Fourteenth Amendment. McLaurin, Vinson wrote, "must receive the same treatment . . . as students of other races" (p. 642).

Augustus M. Burns III

Metro Broadcasting v. Federal Communications Commission, 497 U.S. 547 (1990) argued 28 Mar. 1990, decided 27 June 1990 by vote of 5 to 4; Brennan for the Court, O'Connor, Kennedy, Scalia, and Rehnquist in dissent. In affirming the power of Congress to enact policies that favor African-Americans and other minorities, the Court upheld two federal affirmative action programs intended to increase minority ownership of broadcast licenses. One of the major issues in contention was whether the FCC's desire to promote diversification in programming is served by its policy to integrate broadcast ownership. The majority held that congressional and FCC findings supported a sufficiently strong likelihood that diversity will be promoted by enlarging the numbers of underrepresented groups among owners. The specific groups named by the FCC were persons of "black, Hispanic surnamed, American Eskimo, Aleut, American Indian, and Asiatic American extraction."

For the majority, congressional findings were persuasive not alone because of their authority but because the legislature acts as the expression of the common national interest. The Court's opinion also gave consideration to the historical context in which issues

relating to affirmative action arise. The dissents doubted the sufficiency of the expression of legislative intent and questioned the assumption that an individual minority station owner would structure programming differently than a nonminority owner.

Beyond upholding the two affirmative action programs in question, the ruling was significant because it declared following *Fulli-love* v. *Klutznick* (1980) and rejecting the contrary implications of *Richmond* v. *J. A. Croson Co.* (1989), that the federal government had greater authority than state and local governments to require affirmative action measures in the granting of licenses and other privileges. With this opinion the Court for the first time sustained an affirmative action program not intended as a remedy for past or present unlawful discrimination but as a means of promoting a policy for the future.

Yet the Court continues to demonstrate considerable ambiguity and uncertainty in matters of affirmative action. Hence, the Rehnquist Court in *Adarand Constructors, Inc.* v. *Peña* (1995) held that federal affirmative action programs, like state affirmative action programs, must meet a test of "strict scrutiny" in order to be constitutional.

Herbert Hill

Meyer v. Nebraska, 262 U.S. 390 (1923), argued 3 Feb. 1923, decided 4 June 1923 by vote of 7 to 2; McReynolds for the Court, Holmes, joined by Sutherland, in dissent. The Supreme Court as early as 1923 recognized the right of citizens to conduct their own lives, when it struck down a Nebraska law prohibiting the teaching of modern languages other than English to children who had not passed the eighth grade. Meyer taught in a parochial school and used a German bible history as a text for reading. The Court defined the issue as whether the 1919 statute was a violation of the liberty protected by the Due Process Clause of the Fourteenth Amendment. Seven Justices maintained that it was. Dissenting on the basis of judicial restraint, Justice Oliver W. Holmes, contending that all citizens in the United States should speak a common tongue, argued that the Nebraska "experiment" was reasonable and not an infringement upon Fourteenth Amendment liberty. "That liberty," McReynolds argued for the Court, denotes the right of the individual "to contract, to engage in . . . common occupations, to acquire useful knowledge, to marry, to establish a home and bring up children, to worship God according to the dictates of his own conscience, and generally to enjoy privileges, essential to the orderly pursuit of happiness by free men" (p.399). Such a view marked the emergence of a new branch of substantive due process.

Although *Meyer* languished in doctrinal obscurity for forty years, it resurfaced in the 1960s as an important precedent for a constitutional right of privacy.

Paul L. Murphy

Miami Herald Publishing Co. v. Tornillo, 418 U.S. 241 (1974), argued 17 Apr. 1974, decided 25 June 1974 by vote of 9 to o; Burger for the Court, Brennan, Rehnquist, and White concurring. In this case, the Supreme Court took up the issue of whether a Florida statute that granted a political candidate the right to equal space to reply to newspaper attacks on his personal character or official record violated the First Amendment guarantee of a free press.

In 1972, the *Miami Herald* had twice printed editorials critical of Pat Tornillo, a local teachers' union leader and candidate for the state house of representatives. In response to the newspaper's criticism and in accordance with Florida's 1913 "right to reply" statute, Tornillo demanded that the *Herald* print verbatim his replies to the negative editorials. When the newspaper refused to comply, Tornillo filed suit. After a circuit court declared the statute unconstitutional, the Florida Supreme Court, in *Tornillo v. Miami Herald Publishing Company* (1973), reversed the decision on appeal, upholding the right to reply law as furthering the "broad societal interest in the free flow of information to the public" (p.82).

On appeal to the Supreme Court, the justices reversed the judgment of the state court by holding that the statute was a clear violation of the First Amendment guarantee of a free press. "The choice of material to go into a newspaper, and the decisions made as to limitations on the size and content of the paper," wrote Chief Justice Warren Burger, "and treatment of public issues and public officials—whether fair or unfair—constitute the exercise of editorial control and judgment" (p.258). Government regulation of this crucial process, the Court believed, violated the constitutional guarantees of a free press. In striking down the law, the Court applied precedents that rejected govern-

ment-enforced access to newspapers beginning with *Associated Press* v. *United States* (1945) but over-looked past decisions that upheld "right of reply" regulations in news broadcasting, particularly the Court's opinion in **Red Lion Broadcasting Co.* v. *Federal Communications Commission* (1969).

Timothy S. Huebner

Michael M. v. Superior Court of Sonoma County, 450 U.S. 464 (1981), argued 4 Nov. 1980, decided 23 Mar. 1981 by vote of 5 to 4; Rehnquist for plurality including Burger, Stewart, and Powell; Stewart concurring, Blackmun concurring in judgment; Brennan (with White and Marshall) and Stevens dissenting. This case presented an equal protection challenge to the statutory rape law of California. Under that law, when two people between the ages fourteen and seventeen engaged in heterosexual intercourse, the male was guilty of statutory rape but the female was not. The California Supreme Court, applying strict scrutiny, had nonetheless upheld the law.

The U.S. Supreme Court plurality applied the **Craig* v. *Boren* (1976) test of intermediate scrutiny and upheld the law. The prevention of teenage pregnancy, said the plurality, was an important governmental interest. This interest was "substantially furthered" by this statute, since females and males were not (especially without the "equaling" effects of this law) similarly situated with regard to the burdens of pregnancy. Moreover, the plurality accepted California's convincing argument that a statutory rape law that was neutral with regard to gender would be unenforceable because both culpable parties would be afraid to report the offense. In concurrence Justice Potter Stewart asserted that a law may reasonably treat the sexes differently where, as here, they are not similarly situated.

Justice Harry Blackmun's decisive fifth vote endorsed the plurality's *Craig* reasoning but complained about the Court majority's earlier insensitivity to pregnant women when it had refused to require Medicaid coverage for abortions. He added lengthy excerpts from the trial testimony that seemed to show that this case involved a forcible, but difficult to prove, rape.

The dissents, too, applied *Craig* but found that this statute failed the test. Justice William J. Brennan argued that California had not proved that its law was a greater deterrent to teenage pregnancy than a gender-neutral law would be. Justice John Paul Stevens suggested that a law might punish whichever sex partner was the aggressor, or the more willing, but that to punish only one of two equally willing participants was irrational.

Leslie Friedman Goldstein

Michigan Department of State Police v. Sitz, 496 U.S. 444 (1990), argued 27 Feb. 1990, decided 14 June 1990 by vote of 6 to 3; Rehnquist for the Court, Blackmun concurring, Brennan, Marshall, and Stevens in dissent. Michigan had established a highway sobriety checkpoint program with specific guidelines regarding operation of the checkpoints, site selection, and publicity. In its first operation, state police arrested two persons out of 126 vehicles for driving under the influence of alcohol. Before the program could continue, a group of licensed Michigan drivers sued on the grounds that the checkpoint operation violated the Fourth Amendment, in that it constituted a warrantless and unreasonable search and seizure. The drivers won their case in the lower courts, with the state tribunals ruling that although the state had a legitimate interest in curbing drunken driving, the checkpoint program constituted a substantial intrusion on individual liberties.

The Supreme Court reversed and ruled that the state courts had erred in interpreting the balancing test for administrative searches established in *United States* v. *Martinez-Fuerte* (1976; administrative search at borders for illegal aliens) and *Brown* v. *Texas* (1979; requirements for identification after a lawful stop). Chief Justice William Rehnquist agreed with the lower courts and the state that Michigan had a substantial and legitimate interest in curbing drunken driving.

The lower courts had erred, however, in applying the criteria of fear engendered in administrative searches. For Fourth Amendment purposes, the "fear and surprise" to be considered are not those of drunken drivers apprehensive of arrest but that engendered in law-abiding drivers confronting an administrative search. The majority therefore found the sobriety checkpoint program consistent with Fourth Amendment safeguards.

Melvin I. Urofsky

Michigan v. Long, 463 U.S. 1032 (1983), argued 23 Feb. 1983, decided 6 July 1983

by vote of 6 to 3; O'Connor for the Court, Blackmun concurring, Brennan, Marshall, and Stevens in dissent. The Supreme Court's most recent development of the "independent and adequate state grounds" doctrine arose from a Michigan Supreme Court case holding that both the federal Constitution's Fourth Amendment and the state constitution's counterpart proscribed the search of an automobile. State court opinions like *Long* are often ambiguous about which constitutional provision forms the foundation of their holding. In *Long,* the Supreme Court announced a new presumption of state dependence on federal law, declaring that it will assume the state court relied on federal law when the state court decision "fairly appears to rest primarily on federal law, or to be interwoven with federal law and when the adequacy and independence of any possible state law ground is not clear from the face of the opinion" (pp. 1040–1041). Only when a state court's opinion or judgment incorporates a "plain statement" that "the federal cases are being used only for the purpose of guidance, and do not themselves compel the result that the court has reached" and that the decision rests on "bona fide separate, adequate, and independent" state grounds will the Supreme Court decline to undertake direct review of the decision (p. 1041).

The *Long* decision has generated substantial debate. Some contend that it preserves the integrity and uniformity of federal law by enabling the Supreme Court to review state decisions arguably interpreting the federal Constitution, avoids the potential for issuing advisory opinions, shows respect for the independence of the state courts by abandoning the Court's prior "ad hoc" approach to state court decisions, and provides an opportunity for state courts to develop state law. Others argue that *Long* reflects the Supreme Court's animosity to expansion of individual rights, noting that presumptive jurisdiction extends only to those cases in which a state court affirms rights but not to those in which it rejects rights claims.

Shirley S. Abrahamson and Charles G. Curtis, Jr.

Milkovich v. Lorain Journal Co. 497 U.S. 1 (1990), argued 24 Apr. 1990, decided 21 June 1990 by vote of 7 to 2. Rehnquist for the Court, Brennan, joined by Marshall, in dissent. This case demonstrated the complexity of late twentieth-century defamation law. In 1975 a high school coach sued a sports columnist for suggesting that the coach had lied during an investigation of a post-meet brawl. For nearly fifteen years, the case bounced, back and forth, through Ohio's courts until the Lorain *Journal* finally secured a summary judgment on the grounds that the sports column was a constitutionally protected opinion.

The Supreme Court overturned this holding and sent the case back for trial on the merits. According to Chief Justice William Rehnquist, some courts, such as those in Ohio, mistakenly believed *Gertz* v. *Welch* (1974) created special, First Amendment protection for any libelous statement that might be labeled an "opinion." Nothing in *Gertz*, according to Rehnquist, justified such a constitutionally based defense. Columns that implied any defamatory assertions, statements that could be proved to be true or false, might provide the basis for a libel suit, even by public officials. Plaintiffs, of course, still had to meet all of the strict constitutional protections set forth in other cases, and Rehnquist thus used *Milkovich* to restate the constitutionally based defense available in defamation cases.

Justice William Brennan also rejected claims of a separate privilege for "opinion" but dissented from the holding that the sports column implied any factual claims; it simply offered the writer's "conjecture" about the coach's behavior, not any implications of fact, and was a constitutionally protected publication.

Norman L. Rosenberg

Miller v. California, 413 U.S. 15 (1973), argued 18–19 Jan. and 7 Nov. 1972; **Paris Adult Theatre v. Slaton,** 413 U.S. 49 (1973), argued 19 Oct. 1972, both decided 21 June 1973 by vote of 5 to 4; Burger for the Court, Douglas, Brennan, Stewart, and Marshall in dissent. *Miller* v. *California* articulates the test for obscenity that resolved the dilemma of First Amendment protection for allegedly obscene materials first identified in *Roth* v. *United States* (1957). Chief Justice Warren Burger's majority opinion stated that material could be obscene only if "(a) the average person, applying contemporary community standards, would find that the work, taken as a whole, appeals to the prurient interest; [and] (b) the work depicts or describes, in a patently offensive way, sexual conduct specifically defined by the applicable state

law; and (c) the work, taken as a whole, lacks serious literary, artistic, political, or scientific value" (p. 25). Burger went on to say that under this test "no one will be subject to prosecution for the sale or exposure of obscene materials unless those materials depict or describe patently offensive 'hard core' sexual conduct" (p.27).

One of the most significant contributions of *Miller* was its identification of the geographic criterion of the contemporary community standards against which obscenity was to be measured. Burger held that both prurient interest and patent offensiveness could constitutionally be measured by local rather than national standards. Many persons assumed at the time that the definition of obscenity and thus the coverage of obscenity statutes could vary significantly from place to place. Subsequent cases revealed that this reading of *Miller* was unjustified.

The Court first indicated that the scope of local variation in the identification of prurient interest or patent offensiveness was much narrower than supposed. In *Jenkins* v. *Georgia* (1974) Justice William H. Rehnquist stated that the film "Carnal Knowledge" could not, in light of the First Amendment, be found to appeal to the prurient interest, or be found patently offensive, regardless of the views of the Georgia courts and Georgia's community standards. This established a quite narrow range for permissible variance in local community standards. Moreover, in *Smith* v. *United States* (1977) and in *Pope* v. *Illinois* (1987) the Court required that the third prong of the *Miller* test, lack of serious literary, artistic, political, or scientific value, was to be measured against national standards. A work considered nationally to have literary, artistic, political, or scientific value could not constitutionally be found to be obscene regardless of whether it appealed to prurient interest or was patently offensive, and regardless of the standards of any community smaller than the nation as a whole.

Miller nevertheless remains controversial, in part because of continuing doubts about the extent to which any obscenity regulation can be squared with the First Amendment and in part because the factors identified by *Miller* may not be appropriate for issues of violence against or degradation of women. Feminists' attacks on pornography as a form inciting violence directed at women provide the background for antipornography ordinances such as that struck down by the Seventh Circuit Court of Appeals in *American Booksellers Association, Inc. v. Hudnut* (1985).

Miller's companion case, *Paris Adult Theatre* v. *Slaton,* reaffirmed the *Roth* holding that obscenity was outside the coverage of the First Amendment. Thus its regulation may be tested only against the minimal scrutiny of the rational basis test that the Court uses for regulation not restricting specific constitutional rights. This reaffirmation of *Roth* came as a surprise partly because the development of the right to privacy since 1957 had suggested that state interference with the sexual activities of consenting adults, including watching highly sexually explicit films, was constitutionally suspect. But Chief Justice Burger's majority opinion in *Paris Adult Theatre* rejected the argument, and started a process of restricting the protections for privacy identified in cases such as *Griswold* v. *Connecticut* (1965) and *Roe* v. *Wade* (1973) to matters dealing with marriage, family, and procreation. In dissent, Justice William J. Brennan, the author of the majority opinion in *Roth,* maintained that the Court's inability since 1957 to come up with a workable test for obscenity made the whole enterprise impermissibly vague, especially since that vagueness inhibited the availability of nonobscene materials clearly protected by the First Amendment. Nevertheless, the majority in these two cases reaffirmed the view that, whatever the philosophical permissibility of the regulation of morals and private sexual conduct, the arguments in favor of some regulation were at least plausible enough to satisfy the minimal scrutiny of the rational basis standard.

☐ Frederick Schauer, "Speech and 'Speech'—Obscenity and 'Obscenity': An Exercise in the Interpretation of Constitutional Language," *Georgetown Law Journal* 67 (1979): 899–933.

Frederick Schauer

Miller v. Johnson, 515 U.S. 900 (1995), argued 19 Apr. 1995, decided 29 June 1995 by a vote of 5 to 4; Kennedy for the Court, O'Connor concurring, Stevens and Ginsburg in dissent. In this case, the Supreme Court reaffirmed and attempted to clarify its holding in *Shaw* v. *Reno* (1993) concerning the constitutionality of racial gerrymanders.

According to the 1990 census, Georgia's population was 27 percent black, and the state was entitled to eleven congressional representatives. Under section 5 of the Voting Rights Act of 1965, the Department of Justice refused to approve the legislature's first two redistricting plans because each contained only two majority-black districts. Georgia then passed a congressional redistricting plan that contained three majority-black districts. Five white residents from the additional majority-black district challenged the constitutionality of the revised plan as a racial gerrymander.

The Court found that the burden on plaintiffs in racial gerrymandering cases is to demonstrate that race is the "predominant factor" in the decision to place voters within a particular district; district shape, which was the focus of the inquiry in *Shaw,* was relegated to evidentiary status. The plaintiffs in this case met that burden, primarily by providing evidence that the Georgia legislature had adopted the revised plan only because the Department of Justice had insisted on a third majority-black district. The plan, therefore, was subject to strict scrutiny under the Equal Protection Clause, and was found unconstitutional because section 5 of the Voting Rights Act did not require the existence of a third majority-black district.

The dissenting justices reasserted their view that *Shaw* was wrongly decided, and questioned the continuing wisdom of applying the Court's vague standard in a way that subjected routine redistricting decisions to judicial review. Together, *Shaw* and *Miller* had the effect of placing many of majority-minority districts created in the 1990s in constitutional jeopardy.

Grant M. Hayden

Milligan, Ex parte, 71 U.S. 2 (1866), argued 5–13 Mar. 1866, decided 3 Apr. 1866 by vote of 9 to 0; opinions released 17 Dec. 1866; Davis for the Court, Chase, joined by Miller, Swayne, and Wayne, concurring. The *Milligan* case grew out of restrictions on civil liberties in the North during the Civil War and presented the Court with Fundamental questions concerning military authority over civilians and the government's emergency powers in time of war.

In late 1864, United States army officials in Indiana arrested Lambdin P. Milligan and several other prominent antiwar Democrats, charging them with conspiracy to seize munitions at federal arsenals and to liberate Confederate prisoners held in several northern prison camps. Indiana was not in the theater of military operations, and the defendants could have been tried in federal court for treason. Nevertheless, army officials doubted the reliability of Indiana juries and elected to try the defendants by military commission. This tribunal found Milligan and two other defendants guilty and sentenced them to hang. When Milligan challenged the conviction in the United States Circuit Court in Indianapolis, the two judges disagreed, sending the case to the Supreme Court.

Although the Court announced its decision in April 1866, opinions were not released until December. All nine justices agreed that the military court lacked jurisdiction and that Milligan and the other two prisoners must be released. There was sharp disagreement among the justices, however, on the grounds for the decision.

Writing for the Court, Justice David Davis emphasized that the Constitution was not suspended in time of emergency, eloquently noting that it was "a law for rulers and people, equally in time of war and peace" (pp. 120–121). Therefore, he concluded that military trial of civilians—which violated constitutional guarantees of indictment by grand jury and public trial by an impartial jury—was impermissible where the civil courts remained open. Although the court that had tried Milligan had been established by executive authority, Davis asserted that neither the president nor the Congress could authorize the trial of civilians by military commission as long as the civil courts were open.

A concurrence by Chief Justice Salmon P. Chase, joined by three other justices, agreed that Milligan should be released. Chase, however, rested his conclusion on statutory grounds, arguing that the Habeas Corpus Act of 1863 (which stipulated that civilians detained by the military must be released if grand juries failed to indict them) had been intended to guarantee trial of civilians in the civil courts. Moreover, Chase disagreed with Davis's assertion that Congress could not authorize military trial of civilians if the civil courts were functioning. Under the war power, Chase argued, Congress could enact legislation necessary for prosecution of the war. If it concluded that the civil courts were incapable of punishing treason, Congress could authorize the military to try offenders.

The Court's opinion was controversial. By late 1866, when the opinions were released, violence against southern African-Americans was growing, and most Republicans believed that military courts were essential to afford the slaves security. Consequently, when President Andrew Johnson used *Milligan* as justification to reduce military authority in the occupied states, Republicans denounced the Court. Moreover, Davis's opinion led many Republicans to fear that the Court would declare unconstitutional the Reconstruction Act of 1867, which authorized military trial of civilians in the rebel states.

In the twentieth century many commentators have viewed *Milligan* as a constitutional landmark, and the Court has not repudiated it. Nevertheless, some have criticized *Milligan,* arguing that by categorically prohibiting imposition of martial law when the civil courts are open, it unduly limited the government's ability to protect national security. The Court itself has not always followed *Milligan.* In **Duncan* v. *Kahanamoku* (1946), a case challenging the imposition of martial law in Hawaii during World War II, the Court ruled against the government. The majority, however, rested its decision on congressional legislation governing Hawaii rather than on the constitutional principles established in *Milligan.* Moreover, in acquiescing in the government's internment of Japanese-Americans during World War II, the Court ignored the limits on the government's emergency powers suggested by *Milligan.*

□ Harold M. Hyman and William M. Wiecek, *Equal Justice under Law: Constitutional Development, 1835–1875* (1982).

Donald G. Nieman

Milliken v. Bradley, 418 U.S. 717 (1974), argued 27 Feb. 1974, decided 25 July 1974, by vote of 5 to 4; Burger for the Court, Stewart concurring, Douglas, White, Marshall, and Brennan in dissent. In *School Board of Richmond* v. *State Board of Education* (1973), an equally divided Court—with Justice Lewis Powell not participating—was unable to decide whether a district court could require the merger of three school districts in order to eliminate racial segregation in one. A year later, in *Milliken* v. *Bradley,* a bitterly divided Court ruled 5 to 4 that segregated practices in one district did not warrant relief that included another non-segregating district. Thus, the Court that had implicitly extended *Green* v. *County Board* (1968) integration to the North only thirteen months before in *Keyes* v. *School District No. 1* (1973) drew the remedial line at the offending school district's boundary. For the first time since even before *Brown* v. *Board of Education* (1954), the Court refused to endorse a desegregation remedy sought by the National Association for the Advancement of Colored People (NAACP), which had developed the litigation strategy attacking the constitutionality of Jim Crow schools beginning in the mid-1930s.

The Detroit school district, then fifth largest in the nation, covered 140 square miles; at the time of the suit in 1970, its school population of almost 290,000 was 65 percent black and 35 percent white—a substantial recent growth in black population owing to white flight to nearby suburbs; for the metropolitan area, the proportion of black to white student population was 19 to 81 percent. The district court found that the Detroit school district had engaged in segregative practices and concluded that the only way to achieve *Green*-mandated establishment of a unitary school system was to order busing that included some of the surrounding suburban districts. The court of appeals affirmed, fearing that not to do so would "nullify *Brown* v. *Board of Education* (1954)" and restore the "separate but equal doctrine" of *Plessy* v. *Ferguson* (1896) (p. 249).

Chief Justice Burger, who wrote the *Swann* v. *Charlotte-Mecklenburg County Board of Education* (1971) opinion and affirmed the lower courts on the basis of the fit between constitutional violation and corresponding remedy, wrote for the narrow majority. His statement of the issues in *Milliken* signaled its outcome: "[may a federal court] impose a multi-district, area-wide remedy to a single-district *de jure* segregation problem absent any finding that the other included school districts have failed to operate unitary school systems within their districts, absent any claim or finding that boundary lines of any affected school district were established with the purpose of fostering racial segregation [and] absent any finding that the included districts committed acts which affected segregation within the other districts" (p. 721).

Since the suburban districts had not caused or contributed to the violation, they logically could not be part of the remedy without

a "drastic expansion of the constitutional right itself, an expansion without support in either constitutional principle or precedent" (p. 747). The chief justice may have been right but the difficulty was that the same thing could have been said of the nature of the desegregation cases from the beginning.

The dissenters echoed the anxieties of the court of appeals, but to no avail. The dissent by Justice Thurgood Marshall, who had argued *Brown I* and *II* for the NAACP, bitterly complained that the Court was now turning back the clock in response "to a perceived public mood that we have gone far enough in enforcing the Constitution's guarantee of equal justice" (p. 814).

The gradual ratcheting out of remedies to implement *Brown I* ended as abruptly and as conclusorily as it began, twenty years and two months earlier. Subsequent cases fine-tuned the grounds for identifying constitutional violations and added minor remedial weapons, but *Milliken* v. *Bradley*, by rejecting so-called interdistrict remedies, established the new outer limit of constitutional remedies.

□ J. Harvie Wilkinson, *From Brown to Bakke* (1979).

Dennis J. Hutchinson

Minersville School District v. Gobitis, 310 U.S. 586 (1940), argued 25 Apr. 1940, decided 3 June 1940 by vote of 8 to 1; Frankfurter for the Court, Stone in dissent. The first Flag Salute case, *Minersville School District* v. *Gobitis*, revealed the limits the Supreme Court of the liberal Roosevelt pre-World War II era still put on the religion clauses of the First Amendment. The Court held that a Jehovah's Witness's child could constitutionally be expelled from public school for refusing to participate in the daily ceremony of saluting the American flag and pledging allegiance to it, even though saluting the flag or reciting the pledge violated the child's religious beliefs against serving gods other than the Almighty.

Admittedly, said Justice Felix Frankfurter for the majority, it is only when felt necessities of society compel it that the Constitution's free exercise provision can be overridden. But to say that freedom to follow religious conscience has no limits cannot be reconciled with American history.

National unity, he said, is the basis of national security. True enough, the flag is a symbol, but we live by symbols. To salute it is therefore a constitutionally allowable part of a school program, which may be made mandatory. A claim for exceptional immunity may be refused simply because granting it might weaken the effect of the exercise.

Although only Justice Harlan F. Stone dissented, three years later the decision was reversed, primarily on free speech grounds, in *West Virginia State Board of Education v. Barnette.*

Leo Pfeffer

Minnesota Rate Cases, See INTERSTATE COMMERCE COMMISSION.

Minor v. Happersett, 21 Wall. (88 U.S.) 162 (1875), argued 9 Feb. 1875, decided 9 Mar. 1875 by vote of 9 to 0; Waite for the Court. The Supreme Court held that a state could constitutionally forbid a woman citizen to vote, despite her invocation of the citizenship and privileges or immunities clauses of the Fourteenth Amendment, the Guarantee Clause (Art. IV, sec. 4); the Due Process Clause of the Fifth Amendment, and the prohibition against bills of attainder (Art. I, sec. 9). Noticeably absent from this list, to a modern eye, are the equal protection and due process clauses of the Fourteenth Amendment.

The case is important as near-contemporary interpretation of the Fourteenth Amendment's original intent. It is notable for its narrow definition of citizenship "as conveying the idea of membership of a nation, nothing more" (p. 166) and for its firm, unanimous rejection of the Fourteenth Amendment as a source either of a substantive federal suffrage right or of a federal limit on state control of the franchise. Otherwise, neither section 2 of the Fourteenth Amendment nor, later, the Fifteenth, Nineteenth, Twenty-Fourth, and Twenty-Sixth Amendments would have been necessary. "Certainly," the Court declared, "if the courts can consider any question settled, it is this one.... The Constitution, when it conferred citizenship, did not necessarily confer the right of suffrage" (p. 177). This interpretation was substantially, albeit tacitly, abandoned in *Reynolds v. Sims* (1964) and *Harper v. Virginia State Board of Elections* (1966).

Ward E. Y. Elliott

Miranda v. Arizona, 384 U.S. 436 (1966), argued 28 Feb. 1966, decided 13 June 1966 by vote of 5 to 4; Warren for the Court, Clark,

Harlan, White, and Stewart in dissent. The Warren Court's revolution in American criminal procedure reached its high point (or, depending upon one's perspective, its low point) on 13 June 1966. That day the Court handed down its opinion in *Miranda,* the most famous, and most bitterly criticized, confession case in the nation's history. To some, *Miranda* symbolized the legal system's determination to treat even the lowliest and most despicable criminal suspect with dignity and respect. But to others, especially those who attributed rising crime rates to the softness of judges, the case became a target of abuse.

Background. Prior to the decision in *Miranda,* the admissibility of a confession in a state criminal case was governed by the due process "voluntariness" or "totality of the circumstances" test. Under this approach, the courts decided on a case-by-case basis whether the will of the person who confessed had been "broken" or "overborne" or whether the confession had been "voluntary." But it soon became clear that these terms were not being used as tools of analysis, but as mere conclusions. When a court concluded that the "totality" of a suspect's treatment had not been too bad (e.g., although the police had exerted considerable pressure and used some trickery, they had given the suspect a sandwich and permitted him to have a normal night's sleep), it called the resulting confession "voluntary." On the other hand, when a court concluded that the police methods were too offensive or too heavy-handed (considering such factors as the suspect's youth, poor education, or low intelligence), it labeled the resulting confession "involuntary" or "coerced."

The vagueness and unpredictability of the "voluntariness" test, its application (or manipulation) by lower courts so as to validate confessions of doubtful constitutionality, and the inability of the Supreme Court, because of its heavy workload, to review more than one or two state confession cases a year, led a growing number of the justices to search for a more meaningful and more manageable alternative approach. *Miranda* was the culmination of these efforts.

Facts of the Case. Ernesto Miranda, an indigent twenty-three-year-old who had not completed the ninth grade, was arrested at his home and taken directly to a Phoenix, Arizona, police station. There, after being identified by the victim of a rape-kidnapping, he was taken to an "interrogation room," where he was questioned about the crimes. At first, Miranda maintained his innocence, but after two hours of questioning, the police emerged from the room with a signed written confession of guilt. At his trial, the written confession was admitted into evidence and Miranda was found guilty of kidnapping and rape.

Whether Miranda had been told that anything he said could be used against him was unclear. But the police admitted—and this was to prove fatal for the prosecution—that neither before nor during the questioning had Miranda been advised of his right to consult with an attorney before answering any questions or his right to have an attorney present during the interrogation.

Miranda's confession plainly would have been admissible under the "voluntariness" test. His questioning had been quite mild compared to the objectionable police methods that had rendered a resulting confession "involuntary" or "coerced" in previous cases. But the confession was obtained from Miranda under circumstances that did not satisfy the new constitutional standards the Court was to promulgate in this very case.

A remarkable feature of the American history of confessions law is that until the mid-1960s the privilege against self-incrimination (the Fifth Amendment provision that no person "shall be compelled . . . to be a witness against himself") did not apply to the proceedings in the interrogation room or to in-custody police interrogation.

One reason for this situation was that the privilege was not deemed applicable to the states until 1964 and by that time a large body of law pertaining to "involuntary" or "coerced" state confessions had developed. Moreover, and more important, the prevailing pre-*Miranda* view was that "compelling" someone to testify against himself meant *legal* compulsion. Since a suspect was threatened neither with perjury for testifying falsely nor contempt for refusing to testify at all, it could not be said, ran the argument, that a person undergoing police interrogation was being "compelled" to be "a witness against himself" within the meaning of the privilege—even though under such circumstances a person is likely to assume or to be led by the police to believe that there are legal (or extralegal) sanctions for "refusing to cooperate." Since the police had no lawful authority to make a suspect answer their questions (although, prior to *Miranda*, the police did not have to

tell a person that), there was no legal obligation to answer to which a privilege in the technical sense could apply.

Although this reasoning seems quite strained, it prevailed as long as it did probably because of a widely held view that questioning a suspect without advising him of his rights was "indispensable" to law enforcement work. Moreover, the invisibility of police interrogation made it easy for society to be complacent about what really took place in the interrogation room.

On the eve of *Miranda*, however, there was reason to think that the self-incrimination clause would finally apply to the police station. In **Malloy v. Hogan* (1964), which did not involve a confession, the Court not only held the privilege against self-incrimination fully applicable to the states but stated by way of dictum that the admissibility of a confession in a state or federal court should be controlled by the Fifth Amendment privilege. The confession rules and the privilege had become intertwined in *Malloy*—and they would be fused in *Miranda*.

Decision. There are three parts to the *Miranda* decision:

1. The Fifth Amendment privilege is available outside of court proceedings and other formal proceedings and serves to protect persons in all settings from being compelled to incriminate themselves. Thus, the privilege applies to informal compulsion exerted by law enforcement officers during "custodial interrogation," that is, questioning initiated by the police after a person has been taken into custody.

2. "An individual swept from familiar surroundings into police custody, surrounded by antagonistic forces, and subjected to the techniques of persuasion described in the [standard police interrogation manuals] cannot be otherwise than under compulsion to speak" (p. 461). Because the custodial interrogation environment "carries its own badge of intimidation" that is "at odds" with the privilege, "[u]nless adequate protective devices are employed to dispel the compulsion inherent in custodial surroundings," no statement obtained from a person under these circumstances is admissible (pp. 457–458).

3. The Constitution does not require adherence to any particular system for dispelling the coercion of custodial

interrogation. However, unless the government utilizes other procedures that are at least as effective, in order for a statement to be admissible a suspect must be given the now familiar four-fold *Miranda* warning (set forth below) before being subjected to custodial interrogation and must effectively waive his rights before any questioning.

According to *Miranda,* advising a suspect that he has a right to remain silent and that anything he says can be used against him is not sufficient to assure that the suspect's right to choose between silence and speech will remain unfettered throughout the interrogation process. Therefore, a suspect must also be told of his right to counsel, either retained or (if he is indigent) appointed.

Although the warnings need not be given in the exact form described in the *Miranda* opinion—indeed, they are not described exactly the same way throughout the opinion—the substance of each of the following four warnings must be effectively given: (1) you have the right to remain silent; (2) anything you say can and will be used against you; (3) you have the right to talk to a lawyer before being questioned and to have him present when you are being questioned; and (4) if you cannot afford a lawyer, one will be provided for you before any questioning if you so desire.

Miranda has been widely criticized as a case that tilted the balance heavily in favor of criminal suspects. However, as the Court recently noted in *Moran* v. *Burbine* (1986), the decision "embodies a carefully crafted balance designed to fully protect *both* the defendant's and society's interests" (p. 433, n. 4).

Miranda does not require that a person taken into custody first consult with a lawyer or actually have a lawyer present in order for his waiver of constitutional rights to be valid. The decision's weakness (or saving grace, depending upon one's viewpoint) is that it permits someone subjected to the inherent pressures of police custody to "waive" his rights without actually obtaining the guidance of counsel. That waiver, at least in theory, must be "knowing" and "voluntary."

Miranda allows the police to conduct "general-on-the-scene questioning" without providing the warnings. It also allows the police to interview a suspect in his home or office without advising him of his rights,

provided the questioning takes place in a context that does not restrict the person's freedom to terminate the meeting.

Moreover, *Miranda* leaves the police free to hear and act upon "volunteered" statements even though the "volunteer" has been taken into custody and neither knows nor is informed of his rights. "Custody" alone does not call for the *Miranda* warnings. It is the impact on the suspect of the interplay between police interrogation and police custody that makes "custodial police interrogation" so corrosive and calls for "adequate protective devices" (*Illinois* v. *Perkins,* 1990).

Even when warnings and the waiver of rights are required, *Miranda* permits the police to give the warnings and to obtain waivers without the presence of any disinterested observer and without any tape recording of the proceedings. (This is so even when a tape recording is readily available.)

Whether the promptings of conscience or the desire to get the matter over with usually override the impact of the warnings, or whether the police too often mumble or undermine the warnings, almost all empirical studies indicate that in the quarter century since *Miranda* was decided custodial suspects have continued to make incriminating statements with great frequency. This might not have been the case if a tape recording of police warnings and the suspect's response were required whenever feasible. There is little doubt that it would not have been the case if *Miranda* had required that a suspect first consult with a lawyer or actually have a lawyer present in order for his waiver of rights to be effective.

Future of Miranda. For supporters of *Miranda,* an ominous note was struck in *Michigan* v. *Tucker* (1974), where the Court, speaking through Justice William Rehnquist, viewed the *Miranda* warnings as "not themselves rights protected by the Constitution," but only "prophylactic standards" designed to "safeguard" or to "provide practical reinforcement" for the privilege against self-incrimination (p. 444). A decade later, first in *New York* v. *Quarles* (1984), recognizing a "public safety" exception to *Miranda,* and then in *Oregon* v. *Elstad* (1985), indicating that the prosecution may make considerable derivative use of *Miranda* violations, the Court reiterated *Tucker's* way of looking at, and thinking about, *Miranda.* Both *Quarles* and *Elstad* underscored the distinction between statements that are actually "coerced" or "compelled" and those obtained merely in violation of *Miranda's* "prophylactic rules."

Since the Supreme Court has no supervisory power over state criminal justice and if *Miranda* violations are not constitutional violations, where did the Warren Court get the authority to impose the new confession doctrine on the states? If a confession obtained in violation of *Miranda* does not violate the self-incrimination clause unless "actually coerced," why are the states not free to admit all confessions not the product of actual coercion? *Tucker* and its progeny thus may have prepared the way for the eventual overruling of *Miranda*.

Nevertheless, it would be surprising if the Court did overrule *Miranda*. The Court is well aware of *Miranda's* rather limited scope—indeed, a number of commentators have forcefully argued that it does not go far enough. The Court is also cognizant of the many studies indicating that the decision has had no significant adverse impact on law enforcement. Despite their initial reaction of dismay, the police seem to have adjusted to *Miranda* fairly well. Under these circumstances, the Court is probably willing to "live with" a case that has become part of the American culture, especially if it continues to view it as a serious effort to strike a proper balance between the need for police questioning and the need to protect a suspect against impermissible police pressure.

□ Liva Baker, *Miranda: Crime, Law and Politics* (1983). Gerald Caplan, "Questioning *Miranda*," *Vanderbilt Law Review* 38 (November 1985): 1417–1476. Yale Kamisar, *Police Interrogation and Confessions* (1980). Stephen Schulhofer, "Reconsidering *Miranda*," *University of Chicago Law Review* 54 (Spring 1987): 435–461.

Yale Kamisar

Mississippi v. Johnson, 71 U.S. 475 (1867), argued 12 Apr. 1867, decided 15 Apr. 1867 by vote of 9 to 0; Chase for the Court. In March 1867 Congress enacted the Reconstruction Act over the veto of President Andrew Johnson. The act gave military commanders appointed by the president political authority in the ten unrestored states of the old Confederacy and required these states to adopt new constitutions granting former slaves the right to vote. Mississippi filed a motion in the Supreme Court, challenging the constitutionality of the act and seeking to enjoin the president from enforcing it.

Although Johnson had bitterly opposed the Reconstruction Act, he viewed Mississippi's action as a threat to presidential power and ordered his attorney general to oppose the motion.

Writing for a unanimous Court, Chief Justice Salmon P. Chase held that the judiciary could not enjoin the president from enforcing an allegedly unconstitutional statute. Chase admitted that in **Marbury* v. *Madison* (1803) the Court had asserted its authority to command executive officials to fulfill their legal obligations. He ruled, however, that this extended only to ministerial duties, which involved broad discretion and the exercise of political judgment. Chase asserted that the president's unique position gave him a constitutional responsibility to execute the laws. The courts could not restrain him from carrying out this responsibility, although once he did so, his actions were subject to challenge in the courts.

The decision was not an indication of judicial timidity. Rather it rested on the widely shared belief that enjoining enforcement of a statute threatened separation of powers.

Donald G. Nieman

Mississippi University for Women v. Hogan, 458 U.S. 718 (1982), argued 22 Mar. 1982, decided 1 July 1982 by vote of 5 to 4; O'Connor for the Court, Burger, Blackmun, Powell, and Rehnquist in dissent. Hogan, a male resident of Mississippi, challenged as a violation of equal protection the women-only admission policy of the state-supported Mississippi University for Women nursing school. Justice Sandra Day O'Connor, in her first opinion for the Court, applied the *Craig* v. *Boren* (1976) test of intermediate scrutiny. As its "important interest," the state claimed that this policy compensated for discrimination against women. O'Connor reasoned that the exclusion of men from a nursing college did nothing to compensate women for discriminatory barriers faced by them. Moreover, the state failed to show that the policy "substantially furthered" the alleged objective since men were permitted to attend classes as auditors.

Chief Justice Warren Burger's dissent expressed general agreement with Justice Lewis Powell's but emphasized that the holding applied specifically to a nursing college. Justice Harry Blackmun argued that Hogan had a choice of coed nursing schools elsewhere in the state, that it was valuable to offer women the choice of an all-female school, and that, while the holding applied specifically to nursing colleges, there would be inevitable spillover from the reasoning to other single-sex schools.

Powell (with Justice William Rehnquist) asserted that, in effect, the Court was banning state-provided women-only colleges. He elaborated on Blackmun's educational-choice arguments by focusing on the educational benefits for women of single-sex colleges and claimed that because this was not a case of sex discrimination the *Craig* test was inappropriate, but he maintained that the *Craig* test was nonetheless satisfied. The dissenters argued further that this would lead to the eventual demise of publicly supported colleges exclusively for women, which it did.

Leslie Friedman Goldstein

Missouri ex rel. Gaines v. Canada, 305 U.S. 337 (1938), argued 9 Nov. 1938, decided 12 Dec. 1938 by vote of 6 to 2; Hughes for the Court, McReynolds, joined by Butler, in dissent, Cardozo had died.

This case provided an early test in the campaign, launched by the National Association for the Advancement of Colored People in 1930, to challenge the separate but equal principle that required racial segregation in public educational institutions. Lloyd L. Gaines, an African-American resident, sought admission to Missouri's all-white law school in the absence of a facility for blacks. Predictably, the University of Missouri denied Gaines's application on racial grounds and state courts upheld the denial. Gaines's attorney, Charles H. Houston, then sought from the U.S. Supreme Court a writ of mandamus to compel Gaines's admission to the all-white law school, and the Supreme Court granted certiorari.

Chief Justice Charles Evans Hughes, for the majority, ordered Gaines admitted to the all-white facility, dismissing the state's offer to pay Gaines's tuition to an out-of-state law school as inadequate to the requirements of the Equal Protection Clause of the Fourteenth Amendment. Nor was Hughes persuaded that Missouri's stated intention to develop a law school for blacks at state-supported Lincoln University would meet the separate but equal test.

The Gaines case thus became a pivotal event in the NAACP's campaign to overturn the separate but equal standard. While the Court did not repudiate segregation, the case signaled a new urgency in evaluating the standard. As for Lloyd Gaines, he never enrolled in law school. Shortly after the Court rendered its opinion, he disappeared, never to be heard from again.

Augustus M. Burns III

Missouri v. Holland, 252 U.S. 416 (1920), argued 2 Mar. 1920, decided 19 Apr. 1920 by vote of 7 to 2; Holmes for the Court, Van Devanter and Pitney in dissent. The state of Missouri sought to enjoin a United States game warden from enforcing federal regulations enacted pursuant to the Migratory Bird Treaty Act of 1918 on the grounds that the statute unconstitutionally interfered with rights reserved to the States under the Tenth Amendment. The Bird Treaty Act had been passed to fulfill United States obligations under a treaty with Great Britain to protect migratory birds. Missouri appealed from lower court decisions upholding the statute's constitutionality. An earlier federal statute to regulate the taking of migratory birds, not passed pursuant to an international treaty, had been held unconstitutional in lower courts on the grounds that the birds were owned by the states in their sovereign capacity and were therefore immune from federal regulation under the Tenth Amendment.

Justice Oliver Wendell Holmes concluded that the statute was a "necessary and proper" means of executing the powers of the federal government, valid under Article I, section 8, because the United States had the authority to implement treaty obligations.

The Court held that since the treaty was valid it superseded state authority as the supreme law of the land under Article VI of the Constitution. This was so, Holmes wrote, because migratory birds did not respect national boundaries and were therefore appropriate subjects for regulation by agreement with other countries. Even if the states of the United States were capable of effectively regulating the subject, the Court found nothing in the Constitution to prohibit the federal government from acting by means of a treaty to deal with a "national interest of very nearly the first magnitude ... [that] can be protected only by national action in concert with another power" (p. 435).

Holmes's analysis has been criticized as a bootstrap method to create new federal power by means of international treaty. Fears of an expansive application of this principle were instrumental in encouraging popular support for the "Bricker Amendment" in 1953, which would have amended the constitution to provide that "[a] treaty shall become effective as internal law in the United States only through legislation which would be valid in the absence of treaty." In 1957, the Supreme Court relieved much of this public concern in *Reid* v. *Covert*, when it held that status of forces agreements between the United States and foreign countries could not deprive U.S. civilian dependants of the right to a jury trial by making them subject to military courts-martial while they were stationed abroad. Citing *Missouri* v. *Holland*, the Court wrote, "To the extent that the United States can validly make treaties, the people and the States have delegated their power to the National Government and the Tenth Amendment is no barrier" (p. 18).

The *Holland* opinion has become largely irrelevant because of the greatly expanded scope of national power today over all matters touching interstate or foreign commerce. But the case has continuing importance. First, the opinion contains what has come to be regarded as the classic statement of the "living document" approach to constitutional interpretation in which historic practice, rather than the intent of the framers is given primary emphasis. Second, even though the controversy in this case concerned the scope of the treaty power, rather than treaty supremacy, the theory of the case has provided support for later Court decisions such as *United States* v. *Belmont* (1937) and *United States* v. *Pink* (1942) establishing the supremacy of federal executive agreements over state law.

Last, Holmes's emphasis on the proposition that matters of international concern necessarily give rise to federal power has provided support for later holdings where the Court found that state law may be preempted, even by federal common law, whenever the state rule may interfere with the conduct of foreign affairs by the national government.

Harold G. Maier

Missouri v. Jenkins, 495 U.S. 33 (1990), argued 30 Oct. 1989, decided 18 Apr. 1990 by vote of 9 to 0; White for the Court, Kennedy, joined by Rehnquist, O'Connor, and Scalia, concurring. As a remedy for segregation in the Kansas City, Missouri, school district, the district court ordered a "magnet school" plan to attract suburban students back to the inner city schools—complete with a planetarium, a twenty-five-acre farm, a model United Nations, an art gallery, and swimming pools—at a cost of more than one-half billion dollars. The state had to pay 75 percent and the district 25 percent, but because the district's portion exceeded state law limits the court also ordered a doubling of the district's property tax.

Declining to review the plan, the Supreme Court unanimously disapproved the order directly raising the property tax. Reasoning from principles of equity and comity and thus avoiding a constitutional holding, Justice Byron White and four other justices approved an indirect remedy to set aside the state law tax limits and allow the district itself to raise the necessary future taxes. Justice Anthony Kennedy and three other justices saw this as a distinction without a difference and would have held that a federal court could not impose a state tax, directly or indirectly.

Five years later the case came back to the high court. This time, the justices held that the lower federal courts in Missouri had improperly ordered the state to help pay for the showcase desegregation plan for the Kansas City schools.

Thomas E. Baker

Missouri v. Jenkins, 515 U.S. 70 (1995), argued 11 Jan. 1995, decided 12 June 1995 by vote of 5 to 4; Rehnquist for the Court, O'Connor and Thomas concurring, Souter dissenting, joined by Stevens, Ginsburg, and Breyer, Ginsburg dissenting separately. The case involved school desegregation litigation begun eighteen years earlier in the name of Kalima Jenkins, one of several black students in the Kansas City, Missouri, school district. First the federal district court in Kansas City and then the Court of Appeals for the Eighth Circuit approved a desegregation plan that required the state of Missouri to shoulder more than one-half of the $1.3 billion spent to improve the once-segregated school system. The remedies involved, among other actions, establishing so-called magnet schools, lowering class sizes, drawing students from the surrounding white suburbs, and increasing taxes.

The state of Missouri had failed in its 1990 challenge to overturn the tax increases, but a year later it went back to the Supreme Court seeking an end to the order mandating the other actions. Against the wishes of the school district, the state argued that all vestiges of the formerly segregated system had been eliminated. The federal district court refused to lift its order, and a badly divided Eighth Circuit Court of Appeals agreed. The opinions from the Eighth Circuit indicated, without saying so explicitly, that the remedies would remain in place until standardized student achievement scores had improved to the level of national standards. Missouri argued that such a standard was "outcomes" based and entirely beyond any constitutional requirement to provide equal opportunity under the Equal Protection Clause of the Fourteenth Amendment.

The Supreme Court sided with Missouri. In his opinion for a bare majority of the Court, Chief Justice William H. Rehnquist found that the federal district court in Kansas City and the Eighth Circuit Court had used improper guidelines to justify their sweeping orders. The majority struck particularly hard at that part of the plan that aimed to bring white students from the suburbs into the Kansas City schools. The tactics used by the lower federal courts, the high court concluded, were little more than a subterfuge to get around earlier court decisions that barred such interdistrict remedies. Rehnquist also rejected the lower court's rationale for the use of standardized test scores to mark the progress of the district's students. "This is clearly not the appropriate test to be applied," Rehnquist wrote, since many of the variables influencing poor achievement were beyond the control of the school district (p. 101).

Particularly notable among the concurring opinions was that of Justice Clarence Thomas, an African-American. Thomas issued a deeply personal opinion that directly challenged the lower court's assertion that a largely black district should solve its student quality problems by attracting more white students.

The dissenters were equally adamant, led by Justices David Souter and Ruth Bader Ginsburg. The former argued that the poor state of the segregated schools had originally driven whites from the city and that the state should be made to take actions that would help to bring them back. The latter complained that "[g]iven the deep, inglorious history of segregation in Missouri, to curtail desegregation at this time and in this manner is an action at once too swift and too soon" (p. 176).

The Court's action in *Jenkins* was entirely consistent with its previous rulings over the last several years. The justices broke no new law. Moreover, the justices did not order the plan dismantled and did not find that the vestiges of segregation had been eradicated. They did, however, encourage the lower federal courts handling the case to make such findings. As important, without the considerable annual contribution of the state, the hard-pressed school district was potentially faced with a shortfall of almost $200 million a year.

Kermit L. Hall

Mistretta v. United States, 488 U.S. 361 (1989), argued 5 Oct. 1988, decided 18 Jan. 1989 by vote of 8 to 1; Blackmun for the Court, Scalia in dissent. Federal judges have traditionally exercised considerable discretion in fixing the terms of sentences for convicted offenders. Convinced of a need for more uniformity in sentencing practices, Congress passed the Sentencing Reform Act of 1984, creating the United States Sentencing Commission and giving it authority to establish ranges of sentences for all categories of federal offenses. The commission was established as an independent body within the judicial branch to consist of seven members appointed by the president and removable by him. At least three were required to be federal judges, selected by the president from a list of six judges recommended by the Judicial Conference of the United States.

This statutory challenge to judicial autonomy, plus the unusual provisions for appointment and removal of commission members, raised separation of powers issues. However, in *Mistretta* the Supreme Court upheld the sentencing law in all respects. Though admitting that the commission was "an unusual hybrid in structure and authority," Justice Harry A. Blackmun ruled that locating the commission within the judicial branch did not violate the separation of powers doctrine (p. 412). The commission was not a court nor controlled by the judiciary. Requiring three federal judges to serve on the commission along with non-judges did not affect the integrity or independence of the judicial branch. Giving the president power to remove commission members had no effect on the tenure or compensation of Article III judges. The development of sentencing rules was an "essentially neutral endeavor" in which judicial participation was "peculiarly appropriate" (p. 407).

Justice Antonin Scalia, dissenting, challenged the constitutionality of the commission. He concluded that it was a violation of Article III of the Constitution to have federal judges serve in policy-making positions in the executive branch.

C. Herman Pritchett

Mobile v. Bolden, 446 U.S. 55 (1980), argued 19 Mar. 1979, reargued 29 Oct. 1979, decided 22 Apr. 1980 by vote of 6 to 3; Stewart for the Court, Blackmun concurring in the result, Stevens concurring in the judgment, Brennan, White, and Marshall in dissent. This case was brought on behalf of the black residents of Mobile, Alabama. They alleged that the all-white Mobile City Commission, elected at large, diluted the voting strength of blacks in violation of section 2 of the Voting Rights Act of 1965, and the Fourteenth and Fifteenth Amendments. No black had ever served on the five-member commission since its inception in 1911. The district court found constitutional violations and the court of appeals affirmed. In the Supreme Court the United States argued for the black parties.

The plurality opinion focused on the standard necessary to make out a claim of racial discrimination under the Fourteenth and Fifteenth Amendments where state action, on its face, is racially neutral. Examining the Fifteenth Amendment and reviewing numerous voting rights cases, the Court rejected a discriminatory result standard and concluded that a showing of a discriminatory purpose was required. Similarly, the Court relied on *Washington* v. *Davis* (1976), *Arlington Heights* v. *Metropolitan Housing Development Corp.* (1977), and *Personnel Administrator* v. *Feeney* (1979) for the proposition that a showing of discriminatory intent was necessary under the Fourteenth Amendment. Applying this discriminatory intent standard to Mobile, the Court found no constitutional violation. Mobile's black citizens could register and vote without hindrance, and there were not official obstacles hindering blacks in seeking elective office. Finally, the Court strongly criticized the notion that the Fourteenth Amendment requires or guarantees proportional representation.

Justice Thurgood Marshall, in a lengthy and angry dissent, labeled the Court an accessory to the perpetuation of racial discrimination. He rejected the necessity of finding a discriminatory intent and argued for a discriminatory effects test.

Critics of the decision maintain that the Court's discriminatory purpose test is too burdensome. *Mobile* caused a firestorm of protest. Congress, in its 1982 extension of the Voting Rights Act, incorporated a modified effects test into the act.

Gerald N. Rosenberg

Monell v. Department of Social Services, 436 U.S. 658 (1978), argued 2 Nov. 1977, decided 6 June 1978 by vote of 7 to 2; Brennan for the Court, Powell and Stevens concurring, Rehnquist, joined by Burger, in dissent. In *Monell,* the Court held that New York City's policy of requiring pregnant female city employees to take leave that was not medically necessary subjected the city to liability. It overruled the Court's seventeen-year-old holding, in *Monroe* v. *Pape* (1961), that local governments were wholly immune from suit under Title 42, section 1983 of the U.S. Code. *Monell* enabled civil rights plaintiffs to seek monetary recovery from local governments for constitutional violations.

While overruling *Monroe,* the Court limited the circumstances under which local governments are liable. It rejected imposing municipal liability simply because the municipality employed the person who violated the plaintiff's rights, so-called *respondeat superior* liability. Municipal liability instead depended on finding that the wrong resulted from the "official policy" of the municipality. The "official policy" test, as developed in later cases, requires that the wrongful policy be one made by someone in final policymaking authority. Mere egregious misbehavior by the police, for example, will not support municipal liability.

The Court's reasoning in rejecting *respondeat superior* liability is questionable in light of that doctrine's widespread acceptance in tort law. It relied on congressional rejection of proposed amendments to section 1983 that would have made cities liable for wrongful acts by private persons. The proposed amendments did not, however, address the question of whether cities might be liable for their own employees' wrongful acts.

Theodore Eisenberg

Moore v. Dempsey, 261 U.S. 86 (1923), argued 9 Jan. 1923, decided 19 Feb. 1923 by vote of 6 to 2; Holmes for the Court, McReynolds and Sutherland in dissent, Clarke not participating. *Moore* resulted from a racial clash in Phillips County, Arkansas, in the fall of 1919, in which as many as two hundred blacks and five whites died. The *Moore* case involved six blacks sentenced to death for the murder of whites following the incident. They had petitioned the federal courts for a writ of habeas corpus, contending that their trials had been mob dominated and that witnesses were tortured to force testimony against them. The federal district court, however, dismissed the habeas corpus petition.

On appeal sponsored by the National Association for the Advancement of Colored People, the Supreme Court reversed the district court and ordered that a habeas corpus hearing be held. Speaking for the Court, Justice Oliver Wendell Holmes held that a mob-dominated trial violated the Due Process Clause of the Fourteenth Amendment and that, upon being petitioned for a writ of habeas corpus, the federal courts were duty bound to review claims of mob domination of state trials and to order the release of defendants convicted in mob-dominated trials. In dissent, Justices James McReynolds and George Sutherland contended the Court's decision would result in undue interference by the federal courts in state criminal trials.

Moore v. *Dempsey* marked the beginning of stricter scrutiny of state criminal trials by the Supreme Court and more liberalized use of federal writs of habeas corpus to attack state convictions obtained in violation of federal constitutional rights.

Richard C. Cortner

Moose Lodge v. Irvis, 407 U.S. 163 (1972), argued 28 Feb. 1972, decided 12 June 1972 by vote of 6 to 3; Rehnquist for the Court, Douglas, Brennan, and Marshall in dissent. Irvis, an African-American man, was refused service as the guest of a member of the Moose Lodge in Harrisburg, Pennsylvania. The Pennsylvania Liquor Control Board had issued the Moose Lodge a private club license to dispense liquor, and Irvis contended that this involvement of the state in the racially discriminatory policy of the lodge constituted discriminatory state action in violation of the Equal Protection Clause of the Fourteenth Amendment. Irvis successfully brought suit in federal court against the state liquor authority and the Moose Lodge, winning an injunction that required the liquor authority to suspend the lodge's liquor license as long it continued to discriminate in its guest policies.

On appeal the Supreme Court reversed, holding that there was insufficient governmental involvement by the state of Pennsylvania in the racially discriminatory policies of the Moose Lodge to constitute a violation of the Equal Protection Clause. Justice William Rehnquist noted that the Court had held in the *Civil Rights Cases* (1883) that the Equal Protection Clause prohibited only racial discrimination supported by state action. Under the state action doctrine, acts of racial discrimination resulting from the choices of private individuals and unsupported by any official sanction did not fall within the prohibition of the Equal Protection Clause. The mere licensing of the lodge to dispense liquor and the regulations of the liquor trade enforced by the state, the Court held, did not constitute the official support of the racial discrimination practiced by the lodge necessary to bring its racial policies within the prohibition of the Equal Protection Clause.

The Court additionally distinguished its earlier decision in *Burton* v. *Wilmington Parking Authority* (1961). In *Burton*, the Court had held that the Equal Protection Clause did apply to racial discrimination practiced by a private restaurant that leased its premises from a parking facility owned and financed by the city of Wilmington, Delaware. The circumstances in the *Moose Lodge* case differed from those in *Burton*, the Court pointed out, because the Moose Lodge was located on land and housed in a building owned by the lodge and not by any public authority. Furthermore, the Court held that the liquor license alone did not constitute the kind of "interdependence" between the state and the lodge that had characterized the relationship between the restaurant and the parking authority in *Burton*. Pennsylvania law required that liquor license recipients adhere to all the provisions of their own constitutions and bylaws. At the time Irvis was denied service as a guest, the Moose Lodge constitution only prohibited accepting African-Americans as members. Inexplicably, while the lawsuit was pending, the lodge amended its constitution to prohibit serving African-Americans as guests as well. This entitled Irvis to a decree enjoining the Liquor Control Board from enforcing its regulation requiring recipients to adhere to their own constitutions, Rehnquist held, but not to an injunction dissolving the license itself. Since the liquor board had made no effort to enforce its rule, however, this was a meaningless concession by the Court. So long as the state made no enforcement effort, the lodge, as a private club, was entitled to refuse service to whomever it pleased.

Justice William O. Douglas, in a dissent joined by Justice Thurgood Marshall, agreed that merely issuing a liquor license to a private club with racially discriminatory membership and guest policies might not be sufficient to make the lodge's discrimination unconstitutional. But, Douglas noted, liquor licenses in Pennsylvania were subject to a quota system, and the quota for Harrisburg had been filled for many years. The state-enforced scarcity of liquor licenses thus resulted in restricting the access of African-Americans to liquor, since liquor was available only at private clubs for significant portions of each week. Douglas concluded that the state had in this way put the weight of its liquor licensing and regulatory practices in support of racial discrimination.

Justice William J. Brennan, also joined by Marshall, additionally argued that the state's regulatory scheme for liquor was so intertwined with the racially discriminatory policies of the Moose Lodge as to justify a finding that there was state support for racial discrimination and thus a violation of the Equal Protection Clause.

Moose Lodge marked the end of an expansion of the state action doctrine, which had begun with *Shelley* v. *Kraemer* (1948) and continued with *Burton* and subsequent "sit-in" cases of the 1960s, designed to subject private discrimination to the prohibitions of the Fourteenth Amendment.

Richard C. Cortner

Morehead v. New York ex rel. Tipaldo, 298 U.S. 587 (1936), argued 28–29 Apr. 1936, decided 1 June 1936 by vote of 5 to 4; Butler for the Court, Hughes, Stone, Brandeis, and Cardozo in dissent. Perhaps the most unpopular decision of the 1935–1936 Supreme Court term was *Morehead*, in which a narrow majority struck down a New York minimum-wage law for women and children.

Speaking for the five-member majority, Justice Pierce Butler maintained that the right to contract for wages in return for work "is part of the liberty protected by the due process clause [of the Fourteenth Amendment]" (p. 610). He further argued that a state government should not be permitted to interfere with any contracts for labor. Justice Butler was joined in his *Morehead* majority

by the three other conservative justices on the Court—James McReynolds, George Sutherland, and Willis Van Devanter—and by the quixotic Justice Owen J. Roberts.

In response to Butler's bald assertion that a state was powerless to enact minimum wage legislation—even in the throes of the Great Depression—one of the dissenters, Justice Harlan Fiske Stone, accused the majority of acting on the basis of their "personal economic predilections" (p. 587) and submitted that "there is grim irony in speaking of the freedom of contract of those who, because of their economic necessities, give their services for less than is needful to keep body and soul together" (p. 632).

All but 10 of the 344 newspaper editorials written in response to the *Morehead* decision attacked it. Even the Republican Party Platform of 1936 repudiated the decision, as did the Court in *West Coast Hotel* v. *Parrish* (1937).

John W. Johnson

Morgan v. Virginia, 328 U.S. 373 (1946), argued 27 Mar. 1946, decided 3 June 1946 by vote of 7 to 1. Reed for the Court, Rutledge, Black, and Frankfurter concurring, Burton in dissent, Jackson not participating. This case was one of the constellation of civil rights cases brought to the Supreme Court in the post-World War II years by the National Association for the Advancement of Colored People that challenged the pattern of racial segregation in the American South. Irene Morgan, an African-American woman, boarded an interstate Greyhound bus in Gloucester County, Virginia, bound for Baltimore, Maryland. When ordered by the driver to sit at the rear of the bus, as required by Virginia law, Morgan refused. She was arrested and convicted in Virginia of a misdemeanor, and fined ten dollars. The Supreme Court of Virginia affirmed her conviction.

Attorneys William H. Hastie and Thurgood Marshall carried an appeal to the U.S. Supreme Court, arguing that the Virginia statute, which required segregation on interstate carriers, imposed an improper burden on interstate commerce. Citing *Hall* v. *DeCuir* (1878), in which the justices voided a Louisiana statute prohibiting racial segregation in interstate transportation, Marshall and Hastie urged the Court to reverse the Virginia court and invalidate the statute. Justice Stanley Reed, in his opinion, found their argument convincing and struck down the law. In practice, segregation on southern buses continued on an informal basis, even though it was clear that such practices on interstate bus travel would not survive legal challenge.

Augustus M. Burns III

Morrison v. Olson, 487 U.S. 654 (1988), argued 26 Apr. 1988, decided 29 June 1988 by vote of 7 to 1; Rehnquist for the Court, Scalia in dissent, Kennedy not participating. In this decision, the Supreme Court upheld the statute providing for an independent counsel to investigate possible federal criminal violations by senior executive officials. The independent counsel statute resulted from the Watergate crisis, in which senior officials of the Nixon administration, including the attorney general, were implicated in covering up a politically motivated burglary at the Watergate office complex in Washington, D.C., before the 1972 presidential election.

Adopted in 1978, Title VI of the Ethics of Government Act provides for appointment of an independent counsel by a special court upon the attorney general's application. An independent counsel has more independence from the attorney general than a regular federal prosecutor, in particular because an independent counsel is removable by the attorney general only for good cause, not at will.

The Court held that an independent counsel is an "inferior officer" who can be appointed by a court of law under the Appointments Clause of the Constitution (Art. II, sec. 2). The Court also concluded that the removal limitation did not impermissibly limit executive authority. The decision signaled a renewed willingness by the Court to accept statutory limitations on removal of officers performing executive functions, as it had in *Humphrey's Executor v. United States* (1935).

The Court took account of the practical consequences of the statute's innovations without relying chiefly on abstract formulations of doctrine. In this regard, *Morrison* is widely seen as a less formalistic approach to separation of powers than either *Immigration and Naturalization Service v. Chadha* (1983) or *Bowsher v. Synar* (1986).

Thomas O. Sargentich

Morrison, United States v., 529 U.S. 598 (2000), argued 11 Jan. 2000, decided 15 May 2000 by vote of 5 to 4; Rehnquist for the Court, Thomas concurring, Souter and Breyer in dissent.

The 1994 Violence Against Women Act (VAWA) was the product of four years of congressional hearings that documented the prevalence of violence against women, its impact on the nation, and the states' failure to protect women from such crimes. Citing specific evidence of a substantial effect on the nation's economy and bias in the state justice systems, Congress used its authority under the Commerce Clause and section 5 of the Fourteenth Amendment to enact the Civil Rights Remedy of VAWA (section 3981). The Civil Rights Remedy enabled victims of gender-based violence to sue their assailants in state or federal court for compensatory or punitive damages, declaratory or injunctive relief, and attorney fees.

One of the few women to use the Civil Rights Remedy was Christy Bronzkala. After allegedly being gang raped by Antonio Morrison and James Crawford in a Virginia Polytechnic dorm room, Bronzkala filed a complaint under the school's sexual assault policy. After the school's repeated failure to provide justice or relief, Bronzkala sued her assailants in federal court.

Affirming the decision of the Fourth Circuit Court, the Supreme Court narrowly ruled the Civil Rights Remedy of VAWA unconstitutional. Evaluating the same factors considered in *United States* v. *Lopez* (1995), the majority found violence against women to be noneconomic in nature and outside Congress' legislative jurisdiction. Writing for the Court, Justice William H. Rehnquist emphasized that gender-based violence was a local issue and therefore inappropriate for federal legislation. Additionally, the majority explained that section 5 of the Fourteenth Amendment applied only to states and therefore legislation directed at private persons was outside Congress' section 5 enforcement power.

The dissenting justices argued that Congress had full authority under the Commerce Clause to enact the Civil Rights Remedy. Referring to the "mountain of data" collected by Congress, the Court found that Congress had sufficient support to conclude that gender-based violence affected interstate commerce. Additionally, the dissenters argued that by rejecting Congress' findings and focusing on the noneconomic nature of the activity, the majority was ignoring prior precedent and replacing Congress' judgment with its own. In a separate dissent,

Justice Stephen Breyer argued that a rule that requires an economic/noneconomic distinction for regulated activity is unworkable.

Morrison has played an important role in the continual battle over the balance of federal and state power. Mirroring the decision made in *Lopez*, *Morrison* marked a sharp change in the Court's interpretation of the Commerce Clause. It was the first time since the New Deal the Court rejected congressional findings that an activity affected interstate commerce. Along with limiting Congress' power under the Commerce Clause, the decision also further restrained the use of section 5 of the Fourteenth Amendment for the progression of civil rights.

Mica McKinney

Morse v. Frederick, 127 S. Ct. 2618 (2007), argued 19 Mar. 2007, decided 25 June 2007 by vote of 5 to 4; Roberts for the Court; Thomas concurring; Alito, joined by Kennedy, concurring; Breyer concurring in part and dissenting in part; Stevens, joined by Souter and Ginsburg, dissenting. Joseph Frederick displayed a fourteen-foot banner bearing the phrase "Bong Hits 4 Jesus" as the 2002 Winter Olympic Games torch relay passed his high school. Frederick claimed that the banner was a publicity stunt, calling it "nonsense." The principal of the school disagreed. She confiscated the banner and suspended Frederick for ten days, arguing he had violated school policy by encouraging illegal drug use.

The Court rejected Frederick's contention that his speech was protected by the First Amendment, concluding that "schools may take steps to safeguard those entrusted to their care from speech that can reasonably be regarded as encouraging illegal drug use" (p. 2622). The majority conceded, per *Tinker* v. *Des Moines Independent Community School District* (1969), that students had a right to engage in "non-disruptive speech." But they were unwilling to extend *Tinker* to speech at a "school-sponsored event" in the light of the public interest in deterring the use of illegal drugs. Justice Clarence Thomas, in a provocative concurring opinion, argued that *Tinker* should be overruled. Justice John Paul Stevens, in turn, found little merit in sanctioning what he characterized as, at best, "an oblique" reference to drugs.

The majority opinion is arguably consistent with prior decisions. In **Hazlewood School District* v. *Kuhlmeier* (1988), for example, the Court held that *Tinker* did not extend to speech sponsored by the school, while in **Bethel School District No. 403* v. *Fraser* (1986) it allowed a school to sanction a student for "crude and vulgar" speech at a school event. *Morse* seems to grant school authorities additional latitude, however. The interesting question is how far the holding extends. Where will future lines be drawn if letting students out of school to attend a relay overseen by another organization is deemed a "school-sponsored" event? On what basis does a court determine that a third party's contrary reaction is "reasonable," given a student's avowed intent? The answers to such questions will determine if *Morse* simply clarifies the rules governing student speech or in fact signals a retreat.

Mark R. Killenbeck

Mugler v. Kansas, 123 U.S. 623 (1887), argued 11 Oct. 1887, decided 5 Dec. 1887 by vote of 8 to 1; Harlan for the Court, Field concurring in part and dissenting in part. *Mugler* v. *Kansas* was an important step toward the Court's acceptance of economic due process under the Fourteenth Amendment. Peter Mugler continued manufacturing beer after the Kansas legislature, pursuant to a new provision of the state constitution, enacted a prohibition law, forbidding the manufacture or sale of liquor without a license. For violating the statute, the state fined and imprisoned Mugler and seized his brewery and inventory of beer. On appeal to the Supreme Court, Mugler denied that the police power was so broad to prohibit the manufacture of beer for Mugler's private consumption or for sale outside Kansas. The state law, therefore, deprived Mugler of property without due process. Kansas officials, however, defended their actions against Mugler as a valid exercise of the police power to regulate health and morals.

Under the state's police power the Supreme Court upheld the prohibition statute. Justice John Marshall Harlan held, however, that courts may scrutinize the purpose behind state regulations in order to determine whether the regulation had any real relationship to health, safety, or morals under the police power. Justice Stephen Field's dissent argued that the seizure of the property and prohibition of beer manufactured for export were violations of the due process clause. Taken together Justice Harlan's opinion and Field's dissent helped to lay the foundation for the Court's acceptance of Field's broader property rights theory after 1890.

Tony Freyer

Mulford v. Smith, 307 U.S. 38 (1939), argued 8 Mar. 1939, decided 17 Apr. 1939 by vote of 7 to 2; Roberts for the Court, Butler and McReynolds in dissent. This case involved a challenge to the constitutionality of the Second Agricultural Adjustment Act (1938). In holding this important federal law constitutional, the Court said that its January 1936 decision in United States v. *Butler, which struck down the original Agricultural Adjustment Act (1933), was a mistake. The justice who wrote the majority opinion in Butler was Owen Roberts, the same justice who wrote the decision in Mulford v. Smith.

Both Agricultural Adjustment acts were motivated by Congress's desire to boost the disastrously low prices for agricultural products during the Great Depression. In speaking for the six-member majority in Butler, Roberts had held that the Agricultural Adjustment Act's processing tax, which provided the revenue to underwrite crop subsidies and soil restrictions, was an unconstitutional infringement on the states' rights to regulate agriculture.

Yet in Mulford, Roberts and the Court majority voted to uphold a tobacco quota on production that had been instituted by the Second Agricultural Adjustment Act. In this decision, Roberts concluded that Congress's Article I power "to regulate Commerce . . . among the several states" provided ample justification for the agricultural market restrictions set by the second act. Thus, in 1939 Roberts acknowledged what he had refused to recognize in 1936: that the problems confronting agriculture were national in scope and required national legislative attention.

John W. Johnson

Muller v. Oregon, 208 U.S. 412 (1908), argued 15 Jan. 1908, decided 24 Feb. 1908 by vote of 9 to 0; Brewer for the Court. In February 1903, Oregon set a maximum of ten hours work a day for women employed in factories and laundries. The law differed little from other state statutes passed during the Progressive era and constituted part of the reform drive to ameliorate the harsher aspects of industrialization. The Supreme Court had upheld a similar Utah law for miners in *Holden v. Hardy (1898), but then by a 5-to-4 vote had struck down a New York ten-hour limit for bakery workers as a violation of freedom of contract in *Lochner v. New York (1905).

Shortly after that decision, Joe Haselbock, the foreman of Curt Muller's Grand Laundry in Portland, Oregon, required Mrs. Elmer Gotcher to work more than ten hours on 4 September 1905. Two weeks later a local court found Muller guilty of violating the state ten-hour law and fined him ten dollars. Aware of Lochner, Muller appealed the misdemeanor conviction. The Oregon Supreme Court upheld the statute's constitutionality in 1906, and the following year the Supreme Court agreed to hear the case.

With the permission of the state's attorney general, the National Consumers' League secured Louis D. Brandeis to defend the law before the Supreme Court. Brandeis decided upon a highly innovative strategy yet one firmly grounded in previous decisions of the high court.

In various cases testing protective legislation, the Court had repeatedly upheld the state's police power to guard the health, safety, and welfare of its citizens. The majority opinion by Justice Rufus W. Peckham in Lochner had asserted that no connection existed between the legitimate goals of the police power and the ten-hour bakery law; in his dissent in that case, Justice John Marshall Harlan had suggested that if a valid reason could be found to justify the regulation of hours, such laws could withstand judicial scrutiny.

Brandeis, with the aid of Florence Kelley and Josephine Goldmark of the Consumers' League, set about amassing the evidence to demonstrate the connection between women's health and long hours worked in factories. The two women gathered every medical and government report remotely connected to this issue, and Brandeis assembled the material in a highly unusual brief.

He covered the legal precedents in only two pages, and instead of trying to overturn Lochner, used its assertion that concerns directly related to health, safety, and welfare could justify a state in abridging freedom of contract through limitation of hours. In the next fifteen pages, he included excerpts of other state and foreign statutes to show that Oregon was not alone in its belief that long hours endangered women's health. Part 2 of the brief consisted of ninety-five pages of quotations from American and European factory and medical reports, representing the best data available at the time, supporting the assertion that long hours had a detrimental effect on women's health.

In what observers described as a masterful argument before the Court, Brandeis followed the same strategy, assuming that the law would be upheld if the justices recognized the relationship between the statute and the state's legitimate interest in women's health.

The technique worked, and Justice David J. Brewer, speaking for the Court, not only upheld the law, but in an unusual aside, mentioned Brandeis and the "very copious collection" of data he had filed. The Court acknowledged that "woman's physical structure and the performance of maternal functions place her at a disadvantage in the struggle for subsistence." Long hours of work took a toll on a woman, "and as healthy mothers are essential to vigorous offspring, the physical well-being of women becomes an object of public interest and care" (p. 421).

Brewer took care to note that the decision in *Muller* did not "in any respect" undermine the earlier opinion in *Lochner*, although many people at the time assumed that the Court had *sub silentio* overruled *Lochner*. In the 1920s, however, the conservative majority resurrected *Lochner* and its doctrine of freedom of contract.

Muller became the paradigm for efforts to make courts aware of social and economic conditions underlying reform legislation. Brandeis created an entry into legal argument for social facts; the "Brandeis brief" would now be the norm for advocates defending reform legislation as well as those attacking particular social conditions, such as racial segregation in *Brown v. Board of Education* (1954).

□ Alpheus T. Mason, "The Case of the Overworked Laundress," in *Quarrels That Have Shaped the Constitution,* edited by John Garraty (1975), pp. 176–190.

Melvin I. Urofsky

Munn v. Illinois, 94 U.S. 113 (1877), argued 14, 18 Jan. 1876, decided 1 Mar. 1877 by vote of 7 to 2; Waite for the Court, Field, joined by Strong, in dissent. *Munn v. Illinois* forms with the related Granger Cases a historic ruling that tests the constitutionality of state police power, through legislation, to regulate private business. Coming in the industrial upheaval of the late nineteenth century,

the case gave vitality to the recently enacted Fourteenth Amendment.

In 1875, the Illinois legislature, dominated by representatives sympathetic to the Patrons of Husbandry (the Grange), enacted legislation setting the rates that Illinois grain elevator operators could charge their grain-producing customers—provided the operators did business in any Illinois city larger than 100,000 in population. The law therefore applied to only one Illinois city: Chicago, where farmers were agitated that elevator operators were fixing rates and gouging farmers. The operators argued that the Illinois statute was an unconstitutional infringement on the commerce power of the Congress and that it was violative of the Fourteenth Amendment Due Process Clause, intended to bar any state from depriving persons of property without due process of law.

For the majority, Chief Justice Morrison R. Waite vindicated the Granger forces. He upheld the Illinois law, arguing that such a statute was clearly within the limits of the police power of the state of Illinois. Waite eloquently traced the regulatory principle from its origins in English common law, observing that "[W]hen private property is affected with a public interest," it ceased to be exclusively private (p. 126). He went on to ground his ruling in nineteenth-century American case law regarding bridges, ferries, railroads, and navigable waterways. Waite observed that when one devotes "property to a use in which the public has an interest, he, in effect, grants to the public an interest in that use, and must submit to be controlled by the public for the common good, to the extent of the interest he has created" (p. 126).

Waite next asked if the facts of the case justified the legislature's statutory action—a question he answered affirmatively: "For our purposes we must assume that if a state of facts could exist that would justify such legislation, it actually did exist when the statute under consideration was passed" (p. 132). Moreover, it was the proper function of the judiciary to determine if the legislative power exercised here was a legitimate constitutional power. If so, its exercise was a political question: "For protection against abuses by legislatures, the people must resort to the polls, not to the courts" (p. 134)—Waite's classic statement of nineteenth-century judicial restraint. Finally, Waite noted that the effect of the Illinois statute on interstate commerce was incidental, a local regulation that would stand in the absence of congressional involvement.

Justice Stephen J. Field entered a vigorous dissent in which Justice William Strong concurred. Field found the Illinois statute constitutionally impermissible and argued for a position that would come to be called substantive due process. Field drew a distinction between private rights and public power, basing his dissent in part on the Due Process Clause of the Fourteenth Amendment. Field dismissed the argument that by using their private property to engage in the business of grain storage the private owners had granted the public an interest in that use. "If this be sound law," Field admonished in a celebrated passage, "all property and all business in the state are held at the mercy of the Legislature" (p. 140), a right to property so fragile as to be clearly unacceptable within the property guarantees of the Fourteenth Amendment.

In arguing for a substantive conception of the Due Process Clause—that a hierarchy of rights was embodied in the Constitution that representative bodies could not abridge— Field in dissent announced a position that, over time, a Supreme Court majority would embrace. While Field did not condemn all governmental regulation of business activity, especially in the matter of regulating large corporations, he sought to limit the use of the state police power as an instrument for business regulation. His argument, in addition, foresaw a more activist and interventionist role for the federal judiciary in the economic life of the states—a harbinger of the modern role of federal courts in a broad array of policy questions.

Augustus M. Burns III

Murdock v. Memphis, 20 Wall. (87 U.S.) 590 (1875), argued 21 Jan. and 2 Apr. 1873, decided 11 Jan. 1875 by vote of 5 to 3; Miller for the Court, Bradley, Clifford, and Swayne in dissent, Waite not participating. Section 25 of the 1789 Judiciary Act, the original grant of appellate authority to the Supreme Court over federal question cases from the state courts, excluded questions of state law from review by the Court. This provision established a basic principle of judicial federalism: state courts, not the Supreme Court, have final and unreviewable authority over the interpretation of the state constitutions and laws. In an 1867 reenactment of section 25, Congress omitted the proviso containing

this exclusion. *Murdock* v. *Memphis* presented questions of whether Congress thereby conferred appellate jurisdiction on the Supreme Court over questions of state law, and, if it did, whether such a breach of the bulkheads of federalism was constitutional.

Justice Samuel F. Miller did not reach the second question because he decided the first in the negative. Expressing annoyance at the opacity of congressional intent in the 1867 reenactment, Miller held that such a far-reaching revision of the federal system would require at least a clear statement of Congress's determination to do so. Such a "radical and hazardous change of a policy vital . . . to the independence of the State courts," wrote Miller, could not be inferred from the silences of Congress (p. 630). Thus *Murdock* v. *Memphis* confirmed the modern foundations of American judicial federalism.

William M. Wiecek

Murdock v. Pennsylvania, 319 U.S. 105 (1943), argued 10–11 Mar. 1943, decided 3 May 1943 by vote of 5 to 4; Douglas for the Court, Reed, Frankfurter, Jackson, and Roberts in dissent. The *Murdock* decision was one of a group of World War II–era cases that contributed to the rapid and contentious development of First Amendment doctrine respecting freedom of religion. Justice William O. Douglas, speaking for the majority, stressed that freedom of speech, press, and religion occupied a "preferred position" under the Constitution (p. 115).

*Lovell v. *City of Griffin* (1938), the first of the so-called Jehovah's Witnesses cases establishing specific guidelines for regulating religious communication, struck down a licensing ordinance as applied to religious colporteurs. Thereafter, in a line of decisions the Supreme Court voided ordinances requiring a permit for door-to-door religious pamphleteering and prior approval by a public official for soliciting funds for religious use.

In this context the justices in *Murdock* struck down the application of a city ordinance requiring Jehovah's Witnesses and other religious proselytizers to pay a license tax. Douglas concluded that the license tax "restrains in advance those constitutional liberties of press and religion and inevitably tends to suppress their exercise" (p. 114). Justice Stanley Reed, dissenting, maintained that localities could levy reasonable and nondiscriminatory taxes on the sale of religious literature.

William M. Wiecek

Murphy v. Waterfront Commission of New York, 378 U.S. 52 (1964), argued 5 Mar. 1964, decided 15 June 1964 by vote of 9 to 0; Goldberg for the Court. The main question before the Court was whether a state may compel a witness to answer questions under an immunity statute when those answers might prove incriminating under federal law. *Malloy v. Hogan* (1964), decided on the same day, anticipated the Court's answer. *Malloy* held, for the first time, that the Fifth Amendment's protection against self-incrimination applies to the states through the Due Process Clause of the Fourteenth Amendment.

Having established that the states are now bound by the self-incrimination clause of the Fifth Amendment, the Court in *Murphy* went on to say that incriminating testimony compelled by one government may not be used by another. Thus federal prosecutors would be prohibited from making any use, direct or derivative, of state-compelled incriminating testimony. *Feldman v. United States* (1944), which had held to the contrary, was over-ruled.

The privilege against self-incrimination is, of course, not absolute. The effective administration of justice may require the production of incriminating testimony. Immunizing a witness against the use or derivative use of such testimony is one way of obtaining it. But such immunity, said the Court, must be as broad as the privilege itself. If there is any probability that a defendant's testimony, or the fruits thereof, will be used against him even by prosecutors in another jurisdiction, any such proceeding would be constitutionally invalid unless based on evidence obtained wholly independently of the earlier compelled testimony. This is known as "use" immunity.

Use immunity was an issue in *Kastigar v. United States* (1972) because it did not appear to guarantee absolute protection against a prosecution arising out of the event or transaction in which the witness may have been criminally involved and about which he was forced to testify. "Transactional immunity," which Kastigar claimed, is far broader than use immunity and would virtually amount to a grant of amnesty. This, said the Court in *Kastigar*, would exceed the requirements of the privilege against self-incrimination.

Use immunity is sufficient and coextensive with the privilege because it places the witness and the prosecution in substantially the same position as if the witness had claimed the privilege.

Donald P. Kommers

Murray's Lessee v. Hoboken Land & Improvement Co., 18 How (59 U.S.) 272 (1856), argued 30, 31 Jan., 1, 4 Feb. 1856, decided 19 Feb. 1856 by vote of 9 to 0; Curtis for the Court. Justice Benjamin R. Curtis's opinion in this case provided the Supreme Court's first analysis of the Due Process Clause of the Fifth Amendment. The notorious Samuel Swartwout had embezzled $1.5 million in customs receipts and used the monies to purchase land. The Treasury Department issued distress warrants (a non-judicial procedure) to void the land sales and recover the funds. Swartwout and purchasers of the lands challenged the proceedings as a violation of due process and the separation of powers.

For a unanimous Court, Curtis upheld the constitutionality of this process, holding that the federal government could resort to non-judicial procedures to recover funds embezzled from it. He interpreted the Due Process Clause of the Fifth Amendment to be the equivalent of the "law of the land" provisions that first appeared in Magna Carta's clause thirty-nine (p. 276). His interpretation of the Due Process Clause—"the article is a restraint on the legislative as well as on the executive and the judicial powers of the government, and cannot be construed as to leave Congress free to make any process 'due process of law'"—relied on traditional procedural conceptions of due process, but contained within it an ambiguous hint of the possibility of a substantive interpretation (p. 276). With the New York Court of Appeals' contemporaneous decision in *Wynehamer* v. *People*, *Murray's Lessee* indirectly presaged the late nineteenth-century doctrine of substantive due process. However, Chief Justice Roger B. Taney ignored both opinions in his reliance on the Due Process Clause in his *Dred *Scott* dictum, and Curtis's opinion proved to be a premature anticipation of later doctrinal developments.

Thomas C. Mackey

Muskrat v. United States, 219 U.S. 346 (1911), argued 30 Nov.–2 Dec. 1910, decided 23 Jan. 1911 by vote of 7 to 0; Day for the Court; Van Devanter and Lamar not participating. On 1 March 1907, Congress passed legislation providing that certain named Cherokee Indians, including David Muskrat, were permitted to bring suit against the United States in the Court of Claims, with an appeal to the Supreme Court, to test the constitutionality of previous acts of Congress regulating the lands possessed by the Cherokees. Congress also directed the attorney general to represent the United States in the litigation, and provided that counsel for the Cherokees authorized to initiate the litigation should be paid by the U.S. Treasury.

When litigation reached the Supreme Court, it became obvious that under Article III of the Constitution the judicial power of the United States courts, including the Supreme Court, could only be exercised in the decision of cases and controversies brought to the courts for resolution. The cases and controversies requirement of Article III, the Court noted, had from almost the beginning of the republic been thought to impose limitations upon the exercise of judicial power by the federal courts. The 1907 act of Congress, the Court held, had created a friendly suit, lacking any adverse clash of legal interests between two parties, which a real case or controversy required. The *Muskrat* case was thus not within the Court's legitimate jurisdiction under Article III and was therefore dismissed. *Muskrat v. United States* remains a classic example of the limitations imposed by the cases and controversies requirement upon the exercise of federal judicial power.

Richard C. Cortner

Myers v. United States, 272 U.S. 52 (1926), argued 5 Dec. 1924, reargued 13–14 Apr. 1925, decided 25 Oct. 1926 by vote of 6 to 3; Taft for the Court, Holmes, McReynolds, and Brandeis in dissent. When he was President, William Howard Taft believed that the Constitution strictly limited the chief executive's power. Yet, as chief justice, he penned one of the broadest readings of presidential power in Supreme Court history. Spawning one of the longest decisions in the Court reports, the *Myers* case involved a suit for back pay instituted by a postmaster summarily removed from office by President Woodrow Wilson. The enabling statute provided for removal during the four-year term only with the advice and consent of the Senate. Whether the unpaid salary could be recovered hinged on the Court's interpretation of the power of Congress to limit the president's authority to remove lesser officials appointed by him.

Despite clear congressional authority to establish post offices and provide for the appointment and pay of postal employees, Taft, for the Court, concluded that the statute was an invasion of executive power. Taft found, in the 1789 congressional debates over the office of secretary of state, a legislative understanding that the president inherently possessed an unqualified power to remove government officials he had appointed. Taft accepted this legislative determination because he agreed with the rationale behind the conclusion. Since the president was ultimately responsible for seeing that the laws were faithfully executed, he must have the full discretion to remove all subordinates. To this Taft added that the executive article should be interpreted to promote the separation of powers; the constitutional requirement for Senate advice and consent upon appointment should not be widened by implication. Except for judges, who are appointed during good behavior, the president should have full removal discretion. That was so, Taft said, because political differences between the executive and legislative branches could well prevent the president from performing his constitutional duty of executing the laws.

The dissenters easily exposed the weakness of Taft's opinion. Justice James McReynolds, in an uncharacteristically long and thorough dissent, ridiculed the notion of an inherent executive power to remove governmental employees. Since Congress has the constitutional authority to place the appointment of lesser governmental officials in other hands than the president's and to provide for their removal, McReynolds rejected the view that vesting the president with the authority to appoint inferior officials deprived Congress of the power to limit removal.

In his dissent, Justice Louis D. Brandeis concluded that in dealing with lesser governmental officials the president must act under the authority of Congress and that the president possessed only the power the enabling act provided. Held in check by the entrenched spoils system, Congress began to address the question of the removal of governmental employees only after the Civil War. But Brandeis saw nothing in the earlier period that would contradict the consistent practice since that time. While Taft pushed the concept of separation of powers to its logical extreme, Brandeis emphasized the importance of checks and balances. Congress, Brandeis continued, was not only permitted but was obliged to protect not only government employees but also free government from arbitrary executive action.

The *Myers* decision was too broadly drawn. In a country where administrative agencies were proliferating, an unlimited right of presidential removal threatened the policy-making functions of Congress.

The unanimous Court in *Humphrey's Executor* v. *United States* (1935) repudiated Taft's expansive words and ruled that where government officials performed quasi-legislative and/or quasi-judicial functions, those officials could be protected from arbitrary executive removal by Congress. In regard to officials performing strictly executive functions, however, *Myers* remains good law.

☐ Louis Fisher, *Constitutional Conflicts between Congress and The President* (1985).

John E. Semonche

N

National Association for the Advancement of Colored People v. Alabama ex rel. Patterson, 357 U.S. 449 (1958), argued 15–16 Jan. 1958, decided 30 June 1958 by vote of 9 to 0; Harlan for the Court. In this case, the Supreme Court upheld the right to freedom of association as an integral part of the First Amendment despite the absence of an explicit reference to association in the amendment's wording.

The case arose in the context of the NAACP's noncompliance with Alabama corporate filing laws and its efforts to operate in the face of state legal action to oust it for activities (such as organizing a bus boycott and aiding students seeking to desegregate the state university) that were allegedly causing irreparable injury to the state's citizenry. The Alabama trial court sought to obtain numerous NAACP records and, after some delay, the NAACP produced all the required documentation except its membership list, asserting that to supply such a list would threaten its organizational integrity. Publicizing the names of its members would lead to economic and employment reprisals, harassment, violence, and similar burdens on its members' associational and expressive freedom. A trial judge held the NAACP in contempt and fined it $100,000.

The Supreme Court held that the NAACP could assert the constitutional right of its members as a defense against the contempt charge. To require individual members to come forward and assert their associational rights would, in this instance, effectively negate them. More broadly, the Court found that the membership list was so related to the members' rights to pursue their lawful interests privately, and to associate freely, as to be constitutionally protected. Forced disclosure of the membership list would unduly burden the NAACP's First Amendment freedom of association. Nor had the state demonstrated an interest in the list sufficient to outweigh the NAACP's constitutional objection. The Alabama court's contempt judgment and fine were overturned.

Elliot E. Slotnick

National Association for the Advancement of Colored People v. Button, 371 U.S. 415 (1963), argued 8 Nov. 1961, reargued 9 Oct. 1962, decided 14 Jan. 1963 by vote of 5 to 1 to 3; Brennan for the Court, White concurring in part and dissenting in part, Harlan, Clark, and Stewart in dissent. This case arose in the context of a Virginia "barratry" statute that challenged civil rights groups (such as the NAACP) and their attorneys who utilized the courts to combat racial discrimination through sponsored litigation. Under the statute, attorneys who represented organizations having no "pecuniary interest" in such litigation were subject to disbarment.

The Supreme Court said that the NAACP could assert the rights of its members in defending against the claim that they had engaged in barratry, the illegal solicitation of legal business. Further, the NAACP's efforts to provide attorneys in suits challenging racial discrimination was protected by the First and Fourteenth Amendments. Writing in dissent, Justice John M. Harlan argued that unlike other group activities such as association, discussion, and advocacy, litigation was primarily conduct and not expression. Thus, it was subject to reasonable state regulation. The majority disagreed, however, and held that sponsored litigation might be the only means through which some groups could express the grievances of their members and seek redress. Such group litigation was protected by the First Amendment and, indeed, statutes such as those at issue in this case posed "the gravest danger of smothering all discussion looking to the eventual institution of litigation on behalf of the rights of Negroes" (pp. 416–417). The *Button* decision represents a landmark ruling upholding interest group utilization of the judicial process as a prime component of their political activity.

Elliot E. Slotnick

National Labor Relations Board v. Jones & Laughlin Steel Corp., 301 U.S. 1 (1937), argued 10–11 Feb. 1937, decided 12 Apr. 1937 by vote of 5 to 4; Hughes for the Court, Sutherland, Van Devanter, McReynolds, and Butler in dissent. The *Jones & Laughlin* case was one of the five cases decided on 12 April 1937 that sustained the constitutionality of the National Labor Relations Act (NLRA) and proved to be a crucial turning point in the New Deal constitutional crisis. Passed by Congress in 1935, the NLRA guaranteed the right of workers to organize unions both in businesses operating in interstate commerce and in businesses whose activities affected interstate commerce and prohibited employers from dismissing or otherwise discriminating against their employees because of union membership or activities.

Commonly regarded as the most radical of the legislation enacted by Congress during President Franklin D. Roosevelt's New Deal, the NLRA was regarded at its passage as being of dubious constitutionality. In previous cases, the Court had held that liberty of contract was protected by the Due Process Clause of the Fifth Amendment and that under liberty of contract employers and employees had the right to bargain free of governmental interference. The Court had also held that labor relations associated with

manufacturing or production enterprises only affected interstate commerce indirectly and were thus beyond the legitimate scope of congressional power under the Commerce Clause. The NLRA had been applied to employer-employee relations at Jones & Laughlin's Aliquippa, Pennsylvania, plant, where steel and steel products were manufactured.

Frustrated by the Supreme Court's invalidation of much of the New Deal legislation passed by Congress from 1933 to 1936, President Roosevelt in early 1937 sought legislation authorizing him to appoint additional justices to the Court in order to obtain a pro-New Deal majority. The key issue that spurred the introduction of this so-called court-packing plan was the disagreement between the Supreme Court and the president and Congress over the scope of national power to regulate the economy, with the Court construing such power narrowly, while the President and Congress construed it broadly. The issue was presented to the Court in the *Jones & Laughlin* case, which was argued less than a week after Roosevelt had proposed the court-packing plan.

Dissenting in the *Jones & Laughlin* cases, Justices George Sutherland, Pierce Butler, Willis Van Devanter, and James McReynolds called for invalidation of the NLRA on both liberty of contract and Commerce Clause grounds. Only a year previously, both Chief Justice Charles Evans Hughes and Justice Owen Roberts had also endorsed the view that labor relations associated with production enterprises were local in nature and affected interstate commerce only indirectly. Yet both Hughes and Roberts voted to uphold the NLRA in the *Jones & Laughlin* case, and many observers felt that they had shifted their views because of the court-packing plan.

In his opinion for the Court, Hughes brushed aside the due process and liberty of contract objections to governmental protection of the right of workers to organize unions. Hughes additionally held that the national government could legitimately protect the right of workers in manufacturing and production enterprises to organize and join unions as a means of preventing strikes in those enterprises that would affect interstate commerce. In effect, the Court abandoned the indirect effects test of the validity of Commerce Clause measures and instead adopted what is still the accepted view that, under the Commerce Clause, Congress can reach and regulate not only interstate commerce itself but also any activity affecting commerce, whether directly or indirectly. By upholding the validity of the NLRA on this basis, the Court signaled that it would no longer veto the national government's attempts to regulate the economy, thereby removing the principal reason for the Roosevelt court-packing plan, which was eventually defeated in the Congress.

□ Richard C. Cortner, *The Wagner Act Cases* (1964).

Richard C. Cortner

National League of Cities v. Usery, 426 U.S. 833 (1976), argued 16 Apr. 1975, reargued 2 Mar. 1976, decided 24 June 1976 by vote of 5 to 4; Rehnquist for the Court, Blackmun concurring, Brennan, White, Marshall, and Stevens in dissent. *National League of Cities* struck down a 1974 federal statute that extended the maximum hours and minimum wage provisions of the Fair Labor Standards Act to most state and municipal employees. That the maximum hours and minimum wage provisions of the Fair Labor Standards Act were constitutional as applied to the employees of private corporations was a matter of settled law. However, the Court, seemingly breathing new life into the Tenth Amendment, held that as applied to the "states as states," the provisions were an unconstitutional interference with an essential "attribute of sovereignty attaching to every state government" (p. 845), and thus violated the Tenth Amendment.

The significance of *National League of Cities* lay not so much in the actual impact of the decision itself, but in its symbolic blow in favor of federalism. By invoking the Tenth Amendment as a serious barrier to federal power, the Court revived a provision that had been dormant since the New Deal. The Court struck down the statute in question not because Congress lacked the affirmative power to pass it—the regulation clearly fell under Congress's power to regulate interstate and foreign commerce—but because the act violated "traditional aspects of state sovereignty" and "impermissibly interfere[d] with the integral governmental functions" of the states (pp. 849, 851). For the first time since the New Deal, the Supreme Court had struck down a federal law on the ground that Congress had transgressed the permissible boundaries of federalism.

National League of Cities did not challenge Congress's power to regulate private corporations or individuals involved in interstate commerce or in activities that had a substantial effect on interstate commerce. The decision affected only those cases in which the states themselves—that is, the state governments or their political subdivisions—were so engaged. The Court held that "the States as States stand on a quite different footing from an individual or a corporation when challenging the exercise of Congress'[s] power to regulate commerce" (p. 833). In so holding, the Court overruled *Maryland v. Wirtz* (1968) but left intact the long line of decisions granting broad congressional powers to regulate interstate and foreign commerce.

National League of Cities left unclear exactly where to draw the line between permissible and impermissible federal intrusions on the states. Justice William Rehnquist's formulation of the test varied from "functions essential to separate and independent existence" to "traditional aspects of state sovereignty" to "integral governmental functions" and "traditional operations of state and local governments." As examples of traditional or integral governmental functions the Court listed fire prevention, police protection, sanitation, public health, and parks and recreation. Since *National League of Cities* itself involved a general challenge to the sweeping provisions of the 1974 act, specific determinations of what constituted a traditional governmental function were left to later cases involving more specific congressional actions.

In a brief concurrence, Justice Harry Blackmun suggested that the opinion of the Court adopted "a balancing approach, and does not outlaw federal power in areas such as environmental protection, where the federal interest is demonstrably greater and where state facility compliance with imposed federal standards would be essential" (p. 856).

Four justices dissented. Justice William Brennan pointed out the Court's longstanding deference to congressional regulation in the commerce area and cited its previous holdings that "the sovereign power of the states is necessarily diminished to the extent of the grants of power to the federal government in the Constitution" (p. 859). Brennan accused the majority of creating an "illconceived abstraction . . . as a transparent cover for invalidating a congressional judgment with which they disagree" (p. 867), and of violating the principles of judicial restraint and deference to the political branches. He called the majority's "essential-function" test "conceptually unworkable" and meaningless. The Court's decision, he concluded, "was a catastrophic judicial body blow at Congress'[s] power under the Commerce Clause" (p. 832).

National League of Cities had a brief lifespan. After a decade of drawing fine distinctions between state functions that were or were not "essential" or "traditional," the Court gave up. In *Garcia* v. *San Antonio Metropolitan Transit Authority* (1985), it overruled *National League of Cities* by the same 5-to-4 vote, with Blackmun—who had indicated in *National League of Cities* that he was "not untroubled by certain possible implications of the Court's opinion" (p. 865)—switching his vote (O'Connor voted the same way as Stewart, whom she had replaced in 1981). Yet the Court, led by Chief Justice William H. Rehnquist, continued to stress the theme of local as opposed to federal control in a host of important areas. Thus, in *United States* v. *Lopez* (1995), the justices struck down an act of Congress making it a crime knowingly to possess a firearm within one thousand feet of a public or private school because the act did not flow from any enumerated power.

William Lasser

National Organization of Women v. Scheidler, 510 U.S. 249 (1994), argued 8 Dec. 1993, decided 24 Jan. 1994 by vote of 9 to 0; Rehnquist for the Court, Souter concurring. Perhaps no other issue so roiled American public life in the 1980s as did abortion. While the Court provided broad but incomplete protection for women to seek abortions, opponents of the practice mustered a new strategy aimed at disrupting the business of abortion clinics that had sprung up around the country in the wake of *Roe* v. *Wade* (1973). The most prominent of these antiabortion groups were Operation Rescue and the Pro-Life Action League, led by Joseph Scheidler. The National Organization for Women (NOW) brought suit on behalf of the clinics against Scheidler charging that he and the Pro-Life Action League, along with similar groups, had engaged in a conspiracy of violence, intimidation, and harassment to shut down abortion clinics. Most significantly, NOW's suit relied on the Racketeer Influence and Corrupt Organization Act, commonly known as RICO. The statute, among its many other stiff provisions, called for triple damages and other heavy financial penalties for running an enterprise through a "pattern of racketeering activity."

NOW's use of RICO was both innovative and controversial. Scheidler and other antiabortionists insisted that they were not racketeers but agents of legitimate social protest who should be protected under the First Amendment. Moreover, they asserted that the RICO statute was not applicable, since they were not an economically motivated enterprise. Lower federal courts, however, had split on the question of whether to apply RICO broadly or narrowly when interpreting what was an economically motivated enterprise. The Court of Appeals for the Seventh Circuit adopted a narrow view in sustaining the dismissal of NOW's lawsuit on the ground that, no matter how reprehensible the behavior of the antiabortion groups, they did not fall under the RICO statute's requirement for an economic motive to be present.

A unanimous Supreme Court, however, reversed the Seventh Circuit. Chief Justice William Rehnquist adopted a broad view of the law and of the nature of an economic enterprise. "Nowhere," according to Rehnquist in his analysis of the statute, "is there any indication that an economic motive is required" (p. 257). According to the Court, the law could be applied to any individual or group of individuals, partnerships, corporations, associations, or other legal entities that engaged in a "pattern of racketeering," meaning two or more incidents of criminal activity such as extortion, arson, and kidnapping. While Rehnquist noted that the law had originally been written to deal with organized crime, he refused to read into the law limits that Congress had itself not written. The Court ordered the case remanded to the federal district court in Chicago for trial based on the RICO statute.

While Justice David Souter joined with the majority, he interpreted the scope of the ruling in a somewhat different way. In a concurring opinion joined by Justice Anthony M. Kennedy, Souter concluded that the Court's decision did not bar First Amendment challenges to RICO's application. In this instance, Souter said, the issue had not been properly raised, but it might be in other cases and RICO could not be used to deter advocacy that would otherwise be protected under the First Amendment.

The decision struck a controversial note outside the Court. Anti-abortion groups denounced the justices for siding with abortionists, and civil liberties advocates worried that the RICO statute would be used to undercut the First Amendment freedoms of social-protest groups. Other critics complained that the decision would expose legitimate corporations to suits by environmental groups who could easily show that the business had an economic interest in destroying the environment. At the same time, law enforcement organizations, especially at the federal level, applauded the decision as giving them a new weapon in the fight against terrorism.

Kermit L. Hall

National Treasury Employees Union v. Von Raab, 489 U.S. 656 (1989), argued 2 Nov. 1988, decided 21 Mar. 1989 by vote of 5 to 4; Kennedy for the Court, Marshall, Brennan, Scalia, and Stevens in dissent. At issue in the case, decided along with *Skinner* v. *Railway Labor Executives Association* (1989), was the constitutionality of the United States Custom Service's drug-testing program that analyzed urine samples of employees who sought promotions to positions involving the interdiction of drugs, the carrying of firearms, or access to classified materials.

The program was challenged as violative of the Fourth Amendment by a union of federal employees. A federal district court agreed and enjoined the service from continuing it. The court of appeals vacated the injunction.

The Supreme Court held that the Fourth Amendment's prohibition of unreasonable searches and seizures applied to the program. Balancing the individual's privacy expectations against the government's special needs, the Court acknowledged that such needs can justify a departure from the Fourth Amendment's ordinary warrant, individualized suspicion, and probable cause requirements. In this case, it stressed that the program only applied to those seeking promotions and that it was carefully designed to protect privacy. Given the epidemic of drug abuse, the danger that service personnel using drugs could be bribed and the danger inherent in drug-using service agents misusing their firearms, the Court held that the government had demonstrated a compelling interest in safeguarding the borders and the public safety sufficient to outweigh the privacy expectations of those employees who sought promotions. The

classified material issue was remanded to the lower court for further development of the record.

In dissent, Justices Thurgood Marshall and William Brennan, briefly summarizing their dissent in *Skinner,* found the Court's dismissal of the Fourth Amendment's probable cause requirement unprincipled and unjustifiable. Justices Antonin Scalia and Anthony Kennedy chastised the Court for accepting the service's program based solely on speculation without any showing of actual harm or its likelihood. The Court extended the general principle of *Von Raab* into other areas, notably the public schools. In *Veronia School District* v. *Acton* (1995), the justices held that testing of student athletes for drug use was reasonable, although its decision left open the question of whether other students might also be tested.

Gerald N. Rosenberg

Neagle, In re, 135 U.S. 1 (1890), argued 4–5 Mar. 1890, decided 14 Apr. 1890 by vote of 6 to 2; Miller for the Court, Lamar in dissent, Field not participating. Justice Stephen J. Field had provoked the hostility of David Terry, a popular lawyer and the justice's former colleague on the California Supreme Court by a circuit court opinion invalidating the previous marriage of Terry's wife. When Field returned to California for circuit duty in 1889, he was accompanied by David Neagle, a federal marshal assigned to him. When Terry encountered Field and assaulted him, Neagle shot and killed the assailant. Charged with murder under California law, Neagle sought a writ of habeas corpus from the federal circuit court. Judge Lorenzo Sawyer, who had participated with Field in the decision invalidating Mrs. Terry's marriage, granted the writ.

The Supreme Court had to decide whether a federal court could make a definitive determination of justifiable homicide and thereby preempt the operation of California law. Federal legislation authorized a writ of habeas corpus if the person was held in violation of federal law, which had been understood to mean a statute. To rescue Neagle from the uncertainties of California justice, the Court now defined "law" to include acts done under the authority of the United States. The dissenters condemned this expansion of federal power for its intrusion into the domain of state criminal law.

John E. Semonche

Near v. Minnesota, 283 U.S. 697 (1931), argued 30 Jan. 1931, decided 1 June 1931 by vote of 5 to 4; Hughes for the Court, Butler, Van Devanter, Sutherland, and McReynolds in dissent. Responding to the 1920s burgeoning of yellow journalism, the 1925 Minnesota legislature passed a Public Nuisance Abatement Law, subsequently dubbed the Minnesota Gag Law. It permitted a judge, acting without a jury, to stop the publication of a newspaper if the judge found it "obscene, lewd, and lascivious" or "malicious, scandalous, and defamatory." Periodicals could be abated and publishers enjoined for future violations. Further, the punishment of contempt was available for disobeying an injunction. Minnesota's experiment drew warm national approval as a desirable remedy for these evils.

The first use of the law was against the *Saturday Press,* a hard-hitting weekly newspaper, which focused largely upon corruption and racketeering in Minneapolis. Flamboyant, but still reasonably accurate, its revelations outraged public officials, especially those targeted such as the mayor and police chief. As a result, the local attorney, Floyd B. Olson, successfully sought an injunction to close down this publication. Although the publisher, J. M. Near, was an unsavory character—anti-Catholic, anti-Semitic, anti-black, and anti-labor, the action alarmed many as a form of prior restraint. The American Civil Liberties Union offered to support Near and to challenge the law but was quickly elbowed aside by the conservative Chicago publisher, Col. Robert R. McCormick, who put his legal staff on the case for its appeal to the U.S. Supreme Court. This proved an important test of the First Amendment and an occasion for applying the traditional, historic concept of "no prior restraint" to state laws inhibiting the dispersal of information that a large part of the journalistic world felt the public had a right to know.

Chief Justice Charles Evans Hughes, for the Court, held the law unconstitutional in a decision that firmly established the freedom of the press against censorship. But Hughes went further to say that "this statute . . . raises questions of grave importance, transcending the local interests involved in the particular action. It is no longer open to doubt that the liberty of the press . . . is within the liberty safeguarded by the due process clause of the Fourteenth Amendment from invasion by state action" (p. 706). He also made clear that hostility to prior restraint is at the very core of the First Amendment. Only in exceptional circumstances could the possibility of turning to prior restraint be considered. Thus the "Gag Law" was struck down in its totality.

The Four Horsemen, speaking through Justice Pierce Butler, dissented. Charging that the decision gave to freedom of the press a meaning and scope not heretofore recognized and deploring the fact that the decision put upon the states "a federal restriction that is without precedent," Butler argued strongly that the Minnesota law did not constitute prior restraint (p. 723). The malice, once it was established by reading the published writing, was perfectly susceptible to control through the exertion of the state's police power, a power that the justice viewed as constituting broad authority to prohibit a full range of questionable expression. But his position failed, and freedom of the press was now "incorporated" along with free speech, against the states.

The immediate reaction to the decision was overwhelmingly positive. The nation's press was gratified and relieved. Many newspapers quoted Col. McCormick's statement that "the decision of Chief Justice Hughes will go down in history as one of the great triumphs of free thought."

Near set forth a general principle that came to define freedom of the American press. Possibly, more importantly, the ruling stiffened the backbone of countless editors and publishers and helped stave off periodic attempts by politicians, judges, and prosecutors to muzzle the journalistic watch dog. It further represented an important development in the area of deregulation and decriminalization. It was a form of decontrol, striking at the use of state police power and informal local controls to curtail public information, essential to an informed citizenry.

Paul L. Murphy

Nebbia v. New York, 291 U.S. 502 (1934), argued 4–5 Dec. 1933, decided 5 Mar. 1934 by vote of 5 to 4; Roberts for the Court, McReynolds, Butler, Sutherland, and Van Devanter in dissent. *Nebbia* involved emergency legislation passed by New York State to ease some of the economic hardships brought on by the Great Depression. Leo Nebbia, a grocer in Rochester, New York, broke the Milk Control Act of 1933 by selling a quart of milk for more than the fixed maximum price of nine cents a quart. On appeal to the Supreme Court, Nebbia's conviction was sustained and the New York law was ruled constitutional.

In the majority opinion, Justice Owen Roberts abandoned the "affected with public interest" doctrine that the Court had adhered to since the late nineteenth century and concluded that a state "may regulate a business in any of its aspects, including the prices to be charged for the products or commodities it sells." He added that "a state is free to adopt whatever economic policy may reasonably be deemed to promote public welfare, and to enforce that policy by legislation adapted to its purpose" (pp. 502, 537).

In dissent, Justice James McReynolds voiced the slippery substantive due process argument, maintaining that the Due Process Clause of the Fourteenth Amendment gave the justices license to sustain economic legislation they found reasonable and strike down laws they believed to be unreasonable.

John W. Johnson

Nebraska Press Association v. Stuart, 427 U.S. 539 (1976), argued 19 Apr. 1976, decided 30 June 1976 by vote of 9 to 0; Burger for the Court, Brennan and Stevens concurring. In *Nebraska Press Association,* the Court considered for the first time the permissibility of a gag order on the press to protect a criminal defendant's right to a fair trial. The case involved the murder of six members of one family and the subsequent commission of necrophilia. The trial court prohibited publication of the confession of the accused as well as the contents of a note written by him on the night of the crime. In overturning the gag order, the Supreme Court reiterated its longstanding opposition to prior restraints. It refused to erode established First Amendment press freedoms in order to combat speculative dangers to an accused's fair trial rights.

The Court primarily viewed the gag order from the perspective of the First Amendment and presumptively treated it as unconstitutional. It concluded that most adverse publicity presented few threats to important Sixth Amendment rights. Moreover, the Court observed that the press often guards against miscarriages of justice by subjecting criminal trials to extensive public scrutiny. By employing a version of the clear and present danger test, the Court articulated a First Amendment limit on the means available to trial judges to combat prejudicial publicity.

Patrick M. Garry

New State Ice Co. v. Liebmann, 285 U.S. 262 (1932), argued 19 Feb. 1932, decided 21 Mar. 1932 by vote of 6 to 2; Sutherland for the Court, Brandeis in dissent; Cardozo not participating. In *New State Ice,* the Supreme Court demonstrated its commitment to the protection of entrepreneurial liberty under the Due Process Clause of the Fourteenth Amendment. At issue was a 1925 Oklahoma statute that declared that the manufacture and sale of ice was a public business and forbade the grant of new licenses to sell ice except upon a showing of a necessity for ice in the desired community. The practical effect of the regulation was to shut out new enterprises and thus confer a monopoly on the existing businesses. Under this statute, New State Ice Company brought suit to enjoin Liebmann from selling ice in Oklahoma City without a license.

Concluding that the Oklahoma law unreasonably curtailed the common right to engage in a lawful business, Justice George Sutherland held that the license requirement violated the Due Process Clause. Sutherland insisted that a state legislature could not impose economic regulations simply by declaring that a line of ordinary business was affected with a public use. In a lengthy dissenting opinion, Justice Louis D. Brandeis argued that the need to eliminate destructive competition was primarily a matter for legislative determination. He maintained that federal and state governments must have the power "to remould, through experimentation, our economic practices and institutions to meet changing social and economic needs" (p. 311).

Although *New State Ice* has never been overruled, it has been effectively superseded by decisions that recognize broad legislative authority to regulate business enterprise. Some scholars, however, have defended *New State Ice* on the ground that the Oklahoma statute was classic special interest legislation designed to burden consumers in order to benefit established ice companies.

James W. Ely, Jr.

New York State Club Association v. City of New York, 487 U.S. 1 (1988), argued 23 Feb. 1988, decided 20 June 1988 by vote of 9 to 0; White for the Court, O'Connor, joined by

Kennedy and Scalia, concurring. Following the Supreme Court's decision in *Roberts v. U.S. Jaycees* (1984), New York's city council sought to define clubs that were "not strictly private" and thus subject to the city's human rights law. A club with at least four hundred members, which regularly served meals and regularly received "payment for dues, fees, use of space, facilities, services, meals, or beverages directly or indirectly from or on behalf of non-members for the furtherance of trade or business" was covered and thus prohibited from discriminating on account of race or sex. Benevolent orders and religious corporations were excluded.

The New York State Club Association challenged the law on its face as an unconstitutional restriction on the First Amendment rights of intimate and expressive association of its members and also on equal protection grounds. A unanimous Court rejected this claim, ruling that the private associational rights of each and every club member would not be infringed by the law because many, if not all, had public characteristics. The Court noted that the clubs could still exclude members on the ground of non-shared views but simply could not exclude them on the basis of race or sex. The exemption for benevolent orders and religious corporations was not an equal protection violation because they uniquely exist for the benefit of their members and are not open to commercial activity.

As a result of this decision, many "males only" clubs across the country decided to admit women; these included the Cosmos Club in Washington, D.C., which counted among its members Justices Harry Blackmun and Antonin Scalia.

Inez Smith Reid

New York Times Co. v. Sullivan, 376 U.S. 254 (1964), argued 6 Jan. 1964, decided 9 Mar. 1964 by vote of 9 to 0; Brennan for the Court, Black, Douglas, and Goldberg concurring. In this case, the Supreme Court for the first time considered the extent to which the constitutional guarantee of freedom of speech and the press limits the award of damages in the libel action brought by public officials against critics of their official conduct. Sullivan, an elected commissioner of the city of Montgomery, Alabama, brought a civil libel action against four black clergymen and *The New York Times* alleging that he had been libeled by statements in a full-page advertisement that was carried in

the *Times*. The advertisement, which was entitled "Heed Their Rising Voices," described the civil rights movement in the South and concluded with an appeal for funds.

It was uncontroverted that several statements contained in the text of the advertisement were inaccurate. For example, the advertisement stated that students protesting *racial* segregation sang "My Country, 'Tis of Thee" on the steps of the Alabama State Capitol, but they had actually sung "The Star-Spangled Banner"; it also said that several students were expelled from school for leading that protest, but they were actually expelled for demanding service at a segregated lunch counter in the Montgomery County Courthouse on another day; finally, the advertisement claimed that "the entire student body" of Alabama State College protested the expulsions, but only a majority of the students, not the "entire" student body, had protested the expulsions.

The trial judge submitted the case to the jury under instructions that these statements were libelous per se, that falsity and malice were presumed, and that general and punitive damages could be awarded without direct proof of pecuniary loss. Under these instructions, the jury returned a judgment for Sullivan in the amount of $500,000 against each of the defendants.

The Supreme Court reversed, holding that the rule of law applied by the Alabama court violated the First Amendment. At the outset, the Court confronted its own past declarations to the effect that libelous utterances are no essential part of any exposition of ideas (*Chaplinsky v. New Hampshire*, 1942) and that they are not constitutionally protected speech (*Beauharnais v. Illinois*, 1952). In rejecting these prior declarations, the Court explained that, like "the various other formulae for the repression of expression that have been challenged in this Court, libel can claim no talismanic immunity from constitutional limitations"; to the contrary, libel "must be measured by standards that satisfy the First Amendment" (p. 269).

Turning to the task of articulating these standards, Justice William J. Brennan observed in an oft-quoted passage that "we consider this case against the background of a profound national commitment to the principle that debate on public issues should be uninhibited, robust, and wide-open, and that it may well include vehement, caustic, and sometimes unpleasantly sharp attacks on government and public officials" (p. 270).

Drawing upon history, the Court analogized the civil law of libel, as applied by the Alabama court, to the Sedition Act of 1798, which had been invalidated "in the court of history" because of the restraint it "imposed upon criticism of government and public officials" (p. 276).

The essential difficulty, Brennan explained, was that "erroneous statement is inevitable in free debate," and even false statements must therefore "be protected if the freedoms of expression are to have the 'breathing space' that they 'need . . . to survive'" (pp. 271–72). Thus, the Alabama rule of law could not be "saved by its allowance of the defense of truth," for a "rule compelling the critic of official conduct to guarantee the truth of all his factual assertions" would lead to intolerable "self-censorship." Indeed, under such a rule, "would-be critics of official conduct may be deterred from voicing their criticism, even though it is believed to be true and even though it is in fact true, because of doubt whether it can be proved in court or fear of the expense of having to do so." Such a rule, the Court concluded, "dampens the vigor and limits the variety of public debate" (pp. 278–279).

With these considerations in mind, the Court held that public officials may not recover damages for defamatory falsehood relating to their official conduct unless they can prove actual malice; "that the statement was made with . . . knowledge that it was false or with reckless disregard of whether it was false or not" (pp. 279–280).

New York Times revolutionized the law of libel and, equally importantly, it signaled a critical shift in our general First Amendment jurisprudence. *New York Times* abandoned the traditional approach, which concentrated solely on whether libel was "protected" or "unprotected" speech, and embraced a more speech-protective analysis, which focused on the danger that actions for libel might deter expression that lies at the very heart of First Amendment concern. By fashioning its First Amendment standards in light of these "chilling" effects, the Court took an important step toward a more sensitive, less formulaic mode of analysis, a mode of analysis that is the hallmark of contemporary First Amendment jurisprudence.

Perhaps the most important question remaining after *New York Times* was whether the privilege it recognized governed only libel actions involving the official conduct of public officials or whether it extended to other persons. In *Curtis Publishing Co. v. Butts* (1967) and *Associated Press v. Walker* (1967), the Court, in a sharply divided set of opinions, extended the *New York Times* holding from public officials to figures such as movie stars, athletes, industrialists, and other individuals who, though they are not officials, are nonetheless well known to the public. In reaching this result, the Court rejected the argument that *New York Times* was premised on, and thus limited by, the analogy to seditious libel. Rather, the Court reasoned that *New York Times* rested on a profound national commitment to uninhibited, robust, and wide-open debate on public issues. The Court therefore concluded that libelous utterances concerning public officials, must be governed by the *New York Times* privilege.

Several years later, however, in **Gertz v. Robert Welch, Inc.* (1974), the Court, again sharply divided, recognized an important limitation on the scope of *New York Times*, holding that it did not extend to libel actions brought by private individuals, even where the defamatory statement concerned a matter of "public concern." The Court explained that, unlike public officials and public figures, private individuals are usually unable to rebut the libel effectively and they usually have not gone out of their way to seek the public's attention. The Court reasoned that, because private individuals are more vulnerable to injury and more deserving of recovery than either public officials or public figures, they may recover damages for libel merely by showing that the publisher or broadcaster had acted negligently in disseminating the defamatory material.

New York Times and its progeny have been criticized as both overprotective and under-protective of free expression. Some critics maintain that *New York Times* failed adequately to protect the press because its "reckless disregard" standard implicitly authorized highly intrusive inquiries into the thought processes of reporters and editors and because it failed to preclude large and potentially "chilling" damage awards whenever a jury would find that the press has acted with "reckless disregard." These critics, echoing the views expressed by Justices Hugo Black, William O. Douglas, and Arthur Goldberg in their concurring opinions in *New York Times*, argue that the press should have absolute protection against actions for libel. Other critics maintain that *New York Times* gave too much protection to the press and failed to protect the innocent victims of libel. These critics fault *New York Times* for denying innocent victims reasonable compensation for the harm they suffer and for preventing such victims from obtaining a judicial declaration of falsity, which would at least set the record straight.

Several proposals have been offered in recent years in an effort to "cure" these "deficiencies." The most intriguing of these proposals calls for the creation of a new civil action in which the alleged victim of a defamatory falsehood could sue for a judicial declaration of falsity upon waiving the right to sue for damages. The theory is that such an action would reduce litigation costs and enable the victims of libel to vindicate their reputations without intruding into the editorial process or threatening the press with potentially devastating damage awards. Although this approach would avoid some of the problems identified with *New York Times*, it would effectively empower the judiciary to decide on a case-by-case basis whether specific statements made by the press are "true" or "false." It is questionable whether such a relationship between the judiciary and the press would comport with the underlying theory and assumptions of the First Amendment.

New York Times cannot be fully understood without recognizing that it was driven not only by concerns about free expression but also by the unique historical circumstances in which it arose. *New York Times* was, in short, a product of the civil rights movement of the 1950s and 1960s. Like other devices designed to obstruct the civil rights movement, the libel judgment against the *New York Times* and the African-American clergymen named in the advertisement was designed to dampen the drive for civil rights. After all, if this Alabama jury's massive damage award could be sustained on the basis of such minor inaccuracies, then no person or institution would be free to challenge racial segregation in the South. *New York Times*, one of most important decisions in the history of the First Amendment, was thus not only a triumph for free expression, it was a triumph for civil rights and racial equality as well.

□ David A. Barrett, "Declaratory Judgments for Libel," *California Law Review* 74 (1986): 847–888. Harry Kalven, Jr., "The New York

Times Case: A Note on 'The Central Meaning of the First Amendment,'" *Supreme Court Review* (1964): 191–221. Rodney A. Smolla, *Suing the Press* (1986).

Geoffrey R. Stone

New York Times Co. v. United States, 403 U.S. 713 (1971), argued 26 June 1971, decided 30 June 1971 by vote of 6 to 3; Douglas, Stewart, White, Marshall, Black, and Brennan writing separately, Burger, Blackmun, and Harlan in dissent. On 13 June 1971, the *New York Times* published the first installment of the "Pentagon Papers," a classified, seven thousand page document commissioned by President Lyndon Johnson's secretary of defense, Robert McNamara. It revealed that secrecy had been the handmaiden of deception. Other newspapers quickly serialized the documents, leaked by Daniel Ellsberg, a dissident former bureaucrat in the national security apparatus.

Nixon administration officials initially regarded the documents as embarrassing only to previous administrations. President Richard Nixon himself thought that the "opposition" had an interest in forgetting the papers, but "ours is to play it up." But with National Security Adviser Henry Kissinger, Nixon also realized that publication imperiled his own policies, his patterns of secrecy, and his credibility. Most important, Nixon feared that future presidents would lose control over classified documents and thus potentially embarrass their predecessors.

The administration secured a lower court order on 15 June temporarily restraining publication. Three days later, the judge denied a permanent injunction, but a circuit judge blocked further publication pending the government's appeal. On 25 June the Supreme Court agreed to take an expedited appeal, bypassing the intermediate court, yet did not lift the restraining order. Justices Hugo Black, William Brennan, William O. Douglas, and Thurgood Marshall protested the maintenance of the prior restraint. Arguments were heard the next day, and in conference, the justices voted 6 to 3 to deny the government's request for a permanent order. The Court issued a brief per curiam decision on 30 June, stating that the government had not met the burden of proving a need for prior restraint.

The government had contended that publication would endanger lives, the release of prisoners of war, and the peace process—arguments that most of the justices readily dismissed as transparent. Solicitor General Erwin Griswold himself had serious doubts about the argument the Administration insisted on making; later, he said that the decision "came out exactly as it should."

The haste of hearing arguments and deciding inevitably led to fragmentation among the justices. Black, Brennan, and Douglas insisted that any injunction constituted prior restraint, and the Court never should have allowed any halt to publication. Justices Byron White, Marshall, and Potter Stewart agreed that prior restraint was unnecessary in this case but rejected the absolutist position of their majority colleagues. Chief Justice Warren Burger and Justices Harry Blackmun and John M. Harlan dissented, each objecting to the rush of the proceedings. Burger also emphasized his belief that publishers could be prosecuted for criminal violations of security statutes for printing classified information, but only after publication.

The Court, however divided, largely agreed that prior restraint was extraordinary. Nevertheless, the Burger Court soon allowed the Central Intelligence Agency to require former employees to submit proposed writings to review (*Marchetti* v. *United States*, 1968; *Snepp* v. *United States*, 1980). Criminal statutes abounded for dealing with security breaches; indeed Daniel Ellsberg, who had leaked the documents, eventually was indicted and tried for his role in the case. Ironically, the administration's own illegal behavior resulted in a mistrial and, eventually, the dropping of the indictment.

The Supreme Court's decision legitimated the media's assaults against governmental secrecy and its self-assumed status as the people's paladin against official wrongdoing. The incident intensified an already sharpened adversarial relationship between the press and the administration, a relationship that was to deteriorate even more, and with devastating results for Nixon.

Stanley I. Kutler

New York v. Belton, 453 U.S. 454 (1981), argued 27 Apr. 1981, decided 1 July 1981 by vote of 6 to 3; Stewart for the Court, Brennan and White in dissent. In this case, six members of the Supreme Court agreed to expand the constitutionally permissible scope of a warrantless automobile search incident to a lawful custodial arrest. The circumstances here are similar to many automobile search cases. After the car was stopped for speeding, the occupants were removed and arrested when the police detected the odor of marijuana. A policeman searched the back seat of the car, found a jacket belonging to Belton, unzipped one of the pockets and discovered cocaine. At his trial, Belton moved to suppress admission of the cocaine, arguing that it had been seized in violation of the Fourth and Fourteenth Amendments. Writing for the majority, Justice Potter Stewart argued that to guide police officers it was necessary to adopt the "single familiar standard" articulated in **Chimel* v. *California* (1969). In *Chimel,* the Court said that a lawful custodial arrest justifies a search of the immediate surrounding areas without a warrant. Justice Stewart reasoned that because the jacket was located inside the car where Belton had been just before his arrest, the jacket was "within the arrestee's immediate control" (even though Belton and his companions were no longer in or near the automobile).

The dissenting justices disputed this interpretation of *Chimel,* arguing that its policy justifications for a warrantless search (i.e., to insure the safety of the arresting officer and to prevent evidence from being concealed or destroyed) were deliberately narrow and did not justify the latitude given police officers in this case. The issue in *Chimel,* they concluded, was not whether the arrestee could ever have reached the area that was searched, but whether he could have reached it at the time of the arrest and search.

Christine B. Harrington

New York v. Miln, 11 Pet. (36 U.S.) 102 (1837), argued 27–28 Jan. 1837, decided 16 Feb. 1837 by vote of 6 to 1; Barbour for the Court, Thompson concurring, Story in dissent. *Miln* was the first major Commerce Clause case to come before the Taney Court. It involved an ordinance requiring ships' masters to provide a passenger manifest, to post security for indigent passengers, and to remove undesirable aliens. Because this ordinance involved the states' powers to control the ingress of persons, the ordinance raised delicate and explosive questions implicating the interstate transit of slaves, free blacks, abolitionists, and antislavery propaganda. The recent precedent of **Gibbons* v. *Ogden* (1824) might have suggested the unconstitutionality of such state regulation, but the hidden presence of slavery questions skewed constitutional doctrine.

Justice Philip P. Barbour avoided the dangerous question of concurrent federal-state commerce powers, suggesting only that the Commerce Clause probably encompassed trade in "goods" rather than "persons" (p. 136). For the first time in its history, the Court then invoked state police powers as a constitutionally permissible ground for regulating the contents of vessels plying interstate waterways. Barbour's reading of state police powers alarmed antislavery groups. The statute, he said, was a "regulation, not of commerce, but of police" (p. 132); a state's right to protect the health and welfare of its citizens, unlike the right to regulate interstate commerce, had not been "surrendered or restrained," but was "complete, unqualified, and exclusive" (p. 139). In dissent, Justice Joseph Story insisted that the law infringed federal powers under the Commerce Clause. *Miln* remained good authority until 1941, when the Court ruled that *Miln* erroneously permitted legislators to use economic status as a criterion for limiting personal mobility (*Edwards* v. *California*).

Sandra F. VanBurkleo

Nixon, United States v., 418 U.S. 683 (1974), argued 8 July 1974, decided 24 July 1974 by vote of 8 to 0; Burger for the Court, Rehnquist not participating. A climactic incident in a dramatic event in U.S. history—the only case of a president being driven out of office in disgrace—the decision in *United States* v. *Nixon* was also a major constitutional landmark. It established the conditional nature of presidential immunity and in turn, may have affected the later decision, in *Butz* v. *Economou* (1978), not to follow the plurality view in *Barr* v. *Matteo* (1959) of absolute administrative immunity. Above all, it reined in extravagant assertions of President Richard Nixon's lawyers, who claimed presidential power to be unlimited, especially as to foreign and defense matters, and defined solely by a president's own judgment. In forcefully refuting such claims and proclaiming that no one is above the law, Chief Justice Warren Burger's opinion nevertheless twice quoted Chief Justice John Marshall's words, in *United States* v. *Burr* (1807), to the effect that presidential accountability to the legal order does not mean courts may proceed with the president as with any other citizen. Burger also enunciated a strong presumption of executive immunity and privilege.

The background of the case is the stuff of which books, novels, and movies are (and were) made. In 1972, burglars were discovered breaking into the Democratic campaign headquarters in Washington's Watergate apartment/hotel complex. It gradually emerged that the burglars had CIA and White House connections. The legal (and illegal) efforts to protect the burglars eventually involved President Nixon, though it was never established with whom authority for the break-in ultimately rested nor why the act had been committed.

The effort to sweep matters under the rug generated complex further maneuvers, many involving payments of money to keep the arrested burglars from talking. The proliferation of illegal activity created new rumors and investigations. The courts, the Department of Justice, the FBI, and Congress all conducted investigations, and the media pursued the case thoroughly. Lower-level Nixon aides, many of whom ultimately went to jail, co-operated in order to minimize their sentences. There were flat discrepancies between their testimony and statements of the president. To quiet criticism, Nixon and Attorney General Eliot Richardson set up a special prosecutor's office with a promise of independence. Archibald Cox, who had been solicitor general under President John F. Kennedy, agreed to serve.

Congressional hearings established that Nixon had installed a voice-activated tape recorder in his office, and, armed with this knowledge along with White House appointment records, the special prosecutor sought to obtain certain tapes that he thought would establish the truthfulness or falsity of the president's statements and the testimony of his aides, especially his legal counsel, John Dean.

The president ordered Cox to desist, and, when he refused, ordered the attorney general to remove him. The attorney general and his deputy resigned rather than obey, but on their advice Solicitor General Robert Bork (who had not been a party to the original agreement) did the President's bidding as acting attorney general.

The public outcry was so great, however, that a new special prosecutor, Leon Jaworski, was appointed; Jaworski reinstated the request for tapes. Federal district court judge John Sirica then issued a subpoena to the president, demanding that he produce the tapes.

In the Supreme Court, Nixon's attorneys argued that the matter was nonjusticiable. They reasoned that it was a dispute among departments within the executive branch and that, as such, it was a matter to be resolved by the president, not by the courts; they compared the dispute to one between congressional committees, which would be resolved by Congress without judicial interference. The Court rejected this argument, noting that Bork's agreement with Jaworski had, in fact, included consultation with Congress. The decision also relied on cases such as *Peters* v. *Hobby* (1955) and *United States ex rel. Accardi* v. *Shaughnessy* (1953), which had made clear that executive regulations that were thoroughly repealable nonetheless had legal effect and created rights enforceable in court so long as they were still in effect. The Court's agreement with the special prosecutor thus gave him authority to proceed. The courts had assumed in prior decisions on congressional immunity that they, and not Congress, defined its boundaries, and were in parallel fashion the appropriate forum as to the executive's prerogatives.

On the basic questions of executive immunity and privilege, the Supreme Court held that the president was entitled to great deference, especially in matters of defense and national security, and that all presumptions were in his favor. But the prosecutor had particularized and precisely stated needs for specific tapes, both with respect to credibility of witnesses and for establishing the alleged crime. Too, Nixon's claim of confidentiality had already been weakened by his release of the partial contents of the subpoenaed tapes and others.

At odds, then, were the enfeebled and diffuse claims of the executive branch versus the specific claims of the justice system in prosecuting a criminal case.

Burger's opinion emphasized throughout the need for deference and accommodation and cautioned that courts must not take lightly the presumptions protecting the privilege and immunity of the president. Nonetheless, it unequivocably rendered such privileges conditional, dependent on circumstances. Nixon was ordered to give up the tapes, which, it turned out, contained the "smoking gun" linking him to the conspiracy to obstruct justice. Less than three weeks later, he resigned from office.

Samuel Krislov

Nixon v. Administrator of General Services, 433 U.S. 425 (1977), argued 20 Apr. 1977, decided 28 June 1977, by vote of 7 to 2; Brennan for the Court, White, Stevens, Blackmun, and Powell concurring, Rehnquist and Burger in dissent. Subsequent to President Richard Nixon's resignation in 1974 to avoid impeachment, he reached an agreement with the General Services Administration, by which they shared control of his presidential papers for three years after which they were to be at his disposal. The tapes of his White House meetings, which were a key element in proving his complicity in the Watergate cover up, were to remain with the GSA. Except for those he requested destroyed after five years, all tapes were to be kept for ten years or until his death. Although ex-presidents had exercised full authority over their papers, Congress moved to protect those historically important papers and tapes by vesting complete control in the GSA subject to "any rights, defenses or privileges which the federal government or any person might invoke."

The day after the Presidential Recordings and Materials Act was signed into law, Nixon challenged the Act as violating the separation of powers and his personal privacy rights. Since presidents before had retained rights to their papers, he also claimed the act was a bill of attainder. The district court and court of appeals sustained the act against those challenges.

Justice William Brennan's opinion rejected the government's contention that since President Gerald Ford signed the act and President Jimmy Carter affirmed it, Nixon had no right to assert executive claims. On the merits, though, Nixon's claims were rejected. Reaffirming a flexible doctrine of separation of powers and qualified immunity and privilege, the Court noted the safeguards and opportunity for challenge by Nixon built into the statute. As to both privilege and privacy, archivists were to have access, but this was not more obtrusive than *in camera* inspection by judges, as in *United States* v. *Nixon (1974).

Finally, the Court rejected the bill of attainder argument, finding it neither functionally nor in intent a punishment. Given the circumstances, Congress could reasonably infer a public need to know more and conclude that Nixon was an improper custodian of what historically have been regarded as public papers in ex-presidents' hands.

Justice Byron White concurred but was troubled by the taking of what has in effect been treated as presidential property even though the act preserved Nixon's right to claim compensation. Justice John Paul Stevens also concurred, specifically finding that Nixon constituted "a legitimate class of one."

Chief Justice Warren Burger and Justice William Rehnquist dissented separately. The chief justice emphasized that *U.S.* v. *Nixon* had authorized only narrow, need-to-know incursions on executive privilege. The invasion of privacy here was almost untrammeled and the government seemed to him to have to bear a heavier burden to justify it. Finally, he found the act in form and fact a bill of attainder. Rehnquist's opinion vigorously argued that the decision left all presidential papers available for seizure by future acts of congress, a policy that he opposed.

Samuel Krislov

Nixon v. Condon, 286 U.S. 73 (1932), argued 7 Jan. 1932, reargued 15 Mar. 1932, decided 2 May 1932 by vote of 5 to 4; Cardozo for the Court, McReynolds in dissent. After Reconstruction, the Democratic party dominated southern politics. A Democratic primary victory was tantamount to an election; therefore, state laws barring blacks from participation in primaries were an effective disfranchisement. In *Nixon* v. *Herndon* (1927), the Supreme Court had held that a Texas statute prohibiting blacks from voting in primaries denied them equal protection under the Fourteenth Amendment. Texas responded by granting state party executive committees the power to determine qualifications. The state Democratic committee promptly limited primary participation to whites. When Nixon, a black, was denied a primary ballot he sued, alleging that the committee had acted under the authority of the state statute and violated the Fourteenth Amendment. The defendant election officials argued that the political party was a private association and could define its own membership.

In his first opinion for the Court, Justice Benjamin N. Cardozo held the arrangement unconstitutional. The power to determine membership qualifications rested with the annual state party convention, which had never delegated its authority to the executive committee; instead, the committee's authority was vested by the state statute.

This narrow holding suggested the option—subsequently exercised by Texas—to repeal all primary election statutes thus allowing state party conventions to exclude blacks. This approach to black disfranchisement was permitted until *Smith* v. *Allwright* (1944) established that primary elections were inherently state action and subject to the Constitution.

Thomas E. Baker

Nixon v. Herndon, 273 U.S. 536 (1927), argued 4 Jan. 1927, decided 7 Mar. 1927 by vote of 9 to 0, Holmes for the Court. The collapse of the Republican party in the South after Reconstruction, and then, in 1896, of the Populist party, led to one-party government by the Democratic party in the region. This cut off southern blacks from the one election that counted: the Democratic primary. In the 1920s, Texas blacks sought to register and vote as Democrats. Texas countered with a law barring blacks from voting in the Democratic primary. Dr. L. A. Nixon, a black man from El Paso, attacked the law as a violation of the Fourteenth and Fifteenth Amendments. Though both sides had primarily argued the Fifteenth Amendment, the Court found it unnecessary to consider that issue because it found the Texas law a violation of the Equal Protection Clause of the Fourteenth Amendment.

Whether, in fact, the law violated the Fourteenth Amendment is a harder question than one might have guessed from Justice Oliver Wendell Holmes's brisk, epigrammatic opinion. None of the Fourteenth Amendment's sponsors thought it protected the right to vote; neither had the Supreme Court in *Minor* v. *Happersett* (1875).

Nixon did not end the blacks' exclusion but merely induced Texas to shift that task to the Democratic party. Only in *Smith* v. *Allwright* (1944) did the Court rely on the Fifteenth Amendment to outlaw white primaries altogether and finally permit the integration of blacks into southern politics.

Ward E. Y. Elliott

Nixon v. United States, 506 U.S. 224 (1993), argued 14 Oct. 1992, decided 13 Jan. 1993 by a vote of 9 to 0; Rehnquist for the Court; White, Blackmun, and Souter concurring. On 9 February 1986, U.S. District Judge Walter L. Nixon of Mississippi was convicted in a federal court for lying to a special grand jury concerning allegations that he had accepted an illegal gratuity from a local businessmen. When Nixon refused to resign his judicial office, the House of Representatives approved three articles of impeachment against him on 10 May 1989. Article I, section 2, clause 5 of the Constitution vests in the Senate the "sole power to try all impeachments." Pursuant to its internal rules of operation, the Senate established an evidentiary committee of twelve senators to receive testimony from witnesses and issue findings in Nixon's case. Relying at least in part on the committee's report, the full Senate deliberated for two days on Nixon's fate before voting to convict him on two of the three articles of impeachment on 3 November 1989. Nixon thereafter challenged his removal, claiming that when the Senate delegated to a committee the power to hear testimony, it abandoned its constitutional obligation to "try" the impeachment as a full body. *Nixon v. United States* forced the Supreme Court to once again consider the reach of the controversial Political Question Doctrine—would it preclude judicial interference in the workings of another branch of government? In *Baker v. Carr* (1962) a majority of the Court ruled that the doctrine was applicable whenever there was a "textually demonstrable constitutional commitment of the issue to a coordinate political department." (p. 217) Three decades later, Chief Justice William Rehnquist's majority decision in *Nixon* proved an exercise in judicial pragmatism, as the Court defended invocation of the doctrine in this instance. Certainly the meaning of the word "try" was not so precise as to yield a "workable standard of review" that limited the Senate. Of still greater concern, Rehnquist reasoned, was the lack of finality caused by judicial review of impeachment procedures–such review might threaten the stability of the executive branch and produce political chaos. *Nixon v. United States* thus breathed new life into the Political Question Doctrine, and should provide a significant impediment to courts interested in reviewing impeachment challenges in the future.

David A. Yalof

Nollan v. California Coastal Commission, 483 U.S. 825 (1987), argued 30 Mar. 1987, decided 26 June 1987 by vote of 5 to 4; Scalia for the Court, Brennan, Blackmun, and Stevens in dissent. An important takings decision, *Nollan* involved a challenge to an

effort by California to enhance the public's enjoyment of state beaches. California required the Nollans, owners of a small beachfront bungalow, to dedicate to the state a beach-access easement as a condition for obtaining a state permit to replace and expand their bungalow. The easement would have given the public a permanent right to walk along a narrow strip of the Nollan's beach. The Supreme Court invalidated the state's effort on the ground that California's demand for a public easement amounted to a taking of private property without the payment of just compensation.

Nollan is significant because, in weighing the validity of California's action, the Court required a showing that the easement condition would substantially advance the state's interest in alleviating the congestion caused by beachfront construction. The principal effect of the Nollan's new home was to reduce the public's ability to see and enjoy the beach from the street. The easement that California demanded, however, would only have benefited persons already on the beach and would not have enhanced visual access from a distance. For the majority, this connection or "nexus" between the harm (reduced visual access) and the remedy (enhanced physical access) was too tenuous. Several dissenting justices criticized the majority for requiring more than just a loose, rational connection between harm and remedy.

Eric T. Freyfogle

Nordlinger v. Hahn, 505 U.S. 1 (1992), argued 25 Feb. 1992, decided 18 June 1992 by vote of 8 to 1; Blackmun for the Court, Stevens in dissent.

When Proposition 13 took effect in 1978, it set property taxes in California at 1 percent of the property's value. For property acquired before the proposition took effect, the value was set at the 1975–76 assessment with the additional provision that the tax could not increase more than 2 percent a year. Property bought after 1978 was taxed at essentially the purchase price. In this case, Stephanie Nordlinger discovered that her newly purchased house had a tax on it five times greater than the tax paid by similar houses on her street. She argued that Proposition 13 was unconstitutional because it violated the right to travel by deterring people from moving to California and it violated the Fourteenth Amendment's guarantee of equal protection of the laws.

Justice Harry Blackmun rejected both arguments. Nordlinger had no standing to sue on the first issue, since she was already a state resident when she moved to her new home. California was well within its powers, moreover, to make a public policy decision that favored the preservation of local neighborhoods and prevented rapid turnover of businesses and residences. In any case, new owners knew full well that they would pay more taxes, and if they did not wish to pay such taxes, then they did not have to buy.

Justice John Paul Stevens, the lone dissenter, concluded that the proposition was entirely irrational. It made no sense to treat similarly situated persons differently on the basis of the date they became property owners. Stevens also complained that asking one person to pay five times more for basic services, such as police and fire protection, was clearly unconstitutional. Ironically, efforts by businesses in California to attack the proposition failed, largely because consumers, happy to have their tax breaks, threatened to boycott businesses that sought constitutional relief in the federal courts.

Kermit L. Hall

Norfolk Southern Railway Company v. Shanklin, 529 U.S. 344, argued 1 March 2000, decided 17 Apr. 2000 by a vote of 7 to 2; O'Connor for the Court, Breyer, concurring, Ginsburg and Stevens in dissent. *Norfolk Southern Railway Co.* v. *Shanklin* held that federal law establishing minimum requirements for safety devices installed at railroad grade crossings preempted state tort law actions alleging that those devices were inadequate.

In 1973, Congress enacted the Highway Safety Act, which offered states federal funds to eliminate railroad-highway crossing hazards. The secretary of transportation issued regulations prescribing the adequacy of warning devices installed under the act. In *CSX Transportation, Inc.* v. *Eastwood* (1993), the Court declined to decide whether mere installation of devices under the regulations preempted state tort law. *Norfolk Southern* however, held that while states were "free to install more protective devices," once they "installed federally funded devices at a particular crossing" state tort suits questioning their adequacy were preempted (p. 358).

Justice Ruth Bader Ginsburg, dissenting, would have preempted the suit only if federal employees had specifically determined that warning devices installed in particular locations were adequate, the position adopted by some federal appellate courts.

Norfolk Southern reflects the tendency of the Rehnquist Court to invoke preemption when state law, including tort suits, would disrupt uniformity in a federal regulatory regime. This tendency is sometimes surprising considering the Court's robust enforcement of federalism to limit congressional power. Justices Ginsburg and John Paul Stevens, who often dissent from the Court's federalism decisions, frequently support states in preemption cases, arguing that Congress ought to state its intent to preempt clearly in the statute.

Brannon P. Denning

Norris v. Alabama, 294 U.S. 587 (1935), argued 15 and 18 Feb. 1935, decided 1 Apr. 1935 by vote of 8 to 0; Hughes for the Court, McReynolds not participating. This was the second decision of the Supreme Court in the Scottsboro rape cases. In *Powell* v. *Alabama* (1932), the Court reversed the convictions of African-American youths sentenced to death by the Alabama courts on the ground that the defendants, who lacked effective assistance of counsel, had not received a fair trial as mandated by the Due Process Clause of the Fourteenth Amendment. The Scottsboro cases were then retried by the Alabama authorities, and one of the defendants, Clarence Norris, was again sentenced to death, although defense counsel alleged that African-Americans had been systematically excluded from the grand jury that indicted Norris and from the trial jury that convicted him.

On appeal from a decision of the Alabama Supreme Court affirming Norris's conviction, the U.S. Supreme Court reversed. Speaking for the Court, Chief Justice Charles Evans Hughes held that the systematic exclusion of African-Americans from service on the grand and trial juries denied African-American defendants in the state courts the equal protection of law guaranteed by the Fourteenth Amendment. Since the defense had adduced convincing evidence that African-Americans had been systematically excluded from service on the grand jury that indicted Norris and from the trial jury that convicted him, the Court reversed the conviction.

Richard C. Cortner

Norris v. Boston. See PASSENGER CASES.

Northern Securities Co. v. United States, 193 U.S. 197 (1904), argued 14–15 Dec. 1903, decided 14 Mar. 1904 by vote of 5 to 4; Harlan for the Court, Brewer concurring, White and Holmes in dissent. At the end of the nineteenth century, the Court had begun to find some teeth in the Sherman Antitrust Act. However, it was only when Theodore Roosevelt sought to dissolve the Northern Securities Company, which held the stock of three major railroads, that the question arose whether the statute reached stock ownership.

Reading both congressional power and the law broadly, Justice John Marshall Harlan said that the Court could not properly concern itself with any adverse effects on the business community a decision to dissolve the company would have. A majority was formed when Justice David Brewer, who believed that the Sherman Act should apply only to unreasonable restraints of trade, pronounced the restraint here unreasonable. All the dissenters agreed with Justice Edward White's contentions that the restraint shown here was reasonable, that a broad interpretation of the act would unsettle business, and that congressional control over commerce could not embrace stock ownership. They also joined Justice Oliver Wendell Holmes's opinion, which argued that the Sherman Act must be interpreted strictly to ensure its constitutionality; otherwise the most local of transactions would be brought within the ambit of Congress's control of interstate commerce. In *Standard Oil Co.* v. *United States* (1911), Chief Justice White persuaded the Court to limit the Sherman Act's reach solely to unreasonable restraints of trade.

John E. Semonche

Noto v. United States, 367 U.S. 290 (1961), argued 10–11 Oct. 1960, decided 5 June 1961 by vote of 9 to 0; Harlan for the Court, Brennan, Warren, Black, and Douglas concurring. Like its companion case *Scales* v. *United States* (1961), *Noto* involved the constitutionality of the membership clause of the Smith Act. In this case, however, the Court unanimously reversed the judgment of conviction. Five of the justices rested the decision on the ground that the evidence at the trial was insufficient to show that the Communist party, of which Noto was a member, engaged in advocacy of the doctrine of forcible overthrow of the government and in advocacy of action to that end, as distinguished from advocacy of mere abstract doctrine. There must be substantial evidence, direct or circumstantial, of a call to violence "now or in the future" that is both "sufficiently strong and sufficiently persuasive" to lend color to the "ambiguous theoretical material" regarding Communist party teaching (p. 298) and also substantial evidence to justify the reasonable inference that the call to violence may fairly be imputed to the party as a whole and not merely to a narrow segment of it.

Justice William Brennan and Chief Justice Earl Warren would have directed the trial court to dismiss the indictment under the terms of the Internal Security Act, which they interpreted as granting immunity from prosecution under the membership clause of the Smith Act—an immunity, they said, that extends to "active and purposive membership" no less than to membership that is merely passive or nominal. Justices Hugo Black and William O. Douglas found the conviction invalid as a violation of the First Amendment.

Milton R. Konvitz

O

O'Brien, United States v., 391 U.S. 367 (1968), argued 24 Jan. 1968, decided 27 May 1968 by vote of 7 to 1; Warren for the Court, Harlan concurring, Douglas in dissent, Marshall not participating. David O'Brien burnt his selective service registration certificate ("draft card") on the steps of the South Boston Court-house to communicate his antiwar beliefs and was convicted under a federal statute prohibiting the knowing destruction or mutilation of such certificates. He argued that the statute was unconstitutional because it abridged his rights of free speech. The Court rejected O'Brien's claim and set out a test for determining when governmental regulation was justified in freedom of expression cases involving symbolic speech. This test required the government interest to be a valid and important one, and one unrelated to the suppression of free speech. Further, the restriction of First Amendment freedoms could be no greater than was essential to the furtherance of that interest.

The Court found that the statute here met all the requirements. First, the statute involved the broad and sweeping constitutional power to do what was necessary to raise and support an army. Second, the selective service certificate served a number of valid government interests, such as being proof of registration and facilitating communication between the registrant and the local board. These were interests unrelated

to the suppression of free speech. Finally, the Court held, the statute was limited to preventing harm to the smooth running of the Selective Service System and no alternative means would accomplish this. By his conduct, O'Brien had frustrated the government's valid interest and it was because of this he was convicted.

The test in *O'Brien*, which focuses on whether the regulation is unrelated to content and narrowly tailored to achieve the government interest, is frequently invoked not only in symbolic speech cases, but also cases involving time, place, and manner restrictions.

Keith C. Miller

Ogden v. Saunders, 12 Wheat. (25 U.S.) 213 (1827), argued 18–20 Jan. 1827, decided 19 Feb. 1827 by vote of 4 to 3; majority justices by seriatim opinions, Marshall, Story, and Duvall in dissent. In this decision, a divided Supreme Court held that a New York insolvency law did not impair the obligation of contracts entered into after enactment of the statute, a question that had been left open in *Sturges v. Crowninshield* (1819), which had struck down a retroactive insolvency act. The majority justices agreed that contract rights were not absolute, that commerce required some kind of bankruptcy legislation, that the bankruptcy power conferred on Congress by Article I, section 8 of the Constitution was not exclusive, and that therefore the states had concurrent powers in the area. In dissent, Chief Justice John Marshall contended that the statute violated not only the Contracts Clause but also various nontextual vested rights of individuals. *Ogden* v. *Saunders* removed the Contracts Clause as an absolute bar to state insolvency legislation, an important achievement because Congress was unable to enact permanent bankruptcy legislation until 1898. *Ogden* was the only case where Chief Justice Marshall dissented in an important constitutional decision. On reargument, Justice William Johnson joined the original dissenters to make a new majority for the holding that a state insolvency statute could not be applied to an out-of-state creditor who had no contract with the forum state other than the original contract.

Richard E. Ellis

O'Gorman and Young v. Hartford Fire Insurance Co., 282 U.S. 251 (1930), argued 30 Apr. 1930, reargued 30 Oct. 1930, decided 5 Jan. 1931 by vote of 5 to 4; Brandeis for the Court, Van Devanter, McReynolds, Sutherland, and Butler in dissent. *O'Gorman* is a turning point case in the field of economic due process. One of the last liberty of contract cases, it involved a New Jersey statute regulating the fees paid to local agents by insurance companies. The statute was challenged as a violation of the Fourteenth Amendment's Due Process Clause. Contending that the facts surrounding its origins and operation should be determinative, Justice Louis Brandeis sustained the statute. He found that the presumption of constitutionality must prevail in the absence of some factual foundation of record for overthrowing the statute" (p. 258). Further, legislative judgment must prevail unless it could be demonstrated that the measure was utterly arbitrary. No such demonstration had been made. The business of insurance, he argued further, is so far affected with a public interest that the state may regulate the rates as a subject clearly within the scope of the police power. He further contended that the Court should cease using the Due Process Clause in a "substantive" manner to second guess the legislature.

The four dissenters vigorously propounded freedom of contract, restrictive alteration of the public interest doctrine, and the pressing obligation to check any legislative interference with property. They particularly objected to the idea that the

right to regulate business implied the power to trespass on the duties of private management. The majority opinion, however, made clear that the constitutionality of state regulation of the economy should no longer turn on the question of its unreasonableness.

Paul L. Murphy

Ohio v. Akron Center for Reproductive Health, 110 S.Ct. 2972 (1990), argued 29 Nov. 1989, decided 25 June 1990 by vote of 6 to 3; Kennedy for the Court, Scalia and Stevens concurring, Blackmun, joined by Brennan and Marshall, in dissent. Relying on *Bellotti* v. *Baird* (1979), the Court upheld a statute that required minors seeking abortions either to notify one parent or obtain approval of a court. Less important than other cases indicating that the holding in **Roe* v. *Wade* (1973) was less robust than its supporters wished, the decision turned on whether the state's system of providing judicial approval placed too many burdens on the applicants. There was always a chance that approval would be delayed for more than three weeks because the woman had to prove her maturity or that the abortion was in her best interests by clear and convincing evidence, or because the procedure was unnecessarily complicated. The Court rejected these arguments, finding that the time limits would almost always be much shorter than three weeks, that the burden of proof was permissible, and that the procedures were not overly confusing. The dissenters characterized the procedure as an "obstacle course" and a "labyrinth" and contended that the procedure did place unacceptable burdens on minors desiring abortions. With Justice O'Connor in the majority, the justices invoked the "undue burden" principle in **Planned Parenthood of Southeastern Pennsylvania* v. *Casey* (1992) while sustaining a Pennsylvania law that had many of the same features of the Akron ordinance. The justices refused, however, to renounce their decision in *Roe*.

Mark V. Tushnet

Oklahoma City Board of Education v. Dowell, 111 S.Ct. 630 (1991), argued 2 Oct. 1990, decided 15 Jan. 1991 by vote of 5 to 3; Rehnquist for the Court, Marshall, joined by Blackmun and Stevens, in dissent, Souter not participating. African-American parents and their children brought this suit in 1961 to challenge the racial segregation in Oklahoma City's public schools. The federal district court terminated the case in 1977, declaring that the previously "dual" (intentionally segregated) school district had achieved "unitary" status. In 1985, claiming demographic changes, the school district curtailed busing and reassigned students to neighborhood schools. As a result, thirty-three of the district's sixty-four elementary schools became racially identifiable, with more than 90 percent of their student body of one race. The plaintiffs sought to reopen the case.

The Supreme Court emphasized that court-ordered remedies were always intended to be temporary and not meant to operate in perpetuity. Calling for greater deference to local authorities, the Court held that a desegregation remedy should be terminated when the school district had complied in good faith with all court orders for a reasonable time and when vestiges of past discrimination had been eliminated to the extent practicable. This determination must consider every facet of operation of the schools, including student assignments, faculty, staff, transportation, extracurricular activities, and facilities.

There are more than five hundred school desegregation cases pending in federal courts nationwide, some for more than thirty years. This decision thus could signal a whole new body of case law establishing procedures for ending these lawsuits and the federal judiciary's involvement in school desegregation issues.

Thomas E. Baker

Olmstead v. United States, 277 U.S. 438 (1928), argued 20–21 Feb. 1928, decided 4 June 1928 by vote of 5 to 4; Taft for the Court, Holmes, Brandeis, Butler, and Stone in dissent. Olmstead was convicted of unlawfully transporting and selling liquor under the National Prohibition Act. His petition from the court of appeals provided the Supreme Court with its first opportunity to consider whether the use of evidence obtained by an illegal wiretap in a federal court criminal trial violated the defendant's Fourth and Fifth Amendment rights. Chief Justice William H. Taft held that it did not, finding that conversations are not protected by the Fourth Amendment and that no invasion of the defendant's house was involved in the wiretapping. In dissent, Justice Louis D. Brandeis argued that the Fourth and Fifth Amendments confer a general right to individual privacy rather than mere protection

of material things and that allowing the introduction of evidence illegally acquired by federal officers makes government a lawbreaker. In the 1934 Federal Communications Act, Congress prohibited the interception of any communication and the divulgence of the contents of intercepted communications. The Court extended the exclusionary rule to wiretapping in federal prosecutions in *Nardone* v. *United States* (1937); it overruled *Olmstead* in *Berger* v. *New York* (1967) and **Katz* v. *United States* (1967). In Title III of the Crime Control and Safe Street Act of 1968, Congress prohibited wiretapping for domestic purposes except when authorized by a federal judge following the specific requirements of the act.

Susan E. Lawrence

Oregon v. Mitchell; Texas v. Mitchell; United States v. Arizona, 400 U.S. 112 (1970), argued 19 Oct. 1970, decided 21 Dec. 1970 by vote of 5 to 4; Black for the Court, Douglas, Harlan, Stewart, Brennan, White, Marshall, Burger, and Blackmun concurring in part and dissenting in part. In 1970, Congress passed amendments to the 1965 Voting Rights Act that extended the provisions of the original act for another five years. The amendments also standardized residency requirements for participation in national elections and, dramatically, lowered the voting age to eighteen years for national, state, and local elections. Congress based its action on the enforcement language of the Fifteenth Amendment. The legislation raised the issue of federalism anew because national legislators were attempting to regulate the time and manner of conducting state and local elections, a traditional prerogative of the states. When the issue came to the Supreme Court, the major question was whether Congress had the constitutional authority to lower the national minimum voting age.

In a decision with five opinions and no clearcut majority, the Court ruled that Congress did not have the power to so act with respect to state elections but did have the authority to set the voting age at eighteen in federal elections for Congress and the presidency. Four of the justices believed that Congress had total power to regulate the voting age in any election, while four others believed that Congress had no such absolute power; Justice Hugo Black cast the deciding vote, concluding that Congress could regulate the voting age in national but not in state elections.

To bring the confusion that followed the Court's ruling to a quick end, Congress immediately adopted the Twenty-Sixth Amendment, which was ratified in short order. Reversing the Court's holding regarding voting age in state elections, the amendment states that "the rights of citizens of the United States, who are eighteen years of age or older, to vote shall not be abridged by the United States of any state on account of age."

Howard Ball

Orr v. Orr, 440 U.S. 268 (1979), argued 27 Nov. 1978, decided 5 Mar. 1979 by vote of 6 to 3; Brennan for the Court, Blackmun and Stevens concurring, Rehnquist (with Burger) and Powell in dissent. Orr, a divorced male, challenged the alimony statutes of Alabama. He argued that because the statutory scheme allowed alimony orders only against males, it amounted to unconstitutional sex discrimination in violation of the Equal Protection Clause.

The dissenters focused strictly on the standing question pointing out that Mr. Orr probably had nothing to gain from winning this case: his wife was the needy spouse and he was the spouse able to pay support. The possibility that Alabama would abolish alimony in order to render the laws neutral with regard to gender was, they said, merely fanciful.

The Court majority addressed the standing question by insisting that any person who bears a gender-based financial burden must have standing to challenge it. Justice John Paul Stevens's separate concurring opinion was devoted entirely to elaboration of this point.

The majority applied the *Craig* v. *Boren* (1976) test to invalidate this statutory scheme. The state proffered three goals of the law: to structure family life, with wife at home and husband providing support; to cushion the cost of divorce for needy wives; and to compensate needy wives for economic discrimination attendant upon the traditional marital role. The Court declared the first goal invalid in this era but said that the second two were valid and important. The law, however, failed the second half of the *Craig* test: it was not "substantially related" to these goals. There was no need for blanket gender discrimination, since every alimony award came out of individualized hearings in which any needy spouse could be

identified. Thus, both valid goals could be satisfied by a gender-neutral law.

Leslie Friedman Goldstein

Osborn v. Bank of the United States, 9 Wheat. (22 U.S.) 738 (1824), argued 10–11 March 1824, decided 19 March 1824 by vote of 6 to 1; Marshall for the Court, Johnson in dissent. Originating in a challenge to the constitutionality of the Bank of the United States, *Osborn* produced an elaborate statement by Chief Justice John Marshall concerning the jurisdiction of federal courts. In 1819, Ohio imposed a prohibitive tax on branches of the Bank of the United States. Defying a federal injunction against its collection, Ralph Osborn, the state auditor, ordered his agents to seize the money and deposit it in the state treasury. The bank sued Osborn in federal circuit court for return of the money and prevailed. On appeal by Osborn, the Supreme Court affirmed the judgment; its decision in *McCulloch* v. *Maryland* (1819) had upheld the constitutionality of the bank and inhibited the states' power to tax federal instrumentalities.

At issue in *Osborn* was an unconstitutional state tax levied on a federal corporation. The Constitution extends federal judicial power to all cases "arising under" the Constitution, laws, and treaties of the United States. Marshall, however, used the case to proclaim federal jurisdiction over every case involving the bank, even those seemingly raising only questions of state law. Basing federal jurisdiction on the bare possibility of federal question, Marshall generously construed congressional power to confer jurisdiction, a proposition that Justice William Johnson, writing in dissent, thought risked federalizing too many questions. A further jurisdictional issue concerned the Eleventh Amendment, which restricted suits against states. Although Osborn was acting on behalf of his state, the Court held that he could not assert its immunity from suit, a proposition later reaffirmed in *Ex parte* *Young* (1908).

John V. Orth

Osborne v. Ohio, 495 U.S. 103 (1990), argued 5 Dec. 1989, decided 18 Apr. 1990 by vote of 6 to 3; White for the Court, Blackmun concurring, Brennan, joined by Marshall and Stevens, in dissent. *Osborne* upheld a statute making it illegal to possess child pornography. An earlier case, *Stanley* v. *Georgia* (1969), had invalidated a statute prohibiting the private possession of obscene materials because the government's sole interest in prohibiting such possession, controlling the private thoughts of the owner, was not an interest the government was entitled to advance. The Court in *Osborne* said that banning the possession of child pornography protected the different interest of avoiding the exploitation of children against the harms of being used in pornography. Making private possession of child pornography illegal would reduce demand by destroying the market for exploitative use. The Court also held that the statute did not cover a substantial amount of constitutionally protected conduct because it had been construed to be limited to lewd depictions.

The dissenters argued that the statute remained unconstitutionally overbroad in its scope even after the narrowing construction. *Osborne* reflects the modern Court's discomfort with the prevalence of sexually explicit materials in American society, but its impact is limited because of the obvious importance of controlling the production of child pornography.

Mark V. Tushnet

P

Pacific Mutual Life Insurance Company v. Haslip, 111 S.Ct. 1032 (1991), argued 3 Oct. 1990, decided 4 Mar. 1991 by vote of 7 to 1; Blackmun for the Court, Scalia and Kennedy concurring, O'Connor in dissent, Souter not participating. Concerned about the marked increase in the frequency and size of punitive damage awards by trial juries, the business community in the late 1980s pressed several constitutional challenges to punitive damages. In *Browning-Ferris* v. *Kelco Disposal* (1989), the Supreme Court rejected an Eighth Amendment challenge. In *Pacific Mutual*, an insurance company attacked an Alabama punitive damage award on due process grounds, arguing that the award bore no rational relationship to the plaintiff's actual injuries and that juries had unlimited discretion to assess punitive damages. Stressing that juries have historically determined the imposition and amount of punitive damages, Justice Harry A. Blackmun rebuffed this challenge. He reasoned that the common-law method was not so inherently unfair as to deny due process under the Fourteenth Amendment. Blackmun further concluded that the Alabama procedures at issue reasonably accommodated rational decision making and provided for adequate checks on jury discretion. He did recognize, however, that in some situations unbridled jury discretion in assessing punitive damages might violate due process norms.

Justice Antonin Scalia, in a concurring opinion, maintained that since juries historically had discretion to award punitive damages this traditional practice was not violative of due process. Dissenting, Justice Sandra Day O'Connor argued that the Alabama procedures were "so fraught with uncertainty that they defy rational implementation" (p. 1056) and encouraged inconsistent results. The justices in *Pacific Mutual* left open the possibility that some punitive damage procedures might transcend constitutional limits. In *BMW of North America, Inc.* v. *Gore* (1996) the justices held for the first time that a punitive damages award was excessive under the Due Process Clause. The punitive damages award was $2 million; the actual damages award for the precipitating injury was $4,000.

James W. Ely, Jr.

Pacific States Telephone & Telegraph Co. v. Oregon, 223 U.S. 118 (1912), argued 3 Nov. 1911, decided 19 Feb. 1912 by vote of 9 to 0; White for the Court. Early in the twentieth century, reformers wanted to make government more responsive to the people. In 1902, Oregon led the way by enacting the initiative and referendum, devices that gave citizens the opportunity to directly propose and/or vote on the laws that would govern them. In 1906, Oregonians proposed and passed a tax of 2 percent on the gross revenues of telephone and telegraph companies in the state. Deprived of its lobbying strength in the legislature, one such company refused to pay the tax and was sued by the state. The company lost in the Oregon courts and appealed, arguing that the Constitution's guarantee to the states of a republican government meant that law-making was the exclusive responsibility of the legislature.

That the company could really have expected the Supreme Court to invalidate the initiative procedure and throw Oregon into legal chaos stretched the credulity of the justices. They refused jurisdiction, saying that the matter was political and not judicial. Chief Justice Edward D. White quoted heavily from *Luther* v. *Borden* (1848) in concluding that only Congress could provide a remedy.

John E. Semonche

Palko v. Connecticut, 302 U.S. 319 (1937), argued 12 Nov. 1937, decided 6 Dec. 1937 by vote of 8 to 1; Cardozo for the Court, Butler in dissent. Palko was tried for first-degree murder, but a jury found him guilty of the lesser crime of second-degree murder and sentenced him to life imprisonment. The state appealed this conviction under a Connecticut statute that permitted the prosecution to appeal the judgment of the trial court in certain criminal cases. The state won a new trial, which resulted in Palko being convicted of the greater charge and sentenced to death. Arguing that this chain of events placed him twice in jeopardy for the same offense, Palko appealed the second conviction.

The Fifth Amendment, which provides immunity from double jeopardy, applies only to the federal government, not to the states. Palko's appeal did not rely on the Fifth Amendment alone, however. He claimed the execution of his sentence would violate the Fourteenth Amendment guarantee that no state shall deprive a person of life, liberty, or property without due process of law. The theory of his case was borrowed from Justice John Harlan's dissents in *Twining* v. *New Jersey* (1908) and *Hurtado* v. *California* (1884). Harlan believed that whatever would be a violation of the original Bill of Rights if done by the federal government was equally unlawful under the Fourteenth Amendment if done by the states. In *Twining*, a case involving the Fifth Amendment protection against self-incrimination, the Court rejected this theory, but it later applied other parts of the Bill of Rights to the states. First

Amendment freedoms of speech, assembly, and religion had been applied in this manner, as was the Sixth Amendment guarantee of the right to counsel.

While recognizing this trend, the Court pointedly rejected Palko's thesis. Justice Benjamin Cardozo noted that cases holding the opposite existed as well. Parts of the Bill of Rights had surely been applied to the states, he admitted, but not as the automatic consequence of the first eight amendments being incorporated into the due process guarantee of the Fourteenth Amendment. Rather, some select protections were absorbed into the concept of due process only because they are fundamental to our notions of liberty and justice. In Cardozo's words, these rights imposed limits on the states because "they represented the very essence of a scheme of ordered liberty, . . . principles of justice so rooted in the traditions and conscience of our people as to be ranked fundamental" (p. 325). He concluded that the Connecticut statute did not fall into this category. The state had done no more than seek a trial free of substantial error. It had not subjected the accused to acute and shocking hardships nor attempted to wear him down by multiple trials.

Palko represents the beginning of a struggle to find a test for applying the Due Process Clause of the Fourteenth Amendment as a limit on state power. For more than thirty years the Court had used the doctrine of substantive due process to exercise virtual veto power over all forms of state economic regulation. In 1937, most justices accepted the idea that the Due Process Clause gave the Court authority to review the substance of state legislation as well as the procedure by which laws were enforced. However, in *West Coast Hotel,* v. *Parrish* (1937), decided in the same term as *Palko*, they rejected the uninhibited use of this power and the judicial activism it represented. Now the Court was faced with the problem of replacing an open-ended standard with one that was more restrictive. In this respect, Cardozo's opinion was a precursor of the "incorporation debate" that became so evident later in *Adamson* v. *California* (1947). His rationale for upholding the Connecticut law developed into the "fundamental fairness" test later championed by Justice Felix Frankfurter, while the theory he rejected became known as the incorporation doctrine favored by Justice Hugo Black. A variation of the incorporation doctrine won out, as many of the protections of the Bill of Rights eventually were applied directly to the states. In 1969 *Palko* was overruled by *Benton* v. *Maryland*, and double jeopardy became one of those provisions of the Bill of Rights selectively incorporated into the Fourteenth Amendment.

Paul Kens

Palmer v. Thompson, 403 U.S. 217 (1971), argued 14 Dec. 1970, decided 14 June 1971 by vote of 5 to 4; Black for the Court, Burger concurring, Douglas, White, Marshall, and Brennan in dissent. African-American citizens of Jackson, Mississippi, claimed that the city engaged in unlawful racial discrimination in violation of the Equal Protection Clause of the Fourteenth Amendment when it closed public swimming pools rather than operating them on an integrated basis. The swimming pools were closed when lower courts invalidated racial segregation rules. The city contended that it was closing the pools to preserve public peace and because the pools could not be operated economically on an integrated basis, but black citizens challenged the action as unlawful discrimination on the theory that the decision to close the pools was based on discriminatory intentions, despite the publicly stated reasons. The Supreme Court turned aside the claim, largely on the ground that a legislative act does not violate the Equal Protection Clause simply because the act is adopted by government officials with discriminatory aims, at least when the officials put forth a valid, plausible reason for their actions.

The *Palmer* ruling is significant as an expression of the Court's strong unwillingness at the time to look beyond the surface of a seemingly neutral government act to search for discriminatory intent. Subsequent rulings have diminished the impact of *Palmer* by placing greater emphasis on discriminatory intent in determining equal protection violations. The decision remains important, however, as an indicator of the Court's general reluctance to examine the motives behind legislative acts.

Eric T. Freyfogle

Panama Refining Co. v. Ryan, 293 U.S. 388 (1935), argued 10–11 Dec. 1934, decided 7 Jan. 1935 by vote of 8 to 1; Hughes for the Court, Cardozo in dissent. During the Great Depression of the 1930s, oil prices collapsed because of overproduction and the general economic slowdown. The oil-producing states, unable individually to raise prices by limiting production, demanded congressional controls. The National Industrial Recovery Act (NIRA) of 1934, a wide-ranging effort by the administration of President Franklin Roosevelt to deal with the depression, authorized the president to prohibit the shipment in interstate commerce of petroleum produced in excess of quotas fixed by the states (popularly referred to as "hot oil"). Precedents existed for federal assistance to state law enforcement. For example, the Webb-Kenyon Act of 1913 had prohibited the interstate transportation of liquor into states banning liquor imports.

The "hot oil" program was only one of the many provisions of the NIRA, but it was the first New Deal initiative to be tested before the Supreme Court. *Panama Refining Co.* v. *Ryan* (1935), a decision widely perceived as a threat to the entire New Deal program, held the "hot oil" provision to be an unconstitutional delegation of legislative power to the president.

Separation of powers is a basic principle of the Constitution, but up to 1935 the Supreme Court had never held that Congress had violated this principle by delegating its power to the executive. The reasons for legislative delegation are well understood. When adopting a legislative program, Congress cannot fore-see all the problems that those administering the program will encounter or the adjustments that will be needed as the program develops. As early as 1825 Chief Justice John Marshall, in *Wayman* v. *Southard*, held that officials administering a general statutory program must be permitted to "fill up the details" (p. 43). In previous delegation situations, the Court had insisted that Congress set "standards" to guide administrative discretion, but the justices had typically accepted broad general statements as meeting this requirement. Consequently, that a ruling in the *Panama Refining* case would be based on the delegation issue was so unanticipated by the Roosevelt administration that the government's brief of 427 pages devoted only 13 pages to it.

But in the *Panama* decision, Chief Justice Charles Evans Hughes held the statute invalid because Congress had established no "primary standard," leaving the matter to the president without direction or rule, "to be dealt with as he pleased." The statute, wrote Hughes, established "no criteria to govern the President's course. It does not require any finding by the President as a condition of his action. The Congress . . . thus declares no policy as to the transportation of the excess production" (p. 430).

Justice Benjamin N. *Cardozo was the sole dissenter. He approved the statute because it was framed to meet a "national disaster," presenting problems that only the president could deal with on a day-to-day basis (p. 443). In fact, congressional intention to control the production and transportation of "hot oil" was fairly clear in the statute, and delegations of equal scope in earlier legislation had encountered no judicial ban.

Shortly after the "hot oil" decision, the Supreme Court in *Schechter Poultry Corp. v. U.S. (1935) declared unconstitutional another major feature of NIRA—industry codes of fair competition—also on grounds of unconstitutional delegation of legislative power. The following year legislation regulating prices and labor relations in the bituminous coal industry was ruled unconstitutional on the same grounds in *Carter v. Carter Coal Co. (1936).

After the defeat of Roosevelt's court-packing plan by Congress in 1937, the Court made its peace with the New Deal, and on no subsequent occasion did the justices strike down a statutory program on a charge of unconstitutional delegation of legislative power to the president.

The *Panama* and *Schechter* decisions have never been overruled. In fact, *Panama* (nearly always paired with *Schechter*) has been cited in more than forty subsequent Supreme Court decisions, typically where administrative exercise of delegated power was involved. But in none of these cases was the congressional delegation held invalid. As Justice William H. Rehnquist said in *Hampton* v. *Mow Sun Wong* (1976): "The Court has not seen fit during the forty years following these decisions to enlarge in the slightest their relatively narrow holdings" (p. 122). *Panama* and *Schechter* remain museum pieces from a period of troubled relations between the executive and judicial branches.

C. Herman Pritchett

Parents Involved in Community Schools v. Seattle School District No. 1; Meredith v. Jefferson County Board of Education, 127 S. Ct. 2738 (2007), argued 4 Dec. 2006, decided 28 June 2007 by vote of 5 to 4; Roberts filed an opinion partly for the Court, joined by Scalia, Kennedy, Thomas, and Alito, and partly on behalf of himself, Scalia, Thomas, and Alito; Thomas also concurred separately; Kennedy filed an opinion concurring in part and concurring in the judgment; Breyer filed a dissent, joined by Stevens, Souter, and Ginsburg; Stevens also dissented separately. This case has sometimes been portrayed as a search for the true defender of *Brown* v. *Board of Education* (1954): Was it the school district, which assigned students to schools on account of their race—making sure that at least 49 percent, but no more than 69 percent, of those at each school would be nonwhite? Or was it the parents whose children might have been denied admission to the school of their choice on account of their race?

Seattle tried to ensure that the racial composition of its individual high schools approximated that of its student population as a whole (although only two "races" were recognized by the plan: white and nonwhite). Students could choose which of the district's ten high schools they wished to attend. But when a racially imbalanced school received more applicants than it could accept, students "whose race '[would] serve to bring the school into balance'" were given priority over students whose race would be unhelpful (p. 2747). Of the four oversubscribed schools that were considered imbalanced, nonwhites enjoyed priority at three, while whites had priority at one. The companion case concerned a similar plan for elementary schools in the Louisville area.

The Supreme Court reversed the circuit court decisions, which had ruled in the school districts' favor, and remanded the cases for further proceedings. Following a line of authority that includes *Gratz* v. *Bollinger* (2003), the majority maintained its position that strict scrutiny must be applied to racially discriminatory policies regardless of the victims' racial identity. To be upheld, the plans would have to be narrowly tailored to serve a compelling purpose. The Court concluded that neither of the two lines of authority in which racially discriminatory education policies have been upheld in the past applied here.

First, the discriminatory policies could not be justified as a remedy for a past legal wrong. Seattle had never operated its schools in violation of *Brown*. While Louisville had done so, it had gone through a court-ordered busing phase, which lasted until 2000, when a federal court found that it had eliminated the vestiges associated with its former policy of segregation. As Justice Clarence Thomas's concurrence emphasized, racial imbalance is not in itself a wrong. Thus, unless the state had caused the imbalance by discrimination, there was no Fourteenth Amendment violation to be remedied.

Second, the majority concluded that *Grutter* v. *Bollinger* (2003)—the case in which the University of Michigan Law School's racially discriminatory diversity program was upheld—did not apply. Even assuming that racial diversity could serve as a compelling purpose outside of higher education, the defendants had not complied with *Grutter*, which held that "classification of applicants by race" could be upheld "only as part of a 'highly individualized, holistic review'" (p. 2753). Neither defendant had shown an interest in ensuring that applicants who had exceptional records of community service or had overcome personal adversity would be distributed among its schools. Race was their only concern.

That left the question whether the discriminatory policies served some other compelling purpose. Chief Justice John Roberts's opinion concluded that no such purpose existed, but Justice Anthony M. Kennedy did not join in that conclusion. Instead, a majority united only around Roberts's conclusion that even if a compelling purpose existed, the policies would fail strict scrutiny because they were not narrowly tailored. At most, only 307 students were affected in Seattle. The Court therefore found that the small effect on racial composition at individual schools "casts doubt on the necessity of using racial classifications," especially given the districts' failure to show that they had considered less objectionable methods to achieve their ends (p. 2760).

Justice Kennedy declined to endorse the plurality's position that the districts' goal amounted to simple race balancing and was not compelling. Kennedy wrote that a school district may be "free to devise race-conscious measures" to affect the racial composition of its schools, so long as it avoids doing so at the individual level. To illustrate, he gave a number of examples, including "strategic site selection of new schools," and "drawing attendance zones with general recognition of neighborhood demographics" (p. 2792).

Justice Stephen G. Breyer's dissent argued that the school districts' plans could be justified as remedial, but Roberts's plurality opinion warned that the failure to draw a clear connection between the defendants' wrong and the remedy sought would lead to open-ended discretion to discriminate. Justice John Paul Stevens accused the majority of being disloyal to *Brown*.

In a reverse echo of Justice Harry Blackmun's separate opinion in *Regents of University of California* v. *Bakke* (1978), which stated, "In order to get beyond racism, we must first take account of race," Roberts ended by stating, "The way to stop discrimination on the basis of race is to stop discriminating on the basis of race" (p. 2768).

Gail Heriot

Parker v. Davis. See LEGAL TENDER CASES.

Pasadena Board of Education v. Spangler, 427 U.S. 424 (1976), argued 27–28 Apr. 1976, decided 28 June 1976 by vote of 6 to 2; Rehnquist for the Court, Marshall and Brennan in dissent, Stevens not participating. Whatever doubts remained after *Milliken* v. *Bradley* (1974) that the Supreme Court would exercise a more lenient overview of school desegregation remedies were put to rest two years later in *Pasadena Board of Education* v. *Spangler*. Under a 1970 school desegregation plan, the trial court ordered that pupil assignments guarantee that no school in the district have a majority of minority students. Within four years, five schools were in violation of that provision of the plan. The trial court held that the system was not yet desegregated and that annual reassignments to avoid the prohibited outcome were necessary.

The Supreme Court disagreed, holding that annual reassignments exceeded the district court's authority and emphasizing that the changes in racial proportions were not chargeable to intentional segregative actions by the district. Quoting *Swann* v. *Charlotte-Mecklenburg* (1971), the Court found no constitutional requirement to make annual adjustments "once the affirmative duty to desegregate had been accomplished and racial discrimination through official action [has been] eliminated from the system" (p. 425).

The issue was narrow, but, as Justice Thurgood Marshall's dissent indicated, prior to *Milliken* one might have expected that the district court's ruling would have been sustained as an exercise of sound *Swann*-like discretion.

Dennis J. Hutchinson

Passenger Cases (*Smith* v. *Turner, Norris* v. *Boston*), 7 How. (48 U.S.) 283 (1849), argued 19–22 Dec. 1848, decided 7 Feb. 1849 by vote of 5 to 4; no opinion for the Court (McLean, Wayne, Catron, McKinley, and Grier comprised the majority), Daniel, Woodbury, Taney, and Nelson in dissent. *Smith* v. *Turner* and *Norris* v. *Boston* had each been argued twice separately before being combined as the *Passenger Cases*, by which name they are commonly known. At issue were New York and Massachusetts taxes on incoming passengers, including immigrants, with the proceeds being used to finance hospitals for ships' passengers. The Court's majority invalidated the laws, but the decision produced no useful doctrine. It merely demonstrated the subsurface divisions on the Court caused by the problem of the states' control over slavery, free African-Americans, abolitionists, and antislavery propaganda. The plethora of opinions (eight in all) demonstrated that in the charged atmosphere of the slavery controversy, the Court was unable to deal effectively with issues raised by the Commerce Clause. This problem had manifested itself in Chief Justice Roger B. Taney's maiden term in *New York* v. *Miln* (1837) and would persist until a partial resolution was achieved in *Cooley* v. *Board of Wardens* (1852).

Donald M. Roper

Patterson v. McLean Credit Union, 491 U.S. 164 (1989), argued 29 Feb. 1988, reargued 12 Oct. 1988, decided 15 June 1989 by votes of 9 to 0 on one major issue and 5 to 4 on another; Kennedy for the Court; Brennan, Marshall, and Blackmun concurring in the judgment in part and joining in part in a dissent by Brennan; Stevens concurring in the judgment in part and dissenting in part. *Patterson* formally involved the question whether an African-American woman's claim of racial harassment in employment stated a cause of action under Title 42, section 1981 of the U.S. Code, a surviving portion of the Civil Rights Act of 1866. In *Runyon* v. *McCrary* (1976) and *Jones* v. *Alfred H. Mayer Co.* (1968), section 1981 and a companion provision had been interpreted to reach private racial discrimination in contractual and property relations. After the initial argument, the Court, on its own motion, ordered a reargument and requested that the parties address the question whether *Runyon*'s interpretation of section 1981 should be overruled. *Patterson* thus seemed on the verge of becoming a landmark case reversing the prior twenty years' practice of applying the 1866 act's modern counterparts to cases involving private discrimination.

Few procedural orders in the Supreme Court's history have caused such a volatile reaction. Within the Court, the reargument order itself prompted sharp dissents from Justices Harry Blackmun and John Paul Stevens, both joined by Justices William Brennan and Thurgood Marshall. These dissents moved the majority to take the unusual steps of defending a reargument order in writing. The civil rights community, the press, and scholarly journals focused intense attention on the pending case.

After the second argument, relying on the doctrine of *stare decisis*, the Court unanimously declined to overrule *Runyon*. But, in an unprecedented interpretation of section 1981 that prompted four dissents, the Court held that the right to make contracts does not extend to conduct by an employer after establishment of the contractual relation, including Patterson's claim of posthiring racial harassment. Congress reacted to *Patterson* and other decisions by passing the Civil Rights Act of 1991, which overruled *Patterson*'s narrow reading of section 1981.

Theodore Eisenberg

Paul v. Virginia, 8 Wall. (75 U.S.) 168 (1869), argued 12 Oct. 1869, decided 1 Nov. 1869 by vote of 8 to 0; Field for the Court. During the nineteenth century, fire and life insurance companies were among the first corporations to market products on a national basis. To encourage the development of local enterprise, many states levied discriminatory taxes and license fees against nonresident, or "foreign," insurance companies chartered in other states. Such protectionist legislation was directed chiefly against large corporations in the Northeast. *Paul* v. *Virginia* was a test case financed by the National Board of Fire Under-writers to challenge these discriminatory practices. The case arose when Paul, an agent for a number of New York fire insurance companies, was convicted under a Virginia law for selling insurance without a license.

Company lawyers argued that corporations were "citizens" as defined in the Privileges and Immunities Clause of Article IV and that insurance sales were transactions in interstate commerce under Article I, section 8. A victory on the Commerce Clause issue would have preempted the states from regulating or taxing any aspects of interstate insurance sales.

A unanimous Supreme Court held against the insurance industry on both questions, thereby allowing state projectionist legislation to continue. The decision reflected the nineteenth-century view that corporations were not citizens for purposes of the Privileges and Immunities Clause. The Court ultimately held, in United States v. *South-Eastern Underwriters Association (1944), that the insurance business affected interstate commerce, but by then state regulatory systems were well entrenched. Congress recognized this fact by authorizing the continuation of state insurance regulation through the McCarran-Ferguson Act of 1945.

Philip L. Merkel

Payne v. Tennessee, 501 U.S. 808 (1991), argued 24 Apr. 1991, decided 27 June 1991 by vote of 6 to 3; Rehnquist for the Court, O'Connor, joined by White and Kennedy, concurring; Scalia, joined in part by O'Connor and Kennedy, concurring; Souter, joined by Kennedy, concurring; Marshall, joined by Blackmun, and Stevens, also joined by Blackmun, in dissent.

During the penalty phase of Payne's capital trial, the state presented the grandmother of a surviving victim, who stated that her grandson missed his mother and sister—both of whom were killed in Payne's attack. The prosecutor also referred to the effects of the crimes on the victims' family in his closing argument. Payne was sentenced to death. The Court held that the Eighth Amendment does not prohibit a capital-sentencing jury from considering "victim impact" evidence, even though the defense may often find it prudent not to attempt a rebuttal. In so-doing, the Court overruled Booth v. Maryland (1987), which had disallowed victim-impact testimony, and South Carolina v. Gathers (1989), which had prohibited a prosecutor from even referring to victim impact.

Michael L. Radelet

Payton v. New York, 445 U.S. 573 (1980), argued 26 Mar. 1979, reargued 9 Oct. 1979, decided 15 Apr. 1980 by vote of 6 to 3; Stevens for the Court, Blackmun concurring; Burger, Rehnquist, and White in dissent. Payton resolved a longstanding open question: whether the Fourth Amendment prohibits the police from making a warrantless

nonconsensual entry into a suspect's home in order to accomplish a routine felony arrest. Noting the well-established rule that a nonconsensual warrantless entry of private premises to search for evidence is presumptively unreasonable, the Court concluded the same should be true of an arrest entry, for both types of entries "implicate the same interest in preserving the privacy and the sanctity of the home" (p. 588). Thus a warrant is needed for an arrest entry unless there are "exigent circumstances."

Though some have argued that a search warrant should be necessary for an arrest entry because it would require a judicial officer to focus on the question of whether the wanted person was probably in the specific premises to be entered, the Court in Payton required only an arrest warrant (and thus only an advance judicial determination of grounds to arrest). But in Steagald v. United States (1981), the Court ruled that in the case of entry of premises to arrest a guest a search warrant would be necessary absent exigent circumstances, for in such circumstances it is important to protect the resident's privacy by a preentry judicial determination that the person to be arrested is probably there.

One "exigent circumstance" is where the police are in hot pursuit of the person to be arrested. Beyond that, lower courts often use a difficult-to-apply test that takes into account the magnitude of the crime, the likelihood that the person is armed, the strength of the probable cause to arrest, the likelihood that the person is within, the likelihood of escape absent immediate arrest, whether the entry is peaceable, and whether the entry is at night. In Welsh v. Wisconsin (1984), the Court declined to give express approval to all these factors but, stressing the absence of the first, held that police could not enter a home without a warrant to arrest a person who had minutes earlier been engaged in the civil forfeiture offense of driving while intoxicated. The Court seems to have given insufficient attention to another reason why immediate warrantless entry to arrest is sometimes necessary: to prevent the loss of evidence (in Welsh, the defendant's blood-alcohol level).

In *Wilson v. Arkansas (1995), the justices provided further guidance on such matters, holding that while police are ordinarily required to knock and announce their presence before entering a house to execute a search warrant, there may be "reasonable" exceptions to the rule to account for a likelihood of violence or imminent destruction of evidence.

Wayne R. LaFave

Peirce v. New Hampshire. See LICENSE CASES.

Penn Central Transportation Co. v. City of New York, 438 U.S. 104 (1978), argued 17 Apr. 1978, decided 26 June 1978 by vote of 6 to 3; Brennan for the Court, Rehnquist in dissent. This key decision on the regulatory taking doctrine originated several important principles. New York City's Landmarks Preservation Committee designated Grand Central Terminal a landmark. Consequently, the plaintiff was denied permission to build a fifty-story office building (supported by arches) above the terminal. However, the city allowed "transferable development rights," by which the plaintiff or an assignee could make excess development on certain nearby "transfer" sites. Penn Central challenged the restriction as a denial of due process and a taking.

In a wide-ranging opinion, the Court held that the development restriction was not a taking because it did not impede existing uses or prevent a reasonable return on investment. The opinion emphasized that the restriction did not unduly "frustrate distinct investment-backed expectations" (p. 127), a phrase that appears in subsequent takings decisions. While the Court did not consider the mitigating effect of the transferable development rights, it was suggested that such transferable rights might mitigate loss to prevent a taking or might, if there were a taking, provide a form of compensation. The Court also rejected the argument that airspace be considered a separate parcel of property for taking purposes. Underlying the opinion is the notion that aesthetic values, particularly historic preservation, are important public interests that justify restrictions on private land.

William B. Stoebuck

Pennoyer v. Neff, 95 U.S. 714 (1878), argued 28 Nov. 1877, decided 21 Jan. 1878 by vote of 8 to 1; Field for the Court, Hunt in dissent. *Pennoyer* v. *Neff* provided the Court's earliest consideration of the constitutional and procedural bases for a state's exercise of jurisdiction over an individual who is neither a resident nor a citizen of the state and who is not physically present there. The case involved title to real property located in Oregon owned by a nonresident defendant. To secure judgment in a contract suit against him, the plaintiff attached the property and provided "constructive service" on the defendant by publication of a legal notice in a local newspaper.

For the Court, Justice Stephen J. Field found that this combination of attachment and constructive service was insufficient to give the state jurisdiction over an out-of-state defendant. He laid down two complementary rules: "every State possesses exclusive jurisdiction and sovereignty over persons and property within its territory"; and "no State can exercise direct jurisdiction and authority over persons or property without its territory" (p. 722). His opinion was based both on physical notions of jurisdiction (i.e., physical presence) and concepts of state sovereignty derived from the Tenth Amendment.

Pennoyer proved increasingly inadequate as a comprehensive statement of in personam jurisdiction in the twentieth century, especially because of the revolutions in transportation and communications, and because the idea of physical presence was irrelevant to explain jurisdiction over corporations. The Court articulated a supplemental theory of in personam jurisdiction in *International Shoe Co.* v. *Washington* (1945), based on traditional notions of fair play and substantial justice. But *Burnham* v. *Superior Court* (1990) demonstrated that if the Tenth Amendment basis of *Pennoyer* is obsolete, the concept of physical presence is not, and can still furnish the basis for so-called tag service on a defendant temporarily present in the forum state.

William M. Wiecek

Pennsylvania Coal Co. v. Mahon, 260 U.S. 393 (1922), argued 14 Nov. 1922, decided 11 Dec. 1922 by vote of 8 to 1; Holmes for the Court, Brandeis in dissent. This decision is the origin of the doctrine that a regulation on the use of land may cause a taking of property. The coal company owned underground strata of coal but no surface rights. A Pennsylvania statute, designed to prevent subsidence, had the effect of prohibiting mining the coal strata. The Supreme Court invalidated the statute, because it constituted a taking of property without compensation, as required by the Fifth Amendment. The Court said that a land-use regulation became a taking if it went "too far" in restricting use of land and diminishing its value (p. 415). It remains unclear when a regulation constitutes a taking of property for which compensation is required.

The concept of a regulatory taking is binding upon both the federal government and states. It is the subject of a number of Supreme Court decisions. In *Keystone Bituminous Coal Association v. DeBenedictis* (1987) the Court upheld a Pennsylvania statute that bore some similarity to the statute that *Mahon* struck down, and appeared to limit the taking doctrine to regulations that almost totally prevent use of the regulated land. With the increasing number of land-use and environmental regulations, the taking issue has become the most celebrated question concerning such controls.

William B. Stoebuck

Pennsylvania v. Nelson, 350 U.S. 497 (1956), argued 15–16 Nov. 1955, decided 2 Apr. 1956 by vote of 6 to 3; Warren for the Court, Reed, joined by Burton and Minton, in dissent. During its 1955 term, the Supreme Court began to withdraw from its previous cold war practice of sustaining state and federal anticommunist legislation. Until hostile congressional reaction led a majority to return to self-restraint in internal security matters for the remainder of the 1950s, the Court relied on procedural or statutory grounds to offer some judicial protection to radical dissenters.

In what was probably the most prominent cold war decision of that term, the Court affirmed a judgment of the Pennsylvania Supreme Court that had reversed the conviction of Steve Nelson, a Communist party leader, under the state's antisedition law. Like the state court, the U.S. Supreme Court held that federal legislation (including the Smith Act of 1940) had occupied the field of preventing overthrow of the national government. Thus, state laws on this subject were excluded, the Court said, even though Congress had never expressed any such intention. The Court concluded that Congress had implicitly occupied the field because of the volume and pervasiveness of federal antisubversive legislation, because of the dominant interest of the federal government in protecting itself against overthrow, and because enforcement of state laws could undercut the effectiveness of federal legislation. A powerful congressional effort to overturn this decision ultimately failed when it became tied to proposed general legislation completely barring implied federal exclusion of state laws, a proposal that generated strong political opposition.

Dean Alfange, Jr.

Pennsylvania v. Wheeling and Belmont Bridge Co., 13 How. (54 U.S.) 518 (1852), argued 1 Dec. 1851, decided 6 Feb. 1852 by vote of 7 to 2; McLean for the Court, Taney and Daniel in dissent. To provide access from Wheeling (now in West Virginia) to the western states, the Virginia legislature in 1847 chartered the Wheeling and Belmont Bridge Company to build a suspension bridge across the Ohio River. Pennsylvania brought suit based on the Supreme Court's original jurisdiction to abate the bridge as a public nuisance because it obstructed passage of large steamboats and thus constituted an impediment to interstate commerce and a violation of interstate compacts. At a more basic policy level, the litigation reflected the struggle between older waterborne transportation technology and the newer railroads.

Justice John McLean's majority opinion held that Pennsylvania had standing to sue because of financial losses to its state-owned internal improvements (the Main Line). The Court ordered abatement of the bridge by either removal or elevation to 111 feet. Chief Justice Roger B. Taney and Justice Peter V. Daniel argued in dissent that in the absence of a federal statute declaring an obstruction of the Ohio River to be a public nuisance, the Court lacked jurisdiction.

Six months later Congress designated the bridge lawful at its extant height. In a later suit of the same name in 1856, a divided Court held that because of the federal statute, the bridge did not constitute an obstruction of interstate commerce. The dimensions of the Wheeling bridge were used throughout the nineteenth century to determine clearances of bridges across navigable rivers.

Elizabeth B. Monroe

Penry v. Lynaugh, 492 U.S. 302 (1989), argued 11 Jan. 1989, decided 26 June 1989; O'Connor announced the judgment of the Court and delivered the opinion of the Court, which was joined in part and dissented to in part by the other justices. *Penry* held that the application of the death penalty to persons who are mentally retarded but not legally insane does not violate the Eighth Amendment prohibition against cruel and unusual punishments. The Court also held, however, that jurors in a capital case must be given the opportunity to consider mitigating evidence and to provide a "reasoned moral response" to that evidence in rendering its sentencing decision.

Penry was mildly to moderately mentally retarded, probably from birth but possibly as a result of childhood beatings. Though but a child in mental age and maturity, he was found legally sane and competent to stand trial and was sentenced to death for rape and murder.

Because the Texas jury was not specifically instructed that it could consider mitigating circumstances in deciding whether or not to apply the death penalty, the Supreme Court reversed. The Court, per Justice Sandra Day O'Connor, held that "the jury must be able to consider and give effect to any mitigating evidence relevant to a defendant's background, character, or the circumstances of the crime" (p. 328).

The Court held, however, that the execution of a mildly or moderately retarded person was not automatically barred by the Eighth Amendment, whether viewed in light of the attitudes of its framers or interpreted in accordance with society's evolving attitudes toward crime and punishment. The Court's decision did not affect its previous decision, in Ford v. Wainwright (1986), that execution of an insane person was prohibited by the Eighth Amendment.

William Lasser

Pentagon Papers Case. See NEW YORK TIMES CO. V. UNITED STATES.

Perry v. United States. See GOLD CLAUSE CASES.

Personnel Administrator of Massachusetts v. Feeney, 442 U.S. 256 (1979), argued 26 Feb. 1979, decided 5 June 1979 by vote of 7 to 2; Stewart for the Court, Marshall and Brennan in dissent. The issue in *Feeney* was whether a Massachusetts statute granting an absolute lifetime preference to veterans in public employment discriminated against women in violation of the Equal Protection Clause of the Fourteenth Amendment.

The case was brought in 1975 by a female civil servant who, despite achieving higher grades on civil service examinations than male veterans, was repeatedly passed over for employment and promotion in favor of those veterans. The federal district court twice found the statute unconstitutional.

The state appealed, supported in the Supreme Court by the solicitor general of the United States.

It was undisputed that more than 98 percent of the veterans in Massachusetts were male, that the veterans preference applied to approximately 60 percent of the public jobs in the state, and that its impact on public employment opportunities for women was severe. Relying on *Washington v. Davis* (1976) and *Arlington Heights v. Metropolitan Housing Development Corp.* (1977), however, the Court made clear that the constitutional standard required showing a discriminatory purpose, not merely a disproportionate impact.

Making a twofold inquiry into the legislative purpose, the Court held first that the statute was neutral and not based on gender because it drew a distinction between veterans and nonveterans, not men and women, and thus also burdened significant numbers of male nonveterans. Second, looking at the totality of legislative actions establishing and extending the statute, the Court held that its enactment did not reflect intentional gender-based discrimination. Announcing a tough test for determining discriminatory purpose, the Court held that even if discriminatory results were foreseeable, the constitutional standard required a finding that the legislature acted because of them, not merely in spite of them.

Justices Thurgood Marshall and William Brennan dissented, arguing that because the impact on women was both extreme and foreseeable, the state had the burden of establishing that gender considerations played no role in the legislation, a burden it failed to meet.

Gerald N. Rosenberg

Philip Morris USA v. Williams, 127 S. Ct. 1057 (2007), argued 31 Oct. 2006, decided 20 Feb. 2007 by vote of 5 to 4; Breyer for the Court, Stevens, Thomas, and Ginsburg in dissent. Mayola Williams sued Philip Morris, the manufacturer of Marlboro cigarettes, for the wrongful death (from lung cancer) of her husband Jesse, a lifelong Marlboro smoker. The decedent had allegedly smoked only because he believed Philip Morris's representations that smoking was safe. An Oregon jury awarded the plaintiff $821,000 in compensatory damages (reduced to $521,000 because of a statutory cap on pain and suffering) and $79.5 million in punitive damages (of which 60 percent was diverted to the state government pursuant to another statute). The award was ultimately upheld by the Oregon Supreme Court, even after the U.S. Supreme Court ordered that the punitive component of the award be reconsidered in light of *State Farm Mutual Automobile Insurance Co.* v. *Campbell* (2003). The Oregon Supreme Court sustained the award because it found Philip Morris's behavior to be "extraordinarily reprehensible."

A sharply divided Supreme Court found that the punitive award deprived Philip Morris of property without due process of law. Justice Stephen Breyer's majority opinion declared for the first time that a fact finder may not award punitive damages for harm caused to nonparties. Such harm is, Breyer conceded, relevant to the reprehensibility of the defendant's actions (and thus a legitimate consideration in the decision to award punitive damages), but it cannot directly determine the amount of the award. The majority declined to consider a separate question—whether the 100-to-1 relationship between punitive and compensatory awards met the constitutional standards of *BMW of North America, Inc.* v. *Gore* (1996)—presumably because it expected the amount to be reduced upon remand to the Oregon courts now that nonparties are excluded from calculations.

Justice John Paul Stevens found the majority's distinction between considering third-party harm in order to assess reprehensibility and considering it in order to punish defendants "directly" to be unintelligible. Justice Ruth Bader Ginsburg noted that Philip Morris's proposed jury instruction (the rejection of which was the basis for its appeal) itself allowed the consideration of harm suffered by others. Justice Clarence Thomas insisted that Supreme Court jurisprudence on punitive damages was not susceptible of principled application, and that the Oregon result could not therefore be termed unconstitutional.

Arguably, the most coherent argument for overturning punitive damage awards is the Eighth Amendment's ban on excessive fines, but this option was rejected by the Court in *Browning-Ferris Industries of Vermont, Inc.* v. *Kelco Disposal, Inc.* (1989) on the ground that fines are payable to the government, not to private parties. The fact that 60% of Williams's award will go to Oregon (whose statute declares that the 40% it leaves to plaintiffs is meant to pay attorneys' contingent fees, undercutting the claim that

punitives are not compensatory) makes the "excessive fines" claim more compelling.

In light of *Williams*, judges must tell jurors to assess harm to others in deciding whether a defendant's conduct was sufficiently awful to merit punitive damages. When calculating such damages, however, jurors must consider only the harm to the individual plaintiff. In 2008, on remand of this case, the Supreme Court of Oregon adhered to its prior decision, setting the stage for further Supreme Court consideration of the constitutional limits on punitive damage awards.

Michael I. Krauss

Pierce v. Society of Sisters, 268 U.S. 510 (1925), argued 16–17 Mar. 1925, decided 1 June 1925 by vote of 9 to 0; McReynolds for the Court. In 1922, the voters of Oregon adopted an initiative requiring nearly every parent to send a child between the ages of eight and sixteen to public school. The statute was unique, and the initiative campaign was organized primarily by the Ku Klux Klan and the Oregon Scottish Rite Masons. It was the product of post-World War I fears about Bolshevism and the influx of aliens. Supporters urged that the separation of children of different religions in private schools would cause dissension and discord. Anti-Catholicism also played a major role in the campaign.

A three-judge federal district court declared that the Oregon initiative violated the Due Process Clause of the Fourteenth Amendment and issued an interlocutory injunction restraining the defendants from enforcing the law. The Supreme Court affirmed. Relying on principles of substantive due process, the Court held that under the doctrine of *Meyer v. Nebraska* (1925) the Oregon initiative unreasonably interfered with the liberty of parents and guardians to direct the education and upbringing of their children and that this interference with the schools threatened the destruction of the plaintiffs' businesses and property. The Court indicated, however, that the states have the power to require attendance at "some school" and to regulate all schools to ensure that "certain studies plainly essential to good citizenship . . . be taught . . . and that nothing be taught which is manifestly inimical to the public welfare" (p. 534).

The *Pierce* Court could have adopted any of three standards. First, it could simply have upheld the power of the states to compel attendance at public schools. Second, it might have determined that any compulsory education law violates the liberty of parents to control the education of their children. The standard actually adopted by the Court—the third choice—is that the states may compel attendance at some school, but the parents have a constitutional right to choose between public and private schools. This "Pierce compromise" recognizes that the state has a legitimate interest in socializing the young to citizenship and other virtues, but it denies the state a monopoly over education: "The fundamental theory of liberty . . . excludes any general power of the State to standardize its children by forcing them to accept instruction from public teachers only" (p. 535).

Despite its reliance on now-repudiated doctrines of substantive due process in the economic sphere, *Pierce* has never been overruled and is in fact frequently cited with favor. The modern constitutional basis for the decision is sharply debated. *Board of Education* v. *Allen* (1968) treated *Pierce* as a decision based on the free exercise of religion. This position poses difficulties because one of the petitioners in *Pierce* was not a sectarian school, and because the religion clauses of the First Amendment were not made applicable to the states until *Cantwell* v. *Connecticut* (1940). Others see *Pierce* as involving the fundamental right of parents (not explicitly protected by the Constitution) to raise their children, or as a check on the power of government to indoctrinate children, thereby protecting the personal autonomy essential to freedom of expression. But whatever its rationale, *Pierce* appears to be a permanent feature of American constitutional culture.

The *Pierce* decision has profoundly affected the evolution of civil liberties for more than seventy-five years. In its emphasis on fundamental rights not expressly articulated in the Constitution and on family autonomy, it presaged later privacy decisions protecting, for example, abortion rights (*Roe* v. *Wade*, 1973) and access to contraceptives (*Griswold* v. *Connecticut*, 1965). If, as some scholars have asserted, America has an "unwritten constitution," *Pierce* is a critical example of its invocation. From this perspective, the modern debate over original intent and constitutional interpretation, best exemplified by the Senate's rejection of Judge Robert Bork for the Supreme Court in 1987, is but a continuation of the debate over the premises and implications of *Pierce*.

□ Mark G. Yudof, "When Governments Speak: Toward a Theory of Government Expression and the First Amendment," *Texas Law Review* 57 (1979): 863–918.

Mark G. Yudof

Planned Parenthood of Southeastern Pennsylvania v. Casey, 505 U.S. 833 (1992), argued 22 Apr. 1992, decided 29 June 1992 by vote of 5 to 4; O'Connor, Kennedy, and Souter for the Court, with Blackmun and Kennedy joining in parts; Rehnquist, Scalia, White, and Thomas concurring and dissenting in different parts.

Few issues have roiled American society and the Supreme Court as fully as abortion. In the landmark case of *Roe* v. *Wade* (1973), the justices had established a fundamental constitutional right to abortion and in so doing sparked a continuing controversy not just over the appropriateness of this technique for ending pregnancy but over the role of the Court in deciding the issue. Thereafter, the Court had rendered a number of decisions that suggested that its increasingly conservative ranks would eviscerate the precedent. Such turned out not to be true in *Casey*, although the justices divided sharply.

Casey involved a Pennsylvania law that required women to wait at least twenty-four hours for an abortion after a doctor provided them with specific information about the nature of the procedure, the state of development of the fetus, and the possibilities of using alternatives to abortion. The law also required that minors have the consent of one parent, who was also subject to the informed consent requirements. Married women were required to notify their husbands that they planned to have an abortion, and if they failed to do so, they were subject to up to a year in jail.

Like measures in other states, the Pennsylvania Abortion Control Act aimed to eliminate abortion by imposing time- consuming and potentially embarrassing regulations that would force women to take their pregnancies to term. The chief problem for opponents of abortion was that the Supreme Court, while accepting that the states could impose regulations, had decided in *Webster* v. *Reproductive Health Service* (1989) that such regulations could not create "undue burdens." The *Webster* holding had signaled that the Court was willing to change the standard of constitutional review, moving from the much more demanding requirement that the legislature establish a "compelling state interest" to the less stringent requirement that any regulation not place an "undue burden" on the person seeking the abortion.

Planned Parenthood of Southeastern Pennsylvania brought suit against the law, but the United States Court of Appeals for the Third Circuit, in Philadelphia, upheld all of the provisions save that involving the requirement for married women to notify their husbands. The judges found that this provision did create the kind of undue burden proscribed by *Webster*.

The Supreme Court's decision mirrored the divisions in American society. First President Ronald Reagan and then President George Bush had urged the Court to overturn *Roe*, and in making appointments to the federal courts, they generally insisted on judges that would do just that. In some respects, however, the politicization of the abortion issue may have actually worked against the Court striking boldly at *Roe*.

In an unusual step, three of the justices (Sandra Day O'Connor, Anthony M. Kennedy, and David H. Souter) jointly wrote the opinion for the Court. They were joined in part by Justices Harry A. Blackmun, the author of the *Roe* opinion, and John Paul Stevens. The majority held that the decision in *Roe* had established a rule of law and a component of liberty that the Court would not renounce. The justices made clear that any effort to overturn *Roe* would divide the nation, pose profound questions about the Court's legitimacy, and make it appear that the justices were capitulating to political pressures.

The justices invoked the "undue burden" test of *Webster* to sustain most of the Pennsylvania law, but they refused to take the additional step of striking down *Roe*. The only portion of the Pennsylvania law that they declared unconstitutional was the requirement that a married woman tell her husband of her intent to have an abortion. Justices Blackmun and Stevens argued in dissent that the other four provisions should be struck down as well. At the same time, Chief Justice William H. Rehnquist and Justices Antonin Scalia, Byron R. White, and Clarence Thomas insisted that the Court should overturn *Roe*. The exchange among the justices was among the most intense in the history of the Court.

The case also underscored the important role that Justices O'Connor and Kennedy played in protecting the Court's ideological center. President Ronald Reagan had appointed both of them to the bench, doing so with the hope that on the critical abortion issue they would vote to end the *Roe* precedent. During their initial years on the bench, both justices had given evidence that they would do just that, yet by the time of *Casey* both had moved to a position that permitted state regulation but also perpetuated abortion as a fundamental right. In the end, O'Connor and Kennedy were more concerned with the institutional danger that the case presented to the Court than with settling the abortion issue by outlawing it. The Court's actions in *Casey* were, quite apart from the underlying constitutional issues, a vivid demonstration that the justices know that for their actions to be accepted in a democracy, those actions have to be seen as being different from politics and the justices themselves as different from politicians.

Kermit L. Hall

Plessy v. Ferguson, 163 U.S. 537 (1896), argued 13 Apr. 1896, decided 18 May 1896 by vote of 7 to 1; Brown for the Court, Harlan in dissent, Brewer not participating. In this case, the Supreme Court upheld the constitutionality of a Louisiana statute (1890) that required railroads to provide "equal but separate accommodations for the white and colored races" and barred persons from occupying rail cars other than those to which their race had been assigned. The opinion is one of arresting contrasts: between its relative insignificance at the time and the symbolic importance it would attain during the next six decades, between the petty rationalization of the majority opinion and the abiding appeal of the dissent, and between the begrudging interpretation of the Civil War Amendments as applied to African-Americans and the expansive interpretation of the same amendments as applied to claims of economic right.

The dispute arose as a test case to challenge a statute, an example of the Jim Crow laws then being passed in the South as whites sought to embellish their control of state governments. A New Orleans group of Creoles and blacks organized themselves as the Citizens' Committee to Test the Constitutionality of the Separate Car Law. Their challenge enjoyed some support from the railroads, who objected to the additional costs of providing separate cars. Plessy agreed to initiate the challenge on behalf of the committee. Although he appeared to be white, Plessy was classified as "colored" under the Louisiana code because he was one-eighth black.

A previous decision by the Louisiana Supreme Court had held that the statute could not apply to interstate commerce. Plessy was therefore careful to purchase a ticket for a journey entirely within the state of Louisiana, having insured in advance that the railroad and the conductor knew of his mixed race. He was arrested when he refused to move to the "colored only" section of the coach. Plessy attempted to half the trial, arguing that the statute was unconstitutional under both the Thirteenth and Fourteenth Amendments to the Constitution. After the Louisiana courts rejected his arguments, he sought review by the Supreme Court.

Writing for the Court, Justice Henry Billings Brown rejected both of Plessy's arguments. He continued the Court's practice of construing the Thirteenth Amendment to apply only to actions whose purpose was to reintroduce slavery itself. It did not, he reasoned, reach all distinctions based on color.

He likewise held that the statute did not violate the Fourteenth Amendment's requirement that all citizens be afforded equal protection of the laws. His cardinal postulate was that laws requiring separation of the races did not suggest that one race was inferior. Inferiority, according to Brown, arose only because one race chose to perceive the laws in such a way. It was equally fundamental to Brown that laws could not alter the long-established customs of society. For the Court to mandate that the races be mixed would be futile in the face of strong public sentiment as manifested by statutes requiring separation of the races in educational facilities. To support that proposition Brown pointed to a line of cases beginning with an opinion by Chief Justice Lemuel Shaw of Massachusetts in *Roberts* v. *City of Boston* (1849).

By linking racial separation on trains with that in education, Brown touched one of the most sensitive parts of the efforts to maintain separation of the races. Education was a bug-bear for anyone who suggested legislation mandating racial equality. Brown therefore sought to support his conclusion by implying that transportation was like education. The enduring effect of Brown's analogy was to place the Court's imprimatur on a considerably expanded field in which segregation was justified.

Justice John Marshall Harlan's isolated dissent would later support eloquent rejections of the separate but equal doctrine, especially as applied to education. Harlan refused to restrict the Thirteenth Amendment to slavery itself, preferring to see the amendment as barring all "badge[s] of servitude" (p. 555). In one of the ringing phrases for which he is best known, Harlan argued that the "Constitution is colorblind, and neither knows nor tolerates classes among citizens" (p. 559). The epigram had been suggested in the brief field on behalf of Plessy by Albion Tourgée, a white attorney who was a leader in the campaign for equal rights.

□ Charles A. Lofgren, *The Plessy Case* (1987). Otto H. Olsen, *The Thin Disguise: Turning Point in Negro History; Plessy v. Ferguson: A Documentary Presentation (1864–1896)* (1967).

Walter F. Pratt, Jr.

Plyler v. Doe, 457 U.S. 202 (1982), argued 1 Dec. 1981, decided 15 June 1982 by a vote of 5 to 4; Brennan for the Court, Burger, White, Rehnquist, and O'Connor in dissent. Texas refused to finance the education of undocumented children and authorized local districts to exclude these children from enrollment in free public schools. The Supreme Court held this practice to be repugnant to the Fourteenth Amendment's Equal Protection Clause, which guarantees that "no State shall . . . deny to any person *within its jurisdiction* the equal protection of the laws" [emphasis added]. Texas argued that the phrase "within its jurisdiction" excluded illegal aliens from equal protection guarantees. The Court disagreed, holding that these guarantees extended to each person, regardless of citizenship or immigration status, inside the state's perimeter and subject to state laws.

The Court, however, refused to apply strict scrutiny since education was not a fundamental right and undocumented aliens did not constitute a suspect class because their own conscious actions caused their illegal status. The Court majority, however, did apply an escalated standard of protection ("heightened scrutiny"), appropriate because of education's special and lasting importance relative to other social welfare benefits and because undocumented children, unlike adults, lacked responsibility for their illegal situation. State denial of this especially important benefit to a discrete class of innocents violated equal protection, the Court stated, unless the policy furthered some substantial governmental interest.

Criticizing the majority for employing a result-oriented jurisprudence, flawed reasoning, and an inappropriate standard of review, Chief Justice Warren Burger argued that Texas' exclusionary law was constitutionally valid because it rationally furthered legitimate state interests. Later, many of these children, undocumented in 1982, acquired legal residency under the federal government's amnesty program. The propriety of the majority's jurisprudence, however, is still debated.

Richard A. Gambitta

Pointer v. Texas, 380 U.S. 400 (1965), argued 15 Mar. 1965, decided 5 Apr. 1965 by vote of 9 to 0; Black for the Court, Harlan, Stewart, and Goldberg concurring. The Sixth Amendment provides in part that "[i]n all criminal prosecutions, the accused shall enjoy the right . . . to be confronted with the witness against him." Although the right to confrontation had long been recognized in state law, in this case the Supreme Court ruled that the Sixth Amendment guarantee was applicable to the states via the Due Process Clause of the Fourteenth Amendment.

The case arose when a defendant's attorney objected to the introduction of a transcript of testimony of a robbery victim who had moved out of state between the time he had testified at a preliminary hearing and the trial. In this transcribed testimony the victim identified Pointer as the offender, and Pointer was convicted largely upon the basis of this testimony. In overturning his conviction the Supreme Court held that introduction of such testimony, which had been taken at a proceeding at which Pointer had been present but unrepresented by counsel, constituted a denial of his Sixth Amendment rights to confront witnesses and to cross-examine them by counsel.

In overturning the conviction and extending the right to confrontation to the states, the Court also ruled that this right must be determined by the same standards that hold in federal proceedings. In so doing, the Court also reiterated the underlying reason for the rule, which is to give defendants charged with crimes an opportunity to cross-examine witnesses against them. However, even as the Court embraced a sweeping interpretation of the right, it acknowledged some practical limits, noting for instance that declarations of dying persons and testimony of deceased witnesses who had testified at former trials could still be admissible despite the impossibility of confrontation.

Malcolm M. Feeley

Pollock v. Farmers' Loan & Trust Co., (1) 157 U.S. 429 (1895), argued 7–13 Mar. 1895, decided in three parts on 8 Apr. 1895 by votes of 8 to 0, 6 to 2, and 4 to 4; Fuller for the Court, Field concurring, White, Harlan, Brown, and Shiras in dissent, Jackson not participating. (2) 158 U.S. 601 (1895), rehearing argued 6–8 May 1895, decided 20 May 1895 by vote of 5 to 4; Fuller for the Court, Harlan, Brown, Jackson, and White in dissent. *Pollock* is not important as a precedent, since it was negated by the Sixteenth Amendment and was probably on the way to reversal by the Supreme Court even before that amendment's adoption. Nevertheless, the decision stands as one of the most notorious examples—according to progressive historians—of judicial adherence to laissez-faire constitutionalism.

At issue was the income tax law of 1894, the nation's first peacetime attempt to tax incomes, including those from securities and corporate profits. The tax was itself miniscule—a flat 2 percent on all incomes above four thousand dollars—but the principle was of great significance. On one side, the national government needed additional revenue to support its burgeoning activities. Social reformers also argued that some action was needed to reduce the great disparities of wealth resulting from the rapidly industrializing American economy. On the other side, private individuals and businesses claimed constitutional protection against such measures to redistribute wealth.

Pollock was a contrived case in which a stockholder sued to enjoin his bank from paying a tax that the bank did not wish to pay anyway. The Court agreed to expedite hearings for the case, reflecting the need to have the question settled rapidly.

Lawyers opposing the tax, headed by Joseph H. Choate of New York, argued that the income tax violated the principle of uniformity and that it was a "direct" tax that could be constitutional only if apportioned according to the populations of the several states. Neither argument had any support in precedent; the meaning of direct tax had long been given a narrow interpretation. Moreover, the Supreme Court, in *Springer v. United States* (1881), had sustained the temporary Civil War income tax, holding that an income tax was not a direct tax. Partly for this reason the lawyers freely resorted to hortatory claims that such taxation was an attack on private property rights and the first step on the road to communism.

In the initial decision, the Supreme Court separated the law into three parts, deciding each by a different vote. First, the Court held unanimously that a tax on income from state and municipal bonds was essentially a tax on the state itself, violating the principle of state sovereignty. Next, the Court, in an opinion by Chief Justice Melville Fuller, ruled that a tax on income from real property was a direct tax. The Court split 6 to 2, with Justices Edward D. White and John Marshall Harlan dissenting. Third, the Court divided equally, Justice Howell Jackson being absent, on the question whether the general tax on private and corporate incomes was also a direct tax. Evidence suggests that Justices Henry B. Brown and George Shiras joined White and Harlan in believing the tax constitutional. Thus, a major part of the tax law was left standing.

This situation pleased no one, and the Court immediately agreed to a rehearing on the issue of taxing general income. The terminally ill Jackson struggled to Washington undoubtedly hoping that his vote would settle the question in favor of the tax's validity. But though Jackson voted to support the tax, another justice (probably Shiras) changed position, producing a 5-to-4 vote invalidating the entire tax law because it was a direct tax that had to be apportioned among the states according to their populations.

This barebones description of *Pollock* gives no adequate impression of its emotion-laden context. Both lawyers and judges departed far from constitutional argument; newspapers reported it fully and editorialized acidly. Harlan wrote privately that Justice Stephen J. Field acted like a "madman" throughout the case, but the dissenters' own opinions were similarly emotional. It was doubtless the most controversial case of its era.

Only one part of the decision stood after the adoption of the Sixteenth Amendment in 1913: the ban on the taxation of income from state and municipal bonds. Although Congress has never enacted such a tax, the Court reversed its 1895 objection to such action in *South Carolina v. Baker* (1988).

Loren P. Beth

Powell v. Alabama, 287 U.S. 45 (1932), argued 10 Oct. 1932, decided 7 Nov. 1932 by vote of 7 to 2; Sutherland for the Court, Butler and McReynolds in dissent. *Powell v. Alabama* was the first of the notorious Scottsboro cases decided by the Supreme Court. Nine black youths were arrested near Scottsboro, Alabama, and charged with having raped two white women riding on a freight train in March 1931. The accused youths were hastily indicted and tried for the crime of rape. On the day of the trials, an attorney appeared on behalf of the defendants, but indicated he would not formally represent them. The trial judge then stated that all members of the local bar present in the courtroom should represent the accused. Most of the local bar nevertheless withdrew from the case. Two attorneys did appear on behalf of the accused but had no opportunity to investigate the case and consulted with the defendants for only thirty minutes prior to the trials. Eight of the defendants were convicted and sentenced to death after brief trials, while there was a hung jury in the case of the remaining defendant.

Over the dissent of Chief Justice John C. Anderson, the Alabama Supreme Court affirmed the convictions of seven of the defendants, while reversing the conviction of one of the Scottsboro youths because he was a juvenile. Following a bitter struggle between the National Association for the Advancement of Colored People and the International Labor Defense, the Communist-dominated International Labor Defense won control of the Scottsboro cases, and it was under the sponsorship of that group that *Powell v. Alabama* was appealed to the Supreme Court.

Speaking for the Court, Justice George Sutherland held that the convictions of the Scottsboro defendants must be reversed under the Due Process Clause of the Fourteenth Amendment. Under the Due Process Clause, the states were required to afford criminal defendants fair trials, and the right to counsel was an integral part of due process. Hence, at least under the circumstances existing in the Scottsboro cases, the failure of the trial court to appoint counsel for indigent defendants denied them the right to a fair trial. Dissenting from the Court's reversal of the Scottsboro convictions, Justice Pierce Butler, joined by Justice James McReynolds, argued that the defendants had received the effective assistance of counsel. They contended that the Court, by reversing the convictions, was engaging in an unwarranted interference with the administration of justice in the state courts.

The *Powell* case was the first occasion in which the Supreme Court had held that the Due Process Clause required the appointment of counsel by state courts for indigent defendants in those cases in which lack of representation by counsel would result in an unfair trial. The Court did not rule in *Powell*, however, that the assistance of counsel clause of the Sixth Amendment was applicable to the states. Rather, the Court held only that the Fourteenth Amendment's Due Process Clause required fair trials for state criminal defendants, and that in some cases a fair trial could not be obtained unless the accused was represented by counsel. After the *Powell* decision, the Court thus followed the rule that the Due Process Clause required the state courts to appoint counsel for indigent defendants in all capital cases but that appointed counsel for indigent defendants in noncapital state cases was required only if an unfair trial would result for a defendant unrepresented by counsel. In contrast, the rule the Court enforced under the assistance of counsel clause of the Sixth Amendment, applicable in the federal courts, required the federal courts to appoint counsel for indigent defendants facing serious criminal charges in all cases, capital or noncapital.

In *Gideon* v. *Wainwright* (1963), however, the Court held that the Fourteenth Amendment's Due Process Clause required the appointment of counsel for indigent defendants facing serious criminal charges in all state cases, capital or noncapital. This brought the rule governing the right to counsel in state courts into conformity with the rule applicable in the federal courts under the Sixth Amendment. The *Gideon* case is regarded as having incorporated the assistance of counsel clause of the Sixth Amendment into the Fourteenth Amendment, making it applicable to the states, an expansion of the constitutional right to counsel that began with the Court's decision in *Powell* v. *Alabama* in 1932.

□ Dan T. Carter, *Scottsboro: A Tragedy of the American South*, rev. ed. (1979).

Richard C. Cortner

Powell v. McCormack, 395 U.S. 486, argued 21 Apr. 1969, decided 16 June 1969 by vote of 8 to 1; Warren for the Court, Douglas concurring, Stewart in dissent. In 1966 the flamboyant black congressman, Adam Clayton Powell, Jr., was reelected by Harlem constituency he had served since 1942. Because of allegations about improper use of congressional funds (and because, his supporters contended, he was about to become chairman of the House Labor and Education Committee) the House of Representatives refused to permit Powell to take his seat at the beginning of the Ninetieth Congress. A select committee reported that he met the qualifications of age, residency, and citizenship specified in Article I, section 2, but concluded that he was guilty of various improprieties. It recommended that he be sworn in and seated but fined forty thousand dollars and deprived of his seniority (and thus his chairmanship). This was rejected by the House, which then voted, 307 to 116, to exclude him from the Ninetieth Congress and declare his seat vacant.

Powell and some of his supporters then filed suit in federal court, seeking a declaratory judgment that he had been improperly excluded, an injunction prohibiting the House from excluding him, and back pay. While the suit was pending, Powell was reelected to the Ninety-first Congress. He was permitted to take his seat but fined twenty-five thousand dollars and stripped of his seniority and chairmanship.

The Supreme Court held that a lawsuit against members of Congress, including House Speaker John McCormack, violated the legislative immunity protected by the Speech and Debate Clause of Article I, section 6, and removed them as defendants. But it ruled that the suit could be maintained against employees of the House such as the doorkeeper and sergeant-at-arms.

The government argued that Powell's lawsuit should be dismissed because Congress's decision to exclude one of its members constituted a nonjusticiable political question. Under the doctrine of *Baker* v. *Carr* (1962, political questions that courts should not decide include those where the Constitution has made a "textually demonstrable commitment" to another branch of government to exercise a particular power

(p. 518). Congress, the Court said, had only the exclusive authority to judge the qualifications of its members as specified in Article I, section 2. Powell met those qualifications and thus exclusion for any other reason was reviewable—and, at least in this case, unconstitutional.

The Court also considered whether the vote to exclude could also be taken as a vote to expel, since the two-thirds requirement for expulsion had been met. It observed, however, that the House had been advised by the speaker that it was voting to exclude and that only a majority vote was needed. Furthermore, the rules of the House disfavored expulsion for misbehavior in a prior Congress. Thus a vote to exclude could not be transformed retroactively into a vote to expel; expulsion and exclusion are not equivalents.

If Powell had actually been expelled for misconduct, could the Supreme Court have reviewed the case or would this also have constituted a nonjusticiable political question? The Court gave no formal answer, although Justice William O. Douglas suggested in a footnote that an expulsion would not be reviewable. Also left unanswered was whether a decision to exclude a member because of a disputed finding that he or she was not a citizen or properly a resident of the district would be subject to judicial review.

Powell, following closely on the heels of *Baker* v. *Carr*, seemed to have placed significant limits on the political questions doctrine, thus inviting greater judicial intrusion into the internal processes of the other branches of government. It does not, however, appear to have had that effect. In the many cases in which federal courts declined to address the legality of the war in Vietnam, for example, the political questions doctrine, contrary to the implications in *Baker*, was employed to support judicial restraint.

Joel B. Grossman

Powers v. Ohio, 499 U.S. 400 (1991), argued 9 Oct. 1990, decided 1 Apr. 1991 by vote of 7 to 2; Kennedy for the Court, Scalia in dissent. Clarifying the basis of its decision in *Batson* v. *Kentucky* (1986), the Court ruled that the prosecution in a criminal trial cannot use peremptory challenges to exclude potential jurors on the basis of race, whether or not the defendant and the excluded potential juror are of the same race. Racial discrimination in jury selection, wrote Justice Anthony Kennedy, violates not only the defendant's right to a fair trial but also the potential juror's right "to participate in the administration of justice" (p. 1368). Moreover, the Court held that "a criminal defendant has standing to raise the equal protection rights of a potential juror excluded from service in violation of these principles" (p. 1370).

In dissent, Justice Antonin Scalia argued that the Court's prior holdings sought only to protect criminal defendants from the exclusion of members of their own race from juries and to guarantee that no citizen could be excluded from jury lists on the basis of race. "The sum and substance of the Court's lengthy analysis," he wrote, "is that, since a denial of equal protection to other people occurred at the defendant's trial, though it did not affect the fairness of that trial, the defendant must go free" (p. 1381). Two years later the Court in *Georgia* v. *McCollum* (1992) extended the principle from *Batson* to include both prosecution and defense counsel in civil cases.

William Lasser

Presser v. Illinois, 116 U.S. 252 (1886), argued 23–24 Nov. 1885, decided 4 Jan. 1886 by vote of 9 to 0; Woods for the Court. In *Presser v. Illinois*, the Court sustained an Illinois state statute prohibiting parading with arms by groups other than the organized militia. Herman Presser, who had been convicted of leading armed members of a fraternal organization in a parade, challenged the statute on the grounds that it violated the Second and Fourteenth Amendments. The Court's opinion, written by Justice William B. Woods, rejected Presser's claims holding that the Second Amendment's guarantee of the right to keep and bear arms only applied to the federal government.

Although the opinion in *Presser* is often discussed within the context of the Second Amendment debate, it is probably better viewed as an example of the Court's initial tendency to reject the view that the Fourteenth Amendment applied the Bill of Rights to the states. The Woods opinion noted that the Illinois statute did not interfere with the right to keep and bear arms and that state governments could not disarm their populations because that would interfere with the federal government's ability to raise a militia from the population at large. Despite this the opinion stressed that the Second Amendment only limited action by the federal government.

The modern validity of the holding *Presser* is unclear in light of the Court's application of most provisions of the Bill of Rights to the states through the Fourteenth Amendment in the twentieth century. It has been relied on by lower federal courts but has not been revisited by the Supreme Court, which has generally not looked at Second Amendment claims in recent times.

Robert J. Cottrol

Prigg v. Pennsylvania, 16 Pet. (41 U.S.) 539 (1842), argued and decided Jan. 1842 by vote of 8 to 1; Story for the Court, Taney, Thompson, Baldwin, Wayne, and Daniel concurring, McLean in dissent. In 1837, Edward Prigg, and three other Marylanders, seized Margaret Morgan, a runaway slave living in Pennsylvania. Prigg applied to a justice of the peace for certificates of removal under the federal Fugitive Slave Act of 1793 and Pennsylvania's 1826 personal liberty law. The federal law authorized state magistrates to hear cases involving fugitive slaves. The justice of the peace refused Prigg's request for a certificate of removal. Without any legal authority, Prigg then removed to Maryland Morgan and her children, including one conceived and born in Pennsylvania. Pennsylvania then indicted Prigg for kidnapping under the 1826 state law.

After protracted negotiations, Maryland agreed to extradite Prigg for trial, and Pennsylvania agreed to expedite proceedings so that the case could quickly go to the U.S. Supreme Court so that it might define the power of the states to legislate on the rendition of fugitive slaves.

Speaking for the Court, Justice Joseph Story held (1) that the federal Fugitive Slave Law of 1793 was constitutional; (2) that Pennsylvania's personal liberty law of 1826 (and by extension all similar laws) unconstitutionally added new requirements to the rendition process; (3) that the Constitution's Fugitive Slave Clause (Art. IV, sec. 2, cl. 3) implied a right of recaption, so that under the clause any slave-owner or his agent could capture a fugitive slave without complying with the federal law of 1793 if such a capture could be done without a breach of the peace; and (4) that all state judges and other officials ought to enforce the federal law but that the national government could not force them to do so because the federal government had no power to require state officials to act.

Story held that all state laws that interfered with the enforcement of the Fugitive Slave Act were unconstitutional. Story based much of his decision on an inaccurate analysis of the intentions of the Philadelphia framers, asserting "that it cannot be doubted that it [the Constitution's Fugitive Slave Clause] constituted a fundamental article, without the adoption of which the Union could not have been formed" (p. 611). In fact, the clause was added quite late in the Constitutional Convention, with almost no debate and little thought.

Chief Justice Roger B. Taney concurred in the result in *Prigg*, but objected to Story's conclusion that state judges did not have to enforce the Fugitive Slave Act. In his concurrence (which read more like a dissent), Taney misrepresented Story's opinion by claiming that it prohibited state officials from enforcing the Fugitive Slave Act, when in fact Story actually urged state officials to enforce the law but conceded that the federal government had no power to require them to do so. Taney also complained, again erroneously, that Story's opinion prohibited all supplemental legislation on the rendition of fugitive slaves. Story's opinion actually allowed states to enact legislation aiding the rendition process as long as they did not add requirements beyond what the federal law mandated. Taney complained that under Story's opinion fugitive slave rendition would be virtually impossible, because at the time there were so few federal judges to enforce the federal statute. Taney's complaint became a self-fulfilling prophecy, as some northern judges used his characterization of Story's opinion as a justification for not hearing fugitive slave cases, and some state legislatures also prohibited the use of state facilities for fugitive slave rendition.

Story's son claimed that his father's opinion was an antislavery decision because it allowed the free states to withdraw their support for fugitive rendition. In private correspondence, however, Story urged Congress to create federal commissioners to enforce various federal laws, including the 1793 act. In the Fugitive Slave Act of 1850 Congress adopted Story's recommendation. Rather than being an anti-slavery opinion, Story's effort was actually an attempt to nationalize law, consistent with his opinion from the same term in *Swift* v. *Tyson* (1842).

□ Paul Finkelman, Story Telling on the Supreme Court: Prigg v. Pennsylvania and

Justice Joseph Story's Judicial Nationalism," Supreme Court Review 1994: 247–294.

Paul Finkelman

Printz v. United States, 117 S.Ct. 2365 (1997), argued 3 Dec. 1996, decided 27 June 1997 by vote of 5 to 4; Scalia for the Court, O'Connor and Thomas concurring, Stevens, Souter, Ginsburg, and Breyer in dissent.

In his attempt to assassinate President Ronald Reagan in 1981, John Hinckley gravely wounded White House press secretary James Brady. After years of lobbying, Congress, relying on the Commerce Clause of the Constitution, finally passed in 1993 the Brady Handgun Violence Prevention Act, which required, among other things, a waiting period of five days to purchase a handgun and charged the chief local law enforcement officials, such as county sheriffs, to conduct background checks on persons seeking to purchase weapons. Under these provisions of the law approximately sixty-six hundred applications a month were rejected because the would-be purchasers fell into one of several proscribed categories, such as felons and drug users. Two sheriffs, Jay Printz of Ravalii County, Montana, and Richard Mack of Graham County, Arizona, challenged the law successfully in separate lower federal court lawsuits, arguing that the federal law had placed an undue burden on local law enforcement officials. The United States Court of Appeals for the Ninth Circuit subsequently heard the appeal from the federal government and upheld the law. Printz then appealed.

A bitterly divided Court agreed with Printz. Justice Antonin Scalia's opinion alluded to both the limits of the Commerce Clause and to the Tenth Amendment to the Constitution, which grants to the states powers that the Constitution does not give to the national government. Scalia's opinion, however, rested mostly on his and the majority's understanding of the federal structure of the nation in striking down the background-check provision of the law. Scalia insisted that the federal principle of dividing power between the states and the national government was one of the primary means by which the Constitution protected liberty. As a result, the federal government could no more order state officials to administer federal law than state officials could order federal officials to administer state law. Moreover, Scalia insisted that the principle was categorical, meaning that there could

be no test that would balance state and federal interests in such a way as to advantage the federal government. Scalia's opinion was one of the most remarkable assertions by the Court in favor of state authority in the history of the nation.

The dissenters were diametrically opposed to the majority. Justice John Paul Stevens argued that when Congress acted within one of its express grants of authority, such as the commerce power, it was supreme and had to be obeyed. Indeed, Stevens and the other dissenters could not imagine the American nation in any other way. The legislation passed by Congress, he claimed, was as binding on the states as were laws passed by the legislatures of the states themselves. The federal government, he continued, was entirely within its authority to require local officials to help administer the background-check provisions of the Brady bill. Such enforcement action, Stevens concluded, imposed a minor burden on the states and not the massive incursion that Scalia described in his opinion.

The actual impact of the decision on the administration of justice was limited. The decision did relieve the chief local law enforcement officials from performing background checks, but under the terms of the Brady bill their duties were scheduled to end in 1998 in any case, to be replaced by a federal record-checking system administered by gun dealers. Still, the constitutional importance of the decision was clear enough. It marked the ascension of state power in Supreme Court decision making and a continuation of the aggressive effort by Chief Justice William H. Rehnquist and the conservative majority on the Court to readjust the state-federal balance in favor of the states. Indeed, Justice Clarence Thomas, in a concurring opinion, concluded that, given the Second Amendment's reference to the "right of the people to keep and bear Arms," Congress probably had no authority to regulate intrastate gun sales under any circumstances.

Kermit L. Hall

Prize Cases, 2 Black (67 U.S.) 635 (1863), argued 10–13, 16–20, 23–25 Feb. 1863, decided 10 Mar. 1863 by vote of 5 to 4; Grier for the Court, Nelson, joined by Catron, Clifford, and Taney, in dissent. On 19 April 1861 President Abraham Lincoln ordered a blockade of Confederate ports, and later that month he extended the blockade to the recently seceded states of Virginia and North Carolina. On 13 July Congress authorized Lincoln to declare that a state of insurrection existed, and on 6 August Congress retroactively ratified all of Lincoln's previous military actions.

The *Prize Cases* involved libels against four different ships and their cargoes seized before 13 July. The *Amy Warwick* contained coffee and was en route to Richmond. The Court upheld its seizure as "that of enemies' property" (p. 675). The *Hiawatha* was a British ship caught in Richmond when the Civil War began. The ship's captain was on notice that all neutral ships had to leave Richmond within fifteen days after the blockade began. Because of the failure to obtain a tow the ship was unable to leave port until a few days after the blockade became effective, although its cargo was loaded within the fifteen-day period. The Court affirmed the condemnation of both the ship and its cargo. The *Brilliante* was a Mexican ship that entered New Orleans more than a month after the blockade was established. The ship was captured after leaving New Orleans, and the Court upheld the condemnation. The *Crenshaw*, owned by citizens of Richmond, was captured taking tobacco to England. This ship presented a straightforward question of enemy property. The Court upheld the libel against both the ship and its cargo.

While involving many different technical issues, the cases all turned on one key question: did the president have the power to impose the blockade without Congressional authorization? Lincoln argued that a state of insurrection existed after the firing on Fort Sumter and that he was empowered to take unilateral action against this situation. In supporting Lincoln on this issue, the Supreme Court upheld his theory of the Civil War as an insurrection against the United States government that could be suppressed according to the rules of war. In this way the United States was able to fight the war as if it were an international war, without actually having to recognize the *de jure* existence of the Confederate government.

In the *Prize Cases*, Justice Robert Grier held that "a blockade *de facto* existed" after Lincoln's proclamations and that as "Executive Chief of the Government and Commander-in-Chief of the Army and Navy" Lincoln "was the proper person to make such notifications" (p. 666). Grier argued that a war could exist even if one party did not recognize the sovereignty of another. He noted that, as "civil war is never publicly proclaimed, *eo nomine* against insurgents, its actual existence is a fact in our domestic history which the court is bound to notice and to know" (p. 667). Here the Court took notice of the war and Lincoln's response to it.

In dissent, Justice Samuel Nelson argued that "no civil war existed between this Government and the State in insurrection till recognized by the Act of Congress" on 13 July and that the president did not have the power, under the Constitution, to either declare war "or recognize its existence within the meaning of the law of nations, which carries with it belligerent rights, and thus change the country and all its citizens from a state of peace to a state of war" (p. 698). Nelson believed that only Congress possessed such powers and thus that the seizures under the blockade were illegal.

In the *Prize Cases*, the Court narrowly approved Lincoln's theory of the Civil War as a domestic insurrection with the attributes of an international war. For domestic constitutional purposes the Court affirmed the power of the president to act as if he were merely suppressing an insurrection, while for purposes of international relations, the Court held out to the world that the South was a belligerent and could be legally blockaded. The theory of the war accepted in this case implied that other actions by the president, including the Emancipation Proclamation and the suspension of habeas corpus, were also constitutionally permissible, especially when supported by subsequent congressional approval.

□ Stewart L. Bernath, *Squall across the Atlantic: American Civil War Prize Cases and Diplomacy* (1970).

Paul Finkelman

Providence Bank v. Billings, 4 Pet. (29 U.S.) 514 (1830), argued 11 Feb. 1830, decided 22 Mar. 1830 by vote of 7 to 0; Marshall for the Court. Influenced by the currents of Jacksonian democracy and states' rights sentiment, the Supreme Court in *Providence Bank* limited the amount of protection accorded corporation charters under the Contracts Clause. In 1791, the Rhode Island legislature granted a charter to Providence Bank to conduct a banking business. In 1822, the lawmakers sought to tax the capital stock of every bank in the state. Providence Bank argued that its charter impliedly conferred an exemption from state taxation and that the tax law thus impaired the obligation of contract.

Rejecting this contention, Chief Justice John Marshall stressed that taxing authority "is essential to the existence of government" (p. 560) and could not be relinquished by implication. Only an express grant of immunity from taxation would bind the state. Marshall added that the Constitution "was not intended to furnish the corrective for every abuse of power which may be committed by the state governments" (p. 563). The ruling in *Providence Bank* established the principle that corporate privilege must be expressly set forth in the charter in order to receive constitutional protection. The Court later built upon this doctrine in *Charles River Bridge* v. *Warren Bridge* (1837) to emphasize that corporate grants must be strictly construed.

James W. Ely, Jr.

Prudential Insurance Co. v. Benjamin, 328 U.S. 408 (1946), argued 8 and 11 Mar. 1946, decided 3 June 1946 by vote of 8 to 0; Rutledge for the Court, Black concurring in result without opinion, Jackson not participating. South Carolina imposed a 3 percent tax on the premiums received by out-of-state insurance companies from policies written in the state but did not impose a similar tax on South Carolina corporations. The Prudential, a New Jersey corporation, argued that in light of the Court's decision in *United States* v. *South-Eastern Underwriters Association* (1944), such a discriminatory tax imposed a burden upon interstate commerce and therefore exceeded the powers of the state. Congress, however, had reversed the *South-Eastern* decision in the McCarran Act of 1945 and explicitly delegated to the states the power to regulate and tax insurance companies.

Justice Wiley Rutledge's opinion assumed that a tax discriminating between in-state and foreign corporations constituted a violation of the Commerce Clause, but the Court upheld the tax in this case because Congress had "consented" to state regulation of insurance even if such regulation impinged on interstate commerce. Where earlier cases had held that states could act if Congress had failed to exercise its authority (e.g., *Cooley* v. *Board of Wardens of the Port of Philadelphia*, 1852), here the Court approved a "consent" authority for states to do what they would otherwise be barred from doing, namely regulating some aspect of interstate commerce.

Melvin I. Urofsky

Q

Quirin, Ex Parte, 317 U.S. 1 (1942), argued 29–30 July 1942, decided 31 July 1942 by vote of 8 to 0; per curiam, Murphy not participating; full opinion filed 29 Oct. 1942; Stone for the Court. In early July 1942, President Franklin D. Roosevelt established a military commission to try eight recently captured German saboteurs for alleged violations of the uncodified international law of war and the congressionally enacted Articles of War. During the trial, seven of the accused sought leave to file petitions for habeas corpus. At a special session in late July, the Supreme Court summarily rejected the prisoners' applications, paving the way for the execution of six of the prisoners little more than a week later.

The Court's unanimous full opinion, issued in late October, upheld the prisoners' right to judicial review. The Court declared, however, that a military trial was justified by a combination of the president's power as commander in chief and valid congressional legislation authorizing military trials of those accused of committing offenses against the law of war. The Court upheld congressional adoption of the international common law of war and declared that Congress need not specifically define all the acts that violate that law. The Court further found that the accused had been sufficiently charged with unlawful belligerency and that this offense was within the commission's jurisdiction.

The justices declared that the prisoners were not entitled to grand jury process or a trial by jury. They distinguished *Ex parte *Milligan* (1866), which barred military trials of violations of the law of war when local state courts are in operation, on the ground that Milligan had not been deemed an enemy belligerent.

☐ Michal R. Belknap, "The Supreme Court Goes to War: The Meaning and Implications of the Nazi Saboteur Case," *Military Law Review* 89 (1980): 59–95.

James May

R

Raines v. Byrd, 117 S.Ct. 2312 (1997), argued 27 May 1997, decided 25 June 1997 by vote of 7 to 2; Rehnquist for the Court, Souter concurring, in which Ginsburg joined, Stevens and Breyer in dissent. Congress in 1996 passed the Line-Item Veto Act, which authorized the president to cancel specific items in federal spending and tax bills within five days after signing the legislation. Historically, the president could only veto a measure in its entirety. Senator Robert Byrd, a Democrat of West Virginia, and Senator Daniel Patrick Moynihan, a Democrat of New York, joined with four other sitting or previous members of Congress to bring the suit.

The Supreme Court, however, rejected their case on the grounds that none of them had standing to sue since they had not suffered a personal injury. Chief Justice William H. Rehnquist held that under Article III of the Constitution a federal court can only decide cases where the plaintiffs have a concrete injury and a personal stake in the dispute. In this instance, as members of Congress, they had an institutional interest in the matter of the line-item veto, but the cases and controversies requirement of the Constitution meant that they also had to show personal injury. Even though the Line-Item Veto Act had provided that members of Congress could bring suit to challenge its constitutionality, the chief justice said that Congress could not supersede the Constitution's requirement for an actual case and controversy.

As a result, the Court cleared the way for President Bill Clinton to kill individual spending items, although the justices did not indicate whether the line-item veto would be upheld if a plaintiff with standing brought a case. Justice David Souter made clear in his dissent that he thought the act was unconstitutional, although Justice Stephen Breyer, the other dissenter, offered no such opinion. He did insist that the plaintiffs had a right to sue.

Critics believed that once an appropriate plaintiff could be found, the Court would hold the law unconstitutional as a violation of the doctrine of separation of powers.

Kermit L. Hall

R.A.V. v. City of St. Paul, 505 U.S. 377 (1992), argued 4 Dec. 1991, decided 22 June 1992 by vote of 9 to 0, Scalia for the Court. During the late 1980s and early 1990s, the issue of hate speech became important amid a rash of cross burnings and similar activities. In response more than one-half of the states and the federal government had enacted hate crime statutes, with sixteen of these specifically targeted against cross burnings. The city of St. Paul, Minnesota, in 1989 adopted such a measure, known as the Bias-Motivated Crime Ordinance, which, among other things, made it a misdemeanor for anyone to place "on public or private property a symbol, object, appellation, characterization or graffiti, including, but not limited to, a burning cross or Nazi swastika, which one knows or has reasonable grounds to know arouses anger, alarm or resentment in others on the basis of race, color, creed, religion or gender. . . . "

In the early morning hours of June 21, 1990, Robert A. Viktora (R.A.V.), age seventeen, and Arthur Miller, age eighteen, along with several other teenagers allegedly burned a cross inside the fenced yard of a black family that lived across the street from the house where they were staying. Viktora's counsel in the trial court successfully moved to have the case dismissed on the ground that the St. Paul ordinance was substantially overbroad and impermissibly content-based and hence an unconstitutional limit on freedom of speech guaranteed under the First Amendment. The Minnesota Supreme Court, however, reversed the trial court judge and held that the measure was an appropriate means of accomplishing a compelling governmental interest in protecting the community of St. Paul from bias-motivated threats to public safety and order.

Few high court cases have produced such dissent amid unanimity. Justice Antonin Scalia's opinion for the Court resoundingly condemned the St. Paul ordinance, although some of his colleagues, in various sharply worded concurring opinions, sought to limit the impact of Scalia's pronouncements. Scalia found the measure wholly incompatible with the First Amendment since it aimed to silence speech on the basis of its content. Scalia noted that the St. Paul ordinance singled out for limitation only speech that communicated a message of racial, gender, or religious intolerance. While such speech might be offensive, the actions of the city in punishing it effectively and inappropriately handicapped a particular form of expression. Thus, it was possible for persons to express hostility toward others based on political affiliation, union membership, or homosexuality and not be covered by the ordinance.

Chief Justice William H. Rehnquist and Associate Justices Anthony M. Kennedy, David Souter, and Clarence Thomas agreed with the judgment, but did so on different grounds. For these four justices the ordinance failed because it was "overbroad," meaning that it could be used to limit speech or expression that would otherwise deserve constitutional protection.

The remainder of the Court agreed with Scalia's decision, but they rejected entirely the rationale that he used in reaching it.

Led by Justice Byron White, the three other members of the Court wanted to find a way to sustain the constitutionality of hate crime measures. As Justice Harry Blackmun, a resident of Minnesota, observed, "I see no First Amendment values that are compromised by a law that prohibits hoodlums from driving minorities out of their homes by burning crosses on their lawns, but I see great harm in preventing the people of St. Paul from specifically punishing the race-based 'fighting words' that so prejudice their community" (p. 416). Blackmun's appeal to the concept of "fighting words" invoked *Chaplinsky v. New Hampshire* (1942), where the justices had held that certain words, along with obscenity and defamation, were essentially outside the protection of the First Amendment. Justice Scalia recognized the importance of the fighting words exception but concluded that in this case they did not apply, a matter sharply disputed by White and his supporters. While they could not agree on the reasons, they did unite in the belief that the St. Paul ordinance was constitutionally unacceptable.

The decision cast doubt on the constitutionality of other state and local hate laws along with speech codes at public universities. The most specific outcome was an increasing practice by legislative bodies to write new ordinances in content-neutral ways. The impact of *R.A.V.*, then, was to slow but not altogether end the use of legislatively imposed limitations on hate speech.

Kermit L. Hall

Randall v. Sorrell, 548 U.S. 230 (2006), argued 28 Feb. 2006, decided 26 June 2006 by vote of 6 to 3; Breyer delivered a plurality opinion joined by Roberts and, in most part, Alito, who also filed an opinion concurring in part and concurring in the judgment; Kennedy concurring in the judgment also filed an opinion; Thomas, joined by Scalia, concurring in the judgment as well; Stevens in dissent; Souter, joined by Ginsburg and, in two parts, Stevens, in dissent.

In 1997, Vermont enacted the most severe limitations on campaign contributions in the nation, while also establishing expenditure limitations. The legislation was challenged by former office seekers, campaign contributors, and political parties. Not surprisingly, the case produced another fractured decision by the Supreme Court, characterized by Justice John Paul Stevens, in dissent, as "today's cacophony." The Court's attempts over three decades to reconcile severe restrictions on the influence of money in political campaigns in order to "prevent corruption and the appearance of corruption" has presented the Court with increasingly intrusive congressional and state regulations on the First Amendment freedoms of speech and association.

In *Buckley* v. *Valeo* (1976), the Court permitted restrictions on contributions, maintaining that they presented only "minimal" limitations on a contributor's ability to speak. Expenditure limitations on campaigns were rejected, however, with the Court insisting that they represent a more onerous burden by limiting the total amount of political speech. In Justice Stephen G. Breyer's plurality opinion in *Randall*, no part of which commanded the assent of more than Justices John G. Roberts and Samuel A. Alito, expenditure limits on campaigns ranging from $300,000 over a two-year election cycle for governor to $2,000 for state representative were rejected on the grounds laid out in *Buckley*.

Contribution limits proved a thornier issue for the plurality, since heretofore the Court had never overturned such limitations, with *Buckley* itself upholding a $1,000 limitation. Conceding that deference is usually owed to legislatures in making these decisions, Breyer nevertheless introduced a new, ad hoc test containing two parts to determine whether Vermont's limits on contributions from individuals, PACs, and political parties—ranging from $400 for governor to $200 for state representative— were too meager to satisfy the First Amendment. In assessing the proportionality of the restrictions ("tailoring"), Breyer looked for "danger signs" indicating unusual severity. He noted that the Vermont limits on individual contributions represented, in inflation-adjusted terms, only one-twentieth of the limits on individuals upheld in *Buckley*, and a mere one-hundredth of the limit on political parties. Overall, the Vermont limits were the lowest in the country.

A five-factor test led the plurality to conclude that the restrictions were not narrowly tailored to meet the state's interest, thus violating the First Amendment. The Court found that: (1) the restrictions in the law could impair effective advocacy by challengers; (2) political parties were severely restricted, posing associational freedom concerns; (3) volunteering was unduly burdened; (4) contributions were not indexed for inflation; and (5) Vermont could not justify these disproportionate burdens by any public purpose they were supposed to serve.

The infatuation with *Buckley* as unassailable precedent was shared only by Justices Breyer and Roberts. Justice Alito wished to leave the matter for another day; Justice Anthony Kennedy expressed exasperation with the Court's campaign finance reform jurisprudence; Justice Clarence Thomas, joined by Justice Antonin Scalia, explicitly stated that he would overrule *Buckley* as insufficiently protective of core First Amendment political speech, as incapable of coherent application, and as embodying an untenable distinction between contribution and expenditure limits. The three dissenters were disenchanted with *Buckley*, too, but for different reasons: Justice Stevens would have overruled *Buckley* and held expenditure limits to be constitutional, while Justices Souter and Ginsburg were inclined to have the lower courts reinterpret *Buckley* and find the Vermont expenditure limits acceptable.

Ellen Frankel Paul

Reapportionment Cases, collective name of six cases argued 13 November 1963 and decided 15 June 1964: involving Alabama— *Reynolds* v. *Sims*, 377 U.S. 633 (1964), decided by vote of 8 to 1, Warren for the Court, Harlan in dissent; involving New York— *WMCA* v. *Lomenzo*, 377 U.S. 633 (1964), decided by vote of 6 to 3, Clark and Stewart joining Harlan in dissent; involving Maryland—*Maryland Committee for Fair Representation* v. *Tawes*, 377 U.S. 656 (1964), decided by vote of 7 to 2, Clark concurring, Harlan in dissent, Stewart, refusing either to affirm or reverse, would nonetheless vacate the judgment of the court; involving Virginia— *Davis* v. *Mann*, 377 U.S. 656 (1964), decided by vote of 8 to 1, Warren for the Court, Clark and Stewart concurring, Harlan in dissent; involving Delaware—*Roman* v. *Sincock*, 377 U.S. 695 (1964), decided by vote of 8 to 1, Warren for the Court, Clark and Stewart concurring, Harlan in dissent; and involving Colorado—*Lucas* v. *Forty-Fourth General Assembly of Colorado*, 377 U.S. 713 (1964), decided by vote of 6 to 3, Warren for the Court, Harlan, Clark, and Stewart in dissent.

These cases effectively declared the apportionment of every state legislature unconstitutional.

They were prompted by *Baker* v. *Carr* (1962), which opened federal courts to cases in which state legislatures were challenged for failing to provide equitable legislative districts and thereby depriving citizens of equal protection of the laws. Earlier in its 1963 term, in *Wesberry* v. *Sanders* (1964) the Supreme Court had extended the requirement of population equality (i.e., that districts must be as nearly equal as is practicable) to electoral districts for seats in the House of Representatives; that decision had been based on its reading of Article 1, section 2.

Chief Justice Earl Warren's opinion in *Reynolds* v. *Sims*, which along with *Lucas* was the leading case, reemphasized the "one man, one vote" principle announced the year before in *Gray* v. *Sanders* (1963), a case setting aside Georgia's gubernatorial county unit system. "Legislators represent people," wrote Warren "not trees or acres. Legislators are elected by voters, not farms or cities or economic interests" (p. 562). The Court also rejected the "federal analogy" argument that the states, like Congress, could base only one house on population. As the Court repeatedly stated throughout the opinion, "The Equal Protection Clause requires that the seats in both Houses of a bicameral state legislature must be apportioned on a population basis." Each state legislative district should be "as nearly of equal population as is practicable," as based on the most recent decennial census (p. 577). The Court, however, noted, "Somewhat more flexibility may . . . be constitutionally permissible with respect to state legislative apportionment than in congressional districting" (p. 578).

Warren, responding to Justice John M. Harlan's dissent and to the earlier warnings of Justice Felix Frankfurter, commented: "We are cautioned about the dangers of entering into political thickets and mathematical quagmires. Our answer is this: a denial of constitutional protected rights demands judicial protection" (p. 567).

The other cases applied the doctrines of *Reynolds* to the facts of the involved states, except in *Lucas* v. *Forty-Fourth General Assembly of Colorado*, where the Court held that the fact that the Colorado apportionment plan had been incorporated into the state's Constitution via the initiative process did not protect it from federal constitutional challenge.

Justices Tom Clark and Potter Stewart concurred in *Reynolds* and dissented in *Lucas*.

They objected to the mathematical nicety of *Reynolds* and to extending the requirement of population equality to both chambers of a bicameral legislature. In *Lucas*, Stewart wrote, "The Court's draconian pronouncement . . . finds no support in the words of the Constitution, in any prior decision of this Court, or in the 175-year political history of our Federal Union" (p. 746). Clark would have required only that the legislature avoid "invidious discrimination." As long as one house was based on population, he would have permitted some departure from it in the other chamber "so as to take into account, on a rational basis, other factors in order to afford some representation to the various elements of the State" (p. 588).

Harlan dissented in all the cases, protesting what he characterized as this "placing basic aspects of state political systems under the pervasive overlordship of the federal judiciary" (p. 589). By 1964, he was the lone justice to take the view that federal courts should refuse to review any apportionment issues.

Following these cases, Senator Everett Dirksen of Illinois led a charge for a constitutional amendment to override the holding that both chambers of a state legislature must be based on equal population districts. He came close to securing the necessary petitions from two-thirds of the state legislatures to require Congress to call a convention to consider such an amendment, but by the early 1970s enough state legislatures had been reapportioned to undermine this effort. The newly reapportioned legislatures, after all, had no desire to return to the status quo ante the *Reapportionment Cases*.

J. W. Peltason

Red Lion Broadcasting Co., Inc. v. Federal Communications Commission, 395 U.S. 367 (1969), argued 2–3 April 1969, decided 9 June 1969 by vote of 8 to 0; White for the Court; Douglas not participating. In *Red Lion* the Court upheld the fairness doctrine of the Federal Communications Commission (FCC), which requires broadcast licensees to allow reply time to individuals subjected to personal attacks or political editorials. In this instance, radio station WGCB refused to allow Fred Cook, the author of a book critical of Arizona senator Barry Goldwater, time to respond to an attack by the Rev. Billy James Hargis. The Court utilized the case to explore the different contexts of broadcast and print journalism that result in different

First Amendment considerations. The finite number of broadcast frequencies meant it was "idle to posit an unabridgeable First Amendment right to broadcast comparable to the right of every individual to speak, write, or publish" (p. 388).

The Court asserted that the interests of the listening and viewing public must prevail over those of broadcast licensees when allocating scarce airwaves. This scarcity rationale has met with considerable criticism since cable television (and public access to the airwaves) have proliferated while countless outlets for the printed word have been silenced by mergers and commercial failures. Further, the decision was widely criticized for its possible "chilling effect" on broadcasters who had to censor themselves to avoid controversy and the allowance of response time. Indeed, after President Ronald Reagan vetoed legislation codifying the fairness doctrine, the FCC responded to long-term criticism by eliminating the rule in 1987. In other contexts, however, the Court continues to maintain that critical differences between broadcast and print journalism bring different First Amendment considerations into play.

Elliot E. Siotnick

Reed v. Reed, 404 U.S. 71 (1971), argued 19 Oct. 1971, decided 22 Nov. 1971 by vote of 7 to 0; Burger for the Court, two seats (to be occupied by Rehnquist and Powell) were vacant. This was the first decision in a century of Fourteenth Amendment litigation to rule that statutory gender discrimination violated the Equal Protection Clause. Earlier cases had established that the clause did not forbid group-based discrimination as long as the legislature might have some reason for believing the statutory distinction promoted some aspect of the public good. Under this "rational basis test" the Supreme Court had upheld flat bans on the practice of law by women (*Bradwell* v. *Illinois*, 1873), prohibitions on women's tending bar (*Goesaert* v. *Cleary*, 1948), and blanket exclusions of women from jury service (*Hoyt* v. *Florida*, 1961). In *Reed*, the Court ignored this unbroken line of precedents and explained in an extraordinarily short opinion that this case of gender discrimination presented "the very kind of arbitrary legislative choice forbidden by the the Equal Protection Clause" (p. 76).

The law in question had distinguished categories of preference for selecting administrators of the estates of people deceased intestate. Part of the law preferred spouses to offspring, offspring to parents, parents to siblings, and so on; another preferred males to females within each category. The Reeds were the separated parents of a deceased son. Sally, challenging the statutory gender preference, sued Cecil for the right to administer an estate valued at less than one thousand dollars. After striking down this law in *Reed*, the Court often used the *Reed* precedent during the following decade to strike down many other statutes that discriminated on the basis of gender.

Leslie Friedman Goldstein

Reese, United States v., 92 U.S. 214 (1876), argued 13–14 Jan. 1875, decided 27 Mar. 1876 by vote of 8 to 1; Waite for the Court, Clifford concurring, Hunt in dissent. This was the Supreme Court's first voting rights case under the Fifteenth Amendment and the Enforcement Act of 1870. A Kentucky electoral official had refused to register an African-American's vote in a municipal election and was indicted under two sections of the 1870 act: section 2 required that administrative preliminaries to elections be conducted without regard to race, color, or previous condition of servitude; section 3 forbade wrongful refusal to register votes where a prerequisite step "required as aforesaid" had been omitted. The Court held that the Fifteenth Amendment did not confer the right of suffrage but prohibited exclusion on racial grounds. The justices invalidated the operative section 3 since it did not repeat the words about race, color, and servitude and thus exceeded the scope of the Fifteenth Amendment.

In this case involving local elections the Court, dominated by Lincoln and Grant Republicans, chose not to set an expansive, national stamp on the Constitution. Though the Court was willing to uphold the Enforcement Acts in cases involving federal elections, its cramped, technical treatment of state and local cases crippled the acts for practical purposes. This left southern states free to disfranchise African-Americans during the 1890s with literacy, character, and other tests that, while not based on race, were disproportionately exclusive of African-Americans.

Ward E. Y. Elliott

Regents of the University of California v. Bakke, 438 U.S. 265 (1978), argued 12 Oct.

1977, decided 28 June 1978 by vote of 5 to 4; Powell for the Court, Brennan, White, Marshall, and Blackmun concurring in part and dissenting in part, Stevens, Burger, Stewart, and Rehnquist concurring in part and dissenting in part. Bakke wanted to be a physician. The University of California Medical School at Davis sought greater racial and ethnic diversity in its student body. The conflict between these two goals produced the first major constitutional test of affirmative action. It also posed an intractable conundrum: how to overcome the tension between an individual's claim to equal treatment by a state, and that state's responsibility to foster some degree of equality among its citizens.

Bakke was one of 2,664 applicants for one hundred entering positions at the Davis medical school in 1972. Eighty-four slots were filled through the regular admissions program; sixteen were filled through a special admissions program—a distinct and separate process established in 1970 to address the faculty's concern over the paucity of African-American, Asian, Latino, and Native American students. Grade-point average and standard test score requirements were not as stringent as for students admitted under the regular program.

Rejected twice by the university, Bakke filed a lawsuit alleging that the Davis program violated Title VI of the Civil Rights Act of 1964, forbidding racial or ethnic preferences in programs supported by federal funds, and that the university's practice of setting aside positions for minorities denied him equal protection of the law under the Fourteenth Amendment.

The university agreed that racial classifications are disfavored because racial characteristics are generally irrelevant to permissible state objectives. However, the meritocratic promise of nondiscrimination was offset by the state's equally compelling concern for the victims of past and continuing racial injustice. The university also stressed the program's practical benefits: enriched medical education through a diverse student body, successful role models for minority youth, and improved medical services to minority communities.

Both the state trial court and supreme court ruled that racially exclusionary preferences constituted a quota and that such quotas, absent a finding of prior discrimination by the university itself, were a denial of equal protection.

The U.S. Supreme Court held that a university may consider racial criteria as part of a competitive admissions process so long as "fixed quotas" were not used. But the holding masked a sharply divided Court, with six separate opinions. Four justices (John Paul Stevens, Warren Burger, Potter Stewart, and William Rehnquist) preferred to address the statutory rather than the constitutional issue. The "plain meaning" of Title VI and its "broad prohibition against the exclusion of any individual" (pp. 412–413) on racial grounds from a publicly funded program were sufficient grounds, in their judgment, to order Bakke admitted.

A second group (William J. Brennan, Thurgood Marshall, Byron White, and Harry Blackmun) saw no difference between the commands of the Equal Protection Clause and Title VI. Absent a stigmatizing intent or effect, one "drawn on the presumption that one race is inferior to another" or one that places "the weight of government behind racial hatred and separation" (pp. 357–358), there was no reason to trigger the strictest equal protection test. However, the "mere rationality" test deployed in cases not affecting fundamental rights or suspect classifications was too lenient. Instead, Brennan opted for the middle test of heightened scrutiny. So long as the state can demonstrate an important purpose and the means do not unduly burden "those least well represented in the political process" (pp. 361), race-conscious remedies to help members of groups that had suffered racially motivated injuries were constitutional.

Justice Lewis Powell cast the deciding vote, joining with Stevens's plurality on the illegality of the racial quota and in ordering Bakke admitted, while agreeing with Brennan's plurality on the permissibility of racial considerations in admissions. The decisive factor for Powell was the exclusionary nature of the Davis program. Since Bakke had been "totally foreclosed" (p. 305) from competing for the sixteen special positions, he had been denied equal protection. Racial quotas are allowed only when there was a past constitutional or legal violation identified by a properly authorized governmental body. Powell did find justification for less exclusionary affirmative action programs in the First Amendment's guarantee of academic freedom. In a truly competitive process, racial considerations could be taken into account as part of the university's interest in promoting a "diverse student body" (p. 312).

Despite predictions that the decision would exert a chilling effect on minority admissions to graduate and professional schools, it had little impact. Rather than providing a definitive answer on affirmative action, *Bakke* nibbled at the question, settling only the narrower issue of racial quotas in admissions to state supported schools and leaving later cases to test the propriety of affirmative action in other realms. For example, in *Adarand Constructors, Inc.* v. *Peña* (1995) the justices held that federal affirmative action programs, like state affirmative action programs, must meet a test of "strict scrutiny" in order to be constitutional. The justices also let stand in 1997 a decision by a lower federal court in California that upheld the constitutionality of voter-approved Proposition 209, which bans race-and gender-based affirmative action in that state's employment, education, and public contracting. At the same time, a coalition of civil rights groups joined with the Piscataway, New Jersey, School Board to pay the damages due a white school teacher who had been laid off on the ground that maintaining an equally qualified black teacher on the staff was necessary for purposes of racial diversity and in keeping with affirmative action goals. The civil rights groups believed that if the justices had heard the case, they would almost certainly have decided against the school board and therefore the concept of voluntary affirmative action. As a result, the concept of affirmative action, especially voluntary affirmative action, remains under substantial constitutional and political pressure.

☐ Timothy J. O'Neill, *Bakke and the Politics of Equality* (1985). Susan Welch and John Gruhl, "The Impact of the Bakke Decision on Black and Hispanic Enrollment in Medical and Law Schools," *Social Science Quarterly* 71 (Sept. 1990): 458–473. J. Harvie Wilkinson, *From Brown to Bakke: The Supreme Court and School Integration* (1979).

Timothy J. O'Neill

Reno v. American Civil Liberties Union, 117 S.Ct. 2329 (1997), argued 19 March 1997, decided 26 June 1997 by vote of 9 to 0; Stevens for the Court, O'Connor with Rehnquist concurring.

Without the benefit of hearings, Congress in 1996 passed the Communications Decency Act as a last-minute amendment to the Telecommunications Act. The Decency Act made it a crime either to use a computer to transmit indecent material to someone under eighteen years old or to display such material in a way that would make it available to persons under that age. The statute was an effort by Congress to rein in the growing amount of pornographic and other sexually related material on the rapidly expanding Internet, a global computer network that connects as many as 60 million people. The material to be excluded was not clearly defined, but instead Congress referred in the statute to "patently offensive" descriptions or images of sexual or excretory activities. Persons found in violation of the law could be punished by a fine of $250,000, two years in jail, or both.

The measure passed amid widely expressed doubts about its constitutionality. In order to win approval, therefore, its sponsors agreed to a provision guaranteeing quick Supreme Court review after a hearing by a single three-judge district court panel. The panel in Philadelphia that heard the case, organized as litigation in part by the American Civil Liberties Union, condemned the law as an unconstitutional violation of the First Amendment. So, too, did a unanimous Supreme Court.

Justice John Paul Stevens's opinion makes it unlikely that the government can impose restrictions on the Internet as long as the material going over it has some intrinsic constitutional value. Stevens and his colleagues decided to treat the Internet as similar to newspapers and books, to which the Court gives the highest level of First Amendment protection, rather than broadcast and cable television, to which the Court gives less protection and allows greater governmental regulation. The operation of a television or radio, the justices found, required no technical expertise or training; minors could inadvertently gain access to inappropriate material. That was not true with computers and the Internet, where children would have to search for pornographic material. There was no way for a company to deliver Internet services and identify those persons who were going to use the services, and if the act were allowed to stand, many providers would either be thrown out of business or would be chilled from providing services that adults were entitled to enjoy. The Court's decision did leave in place the Decency Act's prohibition on obscenity, which is outside the First Amendment, but it did so without comment.

The justices held that while the goal of protecting children was laudable, the means to that end was entirely unacceptable. The law was at once too vague and too broad; if allowed to stand, it would lead to the suppression of speech among adults and even between parents and children. Justice Stevens concluded that protecting freedom of speech in a democratic society was far more important than upholding censorship. Stevens also criticized arguments by supporters of the law that unless it was sustained, parents would keep their children from using the Internet and thereby undermine the technological growth of the nation.

Justice Sandra Day O'Connor, joined by Chief Justice William Rehnquist, concurred in the majority opinion. She argued that such a law could be sustained only where it was clear that the party transmitting the material knew that it was intended exclusively for minors.

The decision left the task of regulating the access of minors to the Internet to parents and other caretakers. It also left the Internet to expand free from direct government regulation of its content.

Kermit L. Hall

Republican Party of Minnesota v. White, 536 U.S. 765 (2002), argued 26 March 2002, decided 27 June 2002 by vote of 5 to 4; Scalia for the Court, O'Connor and Kennedy concurring, Ginsburg and Stevens in dissent.

Thirty-nine states have some form of election to select or retain all or some of their judges. Those elections differ in various ways from elections for other state offices, such as restricting political speech during campaigns. In *White*, the Court considered a canon of judicial conduct of the Minnesota Supreme Court that prohibited judicial candidates from announcing their views on disputed legal or political issues. The majority of the Court, speaking through Justice Antonin Scalia, held that the ban violated the First Amendment, because it prohibited political speech at the core of First Amendment protections. The prohibition did not survive a strict scrutiny test, because it was not narrowly tailored to serve a compelling state interest. In particular, a restriction on statements made in a judicial campaign did not serve the purported goal of electing impartial judges. Nor was there a long-established tradition in American history of limiting such speech; judicial codes restricting judicial campaign speech were first

advanced by the American Bar Association (ABA) in the 1920s. States may not mandate judicial elections while simultaneously preventing candidates from discussing issues. The dissenters argued that judges were different than political figures, and that states could restrain candidate speech in the interest of maintaining an impartial judiciary.

The majority opinion disclaimed any holding that the First Amendment requires that judicial campaigns be treated the same way as campaigns for other political offices. Nonetheless, the decision seems to subject other regulation of judicial campaigns, such as campaign finance restrictions, to the same scrutiny of those in nonjudicial contests. The ABA and the states began rewriting codes of judicial campaign conduct in light of the decision while efforts in many states to revisit methods of judicial selection have gathered steam.

Michael E. Solimine

Reynolds v. Sims, 377 U.S. 533 (1964), argued 13 Nov. 1963, decided 15 June 1964 by vote of 8 to 1; Warren for the Court, Stewart and Clark concurring, Harlan in dissent. In June 1964, the Supreme Court handed down a group of decisions—collectively known as the *Reapportionment Cases*—that won immediate recognition as historical landmarks. In cases from six different states, the Court declared that representation in state legislatures must be based substantially on population. One week later, the Court handed down similar rulings (without opinions) for nine additional states. The controlling philosophy for all of these decisions is articulated in the Alabama case of *Reynolds v. Sims*, with the opinion written by Chief Justice Earl Warren.

The 1964 decisions marked the culmination of a two-year period of accelerating litigation involving most states in the wake of the decision in *Baker v. Carr* (1962), which affirmed the justiciability of apportionment suits. While *Baker* furnished no guidelines for lower courts, most of them assertively fashioned decrees mandating more equipopulous legislative districts. In 1963, *Gray v. Sanders* had invalidated Georgia's county unit system and given currency to the phrase "one person, one vote." Then, in *Wesberry v. Sanders* (1964), the Supreme Court invalidated Georgia's grossly unequal congressional districts. While based on Article I rather than the Fourteenth Amendment, *Wesberry* articulated the fundamental constitutional principle of equal representation for equal numbers of people.

The Supreme Court's decisions in *Reynolds* and other 1964 apportionment cases were thus not entirely unexpected. Yet the sweeping nature of the rulings and their forthright language surprised many on both sides of the controversy. As a result of the decisions and their underlying rationale, at least one house in nearly all state legislatures was considered invalid, and both houses in most. The decision portended a vast institutional revolution.

The basis for the 1964 decisions was the holding that the Fourteenth Amendment's Equal Protection Clause guarantees to each citizen an equal weight in the election of state legislators. Speaking for the Court, Warren declared, "Legislators represent people, not trees or acres. Legislators are elected by voters, not farms or cities or economic interests" (p. 562). The opinion went on to reason that any substantial disparity in the populations of legislative districts has the same effect as allotting a different number of votes to different individuals. Hence the Court regarded inequality of representation as a suffrage issue, citing various franchise cases that had invalidated the "dilution" or "debasement" of a citizen's fundamental right to vote.

The Court stated that mathematical exactness or precision is hardly a workable constitutional requirement and declined to suggest any numerical or percentage guidelines. Some deviations from an equal population plan in either or both houses of a state legislature would be constitutionally permissible "so long as the divergences from a strict equal population standard are based on legitimate considerations incident to the effectuation of a rational state policy" (p. 579). There could be some recognition of political subdivisions and community interests, but "population is, of necessity, the starting point for consideration and the controlling criterion for judgment in legislative apportionment controversies" (p. 567).

The Court specifically rejected the "federal analogy," the contention that states may base one legislative house, as in the national Congress, on the equal representation of units of government rather than of people. The opinion dismissed as inapposite the suggested parallel between states in the federal union and local units such as countries or towns within a unitary state. The Court was persuaded by evidence that the origi-

nal constitutions of nearly three-fourths of the states provided that both legislative houses be based entirely or predominantly on population, with most recent support for the federal analogy merely a rationalization of malapportionment.

Dissenting in *Reynolds* as well as the remaining reapportionment cases, Justice John M. Harlan reiterated his view, expressed in *Baker*, that the judiciary was intruding needlessly and dangerously into the political process and that the subject matter was not suitable for the development of judicial standards. A detailed analysis of the history, drafting, language, and ratification of the Fourteenth Amendment convinced Harlan that the Equal Protection Clause was not intended to inhibit states from choosing any democratic method desired in constructing legislative bodies. Thus the decisions, he felt, cut deeply into the fabric of American federalism. Cautioning against judicial activism to cure perceived social ills, Harlan declared, "The Constitution is not a panacea for every blot upon the public welfare, nor should this Court, ordained as a judicial body, be thought of as a general haven for reform movements" (pp. 624–625).

The Supreme Court's choice of *Reynolds* as the lead reapportionment case in 1964 is understandable. Alabama's pattern of legislative representation was among the nation's most egregious departures from the concept of meaningful voter equality. Neither house reflected a population basis, with approximately one-fourth of the state's voters theoretically in a position to elect majorities in both. Population variance ratios in the Alabama senate were 41 to 1, in the house, 16 to 1. Within a few months of the *Baker* decision, litigation brought swift action by a federal district court, the first judicially ordered apportionment in the nation. The court had fashioned what it considered the best of available legislative plans, drawn from a judicially prompted special session. The district court had ordered the plans into effect temporarily, pending further legislative and state constitutional action. The appeal from this judicial order became *Reynolds* v. *Sims*.

Although the Supreme Court decided *Reynolds* (and several other 1964 reapportionment cases) by an overwhelming vote of 8 to 1, the majority was split on the reasoning, best illustrated by its 6-to-3 decision invalidating Colorado's apportionment. The result of an initiative ballot measure overwhelmingly ratified in 1962 by a statewide popular vote that carried all countries, the new state constitutional amendment established a lower house based on population and a senate with population as a prime factor but modified by geographic considerations.

Invalidating this apportionment in *Lucas v. the Forty-Fourth General Assembly of the State of Colorado*, the court relied on its newly expressed philosophy that legislatures must reflect the right of individuals to cast an equally weighted vote, a right that cannot be infringed by popular majorities. In response, Justice Potter Stewart's opinion (joined by Justice Tom C. Clark) rejected the position that the apportionment cases involved the right to vote or the "dilution" or "debasement" of that vote. The Stewart-Clark approach held that the Equal Protection Clause permits states considerable latitude in designing legislative constituencies, provided only that (1) they are rational in the light of each state's own characteristics and needs and (2) they do not systematically prevent "ultimate effective majority rule." Yet Stewart and Clark were unable to agree when applying these guidelines in some other cases.

The Supreme Court majority in *Reynolds* made its own attempt to reconcile the population principle and divergent state interests with various assurances that absolute uniformity was not mandated. While the same basic constitutional logic applied to all states, flexibility to accommodate diverse circumstances was indicated, with the expressed confidence that lower courts could work out specific and appropriate standards on a case-by-case basis.

Such optimism was not borne out by events. Lower courts tended to seek standards that could be applied to apportionment plans, usually in quantifiable ways. The most commonly accepted index was a population deviance range of plus-15 to minus-15 percent of the average population per district, a rule perhaps borrowed from a recommendation made by a committee of the American Political Science Association in 1951, long before judicial entry into apportionment disputes. Furthermore, acceptable ranges of population variances kept shrinking as courts handling apportionment disputes found it difficult to reject plaintiffs' alternative plans that were "more equal" in population.

In *Kirkpatrick* v. *Preisler* (1969) a Supreme Court majority of five, speaking through Justice William J. Brennan, set forth a new population standard requiring states to make a good-faith effort to achieve precise mathematical equality among districts. While this and the companion case of *Wells* v. *Rockefeller* involved congressional districts, presumably controlled by Article I following *Wesberry* v. *Sanders*, the line between that and the Fourteenth Amendment's Equal Protection Clause was increasingly blurred. The 1969 cases found the Court's majority, as well as the concurring and dissenting opinions, all citing *Reynolds* v. *Sims*.

In 1973, the Supreme Court shifted back to the more flexible guidelines of *Reynolds* to govern state redistricting. In **Mahan* v. *Howell*, Virginia's state legislative apportionment, with a total plus-to-minus variance of 16.4 percent, was upheld because state policy consistently followed town and county boundaries. In three subsequent decisions that term, the Court (1) upheld smaller variance ranges of under 10 percent (plus-to-minus) as *de minimis*, needing no state justification, and with the burden of proof shifting to plaintiffs; and (2) emphasized the far more narrow population range expected for congressional districts.

In *Reynolds* Warren had cautioned, "Indiscriminate districting, without any regard for political subdivision or natural or historical boundary lines, may be little more than an open invitation to partisan gerrymandering" (pp. 578–579). This warning was recalled by several observers who suggested that boundary manipulation had been encouraged by increasing judicial preoccupation with equipopulous districts at the expense of various territorial checks (compactness, contiguity, integrity of local boundaries).

Similar judicial concerns have been raised periodically since 1969. In *Karcher* v. *Daggett* (1983) the Court invalidated New Jersey's congressional districting because it lacked a good-faith effort to achieve absolute population equality (the variance percentage from most-to least-populous district was less than 0.7 percent). Five justices (one concurring, four dissenting) objected that partisan gerry-mandering posed a greater threat to fair representation than minor population deviations.

The question whether claims of political gerrymandering were justiciable was answered affirmatively by the Supreme Court in **Davis* v. *Bandemer* (1986). But the Court's plurality opinion confined judicial scrutiny only to boundary manipulations that consistently degraded a voter's, or group of voters', influence on the political process as a whole. The plurality seemed loathe to sanction judicial interference in those instances of partisan advantage subject to correction by genuine electoral competition.

Few Supreme Court decisions have had the impact of *Reynolds* v. *Sims*. Within a period of scarcely two years, the constituency maps of virtually all state legislatures had changed, often dramatically. Patterns of rural and small-town domination in several largely urban states had disappeared. Moreover, the principle of equal representation was soon extended to the local level of county boards and city councils.

In spite of this rapid restructuring, problems and litigation persisted. The question of how precisely equal in population districts must be led to mechanistic approaches maximizing equipopulous districts at the expense of other dimensions of representation and very likely encouraged the proliferation of sophisticated partisan gerrymandering. Ironically, as a result, events appeared to prod the Supreme Court to advance, step by step, further into the political thicket.

In the wake of the 1990 census, several states in the South attempted to extend the principles of *Reynolds* by legislating racially gerrymandered districts, often with bizarre shapes. The justices in several cases, most notably *Shaw* v. *Reno* (1993), *Bush* v. *Vera* (1996), and *Shaw* v. *Hunt* (1996), held that such redistricting violated the Equal Protection Clause of the Fourteenth Amendment and that while such majority-minority congressional districts might be created, such districts had to be "narrowly tailored" and serve a "compelling state interest." The justices in *Abrams* v. *Johnson* (1997) did approve by a narrow 5-to-4 margin the creation of a predominately black congressional district in Georgia, but the decision demonstrated that the Supreme Court remains deeply divided over the appropriate role of race in electoral politics and that the justices will view any use of race in redistricting as constitutionally suspect.

In *Reynolds*, Warren asserted that "the achieving of fair and effective representation for all citizens is concededly the basic aim of legislative apportionment" (pp. 565–566). That goal may be elusive and incapable of complete attainment, but it serves as a continuing challenge to courts and others.

□ Gordon E. Baker, *The Reapportionment Revolution* (1966). Richard C. Cortner, *The Apportionment Cases* (1970). Robert G. Dixon, Jr., *Democratic Representation* (1968). Bernard Grofman, ed., *Political Gerrymandering and the Courts* (1990).

Gordon E. Baker

Reynolds v. United States, 98 U.S. 145 (1879), argued 14–15 Nov. 1878 decided 5 May 1879 by vote of 9 to 0; Waite for the Court, Field concurring. This case grew out of the Grant administration's campaign to stamp out Mormon polygamy. Grant appointed James B. McKean, chief justice of the Utah Territorial Supreme Court, and General J. Wilson Shaffer, territorial governor, with orders to end Mormon polygamy. McKean's United States Marshalls rounded up hundreds of Mormons under a federal antibigamy statute. To test federal law, the Mormon church hierarchy prepared George Reynolds, secretary to Brigham Young, for a test case. Following conviction in territorial district court and appeal to the Utah Territorial Supreme Court, Reynolds appealed before the U.S. Supreme Court.

Anti-Mormon arguments termed polygamy socially destructive and accused the Mormons of constituting a moral menace to the country. Mormons argued that the First Amendment protected religious freedom and that plural marriage was part of religious practice. In the alternative, they argued that polygamy was not bigamy and that it was supportive of mainstream American values such as family and spiritual growth, was not destructive of the social fabric, and clearly did not threaten the public peace.

Chief Justice Morrison R. Waite, for a unanimous court, declared that federal statute constitutionally could punish criminal activity regardless of religious beliefs. Simply, religious practices that impaired the public interest did not fall under the protection of the First Amendment.

In analyzing the original position of the founders on the First Amendment's language on religion, Waite relied heavily upon history and in particular upon Thomas Jefferson. In the process, Waite observed that "a wall of separation between church and state" existed, thus using a metaphor that would trouble the courts for the next century (p. 164).

Gordon Morris Bakken

Rice v. Cayetano, 528 U.S. 495 (2000), argued 6 Oct. 1999, decided 23 Feb. 2000 by vote of 7 to 2; Kennedy for the Court, Breyer and Souter concurring, Stevens and Ginsburg in dissent. Harold F. Rice, a Caucasian citizen of Hawaii precluded by a provision of the Hawaiian Constitution from voting in the statewide election of trustees to the Office of Hawaiian Affairs, an agency responsible for the administration of social programs for the benefit of descendants of the original inhabitants of Hawaii, sued Benjamin Cayetano, governor of Hawaii, claiming violation of his right to vote under the Fifteenth Amendment to the U.S. Constitution. The district court upheld Rice's preclusion on the theory that under the statute granting statehood to Hawaii, Congress intended that the United States and Hawaii assume a trust relationship with Native Hawaiians and that the voting restriction was rationally related to fulfilling this obligation (*Rice* v. *Cayetano*, 1997). The Ninth Circuit Court of Appeals affirmed in 1998.

The Supreme Court reversed, broadly construing the language of the Fifteenth Amendment to preclude not only race-based qualifications on the right to vote but also limitations based on ancestry, which the Court deemed a "proxy for race" and "corruptive of the whole legal order democratic elections seek to preserve" (pp. 514, 517). Although it noted that federal statutes mandating differential treatment of Indian tribes as quasi-sovereign political communities, particularly in fulfillment of treaty obligations, were constitutionally permissible, the majority held that even if Congress had elected to treat Native Hawaiians as a tribe—which it had not—the Fifteenth Amendment prohibited Congress from authorizing Hawaii to create a racially discriminatory voting scheme.

In contrast, the dissent argued that the historical record supported the finding that Native Hawaiians should be considered, for purposes of the Fifteenth Amendment, a tribe of indigenous peoples to whom the United States owed a duty of trust identical to that owed to Indian tribes and that, as a consequence, the provision of the Hawaiian Constitution authorizing differential treatment in regard to voting was rationally related to fulfilling trust obligations and thus constitutionally sound.

In the aftermath, State-funded Native Hawaiian–only educational programs have come under attack on constitutional grounds, and in response efforts to secure federal recognition of a trust responsibil-ity, and thereby constitutional protection for these programs have intensified. The broader process of formal reconciliation between Native Hawaiians and the United States for the role of the latter in the overthrow of the Hawaiian monarchy in 1893 provides what may be a beneficial context for negotiations toward this objective.

William C. Bradford

Richardson, United States v., 418 U.S. 166 (1974), argued 10 Oct. 1973, decided 25 June 1974 by vote of 5 to 4; Burger for the Court, Powell concurring, Douglas, Brennan, Stewart, and Marshall in dissent. Seeking to apply and expand the doctrine of taxpayer standing of *Flast* v. *Cohen* (1968). Richardson challenged the law that prohibited disclosure of CIA expenditures. He claimed a violation of Article I, section 9, which requires publication of *all* public expenditures. The trial court held that Richardson lacked standing under *Flast* because he was not challenging an appropriations act under the Taxing and Spending Clause. The court of appeals reversed, holding that he could first sue to obtain information about the CIA's appropriations that he needed in order to bring suit under the *Flast* doctrine.

The Supreme Court, giving *Flast* the narrowest possible reading, reversed again. It held that Richardson lacked standing because he was not directly alleging the unconstitutionality of an appropriations act and did not allege a specific violation of Congress's taxing and spending power. Chief Justice Warren Burger's opinion reaffirmed a basic principle of *Frothingham. v. Mellon* (1923), which scholars thought *Flast* had modified: a taxpayer cannot use federal courts "as a forum to air his general grievances about the conduct of government or the allocation of power in the federal system" (p. 175). Richardson had suffered no personal injury from the government's failure to disclose the CIA's budget; the issue, Burger said, was clearly not one for the courts to resolve. In dissent, Justices Potter Stewart and Thurgood Marshall insisted that a citizen ought to be able to challenge the failure of the government to carry out an affirmative constitutional duty without any showing of personal harm.

Joel B. Grossman

Richmond Newspapers, Inc. v. Virginia, 448 U.S. 555 (1980), argued 19 Feb. 1980, decided 2 July 1980 by vote of 7 to 1; Burger for the Court, Rehnquist in dissent, Powell not participating. After a series of inconclusive and confusing earlier decisions on the right of access to criminal trials, *Richmond Newspapers, Inc.* v. *Virginia* announced that the public and the press have a First Amendment right to attend criminal trials. This landmark 1980 Supreme Court decision left other issues open, however, some of which have since been resolved.

In a number of cases during the 1970s the Supreme Court supported the media's right, under the First Amendment, to publish whatever information they had in their possession—whether classified and obtained surreptiously (**New York Times Co.* v. *United States*, 1971), or whether obtained in open court (**Nebraska Press Association* v. *Stuart*, 1976). Having established that the press could publish what they knew, the Supreme Court then faced the question of whether the press was constitutionally entitled to access to criminal court proceedings.

In *Gannett* v. *DePasquale* (1979), a newspaper reporter challenged the court-ordered closure of a pretrial hearing on suppression of evidence in a murder case. The closure resulted from the defendants' concern (shared by the prosecutor) that pretrial publicity would jeopardize their right to a fair trial. On appeal, the Supreme Court upheld the exclusion of press and public from pretrial hearings on the ground that only the accused has a Sixth Amendment right to demand an open trial. In contrast, several dissenters in *Gannett* saw the Sixth Amendment as protecting not only the defendant's but also the public's right of access.

The *Gannett* decision was close (5 to 4), fragmented (five separate opinions), and ambiguous in its scope (whether this ruling on pretrials would extend to trials) over the application of the First Amendment to the issue of access (which the Court did not decide) and over the findings needed to justify closure. Despite this uncertainty, *Gannett* gave new power to trial judges who increasingly granted motions to close all types of criminal proceedings. Representatives of the news media protested *Gannett* and urged the Court to reconsider and affirm a public right to access to court.

The Court did so the next year. In *Richmond Newspapers Inc.* v. *Virginia*, it severely limited the defendant's right to a closed courtroom by holding that the First and Fourteenth Amendments guarantee the right of the public (including the press) to attend criminal trials. This case began with the fourth murder trial of a defendant whose earlier trials had been reversed or declared mistrials. Out of concern for pretrial publicity and relying on a Virginia statute, the trial court granted the defendant's motion to exclude the press. Richmond Newspapers challenged the order and sued for access to the trial. The Supreme Court affirmed the First Amendment right of access in its 7-to-1 decision.

The majority view in *Richmond Newspapers* was expressed in six different opinions. Chief Justice Warren Burger wrote for the Court, emphasizing the long history of criminal trials at common law and their presumption of openness. Burger concluded that the press exclusion must be overturned since the trial judge had not pursued alternatives to courtroom closure nor had he made specific findings to support the order. Justices Byron White and John Paul Stevens joined Burger's opinion but also wrote separately. Justice White, a dissenter in *Gannett*, simply noted that this case would have been unnecessary had the Court found a Sixth Amendment right to courtroom access in the earlier decision. Justice Stevens, in his concurrence, extended the principle to prohibit arbitrary governmental restrictions on access to other important and newsworthy information.

In a separate opinion, Justice William Brennan (joined by Justice Thurgood Marshall) developed a different First Amendment theory to balance the important right of public access with opposing interests. He proposed two principles to determine the right of access: the history and tradition of openness of a given proceeding, and the specific structural value or function of the proceeding. Applying these principles to the criminal trial, Brennan found a public right of access and agreed that the Virginia statute was in violation of the First and Fourteenth Amendments.

Justice Potter Stewart concurred in the Court's judgment and, in his separate opinion, stressed limits that could be placed on the right of access, noting that the right is not absolute. Justice Harry Blackmun also wrote separately to reiterate his preference for a Sixth Amendment right of access, but accepted the First Amendment protections as well. In dissent, Justice William Rehnquist argued against Supreme Court intervention in the matter, preferring to let the access issues be resolved by the fifty states without additional constitutional review.

Richmond Newspapers Inc. v. *Virginia* left open key questions. Does the First Amendment right of access to trials extend to pretrial hearings and to civil as well as criminal trials? Does it extend to other governmental proceedings beside the courtroom? What restrictions will be allowed on the right of access? What is the underlying First Amendment theory for the right of access and what standards will be used to guide further cases?

In *Globe Newspaper Co.* v. *Superior Court* (1982), the Court held unconstitutional a Massachusetts statute that required closed trials during testimony of minors who were victims of sexual abuse. For the majority, Justice Brennan emphasized the general functions for self-governance to be served by an open trial and held that a trial might be closed only in specific cases where there was a documented or reasonable fear of harm to such minors. Chief Justice Burger, in dissent, pointed instead to the historical evidence supporting closure of this particular type of trial. The split between these two approaches from *Richmond Newspapers* was also evident in *Press-Enterprise Co.* v. *Superior Court* (1984). Here the Court extended the First Amendment right of access to *voir dire* proceedings.

In *Waller* v. *Georgia* (1984), the Court found that a defendant's Sixth Amendment right to a public trial precluded a trial court from closing a pretrial suppression hearing over the objections of the accused. The question of a public First Amendment right of access to pretrial hearings, left open in *Waller* and in *Richmond Newspapers*, was resolved in *Press-Enterprise Co.* v. *Superior Court* (1986) in favor of allowing public access to preliminary hearings. In this case the Court also reiterated the principle of *Globe Newspaper* that only an overriding governmental interest can justify denial of access. The Court has not yet ruled on the right of access to civil trials, but it is likely that eventually they will also be included.

Lynn Mather

Richmond v. J. A. Croson Co., 488 U.S. 469 (1989), argued 5 Oct. 1988, decided 23 Jan. 1989 by vote of 6 to 3; O'Connor for the Court, Stevens, Kennedy, and Scalia concurring, Marshall, Brennan, and Blackmun in dissent. In *Croson*, a majority of the Supreme Court was finally assembled in support of the application of the strict scrutiny standard to determine the constitutionality of affirmative action plans based on race. However, it is still not possible to determine specifically the content of this standard as applied to affirmative action.

In 1983, the Richmond, Virginia, City Council enacted the Minority Business Utilization Plan requiring prime contractors to subcontract at least 30 percent of the dollar amount of the contract to minority business enterprises. The plan was to remain in effect for five years and contained waiver provisions for cases where every feasible attempt to comply failed.

The Supreme Court found the plan in violation of the Equal Protection Clause of the Fourteenth Amendment. It rejected Richmond's argument that it was legitimately copying an earlier federal minority business set-aside law that had been upheld in *Fullilove* v. *Klutznick* (1980). *Fullilove* was distinguishable, Justice Sandra Day O'Connor wrote, because section 5 of the Fourteenth Amendment granted Congress a unique mandate to enforce its dictates. States, however, are not equally empowered by the Constitution. Justice Antonin Scalia's dissent went even further, declaring that the Constitution is colorblind and that race-conscious plans, presumably even federal ones, are unacceptable.

Because of *Croson* most state or local affirmative action plans will now be judged by the strict scrutiny standard. When combined with two earlier cases, *Wygant* v. *Jackson Board of Education* (1986) and *United States* v. *Paradise* (1987), *Croson* seems to require that these plans demonstrate a compelling interest that requires a showing of past discrimination, not mere reliance on societal discrimination for their justification. They must also choose means that are narrowly tailored to vindicate that interest and must take into account factors such as the necessity of the relief and the efficiency of alternative remedies, the duration of the remedy, the flexibility of the remedy and/or the availability of waivers, the relationship of the numerical goals to minorities within the relevant labor market, and the likely effect on innocent parties. It is uncertain how many of these factors, and in what combination and circumstances, a majority of the Court will require in future cases. What is clear is that the justices remain deeply suspicious of affirmative action. In *Adarand Constructors, Inc.* v. *Peña* (1995), they held that federal affirmative action programs, like state affirmative action programs, must meet a test of "strict scrutiny" in order to be constitutional.

James E. Jones, Jr.

Ring v. Arizona, 536 U.S. 584 (2002), argued 22 Apr. 2002, decided 24 June 2002 by vote of 7 to 2; Ginsburg for the Court, Scalia, Kennedy, Thomas, and Breyer concurring, O'Connor and Rehnquist in dissent. The issue in *Ring* was whether Arizona's capital sentencing scheme violated the Sixth Amendment's jury trial guarantee.

Arizona's capital sentencing scheme, upheld by the Court in *Walton* v. *Arizona* (1990), specified that after a jury found a defendant guilty of first-degree murder, the trial judge alone determined the presence or absence of the aggravating circumstances required by Arizona law for the imposition of the death penalty. Then the defendant could be sentenced to death only if the judge found at least one aggravating circumstance and there were no mitigating circumstances substantial enough to call for mercy. The constitutionality of Arizona's sentencing system became unclear after the Court ruled in *Apprendi* v. *New Jersey* (2000) that the Sixth Amendment did not permit a defendant to be "expose[d] . . . to a penalty exceeding the maximum he would receive if punished according to the facts reflected in the jury verdict alone" (p. 483).

In *Ring*, the Court partially overruled *Walton* and determined that Arizona's sentencing scheme violated the Constitution to the extent that a judge's independent finding of an aggravating circumstance was necessary for the imposition of the death penalty. According to the Court, the Sixth Amendment required that any fact that increased the maximum penalty for a crime had to be submitted to a jury, for the presence of any such fact was effectively equivalent to an element of a greater offense. In a separate concurring opinion, Justice Stephen Breyer argued that jury sentencing in capital cases is simply mandated by the Eighth Amendment. Dissenting, Justice Sandra Day O'Connor argued that *Apprendi* was an erroneous decision and that it rather than *Walton* should be overruled.

Jennifer L. Culbert

Robel, United States v., 389 U.S. 258 (1967), argued 14 Nov. 1966, reargued 9 Oct. 1967, decided 11 Dec. 1967 by vote of 6 to 2; Warren for the Court, White and Harlan in dissent; Marshall not participating. The Court in this case, for only the second time in history, struck down an act of Congress as an infringement of the First Amendment. In **Communist Party* v. *Subversive Activities Control Board* (1961), the Court upheld an order of the Subversive Activities Control Board requiring the Communist party to register as a communistaction organization under the Subversive Activities Control Act of 1950. Robel, a member of the party, was employed at a shipyard that had been officially designated as a defense facility. He was indicted for unlawfully and willfully engaging in employment at the shipyard with knowledge of the order against the party and notice of the shipyard's designation as a defense facility.

The Court held that the relevant section of the act was an unconstitutional abridgment of the right of association protected by the First Amendment. The statute established guilt by association without proof that defendant's association posed a threat to national defense, which includes values and ideals enshrined in the Constitution. The statute was overbroad for proscribing activities that can be punished and membership that cannot be proscribed. The statute disregarded the fact that a person may be a passive or an active member of a registered organization and may be unaware of the party's unlawful aims or may disagree with those aims; or the member may occupy a nonsensitive position in a defense facility.

Milton R. Konvitz

Roberts v. United States Jaycees, 468 U.S. 609 (1984), argued 18 Apr. 1984, decided 3 July 1984 by vote of 7 to 0; Brennan for the Court, Rehnquist and O'Connor concurring, Burger and Blackmun not participating. The Supreme Court held that the application of the Minnesota Human Rights Act to the Minnesota Junior Chamber of Commerce (Jaycees), requiring the Jaycees to admit women as members, did not violate the First and Fourteenth Amendments' guarantee of freedom of association, and that the Human Rights Act was not void on account of vagueness.

For the Court, William J. Brennan recognized two types of associational freedom deserving constitutional protection: freedom of association related to marriage, procreation, contraception, and family and children, and freedom of association related to expressive activities. The Jaycees freedom of association, the Court held, fell outside the first category of associational freedom because of the large, unselective nature of the group. If there was any constitutional claim here, it was the freedom of association related to the expression of collective views and interests. That right of association was not absolute, however, the Court noted. It could be overridden by a compelling governmental interest and Minnesota's interest in prohibiting gender discrimination was such a compelling governmental interest and, as such, was sufficient to override the expressive associational interests of male Jaycee members.

Justice Sandra Day O'Connor concurred, stating that associations could be rationally divided into expressive and nonexpressive associations. The Jaycees were essentially a nonexpressive, commercial association in relation to which greater governmental regulatory power had long been recognized, and the application of the Minnesota Human Rights Act to the Jaycees was thus justified because of the predominantly commercial, non-expressive nature of the group.

Richard C. Cortner

Robinson v. California, 370 U.S. 660 (1962), argued 17 Apr. 1962, decided 25 June 1962 by vote of 7 to 2; Stewart for the Court, White and Clark in dissent. In *Robinson* v. *California* a California law making it a crime to be a drug addict was held to be unconstitutional as cruel and unusual punishment in violation of the Eighth and Fourteenth Amendments. The statute did not require proof that the defendant bought or used drugs or had any in his or her possession. The mere status of being an addict, which could be established, for example, by needle marks on the offender's arm, was sufficient. The U.S. Supreme Court held that addiction is an illness rather than a crime and thought that ninety days in jail for being ill constituted cruel and unusual punishment. Justices Byron White and Tom Clark argued in dissent that detention was a feature of "a comprehensive and enlightened program for the control of narcotism" (p. 679).

The *Robinson* decision was not followed in a 1968 ruling, *Powell* v. *Texas*, where the Court, by a 5-to-4 vote, rejected the contention that criminal conviction for chronic alcoholism was cruel and unusual. The Court majority thought that knowledge about alcoholism and the record in this case were inadequate for a wide-ranging new constitutional principle. Justice Abe Fortas,

writing for the minority in the *Powell* case, insisted that the *Robinson* rule should be followed, and that "criminal penalties may not be inflicted upon a person for being in a condition he is powerless to change" (p. 533).

Controversy has continued concerning whether addiction-related conduct is involuntary and entitled to be regarded as a disease, but the *Robinson* case did establish that the Cruel and Unusual Punishment Clause of the Eighth Amendment applies to the states in appropriate cases by reason of the Due Process Clause of the Fourteenth Amendment.

C. Herman Pritchett

Robinson v. Memphis and Charleston Railroad Co. See CIVIL RIGHTS CASES.

Rochin v. California, 342 U.S. 165 (1952), argued 16 Oct. 1951, decided 2 Jan. 1952 by vote of 8 to 0; Frankfurter for the Court, Minton not participating. Rochin was convicted in a California superior court for possession of a "preparation of morphine," which doctors pumped from his stomach against his will and on the direction of law enforcement officers. Rochin appealed and charged that the manner of extracting the evidence violated the Due Process Clause of the Fourteenth Amendment. Rochin lost his appeal, the California Supreme Court declined to review his case, but the U.S. Supreme Court granted certiorari. The Court reversed Rochin's conviction, holding that stomach-pumping did constitute a method of obtaining evidence that violated the Due Process Clause of the Fourteenth Amendment.

In his opinion for the Court, Justice Felix Frankfurter emphasized that there was no distinction between a "verbal confession extracted by physical abuse and evidence forced from the petitioner's lips, evidence that consisted of real objects" (p. 167). Frankfurter stressed that the Due Process Clause required that the Court review and challenge state procedures when decency and fairness were suspect, but he indicated that this responsibility did not leave judges free to apply their own personal and private conceptions of due process. In Rochin's case, Frankfurter concluded that the use of stomach-pumping to obtain evidence when conducted without the accused's consent "shocks the conscience" and constitutes "methods too close to the rack and the screw to permit constitutional differentiation" (p. 172).

In separate concurring opinions, Justices Hugo Black and William O. Douglas argued that the conviction should have been reversed with reference to the Fifth Amendment privilege against self-incrimination and not the "nebulous standard" employed by Frankfurter (p. 175).

The Supreme Court's eventual incorporation of the Fifth Amendment privilege against self-incrimination in *Malloy* v. *Hogan* (1964) and the application of the exclusionary rule to the states in *Mapp* v. *Ohio* (1961) have rendered moot the majority and minority differences in Rochin, as state criminal procedures can now be reviewed against most provisions of the Bill of Rights.

Susette M. Talarico

Roe. v. Wade, 410 U.S. 113 (1973), argued 13 Dec. 1971, reargued 11 Oct. 1972, decided 22 Jan. 1973 by vote of 7 to 2; Blackmun for the Court, Douglas, Stewart, and Burger concurring, White and Rehnquist in dissent. After the middle of the nineteenth century most states, under the prodding of physicians wishing to establish the scientific stature of their activities, adopted laws severely restricting the availability of abortion. The so-called sexual revolution of the 1950s and 1960s, which fostered increased access to contraceptives and the development of contraceptive drugs, also resulted in an increasing number of situations in which women desired abortions. In the 1960s and early 1970s the discovery that thalidomide, a drug that many women had used in early stages of pregnancy to relieve morning sickness, occasionally caused birth defects, as well as the highly publicized case of Sherry Finkbine, an Arizona broadcasting figure who went to Sweden to obtain an abortion when she feared her baby would be severely handicapped, increased public pressure to relax the abortion laws. Illegal abortions were widespread, though their exact number is impossible to determine, and some women died because of the unsanitary conditions in which illegal abortions were sometimes performed. The revitalized women's movement made change in the abortion laws one of its priority goals.

Abortion reform took two forms. State legislatures began to make it easier to obtain abortions, usually by allowing abortion to protect a woman's health, broadly defined, but also requiring approval of the abortion by a committee of doctors in addition to the woman's own physician. Once some states had begun to relax abortion restrictions, any woman who could afford it found it relatively easy to travel to a state with an unrestrictive law or to find a doctor who would certify that the abortion was necessary to preserve her health.

Court attacks on restrictive abortion laws focused initially on the most restrictive of the traditional laws; challengers argued that such laws, which permitted abortions only to save a woman's life, were so vague that doctors could not know when they were committing an illegal act. The California Supreme Court agreed with such a challenge in *People* v. *Belous* (1969), and the United States Supreme Court in *United States* v. *Vuitch* (1971) avoided a decision on the constitutional question by construing a federal abortion law, applicable in the District of Columbia, to allow abortions when the woman's health, broadly defined, was in danger.

At the time these challenges were being brought, the Court was also developing a law of personal privacy in sexual matters, holding, for example, that a severe restriction on the availability of contraceptives was a violation of a constitutional right to privacy in *Griswold* v. *Connecticut*, 1965. Challenges to restrictive abortion laws relied on *Griswold* as the basis for arguing that such laws violated the right to privacy.

Roe v. *Wade* involved a challenge to a traditional, severely restrictive abortion law (from Texas) as well as a challenge to a more modern abortion law (from Georgia) that allowed abortions to be performed in hospitals, when approved by a hospital committee, to avoid danger to a woman's health. The action was brought in the name of Jane Roe, a procedure adopted to ensure that the plaintiff would not have to reveal the facts surrounding her pregnancy to the Court. Although those facts were irrelevant in light of the Court's analysis of the legal issues, shortly after the case was decided the plaintiff was identified as Norma McCorvey. At first McCorvey stated that her pregnancy had resulted from a gang rape; later she revealed that it resulted from a failed relationship.

Blackmun's Analysis. When the case was first argued, Justice Harry Blackmun, who had once served as counsel to the Mayo Clinic in Rochester, Minnesota, drafted an opinion that would have held both statutes unconstitutionally vague. In part because his analysis was clearly unpersuasive and in part because some justices believed that the case had been improperly assigned to Blackmun to write, the case was set for reargument. During the summer preceding the reargument, Blackmun engaged in an extensive study of medical material relating to abortion.

After reargument, Blackmun circulated an opinion finding both statutes unconstitutional on the ground that they violated the woman's right to privacy, which the opinion located in the Due Process Clause of the Fourteenth Amendment. Justice Potter Stewart's concurring opinion properly pointed out that this invocation of substantive due process meant that the Court was enforcing a right not specifically spelled out in the Constitution.

After finding that the case was not moot despite the fact that there had been no time to secure a decision before the opportunity for obtaining an abortion had passed, Blackmun's opinion acknowledged that states had some valid interests in regulating abortion. The opinion divided pregnancy into three periods, or trimesters. During the first trimester, the woman had an essentially unrestricted right to choose abortion in consultation with her physician; thus, Blackmun held, the hospitalization and committee requirements of the more "liberal" state laws were unconstitutional. During the second trimester, when according to medical experts abortion posed a greater threat to a woman's health, states could regulate abortion to protect her health. Only in the third trimester was the state's interest in protecting the potential life of the fetus great enough to warrant severe restrictions on abortion, and even then, the Court held, states must permit abortions to save a woman's life. In the course of this analysis, Blackmun's opinion stated that because of uncertainty about the medical and moral status of the fetus, the states could not adopt a particular theory of when life begins—they could not decide, for example, that because life begins at conception, fetuses have the same rights as newborn infants.

Although Chief Justice Warren Burger's concurring opinion denied that *Roe* had established a right to abortion on demand, that was its practical effect. Justices Byron White and William Rehnquist, in separate dissents, criticized the Court for enforcing a right not specified in the Constitution to overturn statutes that were no more restrictive than those widely in force when the Fourteenth Amendment was adopted. In addition, they criticized the Court for the trimester framework, which, in their view, was arbitrary. If the state had an interest in protecting the potential life of the fetus, that interest existed, and was equally strong, through the entire pregnancy. Further, they said, the Court's balancing of competing interests and careful laying out of what doctors could do in various circumstances resembled a statute.

Three justices appointed by President Richard Nixon joined the majority in *Roe*, whose outcome appears to be inconsistent with the sort of "strict construction" of the Constitution that they were said to support. In political terms, *Roe* is probably best understood as part of the Court's attempt to respond to and develop support within an important emerging constituency, the organized women's movement. Although the opinion did not treat the issue as one of gender discrimination, there were plainly questions of gender at stake in the abortion controversy, for it was widely understood that the burdens of undesired pregnancy fell exclusively on women. Restrictive abortion laws have typically been enacted by legislatures dominated by men. This practice could have been treated as raising questions of gender discrimination. The Court's failure to present its opinion on these grounds may have been a serious tactical error, for the flaws of Blackmun's privacy analysis, employing a newly discovered constitutional "right," were widely noted after *Roe* was decided.

Criticism and Aftermath of Roe. Academic critics of *Roe* argued that invalidating legislation where there was no constitutional text or history to indicate that the legislation contravened fundamental values protected by the Constitution was reminiscent of the *Lochner* v. *New York* era, when the Court invalidated many statutes aimed at improving the economic conditions of workers on the ground that the statutes violated a "liberty of contract" nowhere spelled out in the Constitution. Critics also pointed out that, given the acknowledged impact of abortion on the fetus and the medical dimensions of the technique, it was silly to treat the case as one involving "privacy" in the way that *Griswold*, which was about the use of contraceptives, involved actions performed in the privacy of the home.

Academic defenders of *Roe* offered two lines of argument. Some suggested that the case should be reconceptualized as a case of gender discrimination, which, they argued, was indeed barred by the Equal Protection Clause of the Fourteenth Amendment. Others agreed that *Roe* resembled *Lochner* but argued that the vice of *Lochner* was not that it enforced values not found in the constitutional text but that it enforced values that were not fundamental according to any well-developed theory of rights, whereas the right to privacy, or to personal autonomy in sexual matters, was fundamental under many uncontroversial versions of liberal political theory.

Roe was even more controversial among the public. It generated a substantial "right to life" movement that lobbied legislatures to adopt regulations that went as far as possible within the *Roe* framework to restrict the availability of abortions and was particularly influential in gaining power within the Republican party, whose presidential candidates in the 1980s agreed not to appoint judges who were sympathetic to the constitutional analysis adopted in *Roe*.

The Court adhered to the *Roe* analysis for the next decade, but in several important cases it upheld legislative attempts to restrict a woman's right to choose an abortion. Perhaps the most important early such decision was *Harris* v. *McRae* (1980), which held that Congress did not violate the Constitution when it prohibited the use of Medicaid funds to pay for nontherapeutic abortions. In an earlier decision, *Maher* v. *Roe* (1977), the Court had held, similarly, that the states were not required to fund abortions for indigent women. (Most states do not fund nontherapeutic abortions, but some do.)

A predicted likely effect of these decisions was the return to the situation that prevailed before *Roe*, in which women who could afford them secured abortions relatively easily, while women without means were forced to rely on illegal abortions or, like Jane Roe, left to carry their unwanted pregnancies to term. The actual impact of *Harris*, however, is uncertain, since despite the absence of public funding legal abortions rose steadily until reaching the present (1991) plateau of about 1.6 million abortions annually. Private charitable sources now fund a majority of those abortions.

Other restrictions the Court upheld were requirements regarding record-keeping about abortions and regulations requiring the notification of the parents of a minor woman seeking an abortion unless the woman could show a court that notifying the parents was inappropriate. The Court, however, did strike down requirements of parental and spousal consent as well as a variety of regulations designed to make the decision to have an abortion more difficult (e.g., *Akron* v. *Akron Center for Reproductive Health*, 1983; *Thornburgh* v. *American College of Obstetricians & Gynecologists*, 1986).

The retirements of Burger and Stewart, both of whom were in the majority in *Roe*, gave President Ronald Reagan the opportunity to begin to reshape the Court's position on the abortion issue, but it was the retirement of Justice Lewis Powell in 1987 that provided the greatest opportunity for change. Reagan nominated Judge Robert Bork to succeed Powell, in part because of Bork's vigorous and well-known opposition to *Roe*. That opposition was a source of great concern to supporters of *Roe*, who formed an important part of the political coalition that defeated Bork's nomination.

In 1989 the Court, with Justice Anthony Kennedy sitting in an abortion case of the first time, came close to overruling *Roe* in *Webster* v. *Reproductive Services*, but in the end a majority of the justices held only that two additional restrictions on abortions were relatively minor extensions of what *Roe* itself allowed. Partisans on both sides of the abortion issue, however, took *Webster* as a signal that further political action was appropriate. Abortion-rights activists, in particular, realized that the right to choose abortion might no longer be adequately protected in the courts, and they revived the sort of political lobbying in which they had engaged prior to *Roe*.

The most significant threat to *Roe* emerged in the 1992 case of *Planned Parenthood of Southeastern Pennsylvania* v. *Casey*. A deeply and bitterly divided Court sustained the Pennsylvania law placing certain restrictions on access to abortions, but the justices refused to overturn the *Roe* precedent. Justice Sandra Day O'Connor's opinion reaffirmed that a woman has a constitutional right to an abortion before the fetus attains viability at roughly six months of pregnancy. In the wake of *Casey*, antiabortion groups turned to new tactics designed to harass persons attempting to use abortion clinics and those who worked in them. The justices in *National Organization of*

Women v. *Scheidler* (1994) held that abortion clinics could deal with these tactics by invoking the Federal Racketeering law (RICO) to sue violent antiabortion protest groups for damages.

□ Marian Faux, *Roe* v. *Wade* (1988). Laurence Tribe, *Abortion: The Clash of Absolutes* (1990).
Mark V. Tushnet

Romer v. Evans, 116 S.Ct. 1620 (1996), argued 10 Oct. 1995, decided 20 May 1996 by vote of 6 to 3; Kennedy for the Court, Scalia, Rehnquist, and Thomas in dissent. As more and more gay people came out of the closet in the 1980s and 1990s, the question of their constitutional status became at once more important and more conflicted. Unlike other groups, such as African-Americans, the Supreme Court had refused to treat gays as a specially protected "suspect" class under the Constitution. In *Bowers* v. *Hardwick* (1986), the justices had refused to overturn a Virginia law that criminalized homosexual sex. Homosexuals nonetheless enjoyed greater public visibility, yet that same visibility brought them into direct conflict with various Christian and family groups that condemned same-sex relations.

The contrast between traditional sexual practices and the gay lifestyle was particularly striking in Colorado, a state whose history as part of the Old West collided with the liberal enclaves of Boulder, Aspen, and Denver. These liberal municipalities passed ordinances banning discrimination based on sexual orientation in housing, employment, education, public accommodations, health and welfare services, and other transactions and activities. In response to these measures, "family values" and fundamentalist religious groups successfully sponsored a statewide referendum—Amendment 2 to the Colorado Constitution—that precluded all legislative, executive, or judicial action at any level of state or local government designed to protect the status of persons based on their sexual orientation and lifestyle. A coalition of gay action groups, liberal religious organizations, the American Civil Liberties Union, and the National Association for the Advancement of Colored People persuaded first a trial court and then the Colorado Supreme Court to enjoin Amendment 2 on the grounds that it violated the Equal Protection Clause of the Fourteenth Amendment. The state of Colorado, through the guise of its governor, Roy

Romer, then appealed to the United States Supreme Court.

The state argued that Amendment 2 did not discriminate against gays but instead simply removed special rights for them that did not apply to other groups. Moreover, since the voters of Colorado had spoken on the issue, the high court was bound to respect the peoples' judgment, especially since the measure followed the common practice of giving state governments broad authority over cities and municipalities. If there was a need for special protection of homosexuals, that protection should come from the state level.

Critics of Amendment 2 denounced it on constitutional grounds as an unacceptable act of discrimination that denied a specific category of people the protection of the laws. In short, counsel for Richard Evans, a gay activist and the coordinator of Denver's HIV resource program, argued that Colorado had failed to show any legitimate objective for this act of discrimination other than a majority of state residents disliked gay people.

Justice Anthony M. Kennedy's majority opinion supported the Colorado Supreme Court in striking down Amendment 2. Kennedy turned to two sources to make his argument. The first was Justice John Marshall Harlan, whose famous dissent in *Plessy* v. *Ferguson* (1896) held that "the Constitution neither knows nor tolerates classes among citizens" (p. 625). The Colorado amendment, Kennedy continued, had no rational or proper legislative purpose; instead, it was designed to "make them [gays] unequal to everyone else" (p. 646). Kennedy, however, avoided establishing homosexuals as a specially protected class, similar to that accorded blacks. He did so by relying on a brief filed by Harvard Law professor Lawrence Tribe, who had a decade before unsuccessfully argued the case of *Bowers* v. *Hardwick*. Tribe told the Court that it did not need to address the issue of special status for gays, since Amendment 2 was a rare example of a per se violation of the Equal Protection Clause of the Fourteenth Amendment. The fact that the other justices in the majority signed on to the opinion, rather than writing concurring opinions, underscored the effort by the majority to demonstrate a unified front over a contentious issue.

The dissenters, however, were blistering in denouncing the majority's actions. Justice

Antonin Scalia, for example, argued that the case was merely another incident in the cultural wars, one in which the majority of the people of Colorado were within their constitutional rights to try and "preserve traditional sexual mores. . . . The people of Colorado have adopted an entirely reasonable provision which does not even disfavor homosexuals . . . " (p. 647).

Romer was a significant victory for gay rights and something of a defeat for states' rights advocates, who had enjoyed strong support from the Rehnquist Court. Most important, however, the majority concluded that the creation of so-called special rights for gays, which prevented discrimination against them, was really just another manifestation of equal rights, to which all persons were entitled. As a result, the decision makes it more difficult for governments at all levels to single out a particular population for a "special burden."

Kermit L. Hall

Roper v. Simmons, 543 U.S. 551 (2005), argued 13 Oct. 2004, decided 1 Mar. 2005 by vote of 5 to 4; Kennedy for the Court, Stevens concurring, O'Connor and Scalia in dissent. Reversing its prior decision in *Stanford* v. *Kentucky* (1989), the Supreme Court in *Roper* held that the death penalty was cruel and unusual punishment, and thus a violation of the Eighth Amendment, when inflicted on persons who were sixteen or seventeen years old at the time of the capital crime. The Court was asked to reconsider *Stanford* in light of *Atkins* v. *Virginia* (2002), in which the Court held that the death penalty could not be imposed on persons who are mentally retarded.

In deciding whether a particular punishment violates the Eighth Amendment, the Court looks to "evolving standards of decency that mark the progress of an evolving society" (*Trop* v. *Dulles* [1958]). Informed by objective indicia of consensus, such as legislative enactments and jury determinations, the Court exercises its own independent judgment as to whether a punishment is disproportionate.

Following the decision in *Stanford*, the general movement among the states was for the abolition of the death penalty for those under eighteen years of age at the time of the capital crime. While this trend was not as dramatic as that against executing persons who are mentally retarded, the Court nonetheless determined that the develop-

ment was significant. Consistent with this trend, the United States was one of only seven countries that had executed juveniles in the years since 1990.

In assessing proportionality, the Court found that neither of the penalogical justifications for the death penalty—retribution and deterrence—could justify inflicting the death penalty on juveniles. It rested this conclusion on three factors that distinguish juveniles from adults: juveniles' lack of maturity, their vulnerability to outside influences, and the fact that their characters are not yet fully developed. Dissenting, Justice Antonin Scalia accused the majority of reaching an implausible result by invoking subjective views about capital punishment to interpret the Eighth Amendment.

Susan L. Kay

Rosenberg v. United States, 346 U.S. 273 (1953), argued 18 June 1953, decided 19 June 1953 by vote of 6 to 3; Vinson for the Court, Black, Douglas, and Frankfurter in dissent. In 1951, Julius and Ethel Rosenberg were convicted of conspiring to violate the Espionage Act of 1917 by transmitting secret atomic and other military information to the Soviet Union. The Rosenbergs' actions relating to atomic secrets occurred before enactment of the Atomic Energy Act of 1946, but other aspects of the conspiracy continued until 1950. The Rosenbergs were sentenced to death. The court of appeals affirmed the judgment, and the U.S. Supreme Court denied certiorari. Several subsequent collateral attacks on the judgment were unsuccessful.

In 1953, counsel for a "next friend" of the Rosenbergs, without their authorization, argued that the Atomic Energy Act of 1946 had superseded the Espionage Act of 1917 and rendered the district court powerless to impose a death sentence without recommendation by a jury. Holding that this claim presented a substantial question of law, Justice William O. Douglas granted a stay of execution. Two days later, the Court vacated the stay on the ground that the Atomic Energy Act did not displace the penalties of the Espionage Act. The Court further concluded that, since most of the activities forming the basis of the conviction had been committed prior to the passage of the Atomic Energy Act, the alleged inconsistency of its penalty provisions with those of the Espionage Act was irrelevant. The dissenting justices maintained that the stay should not be vacated without a full review of the substantive issue. The Rosenbergs were executed on the day of this decision.

Edgar Bodenheimer

Rosenberger v. University of Virginia, 515 U.S. 819 (1995), argued 1 Mar. 1995, decided 29 June 1995 by vote of 5 to 4; Kennedy for the Court, O'Connor and Thomas concurring, Souter, Stevens, Ginsburg, and Breyer in dissent. The bitter cultural wars of the 1980s and early 1990s produced a host of powerful conflicts over religion. Nowhere, however, were these tensions more evident than in *Rosenberger,* a case that pitted religious conservatives against civil libertarians. Ronald W. Rosenberger in 1990 was a student at the University of Virginia and editor of the short-lived Christian publication *Wide Awake.* The magazine included Christian symbols on each page and professed an editorial policy that "challenge[s] Christians to live, in word and deed, according to the faith they proclaim and to encourage students to consider what a personal relationship to Jesus Christ means" (p. 833). Rosenberger requested $6,000 from the Student Activity Fund, a request that first a student advisory group and then the administration of the university denied. They did so on the grounds that *Wide Awake* proselytized religion and violated existing guidelines prohibiting the funding of religious groups. Rosenberger claimed, however, that the university funded other religious groups, including the Jewish Law Students Association and the Muslim Student Association, and that its actions amounted to a violation of his right and that of other Christian students to express a point of view.

There was more than a little irony in the fact that the case arose at the University of Virginia, an institution founded by Thomas Jefferson, whose views on the need to separate church and state were well known, as were his convictions that the marketplace of ideas should be wide open. Behind the case, however, was an important issue: had the Supreme Court's professed position of neutrality in matters involving church-state issues come to allow a pattern of religious discrimination? The issues posed by the case were especially difficult since they implicated not only the Establishment Clause of the First Amendment but the guarantee of freedom of speech in that same amendment.

The lower federal courts found in favor of the University of Virginia. The Court of Appeals for the Fourth Circuit affirmed a summary judgment ruling from a federal district court. The Circuit Court found that the university's invocation of viewpoint discrimination in denying Rosenberger third-party funds had violated the Speech Clause of the First Amendment. The Circuit Court held that in balancing the requirements of the Speech and Establishment Clauses, the university had to do so in favor of the latter. The Fourth Circuit concluded that the Establishment Clause prohibited the university, a state entity, from providing any direct assistance to religion.

The unique set of facts in the case stirred to action all of the major constituencies involved in the debate over church-state relations. Conservative groups, such as Pat Robertson's American Center for Law and Justice, the Christian Legal Society, and the Family Research Council urged the Court to find in favor of Rosenberger and to scrap its "Lemon test," named after the high court's ruling in *Lemon* v. *Kurtzman* (1971). That test mandated that government actions touching on religion must have a secular purpose, must neither advance nor inhibit religion, and must not excessively entangle church and state. The state of Virginia took the unusual step of opposing the position of its own university and siding, instead, with the religious right.

On the other side, Americans United for Separation of Church and State, the American Civil Liberties Union, the American Jewish Council, and the National Council of Churches urged the Court to maintain a bright line separating church and state and to uphold the Lemon test.

Justice Anthony M. Kennedy's ruling for a sharply divided Court found in favor of Rosenberger. To obey the constitutional ban on the establishment of a state religion, Kennedy wrote, "it was not necessary for the university to deny eligibility to student publications because of their viewpoint" (p. 868). Indeed, unlike content discrimination (i.e., discrimination based on the subject matter of the speech), viewpoint discrimination (i.e., discrimination based on a speaker's ideology, opinion, or perspective) was presumed to be unacceptable. By refusing to subsidize the printing of *Wide Awake,* Kennedy continued, the university had violated the free speech rights of the students because it was unconstitutional to silence their particular message about the value of Christian belief. When the Establishment and the Speech Clauses of the First Amendment came into conflict, Kennedy found, the balance had to be tipped in favor of speech, a position that the Fourth Circuit had specifically rejected. The majority, however, left the Lemon Test in place.

Justice David Souter, whose dissent was joined by John Paul Stevens, Ruth Bader Ginsburg, and Stephen Breyer, accused the majority "for the first time" of approving "direct funding of core religious activities by an arm of the government" (p. 898). According to Souter, the ban on establishing a state religion had little meaning if public funds could be used to support activities like *Wide Awake*.

Rosenberger was an important but not a profound constitutional case. It did not establish a new set of principles; instead, it answered an important question: to what extent are public institutions obliged to provide support to religious organizations for the purposes of propagating their viewpoint? The Court answered that question by engaging in a subtle but important shift that weighed the balance between speech and religious freedom somewhat more toward the former.

Kermit L. Hall

Ross, United States v., 456 U.S. 798 (1982), argued 1 Mar. 1982, decided 1 June 1982 by vote of 6 to 3; Stevens for the Court, White and Marshall, joined by Brennan, in dissent. To what extent can the "automobile exception" to the warrant requirement of the Fourth Amendment justify warrantless searches of containers that are placed in automobiles? The Supreme Court first addressed this issue in *United States* v. *Chadwick* (1977). Speaking for a unanimous court, Chief Justice Warren Burger said in that decision that the mere fact that a footlocker, which police officers had probable cause to believe contained narcotics, was placed in the trunk of a car did not render the automobile exception applicable. The Court reaffirmed the general principle that closed packages and containers may not be searched without warrant because a person's expectation of privacy in personal luggage is substantially greater than in an automobile.

Not all police suspicions are directed at a specific container, however. In *Robbins* v. *California* (1981), a companion case to *New York* v. *Belton* (1981), a plurality of the Court invalidated the warrantless search of a closed package found in a car trunk. Only after Robbins, the driver of the automobile, was placed in the police car did the officers search the trunk and discover two packages wrapped in green plastic. The police unwrapped the packages and found marijuana inside. Justice Potter Stewart said that unless the contents of such a package are in plain view, it could not be searched without a warrant.

The rationale of *Robbins* was abandoned a year later in *Ross*. Acting on a tip from a reliable informant that a person known as "Bandit" was selling drugs from the trunk of his car, District of Columbia police stopped the car and arrested the driver. In the trunk they found a closed brown paper bag that contained a white powder later determined to be heroin. At headquarters another search of the trunk revealed a zippered red leather pouch containing cash. Ross's motion to suppress the evidence was denied and he was convicted of possession of heroin with intent to distribute.

Justices John Paul Stevens, writing for six members of the Court, held that police may search compartments and containers within a vehicle even though the contents are not in plain view, so long as the search is based on probable cause, the same standard needed to obtain a search warrant. Stevens said that the "practical consequences of the automobile exception would be largely nullified if the permissible scope of a warrantless search of an automobile did not include containers and packages found inside the vehicle" (p. 820). The Court's holding in *Ross* broadened the automobile exception established in *Carroll* v. *United States* (1925). *Ross* not only held the automobile exception to the minimum probable cause standard for searching containers but effectively placed the power to determine probable cause in the hands of the police rather than a magistrate.

Some observers maintained that with the retirement of Justice Stewart, who wrote the majority opinions in both *Belton* and *Robbins*, and the appointment of Justice Sandra Day O'Connor to the Court, the controversy about warrantless container searches may have ended. The subsequent appointments of Justices Antonin Scalia and Anthony Kennedy will no doubt confirm that result. Police may now conduct warrantless searches incident to an arrest of containers discovered in an automobile and must only demonstrate that they had probable cause to believe contraband was located somewhere in the car. Since police have been granted the power to carry out warrantless searches of automobiles and containers therein so long as they meet the probable cause standard, it is unlikely that they would find it necessary to get a warrant to search a particular container located in an automobile.

Justice Thurgood Marshall's dissent in *Ross*, joined by Justice William J. Brennan and agreed to by Justice Byron White, takes issue with the idea that a police officer should have the same power as a magistrate to determine probable cause. He argued that the majority's position "takes a first step toward an unprecedented 'probable cause' exception to the warrant requirement" (p. 828).

□ Michael A. Jeter, "Constitutional Law— *United States* v. *Ross:* Final Obliteration of Fourth Amendment Protection From Warrantless Searches of Cars and Their Contents," *Black Law Journal* 8 (1983): 306–332.

Christine Harrington

Rostker v. Goldberg, 453 U.S. 57 (1981), argued 24 Mar. 1981, decided 25 June 1981 by vote of 6 to 3; Rehnquist for the Court, White (joined by Brennan) and Marshall (joined by Brennan) in dissent. In 1971, several men facing the draft for the Vietnam War, challenged male-only conscription on the basis of the equal protection principle contained in the Fifth Amendment's Due Process Clause. The draft was discontinued and the case entered legal limbo for several years until 1980, when President Jimmy Carter reinstituted registration (although not actual conscription). The lawsuit was then revived, with Goldberg litigating on behalf of himself and all situated similarly males against Rostker, head of the Selective Service. On 18 July 1980, three days before the new draft registration was to begin, a federal district court declared the act unconstitutional and enjoined the government from requiring registration. Rostker immediately requested a stay pending appeal, and Justice William J. Brennan granted it. Registration began on time.

Rejecting Goldberg's claims, the majority argued that judicial deference is at its peak when the Court, as here, is considering the combined executive-legislative power over national security. The majority further held that the test of "heightened scrutiny" articulated in *Craig* v. *Boren* (1976) for measuring the constitutionality of gender discrimination was satisfied because military flexibility was an important government goal. The exclusion of females from registration for a potential draft substantially furthered that goal, since women, unlike men, could not be rotated from combat into noncombat positions. The Court did not consider the possibility that women could occupy combat roles.

Justice Byron White's dissent read the legislative record differently, and, he urged a remand for hearings on the relation between registering women and military flexibility. Justice Thurgood Marshall's dissent emphasized the distinction between registration for the draft and conscription itself, insisting that the government had failed to demonstrate that excluding women from registration substantially furthered any important governmental interest. Neither dissent challenged the rule of excluding women from combat.

Leslie Friedman Goldstein

Roth v. United States; Alberts v. California, 354 U.S. 476 (1957), argued 22 Apr. 1957, decided 24 June 1957 by vote of 6 to 3; Brennan for the Court, Douglas and Black in dissent, Harlan in dissent in *Roth* only. Laws prohibiting the sale or distribution of obscene literature have existed in the United States since the early part of the nineteenth century. Until 1957, however, neither those laws nor their enforcement was taken to implicate the concerns of freedom of speech or freedom of the press. Obscenity laws were considered to be beyond the province of the First Amendment; the Supreme Court's passing statements to that effect in cases such as *Ex parte Jackson* (1878) and *Near* v. *Minnesota* (1931) were merely restatements of settled understandings. As a result, criminal obscenity convictions based even on works of obvious literary value, such as Theodore Dreiser's *An American Tragedy* (*Commonwealth* v. *Friede*, 1930) and Arthur Schnitzler's *Casanova's Homecoming* (*People* v. *Seltzer*, 1924), were beyond the bounds of constitutional intervention.

After dealing with the issue tangentially in several cases in the late 1940s and early 1950s, the Supreme Court finally turned to the obscenity question in 1957. In *Roth* v. *United States* and its companion case *Alberts* v. *California*, the Court reaffirmed the longstanding view that obscenity was not covered by the First Amendment and that both state and federal obscenity laws were therefore constitutionally permissible. Justice William J. Brennan's majority opinion based this conclusion not only on history and precedent but also on the view that, although the First Amendment protects all ideas with even the slightest social importance no matter how hateful they may be, it does not even cover obscenity because obscenity is "utterly without redeeming social importance" (p. 484).

This conclusion, which both remains the law and remains controversial, likened obscenity to those various other utterances whose regulation need not be measured against a First Amendment standard. By holding that obscenity was to be treated as constitutionally equivalent to conduct rather than speech, the Court allowed obscenity regulation to proceed without the necessity of the kind of showing of particular harm normally required for restrictions on the kinds of speech covered by the First Amendment. Consequently, although there have long been debates on the effect of sexually explicit material on human conduct, the doctrinal exclusion of obscenity from First Amendment coverage made it unnecessary for the Court then (or since) to look at these debates critically.

Although the Court ratified the historical exclusion of obscenity from First Amendment coverage and thus put obscenity into the category of verbal or linguistic activities (such as perjury and price fixing) that lie outside the First Amendment, it also made clear that, unlike in the past, the test for obscenity would have to be tailored to First Amendment concerns in order to ensure that material that did have First Amendment value would not be subject to restriction.

If obscenity was unprotected by the First Amendment because it did not involve the conveyance of ideas, then the test of obscenity would have to guarantee that only material not conveying ideas would be determined to be obscene. The Court did not specify the exact test that would satisfy constitutional standards, but it did specifically rule that the traditional American test, taken from the English case of *Regina* v. *Hicklin* (1868), allowing prosecutions based on the tendency of selected excerpts of the work to "deprave and corrupt" the most susceptible part of an audience, would no longer be tolerated. Henceforth a work could be obscene only if "taken as a whole" it appealed to the "prurient interest" of "the average person" (p. 489).

All of these terms were to cause enormous definitional problems in years to come, but the substitution of "taken as a whole" for the selected-excerpts approach and the substitution of "the average person" for the most susceptible segment of an audience (usually taken to be children) were designed to, and did in fact, remove from the threat of the obscenity laws most works, even those dealing quite explicitly with sex, whose goal was to convey ideas rather than provide sexual stimulation.

Roth accordingly remains important both for having established the doctrinal foundations for the exclusion of obscenity from the coverage of the First Amendment and for providing the constitutional basis for the conclusion that the definition of obscenity must be established primarily on a First Amendment basis rather than that of the common law.

Frederick Schauer

Rumsfeld v. Forum for Academic and Institutional Rights, 547 U.S. 47 (2006), argued 6 Dec. 2005, decided 6 Mar. 2006 by vote of 8 to 0; Roberts for the Court; Alito, who was appointed to the Court after the oral argument in this case, took no part in its consideration or decision. A 1993 federal statute excludes from military service those who have engaged in homosexual acts or announced that they are homosexual. A number of law schools reacted by excluding military recruiters (but not the legislators and president who approved the statute) from their campuses. Congress responded with a statute known as the Solomon Amendment, which cuts off some federal funds to universities that refuse to give military recruiters access to campuses and students equal to that provided to other employers.

An association of law schools brought suit attacking the constitutionality of the Solomon Amendment as an infringement of freedom of speech and association. The Supreme Court rejected the challenge, concluding that the schools had "attempted to stretch a number of First Amendment doctrines well beyond the sort of activities these doctrines protect" (p. 70).

Noting that the Solomon Amendment neither limits what schools or their faculties may say nor requires them to say anything with which they disagree, the Court concluded that the statute is a regulation of conduct, not speech. Congress may forbid racial discrimination or discrimination against military recruiters, and therefore may incidentally forbid a sign reading "White Applicants Only" or require a sign reading "Military Recruiters Available in Room 123 at 11:00 a.m." The government conceded that law schools remain free to post anti-military signs and even "help organize student protests" (p. 60). The Court did not say whether such activities could become so harassing as to violate the Solomon Amendment, nor did it address whether such protests, if they reached that level, would be protected by the First Amendment.

Unlike flag burning, which is constitutionally protected, the exclusion of military recruiters from a university campus is not inherently expressive. The Court found that refusing access to military recruiters is more like refusing to pay taxes—in neither case does such conduct acquire constitutional protection just because it is accompanied by criticism of the government.

The Court also rejected analogies between the Solomon Amendment and statutes through which governments had unconstitutionally required newspapers to publish material to which they objected, required parade organizers to include participants the organizers objected to, or required the Boy Scouts to appoint objectionable scoutmasters. The Court has repeatedly held that high school students can distinguish between speech the school sponsors and speech the school is legally required to permit. Here, the Court acidly noted that students surely "have not lost that ability by the time they get to law school" (p. 65).

Nelson Lund

Runyon v. McCrary, 427 U.S. 160 (1976), argued 26 Apr. 1976, decided 25 June 1976 by vote of 7 to 2; Stewart for the Court, Powell and Stevens concurring, White and Rehnquist in dissent. A surviving remnant of the Civil Rights Act of 1866, Title 42, section 1981 of the U.S. Code provides that all persons shall have the same right to make and enforce contracts. In *Jones v. Alfred H. Mayer Co.* (1968), the Supreme Court held that a closely related portion of the 1866 act, section 1982, applied to private racial discrimination in housing. *Runyon* extended *Jones's* reasoning to section 1981. It held that section 1981 prohibits private, nonsectarian schools from denying admission to African-Americans because of their race. Justices Byron White and William H. Rehnquist dissented

on the ground that *Jones* had been wrongly decided. Justice John Paul Stevens's concurrence agreed that *Jones* may have been incorrect but viewed overruling *Jones* as too much of a step backward in overcoming race discrimination.

Runyon's application of section 1981's right-to-contract provision to private discrimination has had substantial implications for the scope of federal civil rights law. Section 1981, on its face, applies to all contracts. Armed with *Runyon's* holding, lower federal courts applied it to a broad range of behavior, including race-based behavior in security deposit requirements, in admissions to barber school, in banking services, in supply contracts, in amusement park admissions policy, in sales of insurance, and in dealings with mortuaries. Since, as interpreted in *Runyon*, section 1981 outlaws discrimination in many contexts not reached by other federal laws, it, as much as any other statute, supports the generalization that racial discrimination in the United States is unlawful. Even as interpreted in *Runyon*, however, there are limits to section 1981's reach. In close personal relationships such as marriage, for example, few believe that section 1981 prohibits race-conscious behavior.

Because it covers most contracts, section 1981 prohibits racial discrimination in employment and therefore overlaps with Title VII of the Civil Rights Act of 1964. This overlap and continuing concern about *Runyon's* interpretation of the statute led the Court to the brink of overruling it. After oral argument in **Patterson v. McLean Credit Union* (1989), the Supreme Court, on its own motion, requested that the parties brief and argue whether *Runyon's* interpretation of section 1981 should be overruled. *Patterson* did not overrule *Runyon* but held that the right to make contracts does not extend to conduct by an employer after the contractual relation has been established, including breach of the terms of the contract or imposition of discriminatory working conditions. *Patterson* thus severely restricted *Runyon*. Two years later, however, Congress passed the Civil Rights Act of 1991, which overruled *Patterson's* narrow interpretation of section 1981.

□ Theodore Eisenberg and Stewart J. Schwab, "The Importance of Section 1981," *Cornell Law Review* 73 (March 1988): 596–604.

Theodore Eisenberg

Rust v. Sullivan, 500 U.S. 173 (1991), argued 30 Oct. 1990, decided 23 May 1991 by vote of 5 to 4; Rehnquist for the Court, Blackmun, Marshall, Stevens, and O'Connor in dissent. In 1970 Congress passed a statute providing federal funds to support family-planning services. The statute said that no appropriated funds could be used in programs where abortion was a method of family planning. From 1971 to 1986 the government's regulations barred family-planning clinics that received federal assistance from providing abortions. In 1986 it changed the regulations to ensure a stricter separation between abortion providers and family-planning clinics. In 1988, at the end of the Reagan administration, the regulations were tightened even more to impose the so-called gag rule at issue in this case. Under the rule, clinics receiving federal funds may not counsel pregnant women about the availability of abortions; if they refer pregnant women for other services, they may not mention abortion, and if a pregnant woman asks about abortion, the services are directed to say something like, "We do not consider abortion an appropriate method of family planning."

Family-planning services argued that the rule was not authorized by Congress and that it violated their rights under the First Amendment and their clients' rights under *Roe* v. *Wade* (1973). The Court rejected both arguments and found that the statute was ambiguous. By funding family-planning services but prohibiting assistance for abortion, Congress left the precise definition of family-planning services open. The 1988 regulation was, the Court said, a permissible interpretation of the statute by the agency charged with administering it, to which the courts should defer. The four dissenters emphasized that the 1988 regulations were a sharp departure from those originally in force. They also argued that the gag rule raised serious constitutional questions, which the Court could avoid by finding that the rule was unauthorized.

The Court rejected the free speech challenge to the gag rule. In an important discussion of the doctrine of unconstitutional conditions, sometimes known as the doctrine of conditional spending, the Court held that the government could impose conditions on fund recipients designed to assure that the funds were used for the program's purposes. The Court held that this condition did not force clinic doctors to give up their free speech rights; the doctors could continue to advise women about the availability of abortions outside the confines of the program receiving federal funds. The Court suggested that conditions limiting what professionals receiving government money could say to their clients might be unconstitutional, but said that the relationship between a doctor in a family-planning clinic and the clinic's clients was so narrow that limiting the advice the doctor could give did not impair the doctor's free speech rights.

The Court also found that the rules did not impermissibly burden the right to choose to have an abortion. Acknowledging that it would be easier for women to obtain abortions if they could receive information about them from family-planning services, the Court concluded that the right to choose guaranteed by the Constitution did not require the government to "distort the scope of its mandated program" of providing family-planning services (p. 1777).

Justice Harry Blackmun, joined by Justices Thurgood Marshall and John Paul Stevens, argued in dissent that the government could not impose spending conditions that discriminated against a particular viewpoint and that the gag rule distorted the professional relation between doctor and client. Finally, he argued that because many poor pregnant women receive their only information about family planning from federally funded clinics, restricting the information those clinics can provide does significantly impair their ability to choose to have an abortion.

Rust is important as an indicator of the Court's shifting views on abortion; it was the first abortion-related case in which Justice David Souter cast a vote. In addition, it provided some shape to the doctrine of unconstitutional conditions, which is likely to become increasingly important as government funding of controversial activities expands.

Mark V. Tushnet

Rutan v. Republican Party of Illinois, 497 U.S. 62 (1990), argued 16 Jan. 1990, decided 21 June 1990 by vote of 5 to 4; Brennan for the Court; Stevens concurring, Scalia, Rehnquist, Kennedy, and O'Connor in dissent. Following its earlier decisions against dismissals for party-patronage reasons of non-policy-making government employees in *Elrod* v. *Burns* (1976) and *Branti* v. *Finkel* (1980), a sharply divided Court now extended First Amendment protection against party tests covering promotions, transfers, recalls from layoffs, and even hiring itself. The tests, plaintiffs asserted, had been applied in Illinois under a Republican governor's order prohibiting state hiring without his express permission. Speaking for a bare majority Justice William J. Brennan held that denying low-level government jobs on partisan grounds would abridge First Amendment rights and that such infringement served no vital government interests that could not be secured by defining work standards for non-policy makers and choosing or dismissing only certain high-level employees on the basis of political views. Nor, Brennan added, was patronage necessary to preserve the democratic process since, in his view, political parties prosper by other means.

Justice Antonin Scalia's dissent, longer than the Court's opinion, was especially blunt. He described the party-enhancing benefits claimed for traditional patronage and, without endorsing the system, argued that a legislative body, not the Court, should be allowed to weigh such benefits against other values. Scalia's dissent was not merely against extending *Elrod* and *Branti*; he would have overruled them. Supported by three other justices, and written just before Brennan's resignation from the Court, Scalia's dissent commands attention. Justice John Paul Stevens's opinion, concurring with the Court, responds specifically to Scalia's arguments.

Leon D. Epstein

S

San Antonio Independent School District v. Rodriguez, 411 U.S. 1 (1973), argued 12 Oct. 1972, decided 21 Mar. 1973 by vote of 5 to 4; Powell for the Court, Stewart concurring; Douglas, Brennan, White, and Marshall in dissent. In 1968, Demetrio Rodriguez and other parents residing in Texas' property-poor Edgewood school district filed a class-action suit in federal district court contending that their state's school finance law violated the Equal Protection Clause of the Fourteenth Amendment. Under Texas law, the state appropriated funds to provide each child with a minimum education; local school districts then enriched that basic education with funds derived from locally levied ad valorem property taxes. Because the value of taxable property as well as the number of school-aged children differed greatly among the state's more than one thousand districts, significant interdistrict disparities existed in available enhancement revenues, per-pupil expenditures, and tax rates.

In 1971, the district court found that the Texas statute operated for property-poor school districts as a spend-less, tax-more system of school finance, and for rich ones as a spend-less, taxless system. Education, the three-judge panel held unanimously, was a fundamental constitutional right; wealth-based classifications, as Texas had created here, were constitutionally suspect. Applying the test of strict scrutiny, the lower court held that the Texas method of school finance deprived plaintiffs of their equal protection guarantees. It ordered the state to finance its schools so that the amount spent on a child's education did not depend upon the wealth of the neighborhood in which the child resided.

In 1973, a divided Supreme Court reversed the lower court decision and sustained the school finance policy operating in Texas and, in effect, forty-eight other states. Justice Lewis Powell's majority opinion held that education was not a fundamental right, since it was guaranteed neither explicitly nor implicitly in the Constitution. Texas did not, in any case, deprive any class or anyone of an education, but rather assured that each child in the state received a free minimum education. Moreover, no discrete, wealth-based class existed against which the state discriminated, since, among other things, some school children from poor families resided in property-rich school districts expending high per-pupil amounts on their education. Acknowledging its traditional reluctance to meddle in local fiscal affairs, the Court applied the rational basis (or minimal scrutiny) test. It found that the state's method of school finance, incorporating local choice over tax rates and degree of educational enrichment, furthered the state's legitimate interest in fostering local participation in public education while simultaneously providing every child in the state with a free basic education.

Vigorous dissents registered a spectrum of interpretations and objections. Justice Byron White, also applying the minimal scrutiny test, argued that the statute bore no rational relationship to the state's purported goal of local control, since property-poor districts had no meaningful enhancement options available to them. Justice William Brennan argued that a fundamental right to education did exist because of education's importance to the enjoyment of rights that are guaranteed explicitly or implicitly in the Constitution. Hence, strict scrutiny should apply. Justice Thurgood Marshall argued for the adoption of a variable equal protection standard, one that assessed the characteristics of the class and the importance of the governmental benefits to that class, relative to the government's interest in retaining the classification.

During the decade following the *Rodriguez* decision, Texas and numerous other states enacted a series of "equalization" reforms but failed to reduce effectively the inter-district inequities in access to resources, per-pupil expenditures, and tax rates. In 1984, with federal court pathways foreclosed, the Mexican American Legal Defense and Education Fund, on behalf of the Edgewood district, Rodriguez, and other plaintiffs, filed suit in a lower state court alleging that Texas school finance policy violated the Texas constitution.

In October 1989 the Texas Supreme Court held unanimously for the petitioners in *Edgewood* v. *Kirby* (1989). It declared that the legislature had failed "to establish and make suitable provision for . . . an efficient system of public free schools" throughout the state, as mandated by Article VII of the Texas constitution (p. 500). Existent inequality among the districts, the justices held, affronted the constitutional vision of efficiency. The court ordered the legislature to redesign its school finance system by 1 May 1990, so that districts would have access to relatively equal revenues per pupil when making equal tax efforts. With this decision, Texas became the tenth state to have its state supreme court declare a school finance law in violation of the state constitution.

Richard A. Gambitta

Sandin v. Conner, 515 U.S. 472 (1995), argued 28 Feb. 1995, decided 19 June 1995 by vote of 5 to 4; Rehnquist for the Court, Ginsburg in dissent, joined by Stevens, Breyer in dissent, joined by Souter. *Sandin* marked a sharp move by the Court away from its holdings in several earlier prisoner rights cases and made it more difficult for prisoners to bring lawsuits challenging on constitutional grounds the management of prisons.

DeMont R. D. Conner, a convicted murderer serving thirty years to life in Hawaii's maximum security correctional facility, brought suit against Cinda Sandin, a manager in the prison. Conner claimed that Sandin had refused to allow him to call witnesses before being subjected to disciplinary segregation for breaking prison rules, a punishment that placed him in solitary confinement for thirty days. Conner insisted that Sandin's failure to do so amounted to a violation of procedural due process under the Fourteenth Amendment to the Constitution. At issue in the case was the extent to which prison rules dealing with such matters had established a "liberty interest" to be protected under the amendment. The Court had previously recognized that such due process rights as a hearing and the ability to call witnesses came into play when the state's actions had clearly violated a substantive right of the prisoner. For example, if an inmate had behaved well and "earned" time that would shorten his sentence, then he could not be deprived of this substantial right without a hearing. During the 1980s, however, the Court had created considerable uncertainty through its case law about what constituted a substantial and a trivial protection and prompted a flood of litigation by inmates such as Conner.

Chief Justice William H. Rehnquist's goal was to bring clarity to the issue. He concluded that the Court had become far too lenient in accepting assertions by prisoners that their rights had been violated. So-called jailhouse lawyers would comb prison regulations seeking instances of even the smallest procedural violations and then invoke them to charge that prison authorities had denied a liberty interest. The chief justice articulated a standard that required a prisoner to demonstrate that authorities had imposed an atypical and significant hardship rather than carrying out the routine, day-to-day business of the prison. Being placed in solitary confinement at a maximum security prison did not meet this new standard, and the Court rejected Conner's claim. Rehnquist's decision left in place, however, another constitutional provision under the Eighth Amendment that prevents jailers from administering cruel and unusual punishment.

The dissenters also recognized that Conner presented a weak case, and Justice Stephen Breyer went so far as to argue in his dissenting opinion that the inmate did not deserve relief. Yet the dissenters also insisted that Rehnquist's opinion was far too broad and left lower federal courts with little discretion in separating the unimportant complaints brought forward by prisoners from the significant ones. The dissenters also recognized that Rehnquist's opinion fitted neatly with his main objective of curbing prisoners' lawsuits generally.

Kermit L. Hall

Santa Clara County v. Southern Pacific Railroad Co., 118 U.S. 394 (1886), argued 26–29 Jan. 1886, decided 10 May 1886 by vote of 9 to o; Harlan for the Court. This was one of the legion of cases involving railroads and government agencies (at every level) that inundated the courts in the late nineteenth century. The State of California and certain affected counties sought to collect taxes that they claimed were owed by both the Southern Pacific and Central Pacific railroads. Argument focused almost entirely on whether the taxes were barred by the Due Process Clause of the Fourteenth Amendment.

The U.S. Supreme Court did not address the constitutional issues posed by counsel. Instead, it based its ruling on a narrower issue: whether the fences on the railroads' property should have been assessed by either county or state taxing authorities. Justice John Marshall Harlan held that such fences could not be taxed as property subject to taxation under California statute; the Court's ruling upheld that of the California court.

Despite the Court's narrow holding, the case was not without constitutional consequence. In an unusual preface, entered before argument, Chief Justice Morrison R. Waite observed that the Court would not consider the question "whether the provision in the Fourteenth Amendment to the Constitution which forbade a state to deny to any person within its jurisdiction the equal protection of the Constitution, applied to these corporations. We are all of the opinion that it does" (p. 396). It followed that corporations enjoyed the same rights under the Fourteenth Amendment as did natural persons.

Augustus M. Burns III

Santa Clara Pueblo v. Martinez, 436 U.S. 49 (1978), argued 29 Nov. 1977, decided 15 May 1978 by vote of 7 to 1; Marshall for the Court, White in dissent, Blackmun not participating. The 1968 Indian Civil Rights Act applied most of the guarantees of the federal Bill of Rights to Native American tribal governments. It initially provided only a habeas corpus remedy in criminal cases. But lower federal courts developed a series of "implied" civil remedies—actions for declaratory or injunctive relief or mandamus—so that federal courts came to review matters central to tribal self-government, including election procedures, reapportionment cases, the right to vote and hold public office, and proper qualifications for tribal membership.

Martinez was a membership case, filed under the Indian Civil Rights Act on a gender discrimination charge. The case claimed that a tribal rule allowing tribal membership to children of male members who married outside the tribe but not to women who did the same violated the equal protection clause of the act. Justice Thurgood Marshall, writing for the Court, denied the claim and eviscerated the law. Contending that a federal cause of action was not required to extend constitutional norms to tribal governments, he urged that grieving Indians sue in their tribal courts so as to preserve tribal self-determination. Justice Byron White, in his dissent, wrote, "I cannot believe that Congress desired the enforcement of these acts to be left up to the very tribal authorities alleged to have violated them. Extension of constitutional rights to individual citizens is intended to intrude upon the authority of government" (p. 69).

The outcome was that the decision strengthened tribal self-determination, but an Indian with a complaint against a tribal government had little opportunity for relief. Few tribal court decisions were subsequently appealed.

Paul L. Murphy

San Remo Hotel, L.P. v. City and County of San Francisco, 545 U.S. 323 (2005), argued Mar. 28, 2005, decided June 20, 2005 by vote of 9 to 0; Stevens for the Court; Rehnquist concurred in the judgment and filed a separate opinion, joined by O'Connor, Kennedy, and Thomas. In *San Remo Hotel, L.P. v. City and County of San Francisco*, the Supreme Court refused to create an exception to a full faith and credit statute for litigants seeking to advance federal takings claims. The unanimous decision has implications for the resolution of an increasingly common dilemma for litigants attacking land use regulations under the Fifth Amendment's Takings Clause. In particular, when required to seek relief in state court under the two-pronged ripeness requirement articulated in *Williamson County Regional Planning Comm'n v. Hamilton Bank of Johnson City* (1985), the plaintiff property owner is usually precluded from litigating the same issues in federal court.

The ripeness rule in *Williamson County* requires that the landowner: (1) obtain a "final decision" from the relevant state or county agencies on its application for land development, and (2) seek and fail to obtain compensation for the regulatory taking in state court. The *San Remo* decision did not deal directly with either prong, but rather with the preclusion problem faced by litigants who are required to first seek relief in state court under either or both prongs of *Williamson County* and are then barred from relitigating the same claims in federal court.

The petitioners owned and operated a three-story, sixty-two-unit hotel in San Francisco as a bed and breakfast inn when, in 1979, the city passed an ordinance instituting a moratorium on the conversion of residential hotel units into tourist units. The ordinance requires a permit for such conversion, which is obtainable only if an applicant constructs new units, rehabilitates old ones, or pays an "in lieu" fee into a city fund for such construction or rehabilitation. In 1993 the San Francisco City Planning Commission granted the petitioners the permit, but only upon the condition that they paid a $567,000 in lieu fee.

A federal district court ruled that because the petitioners had not sought and been denied just compensation in state court, the claim was unripe under *Williamson County*. The petitioners went to state court, as directed, and eventually the California Supreme Court decided against them on their takings claims. When the petitioners returned to federal court, having satisfied their *Williamson* ripeness obligation, the federal district court held that the full faith and credit statute required federal courts to give preclusive effect to any state court judgment that would, in turn, have preclusive effect under the laws of that state. Because California courts had interpreted the relevant state takings law at the same time as federal

takings law, the petitioners' federal claims were the same as those already resolved in state court. It followed, therefore, that they were precluded from relitigating those claims in federal court.

This narrow issue made its way to the Supreme Court, which ruled that it would not "create an exception to the full faith and credit statute in order to provide a federal forum for litigants who seek to advance federal takings claims that are not ripe" under *Williamson County* (p. 337). The Court also rejected the argument that plaintiffs have a right to try their federal regulatory takings claims in a federal forum. The concurring justices maintained that *Williamson County* should be reconsidered in view of its drastic impact on takings plaintiffs.

David L. Callies

Scales v. United States, 367 U.S. 203 (1961), reargued 10 Oct. 1960, decided 5 June 1961 by vote of 5 to 4; Harlan for the Court, Brennan, Warren, Douglas, and Black in dissent. The Supreme Court had dealt with the conspiracy provisions of the Smith Act in two previous cases: *Dennis v. United States* (1951) and *Yates v. United States* (1957). In *Scales,* as well as in *Noto v. United States* (1961), the Court considered the Smith Act's membership clause. The Court upheld Scales's conviction by interpreting the membership clause as requiring proof of "active" as distinguished from merely "nominal" or "passive" membership in the Communist party.

The Court found in the language of the statute clear warrant for requiring "not only knowing membership, but active and purposive membership, purposive that is as to the organization's criminal ends" (p. 210). As thus construed, it held that the membership clause did not violate the Due Process Clause of the Fifth Amendment nor the free speech guarantee of the First Amendment. Since the Communist party was considered an organization that engaged in criminal activity, the Court saw no constitutional obstacle to the prosecution of a person who actively and knowingly works in its ranks with intent to contribute to the success of its illegal objectives. Even though the evidence disclosed no advocacy for immediate overthrow of the government, the Court held that present advocacy of future action satisfied statutory and constitutional requirements no less than advocacy of immediate action.

Milton R. Konvitz

Schechter Poultry Corp. v. United States, 295 U.S. 495 (1935), argued 2–3 May 1935, decided 27 May 1935 by vote of 9 to 0; Chief Justice Hughes for the Court. The National Industrial Recovery Act (NIRA), adopted by Congress on 16 June 1933, was the Roosevelt administration's first and major instrument for dealing with the Great Depression. Intended to curb unemployment and stimulate business recovery, the statute was wide ranging. But its principal reliance was upon codes of fair competition, which all industry groups were directed to draw up. Within two years more than 750 NIRA codes had been adopted, covering some twenty-three million people. The act declared a national emergency and justified congressional action under the Commerce and General Welfare Clauses of the Constitution.

The codes had some positive effects in raising wages, banning unfair practices, and encouraging business morale. But they were hastily drawn, favored big businesses, and encouraged cartels. The drafting of the codes was done by industry groups, and the role of the president was simply to sign them.

The Department of Justice had recognized from the beginning that the regulatory program's constitutionality might well be difficult to establish before the Supreme Court and made a considerable effort to find an appropriate case to take up to the Court for review. These efforts failed, however, and the commercial activity involved in *Schechter*, considering the issues at stake, was absurdly minor. Certain Brooklyn slaughterhouse operators had been found guilty of violating the wage and hour provisions of their industry's code and, among other offenses, selling an "unfit chicken." While the poultry was brought in from outside the state, the Schechters were only local operators selling in their immediate area.

The Supreme Court was unanimous in rejecting the government's case for the program. First, Chief Justice Charles Evans Hughes disposed of the contention that the legislation was justified by the national economic emergency. Although the Court had recently accepted the claim that the agricultural emergency had justified mortgage relief for Minnesota farmers in *Home Building & Loan Assn.* v. *Blaisdell* (1934), Hughes now held that "extraordinary conditions do not create or enlarge constitutional power" (p. 398).

Hughes's most telling argument, however, was that the statute had unconstitutionally delegated legislative power to the president. Only a few months earlier, in *Panama Refining Co.* v. *Ryan* (1935), the Court had declared unconstitutional another section of the NIRA that authorized the president to ban shipment in interstate commerce of oil produced in excess of state quotas. That decision was by vote of 8 to 1; Justice Benjamin N. Cardozo, dissenting, contended that the law was justified by the economic emergency. But here the statute had given industry groups, with the cooperation of the president, authority to draft regulations covering the entire economic life of the country. "This," said Cardozo, "is delegation run riot" (p. 553).

Hughes's third count against the statute was that the poultry code involved regulation of local transactions, not interstate commerce properly subject to congressional control. The Court had agreed in earlier cases that local commerce could be regulated by Congress if it had a "direct" effect upon interstate commerce. Though the distinction between "direct" and "indirect" effects had always been difficult to draw. Hughes believed that the difference was "clear in principle" and that the effects here were clearly "indirect." Cardozo thought that the distinction was less clear but agreed that the connection of Schechters' business with interstate commerce was remote. If a local poultry dealer could be regarded as engaged in interstate commerce, then all limitations on congressional control would disappear.

By 1988 the *Schechter* decision had been cited in more than seventy Supreme Court cases, nearly always along with *Panama Refining* on the now discredited delegation issue. As Justice Byron R. White noted in *Immigration and Naturalization Service* v. *Chadha* (1983), "restrictions on the scope of the power that could be delegated [have] diminished and all but disappeared" (p. 985). The decision has retained more relevance for its interpretation of the commerce power.

President Franklin D. Roosevelt attacked the Court after the *Schechter* decision for its "horse and buggy" interpretation of the Constitution, but in fact the National Recovery Administration (NRA) program was collapsing, and the Supreme Court's unanimous ruling rescued the administration from an embarrassing failure. However, the lessons of the NRA were of value in the drafting of later New Deal measures such as the National Labor Relations Act and the Fair Labor Standards Act.

C. Herman Pritchett

Schenck v. United States, 249 U.S. 47 (1919), argued 9–10 Jan. 1919, decided 3 Mar. 1919 by vote of 9 to 0; Holmes for the Court. Differences of opinion regarding U.S. involvement in World War I provided the opportunity for the initial Supreme Court consideration of a First Amendment free speech case based on federal law. At issue was whether Charles Schenck and other Socialist party members had violated the 1917 Espionage Act that prohibited obstruction of military recruiting.

Schenck, who served as general secretary of the Socialist party, directed the printing of fifteen thousand antidraft leaflets that were to be mailed to those Philadelphia men who were in the midst of the conscription process. The pamphlets argued that conscripts were victims of the intimidation of war zealots and that young men should assert their individual rights in opposition to the war in Europe. The pamphlets urged people to visit the Socialist party headquarters to sign an anticonscription petition to Congress.

Several recipients of letters complained to Philadelphia postal inspectors, and on 28 August 1917 federal agents searched the Socialist offices, seized files and the party minute book, and arrested Schenck. The defendant pleaded "not guilty" in a trial before Judge J. Whitaker Thompson in the U.S. District Court for the Eastern District of Pennsylvania.

After Schenck's conviction on 20 December 1917, he appealed to the U.S. Supreme Court, questioning the constitutionality of the Espionage Act on First Amendment grounds. He argued that the act prevented full public discussion of the war issue. Schenck's attorneys contended that the law was out of step with Anglo-American legal tradition that in their view distinguished between speech that communicated honest opinion and speech that involved incitement of illegal action. Attorneys for the government contended that the case did not involve the First Amendment but rather congressional draft policy, a question that the Court had settled in favor of the United States in 1918. Therefore, the Supreme Court should refuse to consider the case.

In the Schenck appeal the Court ruled unanimously to uphold the Espionage Act. In his opinion Justice Oliver Wendell Holmes laid out what would become his famous clear and present danger test to determine the limits of First Amendment protection of political speech. Holmes's analysis considered the context of the speech as well as the intent of the persons who sent the leaflets. "The question in every case is whether the words used are used in such circumstances and are of such a nature as to create a clear and present danger that they will bring about the substantive evils that Congress has a right to prevent" (p. 52). Holmes distinguished wartime and peacetime contexts and concluded that Schenck's words constituted such an evil since the statue applied to conspiracies as well as actual obstruction of the military. Under the statute the action did not have to be successful in order to violate the law. His analysis did not, however, explain why Congress could outlaw a conspiracy of words in the first place.

The issues raised in *Schenck* underscored the conflict over the war in the nation at large. American Socialists continued their opposition even after U.S. entry. Other reform groups continued to insist upon their right to criticize the war effort. A number of German-Americans suffered the abuse of superpatriots who feared immigrant ties to the fatherland. Other Americans, including many politicians at all levels of government, insisted upon one hundred percent patriotism and demanded the discontinuance of reform programs in order to maintain full support of the war effort.

Holmes's clear and present danger test attempted to draw a line between protected and unprotected speech in a field of constitutional law where he was pioneering new territory—First Amendment interpretation. Later, in November 1919, Holmes along with Justice Louis D. Brandeis dissented in another free speech case, *Abrams v. United States*. In this dissent Holmes appeared to have modified his earlier view by insisting that a present danger must relate to some immediate evil and specific action. Through the decade of the 1920s, Holmes developed his clear and present danger doctrine in a series of dissents. By the 1930s his persistence had convinced a Court majority to support his thinking, and many aspects of the doctrine remain in First Amendment constitutional interpretation today.

☐ Fred Ragan, "Justice Oliver Wendell Holmes, Jr., Zechariah Chafee, Jr. and the Clear and Present Danger Test for Free

Speech: The First Year, 1919," *Journal of History* 58 (June 1971): 24–45.

Carol E. Jenson

Scott v. Sandford, 19 How. (60 U.S.) 393 (1857), argued 11–14 Feb. 1856 and 15–18 Dec. 1856, decided 6–7 Mar. 1857 by vote of 7 to 2; Taney for the Court, Curtis and McLean in dissent. *Scott* v. *Sandford* (1857) stands as one of the most important cases in American constitutional history. It played a major role in precipitating the Civil War; it provided a basis for far-reaching interpretations of substantive due process; and it stirred deep-seated emotions in the saga of race relations in the United States.

Background. The *Dred Scott Case* began unobtrusively in 1846 in the lower state courts of Missouri. Born in Virginia, the slave Dred Scott moved with his master to St. Louis, where in 1833 he was sold to Dr. John Emerson, an army surgeon. Emerson's military career subsequently took them both, among other places, to the free state of Illinois and to free Wisconsin Territory. While in Wisconsin, Scott married Harriet Robinson, whose ownership was transferred to Emerson. Meanwhile, during a tour of duty in western Louisiana in 1838, Emerson married Eliza Irene Sanford, whose family lived in St. Louis.

In 1842 the army posted Dr. Emerson to Florida, where the Seminole War was being fought. Mrs. Emerson and the family's slaves remained in St. Louis. In 1843, with hostilities winding down, Emerson rejoined his family, but he died shortly thereafter. The slaves continued to work for Mrs. Emerson, and, occasionally, as was common in urban servitude, they were hired out to others.

On 6 Apr. 1846, Dred and Harriet Scott instituted a suit for freedom against Irene Emerson in the Circuit Court of St. Louis County, under Missouri law. (Two separate but similar suits were filed. In 1850, to avoid costly duplication, only Dred Scott's case was pursued, with an agreement that its resolution would apply also to Harriet.) Although some details of the litigation's beginnings remain fuzzy, overwhelming evidence indicates that the slaves sued only for freedom and not, as some charged later, to challenge slavery-oriented political issues. Indeed, based on numerous precedents in Missouri case law—the principal precedent being *Rachael* v. *Walker* (1837)—if a slave returned to Missouri, as

Dred Scott had done, after having sojourned in a free state or territory, that slave was entitled to freedom by virtue of residence in the free state or territory. The established legal principle in Missouri was "once free, always free." In fact, when the suit came to trial in 1847, Scott could have been emancipated had not a problem of hearsay evidence resulted in the judge ordering a mistrial. When the case was retried in 1850 and the problem corrected, the court unhesitatingly ordered Scott freed.

The three-year delay before the second trial proved, however, to be fateful. Pending that trial, Scott's wages were held in escrow until the court determined whether he was free or slave. Meanwhile, Mrs. Emerson remarried, moved to New England with her new husband, and left her affairs in St. Louis in the hands of her businessman brother, John F. A. Sanford. When the court declared Scott free, the possible loss of his accumulated wages led Sanford, acting for his sister, to appeal to the Missouri Supreme Court seeking a reversal.

While the appeal was before the Missouri high court, events associated with the increasingly troublesome slavery issue transformed the litigation from a routine freedom suit to a *cause célèbre*. Asserting that "times now are not as they were" and defiantly exclaiming that Missouri law would not be dictated by antislavery outsiders, the Missouri Supreme Court in 1852 reversed the lower court, overturned numerous legal precedents, and in a manifestly partisan decision proclaimed controversial proslavery rhetoric as the law of Missouri, replacing the principle of "once free, always free" (*Scott* v. *Emerson*, 1852, p. 586).

The Federal Suit. To enable the U.S. Supreme Court to clarify to what degree, if at all, a state court could reverse the "once free, always free" principle, Scott's lawyers began a new suit, *Dred Scott* v. *John F. A. Sandford*, in the federal courts. (Through a clerical error, Sanford's name was misspelled in the court records.) Scott could have appealed directly from the Missouri Supreme Court to the U.S. Supreme Court, but the recent precedent of *Strader* v. *Graham* (1851) might have enabled the U.S. Supreme Court to endorse the state court decision without considering its merits. Mrs. Emerson's brother was named defendant because his New York residency made a federal diversity-of-citizenship case possible.

Sanford's attorneys injected additional issues into the federal litigation, including Scott's ability to sue in a federal court, raising the issue of a black person's claim to be a citizen of the United States. Equally troublesome was their proslavery challenge to the constitutionality of the 1820 Missouri Compromise. The power of Congress to forbid slavery in the territories had been long established but Sanford's attorneys now argued the extreme proslavery doctrine that slaves were private property protected by the United States Constitution and, therefore, that Congress could not abolish slavery in the territories. The issue was no longer whether Missouri could remand Dred Scott to slavery, but rather whether he had ever been free at all. So controversial and delicate were the issues that the Supreme Court requested parties to argue twice, a most unusual procedure, in February 1856 and again the following December.

At first it appeared that judicial restraint would prevail. With *Strader* v. *Graham* as a precedent, the Court was prepared to confirm the Missouri high court as having the final word on its own state law, with no need for the United States court to explore the merits separately. Justice Samuel Nelson was designated to write a Court opinion that would thus avoid any controversial, substantive slavery questions.

But the momentous forces of the time pressured the Court to resolve judicially what political institutions had been unable to do. Justice James M. Wayne of Georgia proposed that a new Court opinion deal with the issues that had until then been sidestepped. Though Wayne made the specific proposal, responsibility falls also on Chief Justice Roger B. Taney and Associate Justices John McLean, Benjamin R. Curtis, and Peter V. Daniel. In conference a bare majority of five justices, all from slave states, approved the Wayne proposal, and Taney wrote a new opinion for the Court. Delivered on 6 March 1857, it became famous (or infamous) as the *Dred Scott* decision.

In its decision the Court divided 7 to 2 along ideological lines. Taney's opinion for the Court declared Scott to be still a slave for several reasons. First, although blacks could be citizens of a given state, they were not citizens of the United States having the concomitant right to sue in federal courts. Scott's suit was therefore dismissed because the Court lacked jurisdiction. Second, aside from not having the right to sue, Scott was still a slave because he had never been free in the first place. Congress exceeded its authority when it forbade or abolished slavery in territories because no such power could be inferred from the Constitution. Furthermore, slaves were property protected by the Constitution. The Missouri Compromise was accordingly declared invalid. Finally, whatever the status of an erstwhile slave might have been in a free state or territory, if the slave voluntarily returned to a slave state, his or her status there depended upon the law of that state as interpreted by its own courts. Since Missouri's high court had declared Scott to be a slave, that was the law that the U.S. Supreme Court would recognize.

Aftermath. The Supreme Court's decision triggered violent reaction, unleashing irreconcilable partisan passions that merged with other forces already building toward the coming national calamity. The press, the pulpit, the political stump, and the halls of Congress reverberated with scathing condemnations and vigorous defenses of the Court's action. Antislavery forces feared the next step, which might be to legalize slavery everywhere. They instituted a furious assault on the Court, charging that Taney's opinion was mostly obiter dictum, attacking the personal integrity of individual justices, and even suggesting a judicial proslavery conspiracy. The decision undermined the prestige of the Court just at the time when the stabilizing influence of a respected national judiciary might have provided the sound guidance so desperately needed. With the intrusion of the Court into the slavery issue, many felt that any compromise over slavery was now impossible, and the North and the South moved inexorably toward civil war.

American legal and constitutional scholars consider the *Dred Scott* decision to be the worst ever rendered by the Supreme Court. Historians have abundantly documented its role in crystalizing attitudes that led to war. Taney's opinion stands as a model of censurable judicial craft and failed judicial statesmanship. It took the Civil War and the Civil War Amendments to overturn the *Dred Scott* decision. The Thirteenth Amendment abolished slavery, and all persons born in the United States, regardless of color or previous condition of servitude, were declared citizens of the United States by the Fourteenth Amendment. Unfortunately Dred Scott himself died in 1858, too soon to reap the benefits of those changes.

□ Walter Ehrlich, *They Have No Rights: Dred Scott's Struggle for Freedom* (1979). Don E. Fehrenbacher, *The Dred Scott Case: Its Significance in American Law and Politics* (1976). David M. Potter, *The Impending Crisis, 1848–1861* (1976).

Walter Ehrlich

Scottsboro Cases. See NORRIS V. ALABAMA; POWELL V. ALABAMA.

Selective Draft Law Cases, 245 U.S. 366 (1918), argued 13–14 Dec. 1917, decided 7 Jan. 1918 by vote of 9 to 0, White for the Court. Not until after the passage of the Selective Service Act of 1917 was the authority of the federal government to draft citizens for military duty tested. Convicted violators of the act appealed to the Supreme Court on grounds that the draft was incompatible with free government and individual liberty, that congressional authority to raise armies was limited by the scope and purposes of the constitutional clause providing for calling the state militia into national service, and that the draft was in conflict with the Thirteenth Amendment's prohibition of involuntary servitude and the First Amendment's religion clauses. Chief Justice Edward D. White, citing Anglo-American history and the common practice of nations, ruled that citizenship carried with it a clear obligation to perform the "supreme and noble duty of contributing to the defense of the rights and honor of the nation" (p. 390). How such service could be characterized as involuntary servitude or how the act with its religious exemption for conscientious objectors could be viewed as establishing religion, White was at a loss to understand. Most of the opinion was addressed to a refutation of the claims that the militia clause imposed limitations on the broad authority of Congress to raise and support armies. Neither in 1918 nor later would the Court challenge congressional authority to institute a draft.

John E. Semonche

Seminole Tribe of Florida v. Florida, 517 U.S. 44 (1996), argued 11 Oct. 1995, decided 27 Mar. 1996 by vote of 5 to 4; Rehnquist for the Court, Stevens, Souter, Ginsburg, and Breyer in dissent. In the 1980s several states rushed to raise revenues by authorizing casino gambling. Perhaps nowhere was the impact of the gambling fever greater than on the lands of Native Americans. By 1995 casino gambling generated more than $4 billion a year in business, with 200 tribes operating 126 casinos in 24 states. In the midst of this rush to gold, Congress in 1988 passed the Indian Gaming Regulatory Act, which permitted tribes to operate gambling casinos, required states to negotiate with tribes, and allowed tribes to file lawsuits in federal courts when they alleged the states failed to negotiate in good faith. The act was a response to a 1987 high court decision, *California v. Cabazon Band of Mission Indians,* which held that the states could not bar high-payoff bingo games on reservations.

Under the act tribes were able to sponsor a wide variety of gambling activities, but only in states that permitted them to do so. The law directed the states and the tribes to negotiate in good faith and to devise "tribal-state compacts" to regulate gambling. The response to the new law was at once more gambling and greater conflict between some tribes and the states, since many states took the position that they would allow on the tribal reservations only those games of chance, such as slot machines, approved for the state as whole.

Nowhere was the conflict greater than in Florida. That state's governor, Lawton Chiles, opposed casino gambling, doing so before and after a statewide vote rejected a proposal to establish casino gambling. Governor Chiles did agree that the Seminoles could offer card games and raffles on their reservations, as well as wagering on racing and jai alai, activities already approved by the state. When Chiles refused to negotiate with the Seminole tribe over casino gambling, the tribe took him into federal court, charging that he had failed to exercise good faith. The Court of Appeals for the Eleventh Circuit ultimately decided that Congress lacked the authority to force the states to negotiate with the tribes. In reaching this opinion, the court of appeals pointed to the Eleventh Amendment, which provided that a state could not be sued without its consent. Hence, what began as an issue involving the right of Native Americans to operate casinos became transformed into a major dispute over the nature of federalism and states' rights.

In its appeal to the high court, Florida was joined by thirty-one other states, all of whom feared that should the Indian Gaming Act stand, Congress would be able in other areas, such as the environment, business practices, health, and safety, to erode their sovereign authority. In arguing before the justices, counsel for Florida insisted that the gaming law directly commanded the states to do certain things in such a way that made them mere subdivisions of the national government.

The Seminole tribe of Florida and the United States government argued that Congress had full authority to pass the legislation under the power of the Indian Commerce Clause. So extensive was that authority that Congress, in this instance, could abrogate the historical immunity that states enjoyed from suit.

The Court upheld the Eleventh Circuit's position and gave proponents of states' rights a stunning victory. Speaking for the Court, Chief Justice Rehnquist said that the Eleventh Amendment restricted federal judicial power and that other constitutional powers allocated to Congress, such as the Indian Commerce Clause, cannot be used to circumvent the constitutional limitations placed on federal jurisdiction. Rehnquist's opinion was important, as well, because it cleared up more than twenty years of dispute about the Eleventh Amendment. One side of the Court had supported the view that Congress had power to enforce federal regulations by subjecting the states to suits in federal courts; the other held that the amendment barred such actions. At least in the case of gambling on Native American reservations, the states were clearly the victors.

The opinion drew a stiff constitutional rebuke from Justice David Souter, who took the unusual step of reading his dissenting opinion aloud to the full Court. Souter and three other justices insisted that Congress had always intended for the states to be subject to the jurisdiction of the federal courts and that, in this light, the Indian Gaming Act was entirely constitutional. "The court today holds for the first time since the founding of the republic," Souter wrote, "that Congress has not authority to subject a state to the jurisdiction of a federal court at the behest of an individual asserting a federal right" (p. 138). Entry into the federal courts had historically been a way for less powerful groups to press their rights, something that was now being denied, according to the dissenters, to Native Americans.

The Court's actions made clear that the Rehnquist Court was determined to revisit some of the most enduring assumptions about the American federal system. That line of development was forecast in *United States v. Lopez* (1995), when the Court held that Congress lacked authority to ban possession of guns near schools. Even the lineup of the justices was the same in the two cases, both of which were decided by 5 to 4 votes.

Yet *Florida Seminole* had a paradoxical result. While it affirmed the right of the states to be free of suits by Native Americans under the Gaming Act, it may have actually made it easier for native tribes to open casinos. With the congressional act voided, all that the tribes now have to do is approach the Department of the Interior to seek authorization to open a casino.

Kermit L. Hall

Shapiro v. Thompson, 394 U.S. 618 (1969), argued 29 Apr. 1968, reargued 23–24 Oct. 1968, decided 21 Apr. 1969 by vote of 6 to 3; Brennan for the Court, Stewart concurring, Warren, joined by Black and Harlan in dissent. This landmark decision considered three separate appeals involving the Connecticut, Pennsylvania, and District of Columbia one-year durational residency requirement for eligibility for welfare benefits. The lead case concerned Vivian M. Thompson, who, at the age of nineteen, was a single mother of one child and pregnant with another. She moved from her residence in Massachusetts to Connecticut to be with her mother and applied for but was denied welfare because she had not lived in Connecticut for one year prior to her application. A three-judge federal district court struck down the requirement as an unconstitutional burden on the right to travel and a violation of the Equal Protection Clause of the Fourteenth Amendment. The two other lower courts decided similarly.

The Supreme Court agreed with the lower courts and emphasized that among fundamental personal liberties is the freedom to travel "throughout the length and breadth of our land uninhibited by statutes, rules, or regulations which unreasonably burden or restrict this movement" (p. 629). It held that the right to travel was a "fundamental" right that required the application of strict scrutiny. The state, however, could not demonstrate a "compelling state interest" in such a restrictive law, or that it had chosen the least restrictive alternative to achieve its legitimate ends. Chief Justice Earl Warren and Justice Hugo Black dissented, seeing no restriction on the right to travel. Justice John

M. Harlan viewed the durational residency requirement as only an indirect and insubstantial inhibition on that right.

This decision provided a precedent for successful attacks on other residency requirements such as those for voting and for practicing law. The impact of the decision on the poor was considerable and as a result, many thousands received welfare assistance who otherwise would not have received it.

Sheldon Goldman

Shaw v. Hunt, 517 U.S. 899 (1996), argued 5 Dec. 1995, decided 13 June 1996 by vote of 5 to 4; Rehnquist for the Court, Stevens and Souter in dissent, joined in various parts by Ginsburg and Breyer. In the 1993 case of *Shaw* v. *Reno*, the Supreme Court struck down a North Carolina plan that relied on race to redistrict congressional districts. A bitterly divided Court had concluded that if the state used race to undertake such redistricting, the plan had to withstand the demanding test of strict scrutiny under the Equal Protection Clause of the Fourteenth Amendment. In *Hunt* the Court returned to the issue of racial gerrymandering, doing so at the same time it decided another case, *Bush* v. *Vera et al.*, which involved Texas. In both instances the justices struck down redistricting measures, although they were hardly of one mind about either the reasons for or the wisdom of doing so.

Of the two cases, North Carolina presented the clearer set of facts. The state legislature had established a narrow 160-mile district that followed the course of Interstate 85, a plan that was intended to overcome the problems identified in *Shaw* v. *Reno* with previous efforts at redistricting. A federal district court in North Carolina approved the plan, holding that it met the demanding requirement under strict scrutiny that the state demonstrate a compelling interest in complying with the Voting Rights Act of 1965 and eradicating the effects of past discrimination. North Carolina, the district court noted, had not sent a black representative to Congress between 1901 and 1992. The district court also found that the remedy of creating the odd-shaped district was "narrowly tailored" and therefore acceptable under the strict scrutiny test for the use of race-based categories.

The Supreme Court, however, overturned the district court finding and held that the North Carolina plan violated the Equal Protection Clause. Chief Justice William Rehnquist's opinion found that whatever justification North Carolina might present in theory, in practice the skinny, 160-mile-long district lacked the compactness associated with acceptable districting plans and therefore was not narrowly tailored to achieve the state's goal. The dissenters, led by Justices John Paul Stevens and David Souter, urged the Court to reverse course and back away from applying the strictest constitutional scrutiny to majority-black districts in order that states such as North Carolina might correct past discrimination. At the same time, the decision, along with that in *Bush*, leaves unanswered the recurring question of whether compliance with the Voting Rights Act provides a sufficiently compelling interest for a state to invoke race-conscious redistricting.

Because the facts in the case were more dramatic than in *Bush*, the Court's action in *Hunt* sent a clearer message. Thus, Chief Justice Rehnquist, along with Associate Justices Antonin Scalia, Clarence Thomas, Sandra Day O'Connor, and Anthony M. Kennedy, were willing to strike down government actions that they considered too race-conscious and that relied too heavily on the federal government to right social wrongs.

Kermit L. Hall

Shaw v. Reno, 509 U.S. 630 (1993), argued 20 Apr. 1993, decided 28 June 1993 by vote of 5 to 4; O'Connor for the Court, White, Blackmun, Stevens, and Souter in dissent. Before 1991 the state of North Carolina had never elected a black to sit in the United States Congress. That history ended, however, when Representatives Eva Clayton and Mel Watt, both Democrats, took their seats in Congress following the 1992 election. The new districts from which these two members of Congress came were drawn after the 1990 census to meet federal standards designed to increase the chances of minority candidates. Moreover, the changes wrought by the reapportionment of districts under the guidelines of the 1965 Voting Rights Act and its 1982 amendments doubled the number of black- and Hispanic-majority districts throughout the country, from twenty-six to fifty-two.

Of these news districts, however, none had an odder history and a stranger shape than the twelfth, which Representative Watt served. Except for a few bulges and detours, the Twelfth Congressional District of North Carolina ran along Interstate 85 for about 160 miles, from Durham to Gastonia, and in some instances the district was no wider than the interstate highway that it followed. Initially, North Carolina had tailored only the Twelfth District to comply with Sections 2 and 5 of the Voting Rights Act, but the Department of Justice rejected the proposal and North Carolina responded by creating a second district, although not in the region that the department had recommended. According to the Department of Justice, that second district and the entire effort to realign voting boundaries for federal elections was necessary because the 22 percent African-American population was not sufficiently represented. The Department of Justice, therefore, gave its blessing not only to the two districts but to the oddly shaped (indeed, even its creators called it "ugly") district.

Ruth Shaw, a white Democrat and resident of the Twelfth District, brought suit against the United States government, represented by Attorney General Janet Reno, and the state of North Carolina. Robinson O. Everett, a Duke University law professor and himself one of the five plaintiffs in the case, argued it before both a special three-judge district court panel and the Supreme Court. In the case of the former, the judges dismissed the complaint, citing *United Jewish Organizations of Williams-burgh* v. *Carey* (1977), which held that a state could redistrict along racial lines to comply with the Voting Rights Act. The Court also said that such race distinctions had a good purpose and therefore were permissible under the Equal Protection Clause of the Fourteenth Amendment.

Shaw and her fellow plaintiffs, however, pressed their claim before the Supreme Court, a court already deeply divided over the constitutionality of affirmative action. According to Shaw and the other plaintiffs, the Department of Justice and North Carolina's legislature had purposefully engaged in race-conscious drawing of district lines. Such "racial redistricting" both discriminated against whites and was an implicit affront to blacks because it implied that they were incapable of organizing coalitions to elect favored candidates of whatever race. In essence, the redistricting plan was a form of reverse discrimination that threatened to balkanize North Carolina into competing racial factions and entrench racial bloc voting. Such actions amounted to the kind of conduct that had led to the passage of the Voting Rights Act in the first place and that had characterized the history of discrimination against black would-be voters in the South during the first half of the twentieth century. The plaintiffs asserted that only by doing what the Voting Rights Act demanded—exercising "color-blind" redistricting—would North Carolina and other states take proper account of all constituencies, such as farmers and political partisans, that would otherwise be barred from effective representation by the effort to draw districts exclusively along racial lines. The Democratic plaintiffs were haunted by another political reality, however. By consolidating the black vote, which had historically been Democratic, the Republican party was better able to make inroads in white districts.

The federal government and the state of North Carolina argued that they had done in the Twelfth District exactly what Sections 2 and 5 of the Voting Rights Act required: used race to establish districts with majority black voting blocks where there had historically been voting discrimination. The government also insisted that the plaintiffs bringing the case had never been injured and they had, as a result, no standing to sue. Moreover, the argument continued, even though white voters had now lost one historically white district, they were still represented in Congress in a proportion that exceeded their numbers in the overall population. While it was clear that the Twelfth District was oddly shaped, there was substantial precedent, according to the government, to permit partisan political goals in redistricting to take precedent over other values, such as cohesiveness and compactness, as long as the configurations were not too extreme.

Shaw came before the Court at a time when Americans were increasingly divided over the issue of how to extend fair opportunities to minorities. On the one hand, many liberal groups argued that minorities had to be given special advantages not only to elect their own representatives but to gain access to higher education and the workplace as well. On the other hand, some moderates and all conservatives complained that racial preferences were dubious and amounted, as was evident in the North Carolina redistricting plan, to little more than reverse discrimination.

By the narrowest of margins and amid sharp disagreement the Supreme Court rejected the North Carolina redistricting plan, rebuffed the arguments of the Department of Justice, and overturned the special three-judge district court ruling. Justice Sandra Day O'Connor's majority opinion brushed aside *United Jewish Organizations* and reiterated another line of the Court's precedents, that dealing with districting plans that had historically excluded blacks. "It is unsettling," O'Connor wrote, "how closely the North Carolina plan resembles the most egregious racial gerrymanders of the past" (p. 641). O'Connor found particularly troubling the odd shape of the Twelfth District, whose residents "may have little in common with one another but the color of their skin bears an uncomfortable resemblance to political apartheid" (p. 670).

Justice O'Connor's opinion, however, did not slam the door shut on the use of racial preferences in redistricting. Rather, she and the majority insisted that the standard of "strict scrutiny" would have to apply to any North Carolina or similar redistricting plan that relied on race. The state would have to show a compelling interest that required it treat some of its citizens differently from others based on race. (That standard, as applied by the Court, has seldom been met in practice.) O'Connor concluded as well that in this instance simply meeting the requirements of the Voting Rights Act was not in and of itself a compelling state interest, leaving open the possibility that it might be in the future. Indeed, O'Connor went on to argue that racial classification can only lead to larger social harms, such as the balkanization of racial groups and the politics of racial identification.

The dissenters, headed by Justice Byron R. White on his last day in Court, took exception to the idea that white voters in North Carolina had been harmed by the redistricting plan. The benefit of the Equal Protection Clause of the Fourteenth Amendement belonged on the side of the minority voters, not the majority white voters. How could discrimination exist, White insisted, if the majority white population continued, even after the redistricting, to command 83 percent of the districts while constituting only 76 percent of the state's people?

When the case was remanded to the lower federal court for rehearing, a three-judge panel decided by a vote of 2 to 1 in favor of the redistricting plan. The two-judge majority ruled that the Twelfth District, though deliberately drawn along racial lines, was nonetheless constitutional under the Equal Protection Clause of the Fourteenth Amendment because it helped remedy past discrimination against blacks. Without such actions, the court held, there was little hope that African-Americans would ever be elected to Congress.

On appeal, however, the Supreme Court once again overturned the federal district court's finding. In *Shaw* v. *Hunt* (1996) the Court threw out the two-district plan for North Carolina and forced the state to redraw the Twelfth District, which it found lacked the compactness and cohesiveness necessary for such districts. Sections 2 and 5 of the Voting Rights Act did not, moreover, require North Carolina or any other state to maximize the number of congressional districts with African-American majorities. The decision meant that North Carolina had to redraw its district boundaries before the 1996 congressional elections. Still, a majority of the Court, while making clear that it harbors grave doubts about the constitutional acceptability of racial redistricting, has not answered the question of whether compliance with the Voting Rights Acts by itself establishes a compelling state interest sufficient to permit such redistricting.

Kermit L. Hall

Shelley v. Kraemer, 334 U.S. 1 (1948), argued 15–16 Jan. 1948, decided 3 May 1948 by vote of 6 to 0; Vinson for the Court, Reed, Jackson, and Rutledge not participating. *Shelley* is one of four cases known collectively as the *Restrictive Covenant Cases*, the others being *McGhee* v. *Sipes*, *Hurd* v. *Hodge*, and *Urciolo* v. *Hodge*. In its decision in these cases, the Court held that state judicial enforcement of agreements barring persons from ownership or occupancy of real property on racial grounds is forbidden by the Equal Protection Clause of the Fourteenth Amendment. The Court also determined that enforcement of racial covenants by federal courts violated the Due Process Clause of the Fifth Amendment.

Agreements to impose restrictions of various sorts on the uses of land are a familiar device in real estate law. Racial covenants, however, sought not to bar specific uses of land but, rather, certain classes of persons from its ownership and occupancy. It was not until municipal zoning laws requiring racial segregation in urban residential housing were invalidated by the Court in *Buchanan v. Warley* (1917) that persons promoting housing segregation turned in significant numbers to the use of racial covenants. By the time that *Shelley v. Kraemer* reached the Supreme Court, racial restrictive agreements were being enforced in many northern cities, and the prospects for the spread of the racial covenant system to other parts of the country were very strong.

In reaching its decision the Supreme Court largely ignored the massive collection of social data submitted by the parties attacking the racial covenants. Instead, the Court's opinion focussed on traditional concepts of "state action" in Fourteenth Amendment law. A sharp distinction was drawn between the creation of the restrictive agreements and their enforcement by courts of equity. According to the Court, those entering into the agreements engaged in merely private behavior, activity not regulated or restricted by constitutional provisions. The judicial enforcement of the covenants, however, was seen as constituting official action violative of rights to equal protection of the laws of minority persons excluded from from occupancy of the land by the covenants. Among the factors cited by the Court to support its result were that in enforcing the covenants the courts applied common-law rules of the jurisdiction in question, that equitable powers were applied directly against minority members subjected to discrimination on racial grounds, and that the transactions being invalidated were those between willing sellers and willing buyers, thus frustrating efforts of sellers to ignore racial criteria in the sale of their land.

The opinion of the Court has been frequently criticized. Ordinarily it is not assumed that the state when enforcing private agreements adopts or is accountable for the various and often conflicting purposes of the contracting parties. Rather, the state is seen as simply providing the means through which a system of private contract can be administered. The facts surrounding the covenant cases, however, suggest that in enforcing the racial covenants the states did more than provide neutral enforcement of private contracts, but had, in fact, adopted policies of racial residential segregation in the supposed interests of protecting property values, suppressing crime, and promoting racial purity. Unfortunately, these matters were not fully canvassed in the Court's opinion, nor were adequate indicia

suggested to determine the point at which enforcement of private agreements becomes transmuted into state action to advance public policies.

Shelley v. Kraemer has not exerted great influence in subsequent civil rights cases. In *Barrows v. Jackson* (1953), the *Shelley* holding was expanded to deny the right of a party to a restrictive agreement to recover damages in a suit at law from one who in violation of the agreement sold his property to a black purchaser. In a number of other cases *Shelley v. Kraemer* has been discussed or cited, but it rarely has appeared dispositive of the outcomes (*Moose Lodger v. Irvis*, 1972; *Black v. Cutter Laboratories*, 1956; *Rice v. Sioux City Memorial Park Cemetery*, 1955). One reason for the comparative neglect of *Shelley* may be the enactment of state and federal civil rights legislation in the 1960s, which provided statutory answers to questions that might otherwise have called *Shelley v. Kraemer* into consideration.

Despite its infrequent citation, the decision constitutes an important event in modern constitutional history. By invalidating enforcement of racial covenants, it destroyed one of the most formidible instruments yet devised to effectuate racial discrimination. The decision provided impetus for further efforts in the civil rights struggle. Finally, by raising the problem of housing segregation to a constitutional level it clothed the issues with greater seriousness and moral concern.

□ Francis A. Allen, "Remembering *Shelley v. Kraemer*," *Washington University Law Quarterly* 67 (1989): 709–735.

Francis A. Allen

Sheppard v. Maxwell, 384 U.S. 333 (1966), argued 28 Feb. 1966, decided 6 June 1966 by vote of 8 to 1; Clark for the Court, Black in dissent. The threat of prejudicial publicity to a criminal defendant's constitutional rights is as old as the media itself. Traditionally, the Court had placed few constraints on the press in reporting on criminal trials. However, in the 1960s, during a decade of expanding constitutional rights for defendants in criminal actions, the courts reassessed this problem.

In *Estes v. Texas* (1965), the Court reversed the conviction of a defendant whose trial proceedings had been televised. A plurality of the Court held that the televised proceedings had deprived the accused of his due process rights and that televising of a trial was inherently prejudicial.

In *Sheppard* the Court reversed the conviction of Dr. Sam Sheppard for the murder of his wife. His case attracted extensive media coverage; after his conviction he served several years in prison before seeking habeas corpus relief in the federal courts. The Supreme Court granted the writ and ordered Sheppard released. It held that Sheppard had been deprived of a fair trial because of the "Roman Holiday" atmosphere surrounding the trial and because the judge failed to minimize the prejudicial impact of massive publicity.

In reversing the conviction, the Court gave heightened consideration to Sixth Amendment interests. Noting that prejudicial news comment on pending trials had become prevalent, it warned trial judges that, when faced with a reasonable likelihood that publicity would prevent a fair trial, they should take certain narrowly tailored measures, such as juror sequestration, to diminish the likelihood of prejudice. Despite the potential dangers of prejudicial publicity recognized in *Sheppard*, the Supreme Court has continued to give the press substantial freedom in reporting.

Patrick M. Garry

Shreveport Rate Cases (*Houston, East and West Texas Railway Co. v. United States, Texas and Pacific Railway Co. v. United States*), 234 U.S. 342 (1914), argued 28–29 Oct. 1913, decided 8 June 1914 by vote of 7 to 2; Hughes for the Court, Lurton and Pitney in dissent (without opinion). These cases are among many that reveal the Supreme Court's willingness to accept the revitalization of the Interstate Commerce Commission (ICC) during the Progressive era. Following mandates of the state railroad commission, Texas railroads imposed rates that discriminated against out-of-state shippers who were located the same distance from markets in Texas as shippers within the state. The intrastate rates were set significantly lower than the federal interstate rates. Thus, freight costs from Shreveport, Louisiana, to points in east Texas were much higher than those from Dallas or Houston to the same locations. The ICC found that the lower intrastate rate had an injurious effect on interstate commerce and ordered it superseded by the higher interstate rates. The Texas railroads made an appeal on the grounds that Congress, through the ICC, lacked the power to control intrastate rates of interstate carriers. The Court sustained the ICC order that set intrastate rates of interstate carriers and asserted that such regulation was within the scope of federal commerce power. Recognizing the interconnected nature of local and interstate commerce, the Court held that the lower, intra-Texas rate had a negative impact on interstate commerce.

Richard F. Hamm

Siebold, Ex parte, 100 U.S. 371 (1880), argued 24 Oct. 1879, decided 8 Mar. 1880 by vote of 7 to 2; Bradley for the Court, Field and Clifford in dissent. Siebold, a Baltimore election judge, was convicted under the Enforcement Acts of 1870–1871 of ballot-box stuffing in a federal congressional election. The Enforcement Acts made it a federal crime for a state official to neglect his duties under state or federal law in a federal election.

Petitioning for a writ of habeas corpus, Siebold argued that, while the federal government was competent to make and enforce its own election laws, it could not adopt existing state laws by reference, far less prospectively adopt state laws not yet in existence, and that it could not punish state officials for neglect of a state duty. Justice Joseph P. Bradley and the majority rejected this invocation of dual sovereignty, holding that a violation of a mixed state and national duty was "an offense against the United States, for which the offender is justly amenable to that government" (p. 388). The Court, however, limited its spacious reading of national powers to federal congressional elections and disavowed federal power over purely state and local elections.

Only Justice Stephen J. Field, in his dissenting opinion, accepted Siebold's arguments. Field reasoned that the federal government had no power to impose duties on a state officer.

Ward E. Y. Elliott

Skinner v. Oklahoma, 316 U.S. 535 (1942), argued 6 May 1942, decided 1 June 1942 by vote of 9 to 0; Douglas for the Court, Stone and Jackson concurring. In 1942 most states authorized sterilization of the "feeble-minded" or habitual criminals. Such laws were justified under theories of eugenics, but critics of compulsory sterilization argued that it was not certain that criminality and mental illness were inheritable. Skinner, convicted once for stealing chickens and twice for armed robbery, was ordered to submit to a vasectomy under the Oklahoma Criminal Sterilization Act.

In deciding Skinner's case, the Court recognized the right to have offspring as a fundamental right but did not declare compulsory sterilization laws totally invalid. Instead, Douglas's majority opinion focused upon an exemption in the Oklahoma law for persons convicted of embezzlement or political crimes. Douglas reasoned that, where a basic right is involved, strict scrutiny of such classifications is essential. He saw no rational basis to conclude that the tendency to commit larceny was inheritable, thus exposing repeat offenders to sterilization, while the tendency to embezzle was not. Therefore, the Oklahoma statute violated the requirements of the Equal Protection Clause of the Fourteenth Amendment and was unconstitutional.

Concurring, Chief Justice Harlan F. Stone argued that the statute violated the Due Process Clause because it did not require a hearing specifically on the question of whether Skinner's criminal traits were inheritable. Justice Robert Jackson, also concurring, recognized that there are limits to the extent to which the state may conduct biological experiments at the expense of the dignity of a minority.

Paul Kens

Skinner v. Railway Labor Executives Association, 489 U.S. 602 (1989), argued 2 Nov. 1988, decided 21 Mar. 1989 by vote of 7 to 2; Kennedy for the Court, Stevens concurring in the judgment, Marshall and Brennan in dissent. At issue in this case, decided along with *National Treasury Employees Union* v. *Von Raab* (1989), was the constitutionality of the drug testing of railroad employees. The case began when the Federal Railroad Administration promulgated regulations requiring blood and urine tests of railroad employees involved in certain major train accidents or incidents and permitting breath or urine tests where employees violated certain safety rules. Railroad labor unions challenged the regulations, arguing that they violated the Fourth Amendment's prohibition of unreasonable searches and seizures.

The Supreme Court held that although the covered workers were employed by private companies, the level of government involvement was such, and the program was intrusive enough, to implicate the Fourth Amendment. As to whether the program was unreasonable under the Fourth Amendment, the Court pointed to the surrounding circumstances. Focusing on the loss of life and property in train accidents, the Court held that the government's interest in ensuring safety presented a special need that made the program reasonable. Further, finding that the employees' expectations of privacy were minimal and that there was little discretion involved, and again stressing the safety aspect, the Court held that the usual Fourth Amendment requirements of a warrant, probable cause, and suspicion of individual wrongdoing were unnecessary.

Dissenting, Justices Thurgood Marshall and William J. Brennan warned that the Court had allowed basic constitutional protections to wither because of hysteria over drugs. They found the Court's special needs approach unprincipled and dangerous, with a resulting cavalier disregard for the constitutional text. Yet the majority of the Court in *Veronica School District* v. *Acton* (1995) held that testing student athletes for drug use was reasonable, leaving open the possibility that all of the student body might be subject to such tests.

Gerald N. Rosenberg

Slaughterhouse Cases, 16 Wall. (83 U.S.) 36 (1873), argued 3–5 Feb. 1873, decided 14 Apr. 1873 by vote of 5 to 4; Miller for the Court, Field, Bradley, Chase, and Swayne in dissent. The *Slaughterhouse Cases* consisted of three suits precipitated by a Louisiana law that incorporated the Crescent City Live-Stock Landing and Slaughtering Company and required that all butchering of animals in New Orleans be done in its facilities. The cases provided the first important opportunity for the Supreme Court to interpret the meaning of the Fourteenth Amendment, ratified in 1870. In an opinion that remains controversial but has never been overruled, the majority of the justices severely limited the meaning of the Privileges or Immunities Clause of the first section of the Fourteenth Amendment.

Louisiana passed the law at issue at a time when many state and local governments were enacting health reforms. Regulations to control the slaughtering of animals were enacted in many localities, because it was a business entailing grave health risks to surrounding neighborhoods in an age before modern refrigeration technology and insect control. Centralizing slaughterhouse operations was one means of regulation.

Although it was conceivable that a state itself might build and operate a new central slaughterhouse, it had been a common practice for states to incorporate privately owned businesses to assume the expense of providing needed public facilities in return for a government-regulated monopoly. Financially strapped after the Civil War, Louisiana chose this alternative. However, this decision presented the problem of choosing who would have the privilege of incorporating the new slaughterhouse company and earning the tidy profit likely to accrue. As was usual in nineteenth-century America, the privilege went to a group of wealthy and politically influential individuals, who brought leading politicians into the concern. Naturally, when governments chose this method to provide public services or facilities, they opened themselves to charges of corruption. Dissatisfied citizens perceived such transactions to confer illicit special privileges on the influential few at the expense of the rest of the people.

This was especially the case in Louisiana. That state was governed by Republicans, elected primarily by black voters enfranchised as part of Reconstruction. Most white Louisianans believed that the white leaders of the Louisiana Republican party were "carpetbaggers" and "scalawags," interested solely in plunder. Democrats charged that the slaughterhouse law was another example of Republican corruption, even though both Democrats and Republicans were among the incorporators of the Crescent City Company.

The slaughterhouse laws imposed by the states seriously inconvenienced butchers. Some of them were accustomed to slaughtering animals on their own property. Others, like those in New Orleans, had formed trade associations that operated slaughterhouses. Now they were required to undertake their business at a distance from the city and often at a single center where they were required to pay fees. In many places affected butchers filed lawsuits challenging the constitutionality of the laws. However, few litigants or counsel in the late 1860s and early 1870s perceived the potential of the Fourteenth Amendment to protect the ordinary rights of white citizens; it had been discussed almost entirely in terms of the slavery controversy. Therefore the butchers brought their suits in state courts, alleging violation of state constitutions. Everywhere they lost, with state courts holding the

laws to be legitimate exercises of the police power—the power to make laws to promote the health, safety, and morals of the community.

However, the Louisiana butchers were blessed with outstanding counsel, among them John A. Campbell, former associate justice of the Supreme Court, who had resigned when his state seceded from the Union. Campbell filed a petition in the local state court for an injunction on behalf of the Butchers' Benevolent Association, which operated a slaughterhouse for its members. He asked the court to bar the Crescent City Company from interfering with the association's slaughterhouse business or that of its members. Although Campbell presented arguments similar to those made by butchers in other states, he added the novel claim that the law contravened the Fourteenth Amendment. The new amendment forbade states from enforcing "any law which shall abridge the privileges or immunities of citizens of the United States," among which, Campbell argued, was the right to labor freely in an honest avocation.

The issue was taken to the Louisiana Supreme Court in 1870. The butchers' lawyers argued that the law went beyond the inherent powers of legislation and violated both the state constitution and the Fourteenth Amendment, because it deprived them of property rights, not for the good of the community, but for the private gain of monopolists. With only one dissent, the judges rejected the butchers' contention that the law worked such a redistribution of property rights.

The butchers appealed to the Supreme Court, based on their Fourteenth Amendment argument. But in the meantime the Crescent City Company secured state court injunctions against the operation of the association slaughterhouse. Campbell petitioned the United States circuit court to issue an injunction forbidding any interference with butchers' activities until the Supreme Court announced its decision. Supreme Court Justice Joseph P. Bradley, sitting on circuit, seized the opportunity to offer his view of the Fourteenth Amendment.

Convinced by the legal and business leaders of New Orleans that the law was designed to enrich the incorporators of the Crescent City Company, he ruled that the law was not a legitimate exercise of the police power in *Live-Stock Dealers and Butchers' Association* v. *Crescent City Live-Stock*

Landing and Slaughter-House Company (1870). In reality the law was designed to confer "a monopoly of a very odious character" (p. 653). Such a law violated the Fourteenth Amendment. Although the framers of the amendment may not have understood the far-reaching character of the amendment, it nonetheless worked a revolutionary change in the federal system, giving the national government the power to intervene to prevent such deprivations of basic rights. Among the privileges and immunities of citizens of the United States was a right to labor, which the Louisiana slaughterhouse law invaded.

Bradley's opinion was important for its articulation of the Fourteenth Amendment rather than for its practical effect. Federal law forbade United States courts from enjoining the action of state courts. Therefore he could only enjoin the Crescent City Company and state officials from bringing new legal actions against the butchers and their association. The state courts enforced the injunctions the company had already obtained.

When the *Slaughterhouse Cases* reached the Supreme Court in 1873, the justices faced a major dilemma. The Republican party, sustained by the people of the North, had framed the Thirteenth, Fourteenth, and Fifteenth Amendments in a political struggle that turned primarily upon the future place of African-Americans in American society. By ratifying the amendments and sustaining the Republican party, the people had indicated that black Americans should be entitled to the same civil and political rights as white Americans. Moreover, the rhetoric of the debates suggested a vague but general belief that all Americans, white and black, had certain fundamental rights that had been violated in the interest of slavery and that should henceforth be secured against infringement. Yet at the same time Republicans were committed to maintaining the essentials of the federal system. The primary responsibility for governing relationships among Americans and for protecting their rights from infringement by others would remain with the states, they had insisted.

Republicans tried to reconcile the two commitments by framing laws and constitutional amendments that authorized the national government to intervene when the states themselves infringed rights or failed to protect them. Furthermore, those laws and amendments carefully avoided making black Americans the special object of protection. They guaranteed the rights of all Americans equally. But in fact Republicans had not solved the problem, and the *Slaughterhouse Cases* made the failure clear. It was not an infringement of black people's civil rights or white unionists' freedom of speech that was at issue, but a health regulation not dissimilar from many passed around the nation. If the Supreme Court agreed that the Fourteenth Amendment authorized it to review such legislation, it could expect similar appeals whenever any person believed a police regulation denied basic rights. Moreover, the Court would in effect be recognizing Congress's power to intervene as well, because the fifth section of the Fourteenth Amendment authorized it to pass legislation appropriate for enforcing the other sections. Yet if the Court declined to review such appeals, how could it avoid undermining the guarantees the Fourteenth Amendment was designed to secure?

The court divided dramatically on the issue. A bare majority ruled that the Privileges or Immunities Clause did not protect such fundamental rights as the right to labor, while four justices trenchantly dissented. Justice Samuel F. Miller delivered the majority opinion. He concluded that "the one pervading purpose" behind the Civil War Amendments was to secure the freedom of black Americans, not to expand or add protections for the rights of whites (p. 71).

In interpreting the Privileges or Immunities Clause, Miller stressed that it barred states from abridging only the "privileges or immunities of citizens of the United States." Even after the Civil War most Americans continued to make a rigid distinction between those areas where the states had jurisdiction and those areas within the jurisdiction of the national government. Miller turned to this distinction to limit the scope of the Fourteenth Amendment. The term "privileges or immunities of citizens of the United States" was meant to differentiate between those rights associated with state citizenship and those associated with United States citizenship, he insisted. The Fourteenth Amendment forbade states only from abridging the latter.

Since the foundation of the Union the states had been conceded to have final authority over such basic rights as the right to labor, Miller said. With that right, the Fourteenth Amendment had nothing to do. To hold otherwise, Miller explained, would make "this court a perpetual censor upon all legislation of the states, on the civil rights of their own citizens," authorized to nullify any law it believed violated those rights (p. 78). Moreover, Congress would have the same right to intervene. With some justification, Miller argued that the American people had no such understanding of the amendment when they discussed and ratified it.

The four dissenting justices wrote three different opinions, although they all joined in that prepared by Justice Stephen J. Field. They denied that the Fourteenth Amendment was designed to secure the rights of black Americans alone. They insisted that the right to labor was among the privileges and immunities of citizens of the United States. Justices Bradley and Noah Swayne also insisted that Louisiana's regulation deprived the butchers of property without due process of law, another of the Fourteenth Amendment's prohibitions.

The *Slaughterhouse Cases* are generally assessed within the context of Reconstruction and the efforts to secure national protection for citizens' rights. They have been heavily criticized by scholars, who argue that Miller artificially narrowed the scope of the Privileges or Immunities Clause. Not only did he impose a distinction between the rights of state and national citizenship that had not been in the minds of the framers, but the language of the opinion implied that the rights of national citizenship were few. Some scholars and twentieth-century Supreme Court justices have argued that the privileges and immunities of the citizens of the United States included at least those listed in the Bill of Rights.

Critics complain that the *Slaughterhouse* decision severely undermined the ability of the government to protect the rights of freedmen. There is ample evidence indicating that the decisions did in fact have that effect. Those who opposed national action to protect the rights of African-American citizens in the 1870s pointed to it to justify their position.

On the other hand, the cases did not involve the rights of black Louisianians. The points at issue were more similar to property rights cases of later years than to the noneconomic civil liberty cases of Reconstruction. From that perspective Miller's opinion may be seen as an articulation of judicial restraint in economic cases rather than an abdication of responsibility to protect human rights. Ultimately the Supreme

Court did overturn state regulations affecting the rights Miller placed within state jurisdiction, by holding them among the liberties and property rights that states could not infringe "without due process of law." Many scholars have perceived a direct line of descent between these decisions and the *Slaughterhouse* dissents.

□ Michael Les Benedict, "Preserving Federalism: Reconstruction and the Waite Court," *Supreme Court Review* 1978: 39–79. Loren Beth, "The Slaughter-House Cases—Revisited," *Louisiana Law Review* 23 (April 1963): 587–605. Charles Fairman, *History of the Supreme Court*, vol. 6, *Reconstruction and Reunion, 1864–1888, Part One* (1971). Robert Kaczorowski, *The Politics of Judicial Interpretation: The Federal Courts, Department of Justice and Civil Rights, 1866–1876* (1985).

Michael Les Benedict

Slochower v. Board of Education of New York City, 350 U.S. 551 (1956), argued 18–19 Oct. 1955, decided 9 Apr. 1956, by vote of 5 to 4; Clark for the Court, Reed, Burton, Minton, and Harlan in dissent. At a hearing of a congressional committee investigating subversion in education, a tenured faculty member at Brooklyn College stated that he was not a communist, that he was willing to testify about his associations since 1941, but claimed the self-incrimination privilege about inquires concerning activities in 1940–1941. The New York City Charter provided that if an employee of the city used the privilege against self-incrimination to avoid answering a question relating to his official conduct, his tenure of employment would terminate. Acting under this provision, the Board of Education discharged Slochower without affording him the usual hearing for tenured faculty members.

The Supreme Court held the provision of the charter was unconstitutional, and that the summary dismissal violated the Due Process Clause. The provision of the charter, as applied in the case, had converted the constitutional privilege into a conclusive presumption of guilt; there was no inquiry into the faculty member's fitness; his dismissal was based solely on events occurring before a congressional committee. The Court held that the action of the Board of Education fell squarely within the prohibition of *Wieman* v. *Updegraff* (1952). The dissenters contended that a state may justifiably conclude that teachers who refuse to answer questions concerning their official conduct are no longer qualified to teach. The case has been limited by *Lerner* v. *Casey* (1958) and *Nelson* v. *County of Los Angeles* (1960), which in turn may have been limited by *Gardner* v. *Broderick* (1968).

Milton R. Konvitz

Smith v. Allwright, 321 U.S. 649 (1944), argued 10 and 12 Nov. 1943, reargued 12 Jan. 1944, decided 3 Apr. 1944 by vote of 8 to 1; Reed for the Court, Roberts in dissent. The history of the "white primary" was a game of constitutional chess waged against blacks and the Supreme Court by whites and the Texas legislature. After Reconstruction, a Democratic primary victory assured success in the general election in Texas and throughout the one-party South. Therefore, exclusion of African-Americans from primary participation had the practical effect of disfranchisement.

Initially, in *Newberry* v. *United States* (1921), the Court concluded that party primary elections were unknown to the framers and therefore were beyond the reach of the Constitution. Two years later, the Texas legislature enacted a statute expressly barring African-Americans from voting in a Democratic primary. The Court in **Nixon* v. *Herndon* (1927) held this measure invalid under the Fourteenth Amendment. The Texas legislature then enacted another statute that authorized the state party executive committee to determine membership qualifications, including race, and again the Court held the statute invalid in **Nixon* v. *Condon* (1932) Next the Texas legislature repealed all state primary election statutes, anticipating that the Democratic state convention would exclude African-Americans, which the Court upheld, in **Grovey* v. *Townsend* (1935), as "private" discrimination beyond the Constitution.

African-American voters were checked until the NAACP saw an opening in *United States* v. **Classic* (1941), which held that Congress could regulate primary as well as general elections for federal office. The NAACP sponsored Smith, who brought suit against Texas Democratic party election officials in a direct challenge on the *Grovey* holding, alleging that he had been unconstitutionally denied a primary ballot because of his race.

Justice Stanley Reed applied the *Classic* reasoning to overrule *Grovey,* and the white primary was checkmated. Since the primary system was an integral part of the state's election procedures, citizens had the right under the Fifteenth Amendment to vote in party primaries free of racial discrimination. The discrimination was not merely "private." First, since state law authorized primary elections and regulated the party's procedures, the party in convention acted as an agent of the state in excluding African-Americans. Second, conducting elections was a state function; therefore, the state was responsible for allowing the private racial discrimination.

Justice Owen J. Roberts, who had written for a unanimous Court only nine years before in *Grovey,* dissented on the grounds that the overruling promoted disrespect for the Court and instability in the law. Justice Reed replied that the Court's decision only required correcting a misapplication of settled principles. Neither opinion noted that seven of the justices had been appointed by President Franklin D. Roosevelt in that interim.

Constitutional scholars cite *Allwright* as one of the seminal cases in the development of the "public function" concept. Certain activities traditionally performed by the government—such as elections—are deemed to be state action under the Constitution even when performed by private actors. This doctrine was extended in **Terry* v. *Adams* (1953) in which the Court invalidated an unofficial primary held by a private, all-white "club" despite the lack of state regulation of the club.

After *Allwright,* the available methods for reducing African-American participation in elections were limited to those directed at individuals rather than groups, such as literacy tests and poll taxes. These methods proved less effective with time. The federal legislative response came in the Civil Rights Acts of 1957, 1960, and 1964, followed by the Twenty-Fourth Amendment, which banned poll taxes in federal elections, and especially in the Voting Rights Act of 1965 with subsequent amendments.

The broader significance of this decision lies in the Court's focus on substance over form in determining voting rights. This approach became the conceptual foundation for later landmark civil rights cases involving such matters as racially restrictive covenants, school segregation, and political reapportionment.

□ Ward E. Y. Elliot, *The Rise of Guardian Democracy—The Supreme Court's Role in Voting*

Rights Disputes, 1845–1969 (1974). Darlene Clark Hine, Black Victory—The Rise and Fall of the White Primary in Texas (1979).

Thomas E. Baker

Smyth v. Ames, 169 U.S. 466, argued 5–7 Apr. 1897, decided 7 Mar. 1898 by vote of 9 to 0; Harlan for the Court. In *Smyth v. Ames,* the Supreme Court voided a schedule of railroad tariffs enacted by Nebraska and defined the constitutional limits of governmental power to set railroad and utility rates. The Court held that regulated industries were constitutionally entitled to earn a "fair return" on the "fair value" of the enterprise. Under the fair value rule a governmental authority was required to determine a "rate base," which was the present value of the enterprise's assets, and to allow the enterprise to charge rates sufficient to earn a normal return on that value.

Smyth v. Ames was emblematic of the Court's protection of the free market economy in the late nineteenth century. Over time, the decision was criticized by jurists who objected to laissez-faire constitutionalism. Critics claimed that the fair value rule was impractical because of the complex administrative proceedings required to determine the current value of utility assets as the rate base. *Smyth's* critics also claimed that the case was illogical because a utility's value is determined by its rates. Rates could not be set according to an enterprise's value since that value cannot be known until the rates are determined.

Despite these criticisms, the conservative Court steadfastly adhered to *Smyth v. Ames,* which set the constitutional limits of rate regulation until it was overruled in *Federal Power Commission v. Hope Natural Gas Co.* (1944).

Stephen A. Siegel

South Carolina v. Katzenbach, 383 U.S. 301 (1966), argued 17–18 Jan. 1966, decided 17 Mar. 1966 by vote of 8 to 1; Warren for the Court, Black dissenting in part. This case, which sustained the constitutionality of the Voting Rights Act of 1965, is a milestone in the development of congressional power to enforce the Civil War Amendments. It established Congress's power to proscribe a class of suspect practices without finding that in every instance the practices would be held by the judiciary to be unconstitutional. In sustaining the 1965 act, *South Carolina v. Katzenbach* contributed to the enfranchisement of millions of nonwhite Americans.

In the Voting Rights Act, Congress relied on its powers under section 2 of the Fifteenth Amendment, which authorizes it by appropriate measures to enforce the amendment's prohibition on racial discrimination in voting. The act prescribed a formula defining the state and political subdivisions to which its novel remedies applied. The remedies applied to a state that maintained a "test or device" as a prerequisite to voting, *and* that had low voter registration or voting rates in the 1964 presidential election. South Carolina was covered by the act and thus was temporarily barred from enforcing a literacy test and a property ownership requirement. New voting requirements could be imposed only if submitted to the attorney general and not disapproved by him. Coverage by the act also authorized federal appointment of voting examiners to place on the state and local voting rolls voters who might otherwise not be listed because of their race.

In an original jurisdiction suit, South Carolina challenged the act's coverage formula, the suspension of voting requirements, the requirement of federal review of new voting requirements, and the authorization of appointment of federal voting examiners. It also asserted that Congress's section 2 power authorized nothing more than legislation forbidding violations of the Fifteenth Amendment in general terms, with remedies necessarily left entirely to the courts. Chief Justice Earl Warren's opinion rejected all these challenges. His opinion addressed both the general power of Congress to enforce the Fifteenth Amendment and each of the challenged provisions.

With respect to the general scope of Congress's section 2 power, the Court relied on the classic statement of congressional legislative power in **McCulloch v. Maryland* (1819). Legitimate ends not banned by the Constitution may be pursued through all appropriate means. Congress's findings that case-by-case litigation proved ineffective in dealing with widespread discriminatory voting practices warranted a sweeping measure not dependent for application on findings of specific discrimination. As Warren wrote, "Congress might well decide to shift the inertia from the perpetrators of the evil to its victims" (p. 328). The Voting Rights Act's selective geographic coverage was permissible because voting discrimination, Congress found, occurred primarily in certain areas of the country. Congress could limit its attention to the most troublesome geographic areas.

In attacking the suspension of existing voting requirements, South Carolina relied on the statement in *Lassiter* v. *Northampton County Board of Elections* (1959) that literacy tests and related devices themselves violate the Fifteenth Amendment. The Court distinguished *Lassiter* on the ground that the Voting Rights Act addressed discriminatory use of tests, a use *Lassiter* itself questioned.

The Court acknowledged that suspension of new voting regulations pending review by federal authorities was an uncommon exercise of congressional power. But Congress knew of past elaborate strategies employed by states to perpetuate voting discrimination despite federal court decrees prohibiting such practices. Congress reasonably feared similar maneuvers in response to the 1965 act and was thus authorized to attack the problem in a decisive manner. The use of federal voting examiners to list qualified voters appropriately countered procedural tactics used to deny African-Americans the franchise.

South Carolina v. *Katzenbach* served as an important precedent in **Katzenbach* v. *Morgan* (1966). The breadth of legislative discretion granted Congress in enforcing the Fifteenth Amendment paved the way for similar treatment of Congress's power under the Fourteenth Amendment. In *Morgan*, the Court rejected New York's argument that Congress may abrogate state laws only if they conflict with the Fourteenth Amendment. These cases, along with **Jones* v. *Alfred H. Mayer Co.* (1968), contributed to a major revitalization of Congress's power to enforce the Civil War Amendments against racial discrimination.

□ Ward E. Y. Elliott, *The Supreme Court's Role in Voting Rights Disputes* (1974).

Theodore Eisenberg

South Dakota v. Dole, 483 U.S. 203 (1987), argued 28 Apr. 1987, decided 23 June 1987 by vote of 7 to 2; Rehnquist for the Court, Brennan and O'Connor in dissent. In this case the Supreme Court upheld congressional legislation that required states to raise their legal drinking age to twenty-one as a condition of receiving their full allotment of federal highway funds. The Court rejected South Dakota's arguments that such a requirement violated congressional power under the spending clause and also under the

Twenty-first Amendment, which repealed prohibition and gave to the states authority over alcoholic beverages.

Congressional restrictions on grants to the states are constitutional, the Supreme Court held, if they meet four requirements. First, the spending must be in the "general Welfare," although "courts should defer substantially to the judgment of Congress" in this regard (p. 207). Second, Congress's conditions on a state's receipt of funds must be "unambiguous." Third, conditions on federal grants must not be unrelated to "the federal interest in particular national projects or programs." Finally, the conditions placed on a grant must not run afoul of "other constitutional provisions . . . [that] provide an independent bar" to Congress's restrictions (p. 207). The last condition, the Court explained, means only that Congress cannot use a conditional grant to induce states to engage in unconstitutional activities.

The Court held that all four conditions had been met. Only the last produced even a serious argument from the Court. O'Connor, in dissent, suggested that Congress's interest in setting a minimum drinking age of twenty-one was insufficiently related to its interest in highway construction under the third part of the test.

William Lasser

South-Eastern Underwriters Association, United States v., 322 U.S. 533 (1944), argued 11 Jan. 1944, decided 5 June 1944 by vote of 4 to 3; Black for the Court, Stone and Frankfurter in dissent, Jackson dissenting in part, Roberts and Reed not participating. Ever since **Paul* v. *Virginia* (1869), the issuance of insurance policies had not been considered a transaction of commerce, and the Court had consistently ruled that, since insurance did not constitute interstate commerce, states could regulate even out-of-state insurance companies doing business within their borders.

Then the Justice Department filed a suit against the South-Eastern Underwriters Association, charging it with collusive price-fixing of premiums for fire insurance in violation of the Sherman Antitrust Act. Despite the long string of cases holding to the contrary, a plurality of the Court agreed that fire insurance companies that conducted substantial parts of their business across state lines were engaged in interstate commerce. Justice Hugo Black explained away previous court decisions on the grounds that all of them had involved state laws; this was the first instance in which a federal law had been applied to insurance, and "Congress wanted to go to the utmost extent of its Constitutional power in restraining trust and monopoly agreements" (p. 558).

Congress immediately responded by passing the McCarran Act of 1945, which explicitly declared that the continued regulation and taxation of insurance companies should remain under state jurisdiction and that no act of Congress, unless specifically addressed to the insurance business, should be interpreted as superseding the states' authority over insurance.

Melvin I. Urofsky

Spallone v. United States, 493 U.S. 265 (1990), argued 2 Oct. 1989, decided 10 Jan. 1990 by vote of 5 to 4; Rehnquist for the Court, Brennan in dissent. After finding that the City of Yonkers, New York, deliberately concentrated public housing in minority neighborhoods, effectively funneling minorities into one quarter, a federal district court ordered that future public housing be dispersed. After losing on appeal, the city accepted a consent decree that included the necessary ordinance, but the defiant city council reneged and failed to enact the ordinance. The district court held the city and the recalcitrant councilmembers in contempt and imposed escalating daily fines. After months of political posturing, the council finally passed the ordinance when the city's daily fines reached nearly one million dollars.

By a 5-to-4 vote, the Court, speaking through Chief Justice William H. Rehnquist, held that the district court abused its discretion under traditional equitable principles by fining the individual councilmembers without first allowing a reasonable time for sanctions against the city alone to obtain compliance. In dissent, Justice William J. Brennan would have deferred to the discretion of the district judge, who was more familiar with local political realities.

Two important issues went undecided: whether the order against the councilmembers violated their freedom of speech to vote in a particular manner and whether they were protected against sanctions by the absolute legislative immunity that applies to state legislators.

Thomas E. Baker

Springer v. United States, 102 U.S. 586 (1881), argued 8–9 Apr. 1880, decided 24 Jan. 1881 by vote of 7 to 0; Swayne for the Court, Hunt and Clifford not participating. At issue in *Springer* was the constitutionality of the 1862 income tax, enacted to help finance the Civil War. William M. Springer refused to pay the income tax on his professional earnings as an attorney. The federal government taxed land belonging to Springer, and the property was eventually sold to the United States for the amount of the unpaid tax. The government brought an action of ejectment against Springer, who argued that the income tax was an invalid direct tax not apportioned among the states according to population as prescribed by the Constitution.

Relying on historical evidence, Justice Noah H. Swayne determined that Congress had only treated taxes on real property and slaves as direct taxes. He accorded great weight to this "uniform practical construction of the Constitution" by Congress (p. 599). Swayne also emphasized the Supreme Court's decision in *Hylton* v. *United States* (1796), upholding a tax on carriages. He concluded that direct taxes included only capitation taxes and taxes on land, and hence the income tax was constitutional. The Civil War income tax remained in force until 1872.

The *Springer* decision was narrowly construed and distinguished by the Court in *Pollock* v. *Farmers' Loan & Trust Co.* (1895), in which the justices invalidated the 1894 income tax as a direct tax not apportioned among the states. The authority of Congress to levy an income tax was not settled until the adoption of the Sixteenth Amendment in 1913.

James W. Ely, Jr.

Standard Oil v. United States, 221 U.S. 1 (1911), argued 14–16 Mar. 1910, reargued 12–17 Jan. 1911, decided 15 May 1911 by vote of 9 to 0; White for the Court, Harlan concurring. The *Standard Oil* case was decided at a time when the Sherman Antitrust Act was being increasingly challenged by big business. The Supreme Court remained divided over the appropriate approach to construing the statute; Congress repeatedly considered (and sometimes enacted) amendments; executive enforcement alternated between trust-busting and regulation.

Responding to a lower court's decree dissolving it under the Sherman Act, Standard Oil appealed to the Supreme Court. Chief Justice Edward D. White resorted to common law and statutory construction to define "restraints of trade" and "monopoly." Emphasizing Congress's intent to protect the right to contract and freedom of commerce, White concluded that the law covered only "unreasonable" restraints of trade and that a common-law standard of reasonableness should be used to identify the actions that the act prohibited. Justice John Marshall Harlan concurred, but he denounced the new "rule of reason" as judicial legislation, imposing on the statute a construction rejected by Congress.

The Court upheld the order to dissolve the Oil Trust, but though its decision was popular, the Court was criticized by progressives for emasculating the law and by business leaders for generating new uncertainties for businesses. The debate over antitrust policy continued through the presidential campaign of 1912, leading to the Clayton Antitrust Act and the Federal Trade Commission Act. The rule of reason, however, remained the judicial standard for interpreting antitrust statutes, allowing considerable flexibility in later cases.

Barbara C. Steidle

Stanford v. Kentucky, 492 U.S. 361 (1989), argued 27 Mar. 1989, decided 26 June 1989 by vote of 5 to 4; Scalia for the Court, joined in whole by Rehnquist, White, and Kennedy and in part by O'Connor, who concurred in the judgment and concurred in part in the opinion; Brennan, Marshall, Blackmun, and Stevens in dissent. *Stanford* rejected the contention that the Eighth Amendment's prohibition of cruel and unusual punishments forbids the execution of those who were juveniles when they committed the crimes for which they were convicted. The Court held that such a practice was not one of "those modes of punishment that had been considered cruel and unusual at the time that the Bill of Rights was adopted" (p. 361) and that it did not violate the "evolving standards of decency that mark the progress of a maturing society" (p. 369). By implication, however, the Court seemed to indicate that it would be unconstitutional for the state to impose the death penalty on a person who was under sixteen at the time of his or her offense.

The Court rejected the first prong of the two-part test outright, since the common law at the time of the Bill of Rights set the minimum age for the application of capital punishment in theory at seven and in practice at fourteen. The Court found that

at least 281 offenders under the age of eighteen, including at least 126 under the age of seventeen, had been executed in the United States.

The Court's rejection of the second argument—that evolving standards of decency were violated—was more involved. Considering the laws of the several states, both as enacted and as applied, Justice Antonin Scalia found that a majority of states allow capital punishment for those above the age of sixteen and rejected as irrelevant the defendants' contention that prosecutors rarely seek and juries rarely apply the death penalty to juveniles.

In dissent, Justice William J. Brennan argued that the evidence from the laws and practices of the states, properly interpreted, suggests that the imposition of the death penalty on juveniles violates "contemporary standards of decency" (p. 388).

William Lasser

Stanley, United States v. See CIVIL RIGHTS CASES.

Stanley v. Georgia, 394 U.S. 557 (1969), argued 14–15 Jan. 1969, decided 7 Apr. 1969 by vote of 9 to 0; Marshall for the Court. From 1957, when the Supreme Court decided *Roth* v. *United States*, to 1973, when it decided *Paris Adult Theatre I* v. *Slaton* and *Miller* v. *California*, obscenity doctrine was in disarray. Different pluralities of the Court used different definitions and employed widely divergent views about the permissibility and scope of obscenity law in light of First Amendment limitations. In *Stanley* v. *Georgia*, the Court decided that the purely private possession in the home of even legally obscene material could not be punished. Justice Thurgood Marshall's opinion is unclear about the basis for this conclusion, subject under one interpretation as being based primarily on Fourth Amendment restrictions on search and seizure, under another as based on freedom of speech and the press, and under still another as based on a more broadly premised right of privacy that makes it impermissible for the state to restrict conduct affecting no one except the actor.

In part because of this uncertainty, question remains about the vitality of *Stanley* as good law. Insofar as it is based on a right of privacy, its holding has been undercut by subsequent decisions, particularly *Bowers* v. *Hardwick* (1986), which allowed state regulation of private sexual conduct. Insofar as the decision is about the limits of obscenity law, there is some question whether the 1973 decisions in *Miller* and *Paris* have rendered it obsolete. In any event the Court is clearly disinclined to extend its implications. In *Obsborne* v. *Ohio* (1990) Justice Byron White for the Court held *Stanley* inapplicable to private possession of child pornography and warned that "*Stanley* should not be read too broadly."

Frederick Schauer

Stanton v. Stanton, 421 U.S. 7 (1975), argued 19 Feb. 1975, decided 15 Apr. 1975 by vote of 8 to 1; Blackmun for the Court, Rehnquist in dissent. *Stanton* was one of several sex discrimination cases decided in the period between *Reed* v. *Reed* (1971) and *Craig* v. *Boren* (1976) in which the Court majority purported to be applying a rational basis test but declared void a statute that legislators and other judges had nonetheless found rational. The statute here declared unconstitutional, as a violation of the Fourteenth Amendment's Equal Protection Clause, had mandated a twenty-one-year age of majority for males and an eighteen-year age of majority for females.

Thelma Stanton, ex-wife of James Stanton, had brought suit when he ceased child support payments for their daughter Sherri upon the latter's eighteenth birthday. The Supreme Court of Utah had rejected her claim on the grounds that the statute had a reasonable basis: girls tend to mature physically, mentally, and emotionally before boys, and also, since men must provide for their families, they need time to acquire an education for that responsibility.

Justice Harry Blackmun, for the Court, denied that the statute was rational. He insisted that coeducation is a fact and that women are increasingly present in business and the professions. He said that the court failed to perceive the "unquestioned truth" of females' tendency to earlier maturity or its relevance to the need for child support (p. 15).

Justice William Rehnquist's dissent argued that Thelma Stanton's claim arose out of a voluntary property settlement at divorce, which could have specified any age whatever to terminate support payments, and therefore the issue of the constitutionality of the age of majority law was not properly before the Court.

Leslie Friedman Goldstein

Steel Seizure Case. See YOUNGSTOWN SHEET & TUBE CO. V. SAWYER.

Steward Machine Co. v. Davis, 301 U.S. 548 (1937), argued 8–9 Apr. 1937, decided 24 May 1937 by vote of 5 to 4; Cardozo for the Court, Butler, McReynolds, Sutherland, and Van Devanter in dissent. One of the centerpieces of the New Deal was the Social Security Act of 1935.

Among other things, this law established mechanism to provide for unemployment compensation and old age benefits.

In *Steward Machine Company* v. *Davis* the unemployment compensation feature of the law was upheld 5 to 4, and in the companion case of *Helvering* v. *Davis* the old age benefits provisions were sustained by a more comfortable 7-to-2 majority. Justice Benjamin Cardozo wrote both opinions.

In *Steward*, the Court held that the payroll tax on employers that generated the revenue to fund Social Security's unemployment compensation was constitutionally permissible under Article I, section 8, which grants Congress the power "to lay and collect taxes. . . to . . . provide . . . for the General Welfare of the United States." In contrast to the majority opinion in *United States* v. *Butler* (1936)—decided prior to Justice Owen Roberts's switch to the liberal side—Cardozo and the Court's majority in *Steward* refused to read the Tenth Amendment as a restriction on Congress's taxing and spending power.

John W. Johnson

Stone v. Mississippi, 101 U.S. 814 (1880), argued 4–5 Mar. 1880, decided 10 May 1880 by vote of 8 to 0; Waite for the Court; Hunt not participating. Chief Justice John Marshall and the early Supreme Court brought both public and private contracts within the scope of the Contract Clause. The dilemma posed by the undifferentiated inclusion of all contracts, public or private, within the clause came before the Court in *Stone*. In 1867, the provisional, post-Civil War government of Mississippi had granted to a corporation, with which John B. Stone was associated, a twenty-five year charter to conduct a lottery. The following year, the state adopted a new Constitution that prospectively and retrospectively prohibited all lottery activity. Stone ignored the new state constitutional provision and the state attorney general obtained an order precluding the lottery, which the Mississippi Supreme Court upheld.

Affirming the judgment, the U.S. Supreme Court stated that it was "too late" to contend that public contracts were not within the prohibition of contractual impairments (p. 816). Instead, the Court held that the state legislature could not bargain away by contract the inalienable police power. Admitting difficulty defining the extent of this reservation the Court concluded that the police power included the prohibition of a lottery that presented a grave injury to public morals. The Court further ruled that persons who ran lotteries pursuant to a state charter had merely a license or privilege, not a contract. Thus, the effect of *Stone* was a narrowing, but not an abandonment, of the application of the clause to public contracts.

Douglas Kmiec

Stone v. Powell, 428 U.S. 465 (1976), argued 24 Feb. 1976, decided 6 July 1976 by vote of 6 to 3; Powell for the Court, Burger concurring, Brennan, joined by Marshall and White in dissent. By an act of Congress (Title 28, sec. 2254 of the U.S. Code), state prisoners may petition a federal court for a writ of habeas corpus and challenge the constitutionality of their state convictions. Generally, a party may not relitigate a matter already presented to or decided by a court. In *Brown* v. *Allen* (1953), however, the Court had held that under section 2254 a state prisoner was entitled to a federal court hearing on all federal constitutional issues.

Writing for the majority in *Stone* v. *Powell*, Justice Lewis Powell reevaluated this interpretation of the statute and held that Fourth Amendment claims once raised and decided in state court could not be heard again in the federal habeas corpus proceeding when the state had provided an opportunity for a full and fair hearing. Applying a cost/benefit analysis, Powell argued that the marginal additional deterrence against police misconduct was insufficient to justify excluding evidence and allowing a guilty defendant to go free. This would only undermine respect for the criminal justice system. Concerns for finality and federalism buttressed his conclusion.

The dissenters disagreed. Habeas corpus, they maintained, protects rights of all persons, including the guilty. Lifetime-tenured federal judges are better situated than state judges to vindicate constitutional rights. Finally, separation of powers considerations weighed against reinterpreting the longstanding statutory language.

While habeas corpus remains an important constitutional provision for those convicted of a crime, the Supreme Court under the leadership of Chief Justice William H. Rehnquist has significantly narrowed access to it in areas beyond the Fourth Amendment. For example, in *Herrera* v. *Collins* (1993) the justices found that a belated claim of innocence, made through a petition for a writ of habeas corpus, does not ordinarily entitle a death-row inmate to a new federal court hearing before being executed. In its push, therefore, to bring finality to the process of administering the death penalty, a majority of the Court has adopted a view similar to what it has taken in Fourth Amendment cases such as *Stone*.

Thomas E. Baker

Strauder v. West Virginia, 100 U.S. 303 (1880), argued 21 Oct. 1879, decided 1 Mar. 1880 by vote of 7 to 2; Strong for the Court, Clifford and Field in dissent. *Strauder* was one of four cases decided in 1880 involving exclusion of African-Americans from jury service that provided guidelines enabling the southern states to evade the Fourteenth Amendment's equal-protection mandate in jury selection. *Strauder* was the easiest of the four to resolve, because it involved a state statute that expressly limited jury service to "all white male persons." The Court had no difficulty in finding that this violated the equal protection clause. In *Ex parte Virginia* and *Neal* v. *Delaware*, the Court held that deliberate exclusion in practice, even if not mandated by express constitutional or statutory provision, also violated the Fourteenth Amendment, thus anticipating its scrutiny of nonfacial discrimination in *Yick Wo* v. *Hopkins* six years later. However, the Court negated any advantages these cases might have held out to African-Americans by holding in *Virginia* v. *Rives* (1880) that their mere absence from juries, no matter how complete, systematic, or obvious, was not in itself a violation of the Fourteenth Amendment. Southern officials took advantage of this concession to create exclusionary systems that did not run afoul of *Strauder's* ban on facial discrimination. In modern times, the Court has held the right of access to jury service a function of the Sixth Amendment's guarantee of civil juries (*Taylor* v. *Louisiana*, 1975), but the *Strauder* rule remains good law.

William M. Wiecek

Strawbridge v. Curtiss, 3 Cranch (7 U.S.) 267 (1806), argued 12 Feb. 1806, decided 13 Feb. 1806 by vote of 6 to 0; Marshall for the Court. Article III of the Constitution provides that federal judicial authority extends to controversies "between Citizens of different States." The *Strawbridge* case raised for the first time the knotty problem of diversity jurisdiction involving multiple parties and produced what is known today as the rule of "complete diversity." Construing section 11 of the Judiciary Act of 1789 (the original grant of diversity jurisdiction) rather than the Constitution itself, Chief Justice John Marshall held that, where multiple parties assert different "interests," each party must have an adequate jurisdictional basis for being in federal court. The practical effect of this holding was to require that all parties on one side must be diverse from all parties on the other. This requirement remains law today, but only as a matter of statutory construction, not as a mandate of the Constitution itself.

William M. Wiecek

Stromberg v. California, 283 U.S. 359 (1931), argued 15 April 1931, decided 18 May 1931 by vote of 7 to 2; Hughes for the Court, Butler and McReynolds in dissent. Yetta Stromberg's summer job teaching at a youth camp for working-class children in rural California led to a court challenge of the previously unenforced 1919 state law that prohibited public use or display of a red flag. The legislature had determined that the presence of red fabric demonstrated opposition to organized government and invited anarchy and sedition.

During the summer of 1929, the Pioneer Summer Camp, maintained by a conference of organizations, some of them communist in ideology, became the target of the Better American Federation (BAF), a group determined to rid California of "dangerous" dissent. The BAF convinced the San Bernardino County sheriff to search the camp, where his men discovered the red flag and arrested Stromberg and other staff members.

After Stromberg's conviction she appealed to the Supreme Court, where her attorneys argued that the California statutes prohibited a symbol of a legally constituted party that had received fifty thousand votes in the previous election. Stromberg's lawyers based much of their argument on Justice Oliver Wendell Holmes's clear and present danger test that maintained that the

circumstances of the act must be considered in testing the law.

Seven members of the Court voted to overturn Stromberg's conviction. In the majority opinion Chief Justice Charles Evans Hughes followed the reasoning of the Holmes doctrine and concluded that the red flag ban was too vague and could be used to interfere with constitutionally based political and partisan opposition to those in power. Therefore, the majority declared the California Red Flag Law unconstitutional because it violated the liberty protected by the Fourteenth Amendment. The legislature repealed the statute in 1933.

Hughes's *Stromberg* opinion is considered a milestone in First Amendment constitutional law, for it was the first ruling in which a Court majority extended the Fourteenth Amendment to include a protection of First Amendment substance—in this case symbolic speech—from state encroachment.

Carol E. Jenson

Stuart v. Laird, 1 Cranch (5 U.S.) 299 (1803), argued 23–24 Feb. 1803, decided 2 Mar. 1803 by vote of 5 to 0; Paterson for the Court, Marshall not participating. *Stuart* v. *Laird* presented two constitutional questions raised by the repeal of the Judiciary Act of 1801. First, could Congress abolish the circuit courts created by the 1801 statute and thereby, in effect, deprive the judges appointed to them of their positions despite the good-behaviour provision of Article III, section 1? Second, could Congress require justices of the Supreme Court to sit as circuit judges? Justice William Paterson's brief opinion answered both questions in the affirmative, but on narrow and technical grounds that avoided rather than resolved the constitutional challenges. Paterson narrowed the first question to the validity of transfer of a pending case from a court existing under the 1801 act to one created under the 1802 repealer and held that Congress had power to require the transfer. As to circuit riding, he stated that the Court had acquiesced in the duty since its inception, so that it was too late in the day to challenge the practice. Implicitly, however, only six days after it had handed down its opinion in *Marbury* v. *Madison* (1803), the Court upheld the 1802 repeal act and thereby avoided a confrontation with the Republican-dominated Congress and executive.

William M. Wiecek

Sturges v. Crowninshield, 4 Wheat. (17 U.S.) 122 (1819), argued 8 Feb. 1819, decided 17 Feb. 1819 by vote of 7 to 0; Marshall for the Court. This case provided the first test of the constitutionality of state insolvency laws, in this instance an 1811 New York statute that freed debtors from imprisonment for debt and discharged their debt if they assigned their property for the benefit of their creditors.

Chief Justice John Marshall rejected a challenge to the state act based on the argument that federal power over bankruptcy was exclusive but warned in dictum that a federal statute would preempt conflicting state legislation. He voided the statute because it discharged a preexisting debt and thus ran afoul of the Contracts Clause (Article I, section 10). Marshall did, however, concede that a state could modify remedies that enforced an obligation (thus the constitutionality of that section of the statute that liberated an insolvent from debtors' prison), provided that it not revise the underlying obligation itself.

The constitutionality of state relief laws remained unsettled until 1827, when the Court ruled in *Ogden* v. *Saunders* that states could discharge debts, provided they did not impair contracts made before the statute was enacted.

Even so, the policy question relating to bankruptcy and insolvency remained unresolved throughout the nineteenth century. Some states, mostly in the North, did create debtor relief systems, but legislators had difficulties in balancing the interests of both debtors and creditors. They wanted to ease the plight of "unfortunate" defaulters, especially during periods of economic hardship, but at the same time they did not want to discourage lenders, whose role they prized as essential to business well being and economic growth. This conflict was largely resolved by enactment of national bankruptcy legislation in 1898.

Peter J. Coleman

Sugar Trust Case. See E. C. KNIGHT CO. V. UNITED STATES.

Swann v. Charlotte-Mecklenburg Board of Education, 402 U.S. 1, argued 12 Oct. 1970, decided 20 Apr. 1971 by vote of 9 to 0; Burger for the Court. A logical extension of *Green* v. *County School Board of New Kent County* (1968), *Swann* nonetheless represented a further—and highly controversial—milestone in the Supreme Court's effort, following *Brown* v. *Board of Education II* (1955), to effectuate the desegregation of southern public schools. *Swann* is best known for its approval of busing as a tool to achieve desegregation. But in thirty pages—the longest school desegregation opinion then to date—the Court, still unanimous, supplied broad guidelines to federal district judges still faced with dual school systems fifteen years after *Brown II*.

Unlike many previous important school desegregation cases involving small rural districts, *Swann* arose from a sprawling, part-urban, part-rural district covering 550 square miles and serving 84,000 pupils in 101 schools. The school population was 29 percent black, and those pupils were concentrated in one quadrant of Charlotte. The district operated under a court-ordered desegregation plan that focused on geographic zoning and free transfers, but even then more than half of the black pupils attended schools without any white students or teachers. After *Green,* the federal district court announced that the rules of the game had changed and adopted a sweeping plan to disperse the highly concentrated black-student population under a program that would transport an additional 13,000 children in more than 100 new buses at an annual operating cost of more than $500,000 and a startup cost of more than $1 million.

The Supreme Court approved the plan in a disarmingly simple opinion. After deploring "deliberate resistance" to *Brown II* and other "dilatory tactics," the Court announced that new guidelines were necessary in light of *Green* (p. 13). Once a constitutional violation was found, the question of the scope of the remedy became a routine issue of the appropriate use of remedial powers in equity. Chief Justice Warren Burger's opinion, which recent evidence has shown to have been the product of desperate and extensive negotiation among the justices, is important mainly for two features: its treatment of "mathematical ratios" for school composition and its approval of the trial court's transportation method for effectuating pupil transfers between schools.

In upholding the trial court's order that efforts be made to reach a 71:29 (white-to-black) ratio in the various schools, the Supreme Court observed that the "constitutional command to desegregate schools does not mean that every school in every community must always reflect the racial composition of the school system as a whole" but only that "the very limited use of mathematical ratios was within the equitable remedial discretion of the District Court" (pp. 24–25). Burger did not explain whether there were any limitations on the use of ratios aimed to achieve racial balance in the schools—absent, hypothetically, the eventual achievement of a unitary system.

The opinion was even more elliptical on the focal point of the case: busing. After noting that 39 percent of public school children nationally are bused to school, Burger declared that freedom of choice would not eliminate the dual system and that busing and other remedial techniques, such as redrawing attendance zones, were within the district court's power to provide equitable relief: "Desegregation plans cannot be limited to the walk-in school" (p. 30). Finally, Burger construed Title VI of the Civil Rights Act of 1964, which appeared to reaffirm *Brown* but seemed inconsistent with *Green*, as not disturbing the Court's rulings and thus as not circumscribing the district court's plan. In a companion case, *North Carolina State Board of Education* v. *Swann* (1971), Burger held that a state could not prohibit racially explicit transportation or assignment of schoolchildren without violating *Brown*.

Despite *Swann's* frank approval of wholesale, districtwide supervision of affected public schools by federal district courts, the opinion did contain two limitations on equitable discretion that would quickly loom large. Burger stated several times, in different words, that the scope of the constitutional violation determined the scope of the remedy. He also declared that the district court's jurisdiction ended when remediation had been achieved to the point where the system was once again "unitary." The former point shaped the decision in *Milliken* v. *Bradley* (1974); the latter presaged *Pasadena Board of Education* v. *Spangler* (1976).

□ Bernard Schwartz, *Swann's Way* (1986).
Dennis J. Hutchinson

Sweatt v. Painter, 339 U.S. 629 (1950), argued 4 Apr. 1950, decided 5 June 1950 by vote of 9 to 0; Vinson for the unanimous Court. *Sweatt* v. *Painter* is a landmark decision in the history of United States race relations. Although the ruling was a more narrow holding than the decision of *Brown* v. *Board of Education of Topeka* (1954), it nonetheless made clear that the separate but equal standard established

by *Plessy* v. *Ferguson* (1896) was unattainable—at least in state-supported higher education. By implication, the principle was not achievable in any area of public life.

Heman Marion Sweatt was a Houston, Texas, mail carrier intent on becoming a lawyer. Having been denied admission to the University of Texas law school in 1946 because he was an African-American, Sweatt sought the assistance of the National Association for the Advancement of Colored People and its chief legal counsel, Thurgood Marshall. An involved legal battle ensued while Texas scrambled to establish an accredited law school for African-Americans within the state, as required by the Supreme Court in *Missouri ex rel. Gaines* v. *Canada* (1938).

Speaking for a unanimous Court, Chief Justice Fred M. Vinson concluded that a newly created state law school for African-Americans in Texas was in no objective way equal to the University of Texas Law School. Even if it were, Vinson wrote, it would still lack the nonmeasurable elements that made a distinguished law school, among which were faculty reputation, alumni prestige, tradition, and history, a test no recent school could meet. The Equal Protection Clause of the Fourteenth Amendment thus required Sweatt's admission to the previously all-white state university law school. The decision made clear that statutory segregation was doomed, whether by piecemeal dismemberment or one sweeping judicial thrust.

Augustus M. Burns III

Swift & Co. v. United States, 196 U.S. 375 (1905), argued 6–7 Jan. 1905, decided 30 Jan. 1905 by vote of 9 to 0; Holmes for the Court. In *Swift*, the most prominent antitrust action against the Beef Trust, the Court abandoned the restrictive interpretations of its earliest antitrust holdings and accepted a broader definition of the federal commerce power. Enjoined under the Sherman Antitrust Act, Swift contended that the statute was vague and that company's activities were wholly intrastate, thus being outside the reach of federal commerce power under the doctrine of *United States* v. *E. C. Knight Co.* (1895). A unanimous Court rejected Swift's argument, holding that a combination that excluded competitors with intent to monopolize interstate commerce violated the Sherman Act. Justice Oliver Wendell Holmes framed the stream of commerce doctrine to produce a "practical," rather than a "technical, legal conception" of commerce (p. 398). The recurring series of acts by which the Beef Trust operated, from shipping to sale of cattle and with only temporary interruptions in the flow, amounted to a current of commerce among the states, however intrastate the nature of the independent acts. Moreover, Swift's anti-competitive impact on commerce was a direct restraint of trade. Noting that intent might render unlawful even independently lawful components of a scheme, Holmes elevated the importance of intent in defining corporate restraints of trade and attempts to monopolize commerce.

As the administration of President Theodore Roosevelt shifted from trust-busting to regulation, the *Swift* decision attracted little notice. The "stream of commerce" doctrine remained an untapped resource until the 1930s, when the New Deal Court restored expansive readings of the commerce power. Under the leadership of Chief Justice William H. Rehnquist, however, the Court has shown an increasing willingness to limit the sweep of the commerce power and with it the stream of commerce doctrine. For example, in *United States* v. **Lopez* (1995), the high court struck down a federal law making it a crime knowingly to possess a firearm within one-thousand feet of a public or private school because the act did not flow from any enumerated power and the Commerce Clause was insufficient to provide the Congress with constitutional authority to do so.

Barbara C. Steidle

Swift v. Tyson, 16 Pet. (41 U.S.) 1 (1842), argued 14 Jan. 1842, decided 25 Jan. 1842 by vote of 9 to 0; Story for the Court. In *Swift* v. *Tyson*, the Supreme Court established the freedom of the federal courts to follow principles of general commercial law, even if those principles were contrary to judicial decisions of the state in which the federal court sat. In *Swift*, New York defendants were sued in a New York federal district court on a bill of exchange made by them and transferred to a nonresident. The defendants invoked New York decisions under which the instrument was defective, but the plaintiffs argued that the general interstate commercial law would uphold the instrument.

The conflict between the New York cases and commercial decisions elsewhere implicated section 34 of the Judiciary Act of 1789, which required federal courts to follow state "laws" whenever they were applicable. Thus

the Court had to decide whether New York decisions were "laws" that federal courts were required to follow. Justice Joseph Story wrote:

In the ordinary use of language, it will hardly be contended that the decisions of courts constitute laws.

[Section 34 does not] . . . apply to questions of a more general nature, not at all dependant local statutes or local usages. . . . As for example, to the construction of ordinary contracts of other written instruments, and especially to questions of general commercial law, where the state tribunals are called upon to perform the like functions as ourselves, that is, to ascertain upon general reasoning and legal analogies, what is the true exposition of the contract or instrument or what is the just rule furnished by the principles of commercial law to govern the case. (pp. 18–19)

Swift was a case falling within the diversity jurisdiction of the federal courts. It did not fall within the exclusive lawmaking authority of New York. The New York decisions cited by the defendants were themselves based upon "general commercial law," that is, the common commercial custom and jurisprudence applicable to multistate business transactions. Thus Story determined that the New York decisions were not "laws" in the sense of being some fixed and definite pronouncement by the sovereign state of New York but were rather attempts by New York courts to articulate the content of commercial custom common to all the states and, as such, were wrong.

A federal court had no reason to regard as a matter of constitutional law the New York decisions as the sole and exclusive governing rule in an interstate commercial transaction. New York opinions addressed multistate general commercial law, as defined by judicially recognized commercial custom. Story compared the New York decisions to the general body of multistate commercial law and found them to be wrong.

Therefore, the *Swift* opinion was not meant to determine the substantive content of New York commercial law but rather was intended to vindicate the plaintiff's reliance on the general and accepted commercial rule. By his skillful handling of the federalism issue, Story limited the ability of local precedent to upset the reasonable expectations of parties in interstate commercial dealings. He affirmed the power of the federal courts as independent tribunals to invoke established general commercial rules already embodied in judicial precedent. He thereby freed interstate commercial transactions from disruptive local aberrations. At a critical time in the nation's commercial development, Story encouraged independent federal courts to nationalize commercial rules and established the law merchant and its mature body of predictable and efficient rules in national and international commerce. The *Swift* decision was thus critical in preventing the balkanization of the commercial law that might have otherwise occurred.

In 1938, the Supreme Court in *Erie Railroad Co. v. Tompkins* repudiated *Swift*. Story's theory of adjudication as the resolution of disputes under customary standards evolved from private conduct was incompatible with Justice Louis D. Brandeis's scientific positivism, under which an applicable legal rule could come only from the command of the state. His rejection of *Swift* thus represented a transition from nineteenth-century liberalism, concerned with a self-ordering society operating within a federal legal system composed of coequal sovereign states subject to traditional choice-of-law rules, to the modern state as exclusive lawgiver.

□ Tony A. Freyer, *Harmony and Discourse: The Swift and Erie Cases in American Federalism* (1981).

Robert Randall Bridwell

T

Tahoe-Sierra Preservation Council, Inc. v. Tahoe Regional Planning Agency, 535 U.S. 302 (2002), argued 7 Jan. 2002, decided 23 Apr. 2002 by vote of 6 to 3; Stevens for the Court, Rehnquist Scalia, and Thomas in dissent. The *Tahoe-Sierra* case involved a regulation that imposed a thirty-two-month moratorium on all development of land in the Lake Tahoe basin while a regulatory agency devised a land use plan. The Court addressed the question whether this temporary moratorium necessarily required compensation under the Fifth Amendment Takings Clause. The landowners argued that, under *Lucas* v. *South Carolina Coastal Council* (1992), a deprivation of all economically viable use of property was, per se, a taking of property, and therefore compensation was required. The *Tahoe-Sierra* Court concluded that the question under *Lucas* was whether a regulation causes a total deprivation of property value. It then held that property should not be divided into temporal segments when considering the impact of a regulation on the ownership of property—all future value, and not merely the thirty-two months at issue, had to be considered. Since there will always be remaining value if a regulation is only temporary, the Court determined that the *Lucas* per se rule was inapplicable to temporary regulations. The Court adopted the multifactor test applied in *Penn Central Transportation Co.* v. *City of New York* (1978). The Court concluded that temporary moratoria could amount to a taking of property, but determined that there was no hard and fast rule for concluding that a temporary regulation is a taking.

The dissenters argued that the ban on development constituted a taking of property under a Lucas analysis. The most significant aspect of the decision may prove to be the Court's preference for an ad hoc examination of circumstances instead of a categorical rule. Regulations that destroy all property value are rare, and accordingly *Penn Central* may cover the majority of future regulatory taking cases.

Andrew S. Gold

Talton v. Mayes, 163 U.S. 376 (1896), argued 16–17 Apr. 1896, decided 18 May 1896 by vote of 8 to 1; White for the Court, Harlan in dissent. *Talton* v. *Mayes* was an appeal by a Cherokee from a homicide conviction by a Cherokee Nation court. He contended that his trial violated the Fifth Amendment because the grand jury that indicted him consisted of only five members, as permitted by Cherokee law. The Supreme Court held that the Fifth Amendment did not apply to legislation of the Cherokee Nation. The Indian tribes have retained the sovereign power to make their own laws, which is binding on tribal members unless in conflict with some provision of federal law specifically applicable to tribal governments.

Talton v. *Mayes* has been interpreted to hold that constitutional limitations on the federal and state governments do not of their own force limit Indian tribes, which are not "states" of the union within the meaning of the Constitution. The Indian Bill of Rights of 1968 modified the *Talton* holding by imposing on tribes certain specified securities for personal liberty copied (sometimes in modified form) from the United States Constitution.

Rennard J. Strickland

Taylor v. Louisiana, 419 U.S. 522 (1975), argued 16 Oct. 1974, decided 21 Jan. 1975 by vote of 8 to 1; White for the Court, Burger concurring, Rehnquist in dissent. *Taylor* was brought by a man charged with rape who had argued unsuccessfully in the Louisiana state courts that its "volunteers only" jury service provision violated his Sixth Amendment right to a jury drawn from a representative cross-section of the community. In *Hoyt* v. *Florida* (1961) the Supreme Court had upheld the conviction of a female defendant who had argued that a similar Florida provision violated her rights to equal protection of the law and to a trial by a jury of her peers. The Florida registration provision had yielded only ten females in a pool of 9,900 jurors, and none of the women were called for her venire.

In *Taylor*, the Court held, first, that the systematic exclusion of women from jury panels violated any defendant's (male or female) fundamental right to a jury trial drawn from a representative cross-section of the community and, second, that women as a class cannot be excluded from jury service or given automatic exemptions if the result is that panels are almost all male. Thus, the Court effectively overruled *Hoyt* v. *Florida*, although it was distinguished as not resting on the Sixth Amendment grounds. Four years later, in *Duren* v. *Missouri* (1979), the Court extended *Taylor* to invalidate a Missouri statute that allowed for the exemption of women from jury service, which had produced juries that generally were at least 85 percent male. In *J.E.B.* v. *Alabama Ex Rel. T.B.* (1994) the Court held that the Constitution's guarantee of equal protection bars the exclusion of potential jurors through peremptory challenges based on their sex.

Karen O'Connor

Terminiello v. Chicago, 337 U.S. 1 (1949), argued 1 Feb. 1949, decided 16 May 1949 by vote of 5 to 4; rehearing denied 13 June 1949; Douglas for the Court, Frankfurter, Vinson, Jackson in dissent. While Terminiello, a priest, was addressing a sympathetic audience inside a packed auditorium, a hostile crowd, which denounced him as anti-Semitic and pro-Fascist, gathered outside. Fearing violence, police arrested him for disorderly conduct. The Illinois courts upheld the conviction under the "fighting words" doctrine of *Chaplinsky* v. *New Hampshire* (1942), but a bare majority of the Supreme Court reversed.

Admittedly deciding the case on a "preliminary question," Justice William O. Douglas held that the trial judge allowed a conviction upon the mere finding that Terminiello's speech had provoked anger and controversy. This violated the First Amendment standard requiring evidence of a clear and present danger of substantial violence and disorder.

All of the dissenters criticized Douglas's opinion for not directly confronting the constitutional status of emotionally charged political expression. Chief Justice Fred Vinson argued that use of "fighting words" in the proximity of a hostile audience could certainly sustain a conviction. In his lengthy dissent, Justice Robert H. Jackson emphasized that the explosive context of the case, a crowded auditorium of sympathizers and a group of angry protestors outside, made Terminiello's speech akin to the deliberate incitement of violence.

Terminiello remains a classic example of the difficulties of applying abstract First Amendment values to situations in which speakers run some risk of inflaming an unfriendly audience.

Norman L. Rosenberg

Terry v. Adams, 345 U.S. 461 (1953), argued 16 Jan. 1953, decided 4 May 1953 by vote of 8 to 1; Black announced the judgment for the Court, Minton in dissent. This was the last of the so-called white primary cases. Beginning in 1889 in Fort Bend County, Texas, the Jaybird Democratic Association, or Jaybird party, held an unofficial primary election to select candidates for county offices. These candidates entered the Democratic party primary and were invariably nominated and then elected in a usually uncontested general election. White voters automatically became members; blacks were excluded. This "self-governing, voluntary, club" thus was purposefully organized to disfranchise blacks and circumvent the Fifteenth Amendment (p. 463).

There was no majority opinion. Justice Hugo Black said that the state could not countenance the exclusion of blacks from the only election that mattered. Justice Felix Frankfurter emphasized the participation of state election officials in the discrimination. Justice Tom Clark maintained that the Jaybird party was an auxiliary of the state-regulated Democratic party. Eight justices seemed to agree that the Jaybird party was performing a public function and was therefore violating the Fifteenth Amendment. Only Justice Sherman Minton dissented, saying that the Jaybird party constitutionally was nothing more than another "pressure group" (p. 494).

Besides marking the last hurrah of the southern white primary, this decision provided a precedent for Congressional proscription of private racial discrimination under the Fifteenth Amendment in later federal legislation such as the Voting Rights Act of 1965.

Thomas E. Baker

Terry v. Ohio, 392 U.S. 1 (1968), argued 12 Dec. 1967, decided 10 June 1968 by vote of 8 to 1; Warren for the Court, Harlan, Black, and White concurring, Douglas in dissent. For years police have engaged in an investigative practice commonly referred to as stop and frisk, involving the stopping of a suspicious person or vehicle for purposes of interrogation or other brief investigation, sometimes accompanied by a patting down of the clothing of the suspect to ensure that the person was not armed. *Terry* was the first in a now-substantial line of Supreme Court cases recognizing stop and frisk as a valid practice.

In *Terry*, a policeman became suspicious of two men when one of them walked up the street, peered into a store, walked on, started back, looked into the same store, and then conferred with his companion. The other suspect repeated this ritual, and between them the two men went through this performance about a dozen times before following a third man up the street. The officer, thinking they were "casing" a stickup and might be armed, confronted the men, asked their names and patted them down, thereby discovering pistols on Terry and his companion. In affirming Terry's conviction for carrying a concealed weapon, the Supreme Court concluded that "where a police officer

observes unusual conduct which leads him reasonably to conclude in light of his experience that criminal activity may be afoot and that the person with whom he is dealing may be armed and presently dangerous, where in the course of investigating this behavior he identifies himself as a policeman and makes reasonable inquiries, . . . he is entitled for the protection of himself and others in the area to conduct a carefully limited search of the outer clothing of such persons in an attempt to discover weapons which might be used to assault him" (p. 30).

This rather cautious holding fell short of resolving all the important legal issues surrounding this practice; many were ultimately answered in subsequent decisions. But *Terry* did settle two fundamental points: stop and frisk neither falls outside the Fourth Amendment nor is subject to the usual Fourth Amendment restraints. In rejecting "the notions that the Fourth Amendment does not come into play at all as a limitation upon police conduct if the officers stop short of something called a 'technical arrest' or a 'full-blown search'" (p. 19), the Court wisely concluded that the protections of the Fourth Amendment are not subject to verbal manipulation. It is the reasonableness of the officer's conduct, not what the state chooses to call it, that counts.

In concluding that a stop and frisk does not require probable cause, the Court in *Terry* explained that because the policeman had acted without a warrant his conduct was not to be judged by the Fourth Amendment's Warrant Clause (which contains an express "probable cause" requirement) but rather "by the Fourth Amendment's general proscription against unreasonable searches and seizures" (p. 20). Dissenting Justice William O. Douglas objected that the majority had held, contrary to earlier rulings of the Court, "that the police have greater authority to make a 'seizure' and conduct a 'search' than a judge has to authorize such action" (p. 36). Douglas was correct in this, but his point casts into question only some of the reasoning in *Terry*, not the result.

The *Terry* result is grounded in the balancing test of *Camara* v. *Municipal Court* (1967), which the Court quoted and specifically relied upon. *Camara*, which concerned the grounds needed to obtain a warrant to conduct a housing inspection, quite clearly involved the Warrant Clause of the Fourth Amendment and its probable cause requirement. Yet the Court adopted a significantly lower probable cause standard for such warrants than is typically required to satisfy the Fourth Amendment, and it did so by "balancing the need to search against the invasion which the search entails" (p. 537). It thus makes sense to view *Terry* as a case in which probable cause is required, albeit a lesser quantum of probable cause than is ordinarily needed to justify Fourth Amendment activity because the intrusion into privacy and freedom is quite limited and the law enforcement interest being served is substantial.

Under the search part of the *Terry* doctrine, policy may pat down the detained suspect on reasonable suspicion that the suspect is armed and may then remove any object from the suspect's clothing that by its size or density might be a weapon. An object so discovered is admissible in evidence whether it turns out to be a gun or something else seizable as contraband or evidence; in *Michigan* v. *Long* (1983), the Court rejected the notion that to ensure against pretext frisks only weapons should be admissible. (*Long* also holds, by rather strained logic, that the protective search allowed by *Terry* may extend to the passenger compartment of a vehicle to which the suspect has access.)

□ George E. Dix, "Nonarrest Investigatory Detention in Search and Seizure Law," *Duke Law Journal* 85 (1985): 849–959.

Wayne R. LaFave

Test Cases. A test case has usually been thought of as one in which an individual, but more likely an interest group, initiates a case in order to challenge the constitutionality, or perhaps a particular disliked interpretation, of a statute. There are other situations that, although somewhat different from this traditional sense of "test case," can also be loosely called "test case." Some people challenge laws, not necessarily with the thought of "going to the Supreme Court," but simply because the laws are thought improper, but their cases end up in the Supreme Court; examples are provided by civil rights demonstrators who sat in at restaurants in the South in the 1950s and 1960s. Their convictions on a variety of misdemeanor charges provided convenient opportunities for the federal courts to speak out against racial discrimination. Others might specifically provoke arrest under a statute, with the intention that the case reach the high court, as occurred after Congress in 1989 passed

a statute against flag burning. In still other situations, when individuals run afoul of a law they did not specifically seek to break, a lawyer taking their case may challenge the statute's validity rather than try to avoid a conviction.

The examples just noted are relatively recent civil liberties or civil rights situations. Instances of test cases are also found in economic regulation: many challenges to New Deal regulatory legislation were intentionally brought by businesses, their trade associations, or conservative interest groups like the Liberty Lobby. Test cases can be found much earlier as well. One example is the famous "separate but equal" case, *Plessy* v. *Ferguson* (1896), which resulted from a concerted effort by some lawyers, joined by railroads, to invalidate Jim Crow statutes; another was an effort by conservatives to challenge the federal income tax through action masked in a collusive suit, *Pollock* v. *Farmers' Loan and Trust Company* (1895).

Interest groups engaging in litigation are now more likely to undertake immediate focused challenges to objectionable laws almost before the ink is dry, rather than waiting for individual cases to arise when the laws are implemented and someone is adversely affected by them.

There are several reasons for frequent contemporary use of test cases. The Supreme Court has broadened access to the courts by those seeking to challenge laws. Judges are also more willing to entertain actions for declaratory judgments, that is, declarations of a party's rights before the person is charged with violation of a law; to entertain attacks on a statute "on its face," that is, on the statute as written, not as applied; to issue injunctions against enforcement of a law; and to grant summary judgments, that is, to rule on the basis of affidavits rather than waiting until extensive testimony has been taken about contested facts. As a result, few new controversial statutes last long before being tested.

Test cases serve to move political issues quickly into a legal setting and to accelerate their arrival at the Supreme Court. Because the Supreme Court is a major political actor likely to confront any major current controversy in due course, test cases are to be expected and are consonant with this view of the Court's role. However, some test cases leave the justices without the benefit of seeing how a statute is applied, and, however it may appear "on its face," whether it might have been applied in a constitutional manner. To the extent our adversary legal system is associated with cases heavily anchored in particular facts, the greater use of facial statutory challenges is a departure from that tradition. The Court itself could make it harder to bring test cases lacking a thorough factual development. One way would be to alter rulings on procedure, as the Burger Court did by tightening rules on access to the courts, for example, limiting who had standing to challenge zoning rules (*Warth* v. *Selden*, 1975). Another would be simply not to grant review in cases where a thorough factual record had not been developed.

Stephen L. Wasby

Texas and Pacific Railway Co. v. United States. See SHREVEPORT RATE CASES.

Texas v. Johnson, 491 U.S. 397 (1989), argued 21 Mar. 1989, decided 21 June 1989 by vote of 5 to 4; Brennan for the Court, Rehnquist, White, O'Connor, and Stevens in dissent. In *Texas* v. *Johnson* a majority of the Supreme Court considered for the first time whether the First Amendment protects desecration of the United States flag as a form of symbolic speech. A sharply divided Court had previously dealt with symbolic speech cases that involved alleged misuses of the flag. While the Court had ruled in favor of the defendants in those cases (*Street* v. *New York*, 1969; *Smith* v. *Goguen*, 1974; *Spence* v. *Washington*, 1974), it had done so on narrow grounds, refusing to confront the ultimate question of the constitutional status of flag desecration.

Johnson had burned a flag in front of a building while protesting policies of the administration of President Ronald Reagan during the 1984 Republican national convention in Dallas. Johnson's act seriously offended several onlookers. He was arrested for violating a Texas statute that made it a crime to intentionally or knowingly desecrate a state or national flag. He was convicted and sentenced to a year in prison and a fine of two thousand dollars. The Texas Court of Criminal Appeals reversed, holding that Johnson's actions were symbolic speech protected by the First Amendment.

Texas asserted two justifications for Johnson's conviction: preventing breaches of the peace triggered by the offense that desecration inflicts and preserving the integrity of the flag as a symbol of national unity. In order to assess the validity of these claims, Justice William J. Brennan had to weigh them against the First Amendment values at stake. Because government has more license to prohibit harmful "conduct" than harmful "speech," the Court first had to decide whether Johnson's desecration was "conduct" or "speech." Brennan ruled that the desecration was "expressive conduct" because it was an attempt to "convey a particularized message" (p. 404).

But First Amendment doctrine also grants the government more power to regulate "expressive conduct" than "pure expression" because, as the Court said in the draft-card burning case *United States* v. *O'Brien* (1968), where "'speech' and 'nonspeech' elements are combined in the same course of conduct, a sufficiently important governmental interest in regulating the nonspeech element can justify incidental limitations of First Amendment freedoms (p. 376). Texas claimed that Johnson's flag burning was a harmful nonspeech element and that he could have made his criticisms of America without resorting to desecration. The state, however, may not use such "incidental" regulation as a pretext for restricting speech because of its controversial content or because it simply causes offense. If the law is ultimately directed at the content of speech itself, it must pass the most stringent First Amendment standards (*Boos* v. *Barry*, 1988, p. 321). Only speech that incites others to imminent lawless or violent conduct may be subject to abridgment on these grounds (**Brandenburg* v. *Ohio*, 1969).

Applying these standards, Brennan concluded that Texas's conviction of Johnson was impermissible. There was no evidence that Johnson's expression threatened an imminent disturbance of the peace, and the statute's protection of the integrity of the flag as a symbol was improperly directed at the communicative message entailed in flag burning. "If there is a bedrock principle underlying the First Amendment," Brennan wrote, "it is that Government may not prohibit the expression of an idea simply because society finds the idea itself offensive or disagreeable" (p. 414).

The majority's opinion reaffirmed central First Amendment doctrine. Nonetheless, four members of the Court dissented because of the special nature of the flag as a symbol. Chief Justice William Rehnquist issued a poetic dissent that celebrated the history of the flag in America. The reaction to *Johnson* spilled into the national political arena. Within a few months Congress passed the Flag Protection Act of 1989, which attempted to challenge legislatively the Supreme Court's ruling in *Johnson*. Following *Johnson*, the Supreme Court declared this act unconstitutional in *United States* v. **Eichman* (1990).

Donald A. Downs

Texas v. White, 74 U.S. 700 (1869), argued 5, 8, and 9 Feb. 1869, decided 12 Apr. 1869 by vote of 5 to 3; Chase for the Court, Grier in dissent. Following the Civil War, the presidentially reconstructed government of Texas brought suit to recover state-owned securities that had been sold by the state's Confederate government. Defendants argued that Texas, which had seceded and had not yet been restored to the Union, was not a state and therefore could not sue in federal courts. Hence the case presented fundamental questions concerning secession, Reconstruction, and the nature of the Union.

Asserting that the Constitution created "an indestructible Union, composed of indestructible States" (p. 725), Chief Justice Salmon P. Chase held that secession was illegal and that Texas had never left the Union. He admitted that participation in the rebellion had left the state without a lawful government and had suspended its rights as a member of the Union. Consequently, under the Guarantee Clause, Congress had authority to reestablish state government. Although Texas had not been restored to its normal position in the Union, Chase noted that Congress had recognized the presidentially reconstructed government as provisional, entitling it to sue in the federal courts. Turning to the merits of the case, Chase ruled that the state's Confederate government had been unlawful, that its acts in support of the rebellion were null and void, and that the state was entitled to recover the securities.

The decision endorsed the Republican position that the Union was perpetual and that Reconstruction was a political problem that lay within the scope of congressional power.

Donald G. Nieman

Thornburgh v. American College of Obstetricians and Gynecologists, 476 U.S. 747 (1986), argued 5 Nov. 1985, decided 11 June 1986 by vote of 5 to 4; Blackmun for the Court, Burger, White, and Rehnquist, joined by O'Connor, in dissent. The Court invalidated several Pennsylvania abortion regulations, including a requirement that women seeking abortions be given detailed information (much like the information required by the ordinance invalidated three years earlier in **Akron* v. *Akron Center for Reproductive Health*, 1983), detailed record-keeping requirements, a requirement that the physician use the technique most likely to protect the fetus in postviability abortions, and a requirement that a second physician be present at such abortions.

As in the law invalidated in *Akron*, the information requirement was viewed as an effort to discourage the woman from having an abortion; furthermore, the Court said, the requirement intruded on the private relationship between the woman and her physician. The record-keeping requirements were invalid because they were too detailed and because they would be available to the public in a way that would make it possible to identify some women who had abortions. The requirements regarding medical care were invalid because they forced the physician to "trade off" the woman's health against that of the fetus and because the statute made no exception to the two-doctor rule for cases in which the woman's life or health would be endangered by waiting for the second doctor to arrive.

The Court expressed impatience at what it regarded as repeated efforts by states to evade the requirements of **Roe* v. *Wade* (1973), and it reasserted the justification for the abortion decision in the face of an argument presented by the solicitor general that *Roe* should be overruled. Chief Justice Warren Burger's dissent stated that because *Roe* had come to stand for a requirement that abortions be available on demand, he was prepared to overrule it.

Justice Byron White's dissent also urged that *Roe* be overruled because it was misguided. His opinion acknowledged that the right to choose an abortion was an aspect of liberty protected by the Due Process Clause of the Fourteenth Amendment but argued that it, like other liberties not specifically identified in the Constitution, could nonetheless be restricted quite substantially. Because states could permissibly regard the interest of the fetus as important, a woman's liberty to choose abortion was not fundamental and did not require strict scrutiny.

Thornburgh was to be the last case in which a firm majority of the Court adhered to the reasoning of *Roe* v. *Wade*. The retirement of Justice Lewis Powell, who had consistently supported *Roe*, and the appointment of Justice Anthony Kennedy led to a substantial assault on the framework established by *Roe* in *Webster* v. *Reproductive Services* (1989). However, in *Planned Parenthood of Southeastern Pennsylvania* v. *Casey* (1992), a sharply divided Court reaffirmed the essential holding in *Roe* that a woman has a constitutional right to an abortion before the fetus attains viability at roughly six months into the pregnancy. At the same time, the justices did sustain several provisions of the Pennsylvania act that placed a greater, but not an undue burden, on women seeking to have abortions.

Mark V. Tushnet

Thornhill v. Alabama, 310 U.S. 88 (1940), argued 29 Feb. 1940, decided 22 Apr. 1940 by vote of 8 to 1; Murphy for the Court, McReynolds in dissent. *Thornhill* v. *Alabama* explicitly placed peaceful labor picketing under the protection of the Free Speech Clause of the First Amendment. In an opinion by Justice Frank Murphy, who had served as governor of Michigan during the 1937 General Motors sitdown strike, the Court struck down an Alabama statute that prohibited all manner of picketing. The Court overturned the statute because it did not regulate specific elements of labor demonstrations, such as the number of pickets, but rather proscribed "every practicable method whereby the facts of a labor dispute may be publicized" (p. 100). Murphy denied, however, that the First Amendment guaranteed an absolute right to picket. The value of picketing lay in its educational function, because public labor demonstrations could inform citizens about economic matters that were "indispensable to the effective and intelligent use of the processes of popular government to shape the destiny of modern industrial society" (p. 103). Thus, the government could properly regulate picketing that interfered with the public's ability to evaluate labor disputes.

Thornhill acknowledged that New Deal reforms had absorbed organized labor into the industrial polity. Protecting labor's freedom of expression served to incorporate the interests of the working class into the formulation of public policy. At the same time, the decision permitted courts to curtail picketing when the activities of picketers went beyond publicizing the issues of a labor dispute. In subsequent cases, the Court specifically invoked the *Thornhill* rationale to limit labor activism that threatened economic production. The *Thornhill* decision, therefore, reflected a balance between the protection of the constitutional rights of workers and the maintenance of economic stability in a changing industrial order.

Eric W. Rise

Thurlow v. Massachusetts. See LICENSE CASES.

Time, Inc. v. Hill, 385 U.S. 374 (1967), argued 27 Apr. 1966, reargued 18–19 Oct. 1966, decided 9 Jan. 1967 by vote of 5 to 4; Brennan for the Court, Black and Douglas concurring, Harlan concurring in part and dissenting in part, Fortas, joined by Warren and Clarke, in dissent. This case concerned a *Life* magazine article describing a Broadway play about the ordeal of a family trapped in their own house by escaped convicts. *Life* claimed that the play described events that had actually happened to the Hill family, which had in fact been held hostage several years before by escaped prisoners. The article was inaccurate in several nondefamatory but nevertheless deeply disturbing respects. Members of the Hill family sued for invasion of privacy under a New York statute.

The Supreme Court's opinion in *Hill* built upon the 1964 decision of *New York Times Co.* v. *Sullivan*, in which the Court had held that plaintiffs who were public officials could not recover damages for defamation unless they could demonstrate that the defamation had been published with actual malice, "that is, with knowledge that it was false or with reckless disregard of whether it was false or not" (pp. 279–280). In *Time, Inc.* v. *Hill* the Court extended the application of the actual malice rule to actions alleging that a plaintiff's privacy had been invaded by "false reports of matters of public interest" (p. 388). In 1974 the Court held in *Gertz v. Robert I. Welch, Inc.* that private plaintiffs did not have to prove actual malice to recover damages in defamation suits, even if the publication at issue concerned matters of public interest. Since then, the courts have divided over the question of whether *Gertz* put limits on the holding in *Time* or whether defendants in false-light privacy actions should receive greater constitutional protection than defendants in defamation actions.

Robert C. Post

Tinker v. Des Moines Independent Community School District, 393 U.S. 503 (1969), argued 12 Nov. 1968, decided 24 Feb. 1969 by vote of 7 to 2; Fortas for the Court, Stewart and White concurring, Black and Harlan in dissent. Some Des Moines, Iowa, high school and junior high school students protested the Vietnam War by wearing black armbands in school. School officials had adopted a policy banning the wearing of armbands two days before the students' action. When the students wore the armbands to school they were sent home and suspended until they returned without them. The students claimed that their First Amendment rights were violated by the schools' action.

The Court's opinion noted that school officials had comprehensive authority to set rules in the schools but that this had to be done consistent with the First Amendment rights of students and teachers, who did not "shed their constitutional rights to freedom of speech or expression at the schoolhouse gate" (p. 506). Wearing an armband as a silent form of expressing an opinion was, according to the Court, "akin to pure speech" and involved "primary First Amendment rights" (p. 508).

Two aspects of the Court's opinion are especially significant. First, the expression of the students who wore the armbands caused no disruption and did not, in the Court's opinion, intrude on the work of the school or the rights of other students. Of the eighteen thousand students in the school system, only a few wore the armbands and only five were suspended. A few students made hostile remarks to the students wearing the armbands, but no acts of violence or threats occurred on school premises. The school officials' actions could not, said the Court, be based merely on an undifferentiated fear of a disturbance, for all unpopular views may create some unpleasantness and discomfort. Such is the price we pay for living in an open and often disputatious society.

Second, the Court stressed the fact that school officials had permitted other political symbols to be worn. For example, some students wore political campaign buttons, and others wore the Iron Cross, a symbol of Nazism. But only the black armbands protesting American involvement in Vietnam were singled out. Thus the regulation was directly related to the suppression of a specific view on a given subject, and the Court struck it down as not constitutionally permissible. As the Court put it, "state-operated schools may not be enclaves of totalitarianism," and "students may not be regarded as closed-circuit recipients of only that which the State chooses to communicate" (p. 511).

Justice Hugo Black, in a notable and bitter dissenting opinion, argued that local officials should be permitted to determine the extent to which freedom of expression should be allowed in their public schools. These officials, Black asserted, knew better than federal judges how to run the schools, and their judgment was also to be preferred to that of the students. Moreover, he disagreed with the majority's finding that there were no disruptions resulting from the students' wearing the armbands. According to Black, there were comments and warnings to the students wearing the armbands, and one mathematics teacher had his lesson period "wrecked" as a result of a dispute with one of the petitioners regarding her armband.

Tinker stands as one of the most significant cases dealing with the constitutional rights of public school students. In stating that the classroom should be a "marketplace of ideas," *Tinker* represents the Court's concern over the role school officials play in indoctrinating students. In other cases (such as *Hazelwood School District* v. *Kuhlmeier*, 1988, and *Bethel School District No. 403* v. *Fraser*, 1986), however, the Court has spoken approvingly of value inculcation in the public schools and has noted the central role schools play in, for example, promoting civic virtues. The tension between these two strains of thought has produced a great deal of inconsistency in Supreme Court and lower court rulings concerning claims of constitutional protection by public school students. The Court has given school officials more extensive powers of regulation where curricular matters are involved or where student expression takes place in a school-sponsored setting such as a school newspaper or assembly.

Keith C. Miller

Trop v. Dulles, 356 U.S. 86 (1958), argued 2 May and 28–29 Oct. 1957, decided 31 Mar. 1958 by vote of 5 to 4; Warren, joined by Black, Douglas, and Whittaker, for the plurality, Brennan concurring, Frankfurter, Burton, Clark, and Harlan in dissent. This case was decided on the same day as *Perez* v. *Brownell*, in which a majority of 5 to 4 affirmed Congress's power to take away the American citizenship of a person who had voted in a foreign election. With Justice William Brennan, who had been in the majority in the *Perez* case, changing sides, the Court in *Trop* held that Congress had no power to withdraw an individual's citizenship for wartime desertion from the military. Chief Justice Earl Warren, who had dissented in *Perez* on the ground that Congress was entirely without power to denationalize anyone without consent, wrote for the plurality in *Trop*, which consisted of the four *Perez* dissenters. Warren reiterated the broad constitutional argument he made in *Perez* and further contended that Congress could not impose expatriation as punishment without violating the Cruel and Unusual Punishments Clause of the Eighth Amendment. Involuntary expatriation, wrote Warren, was cruel and unusual punishment because it constituted "the total destruction of the individual's status in organized society" (p. 101). Brennan, concurring separately, merely concluded that expatriation for wartime desertion was not a rational exercise of the war power. The Eighth Amendment argument, therefore, was not embraced by a majority. Although that argument had no further development in this area of law, its core idea, that the Eighth Amendment "must draw its meaning from the evolving standards of decency that mark the progress of a maturing society" (p. 101), has been accepted as a critical element of constitutional law relating to capital punishment (e.g., *Gregg* v. *Georgia*, 1976).

In *Afroyim* v. *Rusk* (1967), the Court overruled *Perez* and adopted Warren's broad argument that citizenship could only be voluntarily relinquished.

Dean Alfange, Jr.

Truax v. Corrigan, 257 U.S. 312 (1921), argued 29–30 Apr. 1920, reargued 5–6 Oct. 1921, decided 19 Dec. 1921 by vote of 5 to 4; Taft for the Court, Holmes, Pitney (joined by Clarke), and Brandeis in dissent. In the late nineteenth and early twentieth century, courts often ended labor disputes by issuing injunctions against strikers. To redress this judicial favoritism, some states, including Arizona, passed statutes seeking to insulate strikers from labor injunctions. Such statutes did not preclude suits for damages. The Arizona courts upheld a peaceful-picketing, no-injunction law when it was challenged by a local restaurant owner who saw his business decline more than 50 percent when strikers picketed his establishment.

A bare majority of the Supreme Court said that the picketing, despite an absence of violence, invalidated the law. Chief Justice William Howard Taft found that the law abridged the Due Process Clause of the Fourteenth Amendment by depriving the owner of his property and violated the Equal Protection Clause of that same amendment by singling out disputes between an employer and his former employees for special treatment. The probusiness, antiunion bias of the majority was exposed in three dissenting opinions. Justice Oliver Wendell Holmes protested the Court's continuing use of the Fourteenth Amendment to cut off state experimentation; Justice Mahlon Pitney challenged all of Taft's conclusions; and Justice Louis D. Brandeis provided historical and legal justification for the Arizona statute.

The decision in *Truax* v. *Corrigan* is representative of the Taft Court, but its reading of the Due Process and Equal Protection Clauses would not long survive. Specifically, in *Senn* v. *Tile Layers Union* (1937), a similar Wisconsin law was upheld.

John E. Semonche

Turner Broadcasting System, Inc. v. FCC, 520 U.S. 180 (1997), argued 7 Oct. 1996, decided 31 Mar. 1997 by vote of 5 to 4; Kennedy for the Court, joined by Rehnquist and Souter in full, Breyer and Stevens concurring in part or whole; O'Connor filed a dissenting opinion in which Scalia, Thomas, and Ginsburg joined.

The *Turner* case settled a longstanding First Amendment conflict between cable television operators and broadcast television owners. The Cable Television Consumer Protection and Competition Act of 1992 required that cable television operators with more than twelve channels had to set one-third of their capacity aside for use by over-the-air broadcast television stations and to do so without remuneration. This "must-carry" provision was first adjudicated by the high court in 1994 in *Turner Broadcasting System, Inc.* v. *FCC* (512 U.S. 622). In that case, the cable broadcasters argued that the "must-carry" provision of the law forced them to carry material that they did not wish to and that was in direct competition with them. The Court, however, in *Turner I* found the "must-carry" provision content neutral because it protected a particular medium of speech (broadcast television) rather than favoring or disfavoring any specific message. At the same time, the Court concluded that the measure indirectly placed certain burdens on cable operators.

The justices ordered the case back to the lower federal courts for review to see if these indirect burdens were acceptable in advancing an important governmental interest, in this instance providing access by the public to broadcast television transmissions that would not otherwise be available in remote areas of the country. The District Court for the District of Columbia subsequently sustained not only the 1992 law but the "must-carry" provision as well on the ground that this was the most effective way for Congress to advance its goal of preserving broadcast television and that any burden placed on cable operators was minimal. The cable operators, led by media mogul Ted Turner, appealed a second time to the high court.

Justice Kennedy's opinion for a divided Court reiterated the constitutionality of the "must-carry" provision. Kennedy noted that the provision had the considerable benefit of preserving free over-the-air broadcasting, promoting the widespread dissemination of information, and promoting fair competition in television programming. Along with four of the other justices, Kennedy also concluded that cable television had come to so dominate the market that without some government support broadcast television might disappear. Of the approximately five hundred thousand cable television channels available nationwide, Kennedy noted, slightly more than 1 percent were affected by the decision. The dissenters, however, led by Justice Sandra Day O'Connor, argued that federal regulation imposed an inappropriate burden on cable operators by compelling them to carry signals of what could effectively be construed as their competition.

Turner II was a victory for broadcast television and for the idea that Congress can take reasonable steps to address what it believes are important interests, even if they do place some restriction on speech. In this instance, of course, the Court's actions mean that cable television systems with more than twelve channels must make channel capacity available to broadcasters. It also means that subscribers will have more choices of what to watch than would otherwise have been the case.

Kermit L. Hall

Twining v. New Jersey, 211 U.S. 78 (1908), argued 19–20 Mar. 1908, decided 9 Nov. 1908 by vote of 8 to 1; Moody for the Court, Harlan in dissent. Twining and Cornell were convicted of intentionally deceiving a New Jersey state banking examiner. At issue in their appeal was the trial judge's charge to the jury that the defendant's refusal to testify in their own behalf could be considered in determining guilt. New Jersey was among a minority of states that permitted trial judges to make such charges.

The Supreme Court weighed whether the trial judge's instructions violated the Fifth Amendment privilege against self-incrimination and, if so, whether that provision was incorporated by the Fourteenth Amendment against state action. Justice William H. Moody, writing for the majority, rejected the incorporation argument and declined to consider the specific dimensions of Twining's complaint. Moody acknowledged that, for purposes of discussion, the trial court's comment on the defendants' refusal to take the stand in their own defense constituted an "infringement of the privilege against self-incrimination" (p. 114), but he emphasized that the New Jersey courts did not violate their own interpretation of that privilege and, consequently, the "exemption from compulsory self-incrimination in the courts of the States is not secured by any part of the Federal Constitution" (p. 114).

In dissent, Justice John Marshall Harlan argued that the Court should first have considered whether the trial court's action constituted a violation of the privilege against self-incrimination. If so, then the Court had to consider the applicability of federal constitutional provisions to the states. Harlan concluded that the trial court violated the privilege against self-incrimination and that that privilege applied to all citizens as guaranteed by the Fourteenth Amendment.

Although the Court has never explicitly contested Twining's rejection of total incorporation, the process of selective incorporation has been applied to most of the Bill of Rights. *Twining* v. *New Jersey* was reversed in *Malloy* v. *Hogan* (1964).

Susette M. Talarico

Tyson v. Banton, 273 U.S. 418 (1927), argued 6–7 Oct. 1926, decided 28 Feb. 1927 by vote of 5 to 4; Sutherland for the Court, Holmes, Brandeis, Stone, and Sanford in dissent. New York sought to protect theatergoers against the excessive charges demanded by licensed brokers who trafficked in ticket resale. The Court disagreed in this renowned and widely criticized opinion. Theaters were not public utilities or affected with a public interest, the Court ruled. Theaters served only a small percentage of the public and neither they nor that limited public could enjoy special governmental protection or privilege. Writing for the majority, Justice George Sutherland pointed out that a ticket agency did not fall into any of the three categories Chief Justice William H. Taft had listed in *Wolff Packing v. Court of Industrial Relations* (1923), and thereby held the law unconstitutional as a violation of freedom of contract.

There were four dissents. Justice Oliver Wendell Holmes objected strongly to the use of the public interest doctrine in curtailing legitimate social control. The legislature, he argued, when it had sufficient force of public opinion behind it, should have the power to forbid or restrict any business without legal apology. He urged, more broadly, that legislatures should do what they saw fit to do unless restrained by some express prohibition in the Constitution. The concept of public interest, he made clear, was an artificial one, little more than a fiction intended to "beautify what is disagreeable to the sufferers" (p. 446). Justice Louis Brandeis concurred. Justice Harlan F. Stone, in a separate dissent, deplored how far the Court had progressed in destroying the various criteria of social control formerly accepted as valid. In substance, the minority judges were all demanding that the entire concept of public interest be abandoned and replaced by a recognition of the general right of any state legislature to regulate private business whenever it though the public welfare demanded it.

Paul L. Murphy

U

Ullman v. United States, 350 U.S. 422 (1956), argued 6 Dec. 1955, decided 26 Mar. 1956 by vote of 7 to 2; Frankfurter for the Court, Douglas and Black in dissent. A federal district court issued an order under the Immunity Act requiring Ullman to testify before a grand jury that was investigating attempts to endanger the national security. Under the act, a witness could not refuse to testify on the ground that the testimony may have tended to incriminate him. The Immunity Act, however, gave the witness transactional immunity, which prevented state or federal prosecutions for any transactions or matters concerning the compelled testimony. Despite the immunity, Ullman refused to testify and was sentenced to six months imprisonment for contempt.

On appeal to the Supreme Court, Ullman argued that the Immunity Act violated the Fifth Amendment privilege against self-incrimination. He argued that the act did not give him complete immunity because his testimony might lead to practical disabilities, such as loss of job, expulsion from a labor union, and public opprobrium.

The Supreme Court rejected this argument, holding that the act did not violate the Fifth Amendment. It observed that the privilege against self-incrimination protected a witness not from the disabilities described by Ullman but only from giving testimony that might lead to a criminal prosecution. By granting transactional immunity, the act removed exposure to a criminal charge. As a result, the reason for the privilege no longer existed and petitioner could not refuse to answer questions.

Daan Braveman

United Jewish Organizations of Williamsburgh v. Carey, 430 U.S. 144 (1977), argued 6 Oct. 1976, decided 1 Mar. 1977 by vote of 7 to 1; White for the Court, Burger in dissent, Marshall not participating. In this case, the Supreme Court held constitutional a New York State reapportionment plan that was based upon a fixed racial quota. In 1972, the State of New York reapportioned three counties for congressional, state senate, and state assembly seats. Pursuant to provisions of the Voting Rights Act of 1965, New York was required to seek approval of the plan by the United States attorney general. The attorney general found that the state had failed to demonstrate that the plan had neither the purpose nor the effect of abridging the right to vote by reason of race or color with respect to state assembly and senate districts in the Bedford-Stuyvesant area of Kings County (Brooklyn).

The plan for Kings County included the Williamsburgh area, a community whose population included approximately 30,000 Hasidic Jews. Previously, and again in the 1972 plan, the Hasidic community was located entirely in one district for representation in both the state assembly and senate.

Based on representations that only a 65 percent non-white assembly district would be acceptable to the attorney general, the State of New York submitted a revised plan that split the Hasidic community into two state assembly and senate districts.

Before the attorney general gave his approval to the revised reapportionment proposal, the Hasidic community brought suit for injunctive and declaratory relief in district court, alleging that the new plan was discriminatory under the Fourteenth and Fifteenth Amendments. The district court granted motions to dismiss the suit on grounds that Hasidic Jews enjoyed no constitutional right to recognition as a separate community; in re-apportionment, that Hasidic Jews had not been and were not disfranchised, and that under the Voting Rights Act racial considerations could legitimately be invoked in order to correct past discrimination.

The Court of Appeals for the Second Circuit held that the plan did not discriminate against the plaintiffs as white voters, finding no intent by the State of New York to eliminate or to minimize white voting power in Kings County. Because the New York legislature had previously violated the Voting Rights Act, the majority did not consider the constitutional question whether a state legislature could draw district lines on the basis of race in order to achieve a proportional or equal representation of white and non-white voters. Relying on the Voting Rights Act and *Allen* v. *Board of Elections* (1969), the appeals court found that consideration of race was proper in reapportionment cases to correct invidious discrimination against nonwhites.

The Supreme Court held that under the Voting Rights Act the state's action was clearly constitutional. Four members of the Court agreed with the Second Circuit that (1) the use of racial criteria in drawing district lines may be required by section 5 of the Voting Rights Act, (2) under the act, the use of racial criteria is not limited to remedies of explicit prior discrimination, and (3) the use of numerical racial quotas in establishing certain black majority districts does not automatically violate the Fourteenth and Fifteenth Amendments. Writing for the plurality, Justice Byron White agreed with the lower court's interpretation of the Voting Rights Act and its interpretation of the decisions upholding the act's constitutionality. Given the proper conditions for invoking the act,

the use of explicitly racial criteria is appropriate whether or not there is a finding of prior discrimination. Justice Potter Stewart's separate concurring opinion, in which Justice Lewis Powell joined, emphasized the lack of any showing of purposeful discrimination in the New York redistricting.

Chief Justice Warren Burger's dissent opposed any use of quotas or "racial gerrymandering." He also argued that state action not otherwise acceptable is not made constitutionally permissible by attempts to comply with the Voting Rights Act.

In *United Jewish Organizations* the Court moved beyond earlier cases to uphold the use of explicitly numerical racial goals to obtain the attorney general's approval for redistricting under the Voting Rights Act. This approach continues as law, but it applies only to those states or subdivisions covered by the act. More recently, however, the high court has demonstrated considerable wariness when asked to pass on the constitutionality of reapportioned congressional districts based on race. For example, in *Shaw* v. *Reno* (1993), *Bush* v. *Vera* (1996), and *Shaw* v. *Hunt* (1996), the justices have struck down as violations of the Equal Protection Clause of the Fourteenth Amendment the creation of majority-minority congressional districts in Texas and North Carolina. Such redistricting by race, the Court has concluded, must be narrowly tailored and intended to serve a compelling state interest.

Herbert Hill

United Mine Workers, United States v., 330 U.S. 258 (1947), argued 14 Jan. 1947, decided 6 Mar. 1947 by vote of 7 to 2; Vinson for the Court, Frankfurter and Jackson concurring in the judgment, Black and Douglas concurring in part and dissenting in part, Murphy and Rutledge in dissent. After contract negotiations broke down between the miners union and coal operators in the spring of 1946, the federal government determined that the resulting shortage of coal had created a national emergency. President Harry S. Truman seized the mines on 21 May 1946, claiming coal production to be essential to both the war effort and to sustaining the domestic economy in the transition from war to peace. The union, with the silent approval of its president, John L. Lewis, refused to work in government-held mines until a contract had been signed. The government in turn secured an injunction against further work stoppages, and when the workers refused to return to the pits, the district court fined the union $3.5 million and Lewis $10,000 for contempt of court.

The union appealed on the grounds that the Norris-LaGuardia Act of 1932 prohibited federal courts from issuing injunctions against labor during a strike. The government responded that the War Labor Disputes Act of 1942 superseded the Norris-LaGuardia Act in situations in which the president, as commander-in-chief, issued an executive order pursuant to the declaration of a national emergency.

The Court held that the Norris-LaGuardia Act did not apply when the government was the employer and that the district court therefore had jurisdiction in the case. General public approval of this decision led Congress to pass the Taft-Hartley Act later in the year, cutting back some of the privileges labor had been granted during the New Deal, especially by the Wagner Labor Relations Act of 1935.

Melvin I. Urofsky

United Public Workers v. Mitchell, 330 U.S. 75 (1947), argued 3 Dec. 1945, reargued 17 Oct. 1946, decided 10 Feb. 1947 by vote of 4 to 3; Reed for the Court, Frankfurter concurring, Rutledge and Douglas concurring in part and dissenting in part, Black in dissent, Murphy and Jackson not participating. The Hatch Act of 1940 forbade officers and employees of the executive branch, with certain exceptions, from "taking any active part in political management or in political campaigning." Executive-branch employees now came under restrictions concerning political activities as had applied to civil service employees, and violation of those rules required dismissal from their positions. Several members of executive agencies sought a declaratory judgment, claiming that the law unconstitutionally restricted their freedom of speech as protected by the First Amendment.

Justice Stanley Reed pointed out that the Court, in a series of cases going back to *Ex parte Curtis* (1882), had upheld similar restrictions on civil service employees, and he balanced individual speech rights against Congress's decision that the public interest required that government employees be barred from active political participation. "It is accepted constitutional doctrine that these fundamental human rights are not absolute. . . . The essential rights of the

First Amendment in some instances are subject to the elemental need for order without which the grandeur of civil rights to others would be a mockery" (p. 95).

In his partial dissent, Justice William O. Douglas described the statute as too broadly drawn. He did not deny that Congress could restrict the political activity of government workers, but to do so, said Douglas, it had to fashion a more narrowly drawn law aimed at the specific conduct it deemed a clear and present danger. In his dissent, Justice Hugo Black bitterly attacked the Hatch Act as depriving several million people of their constitutional rights to free speech and political participation.

Melvin I. Urofsky

United States v. Booker; United States v. Fanfan, 543 U.S. 220 (2005), argued 4 Oct. 2004, decided 12 Jan. 2005 by vote of 5 to 4; Stevens for the Court in part, joined by Scalia, Souter, Thomas, and Ginsburg; Breyer for the Court in part, joined by Rehnquist, O'Connor, Kennedy, and Ginsburg; Stevens in dissent in part, joined by Souter and Scalia; Scalia and Thomas in dissent in part; Breyer in dissent in part, joined by Rehnquist, O'Connor, and Kennedy. Sentencing guidelines were adopted for federal courts and for many state courts in the mid-1980s, as part of widespread reform efforts to establish a uniform sentencing policy for convicted defendants. In *Apprendi* v. *New Jersey* (2000), the Supreme Court ruled that the Sixth Amendment prohibited judges from increasing criminal sentences beyond statutory maximums based on facts other than those presented to the jury. Four years later, in *Blakely* v. *Washington* (2004), the Court applied this decision to state mandatory sentencing guidelines.

When the Seventh and First Circuits cited *Blakely* in upholding the assignment of lower sentences than required by federal guidelines for two convicted drug dealers—Freddie J. Booker and Ducan Fanfan, respectively—the government appealed, with the Court consolidating the cases. The Court's decision was announced by two groups of justices. Justice John Paul Stevens, for the majority, held that the rule of *Apprendi*, as applied in *Blakely*, governed federal sentencing guidelines. Stevens ruled that the Sixth Amendment prohibited any increase in punishment based on facts not submitted to a jury and proved beyond a reasonable doubt.

Justice Stephen G. Breyer, for a different majority of the Court, addressed the question of how to remedy the constitutional violation in U.S. v. Fanfan. The federal sentencing statute that required district courts to impose a sentence within the range mandated by the law was judged incompatible with the constitutional holding in Booker and had to be severed and excised from the statute, as did a similar provision that governed the handling of appeals. Thus, under this ruling, federal sentencing guidelines are discretionary. Judges may follow them, but they cannot be required to do so.

David J. Bodenhamer

United States District Court, United States v., 407 U.S. 297 (1972), argued 24 Feb. 1972, decided 19 June 1972 by vote of 8 to 0; Powell for the Court, Burger, Douglas, and White concurring, Rehnquist not participating. In the early 1970s, the nation was in a state of civil unrest. Various groups were accused of bombing buildings and plotting against the government. In the name of national security, the administration of President Richard Nixon claimed authority to use electronic surveillance to monitor American citizens allegedly involved in subversive activities without, as customarily required by the Fourth Amendment, first obtaining a warrant from a magistrate on a showing of probable cause.

The government argued that the vesting of executive power in the president in Article II of the Constitution implied authority to use electronic surveillance to secure information necessary to protect the government from destruction. A judicial warrant requirement would interfere with the executive's responsibility by increasing the risk that sensitive information would be disclosed. Moreover, judges would not be able to evaluate domestic intelligence involving issues beyond judicial expertise.

A unanimous Court rejected the administration's claim. The Court emphasized that the case involved First Amendment as well as Fourth Amendment values because political organizations antagonistic to prevailing policies are the organizations most likely to be suspected by government of raising domestic national-security dangers. In light of these First Amendment values and the vagueness of the concept of national security, the Court concluded that to permit official surveillance of domestic groups on the basis of a presidential decision without

prior judicial warrant would create undue dangers of abuse.

Two days before this opinion was rendered, five men were arrested for attempting to plant electronic surveillance devices in the Democratic National Committee Headquarters in Washington, D.C., an event that initiated the Watergate affair.

Stanley Ingber

United States v. _____. See under latter part of case name.

United Steelworkers of America v. Weber, 443 U.S. 193 (1979), argued 28 Mar. 1979, decided 27 June 1979 by vote of 5 to 2; Brennan for the Court, Burger and Rehnquist in dissent, Powell and Stevens not participating. Despite earlier opportunities, *Weber* was the first case in which the Supreme Court specifically addressed affirmative action in employment.

The master collective bargaining agreement for the Kaiser Aluminum Company had been adapted from a settlement of employment discrimination claims in the steel industry. Craft hiring goals for blacks were set at each Kaiser plant equal to the percentage of blacks in the respective local labor forces. On the job training programs were established for unskilled production workers, both black and white. Admission to the programs was based on seniority, with 50 percent of the openings in these newly created in-plant training jobs available for whites.

Weber, an unskilled white employee at the Kaiser plant in Gramercy, Louisiana, had more service than some of the black employees selected for the program but less than any of the successful white applicants. He sued the company and the union, alleging that the program's racial classification for admission violated Title VII of the Civil Rights Act of 1964.

Acknowledging that Weber's literal interpretation of the act was not without force, Justice William J. Brennan, for the majority, emphasized the significance of the fact that the program was voluntarily adopted by private parties to eliminate traditional patterns of racial segregation. He noted that judicial findings of exclusion from crafts on racial grounds are so numerous as to make such exclusion a proper subject for judicial notice.

The court rejected Weber's argument that Title VII specifically prohibited *any* grant of preferential treatment to racial minorities. It held that Title VII's prohibitions against racial discrimination do not condemn all private, voluntary, race-conscious affirmative action plans.

The Court declined to define in detail the line of demarcation between permissible and impermissible affirmative action plans. But this plan did not unnecessarily trammel the interests of white employees, did not require the discharge of whites to make room for blacks, and did not permanently bar the advancement of white employees. The plan was temporary, and it was not intended to maintain racial balance but simply to eliminate a manifest racial imbalance. Therefore, it fell within the area of discretion left by Title VII to the private sector voluntarily to adopt affirmative action plans designed to eliminate conspicuous racial imbalance in traditionally segregated job categories. More recently, the Court has taken a somewhat tougher stance on affirmative action programs, holding in *Adarand Constructors, Inc. v. Peña (1995) that federal programs of this sort must meet a test of "strict scrutiny" in order to be constitutional.

James E. Jones, Jr.

U.S. Term Limits, Inc. v. Thornton, 514 U.S. 779 (1995), argued 29 Nov. 1994, decided 22 May 1995 by vote of 5 to 4; Stevens for the Court, Kennedy concurring, Thomas, Rehnquist, O'Connor, and Scalia in dissent. By the late 1980s and early 1990s the perceived advantages held by incumbents in Congress and in state legislatures stimulated a nationwide movement to place restrictions on the number of terms that elected officials could serve. Between 1990 and 1993, for example, twenty-three states placed such restrictions on members of their congressional delegations and an even larger number imposed limitations on their state legislators. Moreover, in 1994 Republican candidates for Congress pledged in their "Contract with America" to bring a proposed term limit amendment to a vote. The entire term limits debate evoked images of citizen lawmakers versus corrupt professional politicians.

At the general election in 1992, the voters of Arkansas adopted Amendment 73. This ballot initiative applied term limits to three groups: elected officials in the executive branch, members of the state legislature, and the Arkansas congressional delegation. In the case of the third group, the new amendment restricted persons serving in

the Congress to three terms and persons serving in the United States Senate to two terms. The amendment provided that persons who exceeded these limits would not be certified to be on the ballot, although this arrangement did not restrict a candidate from running a write-in campaign. The sponsors of the amendment argued that the states alone had authority to determine who they wished to send to Congress and that the question of election qualifications was the business of the states and not of the federal government.

The proponents of Amendment 73 insisted that the regulation was not a qualification to hold office but simply a ballot access measure of the sort authorized by the federal Constitution's "elections clause." The Arkansas measure simply continued a practice reaching back to the colonial era in which the states were fully empowered to set nominating rules and procedural limits. Moreover, the framers of the federal Constitution had intended as much, since they wanted, above all else, a Congress of citizen legislators, who would not want to stay in office indefinitely. While supporters of the term limit concept differed over whether Congress or the states alone could pass these measures, they all agreed that better government required higher turnover in office.

The critics of Amendment 73 insisted that the states could regulate the integrity of the electoral process only within a single electoral cycle, and that the states could not supersede the provisions of Article I, section 2, clause 3 (House of Representatives) and Article I, section 3, clause 3 (Senate), which laid out the qualifications for office. They complained that the Arkansas amendment had established a qualification for serving in Congress by limiting the terms of service that a candidate could offer to the public. The replacement of incumbent congressmen was the function of the electoral process; provisions dealing with membership in Congress were beyond the reach of the states.

Justice John Paul Stevens's majority opinion was direct. According to Stevens, the framers of the Constitution had intended for there to be a uniform national legislature that represented the people of the United States. Such a requirement could not be met through Amendment 73, since the states were prohibited from establishing their own qualifications for congressional service. The assertion that the Arkansas amendment was a ballot access measure was simply wrong, both as a matter of history and good constitutional sense. Amendment 73 was nothing more than an indirect attempt to circumvent the clear requirements of the federal Constitution and to trivialize the basic democratic principles upon which that document rested. Even Congress, Stevens observed, could not summarily change the terms of Article I, section 4, which allowed the states to establish the times, places, and manner of holding elections for senators and representatives but gave Congress the authority at any time to alter such regulations. Stevens noted that such an arrangement would put Congress in the position of setting its own qualifications, something that the framers had rejected. As Justice Stevens reminded his colleagues, the Tenth Amendment could only reserve that which existed before. While the Articles of Confederation had contained a term limits provision, the framers of the Constitution in Philadelphia had specifically rejected a proposal to require "rotation" in office. Although the possibility of the states setting their own term limits was not discussed at the constitutional convention, the absence of such a discussion meant, according to the majority, that it was implicitly rejected. "Permitting individual states to formulate diverse qualification for their representatives," Stevens concluded, "would result in a patchwork of state qualifications, undermining the uniformity and the national character that the framers envisioned and sought to insure" (p. 850). The framers of the Constitution, in short, never intended that the states would be allowed to exclude from congressional service whole classes of people, such as those who had already served three terms in the House or two terms in the Senate. Any change in these provisions could be accomplished only through the federal amending process.

Justice Clarence Thomas's forceful dissent argued in support of the constitutional and political wisdom of Amendment 73.

Thomas noted that more than 60 percent of the voters in Arkansas had approved the ballot initiative and that it had passed in every congressional district. By failing to accept the Arkansas measure, the Court had, according to Thomas, misrepresented the nature of the federal union. That union, he declared, was based on the consent of the people of each individual state, not the consent of the un-differentiated people of the nation as a whole. Thomas's opinion served as a dramatic reminder of how the conservative members of the Court wanted to rewrite the script of modern constitutional law by resurrecting the idea that the states were the authentic organs of democratic government. Since the Constitution had not specifically enumerated the powers of the federal government to set qualifications, then the power to do so was specifically reserved under the Tenth Amendment to the states.

Justice Anthony M. Kennedy's concurring opinion was particularly important, since it represented the views of the critical swing vote in the case. Kennedy reminded the dissenters, with whom he often sided, that citizens of the United States had a dual identity, one state and one federal, which formed the major "discovery" of the American constitutional system. The power to add qualifications for membership in Congress could not be seen as a power "reserved" to the states by the Tenth Amendment because it was never part of the states' original powers.

The Court's decision was among the most important of the modern era dealing with the structure of the federal government. The decision effectively wiped off the books congressional term limit provisions in twenty-three states, although it left intact measures that limited state legislators and executive branch officials. Most important, the Court affirmed the right of the people as a whole and not the states individually to serve as the building blocks of American representative government.

Kermit L. Hall

V

Van Orden v. Perry, 545 U.S. 677 (2005), argued 2 March 2005, decided 27 June 2005 by vote of 5 to 4; Rehnquist for the Court; Scalia, Thomas, and Breyer concurring; Stevens, O'Connor, Souter, and Ginsburg in dissent. On the grounds of the Texas State Capitol there are seventeen monuments and twenty-one memorials; among them is a six-foot tall monument inscribed with the Ten Commandments. The monument also includes several nonreligious symbols, such as an eagle with an American flag. At the bottom, the monument has an inscription indicating that it was a gift in 1961 from the Fraternal Order of Eagles of Texas, a civic organization. A citizen challenged the monument's placement on the capitol grounds under the Establishment Clause of the First Amendment.

The Supreme Court held that the monument did not violate the Establishment Clause. Finding the test from *Lemon* v. *Kurtzman* (1971) unhelpful in analyzing this sort of passive monument, the Court instead examined the nature of the monument and the history of the nation. It observed that acknowledgements of the role of religion, including the Ten Commandments, are common in our nation's tradition. The Court did not discount the religious message of the Ten Commandments, but it found that the existence of a religious message is insufficient to violate the Establishment Clause. The Ten Commandments also has

a historical significance, and the monument serves both a religious and historical function. Furthermore, the monument did not violate other Establishment Clause principles. In particular, it had no improper religious purpose; it was not in a location that raises special concerns, such as a public elementary or secondary school; and it manifested a relatively passive use of the religious text, which passers-by confronted only occasionally.

Justice Antonin Scalia concurred, maintaining that the Establishment Clause should allow a state to favor religion generally, through public prayer and an acknowledgement of God. Also concurring, Justice Clarence Thomas insisted that the Establishment Clause should not apply to the states and, in any event, should not prohibit government actions unless they coerce individual religious belief or practice.

Justice Stephen Breyer concurred, arguing against rigid reliance on doctrinal tests and in favor of the exercise of legal judgment according to the basic purposes of the Establishment Clause. Finding this to be a borderline case, Justice Breyer nevertheless concluded that the text of the Ten Commandments was not used in a manner that suggested government endorsement of its religious message, given its physical setting, the circumstances surrounding its placement, and its forty-year history on the capitol grounds. Justice Breyer distinguished the Ten Commandments display that the Court held unconstitutional in a case decided the same day, McCreary Country v. ACLU of Kentucky. He joined the majority, comprised of the dissenters in this case, to reject the McCreary County display because, in his view, the history of that display revealed the religious objectives of those who mounted it. It was therefore an effort to promote religion not to reflect the secular impact of a religiously inspired document.

Justices John Paul Stevens, Sandra Day O'Connor, David H. Souter, and Ruth Bader Ginsburg dissented in various combinations, finding, for different reasons, that the monument conveyed a religious message.

Lisa Bressman

Veazie Bank v. Fenno, 8 Wall. (75 U.S.) 533 (1869), argued 18 Oct. 1869, decided 13 Dec. 1869 by vote of 7 to 2; Chase for the Court, Nelson, joined by Davis, in dissent. This important case arose out of the need for revenue to finance the Union effort in the Civil War. In 1866, Congress enacted a statute that increased a 1 percent tax on state bank notes to a rate of 10 percent. The Veazie Bank of Maine refused to pay the increased tax, and a case ensued between the bank and Fenno, a collector of internal revenue. The bank contended that the 10-percent levy was excessive and threatened it with extinction. Congress, the bank argued, could not use its taxing power to destroy the bank. Such an action was an unconstitutional use of Congress's power to tax because the levy was a direct tax forbidden by the Constitution and because the levy was a tax on a state agency, as Veazie Bank had been chartered by the State of Maine.

Justice Salmon P. Chase held that, consistent with *Hylton* v. *United States* (1796), the tax on bank notes did not constitute a direct tax within the meaning of the Constitution. Nor was the levy a tax on a state instrumentality. Finally, he ruled that the tax was not unconstitutional simply because Veazie Bank thought the tax excessive. Congress's authority in this matter was clear, Chase concluded, and the remedy for excessive taxes was through the political process, not the courts. Indeed, Chase concluded that the act could be viewed not as a tax but as an action to control the national currency, clearly a congressional function. Chase's explanation of the power to tax would prove to be an important landmark in the years ahead, as

the taxing power became a powerful instrument of public policy.

In dissent, Justice Samuel Nelson insisted that Congress had overreached its authority. Nelson thought that the statute impaired the authority of the states, as constitutionally sovereign bodies, to incorporate and control the banks that operated within their borders.

Augustus M. Burns III

Veronia School District v. Acton, 515 U.S. 646 (1995), argued 28 Mar. 1995, decided 26 June 1995 by vote of 6 to 3; Scalia for the Court, Ginsburg concurring, O'Connor in dissent. *Veronia* was yet another example of the ways in which the war on drugs raised seminal questions about the scope of individual liberty and the extent of the government's authority to limit that liberty in the name of reduced drug use. In this instance, a school district in a small (population three thousand) Oregon logging town. Veronia, decided on a new way to attack the problem of student drug use after a host of other approaches proved unsatisfactory. Faced with what they believed was rampant use by students, especially athletes, of drugs, the Veronia School Board in 1989 approved a program of random drug testing of all athletes. The school board reasoned that if drug use could be cut among the athletes and if they could become wholesome role models, then drug use as a whole would decline. At the start of each season, the new rule provided, school authorities would collect and analyze urine samples from middle and high school athletes to see if drugs were present. Throughout the remainder of the season all athletes would be susceptible to testing at random intervals. The school board sent the samples to a private firm, whose analysis was valid 99.4 percent of the time. Any athlete that refused to take the test was prohibited from participating in athletics for two years, while those who tested positive had to agree to drug counseling and a period of suspension from organized athletics.

James Acton was a twelve-year-old seventh grader in 1991 who wanted to try out for the football team. His parents, however, refused to sign a urinalysis consent form. There was never any suspicion that James, a model student, either had used or was using drugs. His parents objected to the policy as an interference with his and their privacy and, in essence, an unreasonable search of his body prohibited by the Fourth

Amendment to the Constitution. They insisted that the responsibility for drug testing rested with them, not the school board.

The Supreme Court and lower federal courts had previously dealt with issues of random drug testing for workers in areas vital to safety, such as railroads, and national security. Never before had the high court entertained the questions of whether schools might engage in such testing and whether such testing might be random. After the federal district court in Oregon dismissed the Actons' suit, the Court of Appeals for the Ninth Circuit proceeded to reverse this decision and strike down the drug testing program as an unjustified violation of the privacy of students not suspected of drug use and an unreasonable search precluded by the Fourth Amendment. That Ninth Circuit opinion, however, conflicted with a Fifth Circuit Court of Appeals decision in 1988 that permitted random drug testing in the schools of Indiana, Illinois, and Wisconsin. The Supreme Court then stepped in to settle, for the first time, the constitutional law of drug testing in schools.

The justices gave a clear victory to the supporters of such testing. Justice Antonin Scalia's opinion for the Court affirmed the school district's policy as a "reasonable and hence constitutional" practice on three grounds (p. 680). First, Scalia found that students generally and student athletes in particular had lower expectations of privacy in communal locker rooms and rest rooms. In any case, the Court had already settled the matter that school officials could exercise "a degree of supervision and control that could not be exercised over free adults" (p. 663). Second, because the samples were taken in relative privacy and with a high level of confidence in the laboratory testing, there could be no concerns about the school's actions being overly obtrusive. Third, and perhaps most important, Scalia concluded that the school board had identified an important interest in attacking drug use in the schools and that its program, of making sure that important leaders on campus were drug-free, was likely to be effective. The school system did not, in Scalia's eyes, have to fulfill the traditional Fourth Amendment requirement of individualized suspicion before the government could act to conduct a search, since the state had identified a compelling state interest and students were not, in the end, accorded the same rights as were adults under the Fourth Amendment.

Justice O'Connor's dissent actually supported the idea of random drug testing, but it took strong exception to Scalia's willingness to set aside the traditional requirement of individualized suspicion. According to O'Connor, the actions of the Veronia School Board amounted to a mass, suspicionless search that was, on its face, unreasonable. What would have been reasonable? According to O'Connor it would have been "far more reasonable" for school officials to limit drug testing to those students who were disciplinary problems. Justice Ruth Bader Ginsburg argued in her concurring opinion that the decision applied only to student athletes, but none of the other members of the Court joined her in drawing that distinction.

The Court essentially found that the importance of the schools' interest in deterring drug use by students outweighed the students' limited privacy rights. Civil libertarians condemned the decision for making students second-class citizens and sacrificing individual rights at the altar of the drug war. Proponents, including the administration of President Bill Clinton, hailed the decision as another way of combating drug use among America's young people.

Kermit L. Hall

Virginia, United States v., 518 U.S. 515 (1996), argued 17 Jan. 1996, decided 26 June 1996 by vote of 7 to 1; Ginsburg for the Court, Scalia in dissent; Thomas took no part in the consideration or the decision of the case since his son was a student at the Virginia Military Academy (VMI). By 1995 only two state-supported all-male military colleges existed in the United States—The Citadel, in Charleston, South Carolina, and VMI, in Lexington, Virginia. In both instances, the colleges had excluded women from their ranks. VMI did so on the grounds that its "adversative" method of training was not appropriate for women. The Court of Appeals for the Fourth Circuit had concluded that excluding women from a state-supported military education violated the Fourteenth Amendment's guarantee of equal protection of the laws. In the case of VMI, however, the Fourth Circuit had accepted Virginia's plan to offer a military-style education for women in the Virginia Women's Institute for Leadership (VWIL) at Mary Baldwin College in nearby Staunton, Virginia. The Clinton administration then appealed this decision on the grounds that

Virginia had actually made the situation worse by not even meeting the constitutionally discredited standard of "separate but equal" in *Plessy v. Ferguson* (1896).

Counsel for Virginia argued to the Supreme Court that single-sex education offered distinctive advantages for men that would be fundamentally altered if women were admitted to the program. Women, Virginia argued, differed from men in their psychological and physical makeups. Men were better equipped for self-reliance; women were better suited to relationships. Women could not and would not be able to perform under the "adversative" method of training that had become the hallmark of an education at VMI.

The United States countered by arguing that the constitutional guarantee of equal protection of the laws under the Fourteenth Amendment prohibited a state from limiting individual rights by resorting to stereotypes. The government struck especially hard at the VWIL program set up for women who wanted military training, insisting that such a program not only denied the women the same facilities and training methods used by the men but it prevented them from demonstrating that they could ever succeed in the more rigorous environment of VMI. Finally, the government insisted that the Court should apply a standard of strict scrutiny, which had been applied to racial categories, in dealing with matters of gender discrimination.

Justice Ruth Bader Ginsburg's opinion for the Court brought an end to the 157-year tradition of all-male education at VMI. Ginsburg held that the practice violated the Equal Protection Clause of the Fourteenth Amendment. "While Virginia serves the state's sons," Ginsburg wrote, "it makes no provision whatever for her daughters. That is not equal protection" (pp. 2307–2308). Ginsburg also dismissed VWIL at Mary Baldwin College as distinctly inferior based on the quality of the faculty, the academic skills of the student body, and the physical facilities. The justice also reminded Virginia that women already attended the nation's military academies. "There is no reason," Ginsburg concluded, "to believe that the admission of women capable of all the activities required of V.M.I. cadets would destroy the Institute rather than enhance its capacity ... " (p. 2336).

Justice Antonin Scalia denounced the majority for destroying VMI, "an institution

that has served the people of the Commonwealth of Virginia with pride and distinction for over a century and half. . . . I do not think any of us, women included, will be better off for its destruction" (p. 2350). Chief Justice William Rehnquist, who refused to sign Ginsburg's opinion, authored a concurring opinion that accepted the outcome but rejected the majority's rationale for reaching it. If, according to Rehnquist, VWIL had offered a program comparable to VMI's he likely would have voted in support of it.

The VMI decision was viewed at the time as a test case for all single-sex education, even private schools that receive public funds. Whether it will prove to be that sweeping, as Scalia warned in his dissent, remains to be seen. Strikingly, the Court refused to adopt a new standard for deciding the legality of any classification based on sex, continuing as a result to adhere to the "intermediate scrutiny" test rather than replacing it with a strict scrutiny standard. At the same time, Justice Ginsburg's decision does make clear that the traditional standard will be applied in a more forceful way. Government has, therefore, to produce an "exceedingly persuasive justification" for any classification based on sex. This principle is what Ginsburg termed "skeptical scrutiny" (p. 2292).

Kermit L. Hall

Virginia v. Tennessee, 148 U.S. 503 (1893), argued 8–9 Mar. 1893, decided 3 Apr. 1893 by vote of 8 to 0; Field for the Court, Harlan not participating. Virginia invoked the original jurisdiction of the Supreme Court, asking it to set aside a survey that both Virginia and Tennessee had recognized in 1803 as correctly marking their boundary. Virginia argued that the joint recognition was unenforceable because it had not received the approval of Congress as required by the Compact Clause of Article I, section 10, which states that "no state shall, without the consent of Congress, . . . enter into any agreement or compact with another state, or with a foreign power." The "compact" was said to arise from each state's ratification of the line in consideration of the ratification by the other.

Justice Stephen J. Field rejected Virginia's argument. In Field's pragmatic view, the clause did not require congressional approval of every compact. Instead, Congress need approve only those that threatened to increase the powers of the states at the expense of the national government. Furthermore, Field reasoned that the approval need not be explicit; approval could be found, as it was here, in successive Congressional acts recognizing the result of the pact.

Field's opinion had two obvious advantages: it fit well within the Court's continuing effort to preserve a place for the states in the federal scheme, and it rid Congress of the burden of considering every joint action taken by two or more states. The interpretation is still followed and continues to allow states considerable freedom to contract with each other to deal with regional problems.

Walter F. Pratt, Jr.

Virginia v. West Virginia, 206 U.S. 290 (1907), argued 11–12 Mar. 1907, decided 27 May 1907 by vote of 9 to 0; Fuller for the Court. The first of nine cases concerning the division of fiscal responsibilities between one state and another formed from its territory, *Virginia* v. *West Virginia* sorely tested the power of the Supreme Court to enforce decrees against a state. When West Virginia separated from Virginia in 1863 during the Civil War, no settlement was made concerning its respective share of its parent's prewar state debt. Delayed by Virginia's disputes with the state bondholders even as to the share it concededly owed, negotiation on West Virginia's portion did not begin until 1894. Virginia attributed one-third of its debt to West Virginia since the latter had succeeded to one-third of its territory, while West Virginia offered to pay a much smaller share based on the proportion of the borrowed money actually expended within its borders. Negotiation proved fruitless, and in 1906 Virginia commenced an original action in the Supreme Court on behalf of the bondholders. After fact-finding by a court-appointed master, a decree was issued in 1911 apportioning West Virginia's share on the basis of property values (exclusive of slaves) at the time of separation; by this reckoning West Virginia owed less than a quarter of the original debt, plus accrued interest. When West Virginia failed to pay, Virginia—in marked contrast to its usual states' rights position—asked the Court to consider means of coercion. The possibility was raised that the Supreme Court might order the West Virginia legislature to levy a tax, or even that the Court might levy the tax itself. In 1919 West Virginia admitted liability and began payment on its share of the debt, which was completed in 1939.

John V. Orth

W

Wabash, St. Louis & Pacific Railway Co. v. Illinois, 118 U.S. 557 (1886), argued 14–15 Apr. 1886, decided 25 Oct. 1886 by vote of 6 to 3; Miller for the Court, Bradley, Waite, and Gray in dissent. In *Wabash*, the Supreme Court held that the states have no power to regulate railroad rates for interstate shipments. Substantially modifying the standard employed since *Cooley* v. *Board of Wardens* (1852), the Court said the Commerce Clause allows the states to enact "indirect" but not "direct" burdens on interstate commerce. State rate regulations were "direct" burdens on commerce and therefore could not govern interstate transportation.

Wabash did not deny the states all power over interstate railroading. The Court, for example, upheld state safety regulations as permissible "indirect" burdens. Yet *Wabash* created an important regulatory void by making rate regulation of interstate shipments an exclusive federal power. Prior to *Wabash*, the federal government had left the subject of railroad regulation almost entirely to the states. In response to the decision, Congress established the Interstate Commerce Commission (1887). Thus, *Wabash* precipitated the advent of the modern independent regulatory agency and initiated the shift of governmental responsibility for economic affairs from the states to the national government. *Wabash* remains a landmark even though the "direct" versus "indirect" test it propounded to define the

domain of exclusive federal power over interstate commerce was abandoned in the 1930s in favor of a functional balancing approach.

Stephen A. Siegel

Wade, United States v., 388 U.S. 218 (1967), argued 16 Feb. 1967, decided 12 June 1967 by vote of 5 to 4; Brennan for the Court; White, joined by Harlan and Stewart, dissented from the second part of the holding (see below) and would have upheld the conviction; Black dissented from the first part of the holding but would have upheld the conviction; Fortas, joined by Warren and Douglas, concurred in overturning the conviction, but dissented from the first part of the holding. Wade was indicted for bank robbery, and the FBI put him in a lineup without notifying his attorney. Everyone in the lineup was required to wear a mask and say "put the money in the bag." The Supreme Court held that (1) putting defendants in a lineup and having them wear certain items and utter words used in the crime is not compelled self-incrimination because it is not testimonial evidence, but also that (2) lineups are a "critical stage" of the prosecution and defendants are entitled to have counsel present. The Court thought that prejudicial conditions, perhaps created unintentionally, existed at lineups for unrepresented defendants. Wade's conviction was overturned on that basis. This holding

369

enlarged the right to counsel, already greatly expanded in *Miranda* v. *Arizona* (1966).

Many saw *Wade* as epitomizing the Warren Court's "softness" on crime. In the Crime Control and Safe Streets Act of 1968, Congress allowed use of lineup identification evidence obtained without counsel present in the federal courts. The Burger Court undermined *Wade* in *Kirby* v. *Illinois* (1972) by ruling that the right to counsel at lineups did not take effect until after indictment or its equivalent. In *United States* v. *Ash* (1973), it ruled that counsel was unnecessary when witnesses were shown photographs of the defendant.

Bradley C. Canon

Wallace v. Jaffree, 472 U.S. 38 (1985), argued 4 Dec. 1984, decided 4 June 1985 by vote of 6 to 3; Stevens for the Court, Powell concurring, O'Connor concurring in the judgment, Burger, White, and Rehnquist in dissent. Public opinion has never endorsed the Supreme Court's school prayer decisions. Since 1961, more than 75 percent of those questioned by the Gallup Poll have consistently supported reintroduction of formal prayer into the public schools. Constitutional amendments to this end were periodically but unsuccessfully introduced in Congress. The constitutional doctrine of *Engel* v. *Vitale* (1962) and *Abington* v. *Schempp* (1963) remained in force. *Wallace* was the first serious test of its continuing vitality.

The Alabama statute at issue in *Wallace*, as initially enacted in 1978, authorized schools to provide a minute of silence for "meditation." A 1981 amendment provided a similar period for "meditation or voluntary prayer," and in 1982 the law was changed to allow teachers to lead "willing students" in a specified prayer to "Almighty God." Upon challenge by Ishmael Jaffree and various separationist groups, a federal district court held that *Engel* and *Schempp* were wrong; states did have the authority to establish religion. A court of appeals reversed, and the Supreme Court granted certiorari to decide the constitutionality of only the 1981 amendment: Can a state provide a moment of silence at the beginning of a school day for the express purpose of facilitating "meditation or prayer"?

There were reasons to believe that the Court would be amenable to opening a crack in the "wall of separation" on this question. The public's support for school prayer was translated by various state legislatures into statutes aiding religious schools and practices. The election of Ronald Reagan and the legal mobilization of accommodationist forces—seven groups, including the Moral Majority, the Christian Legal Society, and the Legal Foundation of America, filed amicus curiae briefs in *Wallace*—also augured ill for separationist precedents. The Administration was dedicated to an interpretation of the Establishment Clause that would lower or abandon the "wall." It filed numerous amicus briefs before the Court and split oral argument with states sympathetic to its view (as in *Wallace*) to advance this argument.

There were also signs from the Court that it was ready to reject its earlier approach. Even before Reagan's election, it adopted an accommodationist posture in affirming, for the first time, direct payment of public funds to religious schools (*Committee for Public Education and Religious Liberty* v. *Regan*, 1980). In subsequent cases, it upheld tax credits and deductions to parents of all school children (*Mueller* v. *Allen*, 1983), state-paid legislative chaplains (*Marsh* v. *Chambers*, 1983), and a publicly sponsored nativity creche (*Lynch* v. *Donnelly*, 1984). The time seemed ripe for a reconsideration of *Engel/Schempp*. However, it proved not to be.

Justice John Paul Stevens's majority opinion striking down the law was short, to the point, and girded by separationist precedents. Applying the *Schempp* test as it had been reworked in *Lemon* v. *Kurtzman* (1971), he found the practices sanctioned by the statute to lack a "secular purpose"—one not grounded in a desire to "advance" religion. Although the meditation and prayer statute failed constitutional scrutiny, the Court left open the possibility that one confined to an undefined moment of silence might pass muster; Powell's concurrence emphasized that point. Justice Sandra Day O'Connor concurred separately to reiterate her "endorsement" standard, first articulated in her *Lynch* concurrence, and to note that a neutral moment of silence law would not be controlled by the doctrine of *Engel* and *Schempp*.

The dissents of Chief Justice Warren Burger and Justice Byron White held that the Alabama act was an example of "benevolent neutrality" and was thus constitutional under the Court's accommodationist precedents (p. 89). Justice William Rehnquist's dissent was more pointed. He contended that any decision based on *Everson* v. *Board of Education* (1947) was wrong; the

Constitution does not impose a "wall of separation" between church and state. After an extended analysis of the intent of the framers of the First Amendment, he concluded that the Establishment Clause merely forbids state establishment of a national church or preference of one sect over others and most certainly does not require a state to be neutral between religion and "irreligion."

In *Lee* v. *Weisman* (1992) the Court once again considered the issue of prayer in the schools. In this instance, the justices overturned the practice of prayer at public school graduations as transgressing the constitutional boundary between church and state.

Joseph F. Kobylka

Ward's Cove Packing Co. v. Atonio, 490 U.S. 642 (1989), argued 18 Jan. 1989, decided 5 June 1989 by vote of 5 to 4; White for the Court, Stevens (joined by Brennan, Marshall, and Blackmun) and Blackmun (joined by Brennan and Marshall) in dissent. Plaintiffs alleging employment discrimination in Alaskan salmon canneries showed a high percentage of nonwhite workers in low-paying jobs and a low percentage of nonwhite workers in high-paying jobs. The nonwhite workers relied on this disproportion in the workforce to help establish a violation of Title VII of the Civil Rights Act of 1964. The Supreme Court held that the comparison between the racial composition of the high-and low-paying jobs was flawed because the data failed to take into account the pool of qualified job applicants.

Three additional rulings in *Ward's Cove* overshadowed this holding and arguably shifted legal standards in favor of Title VII defendants. First, building on *Watson* v. *Fort Worth Bank and Trust* (1988), the Court held that, in Title VII disparate-impact cases, plaintiffs must show which specific employment practice led to the statistical disparity. Second, even if plaintiffs make a satisfactory statistical showing, if defendants supply a business justification for the practice, the ultimate burden of persuading the decision maker that discrimination occurred rests with the plaintiffs. Third, the business justification offered by the defendants must show that the "challenged practice serves, in a significant way, the legitimate employment goals of the employer" (p. 659). *Ward's Cove* was overturned by the Civil Rights Act of 1991, which shifted the burden of proof back to the employers, thereby making it easier for plaintiffs to win employment discrimination suits.

Theodore Eisenberg

Ware v. Hylton, 3 Dall. (3 U.S.) 199 (1796), argued 6–12 Feb. 1796, decided 7 March 1796 by vote of 4 to 0; Chase, Paterson, Wilson, and Cushing delivered seriatim opinions; Ellsworth and Iredell not participating (Iredell later submitted an opinion for the record). *Ware* established the supremacy of national treaties over conflicting state laws. It was representative of numerous cases brought by British creditors to recover pre-Revolutionary War debts owed them by Americans. The Treaty of Paris (1783) provided that creditors should meet with no legal impediment to the recovery of such debts. Virginia, however, enacted legislation enabling its citizens to pay debts owed to British subjects into the state treasury in depreciated currency and thereby obtain a certificate of discharge.

In losing the only case he argued before the Supreme Court, future Chief Justice John Marshall, then an attorney representing a Virginia debtor, contended that the state had a "sovereign right" to confiscate British debts during the war, that the debtor's payment into the state treasury was a lawful discharge of the debt, and that the peace treaty could not revive the debt without violating the "plighted" faith of the state and destroying vested rights accruing under state law. The Supreme Court rejected his arguments, holding that the treaty nullified the inconsistent state statute. Justice Samuel Chase set forth a sweeping nationalist interpretation of the Supremacy Clause of Article VI as operating retrospectively to "prostrate" all state laws in conflict with national treaties.

Charles F. Hobson

Washington v. Davis, 426 U.S. 229 (1976), argued 1 Mar. 1976, decided 7 June 1976 by vote of 7 to 2; White for the Court, Brennan and Marshall in dissent. This case involved the standard required to show unconstitutional racial discrimination, specifically the distinction between laws having a racially disproportionate impact and laws adopted with a racially discriminatory purpose or intent.

The case originated in 1970 as a suit by African-American police officers and unsuccessful applicants against the District of Columbia's Metropolitan Police

Department. The suit alleged that the department's promotion and hiring policies were racially discriminatory. The rejected applicants contended that the department's use of a written personnel test (Test 21), which a disproportionately high number of African-American applicants failed, violated the equal protection component of the Due Process Clause of the Fifth Amendment as well as several federal and District of Columbia statutes.

The district court held for the police department. On appeal, the decision was reversed. The court of appeals, in examining whether Test 21 unconstitutionally discriminated against African-Americans, relied on an earlier Supreme Court decision, *Griggs v. Duke Power Co.* (1971). Under *Griggs*, which developed standards for interpreting the prohibition on employment discrimination in Title VII of the 1964 Civil Rights Act, a showing of disproportionate impact was sufficient to make out a rebuttable case of unconstitutional race discrimination. Applying the *Griggs* standard, the court of appeals held that because four times as many blacks as whites failed Test 21 and because the test had not been shown to be an adequate measure of job performance, the Constitution had been violated. It found that Test 21 had a racially discriminatory impact with no adequate justification for its use.

The Supreme Court reversed the court of appeals' decision, finding that it had erroneously applied standards developed for Title VII to the Constitution. It flatly rejected the disproportionate impact claim as sufficient to make out a case of unconstitutional racial discrimination. Rather, the Court held that an intent or purpose to discriminate had to be present for there to be a constitutional violation. The Court cited numerous opinions in jury discrimination, legislative apportionment, and school desegregation cases to show that its decisions had always required a showing of racially discriminatory intent or purpose for a holding of unconstitutional discrimination. Thus, the Title VII requirement for a showing of unlawful race discrimination differed from the showing required to make such a case under the Constitution.

The Court also addressed the question of what might count as proof of a racially discriminatory purpose or intent. It held that a racially discriminatory purpose could be inferred from the totality of relevant facts, including disproportionate impact.

This relatively weak test was considerably strengthened, to the disadvantage of civil rights litigants, in *Personnel Administrator v. Feeney* (1979).

Focusing on Test 21, the Court argued that the fact that many more blacks failed the test than whites did not demonstrate that the original plaintiffs were being denied equal protection. It found the test neutral on its face and rationally related to a legitimate government purpose, the modest upgrading of the communicative skills of government employees. The Court took note of the efforts of the department to recruit black officers and the changing racial composition of the recruit classes. Putting the totality of the circumstances together, no constitutional violation was found.

In their dissenting opinion, Justices William J. Brennan and Thurgood Marshall argued that the department failed to show that Test 21 was sufficiently related to the job of a police officer.

While the case remains good law, it has been criticized on several grounds. First, the Court gave little indication of how discriminatory purpose or intent is to be shown. Aside from the very few cases where statutes or policies discriminate on their face or are administered in a racially discriminatory fashion, what serves as proof? Second, as Justice John Paul Stevens suggested in his concurring opinion, the distinction between discriminatory purpose and discriminatory impact is not always clear. Indeed, if racially discriminatory impact is evidence of racially discriminatory intent, as the Court states, the two standards collapse toward each other. Third, as is often argued, the decision ignores the fact that a statute or policy lacking discriminatory intent or purpose can build on the present effects of past discrimination to produce identical results. For example, if Test 21 was intended to discriminate, and four times as many blacks failed it as whites, it would be unconstitutional, but if there were no such intent, and the result were identical because of a history of school segregation that was still being felt, no constitutional violation would occur.

Gerald N. Rosenberg

Washington v. Glucksberg, 117 S.Ct. 2258 (1997) and **Vacco v. Quill,** 117 S.Ct. 2293 (1997), argued 8 Jan. 1997, decided 26 June 1997 by vote of 9 to 0; Rehnquist for the Court, O'Connor concurring, joined in part by Ginsburg and Breyer; Stevens, Souter,

Ginsburg, and Breyer filed opinions concurring in the judgment.

As the American population has grown older and medical technology more sophisticated, the question of how and when life can be ended has become increasingly controversial. Dr. Jack Kevorkian of Michigan, for example, presided over several widely publicized incidents in which he helped people suffering from serious illnesses to kill themselves. Critics of Kevorkian argued that should the practice become widespread, it would cheapen life and fall disproportionately on those most vulnerable. At the same time, several groups eager to make the practice legal pressed lawsuits insisting that state laws banning persons from assisting in suicides were unconstitutional. Both New York and Washington state, for example, made it a felony for one person to assist another in committing suicide, although both states permitted competent persons to refuse or have withdrawn life-sustaining treatment. The Supreme Court, moreover, in *Cruzan* v. *Director, Missouri Department of Health* (1990), with Chief Justice William H. Rehnquist writing for the majority, found that persons can refuse medical treatment or stop medical care that is intrusive, even if the outcome of that decision is expected to be life-ending.

Physicians in both New York and Washington, along with several of their terminally ill patients, filed suits challenging the constitutionality of the law prohibiting assisted suicide. In New York, Dr. Timothy Quill, on behalf of two AIDS patients, claimed that there was no essential legal difference between ending a life by terminating medical treatment, as permitted by *Cruzan*, and a doctor proactively administering life-ending drugs. The United States Court of Appeals for the Second Circuit ruled, in what came to be the case of *Vacco* v. *Quill*, in favor of the plaintiffs on the grounds that the state's assisted-suicide ban violated the Equal Protection Clause of the Fourteenth Amendment. The court reasoned that while New York law permitted competent terminally ill persons to hasten their own deaths by ordering the withdrawal of life-sustaining treatment, these same persons were unconstitutionally prohibited from engaging the services of a physician to administer a lethal drug overdose.

The suit from Washington state, *Glucksburg* v. *Washington*, took a different tack. The plaintiffs there argued that the state's ban on assisted suicide violated the Due Process Clause of the Fourteenth Amendment. The United States Court of Appeals for the Ninth Circuit sustained this argument and overturned the Washington statute banning assisted suicide. The federal circuit court found that every person had a fundamental liberty interest in controlling the time and manner of their death, an interest protected by the Due Process Clause.

The high court issued two separate opinions in these cases, but it acted in essentially the same manner in dealing with both of them. Chief Justice Rehnquist spoke for the Court in both opinions, although in each case the seeming unanimity of the Court was broken by the realization that only five of the nine justices agreed that an absolute ban on assisted suicide was acceptable.

Rehnquist drew a sharp distinction between ending life by refusing treatment and ending life by assisted suicide. Thus, in *Vacco*, the chief justice concluded that as a matter of history and professional medical practice the law had correctly treated these two practices as different. Rehnquist also found that such differences were entirely rational and therefore supportable as a matter of state legislative prerogative. The government, Rehnquist observed, had a legitimate interest in banning assisted suicide, since failing to do so would undermine the role of the physician as healer, expose the vulnerable to abuse, and initiate a steady slide toward euthanasia.

Rehnquist was even more forceful in dealing with *Glucksburg* v. *Washington*. He rejected the claim that an abstract concept of personal autonomy, akin to that described in the abortion decision *Roe* v. *Wade* (1973), provided a sufficient basis to assert a due process right to commit suicide or to have someone assist in a suicide. There was not, Rehnquist made clear, a fundamental right to assisted suicide because it was not deeply rooted in the nation's history and traditions. The Washington ban on assisted suicide was acceptable because it was related to a number of important governmental interests, including protecting the integrity and ethics of the medical profession, protecting the vulnerable from mistakes, and reaffirming the value of life.

Various justices weighed in with concurring opinions, all of which suggested that the issue of assisted suicide was not entirely foreclosed from further discussion by the Court. Justice Sandra Day O'Connor, for example, speculated that a mentally competent person experiencing great suffering might be able to secure help in shaping the circumstances of his or her imminent death. Even Chief Justice Rehnquist noted that the decisions in both cases left open the possibility for further debate on the issue. Yet both decisions made a constitutional challenge unlikely to succeed without a state first enacting legislation that would permit assisted suicide. As in many other areas of the law, the Rehnquist Court decided to return the issue to the states and their legislative processes rather than imposing a federally mandated judicial solution.

Kermit L. Hall

Watkins v. United States, 354 U.S. 178 (1957), argued 7 Mar. 1957, decided 17 June 1957 by vote of 6 to 1; Warren for the Court, Clark in dissent, Burton and Whittaker not participating. Watkins, a labor union officer, appeared as a witness before a subcommittee of the Un-American Activities Committee of the House of Representatives. He was willing to answer any questions about himself and also about others whom he knew to be members of the Communist party, but he refused to answer questions about persons who may in the past have been, but were no longer, members of the party.

Watkins's conviction for contempt of Congress was set aside. Though the rationale for the decision may have been limited to the sub-committee as failure to state the subject under inquiry or to show the pertinence of the questions to the investigation, *Watkins* is especially important for its articulation of broad constitutional principles that place limits on the congressional power of investigation. The power of inquiry is not unlimited; there is no authority to expose the private affairs of individuals unless justified by a function of Congress; and it is not a function of Congress to engage in law enforcement (an executive function) nor to act as a trial agency (a judicial function). An inquiry may not be an end in itself but it must be in furtherance of a legitimate task of Congress. The Bill of Rights, said the Court, is applicable to congressional investigations. The public is entitled to be informed as to the workings of government, but this does not mean that Congress has the power to invade the private lives of individuals.

Milton R. Konvitz

Webster v. Reproductive Health Services, 492 U.S. 490 (1989), argued 29 Apr. 1989, decided 3 July 1989 by vote of 5 to 4; Rehnquist for the plurality, concurrences by Scalia and O'Connor, Blackmun, joined by Brennan and Marshall, and Stevens in dissent. *Webster* upheld various restrictions on the availability of abortion, but, more importantly, the decision was taken by partisans in the political battles over abortion as a signal that the Court was willing to accept substantially more restrictive regulation than it had earlier. As a result, interest groups, especially those supporting the abortion rights, began to mobilize more vigorously for political action in state legislatures and election campaigns.

Webster involved several restrictions imposed on abortions by Missouri. A preamble to the statute stated that life begins at conception; a majority of the Court held that this statement had no operative legal effect and therefore did not conflict with the statement in **Roe v. Wade* (1973) that a state may not adopt a particular theory of when human life begins. Another provision barred the use of state property for abortions; as a result, no public hospital in the state could perform an abortion even if the patient paid for it herself. The provision, if read broadly, might have barred private hospitals located on land leased from the state from performing abortions. A majority of the Court did not decide whether this provision would be constitutional if read broadly, holding that in its core application the provision was indistinguishable from the ban on public funding of abortions whose constitutionality had been upheld in **Harris v. McRae* (1980).

The third provision at issue required physicians to perform medically appropriate tests to determine the viability of the fetus in cases where, in the doctor's judgment, the fetus was twenty or more weeks of gestational age. In the framework established by *Roe v. Wade*, twenty weeks falls within the second trimester and, under *Roe*, regulation was permissible only to assure the health of the woman. Justice Sandra Day O'Connor, who agreed that the medical test provision was constitutional, noted that there was roughly a four-week margin of error in determining gestational age. Thus, when a doctor believes a fetus to be twenty weeks old, it might be twenty-four weeks old, which would place the pregnancy in its third trimester. Because, under *Roe*, states can regulate third-trimester abortions to protect fetuses if they are viable, O'Connor argued that the medical testing provision was consistent with *Roe*.

The plurality opinion by Chief Justice William Rehnquist argued, in contrast, that the provision was a second-trimester regulation and therefore could not be upheld unless *Roe* were modified. The opinion would have modified *Roe*. It acknowledged that the woman's interest in choosing abortion or not was a "liberty" interest protected by the Due Process Clause. But, the plurality said, that interest could be affected, consistent with the Constitution, whenever the state had a sufficient countervailing interest. *Roe* had said that the state's interest in protecting potential life increased in weight as the pregnancy advanced. The plurality rejected that analysis and insisted that the state's interest in protecting potential life was of equal weight throughout the pregnancy. Because the medical test requirement promoted the state's interest, it was constitutional.

The plurality opinion did not explicitly overrule *Roe* v. *Wade*, although the analytic framework it established appears to authorize states to adopt any regulations they desire to promote the interest in protecting potential life, including criminal bans on performing or obtaining abortions. The plurality disclaimed that it envisioned such an outcome, saying that it had confidence that state legislatures would not return to the "dark ages" of such severe restrictions on the availability of abortions. Justice Antonin Scalia concurred in the result but chastised the plurality and particularly O'Connor for failing to take the step of overruling *Roe*.

Justice Harry Blackmun, the author of *Roe*, wrote a vigorous dissent, whose tone indicates that the Court had come close to overruling *Roe*. Like the plurality, he took the medical test provision to be a second-trimester regulation that was not designed to protect the health of the woman, and he would have held that it was therefore unconstitutional.

As a matter of legal analysis, *Webster* might have been treated as unexceptional. Blackmun indicated that he agreed with the main lines of O'Connor's analysis of the medical test requirement if it was treated as a requirement to find out whether the pregnancy was in the second or third trimester. The ban on the use of public facilities was not significantly different in law, and probably not in practical impact, from the ban on the use of public funds to pay for abortions

that the Court had upheld almost a decade earlier.

Interest groups organized around the abortion issue, however, interpreted *Webster* as a major assault on *Roe*. Both sides in the abortion controversy saw political advantage to be gained by representing it as a major change in the law. Proponents of increased restrictions on the availability of abortions used the decision to prod state legislatures into doing more than they had already done; some state legislatures enacted laws that were clearly unconstitutional under *Roe*. Opponents found that they could mobilize a good deal of latent support for their position by presenting the decision as a major threat to the right to choose abortion; courts could no longer be relied on to block restrictions on the availability of abortions.

In **Planned Parenthood of Southeastern Pennsylvania* v. *Casey* (1992) the justices came to grips with *Roe* in light of their holding in *Webster*. Amid bitter division and with Justice O'Connor playing a particularly critical role, the justices reaffirmed the essential holding in *Roe* that a woman has a constitutional right to an abortion before the fetus attains viability at roughly six months into the pregnancy. As in *Webster*, however, the justices also accepted that the states might impose certain unburdensome requirements on women seeking abortions.

Mark V. Tushnet

Weeks v. United States, 232 U.S. 383 (1914), argued 2–3 Dec. 1913, decided 24 Feb. 1914 by vote of 9 to 0; Day for the Court. *Weeks* marked the birth of the federal exclusionary rule. Prior to *Weeks*, courts admitted illegally seized evidence on the premise that the individual's right of possession was secondary to the needs of justice. Subjected to warrantless arrest and searches by state officers and a federal marshal, Weeks was convicted on charges of using the mails to transport lottery tickets. His pretrial petition for return of his effects and subsequent objection to their introduction at trial laid the grounds for challenges in the Supreme Court based on the Fourth and Fifth amendments.

Narrowing the issue, Justice William R. Day emphasized the obligation of federal courts and officers to effectuate the guarantees of the Fourth Amendment. Drawing upon **Boyd* v. *United States* (1886), he suggested that the essential violation was the invasion of Weeks's right of personal security, personal liberty, and private property. The original warrantless search by the federal marshal and the trial court's subsequent refusal to return the materials violated the plaintiff's constitutional rights. Day relied exclusively on Fourth Amendment grounds to order the judgment reversed.

Weeks attracted little attention until the enforcement of prohibition compounded issues of search and seizure.

Barbara C. Steidle

Weems v. United States, 217 U.S. 349 (1910), argued 30 Nov.-1 Dec. 1909, decided 2 May 1910 by vote of 4 to 2; McKenna for the Court, White in dissent, Lurton and Moody not participating, Brewer's seat vacant. American control of the Philippines gave the Court a rare opportunity to define the protections the Bill of Rights afforded individuals. This was so because the Philippine Bill of Rights contained much of the wording of its American model.

Under Philippine law, an American disbursing officer was convicted of falsifying official documents. He was sentenced to a heavy fine and to fifteen years of hard labor while in chains. Confronted with this graphic example of Philippine justice, the Court seized on an argument first made in the defendant's brief—that the punishment was cruel and unusual. Realizing that any interpretation of the Philippine protection against such punishment would also interpret the Eighth Amendment to the American Constitution, the majority did not flinch. What was cruel and unusual, Justice Joseph McKenna said, should be determined by current sensibilities and not fixed by "impotent and lifeless formulas" (p. 373). Because the penalty was disproportionate when compared to that levied for more serious crimes, the Court ordered Weems freed because the Philippine law, which prescribed the harsh penalties, violated the ban on cruel and unusual punishment. Justice Edward White, joined by Justice Oliver Wendell Holmes, protested against judicial interference with the legislative function and against the expansive reading of constitutional protections.

John E. Semonche

Weinberger v. Wiesenfeld, 420 U.S. 636 (1975), argued 20 Jan. 1975, decided 19 Mar. 1975 by vote of 8 to 0; Brennan for the Court, Powell, joined by Burger, and Rehnquist concurring; Douglas not participating.

Following its initial decision to void a gender classification as a denial of equal protection in **Reed* v. *Reed* (1971), the Supreme Court faced a dilemma. Many sex-based classifications benefited women but not men. Should the justices consider these "benign" classifications to be equivalent to those that disfavored women? Such laws could be said to foster stereotypes ultimately harmful to women, not to mention their discrimination against men. In *Kahn* v. *Shevin* (1974), the Court had badly splintered on this question in sustaining an old Florida law that granted a property tax exemption to widows but not to widowers.

In *Weinberger*, though, a unanimous eight-member Court overturned a provision of the federal Social Security Act that awarded survivor's benefits to widows but not to widowers. The Court achieved unanimity for two reasons. First, it treated the statute not as a benevolent aid for widows, as the government had urged, but rather as a denial of equality to the deceased wife: the Fifth Amendment's equal protection principle no more allowed Congress now "to deprive women of protection for their families which men receive as a result of their employment" (p. 645) than it had in the statute voided by **Frontiero* v. *Richardson* (1973). Second, no justice believed the classification satisfied even the minimum "rational basis" test for equal protection. The clear purpose of the benefits was to help the surviving parent to raise a child. For this goal, the law's gender distinction was "entirely irrational."

G. Roger McDonald

Wesberry v. Sanders, 376 U.S. 1 (1964), argued 18–19 Nov. 1963, decided 17 Feb. 1964 by vote of 7 to 2; Black for the Court, Clark concurring in part and dissenting in part, Harlan in dissent. This is the second of the "reapportionment decisions" of the 1960s, which established that federal courts have jurisdiction to enforce the constitutional requirement that representation in governmental bodies be based on equal-population districts. The first, **Baker* v. *Carr* (1962), was not a ruling on the merits but a holding that the question of the apportionment of a state legislature is a justiciable question.

Wesberry dealt with the apportionment of congressional districts in Georgia, which were challenged under Article I, section 2, which provides that "The House of Representatives shall be composed of Members chosen every second Year by the People of the several states," and the part of section 2 of the Fourteenth Amendment that provides that "Representatives shall be apportioned among the several states according to their respective numbers."

In *Baker*, Justice William J. Brennan had argued for the Court that since the question of whether the Tennessee legislature's reapportionment of its own legislative districts did not present the Court with the possibility of a conflict with a coordinate branch of the national government, the Court could handle the matter as a justiciable issue. In *Wesberry*, however, the Court was faced with such a conflict. Congress had made a deliberate decision in 1929, reaffirmed after each decennial apportionment, to drop any requirement that state legislatures create congressional districts that were compact, contiguous, and equal in population.

Wesberry involved a challenge by voters in Georgia's Fifth Congressional District, the population of which was two to three times greater than that of other congressional districts. Claiming that their vote had been debased by the Georgia legislature's failure to realign congressional districts on a population basis, they brought a class action asking that the apportionment statute be declared unconstitutional and that the Georgia officials be enjoined from conducting elections under it. A three-judge district court, although recognizing a constitutional issue, dismissed the complaint for "want of equity," primarily relying on Justice Felix Frankfurter's opinion in *Colegrove* v. *Green* (1946).

Justice Hugo Black promptly disposed of the political question issue on the grounds that the "right to vote is too important in our free society to be stripped of judicial protection" (p. 7). He also completely ignored prior actions of Congress and construed Article I, section 2, as commanding that "as nearly as is practicable one man's vote in a congressional election is to be worth as much as another's." Hence, "[w]hile it may not be possible to draw congressional districts with mathematical precision," the "Constitution's plain objective" is that "equal representation for equal numbers of people" is a fundamental goal for the House of Representatives (p. 18).

Justice John M. Harlan, in dissent, rather persuasively pointed out that such a conclusion could hardly be drawn from the intent of the framers—as Black had argued—or from Congressional actions that had, rather

pointedly in the 1929 reapportionment act, deleted the requirement of five previous acts that congressional districts be equal in population.

With the coming of computers it became possible, contrary to Black's observation, to draw congressional districts with mathematical precision, and, in *Kirkpatrick* v. *Preisler* (1969), that quickly became the Court's constitutional standard for congressional apportionment. State legislatures and other governmental bodies were held to a less rigidly precise mathematical standard in *Mahan* v. *Howell* (1973). Later cases have made it clear that the Supreme Court will now tolerate substantial deviations (of as much as 20 percent or more) in state districting. The Court has, however, maintained the "near precision" requirement for congressional districts.

J. W. Peltason

West Coast Hotel Co. v. Parrish, 300 U.S. 379 (1937), argued 16–17 Dec. 1936, decided 29 Mar. 1937 by vote of 5 to 4; Hughes for the Court, Sutherland in dissent. In *West Coast Hotel Co.* v. *Parrish*, the Supreme Court supposedly made "the switch in time that saved nine." The decision was handed down less than two months after President Franklin D. Roosevelt announced his plan to pack the Supreme Court with justices supportive of New Deal economic regulation. Yet the circumstances surrounding the *Parrish* decision have made it seem more of a direct reaction to the court-packing plan than it probably was.

Parrish heralded greater Supreme Court deference to economic regulation by upholding a Washington State minimum wage law for women. In doing so, the Court ratified a policy that many argued was desperately needed by underpaid women workers. However, because the minimum wage for women rested on a theory of women's inequality, and because labor restrictions based on gender interfered with women's employment opportunities, many feminists opposed minimum wage laws.

In *Lochner* v. *New York* (1905), the Court had struck down a statute restricting the number of hours bakers could work on the basis that it violated the due process rights of employers and employees to freedom of contract. In *Muller* v. *Oregon* (1908), however, the Court had upheld a statute limiting the number of hours women could work under the theory that states had a greater interest in regulating the employment of women because their central role as childbearers meant that women's health was essential to the well-being of future generations. The Court distinguished maximum hours legislation from minimum wage legislation, and ruled in *Adkins* v. *Children's Hospital* (1923) that a minimum wage law for women and children violated freedom of contract. Just one year before *Parrish* was decided, the Court had applied *Adkins* and struck down a minimum wage for women in *Morehead* v. *New York ex rel. Tipaldo* (1936).

In *Parrish*, the Court overturned the *Adkins* decision. Chief Justice Charles Evans Hughes, writing for a majority of five, argued that the concept of freedom of contract was not unlimited. "What is this freedom?" Hughes asked. "The Constitution does not speak of freedom of contract" (p. 391). The Constitution protected liberty, but subject to reasonable regulation in the interest of the community. Hughes found that state power to restrict freedom of contract was especially evident in the area of protective labor legislation for women. Relying on *Muller*, he argued that women's physical structure and their role as mothers required that the state protect them in order to "preserve the strength and vigor of the race" (p. 394). Hughes could find no relevant difference between laws regulating hours and those regulating wages, and suggested that state legislatures could address the abuses of unconscionable employers who paid their workers less than a living wage. Hughes adopted a posture of deference to legislative judgment, suggesting that even if the wisdom of a policy was debatable, the legislature was entitled to enact it as long as it was not arbitrary or capricious.

Justice George Sutherland wrote a vigorous dissent. He argued, in part, that women and men were equal under the law and that, consequently, legislation that treated them differently with respect to the right to contract constituted arbitrary discrimination.

Because Justice Owen Roberts, who voted with the majority in *Morehead*, provided the fifth vote in *Parrish*, his role in the decision has received much attention. There has been much speculation as to whether Roberts switched his vote in response to President Roosevelt's pressure. Two factors militate against such a conclusion. First, because the *Morehead* majority rested on very narrow grounds, Roberts could argue that

he had not changed his position because he had never expressed an opinion on the substantive issue in *Adkins*. More importantly, a vote on *Parrish* was taken in December 1936, before the court-packing plan, and Roberts voted to sustain the minimum wage law. Consequently, the court-packing plan seems not to have directly affected Roberts's vote. Harsh criticism of the Court preceded the court-packing plan, however, so it remains likely that Roberts's vote in *Parrish* was to some degree responsive to the concerns and pressures of the times.

□ Charles A. Leonard, *A Search for a Judicial Philosophy: Mr. Justice Roberts and the Constitutional Revolution of 1937* (1971)

Mary L. Dudziak

Weston v. Charleston, 2 Pet. (27 U.S.) 449 (1829), argued 28 Feb. and 10 Mar. 1829, decided 18 Mar. 1829 by vote of 4 to 2; Marshall for the Court, Johnson and Thompson in dissent, Trimble deceased. *Weston* involved an attempt by the city of Charleston (a political subdivision of the state of South Carolina), to tax "stock of the United States," that is, debt certificates held by creditors of the federal government. The Court struck down the tax as an interference with the Article I, section 8 power "To borrow Money on the credit of the United States." Chief Justice John Marshall reaffirmed *McCulloch* v. *Maryland* (1819), which had vigilantly guarded federal powers against state encroachment by invoking the maxim "the power to tax involves the power to destroy."

William M. Wiecek

West River Bridge Co. v. Dix, 6 How. (47 U.S.) 507 (1848), argued 5–7 Jan. 1848, decided 31 Jan. 1848 by vote of 7 to 1. Daniel for the Court, McLean and Woodbury concurring, Wayne in dissent, McKinley not participating. In *West River Bridge Co.* the Supreme Court established that the exercise of eminent domain power to extinguish a franchise did not violate the Contract Clause. In 1795 the Vermont legislature invested a corporation with the exclusive privilege of maintaining a toll bridge over West River for one hundred years. The state subsequently decided to lay out a free public highway over the toll bridge. The bridge company was awarded compensation for the appropriation of its property and franchise. The bridge company, however, objected that the state proceeding violated the

Contract Clause. Daniel Webster, appearing for the bridge company, contended that the state's action constituted an impairment of the grant to erect a toll bridge. He also argued that unrestrained use of eminent domain would allow the states despotic authority over private property.

Rejecting Webster's arguments, Justice Peter V. Daniel reasoned that all private property rights were subordinate to the paramount power of eminent domain. He emphasized that a franchise was simply a form of property. Daniel concluded that the exercise of eminent domain power did not abrogate any contractual rights protected by the Contract Clause. This decision established the principle that a grant or franchise does not divest a state of eminent domain authority and pointed the way for later rulings that a state cannot contract away certain police powers. As a result, states could use eminent domain broadly to promote public welfare.

James W. Ely, Jr.

West Virginia State Board of Education v. Barnette, 319 U.S. 624 (1943), argued 11 Mar. 1943, decided 14 June 1943 by vote of 6 to 3; Jackson for the Court, Black, Douglas, and Murphy concurring, Frankfurter, Roberts, and Reed in dissent. In 1940, in *Minersville School District* v. *Gobitis*, the Supreme Court had upheld a law mandating flag salute and recitation of the Pledge of Allegiance in public schools, rejecting a challenge brought on grounds of religious conscience by a member of the Jehovah's Witnesses. Only one dissent, that of Justice Harlan Stone, had been registered in the *Gobitis* decision. Only three years later, the Court ruled to the contrary. The majority opinion in *West Virginia State Board of Education* v. *Barnette*, written by Justice Robert Jackson, became one of the great statements in American constitutional law and history.

The Court's opinion in *Gobitis* had been taken as a signal by many that further attacks on flag salute and the pledge by Jehovah's Witnesses would now be futile. The onset of World War II made refusal to pledge loyalty to the flag even more suspect. In one week alone the Justice Department received reports of hundreds of physical assaults on Jehovah's Witnesses. Officials threatened to send nonconformist Witnesses' children to reformatories for juvenile delinquents. Witnesses' meeting places were burned and their leaders driven out of town.

In turn, these actions aroused a backlash. The *Gobitis* decision was widely criticized by scholars, and even organizations as staunchly patriotic as the American Legion supported enactment of a 1942 law making flag observance voluntary at the federal level. When Walter Barnette and other Jehovah's Witnesses brought suit challenging a compulsory flag-salute law in the schools of West Virginia, a law patterned directly on the rationale of the Supreme Court's opinion in *Gobitis*, the lower court simply rejected the *Gobitis* holding and ruled for the parents.

None of this was lost on the Supreme Court, which overruled *Gobitis* and held the West Virginia statute unconstitutional. But it did so by invoking the broad Free Speech Clause of the First Amendment rather than relying primarily on the Religion Clause.

The flag salute, said the Court, was a form of speech. The government could not compel citizens to express beliefs without violating freedom of speech. Hence, regardless of whether objections to saluting the flag were religiously based or not, that freedom had to be respected.

In a sense, the *Barnette* decision marked the end of an era. Not only was it the last of the major Supreme Court victories of the Jehovah's Witnesses, it was also the last case for many years to subsume claims for religious liberty under the free speech clause. Indeed, beginning with *Sherbert* v. *Verner* (1963), the Court began carving out constitutional exemptions exclusively for religious believers. This trend has continued, although the Court still resorts on occasion to dealing with religious issues in terms of free speech.

The true legacy of *Barnette* is less its jurisprudence than its defense of the principles of freedom. The opinion's eloquent closing has been cited in both religious and secular contexts. Thus, it said, in part: "The very purpose of a Bill of Rights was to withdraw certain subjects from the vicissitudes of political controversy, to place them beyond the reach of majorities and officials and to establish them as legal principles to be applied by the courts (p. 1185).

Leo Pfeffer

Whitney v. California, 274 U.S. 357 (1927), argued 18 Mar. 1926, decided 26 May 1927 by vote of 9 to 0; Sanford for the Court, Brandeis and Holmes concurring. In 1919, California passed a criminal syndicalism law designed to restrict the activities of the Industrial Workers of the World (IWW), a union long active in the state's agricultural fields and lumber camps. The statute prohibited advocacy of changes in the system of industrial ownership or political control.

The first significant prosecution under the law involved Charlotte Anita Whitney, social activist and prominent member of the Socialist party. In late 1919 authorities arrested her for participating in a November convention of the Communist Labor party (CLP), an organization from which she had recently resigned. At Whitney's trial, the prosecution introduced considerable IWW literature in an attempt to tie the organization to the CLP, which had generally endorsed IWW objectives. Whitney did not deny her short-lived CLP membership, and the jury convicted her solely on that count— a classic example of guilt by association.

Subsequently, the U.S. Supreme Court unanimously upheld the California statute on the basis of the state's power to protect the public from violent political action. However, in his concurrence, Justice Louis Brandeis, joined by Justice Oliver Wendell Holmes, contended that Whitney's attorneys should have argued for a clear and present danger test to distinguish between membership and dangerous action. They reasoned that the liberty protection of the Fourteenth Amendment Due Process Clause joined with the First Amendment to protect freedom of assembly from state regulation.

The Brandeis concurrence became an important step in the Court's eventual acceptance of the clear and present danger test. In *Brandenburg v. Ohio* (1969), the Supreme Court overturned *Whitney*, but a modified version of the law remains in force.

Carol E. Jenson

Wickard v. Filburn, 317 U.S. 111 (1942), argued 4 May 1942, decided 9 Nov. 1942 by vote of 9 to 0; Jackson for the Court. Perhaps the decision that best indicated how completely the Supreme Court had come in acquiescing to the nationalist economic philosophy of President Franklin Roosevelt and the Democratic majorities in both houses of Congress was *Wickard v. Filburn*. In this case, a unanimous court, speaking through Justice Robert Jackson, upheld important features of the Second Agricultural Adjustment Act (1938).

Previously, in *Mulford v. Smith* (1939), the Supreme Court had upheld the tobacco quotas set by the Second Agricultural Adjustment Act. Now the Court was asked to examine problems involving a more commonly grown crop—wheat. The specific question presented in *Wickard* was whether wheat that never left the farm should be subject to the marketing quotas established by the act.

The man who challenged the act's wheat quotas was Roscoe C. Filburn, a small Ohio farmer. Filburn maintained a herd of dairy cattle, raised poultry, and sold milk, poultry, and eggs in the open market. He planted a small acreage of winter wheat that he fed to his chickens and cattle, ground into flour for his family's consumption, and saved for the following year's seed. Filburn did not sell a single bushel of wheat in the open market. In 1941, Filburn sowed twelve acres of wheat more than he was permitted by Second Agricultural Adjustment Act's regulations. This unauthorized planting yielded 239 bushels of wheat, on which the federal government imposed a penalty of 49 cents a bushel. Filburn contested the government's assessment, arguing that the federal power to regulate commerce did not extend to the production and consumption of wheat that was never marketed.

When Filburn's challenge reached the Supreme Court in 1942, the tribunal had been dramatically refashioned by the appointments of President Roosevelt. The only justice whom Roosevelt had no hand in appointing to the Court that reviewed Filburn's case was Owen Roberts, the individual who had undergone the famous "switch in time that saved nine" in 1937. So, by 1942 the Supreme Court was very much "the Roosevelt Court."

Following the logic of the important Commerce Clause case of *United States v. *Darby Lumber Co.* (1941), Jackson held for the Court in *Wickard* that the quota on wheat authorized by the Second Agricultural Adjustment Act was constitutional under Article I, section 8 of the Constitution, which permitted Congress to "regulate Commerce . . . among the several States." Jackson maintained that wheat consumed but not marketed still had an effect upon interstate commerce and thus could be regulated. Filburn's 239 bushels of home-consumed wheat might by itself have seemed trivial, but it was part of a much larger story. In the early 1940s more than 20 percent of all the wheat grown in the country never left the farm. By consuming their own grain, Filburn and thousands of farmers like him cut the overall demand and depressed the market price of wheat. Their actions clearly affected interstate commerce and were, Jackson concluded, subject to federal regulation.

In several previous Commerce Clause cases, the Supreme Court had struggled to find an appropriate standard to determine what could be constitutionally regulated. In one line of cases, the Court held production could not be regulated. In another, it determined that intrastate commerce could be regulated only if it placed a direct burden on interstate commerce. Jackson's ruling in *Wickard* further extended the federal commerce power and, more importantly, stipulated that economic realities—not deceptive terminology like "direct" and "indirect"—should henceforth determine what matters would fall within the ambit of the Commerce Clause.

John W. Johnson

Wiener v. United States, 357 U.S. 349 (1958), argued 18 Nov. 1957, decided 30 June 1958 by vote of 9 to 0; Frankfurter for the Court. The Constitution is silent on the removal powers of the president. In *Myers* v. *United States* (1926), the Supreme Court had held that a president had the absolute right, without concurrence by the Senate, to remove executive-branch officers whom he had appointed and that Congress had no authority to limit this removal power. In dicta, Chief Justice William Howard Taft also claimed that the president had constitutional authority to remove administrators "who perform duties of a quasi-judicial character" (p. 352). In *Humphrey's Executor* v. *United States* (1935) this far-reaching claim of inherent presidential power was curtailed; the Court held that Congress could protect the independence of agencies that exercised "quasi-legislative" and "quasi-judicial" functions by prohibiting the president from removing commissioners "except for cause" (p. 629).

The facts in *Wiener* were strikingly similar to those in *Humphrey's Executor,* and so was the result. Wiener was appointed to the War Claims Commission by President Harry Truman. Under the War Claims Act, commissioners were to serve for the life of the commission; there was no provision made for removal. In 1953 President Dwight Eisenhower asked Wiener to step down. Wiener declined, and Eisenhower removed him. Wiener then filed suit with the Court of Claims for back pay from the date of his

removal to the end of the life of the commission. The Court of Claims dismissed his suit, but the Supreme Court unanimously reversed.

Writing for the Court, Justice Felix Frankfurter solidly endorsed both the philosophy and the holding of *Humphrey's Executor.* The War Claims Commission, like the Federal Trade Commission in the earlier case, was a quasi-judicial body whose officials were protected from removal by the president without good cause.

Joel B. Grossman

Williams v. Florida, 399 U.S. 78 (1970), argued 4 Mar. 1970, decided 22 June 1970 by vote of 7 to 1; White for the Court, Marshall in dissent, Blackmun not participating. Pursuant to state law, Williams was tried and convicted of a felony by a jury of six persons—the six-person jury having been adopted by Florida for all but capital cases in 1967. Williams had filed a pretrial motion to impanel a jury of twelve, arguing that the smaller jury would deprive him of his Sixth Amendment right to trial by jury. Williams was sentenced to life imprisonment. The Supreme Court approved the use of six-person juries in state criminal cases and affirmed the judgment.

Williams was the first in a series of cases decided by the Court during the 1970s that overturned centuries of legal tradition, namely, the long-established universal practice and common understanding that the constitutionally required trial jury consisted of twelve persons who decided unanimously: *Landry* v. *Hoepfner* (1988), *Colgrove* v. *Battin* (1973), *Ballew* v. *Georgia* (1978), *Johnson* v. *Louisiana* (1972), *Apodaca* v. *Oregon* (1972), and *Burch* v. *Louisiana* (1979). *Williams* held that six-person state criminal juries were constitutionally adequate because they were functionally equivalent to twelve-person juries. The ruling was particularly unexpected because only two years earlier the Court had extended the Sixth Amendment right to trial by jury to the states in *Duncan* v. *Louisiana* (1968).

Nearly all commentators on *Williams* regarded the Court's reasoning and sense of evidence as bizarre. A close reading of Justice Byron White's opinion made it clear that there was no constitutional or factual support for the ruling. The Court cited several items of "evidence" to support its assertion of functional equivalence—ranging from a statement that "it could be argued that there would be no differences," to a trial judge's thought on the economies of smaller juries. None of the items were competent evidence and most of them were not even relevant to the issue at hand.

The reviews of *Williams* were scathing. The only difference in opinion was whether the Court had been willfully or naively ignorant. Three years later in *Colegrove* v. *Battin* (1973), which authorized six-person civil juries for the federal courts, the Court answered the question in favor of willfulness. It boldly reasserted the *Williams* "proofs," added further flawed materials to the evidentiary array, and rebuked the critics of *Williams* as unpersuasive. For whatever reasons, the Court wanted smaller juries and got them.

Peter W. Sperlich

Williams v. Mississippi, 170 U.S. 213 (1898), argued 18 Mar. 1898, decided 25 Apr. 1898 by vote of 9 to 0; McKenna for the Court. An all-white grand jury indicted Williams, a Mississippi black man, for murder. An all-white petit jury convicted him and sentenced him to be hanged. Williams attacked the indictment and trial for violating the Equal Protection Clause of the Fourteenth Amendment because blacks had been excluded from jury service. Only qualified voters could serve on juries, and a Mississippi constitutional convention in 1890 had adopted literacy and poll-tax qualifications for voting, drastically reducing the number of registered black voters and effectively eliminating blacks from jury rolls after 1892. Nevertheless, the U.S. Supreme Court unanimously rejected Williams's contention, distinguishing the principle of *Yick Wo* v. *Hopkins*, (1886) that a law fair on its face would be voided if it was administered by public authorities in an unequal manner. Williams had not shown that the actual administration of the Mississippi suffrage provisions was discriminatory.

Other southern states followed Mississippi's lead, and the new laws, together with white primary elections, effectively disfranchised southern blacks until the white primaries were ended in the 1940s. *Williams* was, for practical purposes, superseded by the Civil Rights Act of 1964 and the Voting Rights Act of 1965, which banned exclusionary tests and devices in states and areas where minority turnout was unusually low.

Ward E. Y. Elliott

Willson v. Blackbird Creek Marsh Co., 2 Pet. (27 U.S.) 245 (1829), argued 17 Mar. 1829, decided 20 Mar. 1829 by vote of 6 to 0; Marshall for the Court; Trimble had died. The *Willson* decision had a double significance: it suggested what has since come to be known as the doctrine of the dormant commerce power; and it was one of several post-1824 cases that constituted Chief Justice John Marshall's retreat from the uncompromising nationalism that characterized the earlier period of his Court.

In **Gibbons* v. *Ogden* (1824), Marshall had upheld expansive congressional power under the Commerce Clause and given a broad reading of a federal coastal licensing statute. The Delaware statute challenged in *Willson,* which permitted a company to erect a dam across a minor navigable stream to drain a swamp, might have been invalidated on the same grounds. Marshall, however, upheld it. He observed in passing that Congress had not enacted any directly pertinent legislation. Hence, Marshall suggested that when Congress chose to allow its commerce power to lie dormant, states could exercise a concurrent power to regulate commerce. This indirectly repudiated an ambiguous hint in Marshall's *Gibbons* opinion that congressional power over interstate commerce was always exclusive, even when unexercised. The difference in result between the two cases may be explained in several ways. The waterway in *Willson* was insignificant, the doctrine of state police power was emergent, and the Delaware statute was defensible as a public health measure.

William M. Wiecek

Wilson v. Arkansas, 514 U.S. 927 (1995), argued 28 Mar. 1995, decided 22 May 1995 by vote of 9 to 0; Thomas for the Court. Throughout the 1980s and 1990s the so-called war on drugs posed an increasing number of new constitutional issues. From the perspective of law enforcement agencies, the "war" required the fullest possible exertion of their authority; from the vantage point of civil libertarians, the rights of suspects were likely to be the first casualties of the war. One area of particular importance was the extent to which the police might break into a residence without announcing themselves. English common law provided for the "knock-and-announce" rule, which required the sheriff to announce his presence before entering a premises. The Supreme Court in **Ker* v. *California* (1963) issued a split decision on the matter, although many states and the federal government subsequently acted in response to it by requiring police to announce themselves. However, prosecutors in many of these same states had responded to the rising tide of drug-related crimes by attempting to carve out exceptions when there was a likelihood that the delay caused by the announcement would result in the destruction of evidence.

Arkansas was one of a handful of states that had no knock-and-announce statute. Hence, on New Year's Eve 1992 the Arkansas State Police burst unannounced into the home of Sharlene Wilson of Malvern, Arkansas. Through an informant, the police had made a number of narcotics purchases from Wilson in the days before the raid. Without knocking, the police entered Wilson's home and found a large quantity of narcotics, a gun, and ammunition and discovered Wilson busily flushing drugs down the toilet. She was arrested and ultimately sentenced to thirty one years in jail. She appealed to the Arkansas Supreme Court, claiming that the search warrant was invalid because the police had failed to follow the common-law rule of knock and announce, a rule that Wilson claimed was enshrined in the Fourth Amendment to the federal Constitution. The Arkansas Supreme Court rejected this argument and concluded that the Fourth Amendment did not include the knock-and-announce principle. The United States Supreme Court agreed to hear the case because of the conflicting views held among the lower federal courts on the subject of whether the Fourth Amendment did include the common-law rule.

Justice Clarence Thomas overturned the state court ruling and remanded the case back to the Arkansas courts for a determination of the facts. Most significantly, however, Thomas found that the Fourth Amendment's protection against unreasonable searches and seizures included the common-law principle of knock and announce. Thomas relied on a reading of the history of the Fourth Amendment to reach his conclusion, but he also found that the framers of the amendment never intended that the police must always knock and announce themselves before entering. Far from mandating a rigid rule, Thomas held, the framers wanted to make certain that the police had sufficient discretion to prevent evidence from being destroyed, police officers from being put in harm's way, and suspects from escaping. The question of how to apply this discretion was left by the high court to lower courts to decide on a factual basis.

The ruling was a rare victory in the era of the Rehnquist Court for defendants in criminal cases. In light of *Wilson*, the police now have to have some good reason before they start knocking down doors.

Kermit L. Hall

Winship, In re, 397 U.S. 358 (1970), argued 20 Jan. 1970, decided 31 Mar. 1970 by vote of 6 to 3; Brennan for the Court, Harlan concurring, Burger, Stewart, and Black in dissent. The Supreme Court's extension of criminal defendants' rights to juveniles faced with possible incarceration revealed the inconsistencies between existing juvenile procedures in the states and the adversary standards implied by In re *Gault (1967). Winship addressed one of these and, in the process, raised significant jurisprudential questions about the nature of due process in a constitutional system.

At issue was the standard of proof necessary to commit a twelve-year-old boy to a training school for an act that would have constituted larceny if committed by an adult. Under New York juvenile law at the time, a family court judge needed only a "preponderance of the evidence" to justify juvenile detention, rather than the criminal standard of proof "beyond a reasonable doubt."

On appeal, the Court ventured beyond the explicit guarantees of the Constitution (since the reasonable doubt standard is nowhere specified) to assert that such a standard, accepted at common law and historically by the Court for determining guilt, was essential for due process and the fair treatment of juveniles facing incarceration; furthermore, it would not disturb the distinctiveness and flexibility of juvenile adjudication. The Court thus "constitutionalized" the reasonable doubt standard for adult criminal defendants as well as juveniles.

Significantly, Chief Justice Warren Burger's dissent foreshadowed the emergence of a more conservative attitude toward the procedural protections afforded minors. A year later, the Court sharply curtailed the expansion of due process. In *McKeiver* v. *Pennsylvania* (1971) it narrowly interpreted *Gault* and *Winship* and denied juveniles the right to trial by jury.

Albert R. Matheny

Winstar Corporation, United States v., 518 U.S. 839 (1996), argued 24 Apr. 1996, decided 1 July 1996 by vote of 7 to 2; Souter for the plurality, Breyer concurring, Scalia concurring in the judgment, Rehnquist, dissenting, joined in part by Ginsburg. This complex and highly fragmented case had its genesis in the savings and loan industry debacle of the late 1970s and early 1980s. In an effort to resolve the problem of failing thrifts, the federal government induced healthy thrift institutions to acquire them by promising special accounting treatment that would permit the acquiring thrifts to claim notional "goodwill" as part of their required "regulatory capital."

However, subsequent legislation forbidding thrifts to count goodwill toward regulatory capital made no exception for those relying on earlier promises. Winstar, for instance, was seized by regulators because it failed to meet capital requirements under the new rules. The United States court of appeals held that the promises constituted valid contracts.

In the Supreme Court, the government stressed two constitutional issues. Under the "unmistakability doctrine," the government had to waive its sovereign power and agree to be liable for a breach of contract "in unmistakable terms." Under the "sovereign acts" doctrine, "public" acts of government would not be deemed to modify its contractual obligations.

Justice David Souter, writing for the plurality, stated that the unmistakability doctrine was inapplicable because the United States was not waiving its sovereignty—it could enact new banking regulations and pay damages. Respecting sovereign acts, he concluded that the promise to permit acquiring thrifts to count goodwill as regulatory capital was not a public act. Furthermore, treating the government as a private contracting party, it could not show "impossibility" of performance to excuse breaching its agreement.

While nuances in the various opinions limit *Winstar*'s clarity as precedent, the case supports the proposition that government contracts should be adjudicated under normal contract principles.

Steven J. Eagle

Wisconsin v. Mitchell, 508 U.S. 476 (1993), argued 21 Apr. 1993, decided 11 June 1993 by vote of 9 to 0; Rehnquist for the Court.

Wisconsin was one of several states to pass so-called hate crime statutes, measures designed to inflict greater punishment on persons who committed crimes motivated by racial or other bias. The Wisconsin legislature had authorized stiffer sentences for crimes already on the books if the defendant had intentionally selected the person or property based on race, religion, color, disability, sexual orientation, national origin, or ancestry. Such measures came under increasing scrutiny in the early 1990s as defendants claimed that, among other things, these laws violated their freedom of expressive conduct under the First Amendment. For example, in *R.A.V.* v. *City of St. Paul* (1992) the justices held that government could not selectively silence speech on the basis of its content even if that expression was based on racial, religious, or gender bigotry. The justices in *Mitchell*, however, took a decidedly different tack.

The case involved Todd Mitchell, a black teenager from Kenosha, Wisconsin. He was convicted of leading an assault in October 1989 on a white teenager with the words, "There goes a white boy; go get him." The incident, which left the victim in a coma for four days, flowed directly from a scene in the movie *Mississippi Burning*, in which similar treatment was accorded a black teenager. Mitchell was convicted and sentenced to a four-year term, twice the length ordinarily imposed, because the victim had been selected based on his race. Mitchell appealed the sentence and the Wisconsin Supreme Court overturned the law on the grounds that it had the effect of punishing thought.

In a rare show of unanimity meant to underscore the strength of their purpose, the justices acted without either dissent or concurrence in reversing the Wisconsin Supreme Court. Chief Justice William H. Rehnquist held that the abstract thoughts of a defendant could not be taken into account in sentencing, but that once belief had turned into action it could be punished. "A physical assault is not by any stretch of the imagination expressive conduct protected by the First Amendment," the chief justice wrote (p. 484). A judge was entirely justified, moreover, in taking into account a defendant's motive in committing an offense, a long-established practice in criminal sentencing.

Kermit L. Hall

Wisconsin v. Yoder, 406 U.S. 205 (1972), argued 8 Dec. 1971, decided 15 May 1972 by vote of 6 to 1; Burger for the Court, Douglas in dissent, Powell and Rehnquist not participating. In this case the Supreme Court decided that the application of Wisconsin's compulsory high school attendance law to children of members of the Conservative Amish Mennonite Church violated the parents' rights under the Free Exercise Clause of the First Amendment.

The Court decided that a state's interest in universal education is not totally free from a balancing process when it impinges on other fundamental rights, such as those specifically protected by the Free Exercise Clause and the traditional liberty interests of the parents with respect to the upbringing of their children. The Amish had argued that enforcement of this law after the eighth grade would gravely endanger if not destroy their religious beliefs. They pointed to their long history as a self-sufficient religious community, the sincerity of their beliefs, and the interrelationship of those beliefs with a unique way of life, and the need to continue that interplay for the survival of the sect.

The majority concluded that the Amish met the difficult burden of demonstrating that their alternative mode of informal vocational education did not violate the objectives and important state interests upon which the Wisconsin Supreme Court had relied in sustaining the state's program of compulsory high school attendance. The Amish demonstrated that forgoing one or two additional years of compulsory education would not impair the physical or mental health of their children or their ability to become self-supporting and productive citizens. Moreover, the Amish argued that high school attendance emphasizes intellectual and scientific accomplishments, self-distinction, and competitiveness—all values opposed to Amish concerns for learning through doing, a life of goodness, support for community welfare, and separation rather than integration into worldly society.

The Court decided that genuine religious beliefs, not mere personal preference or philosophical wants, were behind the Amish claims. Also important to the Court was the breadth and historical constancy of Amish religious culture; the Court acknowledged that secondary school life would present a far greater threat to their religious community than grammar school. Compulsory high school attendance, the Court found, would undermine the Amish religious community by forcing young adherents to abandon the free exercise of their religion or move to more tolerant environs.

The Court rejected the State's claims that only religious beliefs, not actions, even though religiously grounded, are within the protection of the First Amendment. The Court drew on *Sherbert* v. *Verner* (1963) to argue that a regulation neutral on its face may in its application offend the constitutional requirement for government neutrality if it unduly burdens the free exercise of religion. Where parents' interests in their children's religious upbringing are combined with a valid free exercise claim, more than the usual reasonableness basis test is needed to sustain the law.

The Court repeatedly emphasized the historical uniqueness and self-sufficiency of the Amish community. Indeed, it went out of its way to suggest that without such a long history, courts should not grant the exemption from compulsory school attendance laws. Few other groups, the Court said, will be able to carry the burden of showing that informal vocational education or other training will meet valid state interests in compulsory school attendance.

Justice William O. Douglas's dissent focused on the narrowness of the Court's framework, which encompassed only the interests of the parents and the state. He argued that the child must first be heard as to his or her desire for a high school education and emancipation from the Amish religion and community. In addition, he questioned whether only formal religious communities can seek an exemption from compulsory high school for their adherents.

Many scholars believe, as Douglas did, that the Court made a content-based choice in violation of a cardinal principle of the First Amendment. They question the Court's reasoning in choosing to grant exemptions from attending high school to those with prescribed religious beliefs and long-standing membership in religious communities, while apparently withholding such opportunities from citizens and groups whose independent and individualistic moral choices are based on secular grounds. In addition, many scholars agree with Douglas that children have constitutional rights of religious beliefs and liberty interests that may be different from those of their parents and that they need a neutral legal forum for their protection.

□ Jesse H. Choper, "Defining 'Religion' in the First Amendment," *University of Illinois Law Review* (1984): 579–613.

Ronald Kahn

Wolf v. Colorado, 338 U.S. 25 (1949), argued 19 Oct. 1948, decided 27 June 1949 by vote of 6 to 3; Frankfurter for the Court, Douglas and Murphy in dissent. Wolf was convicted of conspiracy to commit abortion in Colorado. The Colorado Supreme Court affirmed the conviction against Wolf's challenge to the constitutionality of the seizure and the use of evidence in criminal proceedings. Granting certiorari, the U.S. Supreme Court considered whether the Fourth Amendment search and seizure protection was incorporated by the Fourteenth Amendment's Equal Protection Clause and thereby applicable to the states as well as the federal government. The Court also considered whether incorporation required the application of the exclusionary rule as defined and applied to federal court in *Weeks v. United States* (1914). The Court responded in the affirmative to the first question but rejected the extension of the exclusionary rule to state courts.

Writing for the majority, Justice Felix Frankfurter argued that protection from arbitrary intrusion by law enforcement is implied in the "concept of ordered liberty" and thereby incorporated by the Fourteenth Amendment and applicable to the states (p. 27). He rejected, however, the claim that illegally or unconstitutionally obtained evidence had to be excluded in state criminal proceedings. Frankfurter acknowledged that such a rule could deter police from unreasonable searches but stressed that there were other means of enforcing such a basic right and that state courts were resistant to the rule defined in the *Weeks* decision. Much the same arguments were offered by Justice Hugo Black in a concurring opinion in which he emphasized that incorporation did not require the application of a "judicially created rule of evidence" (p. 40).

Two dissenting opinions were filed in the case: one by Justice William O. Douglas and one by Justice Frank Murphy with Wiley B. Rutledge in agreement. Douglas observed that the Fourth Amendment protection is rendered ineffective without the exclusion of evidence seized in an unconstitutional fashion, while Murphy stressed that few states would devise practically efficient means of redressing Fourth Amendment violations.

Wolf has since been overruled by *Mapp v. Ohio,* (1961). The Supreme Court accepted the minority position in *Wolf* and required states not only to abide by Fourth Amendment provisions but to exclude evidence seized in violation of such protections.

Susette M. Talarico

Wolff Packing Co. v. Court of Industrial Relations, 262 U.S. 522 (1923), argued 27 Apr. 1923, decided 11 June 1923 by vote of 9 to 0; Taft for the Court. Kansas startled the nation in 1920 by enacting the Industrial Relations Act, which provided for the compulsory arbitration of all disputes in key industries—food, clothing, fuel—through a specially appointed court. This court had the right to restrict strikes and employer lockouts, and also had the power to fix wages and oversee working conditions. The measure proved to be unpopular with both management and labor.

Ruling the law unconstitutional, Chief Justice William Howard Taft used the occasion to formulate definitive guidelines for freedom of contract and to settle precisely which businesses could be regulated on the basis of being "affected with a public interest." These included businesses carried on under the authority of a public grant (i.e., public utilities that rendered public services; occupations traditionally recognized as vested with a public service dimension, such as inns, cabs, grist mills; and businesses where natural economic laws did not operate, such as monopolies or businesses whose operations had changed toward public service so as to warrant some governmental regulation.

The ruling negated a half-century of legal development since *Munn v. Illinois* (1877) by putting the majority of businesses outside the reach of state regulation. Economic freedom became the rule, and restraint the exception. Affording the legal rationale for even more vigorous assaults upon statutes directly regulating business behavior, the case led to the voiding of a series of state measures enacted to impose social controls upon a variety of private businesses.

Paul L. Murphy

Wong Kim Ark, United States v., 169 U.S. 649 (1898), argued 5–8 Mar. 1897, decided 28 Mar. 1898 by vote of 6 to 2; Gray for the Court, Fuller and Harlan in dissent, McKenna not participating. This case arose out of the debate over the exclusion of Chinese from the United States in the late nineteenth century. At issue was the citizenship status of persons of Chinese descent born in the United States. Chinese had already been denied the privilege of becoming naturalized citizens under an 1882 act. Exclusionists urged that persons of Chinese descent should be denied birthright citizenship as well and pushed for a definition of citizenship based upon the nationality of the parents ("jus sanguinis") rather than upon place of birth ("jus soli").

The issue came before the Supreme Court when Wong Kim Ark, born to Chinese parents in San Francisco in 1873, was denied admission to the United States after traveling to China for a visit. The decision hinged upon the interpretation of the first clause of the Fourteenth Amendment, which provided that "all persons born or naturalized in the United States, and subject to the jurisdiction thereof, are citizens of the United States." The government argued that Wong Kim Ark was not a citizen because his Chinese parentage made him subject to the emperor of China. The Supreme Court, however, ruled in favor of Wong Kim Ark, holding that the common law and the Fourteenth Amendment guaranteed citizenship to all persons born in the United States, regardless of their ethnic heritage. The case proved to be an important legal victory for Chinese-Americans as well as other persons of Asian descent during a period of intense anti-Asian sentiment.

Lucy E. Salyer

Woodruff v. Parham, 8 Wall. (75 U.S.) 123 (1869), argued 13 Oct. 1869, decided 8 Nov. 1869 by vote of 8 to 1; Miller for the Court, Nelson in dissent. The plaintiffs refused to pay the Mobile, Alabama, tax on sales of goods at auction, contending that, since their goods were brought in from other states and sold in original packages they were exempt from taxation. They invoked the Constitution's prohibition against state taxation of imports and the Commerce Clause, stressing the original package doctrine established in *Brown* v. *Maryland* (1827). In *Brown*, the Court held that state power over commerce attached when a commodity lost its character as an import. While in its original package it remained a part of interstate commerce. In *Woodruff* the Court read the *Brown* precedent narrowly, holding that the Constitution did not prohibit one state from taxing articles imported from another provided the taxing state did not discriminate against such goods. As this case concerned a tax imposed on all sales made in Mobile, it did not discriminate against interstate commerce. Conversely, the opinion underscored

the limitations of state power. States could not tax products of other states so as to drive them out of the jurisdiction or interfere with commerce between the states; a tax that attempted to fetter interstate commerce would be unconstitutional. Thus, the *Woodruff* decision helped to establish the principle that state discrimation against interstate commerce violated the Commerce Clause.

Richard F. Hamm

Woodson v. North Carolina, 428 U.S. 280 (1976), argued 31 Mar. 1976, decided 2 July 1976 by vote of 5 to 4; Stewart for the Court, Brennan and Marshall concurring, White, Burger, Blackmun, and Rehnquist in dissent. Woodson, an accomplice in a robbery/murder, had been convicted of first-degree murder. Under North Carolina law, he received a mandatory death sentence. Following **Furman* v. *Georgia* (1972), North Carolina had replaced its discretionary sentencing system with a mandatory death sentence for first-degree murder. This case, decided on the same day as **Gregg* v. *Georgia* (1976), reversed the lower court's approval of mandatory sentencing on Eighth Amendment grounds.

Justice Potter Stewart's opinion held that the constitutional proscription of cruel and unusual punishments required the state to exercise its power to punish within the limits of civilized standards. Stewart insisted that evolving standards of decency have moved away from mandatory sentencing and that most death penalty laws reenacted after *Furman* did not provide for automatic death sentences. Those that did treated people not as unique individuals but as part of a faceless and inhuman mass, in violation of the Eighth Amendment. Stewart also noted that, in light of evidence that juries will tailor the death penalty to individual circumstances, the North Carolina statute might encourage juries to find a defendant innocent only to avoid mandatory capital punishment. Such choices would necessarily be made without specific statutory guidance and would thus violate the requirements set out in *Gregg*. William J. Brennan and Thurgood Marshall concurred by reiterating their view that the death penalty violated the Eighth Amendment per se. The dissenters questioned the Court's capacity to determine that mandatory sentencing was less evenhanded than a system of statutory guides to discretionary sentencing.

Lief H. Carter

Worcester v. Georgia. See CHEROKEE CASES.

Y

Yakus v. United States, 321 U.S. 414 (1944), argued 7 Jan. 1944, decided 27 Mar. 1944 by vote of 6 to 3, Stone for the Court, Roberts, Rutledge, and Murphy in dissent. The Court upheld congressional power to fetter judicial review and to delegate broad and flexible lawmaking power to an administrative agency in this constitutional challenge to the Emergency Price Control Act of 1942. The wartime anti-inflation measure, intended to expedite price control enforcement, conferred on the lower federal courts jurisdiction over violations of Office of Price Administration (OPA) regulations made under the act. But judicial power to consider the validity of such regulations was excepted. Congress specified that challenges to them be initially reviewed under stringent time limitations by the OPA and on appeal exclusively by a special Article III tribunal in the District of Columbia—the Emergency Court of Appeals and thereafter by the Supreme Court. Massachusetts meat dealer Albert Yakus, criminally prosecuted for violating the wholesale beef price ceiling, had failed to launch a procedurally difficult preenforcement attack on the regulation's constitutionality. The Court affirmed his conviction, holding that "so long as there is an opportunity . . . for judicial review which satisfies the demands of due process," the bifurcated enforcement and constitutional proceedings were permissible (p. 444).

In dissent, Wiley Rutledge, with Frank Murphy, asserted that once Congress conferred jurisdiction, it could not compel the justices to ignore *Marbury* v. *Madison* nor to violate the Constitution by criminally enforcing unconstitutional regulations. A *Yakus*-like incontestability provision reached the Court in *Adamo Wrecking Co.* v. *United States* (1978). Statutory construction facilitated evasion of the constitutional issue, but Lewis Powell, concurring, questioned the validity of *Yakus*.

Owen Roberts's dissent in *Yakus* contended that the OPA had exercised unconstitutionally delegated congressional powers. The New Deal Court majority reacted by stipulating that statutory standards need only be sufficiently defined to permit ascertainment of the administrative agency's obedience to the congressional will.

Peter G. Fish

Yarbrough, Ex parte, 110 U.S. 651 (1884), argued 23–24 Jan. 1884, decided 3 Mar. 1884 by vote of 9 to 0; Miller for the Court. The *Yarbrough* decision is the one instance during Reconstruction in which the Supreme Court upheld federal power to punish private obstruction of someone's voting rights. Yarbrough and a band of Ku Klux Klansmen were convicted of beating and wounding Saunders, a Georgia black man, to prevent him from voting in a federal congressional election. The Court unanimously upheld the conviction against claims that there was no constitutional provision authorizing the pertinent statute, which forbade conspiring to injure or intimidate any citizen in the exercise of a federal right.

Justice Samuel F. Miller considered implied powers and the "times, places, and manner clause" (Art. I, sec. 4), and observed that the Fifteenth Amendment "does, *proprio vigore*, substantially confer on the negro the right to vote" (p. 665). He justified his extremely broad interpretation of these clauses on practical grounds. Otherwise, he argued, the country would be "at the mercy of the combinations of those who respect no right but brute force" (p. 667).

This broad interpretation, however, proved to be exceptional in its time. In a similar case, *James* v. *Bowman* (1903), the Court ignored *Yarbrough* and voided the federal act for attempting to control private action.

Ward E. Y. Elliott

Yates v. United States, 354 U.S. 298 (1957), argued 8–9 Oct. 1956, decided 17 June 1957 by vote of 6 to 1; Harlan for the Court, Clark in dissent, Burton, Black, and Douglas dissenting in part, Brennan and Whittaker not participating. Fourteen Communist party leaders had been convicted under the conspiracy provisions of the Smith Act just as were the eleven defendants in *Dennis* v. *United States* (1951). But in this case the Court found two decisive differences and reversed the convictions of all defendants; however, the cases of nine of the defendants were sent back for new trials.

One of the charges was that the defendants had conspired to organize the Communist party to advocate and teach the duty and necessity of overthrowing the Government of the United States by force and violence as speedily as circumstances would permit. Although the American Communist Party was first organized in 1919, the conspiracy was alleged to have originated in 1940, when the Smith Act was enacted, and continued down to the date of the indictment in 1951. The government's contention was that the term "organize" meant a continuing process that went on throughout the life of an organization and included recruitment of new members, forming new units, organizing clubs and classes. The defense, however, contended that the party had disbanded and was reformed in 1945 and that "to organize" means to establish,

to found, to bring into existence, and that under this meaning of the term the prosecutions were barred by the three-year statute of limitations.

The Court, conceding that the term "organize" was ambiguous, held that the statute was defective for lack of precision in its definition of a crime. It held that the term "organize" as used in the Smith Act referred only to acts involving the creation of a new organization and did not connote a continuing process.

The indictment also charged the defendants with conspiring to advocate and teach the duty and necessity of overthrowing the government of the United States by force and violence. The Court found that the charge to the jury with respect to advocacy was constitutionally defective because it failed to distinguish between advocacy of forcible overthrow as an abstract doctrine and advocacy of action to that end. The Court said that *Dennis* did not obliterate that distinction. There may be advocacy of violent action to be taken immediately or at some future date. The latter case must involve the establishment of a seditious group that is maintained in readiness for action at a propitious time. Interpreting *Dennis*, the Court now said,

[T]hat indoctrination of a group in preparation for future violent action, as well as exhortation to immediate action, by advocacy found to be directed to "action for the accomplishment" of forcible overthrow, [directed] to violence "as a rule or principle of action," and employing "language of incitement," . . . is not constitutionally protected when the group is of sufficient size and cohesiveness, is sufficiently oriented towards action, and other circumstances are such as reasonably to justify apprehension that action will occur. (p. 321)

The trial court had not read *Dennis* as having this meaning. In the view of the trial court, mere doctrinal justification of forcible overthrow, if engaged in with the intent to accomplish overthrow, was punishable per se under the Smith Act. The charge to the jury—at best ambiguous or equivocal—thus blurred the essential distinction between the advocacy or teaching of abstract doctrine and the advocacy or teaching of action. The advocacy to act, however, the Court held, again interpreting *Dennis*, did not need to be incitement to take immediate action. It could have been advocacy to do something in the future, as having a group in readiness for action at an appropriate time—a time to strike when the leaders feel the circumstances permit.

The case is chiefly important as a gloss on *Dennis*. The opinion for the Court clarifies the distinction between advocacy of action and advocacy of doctrine or belief, a distinction, the Court said, that can be found in the free speech and free press cases of the 1920s, especially in *Gitlow* v. *New York* (1925). The case also elucidates the point that was so essential to the decision in *Dennis*, namely, advocacy of action in the future when circumstances will permit the action that the Smith Act proscribes.

Justices Hugo Black and William O. Douglas would have directed that all defendants be acquitted and argued that the Court should hold the Smith Act unconstitutional as a violation of the First Amendment. As a practical matter, its interpretation of *Dennis* rendered the Smith Act's conspiracy provisions virtually unusable, and no futher prosecutions were ever brought under them.

□ Milton R. Konvitz, *Expanding Liberties: Freedom's Gains in Postwar America* (1966), chap. 4. Laurence H. Tribe, *American Constitutional Law*, 2d ed. (1988), chap. 12.

Milton R. Konvitz

Yick Wo v. Hopkins, 118 U.S. 356 (1886), argued 14 Apr. 1886, decided 10 May 1886 by vote of 9 to 0; Matthews for the Court. During the summer of 1885, many Chinese in San Francisco, including Yick Wo, violated a municipal laundry ordinance to test its validity. This local law allowed only the city's Board of Supervisors to approve laundry operating licenses. Failure to secure a license and continuing to do business could result in a misdemeanor conviction, a thousand-dollar fine, and a jail term of up to six months. The ordinance did not apply to laundries located in brick buildings.

This ordinance was clearly aimed at Chinese businesses since Chinese laundries were invariably located in wooden buildings. The law followed several other attempts by San Francisco to discourage Chinese settlement. In 1870 the Cubic Air Ordinance restricted the number of occupants in Chinese apartment buildings based upon certain space requirements. The Queue Ordinance of 1876 stipulated that all Chinese prisoners had to have their hair cut, and the No Special Police for Chinese Quarter Ordinance of 1878 denied Chinatown police protection.

In addition, Chinese laundries had to pay a special fee if they used horse-drawn delivery vehicles.

The laundry ordinance was also drafted with white Californians' concern about the Chinese presence in mind. From 1820 up to 1882, the year the first Chinese Exclusion Act was passed by Congress, open immigration brought many Chinese to California. In 1880 approximately 75,000 Chinese lived in California, amounting to 10 percent of that state's population. Nearly half of California's Chinese were concentrated in the San Francisco area.

According to an 1881–1882 labor census taken in San Francisco, Chinese were primarily employed in four businesses: making cigars, shoes, and clothes, and operating laundries. Most laundries in San Francisco were owned by Chinese. Yick Wo had lived in California since 1861 and had been in the laundry business for twenty-two years. His laundry had been inspected by local authorities as late as 1884 and found safe. But in 1885 the Board of Supervisors denied him and two hundred other Chinese laundry owners their licenses. Only one Chinese laundry owner was given a license, and she had probably not been identified as Chinese. The Board was obviously seeking to wipe out the Chinese laundry business.

After Yick Wo was denied his license, he continued to operate and was arrested. In police court Yick Wo was found guilty, and fined ten dollars. He refused to pay and was ordered to jail for ten days. Yick Wo then petitioned the California Supreme Court for a writ of habeas corpus. The petition was denied, and he appealed to the U.S. Supreme Court, naming the sheriff, a man named Hopkins, in the suit.

Yick Wo claimed that the ordinance abrogated his Fourteenth Amendment rights because of the blatant discriminatory results of its implementation. He presented statistical evidence showing the discrimination to San Francisco's Chinese community. Only 25 percent of San Francisco laundries could operate under the Board of Supervisors' licensing requirements, seventy-nine of them owned by non-Chinese and only one owned by a Chinese. His attorneys also contended that the ordinance violated China's 1880 treaty with the United States. San Francisco argued that the Fourteenth Amendment could not infringe upon the police powers granted to cities and states.

In a unanimous opinion, the Supreme Court found for Yick Wo and directed his discharge. Justice Stanley Matthews wrote that the ordinances as enforced conferred an authority broader than the traditional police power to regulate the use of property. This power was discriminatory and constituted class legislation prohibited by the Fourteenth Amendment. Matthews held that the Fourteenth Amendment applied to all persons, citizens and aliens alike. For Matthews, legitimate police power had to regulate safety and health practices with specificity, and the power had to be applied in good faith. Such was not the circumstance for the Chinese in San Francisco.

The Court had clearly expanded the meaning of the Fourteenth Amendment. State police powers had been limited and the Due Process Clause was now available to apply to local governmental discriminatory actions. Although the Yick Wo decision was potentially sweeping, it did not achieve instant recognition. After 1886 the Supreme Court's composition changed, and the Court did not build upon this precedent until the mid-twentieth century.

□ William L. Tang, "The Legal Status of the Chinese in America," in The Chinese in America, edited by Paul K. T. Sih and Leonard B. Allen (1976), pp. 3–15.

John R. Wunder

Young, Ex parte, 209 U.S. 123 (1908), argued 2–3 Dec. 1907, decided 23 Mar. 1908 by vote of 8 to 1; Peckham for the Court, Harlan in dissent. One incident in the long contest over state legislation to control the power of railroads, Ex parte Young became a landmark in federal jurisdiction over state officers. A 1907 Minnesota law reduced railroad rates and imposed Draconian penalties on violators. Illustrating Oliver Wendell Holmes's maxim that "people who no longer hope to control the legislatures . . . look to the courts," railroad shareholders brought a derivative action in federal court seeking to enjoin their companies from complying with the law and state officers from enforcing it. The reduced rates were alleged to be confiscatory, depriving the companies of their property without due process of law in violation of the Fourteenth Amendment. The petitioners claimed that an injunction was needed because the penalties were so severe that the companies could not afford to violate the law in order to test its

constitutionality directly. Although a temporary injunction was granted, Young, the Minnesota attorney general, violated it by seeking to enforce the new rates in state court. Jailed for contempt, he petitioned the Supreme Court for a writ of habeas corpus.

Holding against Young, the Court, in an opinion by Justice Rufus Peckham, completed the jurisdictional circle. Although the Eleventh Amendment restricts the power of federal courts to hear suits against states, Peckham wrote that a state officer seeking to enforce an unconstitutional statute is "in that case stripped of his official or representative character and is subjected in his person to the consequences of his individual conduct" (p. 160). Peckham left unanswered the question how, if "stripped of his official or representative character," the officer was threatening state action for purposes of the Fourteenth Amendment (p. 160). In In re Ayers (1887), a procedurally similar case, the Court had discharged another state attorney general who had been imprisoned for seeking to enforce state law in violation of a federal injunction. Peckham put to rest the embarrassment by limiting Ayers, a state bond repudiation case, to cases involving an attempt to compel a state to perform its contract.

In a lengthy dissent Justice John Marshall Harlan argued that the Court's decision would "practically obliterate the Eleventh Amendment" (p. 204). He too was embarrassed since he had dissented in Ayers. "I propose," Harlan wrote, "to adhere to former decisions of the court, whatever may have been once my opinion as to certain aspects of this general question" (p. 169). In a final irony the Court subsequently determined, in Simpson v. Shepard (1913), that the Minnesota railroad rates were not unconstitutional, so Young had not committed a wrong after all.

In its day, Ex parte Young was an unpopular decision. The same Court and the same justice who decided *Lochner v. New York (1905), invalidating a state regulation of the hours of labor, had again sided with the monied interests against the public. "Government by injunction" was condemned, and Congress, fending off bills to curtail the power of federal courts, responded with the cumbersome and inefficient Three-Judge Court Act of 1910, which created a special court of three judges and a direct appeal to the Supreme Court to handle suits for injunctions against state officers. (The act was largely repealed in 1976, long after it had outlived it usefulness.) Among legal scholars, especially in recent years, the case of *Ex parte Young* has been widely criticized and its illogicality regularly demonstrated. The Supreme Court, too, had been loath to extend the case, refusing in *Pennhurst State School and Hospital* v. *Halderman* (1984) to apply "the fiction of *Young*" to official violations of state law (p. 105). Notwithstanding its illogicality, *Ex parte Young* has long survived *Lochner* and substantive due process because of its indispensability to the federal scheme of government. As Holmes (who joined the majority in *Young*) elsewhere observed, "the Union would be imperiled" if the Supreme Court could not declare unconstitutional the laws of the several states. The power to enjoin state officers from violating federal law seems a necessary adjunct to that ability. Ironically, this power, forged by corporate shareholders and a conservative Court, is today regularly exercised on behalf of private (and otherwise powerless) parties in conflict with state governments.

□ William F. Duker, "Mr. Justice Rufus W. Peckham and the Case of *Ex parte Young*: Lochnerizing *Munn* v. *Illinois*," *Brigham Young University Law Review* (1980): 539–558.

John V. Orth

Younger v. Harris, 401 U.S. 37 (1971), argued 1 Apr. 1969, reargued 29 Apr. and 6 Nov. 1970, decided 23 Feb. 1971 by vote of 8 to 1; Black for the Court, Stewart, Harlan, Brennan, White, and Marshall, concurring, Douglas in dissent. Harris was indicted in a California court for violation of the state's criminal syndicalism act. The U.S. Supreme Court had held the act valid in *Whitney* v. *California* (1927), but an identical statute had been found unconstitutional in *Brandenburg* v. *Ohio* (1969), and *Whitney* was overruled. Harris therefore sought an injunction in the federal courts to prohibit his prosecution under an almost certainly unconstitutional statute. He claimed that both the prosecution and the act violated his rights under the First and Fourteenth Amendments and that *Dombrowski* v. *Pfister* (1965) permitted federal intervention.

Without discussing the implications of *Brandenberg*, and despite the alleged threat to freedom of expression, the Supreme Court reversed the federal district court and lifted the federal injunction.

For Justice Hugo Black, the issue turned on the nature of federalism. Long-established policy prohibited federal courts from intervening in state court proceedings except (1) when authorized by Congress, (2) when necessary to "aid in its jurisdiction," (3) when necessary "to protect or effectuate its judgments," and (4) when those being prosecuted by states will "suffer irreparable damages" (p. 43).

The policy was designed to protect the principle of comity. The legitimate concerns of both state and federal governments must be carefully balanced. Consequently, federal courts should interfere with pending state prosecutions only under extraordinary circumstances, when the danger of irreparable injury is both substantial and imminent. Even then, intervention is warranted only if the threat to protected federal rights could not be resolved at the state criminal trial. According to Black, none of these reasons for intervention was present in *Harris*.

Unlike *Dombrowski*, Harris was not threatened with continued bad-faith prosecutions or harassment that created a "chilling effect" on freedom of expression. Neither was any irreparable injury to Harris, beyond the ordinary consequences of a criminal trial, foreseen. And, according to Black, the validity of the threat to Harris's federally protected rights could well be determined in his state trial.

Black admitted that the First Amendment issues involved in *Dombrowski* suggested that even absent bad faith and harassment, a "chilling effect" might result from the enforcement of statutes that are on their face unconstitutional. Such a suggestion, however, was not directly relevant to the earlier decision and a possible "chilling effect" by itself was not enough to justify federal injunctive intervention here. Black also maintained that injunctive intervention in pending prosecutions involving constitutional issues places the federal judiciary in an inappropriate role. Federal courts ought not to pass judgment on state statues without benefit of state court interpretation. Such judgment would constitute a form of advisory opinion and would fail to meet requirements of true cases and controversies under Article III.

In separate concurring opinions, Justice Potter Stewart carefully outlined the limited reach of the decision, and Justice William Brennan emphasized those factors that distinguished the case from *Dombrowski*.

Justice William O. Douglas, however, praised the wisdom of *Dombrowski* in his dissent. During times of repression, Douglas wrote, the federal judiciary has a special obligation to protect constitutional rights, and the circumstances in *Harris* called for such protection. A threatened prosecution under an unconstitutionally overbroad and vague state criminal statute created a "chilling effect" on the exercise of federal rights and thus required the exercise of federal equity power. Otherwise, when "criminal prosecution can be leveled against [persons] because they express unpopular views, the society of the dialogue is in danger" (p. 65).

Charles H. Sheldon

Youngstown Sheet & Tube Co. v. Sawyer, 343 U.S. 579 (1952), argued 12 and 13 May 1952, decided 2 June 1952 by vote of 6 to 3; Black for the Court, Frankfurter, Douglas, Jackson, Burton, and Clark concurring, Vinson, Reed, and Minton in dissent. This decision rejected the argument that President Harry Truman had inherent constitutional authority to issue an executive order seizing private steel mills in 1952.

Apprehensive that an impending strike by steelworkers would harm the country's participation in the United Nations' police action in Korea, President Truman issued an executive order instructing Secretary of Commerce Charles Sawyer to seize and operate the nation's steel mills. Secretary Sawyer directed the companies' presidents to operate the facilities in compliance with government regulations. The president immediately gave Congress formal notice of his action, but Congress took no action. Although the seizure lacked statutory authority, Truman took the view that his action was valid under the powers invested in him as president and commander in chief. He relied upon the many historical precedents of executive seizure without the consent of Congress.

The steel industry argued that the purpose of the Labor Management Relations Act of 1947 (Taft-Hartley Act) was to allow the parties to arrive at a settlement and to permit Congress to become involved if collective bargaining was unsuccessful. The fact that Congress had specifically rejected a seizure provision during the debate of this act could only be interpreted as a prohibition against executive seizure.

The opinions of the justices reflected the two polar interpretations of the first clause

of Article II of the Constitution—"The executive Power shall be vested in a President of the United States."

Justice Hugo Black, writing for the Court, held that inasmuch as Congress could have directed the seizure of the steel mills, the president had no power to do so without an express prior congressional authorization. Black insisted that each of the popular branches must be left to carry out its duties according to the original constitutional understanding. The power exercised by Truman clearly was a lawmaking task that properly belonged only to Congress.

Concurring, Justice Felix Frankfurter suggested that long-standing executive practices, with the silent acquiescence of Congress, might provide an additional gloss on the executive powers. Justice William O. Douglas concurred, observing that Congress has the power to pay compensation and is the only branch able to authorize a lawful seizure.

Justice Robert Jackson also concurred and distinguished constitutional situations in which presidential powers fluctuate: strongest with a congressional authorization, weakest against a congressional prohibition, and uncertain alongside a congressional silence. Jackson concluded that the president acted unconstitutionally because Congress had refused to authorize the seizure.

Justice Harold Burton concurred because Congress had prescribed specific procedures exclusive of seizure. Justice Tom Clark, who as attorney general had earlier advised Truman, concurred because the president's authority to act in times of national emergency was subject to the limitations expressly prescribed by Congress.

Chief Justice Fred Vinson dissented, joined by Justices Stanley Reed and Sherman Minton, and surveyed the elements of the emergency: the Korean military involvement, the importance of steel as a war material, and the impasse in the labor negotiation. Presidential emergency action had been allowed in the past and the dissent concluded that the president acted constitutionally.

This decision, especially Justice Jackson's concurring opinion, has provided an important precedent for resisting subsequent claims of presidential inherent authority in areas such as impoundment, executive privilege, electronic surveillance, and national security. The holding has come to be generally understood as an interpretive effort to restrain the executive branch within a proper separation of power.

☐ Maeva Marcus, *Truman and the Steel Seizure Case—the Limits of Presidential Power* (1977). Alan F. Westin, *The Anatomy of A Constitutional Law Case* (1958).

Thomas E. Baker

Young v. American Mini Theatres, Inc., 427 U.S. 50 (1976), argued 24 Mar. 1976, decided 24 June 1976 by vote of 5 to 4; Stevens for a plurality of the Court, Powell concurring, Stewart, Brennan, Marshall, and Blackmun in dissent. Although most legal questions about the control of sexually explicit material turn into questions about criminal prosecution and obscenity law, *Young* v. *American Mini Theatres* is the most important case on the issue of zoning of "adult" establishments, that is, businesses specializing in the sale of sexually oriented films, magazines, and other items sold only to adults. The case arose when the city of Detroit attempted, through zoning, to prevent concentrations of such businesses, although other constitutionally indistinguishable zoning approaches focus on concentration rather than dispersal of adult establishments.

The case's importance lies in the fact that the Detroit ordinance did not require a finding that the establishment dealt in legally obscene materials as a prerequisite to legal action. Under the then-existing doctrine of *Erznoznik* v. *City of Jacksonville* (1975), this would seem to have rendered the restriction impermissible, for all sexually oriented material not legally obscene was thought to be entitled to complete First Amendment protection. But Justice John Paul Stevens's plurality opinion held that some degree of content regulation within the First Amendment was permissible and that the regulation here was constitutional for three reasons. First, the material was so sexually explicit as to be entitled to less protection than other speech more central to the First Amendment; as Stevens wrote, "[F]ew of us would march our sons and daughters off to war to preserve the citizen's right to see 'Specified Sexual Activities' exhibited in the theaters of our choice" (p. 70). Second, the zoning restriction was not a total prohibition on the availability of the material. Third, the material would be considered highly offensive by many people.

These conclusions, which represent current law (as in *City of Renton* v. *Playtime Theatres, Inc.,* 1986), remain especially important because they have been the basis for a number of other restrictions that fall short of outright prohibition of sexually explicit but nonobscene communication, such as *Federal Communications Commission* v. *Pacifica Foundation* (1978), and because they represent the beginnings of the increasingly influential First Amendment approach of Justice Stevens, in which distinctions among forms of constitutionally protected speech are permissible depending on the offensiveness of the material and the form of the restriction.

Frederick Schauer

Z

Zelman v. Simmons-Harris, 536 U.S. 639 (2002), argued 20 Feb. 2002, decided 27 June 2002 by vote of 5 to 4; Rehnquist for the Court, O'Connor and Thomas concurring, Souter, Stevens, and Breyer in dissent. As part of a plan to improve educational opportunities in Cleveland, the state of Ohio enacted legislation providing tuition aid to low-income parents. These parents, rather than send their children to the usual public school, could make use of a state-subsidized voucher to send their children to participating public or private schools. In the 1999–2000 school year, no suburban public school participated in the program; instead, 82 percent of the participating schools were religious and 96 percent of the students participating in the program attended these religiously affiliated schools.

In 1999 and 2000, a federal district judge in the Northern District of Ohio and a divided panel of the Sixth U.S. Circuit Court of Appeals concluded that the Ohio law had the primary effect of advancing religion and therefore violated the Establishment Clause of the First Amendment. The Supreme Court overturned this finding, contending that previous decisions have drawn a "consistent distinction between government programs that provide aid directly to religious schools, and programs of true private choice, in which government aid

reaches religious schools only as a result of the genuine and independent choice of private individuals" (p. 649). It did not matter that nearly all students attended religiously affiliated schools and that there were few options available for parents who did not want to send their child to a religiously affiliated school. Instead, the Court emphasized that the program was facially "neutral in all respects toward religion" (p. 653) and that the number of students attending religiously affiliated schools varies from year to year. The dissenters, in contrast, stressed these enrollment patterns. Noting that two-thirds of the parents participating in the program sent their children to schools who "proselytized in a religion not their own" (p. 704), Justice David Souter accused the majority of "ignoring the meaning of neutrality and private choice."

Neal Devins

Zorach v. Clauson, 343 U.S. 306 (1952), argued 31 Jan.-1 Feb. 1952, decided 28 Apr. 1952 by vote of 6 to 3; Douglas for the Court, Black, Frankfurter, and Jackson in dissent. *Zorach* v. *Clauson* was the Supreme Court's second decision on "released time" plans that allow religious instruction for public school students during the school week. In *Illinois ex rel. McCollum* v. *Board of Education*, (1948), a plan, including instruction within school buildings, had been held to violate

395

the First Amendment's Establishment Clause. In *Zorach*, the Court, stressing the desirability of accommodation to religious needs, approved New York City's program for religious instruction taking place outside the public schools.

According to Justice William O. Douglas's opinion for the Court, the result in *McCollum* was to be explained by the use of school buildings for religious instruction. New York, by contrast, had not violated separation of church and state. In language often quoted by those who oppose strict separationist approaches to the Establishment Clause, Justice Douglas wrote, "We are a religious people whose institutions presuppose a Supreme Being" (p. 313).

The three justices who had written in favor of the result in *McCollum* dissented in *Zorach*. Justice Hugo Black protested that his opinion for the Court in *McCollum* had not emphasized the location of the religious instruction. He contended, as did Justices Felix Frankfurter and Robert Jackson, that New York, like Illinois, had impermissibly placed the coercive apparatus of the public school laws behind religious instruction, receiving attendance reports for those released and treating as truants students who failed to go to religious instruction.

The Court's language in *Zorach* does not comport comfortably with its language in *McCollum*. Some justices who did not write in *McCollum* may have thought the school location of the religious instruction mattered more than the opinions reflected, or they may have come to that view on further reflection, perhaps partly in response to criticism of the Court's "hostility" to religion. In subsequent cases, *Zorach* has been used to advocate permissible accommodation to religion; ironically, Douglas later adopted strictly separationist positions and disavowed the result his language eloquently justifies.

In the landmark case of *Agostini* v. *Felton* (1997), the justices overturned their previous decision in *Aguilar* v. *Felton* (1985) and held that they would no longer presume that public employees will inculcate religion simply because they happen to be in a sectarian environment. Thus the decision in *Agostini* may well have created a more conducive environment for such programs as school vouchers.

Kent Greenawalt

Zurcher v. The Stanford Daily, 436 U.S. 547 (1978), argued 17 Jan. 1978, decided 31 May 1978 by vote of 5 to 3; White for the Court, Stewart, Marshall, and Stevens in dissent, Brennan not participating. In April 1971, violence and injuries resulted when police from Palo Alto, California, confronted demonstrators at Stanford University Hospital. Subsequently, officers obtained a warrant and searched the offices of the student newspaper, which had printed a photograph of the incident. Police found no additional pictures, but in the process they read a number of confidential files. *The Stanford Daily* brought civil charges against the police, contending that the search violated the First Amendment's guarantee of freedom of the press and the Fourth Amendment's protection against unreasonable searches.

The U.S. District Court for the Northern District of California ruled that a warrant was not appropriate for searching press offices unless a subpoena was shown to be impractical and the Ninth Circuit Court of Appeals affirmed. In the Supreme Court Justice Byron White argued that the Fourth Amendment did not provide special search provisions for press offices. He rejected the argument that the search interfered with the *Daily's* sources and created a chilling atmosphere that would contribute to self-censorship. He held that requiring a subpoena prior to authorization of a search warrant would undermine law enforcement efforts.

Justice Potter Stewart, dissenting for himself and Justice Thurgood Marshall, concluded that, under these circumstances, the warrant impermissibly burdened freedom of the press because it threatened physical disruption of newspaper operations and might force disclosure of confidential sources essential to news gathering. Justice John Paul Stevens argued that the search did not meet the Fourth Amendment's standards for reasonableness because the newspaper was not itself under suspicion.

The *Zurcher* ruling caused a furor in the press community and led to congressional passage of a provision in the Privacy Protection Act of 1980 limiting the use of search warrants in newsrooms where neither the organization nor its members were suspected of wrongdoing.

Carol E. Jenson

Glossary of Terms

Affirmative Action is a term of general application referring to government policies that directly or indirectly award jobs, admission to universities and professional schools, and other social goods and resources to individuals on the basis of membership in designated protected groups, in order to compensate those groups for past discrimination caused by society as a whole.

Amicus Brief stems from the phrase *amicus curiae* ("friend of the court") and is a brief filed by a person not a party to the case but interested in the legal doctrine to be developed there because of the relevance of that doctrine to their own preferred policy or later litigation.

Amicus Curiae, literally "friend of the court," is a designation give to an individual or an organization, other than a party's counsel, who files a legal brief with the Court.

Appeal means to have a lower court proceeding reviewed by a superior court, such as the Supreme Court. The party making the appeal is known as the "appellant" or "petitioner," and the opposing party is known as the "appellee" or "respondent."

Bad Tendency Test is a test used by the Court to analyze free speech issues. This test measures the legality of the speech by its tendency to cause an illegal action.

Bail relates to the defendant's right to freedom during the period following arrest but before the trial begins. It involves a pledge of money, property, or a "signature bond" as security that the person will be available for trial when requested to appear. The right to bail is enshrined in the Eighth Amendment to the Constitution.

Bill of Rights is commonly viewed as consisting of the first ten amendments to the Constitution of the United States, although the substantive protections set forth in the first eight amendments are often distinguished from the Ninth and Tenth Amendments, which are statements depicting constitutional structural divisions of power rather than specific, identifiable guarantees on behalf of the individual versus the state. State constitutions often contain their own bill of rights.

Briefs are written statements setting forth the factual background and legal contentions of a party in appellate litigation.

Capital Punishment penalizes those convicted of certain classes of crimes by killing them.

Cases and Controversies are two words that impose important restraints on the power of the federal judiciary. These words require the federal courts to adjudge only issues that present a real rather than a hypothetical or abstract dispute and that are subject to the adversarial process of litigation.

Certification is the process by which a U.S. court of appeals can certify questions of law at issue in a case to the Supreme Court for binding instruction. Only questions of law and not fact can be certified by the court.

Certiorari, Writ of, is the primary means by which a case comes before the Supreme Court. Litigants seeking review by the justices must petition the Court for a writ to bring their case forward for review. The Court receives the vast majority of its cases through this process.

Citation is a term that has several meanings. It can be a writ or order, analogous to a summons, that is issued by a court commanding a person to appear before the court. Or it may refer to the way in which opinions of the Supreme Court are cited, such as *Brown* v. *Board of Education*, 347 U.S. 483, 74 S.Ct. 686, 98 L.Ed. 873 (1954). The antecedent number refers to the volume in *United States Reports, Supreme Court Reporter*, and *Lawyers' Edition*, respectively, while the subsequent number is the page on the which the report begins.

Civil Law has two distinct meanings. As used within the American legal system, "civil law" is noncriminal law such as the law of property, commercial law, administrative law, and the rules governing procedure in civil cases. But "civil law" also refers to a body of law used throughout much of the world that is distinct from common law.

Class Actions refer to multiparty litigation brought in unison by plaintiffs that share some common condition, such as the violation of their civil rights, or where hazardous environmental conditions, such as asbestos, have affected a large number of people.

Clear and Present Danger Test was first developed by Justice Oliver Wendell Holmes, Jr., to determine whether speech is protected by the First Amendment. It has been given various meanings by generations of justices, but it has generally come to mean that speech cannot be restricted unless it would imminently threaten an illegal act.

Collusive Suits are brought by "friendly" parties having no antagonistic interest. Such suits seek to secure an opinion on the constitutionality of a statute by concocting a test case rather than pitting genuinely hostile parties against one another.

Comity is the courtesy that one jurisdiction gives by enforcing the laws of another jurisdiction.

Commercial Speech is a separate level of First Amendment activity that involves commercial advertising rather than political advocacy. Historically, it has received less protection than political advocacy, although in recent years the justices have given more and more protection to it.

Common Carriers are characterized as public transportation businesses, such as trains and planes. These carriers are distinguished from ordinary carriers because they are available to the public for general use. Sometimes referred to as public carriers.

Common Law is that body of law made not by legislatures but by courts and judges and that relies heavily on precedent found in the published reports of court decisions. It developed in the royal courts of England and came to be known as the general and customary law of the realm. In American practice, the common law is one of two legal systems (the other being equity), now merged in all jurisdictions, including the federal, that are the basis of the American legal order.

Compulsory Process provides under the common law that parties to a suit and others who possess information about it have a duty to come forward and cooperate with the court when ordered to do so. The Sixth Amendment regards compulsory process as a fundamental right for the accused in criminal proceedings.

Concurrent Power in American federalism means the power shared between the states and the federal government. The Supreme Court has often acted as an arbiter in defining the scope of a particular power and whether it resides in the state or the nation.

Concurring Opinions are written by justices who agree with the outcome or the decision in a case, but disagree with the logic or the reasons for that decision.

Conference, The is a private meeting of the justices of the Supreme Court to deliberate cases currently on the docket while the Court is in session.

Consent Decree is a final judgment of a court entered by agreement of the parties. A consent decree terminates litigation but binds only the parties, not persons who were not parties to the litigation.

Contempt Power is the power of a court to punish summarily disobedience to its order or disrespect to its authority, either in or out of court.

Contract, Freedom of, is a doctrine that holds that parties capable of entering into a contract and giving their consent to its terms ought not to be curbed by the state, save to protect the health, welfare, and morals of the community or to prevent criminal activities. Often referred to as liberty of contract, it had its heyday in the late nineteenth and early twentieth centuries.

Contracts Clause is found in Article I, section 10, clause 1 of the Constitution and provides that "No State shall … pass any Law impairing the Obligation of Contracts."

Cooperative Federalism is a constitutional concept that refers, among other things, to federal grant-in-aid programs that established during the New Deal era national regulatory programs administered by the states and funded by Congress.

Coram Nobis is a Latin phrase meaning "before us." It was used as a writ addressed to a court to call attention to errors of fact that would vitiate a judgment already given. It has been abolished by the Federal Rules of Civil Procedure.

Courts of Appeals are the intermediate courts in the federal judicial system, sitting between the lower federal district court and the higher Supreme Court of the United States.

Criminal Syndicalism Laws are statutes making it a crime to defend, advocate, or set up an organization committed to the use of crime, violence, sabotage, or other unlawful means to bring about a change in the form of government or in industrial ownership or control.

Cruel and Unusual Punishment is a provision of the Eighth Amendment to the Constitution that prohibits punishments such as burning at the stake, crucifixion, or breaking on the wheel but permits the death penalty if administered properly.

Declaratory Judgment is a passive relief given by a court to define legal relations rather than an active relief, such as an award of money damages or an injunction.

Discriminatory Intent provides that the Equal Protection Clause of the Fourteenth Amendment is violated only by government actions that were taken with an intent to injure the group adversely affected.

Disparate Impact covers those actions that are fair in form but discriminatory in operation. Thus an employment practice might on its face seem neutral although in practice it had discriminatory effect.

Dissent is the disagreement registered by those justices who reject the position taken by the majority of justices and express their differences through dissenting opinions.

Diversity Jurisdiction refers to cases in federal courts involving parties who are citizens of different states.

Double Jeopardy refers to the clause of the Fifth Amendment that provides: "nor shall any person be subject for the same offense to be twice put in jeopardy of life or limb."

Dual Federalism is a concept that derives from the view that the Constitution is a compact made by sovereign states for the limited purpose of giving the national government an explicitly limited range of enumerated powers.

Due Process, Procedural, refers in the Fifth and the Fourteenth Amendments to the doctrine that in order for government to impose a burden on an individual it must do so through fair procedures. The doctrine seeks to prevent the arbitrary use of power by government, although it does not prevent government from ultimately depriving a person of life or liberty.

Due Process, Substantive, refers in the Fifth and the Fourteenth Amendments to the doctrine that requires the justices to examine whether the right being denied or the obligation being created is reasonable rather than whether it has been imposed in a procedurally appropriate way. The doctrine gives the justices broad powers to adapt constitutional law to changing social circumstances.

Eminent Domain is the power of a government to compel owners of real or personal property to transfer it, or some interest in it, to the government.

Equal Protection refers to the Equal Protection Clause of the Fourteenth Amendment, adopted in 1868, which provides that government cannot discriminate in its application of the laws. For example, the Clause prohibits states from segregating students by race.

Error, Writ of, is a common law writ from an appellate to an inferior court, commanding the latter to send up the record of a case for review of alleged errors of law but not fact.

Exclusionary Rule is the name commonly given to the principle that evidence obtained by the government in violation of a defendant's constitutional rights may not be used against him or her.

Executive Immunity is the principle that holds that a president enjoys some shield from both judicial and congressional control, although, unlike Congress, the Constitution provides no exemption for the presidency from the legal processes of the other branches.

Executive Privilege holds that the president has the authority, nowhere explicitly provided in the Constitution, to withhold information from the other branches.

Exhaustion of Remedies is a judicially created doctrine that requires a litigant to seek relief elsewhere before bringing an action in federal court.

Ex Parte is a Latin term meaning "on behalf of" and is generally used in the law to refer to action taken without notice to the adverse party or without participation by that party in the hearing.

Ex Post Facto Laws are statutes that make an act punishable as a crime when such an act was not an offense when committed. The Constitution prohibits both state and national governments from passing such laws.

Ex Rel. is a Latin term meaning *ex relatione* or "on the relation of." When the phrase appears in the title of a case, it indicates that the case was brought by the attorney general in the name of the state but at the behest of a private party having an interest in the subject of the suit.

Federalism is the constitutional principle that the power to govern is shared between the national and the state governments. The exact balance to be struck between state and nation has varied over time and in relationship to the substantive issues in controversy.

Federal Questions are those cases that arise under the Constitution, the laws of the United States, and treaties made under the Constitution's authority. Such matters are the exclusive domain of the federal courts.

Fighting Words are those words used in speech that are offensive, derisive, and insulting and that, as such, do not contribute to the expression of ideas nor possess any social value in the search for truth. As such, they are not protected by the First Amendment.

Fundamental Rights are those freedoms deemed the most important to Americans. These include, but are not limited to, property, speech, and more recently privacy.

Gerrymandering, named for a salamander-shaped district devised by Massachusetts governor Elbridge Gerry in 1812, is the practice of drawing the boundaries of a political district to the advantage or disadvantage of some person, party, or other group.

Grandfather Clause is an exemption of current rights holders and sometimes their descendants from a new regulation or legal qualification.

Guarantee Clause is found in Article IV, section 4 of the Constitution. It provides that "The United States shall guarantee to every State in this Union a Republican Form of Government."

Habeas Corpus, or the "Great Writ," is available so that a judge may inquire into the legality of any form of loss of personal liberty.

Headnotes are syllabuses, or summaries, found at the beginning of court decisions.

Higher Law is unwritten law that binds government or provides a standard by which to judge written statute law. Sometimes called fundamental law.

Holding is a statement of law in a judicial opinion that is necessary to the resolution of the legal problem presented in the case. It can be contrasted with "dictum," which is a gratuitous statement of opinion in a decision not necessary to the result in the case.

Implied Powers are those powers that allow Congress to exercise authority that is implied by the enumeration of specific powers, such as in Article I, section 8 of the Constitution.

In Camera is a Latin term meaning "in the chamber." It is applied to hearings held either in a justice's private chambers or in a courtroom from which spectators have been excluded, the purpose being to protect privacy, confidentiality, or secrets.

Incorporation Doctrine provides, according to the Supreme Court of the United States, that most, but not all, guarantees in the federal Bill of Rights limit state and local governments as well as the federal government through the Due Process Clause of the Fourteenth Amendment.

Independent and Adequate State Grounds Doctrine provides that if a state court judgment rests on two grounds, one federal and the other nonfederal, the Supreme Court will not accept jurisdiction if the nonfederal ground is independent of the federal ground and adequate to support the judgment.

In Forma Pauperis is Latin for "in the form of a pauper" and is applied to criminal defendants who do not have the resources to pay court costs.

In Personam Jurisdiction refers to the Supreme Court's requirement that in order for it to take jurisdiction of a cause, it must have jurisdiction over the person of the defendant as well as subject-matter jurisdiction over the case itself.

In Re is Latin for "in the matter of," a phrase used to designate cases lacking formally adversarial parties. It refers to the thing that is the subject of litigation, such as physical object.

In Rem Jurisdiction extends to things (that is, physical objects or real property) rather than to persons, which is termed in personam jurisdiction.

Intermediate Scrutiny is the standard under the Equal Protection Clause that federal courts use to assess the constitutionality of government action based on sex and illegitimacy. Also known as heightened or semisuspect scrutiny, the standard requires that governmental action be "substantially" related to an "important" government interest.

Interposition is a constitutional doctrine that holds that the states have a right to interpose their authority to protect their citizens from the unconstitutional measures of the federal government.

Inverse Condemnation is a cause of action that can be brought by a property owner when a governmental entity allegedly has taken property without initiating any formal eminent domain proceedings.

Judicial Review is a distinctive power associated with the Supreme Court that is nowhere specifically mentioned in the Constitution. This power permits the Court to review acts of the other branches of the federal government and state laws and judicial decisions that involve the federal Constitution.

Just Compensation is the amount government must pay the owner to take property by exercise of the power of eminent domain.

Laissez-Faire Constitutionalism refers to an ideological attitude that characterized some justices of the Supreme Court between the Civil War and the New Deal. It reflected classical liberal economics, with its commitment to market control of the economy, a preference for entrepreneurial liberty, and hostility to government regulation.

Least Restrictive Means Test refers to the limits placed on speech by government and holds that where any choice exists, government must use those means that least severely inhibit expression.

Lemon Test is a three-pronged test employed by the Supreme Court in Establishment Clause disputes that provides that for a law to violate that clause (1) it must have secular legislative purpose, (2) its primary effect must be one that neither advances nor inhibits religion, and (3) it must not foster an excessive entanglement with religion.

Mandamus, Writ of, is an order by a court to some officer, corporation, or inferior court requiring the performance of a duty prescribed by law.

Martial Law is rule by a military rather than a civilian authority.

Miranda Warning derives from the case of *Miranda* v. *Arizona* (1966), in which the Warren Court required that police must advise criminal suspects of their constitutional rights prior to interrogation. Suspects must be advised that (1) they can remain silent, (2) anything said could be used against them, (3) they have a right to counsel, and (4) that in the case of indigents they will be provided counsel.

Mootness arises when the issue that is being litigated has become resolved in one way or another, thus leaving the plaintiff with no current complaint. The Cases and Controversies Clause of Article III requires that the justices hear and decide only live rather than moot issues.

Natural Law is a philosophic doctrine holding that there is a certain order in nature that provides norms for human conduct.

Nonverbal Expression is conduct, rather than spoken or written words, covered by the First Amendment to the Constitution. Art, drama, and music, for example, serve to convey ideas just as much as words do and, therefore, require protection from governmental interference.

Nullification is the doctrine by which states claim power to declare a law of the federal government unconstitutional.

Obiter Dictum is Latin for "said in passing" and refers to an assertion in an opinion that is not necessary to the result but is merely the gratuitous opinion of the judge.

Original Intent is a method of constitutional interpretation that seeks to discern the original meaning of the words being construed as that meaning is revealed in the intentions of those who created the constitutional provision in question.

Original Jurisdiction is the jurisdiction exercised by the court that initially hears a lawsuit.

Per Curiam is Latin for "by the court" and is an opinion rendered by the whole court or a majority of it, rather than being attributed to an individual judge.

Peremptory Challenges are those challenges used to disqualify a potential juror without giving a cause for doing so.

Plea Bargaining is a process whereby persons accused of a crime plead guilty to specified charges in return for an agreed-upon sentence, a sentence recommendation to the judge, or the dismissal or reduction of other charges.

Plurality Opinion is one that announces the judgment of the Court but that does not have the assent of a majority of the participating justices.

Police Powers are those powers of the state to deal with questions of health, safety, morals, and welfare.

Political Questions are controversies that the Supreme Court has historically regarded as nonjusticiable and inappropriate for judicial resolution. While the Court may have jurisdiction over such questions, it has often chosen not to decide them, preferring instead to allow them to be resolved by the political branches of government.

Political Thicket is a term once applied narrowly to questions involving legislative re-apportionment but more recently to any question that would ensnare the Supreme Court in political controversy.

Poll Taxes are head taxes usually levied by local governments on adults within their jurisdiction.

Precedent is a doctrine that holds that judges should look to past decisions for guidance and answer questions of law in a manner consistent with precedent.

Preferred Freedoms Doctrine holds that some constitutional freedoms, principally those guaranteed by the First Amendment, are fundamental in a free society and consequently are entitled to more judicial protection than other constitutional values. Justice Oliver Wendell Holmes, Jr., was the first to make this distinction.

Prior Restraint is a doctrine that holds that the state must approve the publication of any material before it reaches the public. The First Amendment was designed to eliminate prior restraint on speech and press, although the high court has accepted some very narrow exceptions.

Prohibition, Writ of, is the negative counterpart of the writ of mandamus and is an extraordinary writ issued by a superior court to an inferior court commanding it to abandon a cause pending before it over which it lacks jurisdiction.

Pro Se Petition is a written application submitted to a court by a litigant in his or her own behalf, rather than by legal counsel.

Public Forum Doctrine was established by the Supreme Court in 1939, when it ruled in *Hague* v. *Congress of Industrial Organizations* that government may not prohibit speech-related activities such as demonstrations, leafleting, and speaking in public areas traditionally provided for speech.

Public Use Doctrine establishes a limit on the purposes for which the government can exercise the power of eminent domain. Any takings must be, according to this doctrine, for a public rather than a private purpose.

Quo Warranto is the Latin for "by what warrant" and is a writ brought by the state or federal government against any person alleged to exercise an office or authority without the lawful right to do so.

Recuse is from the Latin *recusare*, or "to refuse," and applies to judges who refuse to participate in a hearing or decision of a case because of interest or bias in the matter.

Regulatory Taking occurs when land use restrictions substantially interfere with an owner's beneficial enjoyment of property even though the owner's title is undisturbed.

Released Time is the practice of permitting public school students to receive religious instruction during school hours.

Removal of Cases is a feature of the American federal system that permits, under certain circumstances, a party to a case to remove it from a state to a federal court.

Res Judicata is the Latin for "the matter adjudged" and is a principle of the common law that holds that a final judgment on the merits by a jurisdictionally competent court is conclusive of the rights of the parties in all subsequent litigation on the issues resolved.

Restrictive Covenants are contracts among home owners that prohibit the sale of real estate to certain groups, such as African-Americans or Jews. Such agreements for these purposes are no longer constitutional.

Ripeness is a doctrine that applies to litigation in the federal courts and requires that controversies have matured sufficiently that there is a real threat to an individual's property, liberty, or other rights.

Rule of Four is the term that describes the Supreme Court's long-standing practice of reviewing a case if four justices favor granting the petition for certiorari.

Segregation, De Facto, is segregation that exists in fact but is neither created by specific statutes nor enforced by statutes of judicial decrees.

Segregation, De Jure, is segregation that is required by law.

Separate but Equal Doctrine derived from *Plessy* v. *Ferguson* (1896) and provided that so long as the facilities provided for a segregated race were equal, there was no violation of the Equal Protection Clause of the Constitution.

Separation of Powers is the constitutional proposition that requires that the legislative, executive, and judicial branches be structurally distinct from one another.

Silver Platter Doctrine was an exception to the exclusionary rule until 1960. It provided that federal courts could accept evidence seized illegally by state officers in searches that involved neither federal participation nor federal direction.

Sovereign Immunity is the principle that government officers acting in their official capacities are free from being sued by citizens.

Standing is a doctrine that identifies who may bring claims that some government action violates the Constitution.

Stay is an order to arrest or suspend a judicial proceeding or the execution of a judgment resulting from that proceeding.

Stop and Frisk is a phrase that refers to the authority of a police officer to stop and search a person for concealed weapons without a warrant.

Strict Scrutiny is the standard under the Equal Protection Clause that federal courts use to assess the constitutionality of governmental classifications, such as race, that impose on fundamental constitutional rights. To pass muster, a challenged governmental action must be "closely" related to a "compelling" governmental interest.

Subpoena is Latin for "under penalty" and is an order of a court to a person commanding him or her to appear as a witness or to produce documents in his or her possession (*subpoena duces tecum*).

Suspect Classifications are categories that the Supreme Court has determined are unacceptable and therefore suspect, such as race and religion, because they are arbitrary, invidious, and irrational.

Symbolic Speech is nonverbal expression, such as the wearing of an armband or the flying of a flag, that is protected by the First Amendment under certain circumstances.

Takings Clause is more accurately called the Eminent Domain Clause and is part of the Fifth Amendment to the Constitution.

Test Case is one in which an individual, but more likely an interest group, initiates a case in order to challenge the constitutionality, or perhaps a particular disliked interpretation, of a statute.

Time, Place, and Manner Rule provides that government may protect society by controlling the harmful incidental effects of speech so long as such regulation is neutral concerning the content of the expression and it does not burden the flow of ideas to a substantial extent.

Tort is a harmful wrong (other than a breach of a contract) for which courts will provide a remedy, usually damages, to a private party.

Vested Rights is a phrase that connotes a legal regime that protects property rights both from private interference and from taking by government without compensation.

War Powers involve the power to deploy United States troops abroad in hostile situations.

Writ in modern practice means a formal written order of a court commanding someone to do something or refrain from doing something.

Zoning is the process by which a local government regulates the use of privately owned land within its jurisdiction.

APPENDIX ONE

The Constitution of the United States

WE THE PEOPLE OF THE UNITED STATES, in order to form a more perfect Union, establish Justice, insure domestic Tranquility, provide for the common defence, promote the general Welfare, and secure the Blessings of Liberty to ourselves and our Posterity, do ordain and establish this Constitution for the United States of America.

ARTICLE. I.

Section 1. All legislative Powers herein granted shall be vested in a Congress of the United States, which shall consist of a Senate and House of Representatives.

Section 2. The House of Representatives shall be composed of Members chosen every second Year by the People of the several States, and the Electors in each State shall have the Qualifications requisite for Electors of the most numerous Branch of the State Legislature.

No Person shall be a Representative who shall not have attained to the Age of twenty five Years, and been seven Years a Citizen of the United States, and who shall not, when elected, be an Inhabitant of that State in which he shall be chosen.

Representatives and direct Taxes shall be apportioned among the several States which may be included within this Union, according to their respective Numbers, which shall be determined by adding to the whole Number of free Persons, including those bound to Service for a Term of Years, and excluding Indians not taxed, three fifths of all other Persons. The actual Enumeration shall be made within three Years after the first Meeting of the Congress of the United States, and within every subsequent Term of ten Years, in such Manner as they shall by Law direct. The Number of Representatives shall not exceed one for every thirty Thousand, but each State shall have at Least one Representative; and until such enumeration shall be made, the State of New Hampshire shall be entitled to chuse three, Massachu-

setts eight, Rhode-Island and Providence Plantations one, Connecticut five, New-York six, New Jersey four, Pennsylvania eight, Delaware one, Maryland six, Virginia ten, North Carolina five, South Carolina five, and Georgia three.

When vacancies happen in the Representation from any State, the Executive Authority thereof shall issue Writs of Election to fill such Vacancies.

The House of Representatives shall chuse their Speaker and other Officers; and shall have the sole Power of Impeachment.

Section 3. The Senate of the United States shall be composed of two Senators from each State, chosen by the Legislature thereof, for six Years; and each Senator shall have one Vote.

Immediately after they shall be assembled in Consequence of the first Election, they shall be divided as equally as may be into three Classes. The Seats of the Senators of the first Class shall be vacated at the Expiration of the second Year, of the second Class at the Expiration of the fourth Year, and of the third Class at the Expiration of the sixth Year, so that one third may be chosen every second Year; and if Vacancies happen by Resignation, or otherwise, during the Recess of the Legislature of any State, the Executive thereof may make temporary Appointments until the next Meeting of the Legislature, which shall then fill such Vacancies.

No Person shall be a Senator who shall not have attained to the Age of thirty Years, and been nine Years a Citizen of the United States, and who shall not, when elected, be an Inhabitant of that State for which he shall be chosen.

The Vice President of the United States shall be President of the Senate, but shall have no Vote, unless they be equally divided.

The Senate shall chuse their other Officers, and also a President pro tempore, in the Absence of the Vice President, or when he shall exercise the Office of President of the United States.

The Senate shall have the sole Power to try all Impeachments. When sitting for that Purpose, they shall be on Oath or Affirmation. When the President of the United States is tried, the Chief Justice shall preside: And no Person shall be convicted without the Concurrence of two thirds of the Members present.

Judgment in Cases of Impeachment shall not extend further than to removal from Office, and disqualification to hold and enjoy any Office of honor, Trust or Profit under the United States: but the Party convicted shall nevertheless be liable and subject to Indictment, Trial, Judgment and Punishment, according to Law.

Section 4. The Times, Places and Manner of holding Elections for Senators and Representatives, shall be prescribed in each State by the Legislature thereof, but the Congress may at any time by Law make or alter such Regulations, except as to the Places of chusing Senators.

The Congress shall assemble at least once in every Year, and such Meeting shall be on the first Monday in December, unless they shall by Law appoint a different Day.

Section 5. Each House shall be the Judge of the Elections, Returns and Qualifications of its own Members, and a Majority of each shall constitute a Quorum to do Business; but a smaller Number may adjourn from day to day, and may be authorized to compel the Attendance of absent Members, in such Manner, and under such Penalties as each House may provide.

Each House may determine the Rule of its Proceedings, punish its Members for disorderly Behavior, and, with the Concurrence of two thirds, expel a Member.

Each House shall keep a Journal of its Proceedings, and from time to time publish the same, excepting such Parts as may in their Judgment require Secrecy; and the Yeas and Nays of the Members of either House on any question shall, at the Desire of one fifth of those Present, be entered on the Journal.

Neither House, during the Session of Congress, shall, without the Consent of the other, adjourn for more than three days, nor to any other Place than that in which the two Houses shall be sitting.

Section 6. The Senators and Representatives shall receive a Compensation for their Services, to be ascertained by Law, and paid out of the Treasury of the United States. They shall in all Cases, except Treason, Felony and Breach of the Peace, be privileged from Arrest during their Attendance at the Session of their respective Houses, and in going to and returning from the same; and for any Speech or Debate in either House, they shall not be questioned in any other Place.

No Senator or Representative shall, during Time for which he was elected, be appointed to any civil Office under the Authority of the United States, which shall have been created, or the Emoluments whereof shall have been encreased during such time; and no Person holding any Office under the United States, shall be a Member of either House during his Continuance in Office.

Section 7. All Bills for raising Revenue shall originate in the House of Representatives; but the Senate may propose or concur with Amendments as on other Bills.

Every Bill which shall have passed the House of Representatives and the Senate shall, before it become a Law, be presented to the President of the United States; if he approve he shall sign it, but if not he shall return it, with his Objections to that House in which it shall have originated, who shall enter the Objections at large on their Journal, and proceed to reconsider it. If after such Reconsideration two thirds of the House shall agree to pass the Bill, it shall be sent, together with the Objections, to the other House, by which it shall likewise be reconsidered, and if approved by two thirds of that House, it shall become a Law. But in all such Cases the Votes of both Houses shall be determined by yeas and Nays, and the Names of the Persons voting for and against the Bill shall be entered on the Journal of each House respectively. If any Bill shall not be returned by the President within ten Days (Sundays excepted) after it shall have been presented to him, the Same shall be a Law, in like Manner as if he had signed it, unless the Congress by their Adjournment prevent its Return, in which Case it shall not be a Law.

Every Order, Resolution, or Vote to which the Concurrence of the Senate and House of Representatives may be necessary (except on a question of Adjournment) shall be presented to the President of the United States; and before the Same shall take Effect, shall be approved by him, or being disapproved by him, shall be repassed by two thirds of the Senate and House of Representatives, according to the Rules and Limitations prescribed in the Case of a Bill.

Section 8. The Congress shall have Power To lay and collect Taxes, Duties, Imposts and Excises, to pay the Debts and provide for the common Defence and general Welfare of the United States; but all Duties, Imposts and Excises shall be uniform throughout the United States.

To borrow Money on the credit of the United States;

To regulate Commerce with foreign Nations, and among the several States, and with the Indian Tribes;

To establish an uniform Rule of Naturalization, and uniform Laws on the subject of Bankruptcies throughout the United States;

To coin Money, regulate the Value thereof, and of foreign Coin, and fix the Standard of Weights and Measures;

To provide for the Punishment of counterfeiting the Securities and current Coin of the United States;

To establish Post Offices and Post Roads;

To promote the Progress of Science and useful Arts, by securing for limited Times to Authors and Inventors the exclusive Right to their respective Writings and Discoveries;

To constitute Tribunals inferior to the supreme Court;

To define and punish Piracies and Felonies committed on the high Seas, and Offences against the Law of Nations;

To declare War, grant Letters of Marque and Reprisal, and make Rules concerning Captures on Land and Water;

To raise and support Armies, but no Appropriation of Money to that Use shall be for a longer Term than two Years;

To provide and maintain a Navy;

To make Rules for the Government and Regulation of the land and naval Forces;

To provide for calling forth the Militia to execute the Laws of the Union, suppress Insurrections and repel Invasions;

To provide for organizing, arming, and disciplining, the Militia, and for governing such Part of them as may be employed in the Service of the United States, reserving to the States respectively, the Appointment of the Officers, and the Authority of training the Militia according to the discipline prescribed by Congress;

To exercise exclusive Legislation in all Cases whatsoever, over such District (not exceeding ten Miles square) as may, by Cession of particular States, and the Acceptance of Congress, become the Seat of the Government of the United States, and to exercise like Authority over all Places purchased by the Consent of the Legislature of the State in which the Same shall be, for the Erection of Forts, Magazines, Arsenals, dock-Yards, and other needful Buildings;—And

To make all Laws which shall be necessary and proper for carrying into Execution the foregoing Powers, and all other Powers vested by this Constitution in the Government of the United States, or in any Department or Officer thereof.

Section 9. The Migration or Importation of such Persons as any of the States now existing shall think proper to admit, shall not be prohibited by the Congress prior to the Year one thousand eight hundred and eight, but a Tax or duty may be imposed on such Importation, not exceeding ten dollars for each Person.

The Privilege of the Writ of Habeas Corpus shall not be suspended, unless when in Cases of Rebellion or Invasion the public Safety may require it.

No Bill of Attainder or ex post facto Law shall be passed.

No Capitation, or other direct, Tax shall be laid, unless in Proportion to the Census or Enumeration herein before directed to be taken.

No Tax or Duty shall be laid on Articles exported from any State.

No Preference shall be given by any Regulation of Commerce or Revenue to the Ports of one State over those of another: nor shall Vessels bound to, or from, one State, be obliged to enter, clear, or pay Duties in another.

No Money shall be drawn from the Treasury, but in Consequence of Appropriations made by Law; and a regular Statement and Account of the Receipts and Expenditures of all public Money shall be published from time to time.

No title of Nobility shall be granted by the United States: And no Person holding any Office of Profit or trust under them, shall, without the Consent of the Congress, accept of any present, Emolument, Office, or title, of any kind whatever, from any King, Prince, or foreign State.

Section 10. No State shall enter into any Treaty, Alliance, or Confederation; grant Letters of Marque and Reprisal; coin Money; emit Bills of Credit; make any Thing but gold and silver Coin a Tender in Payment of Debts; pass any Bill of Attainder, ex post facto Law, or Law impairing the Obligation of Contracts, or grant any Title of Nobility.

No State shall, without the Consent of the Congress, lay any Imposts or Duties on Imports or Exports, except what may be absolutely necessary for executing it's inspection Laws: and the net Produce of all Duties and Imposts, laid by any State on Imports or Exports, shall be for the Use of the Treasury of the United States; and all such Laws shall be subject to the Revision and Controul of the Congress.

No State shall, without the Consent of Congress, lay any Duty of Tonnage, keep Troops, or Ships of War in time of Peace, enter into any Agreement or Compact with another State, or with a foreign Power, or engage in War, unless actually invaded, or in such imminent Danger as will not admit of delay.

ARTICLE. II.

Section 1. The executive Power shall be vested in a President of the United States of America. He shall hold his Office during the term of four Years, and, together with the Vice President, chosen for the same Term, be elected, as follows.

Each State shall appoint, in such Manner as the Legislature thereof may direct, a Number of Electors, equal to the whole Number of Senators and Representatives to which the State may be entitled in the Congress: but no Senator or Representative, or Person holding an Office of Trust or Profit under the United States, shall be appointed an Elector.

The Electors shall meet in their respective States, and vote by Ballot for two Persons, of whom one at least shall not be an Inhabitant of the same State with themselves. And they shall make a List of all the Persons voted for, and of the Number of Votes for each; which List they shall sign and certify, and transmit sealed to the Seat of the Government of the United States, directed to the President of the Senate. The President of the Senate shall, in the Presence of the Senate and House of Representatives, open all the Certificates, and the Votes shall then be counted. The Person having the greatest Number of Votes shall be the President, if such Number be a Majority of the whole Number of Electors appointed; and if there be more than one who have such Majority, and have an equal Number of Votes, then the House of Representatives shall immediately chuse by Ballot one of them for President; and if no Person have a Majority, then from the five highest on the List the said House shall in like Manner chuse the President. But in chusing the President, the Votes shall be taken by States, the Representation from each State having one Vote; A quorum for this Purpose shall consist of a Member or Members from two thirds of the States, and a Majority of all the States shall be necessary to a Choice. In every Case, after the Choice of the President, the Person having the greatest Number of Votes of the Electors shall be the Vice President. But if there should remain two or more who have equal Votes, the Senate shall chuse from them by Ballot the Vice President.

The Congress may determine the Time of chusing the Electors, and the Day on which they shall give their Votes; which Day shall be the same throughout the United States.

No Person except a natural born Citizen, or a Citizen of the United States, at the time of the Adoption of this Constitution, shall be eligible to the Office of President, neither shall any Person be eligible to that Office who shall not have attained to the Age of thirty-five Years, and been fourteen Years a Resident within the United States.

In Case of the Removal of the President from Office, or of his Death, Resignation, or Inability to discharge the Powers and Duties of the said Office, the Same shall devolve on the Vice President, and the Congress may by Law provide for the Case of Removal, Death, Resignation or Inability, both of the President and Vice President, declaring what Officer shall then act as President, and such Officer shall act accordingly, until the Disability be removed, or a President shall be elected.

The President shall, at stated Times, receive for his Services, a Compensation, which shall neither be encreased or diminished during the Period for which he shall have been elected, and he shall not receive within that Period any other Emolument from the United States, or any of them.

Before he enters on the Execution of his Office, he shall take the following Oath or Affirmation:—"I do solemnly swear (or affirm) that I will faithfully execute the Office of President of the United States, and will to the best of my Ability, preserve, protect and defend the Constitution of the United States."

Section 2. The President shall be Commander in Chief of the Army and Navy of the United States, and of the Militia of the several States, when called into the actual Service of the United States; he may require the Opinion, in writing, of the principal Officer in each of the executive Departments, upon any Subject relating to the Duties of their respective Offices, and he shall have Power to grant Reprieves and Pardons for Offences against the United States, except in Cases of Impeachment.

He shall have Power, by and with the Advice and Consent of the Senate, to make Treaties, provided two thirds of the Senators present concur; and he shall nominate, and by and with the Advice and Consent of the Senate, shall appoint Ambassadors, other public Ministers and Consuls, Judges of the supreme Court, and all other Officers of the United States, whose Appointments are not herein otherwise provided for, and which shall be established by Law; but the Congress may by Law vest the Appointment of such inferior Officers, as they think proper, in the President alone, in the Courts of Law, or in the Heads of Departments.

The President shall have Power to fill up all Vacancies that may happen during the Recess of the Senate, by granting Commissions which shall expire at the End of their next Session.

Section 3. He shall from time to time give to the Congress Information of the State of the Union, and recommend to their Consideration such Measures as he shall judge necessary and expedient; he may, on extraordinary Occasions, convene both Houses, or either of them, and in Case of Disagreement between them with Respect to the Time of Adjournment, he may adjourn them to such Time as he shall think proper; he shall receive Ambassadors and other public Ministers; he shall take Care that the Laws be faithfully executed, and shall Commission all the Officers of the United States.

Section 4. The President, Vice President and all civil Officers of the United States, shall be removed from Office on Impeachment for, and Conviction of, Treason, Bribery, or other high Crimes and Misdemeanors.

ARTICLE. III.

Section 1. The judicial Power of the United States, shall be vested in one supreme Court, and in such inferior Courts as the Congress may from time to time ordain and establish. The Judges, both of the supreme and inferior Courts, shall hold their Offices during good Behavior, and shall, at stated Times, receive for their Services, a Compensation, which shall not be diminished during their Continuance in Office.

Section 2. The judicial Power shall extend to all Cases, in Law and Equity, arising under this Constitution, the Laws of the United States, and Treaties made, or which shall be made, under their Authority;—to all Cases affecting Ambassadors, other public Ministers and Consuls;—to all Cases of admiralty and maritime Jurisdiction;—to Controversies to which the United States shall be a Party;—to Controversies between two or more States;—between a State and Citizens of another State;—between Citizens of different States;—between Citizens of the same State claiming Lands under Grants of different States, and between a State, or the Citizens thereof, and foreign States, Citizens or Subjects.

In all cases affecting Ambassadors, other public Ministers and Consuls, and those in which a State shall be Party, the supreme Court shall have original Jurisdiction. In all the other Cases before mentioned, the supreme Court shall have appellate Jurisdiction, both as to Law and Fact, with such Exceptions, and under such Regulations as the Congress shall make.

The Trial of all Crimes, except in Cases of Impeachment, shall be by Jury; and such Trial shall be held in the State where the said Crimes shall have been committed; but when not committed within any State, the Trial shall be at such Place or Places as the Congress may by Law have directed.

Section 3. Treason against the United States, shall consist only in levying War against them, or in adhering to their Enemies, giving them Aid and Comfort. No Person shall be convicted of Treason unless on the Testimony of two Witnesses to the same overt Act, or on Confession in open Court.

The Congress shall have Power to declare the Punishment of Treason, but no Attainder of Treason shall work Corruption of Blood, or Forfeiture except during the Life of the Person attainted.

ARTICLE. IV.

Section 1. Full Faith and Credit shall be given in each State to the public Acts, Records, and

412 □ The Constitution of the United States

judicial Proceedings of every other State. And the Congress may by general Laws prescribe the Manner in which such Acts, Records, and Proceedings shall be proved, and the Effect thereof.

Section 2. The Citizens of each State shall be entitled to all Privileges and Immunities of Citizens in the several States.

A person charged in any State with Treason, Felony, or other Crime, who shall flee from Justice, and be found in another State, shall on Demand of the executive Attorney of the State from which he fled, be delivered up, to be removed to the State having Jurisdiction of the Crime.

No Person held to Service or Labour in one State, under the Laws thereof, escaping into another, shall, in Consequence of any Law or Regulation therein, be discharged from such Service or Labour, but shall be delivered up on Claim of the Party to whom such Service or Labour may be due.

Section 3. New States may be admitted by the Congress into this Union; but no new State shall be formed or erected within the Jurisdiction of any other State; nor any State be formed by the Junction of two or more States, or Parts of States, without the consent of the Legislatures of the States concerned as well as of the Congress.

The Congress shall have Power to dispose of and make all needful Rules and Regulations respecting the Territory or other Property belonging to the United States; and nothing in this Constitution shall be so construed as to Prejudice any Claims of the United States, or of any particular States.

Section 4. The United States shall guarantee to every State in this Union a Republican Form of Government, and shall protect each of them against Invasion; and on Application of the Legislature, or of the Executive (when the Legislature cannot be convened) against domestic Violence.

ARTICLE. V.

The Congress, whenever two thirds of both Houses shall deem it necessary, shall propose Amendments to this Constitution, or, on the Application of the Legislatures of two thirds of the several States shall call a Convention for proposing Amendments, which, in either Case, shall be valid to all Intents and Purposes, as Part of this Constitution, when ratified by the Legislatures of three fourths of the several States, or by Conventions in three fourths thereof, as the one or the other Mode of Ratification may be proposed by the Congress; Provided that no Amendment which may be made prior to the Year One thousand eight hundred and eight shall in any Manner affect the first and fourth Clauses in the Ninth Section of the first Article; and that no State, without its Consent, shall be deprived of its equal Suffrage in the Senate.

ARTICLE. VI.

All Debts contracted and Engagements entered into, before the Adoption of this Constitution, shall be as valid against the United States under this Constitution, as under the Confederation.

This Constitution, and the Laws of the United States which shall be made in Pursuance thereof; and all Treaties made, or which shall be made, under the Authority of the United States, shall be the supreme Law of the Land; and the Judges in every State shall be bound thereby, any Thing in the Constitution or Laws of any State to the Contrary notwith-standing.

The Senators and Representatives before mentioned, and the Members of the several State Legislatures, and all executive and judicial Officers, both of the United States and of the several States, shall be bound by Oath or Affirmation, to support this Constitution; but no religious Test shall ever be required as a Qualification to any Officer or public Trust under the United States.

ARTICLE. VII.

The Ratification of the Conventions of nine States, shall be sufficient for the Establishment of this Constitution between the States so ratifying the Same.

Done in Convention by the Unanimous Consent of the States present the Seventeenth Day of September in the Year of our Lord one thousand seven hundred and Eighty seven and of the Independence of the United States of America the Twelfth. In witness thereof We have hereunto subscribed our Names,

G°: Washington
Presid' and deputy from Virginia

AMENDMENT I.

Congress shall make no law respecting an establishment of religion, or prohibiting the free exercise thereof; or abridging the freedom of speech, or of the press; or the right of the people peaceably to assemble, and to petition the Government for a redress of grievances.

AMENDMENT II.

A well regulated Militia, being necessary to the security of a free State, the right of the people to keep and bear Arms, shall not be infringed.

AMENDMENT III.

No Soldier shall, in time of peace be quartered in any house, without the consent of the Owner, nor in time of war, but in a manner to be prescribed by law.

AMENDMENT IV.

The right of the people to be secure in their persons, houses, papers, and effects, against unreasonable searches and seizures, shall not be violated, and no Warrants shall issue, but upon probable cause, supported by Oath or affirmation, and particularly describing the place to be searched, and the persons or things to be seized.

AMENDMENT V.

No persons shall be held to answer for a capital, or otherwise infamous crime, unless on a presentment or indictment of a Grand Jury, except in cases arising in the land or naval forces, or in the Militia, when in actual service in time of War or public danger; nor shall any person be subject for the same offence to be twice put in jeopardy of life or limb; nor shall be compelled in any criminal case to be a witness against himself, nor be deprived of life, liberty, or property, without due process of law; nor shall private property be taken for public use, without just compensation.

AMENDMENT VI.

In all criminal prosecutions, the accused shall enjoy the right to a speedy and public trial, by an impartial jury of the State and district wherein the crime shall have been committed, which district shall have been previously ascertained by law, and to be informed of the nature and cause of the accusation; to be confronted with the witnesses against him; to have compulsory process for obtaining witnesses in his favor, and to have the Assistance of Counsel for his defence.

AMENDMENT VII.

In Suits at common law, where the value in controversy shall exceed twenty dollars, the right of trial by jury shall be preserved, and no fact tried by a jury, shall be otherwise re-examined in any Court of the United States, than according to the rules of the common law.

AMENDMENT VIII.

Excessive bail shall not be required, nor excessive fines imposed, nor cruel and unusual punishments inflicted.

AMENDMENT IX.

The enumeration in the Constitution, of certain rights, shall not be construed to deny or disparage others retained by the people.

AMENDMENT X.

The powers not delegated to the United States by the Constitution, nor prohibited by it to the States, are reserved to the States respectively, or to the people.

AMENDMENT XI.

The Judicial power of the United States shall not be construed to extend to any suit in law or equity, commenced or prosecuted against one of the United States by Citizens of another State, or by Citizens or Subjects of any Foreign State.

AMENDMENT XII.

The Electors shall meet in their respective states, and vote by ballot for President and Vice-President, one of whom, at least, shall not be an inhabitant of the same state with themselves; they shall name in their ballots the person voted for as President, and in distinct ballots the person voted for as Vice-President, and they shall make distinct lists of all persons voted for as President, and of all persons voted for as Vice-President, and of the number of votes for each, which lists they shall sign and certify, and transmit sealed to the seat of the government of the United States, directed to the President of the Senate;—The President of the Senate shall, in the presence of the Senate and House of Representatives, open all the certificates and the votes shall then be counted;—The person having the greatest number of votes for President, shall be the President, if such number be a majority of the whole number of Electors appointed; and if no person have such majority, then from the persons having the highest numbers not exceeding three on the list of those voted for as President, the House of Representatives shall choose immediately, by ballot, the President. But in choosing the President, the votes shall be taken by states, the representation from each state having one vote; a quorum for this purpose shall consist of a member or members from two-thirds of the states, and a majority of all the states shall be necessary to a choice. And if the House of Representatives shall not choose a President whenever the right of choice shall devolve upon them, before the fourth day of March next following, then the Vice-President shall act as President, as in the case of the death or other constitutional disability of the President.—The person having the greatest number of votes as Vice-President, shall be the Vice-President, if such number be a majority of the whole number of Electors appointed, and if no person have a majority, then from the two highest numbers on the list, the Senate shall choose the Vice-President; a quorum for the purpose shall consist of two-thirds of the whole number of Senators, and a majority of the whole number shall be necessary to a choice. But no person constitutionally ineligible to the office of President shall be eligible to that of Vice-President of the United States.

AMENDMENT XIII.

Section 1. Neither slavery nor involuntary servitude, except as a punishment for crime whereof the party shall have been duly convicted, shall exist within the United States, or any place subject to their jurisdiction.

Section 2. Congress shall have power to enforce this article by appropriate legislation.

AMENDMENT XIV.

Section 1. All persons born or naturalized in the United States, and subject to the jurisdiction thereof, are citizens of the United States and of the State wherein they reside. No State shall make or enforce any law which shall abridge the privileges or immunities of citizens of the United States; nor shall any State deprive any person of life, liberty, or property, without due process of law; nor deny to any person within its jurisdiction the equal protection of the laws.

Section 2. Representatives shall be apportioned among the several States according to their respective numbers, counting the whole number of persons in each State, excluding Indians not taxed. But when the right to vote at any election for the choice of electors for President and Vice President of the United States, Representatives in Congress, the Executive and Judicial officers of a State, or the members of the Legislature thereof, is denied to any of the male inhabitants of such State, being twenty-one years of age, and citizens of the United States, or in any way abridged, except for participation in rebellion, or other crime, the basis of representation therein shall be reduced in the proportion which the number of such male citizens shall bear to the whole number of male citizens twenty-one years of age in such State.

Section 3. No person shall be a Senator or Representative in Congress, or elector of President and Vice President, or hold any office, civil or military, under the United States, or under any State, who, having previously taken an oath, as a member of Congress, or as an officer of the United States, or as a member of any State legislature, or as an executive or judicial officer of any State, to support the Constitution of the United States, shall have engaged in insurrection or rebellion against the same, or given aid or comfort to the enemies thereof. But Congress may be a vote of two-thirds of each House, remove such disability.

Section 4. The validity of the public debt of the United States, authorized by law, including debts incurred for payment of pensions and bounties for services in suppressing insurrection or rebellion, shall not be questioned. But neither the United States nor any State shall assume or pay any debt or obligation incurred in aid of insurrection or rebellion against the United States, or any claim for the loss or emancipation of any slave; but all such debts, obligations and claims shall be held illegal and void.

Section 5. The Congress shall have power to enforce, by appropriate legislation, the provisions of this article.

AMENDMENT XV.

Section 1. The right of citizens of the United States to vote shall not be denied or abridged by the United States or by any State on account of race, color, or previous condition of servitude.

Section 2. The Congress shall have power to enforce this article by appropriate legislation.

AMENDMENT XVI.

The Congress shall have power to lay and collect taxes on incomes, from whatever source derived, without apportionment among the several States, and without regard to any census or enumeration.

AMENDMENT XVII.

The Senate of the United States shall be composed of two senators from each State, elected by the people thereof, for six years; and each Senator shall have one vote. The electors in each State shall have the qualifications requisite for electors of the most numerous branch of the State legislature.

When vacancies happen in the representation of any State in the Senate, the executive authority of such State shall issue writs of election to fill such vacancies: *Provided,* That the legislature of any State may empower the executive thereof to make temporary appointments until the people fill the vacancies by election as the legislature may direct.

This amendment shall not be so construed as to affect the election or term of any senator chosen before it becomes valid as part of the Constitution.

AMENDMENT XVIII.

After one year from the ratification of this article, the manufacture, sale, or transportation of intoxicating liquors within, the importation thereof into, or the exportation thereof from the United States and all territory subject to the jurisdiction thereof for beverage purposes is hereby prohibited.

The Congress and the several States shall have concurrent power to enforce this article by appropriate legislation.

This article shall be inoperative unless it shall have been ratified as an amendment to the Constitution by the legislatures of the several States, as provided in the Constitution, within seven years from the date of the submission thereof to the States by Congress.

AMENDMENT XIX.

The right of citizens of the United States to vote shall not be denied or abridged by the United States or by any State on account of sex.

The Congress shall have power by appropriate legislation to enforce the provisions of this article.

AMENDMENT XX.

Section 1. The terms of the President and Vice-President shall end at noon on the twentieth day of January, and the terms of Senators and Representatives at noon on the third day of January, of the years in which such terms would have ended if this article had not been ratified; and the terms of their successors shall then begin.

Section 2. The Congress shall assemble at least once in every year, and such meeting shall begin at noon on the third day of January, unless they shall by law appoint a different day.

Section 3. If, at the time fixed for the beginning of the term of the President, the Presidentelect shall have died, the Vice-President-elect shall become President. If a President shall not have been chosen before the time fixed for the beginning of his term, or if the President-elect shall have failed to qualify, then the Vice-President-elect shall act as President until a President shall have qualified; and the Congress may by law provide for the case wherein neither a President-elect nor a Vice-President-elect shall have qualified, declaring who shall then act as President, or the manner in which one who is to act shall be selected, and such person shall act accordingly until a President or Vice-President shall have qualified.

Section 4. The Congress may by law provide for the case of the death of any of the persons from whom the House of Representatives may choose a President whenever the right of choice shall have devolved upon them, and for the case of the death of any of the persons from whom the Senate may choose a Vice-President whenever the right of choice shall have devolved upon them.

Section 5. Sections 1 and 2 shall take effect on the 15th day of October following the ratification of this article.

Section 6. This article shall be inoperative unless it shall have been ratified as an amendment to the Constitution by the legislatures of three-fourths of the several States within seven years from the date of its submission.

AMENDMENT XXI.

Section 1. The eighteenth article of amendment to the Constitution of the United States is hereby repealed.

Section 2. The transportation or importation into any State, Territory, or possession of the United States for delivery or use therein of intoxicating liquors, in violation of the laws thereof, is hereby prohibited.

Section 3. This article shall be inoperative unless it shall have been ratified as an amendment to the Constitution by convention in the several States, as provided in the Constitution, within seven years from the date of the submission thereof to the States by the Congress.

AMENDMENT XXII.

Section 1. No person shall be elected to the office of the President more than twice, and no person who has held the office of President, or acted as President, for more than two years of a term to which some other person was elected President shall be elected to the office of the President more than once. But this Article shall not apply to any person holding the office of President when this Article was proposed by the Congress, and shall not prevent any person who may be holding the office of President, or acting as President, during the term within which this Article becomes operative from holding the office of President or acting as President during the remainder of such term.

Section 2. This article shall be inoperative unless it shall have been ratified as an amendment to the Constitution by the legislatures of three-fourths of the several States within seven years from the date of its submission to the States by the Congress.

AMENDMENT XXIII.

Section 1. The District constituting the seat of government of the United States shall appoint in such manner as the Congress may direct:

A number of electors of President and Vice-President equal to the whole number of Senators and Representatives in Congress to which the District would be entitled if it were a State, but in no event more than the least populous State; they shall be in addition to those appointed by the States, but they shall be considered, for the purposes of the election of President and Vice-President, to be electors appointed by a State; and they shall meet in the District and perform such duties as provided by the twelfth article of amendment.

Section 2. The Congress shall have the power to enforce this article by appropriate legislation.

AMENDMENT XXIV.

Section 1. The right of citizens of the United States to vote in any primary or other election for President or Vice President, for electors for President or Vice President, or for Senator or Representative in Congress, shall not be denied or abridged by the United States or any State by reason of failure to pay any poll tax or other tax.

Section 2. The Congress shall have power to enforce this article by appropriate legislation.

AMENDMENT XXV.

Section 1. In case of the removal of the President from office or of his death or resignation, the Vice President shall become President.

Section 2. Whenever there is a vacancy in the office of Vice President, the President shall nominate a Vice President who shall take office upon confirmation by a majority vote of both Houses of Congress.

Section 3. Whenever the President transmits to the President pro tempore of the Senate and the Speaker of the House of Representatives his written declaration that he is unable to discharge the powers and duties of his office, and until he transmits to them a written declaration to the contrary, such powers and duties shall be discharged by the Vice President as Acting President.

Section 4. Whenever the Vice President and a majority of either the principal officers of the executive departments or of such other body as Congress may by law provide, transmit to the President pro tempore of the Senate and the Speaker of the House of Representatives their written declaration that the President is unable to discharge the powers and duties of his office, the Vice President shall immediately assume the powers and duties of the office as Acting President.

Thereafter, when the President transmits to the President pro tempore of the Senate and the Speaker of the House of Representatives his written declaration that no inability exists, he shall resume the powers and duties of his office unless the Vice President and a majority of either the principal officers of the executive departments or of such other body as Congress may by law provide, transmit within four days to the President pro tempore of the Senate and the Speaker of the House of Representatives their written declaration that the President is unable to discharge the powers and duties of his office. Thereupon Congress shall decide the issue, assembling within forty-eight hours for that purpose if not in session. If the Congress, within twenty-one days after receipt of the latter written declaration, or, if Congress is not in session, within twenty-one days after Congress is required to assemble, determines by two-thirds vote of both Houses that the President is unable to discharge the power and duties of his office, the Vice President shall continue to discharge the same as Acting President; otherwise, the President shall resume the powers and duties of his office.

AMENDMENT XXVI.

Section 1. The right of citizens of the United States, who are eighteen years of age or older, to vote shall not be denied or abridged by the United States or by any State on account of age.

Section 2. The Congress shall have power to enforce this article by appropriate legislation.

AMENDMENT XXVII.

No law, varying the compensation for the services of the Senators and Representatives, shall take effect, until an election of Representatives shall have intervened.

APPENDIX TWO

Nominations and Succession of the Justices

Supreme Court Nominations, 1789–2006

1 President/ Nominee	2 Appointed	3 Action (vote)	4 Oath Taken	5 Term End	6 Yrs. of Service
Washington					
John Jay*	24 Sep. 1789	C 26 Sep. 1789	19 Oct. 1789	R 29 June 1795	6
John Rutledge	24 Sep. 1789	C 26 Sep. 1789	15 Feb. 1790	R 5 Mar. 1791	1
William Cushing	24 Sep. 1789	C 26 Sep. 1789	2 Feb. 1790	D 13 Sep. 1810	21
Robert Harrison	24 Sep. 1789	C 26 Sep. 1789			
James Wilson	24 Sep. 1789	C 26 Sep. 1789	5 Oct. 1789	D 21 Aug. 1798	9
John Blair, Jr.	24 Sep. 1789	C 26 Sep. 1789	2 Feb. 1790	R 25 Oct. 1795	6
James Iredell	8 Feb. 1790	C 10 Feb. 1790	12 May 1790	D 20 Oct. 1799	9
Thomas Johnson*	R 5 Aug. 1791		19 Sep. 1791		
	31 Oct. 1791	C 7 Nov. 1791	6 Aug. 1792	R 16 Jan. 1793	1
William Paterson	27 Feb. 1793	W 28 Feb. 1793			
William Paterson	4 Mar. 1793	C 4 Mar. 1793	11 Mar. 1793	D 9 Sep. 1806	13
John Rutledge*†	R 1 July 1795		12 Aug. 1795		
		R 15 Dec. 1795 (10–14)			
William Cushing*	26 Jan. 1796	D 27 Jan. 1796			
Samuel Chase	26 Jan. 1796	C 27 Jan. 1796	4 Feb. 1796	D 19 June 1811	15
Oliver Ellsworth	3 Mar. 1796	C 4 Mar. 1796 (21–1)	8 Mar. 1796	R 15 Dec. 1800	4
Adams					
Bushrod Washington	R 29 Sep. 1798		9 Nov. 1798		
	19 Dec. 1798	C 20 Dec. 1798	4 Feb. 1799	D 26 Nov. 1829	31
Alfred Moore	4 Dec. 1799	C 10 Dec. 1799	21 Apr. 1800	R 26 Jan. 1804	4
John Jay	18 Dec. 1800	D 19 Dec. 1800			
John Marshall*	20 Jan. 1801	C 27 Jan. 1801	4 Feb. 1801	D 6 July 1835	34
Jefferson					
William Johnson	22 Mar. 1804	C 24 Mar. 1804	8 May 1804	D 4 Aug. 1834	30

Column 1. * = chief justice. † = nomination for promotion to chief justice; years of service, where applicable, are as chief justice only; see prior listing for nomination and service as associate justice. *Column 2.* R = recess appointment. *Column 3.* C = confirmed. D = declined. P = postponed. R = rejected. W = withdrawn. *Column 5.* D = died. P = promoted to chief justice (see separate listing for service as chief justice). R = retirement/resignation.

1	2	3		4	5	6
President/ Nominee	**Appointed**	**Action (vote)**		**Oath Taken**	**Term End**	**Yrs. of Service**
Brockholst Livingston	R 10 Nov. 1806			20 Jan. 1807		
	13 Dec. 1806	C	17 Dec. 1806	2 Feb. 1807	D 18 Mar. 1823	16
Thomas Todd	28 Feb. 1807	C	3 Mar. 1807	4 May 1807	D 7 Feb. 1826	19
Madison						
Levi Lincoln	2 Jan. 1811	D	3 Jan. 1811			
Alexander Wolcott	4 Feb. 1811	R	13 Feb. 1811 (9–24)			
John Quincy Adams	21 Feb. 1811	D	22 Feb. 1811			
Joseph Story	15 Nov. 1811	C	18 Nov. 1811	3 Feb. 1812	D 10 Sep. 1845	34
Gabriel Duvall	15 Nov. 1811	C	18 Nov. 1811	23 Nov. 1811	R 14 Jan. 1835	23
Monroe						
Smith Thompson	R 1 Sep. 1823					
	8 Dec. 1823	C	19 Dec. 1823	10 Feb. 1824	D 18 Dec. 1843	20
J. Q. Adams						
Robert Trimble	11 Apr. 1826	C	9 May 1826 (27–5)	16 June 1826	D 25 Aug. 1828	2
John Crittenden	17 Dec. 1828	P	12 Feb. 1829			
Jackson						
John McLean	6 Mar. 1829	C	7 Mar. 1829	11 Jan. 1830	D 4 Apr. 1861	32
Henry Baldwin	4 Jan. 1830	C	6 Jan. 1830 (41–2)	18 Jan. 1830	D 21 Apr. 1844	14
James M. Wayne	6 Jan. 1835	C	9 Jan. 1835	14 Jan. 1835	D 5 July 1867	32
Roger B. Taney*	15 Jan. 1835	P	3 Mar. 1835			
	28 Dec. 1835	C	15 Mar. 1836 (29–15)	28 Mar. 1836	D 12 Oct. 1864	28
Philip P. Barbour	28 Dec. 1835	C	15 Mar. 1836 (30–11)	12 May 1836	D 25 Feb. 1841	5
William Smith	3 Mar. 1837	D	8 Mar. 1837 (23–18)			
John Catron	3 Mar. 1837	C	8 Mar. 1837	1 May 1837	D 30 May 1865	28
Van Buren						
John McKinley	R 22 Apr. 1837					
	18 Sep. 1837	C	25 Sep. 1837	9 Jan. 1838	D 19 July 1852	15
Peter V. Daniel	26 Feb. 1841	C	2 Mar. 1841 (22–5)	10 Jan. 1842	D 31 May 1860	19

Column 1. * = chief justice. † = nomination for promotion to chief justice; years of service, where applicable, are as chief justice only; see prior listing for nomination and service as associate justice. *Column 2.* R = recess appointment. *Column 3.* C = confirmed. D = declined. P = postponed. R = rejected. W = withdrawn. *Column 5.* D = died. P = promoted to chief justice (see separate listing for service as chief justice). R = retirement/resignation.

1 President/ Nominee	2 Appointed		3 Action (vote)	4 Oath Taken	5 Term End		6 Yrs. of Service
Tyler							
John C. Spencer	9 Jan. 1844	R	31 Jan. 1844 (21–26)				
Reuben H. Walworth	13 Mar. 1844	W	17 June 1844				
Edward King	5 June 1844	P	15 June 1844 (29–18)				
	4 Dec. 1844	W	7 Feb. 1845				
Samuel Nelson	4 Feb. 1845	C	14 Feb. 1845	27 Feb. 1845	R	28 Nov. 1872	27
John M. Read	7 Feb. 1845		No action				
Polk							
George W. Woodward	23 Dec. 1845	R	22 Jan. 1846 (20–29)				
Levi Woodbury	R 20 Sep. 1845			23 Sep. 1845			
	23 Dec. 1845	C	3 Jan. 1846	3 Jan. 1846	D	4 Sep. 1851	5
Robert C. Grier	3 Aug. 1846	C	4 Aug. 1846	10 Aug. 1846	R	31 Jan. 1870	23
Fillmore							
Benjamin R. Curtis	R 22 Sep. 1851			10 Oct. 1851			
	11 Dec. 1851	C	20 Dec. 1851		R	30 Sept. 1857	5
Edward A. Bradford	16 Aug. 1852		No action				
George E. Badger	10 Jan. 1853	P	11 Feb. 1853				
William C. Micou	24 Feb. 1853		No action				
Buchaman							
Pierce							
John A. Campbell	22 Mar. 1853	C	25 Mar. 1853	11 Apr. 1853	R	30 Apr. 1861	8
Nathan Clifford	9 Dec. 1857	C	12 Jan. 1858 (26–23)	21 Jan. 1858	D	25 July 1881	23
Jeremiah S. Black	5 Feb. 1861	R	21 Feb. 1861 (25–26)				
Lincoln							
Noah H. Swayne	22 Jan. 1862	C	24 Jan. 1862 (38–1)	27 Jan. 1862	R	24 Jan. 1881	19
Samuel F. Miller	16 July 1862	C	16 July 1862	21 July 1862	D	13 Oct. 1890	28
David Davis	R 17 Oct. 1862						
	1 Dec. 1862	C	8 Dec. 1862	10 Dec. 1862	R	4 Mar. 1877	14
Stephen J. Field	6 Mar. 1863	C	10 Mar. 1863	20 May 1863	R	1 Dec. 1897	34
Salmon P. Chase*	6 Dec. 1864	C	6 Dec. 1864	15 Dec. 1864	D	7 May 1873	8
A. Johnson							
Henry Stanbery	16 Apr. 1866		No action				
Grant							
Ebenezer R. Hoar	15 Dec. 1869	R	3 Feb. 1870 (24–33)				

1	2	3		4	5		6
President/ Nominee	**Appointed**	**Action (vote)**		**Oath Taken**	**Term End**		**Yrs. of Service**
Edwin M. Stanton	20 Dec. 1869	C	20 Dec. 1869 (46–11)	(Died 24 Dec. 1869)			
William Strong	7 Feb. 1870	C	18 Feb. 1870	14 Mar. 1870	R	14 Dec. 1880	10
Joseph P. Bradley	7 Feb. 1870	C	21 Mar. 1870 (46–9)	23 Mar. 1870	D	22 Jan. 1892	21
Ward Hunt	3 Dec. 1872	C	11 Dec. 1872	9 Jan. 1873	R	27 Jan. 1882	9
George H. Williams	1 Dec. 1873	W	8 Jan. 1874				
Caleb Cushing	9 Jan. 1874	W	13 Jan. 1874				
Morrison R. Waite*	19 Jan. 1874	C	21 Jan. 1874 (63–0)	4 Mar. 1874	D	23 Mar. 1888	14
Hayes							
John Marshall Harlan	16 Oct. 1877	C	29 Nov. 1877	10 Dec. 1877	D	14 Oct. 1911	34
William B. Woods	15 Dec. 1880	C	21 Dec. 1880 (39–8)	5 Jan. 1881	D	14 May 1887	6
Garfield							
Stanley Matthews	26 Jan. 1881		No action				
	14 Mar. 1881		12 May 1881 (24–23)	17 May 1881	D	22 Mar. 1889	7
Arthur							
Horace Gray	19 Dec. 1881	C	20 Dec. 1881 (51–5)	9 Jan. 1882	D	15 Sep. 1902	20
Roscoe Conkling	24 Feb. 1882	D	2 Mar. 1882 (39–12)				
Samuel Blatchford	13 Mar. 1882	C	27 Mar. 1882	3 Apr. 1882	D	7 July 1893	11
Cleveland							
Lucius Q. C. Lamar	6 Dec. 1887	C	16 Jan. 1888 (32–28)	18 Jan. 1888	D	23 Jan. 1893	5
Melville W. Fuller*	30 Apr. 1888	C	20 July 1888 (41–20)	8 Oct. 1888	D	4 July 1910	22
Harrison							
David J. Brewer	4 Dec. 1889	C	18 Dec. 1889 (53–11)	6 Jan. 1890	D	28 Mar. 1910	20
Henry B. Brown	23 Dec. 1890	C	29 Dec. 1890	5 Jan. 1891	R	28 May 1906	15
George Shiras	19 July 1892	C	26 July 1892	10 Oct. 1892	R	23 Feb. 1903	10
Howell E. Jackson	2 Feb. 1893	C	18 Feb. 1893	4 Mar. 1893	D	8 Aug. 1895	2

Column 1. * = chief justice. † = nomination for promotion to chief justice; years of service, where applicable, are as chief justice only; see prior listing for nomination and service as associate justice. *Column 2.* R = recess appointment. *Column 3.* C = confirmed. D = declined. P = postponed. R = rejected. W = withdrawn. *Column 5.* D = died. P = promoted to chief justice (see separate listing for service as chief justice). R = retirement/resignation.

1	2	3	4	5	6
President/ Nominee	Appointed	Action (vote)	Oath Taken	Term End	Yrs. of Service
Cleveland					
William B. Hornblower	19 Sep. 1893	R 15 Jan. 1894 (24–30)			
Wheeler H. Peckham	23 Jan. 1894	R 16 Feb. 1894 (32–41)			
Edward D. White	19 Feb. 1894	C 19 Feb. 1894	12 Mar. 1894	P 18 Dec. 1910	17
Rufus W. Peckham	3 Dec. 1895	9 Dec. 1895	6 Jan. 1896	D 24 Oct. 1909	13
McKinley					
Joseph McKenna	16 Dec. 1897	C 21 Jan. 1898	26 Jan. 1898	R 5 Jan. 1925	26
T. Roosevelt					
Oliver Wendell Holmes	R 11 Aug. 1902				
	2 Dec. 1902	C 2 Dec. 1902	8 Dec. 1902	R 12 Jan. 1932	29
William R. Day	2 Mar. 1903	C 23 Feb. 1903	2 Mar. 1903	R 13 Nov. 1922	19
William H. Moody	3 Dec. 1906	C 12 Dec. 1906	17 Dec. 1906	R 20 Nov. 1910	3
Taft					
Horace H. Lurton	13 Dec. 1909	C 20 Dec. 1909	3 Jan. 1910	D 12 July 1914	4
Charles E. Hughes	25 Apr. 1910	C 2 May 1910	10 Oct. 1910	R 10 June 1916	6
Edward D. White*†	12 Dec. 1910	C 12 Dec. 1910	19 Dec. 1910	D 19 May 1921	10
Willis Van Devanter	12 Dec. 1910	C 15 Dec. 1910	3 Jan. 1911	R 2 June 1937	26
Joseph R. Lamar	12 Dec. 1910	C 15 Dec. 1910	3 Jan. 1911	D 2 Jan. 1916	5
Mahlon Pitney	19 Feb. 1912	C 13 Mar. 1912 (50–26)	18 Mar. 1912	R 31 Dec. 1922	10
Wilson					
James C. McReynolds	19 Aug. 1914	C 29 Aug. 1914 (44–6)	5 Sep. 1914	R 1 Feb. 1941	26
Louis D. Brandeis	28 Jan. 1916	C 1 June 1916 (47–22)	5 June 1916	R 13 Feb. 1939	22
John H. Clarke	14 July 1916	C 24 July 1916	1 Aug. 1916	R 18 Sep. 1922	6
Harding					
William H. Taft*	30 June 1921	C 30 June 1921	11 July 1921	R 3 Feb. 1930	8
George Sutherland	5 Sep. 1922	C 5 Sep. 1922	2 Oct. 1922	R 17 Jan. 1938	15
Pierce Butler	23 Nov. 1922		No action		
	5 Dec. 1922	C 21 Dec. 1922 (61–8)	2 Jan. 1923	D 16 Nov. 1939	17
Edward T. Sanford	24 Jan. 1923	C 29 Jan. 1923	5 Feb. 1923	D 8 Mar. 1930	7
Coolidge					
Harlan F. Stone	5 Jan. 1925	C 5 Feb. 1925 (71–6)	2 Mar. 1925	P 2 July 1941	16

1	2	3	4	5	6
President/ Nominee	Appointed	Action (vote)	Oath Taken	Term End	Yrs. of Service
Hoover					
Charles E. Hughes*†	3 Feb. 1930	C 13 Feb. 1930 (52–26)	24 Feb. 1930	R 1 July 1941	11
John J. Parker	21 Mar. 1930	R 7 May 1930 (39–41)			
Owen J. Roberts	9 May 1930	C 20 May 1930	2 June 1930	R 31 July 1945	15
Benjamin N. Cardozo	15 Feb. 1932	C 24 Feb. 1932	14 Mar. 1932	D 9 July 1938	6
F. D. Roosevelt					
Hugo L. Black	12 Aug. 1937	C 17 Aug. 1937 (63–16)	19 Aug. 1937	R 17 Sep. 1971	34
Stanley F. Reed	15 Jan. 1938	C 25 Jan. 1938	31 Jan. 1938	R 25 Feb. 1957	19
Felix Frankfurter	5 Jan. 1939	C 17 Jan. 1939	30 Jan. 1939	R 28 Aug. 1962	23
William O. Douglas	20 Mar. 1939	C 4 Apr. 1939 (62–4)	17 Apr. 1939	R 12 Nov. 1975	36
Frank Murphy	4 Jan. 1940	C 16 Jan. 1940	18 Jan. 1940	D 19 July 1949	9
Harlan F. Stone*†	12 June 1941	C 27 June 1941	3 July 1941	D 22 Apr. 1946	5
James F. Byrnes	12 June 1941	C 12 June 1941	8 July 1941	R 3 Oct. 1942	1
Robert H. Jackson	12 June 1941	C 7 July 1941	11 July 1941	D 9 Oct. 1954	13
Wiley B. Rutledge	11 Jan. 1943	C 8 Feb. 1943	15 Feb. 1943	D 10 Sep. 1949	6
Truman					
Harold H. Burton	18 Sep. 1945	C 19 Sep. 1945	1 Oct. 1945	R 13 Oct. 1958	13
Fred M. Vinson*	6 June 1946	C 20 June 1946	24 June 1946	D 8 Sep. 1953	7
Tom C. Clark	2 Aug. 1949	C 18 Aug. 1949 (73–8)	24 Aug. 1949	R 12 June 1967	18
Sherman Minton	15 Sep. 1949	C 4 Oct. 1949 (48–16)	12 Oct. 1949	R 15 Oct. 1956	7
Eisenhower					
Earl Warren*	R 2 Oct. 1953		5 Oct. 1953		
	11 Jan. 1954	C 1 Mar. 1954	2 Mar. 1954	R 23 June 1969	15
John M. Harlan II	9 Nov. 1954		No action		
	10 Jan. 1955	C 16 Mar. 1955 (71–11)	28 Mar. 1955	R 23 Sep. 1971	16
William J. Brennan, Jr.	R 15 Oct. 1956			16 Oct. 1956	
	14 Jan. 1957	C 19 Mar. 1957	22 Mar. 1957	R 20 July 1990	33
Charles E. Whittaker	2 Mar. 1957	C 19 Mar. 1957	25 Mar. 1957	R 1 Apr. 1962	5
Potter Stewart	R 14 Oct. 1958		14 Oct. 1958		
	17 Jan. 1959	C 5 May 1959 (70–17)	15 May 1959	R 3 July 1981	22

Column 1. * = chief justice. † = nomination for promotion to chief justice; years of service, where applicable, are as chief justice only; see prior listing for nomination and service as associate justice. *Column 2.* R = recess appointment. *Column 3.* C = confirmed. D = declined. P = postponed. R = rejected. W = withdrawn. *Column 5.* D = died. P = promoted to chief justice (see separate listing for service as chief justice). R = retirement/resignation.

1	2	3	4	5	6
President/ Nominee	Appointed	Action (vote)	Oath Taken	Term End	Yrs. of Service
Kennedy					
Byron R. White	3 Apr. 1962	C 11 Apr. 1962	16 Apr. 1962	R 28 June 1993	31
Arthur J. Goldberg	31 Aug. 1962	C 25 Sep. 1962	1 Oct. 1962	R 25 July 1965	3
L. B. Johnson					
Abe Fortas	28 July 1965	C 11 Aug. 1965	4 Oct. 1965	R 14 May 1969	4
Thurgood Marshall	13 June 1967	C 30 Aug. 1967 (69–11)	2 Oct. 1967	R 1 Oct. 1991	24
Abe Fortas[†]	26 June 1968	W 4 Oct. 1968			
Homer Thornberry	26 June 1968	W 2 Oct. 1968			
Nixon					
Warren E. Burger*	21 May 1969	C 9 June 1969 (74–3)	23 June 1969	R 26 Sep. 1986	17
Clement Haynsworth, Jr.	18 Aug. 1969	R 21 Nov. 1969 (45–55)			
G. Harrold Carswell	19 Jan. 1970	R 8 Apr. 1970 (45–51)			
Harry A. Blackmun	15 Apr. 1970	C 12 May 1970 (94–0)	9 June 1970	R 3 Aug. 1994	24
Lewis F. Powell, Jr.	22 Oct. 1971	C 6 Dec. 1971 (89–1)	7 Jan. 1972	R 26 June 1987	16
William H. Rehnquist	22 Oct. 1971	C 10 Dec. 1971 (68–26)	7 Jan. 1972	P 26 Sep. 1986	15
Ford					
John Paul Stevens	28 Nov. 1975	C 17 Dec. 1975 (98–0)	19 Dec. 1975		
Reagan					
Sandra Day O'Connor	7 July 1981	C 21 Sep. 1981 (99–0)	25 Sep. 1981	R 31 Jan. 2006	24
William H. Rehnquist*†	17 June 1986	C 17 Sep. 1986 (65–33)	26 Sep. 1986	D 3 Sept. 2005	19
Antonin Scalia	17 June 1986	C 17 Sep. 1986 (98–0)	26 Sep. 1986		
Robert H. Bork	1 July 1987	R 23 Oct. 1987 (42–58)			
Douglas Ginsburg	29 Oct. 1987	W 7 Nov. 1987			
Anthony M. Kennedy	24 Nov. 1987	C 3 Feb. 1988 (97–0)	18 Feb. 1988		
Bush					
David H. Souter	25 July 1990	C 2 Oct. 1990 (90–9)	9 Oct. 1990		
Clarence Thomas	1 July 1991	C 15 Oct. 1991 (52–48)	1 Nov. 1991		

1 President/ Nominee	2 Appointed	3 Action (vote)	4 Oath Taken	5 Term End	6 Yrs. of Service
Clinton					
Ruth B. Ginsburg	14 June 1993	C 3 Aug. 1993 (96–3)	10 Aug. 1993		
Stephen G. Breyer	13 May 1994	C 29 July 1994 (87–9)	3 Aug. 1994		
G. W. Bush					
John G. Roberts Jr.	19 July 2005	C 29 Sept. 2005 (78–22)	29 Sept. 2005		
Samuel A. Alito Jr.	10 Nov. 2005	C 31 Jan. 2006 (58–42)	31 Jan. 2006		

Appointments, by Presidential Term

In this chart, arrows pointing out from presidents indicated appointments of justices; arrows pointing in from chief justices indicate administration of presidential oath of office

Chief Justices Appointment date	Presidents Inauguration date	Associate Justices Appointment date

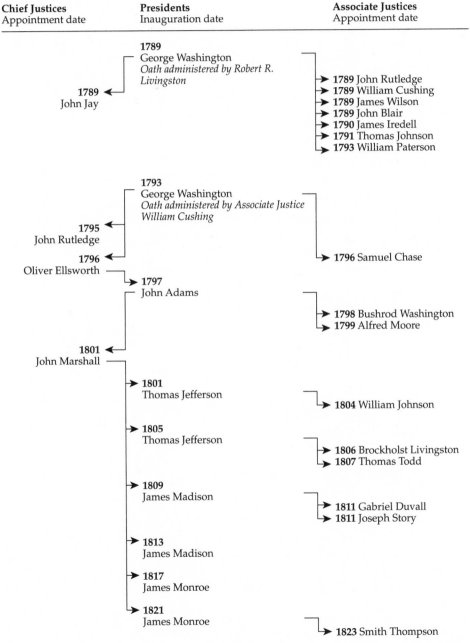

1789
George Washington
Oath administered by Robert R. Livingston

1789 ◄
John Jay

➤ **1789** John Rutledge
➤ **1789** William Cushing
➤ **1789** James Wilson
➤ **1789** John Blair
➤ **1790** James Iredell
➤ **1791** Thomas Johnson
➤ **1793** William Paterson

1793
George Washington
Oath administered by Associate Justice William Cushing

1795 ◄
John Rutledge

1796 ◄
Oliver Ellsworth

➤ **1796** Samuel Chase

➤ **1797**
John Adams

➤ **1798** Bushrod Washington
➤ **1799** Alfred Moore

1801 ◄
John Marshall

➤ **1801**
Thomas Jefferson

➤ **1804** William Johnson

➤ **1805**
Thomas Jefferson

➤ **1806** Brockholst Livingston
➤ **1807** Thomas Todd

➤ **1809**
James Madison

➤ **1811** Gabriel Duvall
➤ **1811** Joseph Story

➤ **1813**
James Madison

➤ **1817**
James Monroe

➤ **1821**
James Monroe

➤ **1823** Smith Thompson

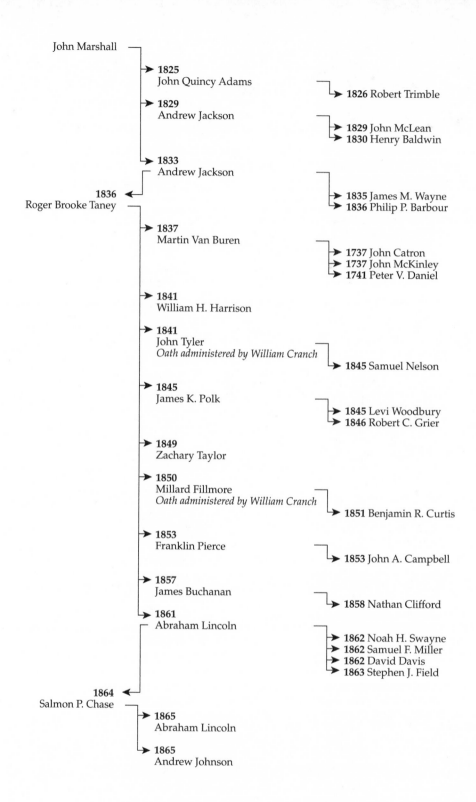

John Marshall

1825
John Quincy Adams

1826 Robert Trimble

1829
Andrew Jackson

1829 John McLean
1830 Henry Baldwin

1833
Andrew Jackson

1836
Roger Brooke Taney

1835 James M. Wayne
1836 Philip P. Barbour

1837
Martin Van Buren

1737 John Catron
1737 John McKinley
1741 Peter V. Daniel

1841
William H. Harrison

1841
John Tyler
Oath administered by William Cranch

1845 Samuel Nelson

1845
James K. Polk

1845 Levi Woodbury
1846 Robert C. Grier

1849
Zachary Taylor

1850
Millard Fillmore
Oath administered by William Cranch

1851 Benjamin R. Curtis

1853
Franklin Pierce

1853 John A. Campbell

1857
James Buchanan

1858 Nathan Clifford

1861
Abraham Lincoln

1862 Noah H. Swayne
1862 Samuel F. Miller
1862 David Davis
1863 Stephen J. Field

1864
Salmon P. Chase

1865
Abraham Lincoln

1865
Andrew Johnson

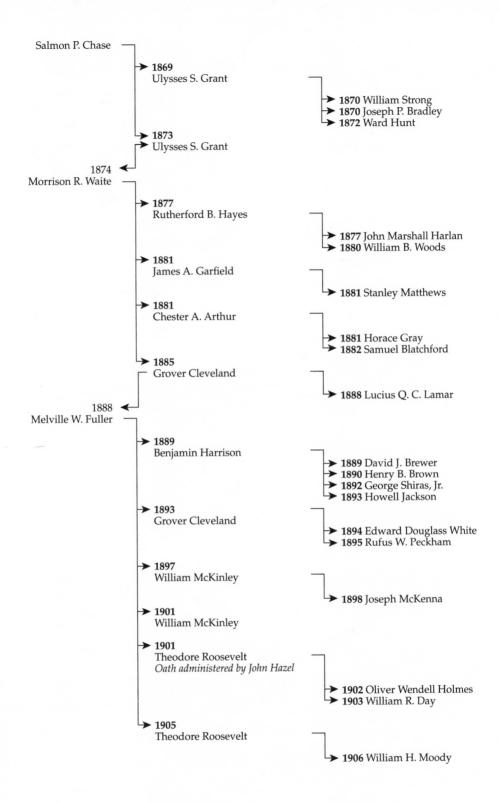

Salmon P. Chase

1869
Ulysses S. Grant

1870 William Strong
1870 Joseph P. Bradley
1872 Ward Hunt

1873
Ulysses S. Grant

1874
Morrison R. Waite

1877
Rutherford B. Hayes

1877 John Marshall Harlan
1880 William B. Woods

1881
James A. Garfield

1881 Stanley Matthews

1881
Chester A. Arthur

1881 Horace Gray
1882 Samuel Blatchford

1885
Grover Cleveland

1888 Lucius Q. C. Lamar

1888
Melville W. Fuller

1889
Benjamin Harrison

1889 David J. Brewer
1890 Henry B. Brown
1892 George Shiras, Jr.
1893 Howell Jackson

1893
Grover Cleveland

1894 Edward Douglass White
1895 Rufus W. Peckham

1897
William McKinley

1898 Joseph McKenna

1901
William McKinley

1901
Theodore Roosevelt
Oath administered by John Hazel

1902 Oliver Wendell Holmes
1903 William R. Day

1905
Theodore Roosevelt

1906 William H. Moody

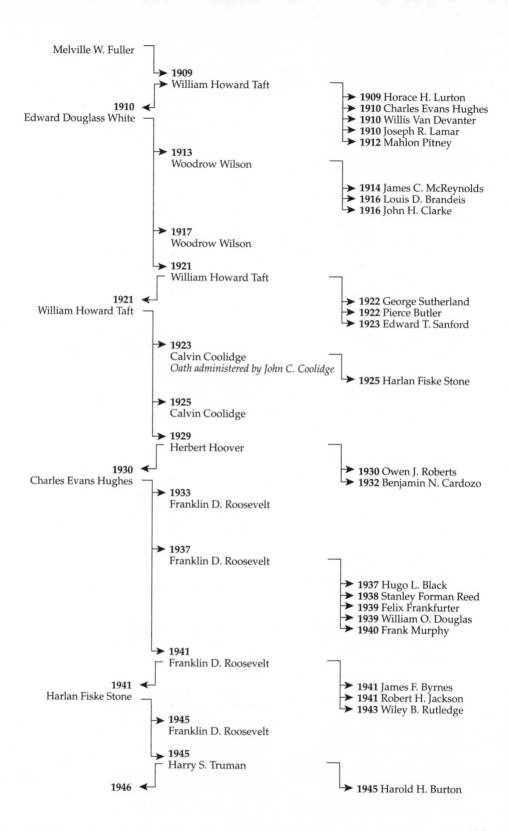

Melville W. Fuller

1909
William Howard Taft

1910
Edward Douglass White

→ **1909** Horace H. Lurton
→ **1910** Charles Evans Hughes
→ **1910** Willis Van Devanter
→ **1910** Joseph R. Lamar
→ **1912** Mahlon Pitney

1913
Woodrow Wilson

→ **1914** James C. McReynolds
→ **1916** Louis D. Brandeis
→ **1916** John H. Clarke

1917
Woodrow Wilson

1921
William Howard Taft

1921
William Howard Taft

→ **1922** George Sutherland
→ **1922** Pierce Butler
→ **1923** Edward T. Sanford

1923
Calvin Coolidge
Oath administered by John C. Coolidge

→ **1925** Harlan Fiske Stone

1925
Calvin Coolidge

1929
Herbert Hoover

1930
Charles Evans Hughes

→ **1930** Owen J. Roberts
→ **1932** Benjamin N. Cardozo

1933
Franklin D. Roosevelt

1937
Franklin D. Roosevelt

→ **1937** Hugo L. Black
→ **1938** Stanley Forman Reed
→ **1939** Felix Frankfurter
→ **1939** William O. Douglas
→ **1940** Frank Murphy

1941
Franklin D. Roosevelt

1941
Harlan Fiske Stone

→ **1941** James F. Byrnes
→ **1941** Robert H. Jackson
→ **1943** Wiley B. Rutledge

1945
Franklin D. Roosevelt

1945
Harry S. Truman

1946

→ **1945** Harold H. Burton

430

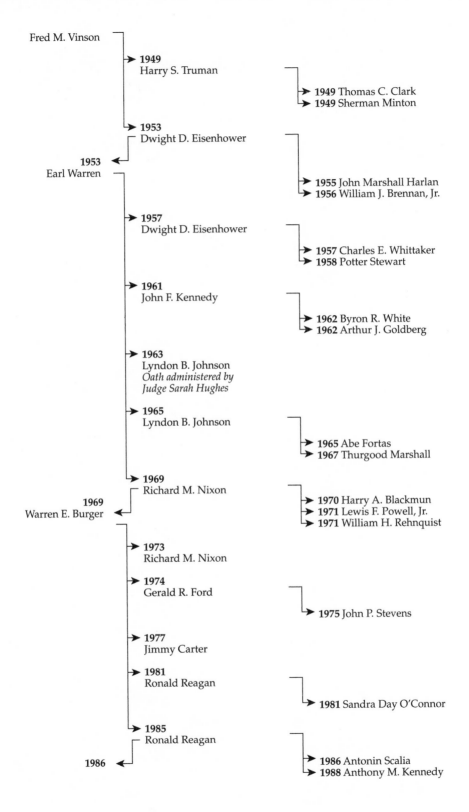

Fred M. Vinson

1949
Harry S. Truman

> **1949** Thomas C. Clark
> **1949** Sherman Minton

1953
Dwight D. Eisenhower

1953
Earl Warren

> **1955** John Marshall Harlan
> **1956** William J. Brennan, Jr.

1957
Dwight D. Eisenhower

> **1957** Charles E. Whittaker
> **1958** Potter Stewart

1961
John F. Kennedy

> **1962** Byron R. White
> **1962** Arthur J. Goldberg

1963
Lyndon B. Johnson
*Oath administered by
Judge Sarah Hughes*

1965
Lyndon B. Johnson

> **1965** Abe Fortas
> **1967** Thurgood Marshall

1969
Richard M. Nixon

1969
Warren E. Burger

> **1970** Harry A. Blackmun
> **1971** Lewis F. Powell, Jr.
> **1971** William H. Rehnquist

1973
Richard M. Nixon

1974
Gerald R. Ford

> **1975** John P. Stevens

1977
Jimmy Carter

1981
Ronald Reagan

> **1981** Sandra Day O'Connor

1985
Ronald Reagan

1986

> **1986** Antonin Scalia
> **1988** Anthony M. Kennedy

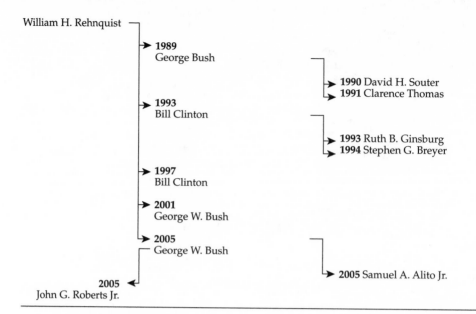

William H. Rehnquist

1989
George Bush

1990 David H. Souter
1991 Clarence Thomas

1993
Bill Clinton

1993 Ruth B. Ginsburg
1994 Stephen G. Breyer

1997
Bill Clinton

2001
George W. Bush

2005
George W. Bush

2005 Samuel A. Alito Jr.

2005
John G. Roberts Jr.

Chronology of the Justices' Succession

Date[1]	Justice	Action
5 Oct. 1789	James Wilson	Oath of Office
19 Oct. 1789	John Jay*	Oath of Office
2 Feb. 1790	William Cushing	Oath of Office
2 Feb. 1790	John Blair	Oath of Office
15 Feb. 1790	John Rutledge	Oath of Office
12 May 1790	James Iredell	Oath of Office
5 Mar. 1791	John Rutledge	Resigned
6 Aug. 1792	Thomas Johnson	Oath of Office
16 Jan. 1793	Thomas Johnson	Resigned
11 Mar. 1793	William Paterson	Oath of Office
29 June 1795	John Jay*	Resigned
12 Aug. 1795	John Rutledge*	Oath of Office
25 Oct. 1795	John Blair	Resigned
15 Dec. 1795	John Rutledge*	Rejected
4 Feb. 1796	Samuel Chase	Oath of Office
8 Mar. 1796	Oliver Ellsworth*	Oath of Office
21 Aug. 1798	James Wilson	Death
4 Feb. 1799	Bushrod Washington	Oath of Office
20 Oct. 1799	James Iredell	Death
21 Apr. 1800	Alfred Moore	Oath of Office
15 Dec. 1800	Oliver Ellsworth*	Resigned
4 Feb. 1801	John Marshall*	Oath of Office
26 Jan. 1804	Alfred Moore	Resigned
8 May. 1804	William Johnson	Oath of Office
9 Sep. 1806	William Paterson	Death
20 Jan. 1807	Brockholst Livingston	Oath of Office
4 May 1807	Thomas Todd	Oath of Office
13 Sep. 1810	William Cushing	Death
19 June 1811	Samuel Chase	Death
23 Nov. 1811	Gabriel Duvall	Oath of Office
3 Feb. 1812	Joseph Story	Oath of Office
18 Mar. 1823	Brockholst Livingston	Death
10 Feb. 1824	Smith Thompson	Oath of Office
7 Feb. 1826	Thomas Todd	Death
16 June 1826	Robert Trimble	Oath of Office
25 Aug. 1828	Robert Trimble	Death
26 Nov. 1829	Bushrod Washington	Death
11 Jan. 1830	John McLean	Oath of Office

---

* Denotes chief justice
[1] In some instances, justices were appointed to the Court while the Senate was not in session, and a handful of these "recess appointees" took their judicial oaths before their names had been formally submitted to the Senate. The dates of oaths listed in this table refer to oaths taken *after* Senate confirmation. For other information regarding recess appointees, see the table of nominations, above.

Date[1]	Justice	Action
18 Jan. 1830	Henry Baldwin	Oath of Office
4 Aug. 1834	William Johnson	Death
14 Jan. 1835	Gabriel Duvall	Resigned
14 Jan. 1835	James Moore Wayne	Oath of Office
6 July 1835	John Marshall*	Death
28 Mar. 1836	Roger Brooke Taney*	Oath of Office
12 May 1836	Philip Pendleton Barbour	Oath of Office
1 May 1937	John Catron	Oath of Office
9 Jan. 1838	John McKinley	Oath of Office
25 Feb. 1841	Philip Pendleton Barbour	Death
10 Jan. 1842	Peter Vivian Daniel	Oath of Office
18 Dec. 1843	Smith Thompson	Death
21 Apr. 1844	Henry Baldwin	Death
27 Feb. 1845	Samuel Nelson	Oath of Office
10 Sep. 1845	Joseph Story	Death
3 Jan. 1846	Levi Woodbury	Oath of Office
10 Aug. 1846	Robert Cooper Grier	Oath of Office
4 Sep. 1851	Levi Woodbury	Death
10 Oct. 1851	Benjamin Robbins Curtis	Oath of Office
19 July 1852	John McKinley	Death
11 Apr. 1853	John Archibald Campbell	Oath of Office
30 Sep. 1857	Benjamin Robbins Curtis	Resigned
21 Jan. 1858	Nathan Clifford	Oath of Office
31 May 1860	Peter Vivian Daniel	Death
4 Apr. 1861	John McLean	Death
30 Apr. 1861	John Archibald Campbell	Resigned
27 Jan. 1862	Noah Haynes Swayne	Oath of Office
21 July 1862	Samuel Freeman Miller	Oath of Office
10 Dec. 1862	David Davis	Oath of Office
20 May 1863	Stephen Johnson Field	Oath of Office
12 Oct. 1864	Roger Brooke Taney*	Death
15 Dec. 1864	Salmon Portland Chase*	Oath of Office
30 May 1865	John Catron	Death
5 July 1867	James Moore Wayne	Death
31 Jan. 1870	Robert Cooper Grier	Retired
14 Mar. 1870	William Strong	Oath of Office
23 Mar. 1870	Joseph P. Bradley	Oath of Office
28 Nov. 1872	Samuel Nelson	Retired
9 Jan. 1873	Ward Hunt	Oath of Office
7 May 1873	Salmon Portland Chase*	Death
4 Mar. 1874	Morrison Remick Waite*	Oath of Office
4 Mar. 1877	David Davis	Resigned
10 Dec. 1877	John Marshall Harlan	Oath of Office
14 Dec. 1880	William Strong	Retired
5 Jan. 1881	William Burnham Woods	Oath of Office
24 Jan. 1881	Noah Haynes Swayne	Retired
17 May 1881	Stanley Matthews	Oath of Office
25 July 1881	Nathan Clifford	Death
9 Jan. 1882	Horace Gray	Oath of Office

Date[1]	Justice	Action
27 Jan. 1882	Ward Hunt	Disabled
3 Apr. 1882	Samuel Blatchford	Oath of Office
14 May 1887	William Burnham Woods	Death
18 Jan. 1888	Lucius Quintus C. Lamar	Oath of Office
23 Mar. 1888	Morrison Remick Waite*	Death
8 Oct. 1888	Melville Weston Fuller*	Oath of Office
22 Mar. 1889	Stanley Matthews	Death
6 Jan. 1890	David Josiah Brewer	Oath of Office
13 Oct. 1890	Samuel Freeman Miller	Death
5 Jan. 1891	Henry Billings Brown	Oath of Office
22 Jan. 1892	Joseph P. Bradley	Death
10 Oct. 1892	George Shiras, Jr.	Oath of Office
23 Jan. 1893	Lucius Quintus C. Lamar	Death
4 Mar. 1893	Howell Edmunds Jackson	Oath of Office
7 July 1893	Samuel Blatchford	Death
12 Mar. 1894	Edward Douglass White	Oath of Office
8 Aug. 1895	Howell Edmunds Jackson	Death
6 Jan. 1896	Rufus Wheeler Peckham	Oath of Office
1 Dec. 1897	Stephen Johnson Field	Retired
26 Jan. 1898	Joseph McKenna	Oath of Office
15 Sep. 1902	Horace Gray	Death
8 Dec. 1902	Oliver Wendell Holmes	Oath of Office
23 Feb. 1903	George Shiras, Jr.	Retired
2 Mar. 1903	William Rufus Day	Oath of Office
28 May 1906	Henry Billings Brown	Retired
17 Dec. 1906	William Henry Moody	Oath of Office
24 Oct. 1909	Rufus Wheeler Peckham	Death
3 Jan. 1910	Horace Harmon Lurton	Oath of Office
28 Mar. 1910	David Josiah Brewer	Death
4 July 1910	Melville Weston Fuller*	Death
10 Oct. 1910	Charles Evans Hughes	Oath of Office
20 Nov. 1910	William Henry Moody	Disabled
18 Dec. 1910	Edward Douglass White	Promoted
19 Dec. 1910	Edward Douglass White*	Oath of Office
3 Jan. 1911	Willis Van Devanter	Oath of Office
3 Jan. 1911	Joseph Rucker Lamar	Oath of Office
14 Oct. 1911	John Marshall Harlan	Death
18 Mar. 1912	Mahlon Pitney	Oath of Office
12 July 1914	Horace Harmon Lurton	Death
5 Sep. 1914	James Clark McReynolds	Oath of Office
2 Jan. 1916	Joseph Rucker Lamar	Death
5 June 1916	Louis Dembitz Brandeis	Oath of Office
10 June 1916	Charles Evans Hughes	Resigned
1 Aug. 1916	John Hessin Clarke	Oath of Office
19 May 1921	Edward Douglass White*	Death
11 July 1921	William Howard Taft*	Oath of Office
18 Sep. 1922	John Hessin Clarke	Resigned
2 Oct. 1922	George Sutherland	Oath of Office
13 Nov. 1922	William Rufus Day	Retired

Date[1]	Justice	Action
31 Dec. 1922	Mahlon Pitney	Disabled
2 Jan. 1923	Pierce Butler	Oath of Office
5 Feb. 1923	Edward Terry Sanford	Oath of Office
5 Jan. 1925	Joseph McKenna	Retired
2 Mar. 1925	Harlan Fiske Stone	Oath of Office
3 Feb. 1930	William Howard Taft*	Retired
24 Feb. 1930	Charles Evans Hughes*	Oath of Office
8 Mar. 1930	Edward Terry Sanford	Death
2 June 1930	Owen Josephus Roberts	Oath of Office
12 Jan. 1932	Oliver Wendell Holmes	Retired
14 Mar. 1932	Benjamin Nathan Cardozo	Oath of Office
2 June 1937	Willis Van Devanter	Retired
19 Aug. 1937	Hugo Lafayette Black	Oath of Office
17 Jan. 1938	George Sutherland	Retired
31 Jan. 1938	Stanley Forman Reed	Oath of Office
9 July 1938	Benjamin Nathan Cardozo	Death
30 Jan. 1939	Felix Frankfurter	Oath of Office
13 Feb. 1939	Louis Dembitz Brandeis	Retired
17 Apr. 1939	William Orville Douglas	Oath of Office
16 Nov. 1939	Pierce Butler	Death
18 Jan. 1940	Frank Murphy	Oath of Office
1 Feb. 1941	James Clark McReynolds	Retired
1 July 1941	Charles Evans Hughes*	Retired
2 July 1941	Harlan Fiske Stone	Promoted
3 July 1941	Harlan Fiske Stone*	Oath of Office
8 July 1941	James Francis Byrnes	Oath of Office
11 July 1941	Robert Houghwout Jackson	Oath of Office
3 Oct. 1942	James Francis Byrnes	Resigned
15 Feb. 1943	Wiley Blount Rutledge	Oath of Office
31 July 1945	Owen Josephus Roberts	Resigned
1 Oct. 1945	Harold Hitz Burton	Oath of Office
22 Apr. 1946	Harlan Fiske Stone*	Death
24 June 1946	Fred Moore Vinson*	Oath of Office
19 July 1949	Frank Murphy	Death
24 Aug. 1949	Thomas Campbell Clark	Oath of Office
10 Sep. 1949	Wiley Blount Rutledge	Death
12 Oct. 1949	Sherman Minton	Oath of Office
8 Sep. 1953	Fred Moore Vinson*	Death
5 Oct. 1953	Earl Warren*	Oath of Office
9 Oct. 1954	Robert Houghwout Jackson	Death
28 Mar. 1955	John Marshall Harlan II	Oath of Office
15 Oct. 1956	Sherman Minton	Retired
25 Feb. 1957	Stanley Forman Reed	Retired
22 Mar. 1957	William J. Brennan, Jr.	Oath of Office
25 Mar. 1957	Charles Evans Whittaker	Oath of Office
13 Oct. 1958	Harold Hitz Burton	Retired
14 Oct. 1958	Potter Stewart	Oath of Office
1 Apr. 1962	Charles Evans Whittaker	Disabled
16 Apr. 1962	Byron Raymond White	Oath of Office

Date[1]	Justice	Action
28 Aug. 1962	Felix Frankfurter	Retired
1 Oct. 1962	Arthur Joseph Goldberg	Oath of Office
25 July 1965	Arthur Joseph Goldberg	Resigned
4 Oct. 1965	Abe Fortas	Oath of Office
12 June 1967	Thomas Campbell Clark	Retired
2 Oct. 1967	Thurgood Marshall	Oath of Office
14 May 1969	Abe Fortas	Resigned
23 June 1969	Earl Warren*	Resigned
23 June 1969	Warren Earl Burger*	Oath of Office
9 June 1970	Harry A. Blackmun	Oath of Office
17 Sep. 1971	Hugo Lafayette Black	Retired
23 Sep. 1971	John Marshall Harlan II	Retired
7 Jan. 1972	Lewis F. Powell, Jr.	Oath of Office
7 Jan. 1972	William H. Rehnquist	Oath of Office
12 Nov. 1975	William Orville Douglas	Retired
19 Dec. 1975	John Paul Stevens	Oath of Office
3 July 1981	Potter Stewart	Retired
25 Sep. 1981	Sandra Day O'Connor	Oath of Office
26 Sep. 1986	Warren Earl Burger	Retired
26 Sep. 1986	William H. Rehnquist	Promoted
26 Sep. 1986	William H. Rehnquist*	Oath of Office
26 Sep. 1986	Antonin Scalia	Oath of Office
26 June 1987	Lewis F. Powell, Jr.	Retired
18 Feb. 1988	Anthony M. Kennedy	Oath of Office
20 July 1990	William J. Brennan, Jr.	Retired
9 Oct. 1990	David H. Souter	Oath of Office
1 Oct. 1991	Thurgood Marshall	Retired
1 Nov. 1991	Clarence Thomas	Oath of Office
28 June 1993	Byron R. White	Retired
10 Aug. 1993	Ruth B. Ginsburg	Oath of Office
3 Aug. 1994	Harry A. Blackmun	Retired
3 Aug. 1994	Stephen G. Breyer	Oath of Office
3 Sep. 2005	William H. Rehnquist	Death
29 Sep. 2005	John G. Roberts Jr.	Oath of Office
31 Jan. 2006	Sandra Day O'Connor	Retired
31 Jan. 2006	Samuel A. Alito Jr.	Oath of Office

Succession of the Justices

Departing Justice/ Date of Vacancy	Replacement Justice/ Date of Arrival[1]	Days without Full Court[2]
John Rutledge 5 Mar. 1791	Thomas Johnson 6 Aug. 1792	519
Thomas Johnson 16 Jan. 1793	William Paterson 11 Mar. 1793	54
John Jay* 29 June 1795	John Rutledge* 12 Aug. 1795	44
John Rutledge* 15 Dec. 1795	Oliver Ellsworth* 8 Mar. 1796	83
John Blair 25 Oct. 1795	Samuel Chase 4 Feb. 1796	102
James Wilson 21 Aug. 1798	Bushrod Washington 4 Feb. 1799	167
James Iredell 20 Oct. 1799	Alfred Moore 21 Apr. 1800	183
Oliver Ellsworth* 15 Dec. 1800	John Marshall* 4 Feb. 1801	51
Alfred Moore 26 Jan. 1804	William Johnson 8 May 1804	102
William Paterson 9 Sep. 1806	Brockholst Livingston 20 Jan. 1807	133
William Cushing 13 Sep. 1810	Joseph Story 3 Feb. 1812	508
Samuel Chase 19 June 1811	Gabriel Duvall 23 Nov. 1811	
Brockholst Livingston 18 Mar. 1823	Smith Thompson 10 Feb. 1824	330
Thomas Todd 7 Feb. 1826	Robert Trimble 16 June 1826	129
Robert Trimble 25 Aug. 1828	John McLean 11 Jan. 1830	505

---

*Denotes chief justice

[1]In some instances, justices were appointed to the Court while the Senate was not in session, and a handful of these "recess appointees" took their judicial oaths before their names had been formally submitted to the Senate. The dates and numbers of days listed in this table refer to the official arrival of a justice on the Supreme Court, that is, the date of oath *after* Senate confirmation, even though the justice may already have taken his or her seat and participated in decisions. For further information regarding recess appointees, see the table of nominations, above.

[2]Braces indicate periods when a new vacancy occurred before all existing vacancies were filled. Thus, the number of days without a full court continues to increase until all vacancies are filled, although the succession was not broken. In this instance, before Justice Cushing could be replaced, Justice Chase retired and was replaced by Justice Duvall. Justice Story finally took Justice Cushing's seat 508 days after it had been vacated.

Departing Justice/ Date of Vacancy	Replacement Justice/ Date of Arrival[1]	Days without Full Court[2]
Bushrod Washington 26 Nov. 1829	Henry Baldwin 18 Jan. 1830	
William Johnson 4 Aug. 1834	James Moore Wayne 14 Jan. 1835	
Gabriel Duvall 14 Jan. 1835	Philip P. Barbour 12 May 1836	646 (between Johnson's departure and Taney's arrival)
John Marshall* 6 July 1835	Roger Brooke Taney* 28 Mar. 1836	
Philip P. Barbour 25 Feb. 1841	Peter Vivian Daniel 10 Jan. 1842	319
Smith Thompson 18 Dec. 1843	Samuel Nelson 27 Feb. 1845	
Henry Baldwin 21 Apr. 1844	Robert Cooper Grier 10 Aug. 1846	965 (between Thompson's departure and Grier's arrival)[3]
Joseph Story 10 Sep. 1845	Levi Woodbury 3 Jan. 1846	
Levi Woodbury 4 Sep. 1851	Benjamin Robbins Curtis 10 Oct. 1851	36
John McKinley 19 July 1852	John Archibald Campbell 11 Apr. 1853	266
Benjamin Robbins Curtis 30 Sep. 1857	Nathan Clifford 21 Jan. 1858	113
Peter Vivian Daniel 31 May 1860	Samuel Freeman Miller 21 July 1862	
John McLean 4 Apr. 1861	Noah Haynes Swayne 27 Jan. 1862	923 (between Daniel's departure and Davis's arrival)
John Archibald Campbell 30 Apr. 1861	David Davis 10 Dec. 1862	
Roger Brooke Taney* 2 Oct. 1864	Salmon Portland Chase* 15 Dec. 1864	64
John Catron 30 May 1865	No Replacement[4]	
James Moore Wayne 5 July 1867	No Replacement[4]	
Robert Cooper Grier 31 Jan. 1870	William Strong 14 Mar. 1870	42
Samuel Nelson 28 Nov. 1872	Ward Hunt 9 Jan. 1873	42
Salmon Portland Chase* 7 May 1873	Morrison Remick Waite* 4 Mar. 1874	301

[3]Although Justice Baldwin left the bench before Justice Story, his replacement, Justice Grier, did not arrive until after Justice Story's replacement did. Therefore, at least one seat was vacant for 965 days, from Justice Thompson's departure to Justice Grier's arrival.

[4]Under the provisions of the judiciary Act of 1866, the size of the Court was to decrease from ten to seven by attrition; the Judiciary Act of 1869 reestablished the number of justices at nine.

Departing Justice/ Date of Vacancy	Replacement Justice/ Date of Arrival[1]	Days without Full Court[2]
David Davis 4 Mar. 1877	John Marshall Harlan 10 Dec. 1877	281
William Strong 14 Dec. 1880	William Burnham Woods 5 Jan. 1881	22
Noah Haynes Swayne 24 Jan. 1881	Stanley Matthews 17 May 1881	113
Nathan Clifford 25 July 1881	Horace Gray 9 Jan. 1882	168
Ward Hunt 27 Jan. 1882	Samuel Blatchford 3 Apr. 1882	66
William Burnham Woods 14 May 1887	Lucius Quintus C. Lamar 18 Jan. 1888	249
Morrison Remick Waite* 23 Mar. 1888	Melville Weston Fuller* 8 Oct. 1888	199
Stanley Matthews 22 Mar. 1889	David Josiah Brewer 6 Jan. 1890	290
Samuel Freeman Miller 13 Oct. 1890	Henry Billings Brown 5 Jan. 1891	84
Joseph P. Bradley 22 Jan. 1892	George Shiras, Jr. 10 Oct. 1892	261
Lucius Quintus C. Lamar 23 Jan. 1893	Howell Edmunds Jackson 4 Mar. 1893	40
Samuel Blatchford 7 July 1893	Edward Douglass White 12 Mar. 1894	248
Howell Edmunds Jackson 8 Aug. 1895	Rufus Wheeler Peckham 6 Jan. 1896	151
Stephen Johnson Field 1 Dec. 1897	Joseph McKenna 26 Jan. 1898	56
Horace Gray 15 Sep. 1902	Oliver Wendell Holmes 8 Dec. 1902	84
George Shiras, Jr. 23 Feb. 1903	William Rufus Day 2 Mar. 1903	7
Henry Billings Brown 28 May 1906	William Henry Moody 17 Dec. 1906	203
Rufus Wheeler Peckham 24 Oct. 1909	Horace Harmon Lurton 3 Jan. 1910	71
David Josiah Brewer 28 Mar. 1910	Charles Evans Hughes 10 Oct. 1910	281 (between Brewer's departure and Lamar's arrival)
Melville Weston Fuller* 4 July 1910	Edward Douglass White* 19 Dec. 1910	
William Henry Moody 20 Nov. 1910	Willis Van Devanter 3 Jan. 1911	
Edward Douglass White[5] 18 Dec. 1910	Joseph Rucker Lamar 3 Jan. 1911	
John Marshall Harlan 14 Oct. 1911	Mahlon Pitney 18 Mar. 1912	155

Departing Justice/ Date of Vacancy	Replacement Justice/ Date of Arrival[1]	Days without Full Court[2]
Horace Harmon Lurton 12 July 1914	James Clark McReynolds 5 Sep. 1914	55
Joseph Rucker Lamar 2 Jan. 1916	Louis Dembitz Brandeis 5 June 1916	154
Charles Evans Hughes 10 June 1916	John Hessin Clarke 1 Aug. 1916	51
Edward Douglass White* 19 May 1921	William Howard Taft* 11 July 1921	53
John Hessin Clarke 18 Sep. 1922	George Sutherland 2 Oct. 1922	14
William Rufus Day 13 Nov. 1922	Pierce Butler 2 Jan. 1923	84 (between Day's departure and Sanford's arrival)
Mahlon Pitney 31 Dec. 1922	Edward Terry Sanford 5 Feb. 1923	
Joseph McKenna 5 Jan. 1925	Harlan Fiske Stone 2 Mar. 1925	56
William Howard Taft* 3 Feb. 1930	Charles Evans Hughes* 24 Feb. 1930	21
Edward Terry Sanford 8 Mar. 1930	Owen Josephus Roberts 2 June 1930	86
Oliver Wendell Holmes 12 Jan. 1932	Benjamin Nathan Cardozo 14 Mar. 1932	61
Willis Van Devanter 2 June 1937	Hugo Lafayette Black 19 Aug. 1937	78
George Sutherland 17 Jan. 1938	Stanley Forman Reed 31 Jan. 1938	14
Benjamin Nathan Cardozo 9 July 1938	Felix Frankfurter 30 Jan. 1939	205
Louis Dembitz Brandeis 13 Feb. 1939	William Orville Douglas 17 Apr. 1939	63
Pierce Butler 16 Nov. 1939	Frank Murphy 18 Jan. 1940	61
James Clark McReynolds 1 Feb. 1941	James Francis Byrnes 8 July 1941	160 (between McReynolds's departure and Jackson's arrival)
Charles Evans Hughes* 1 July 1941	Harlan Fiske Stone* 3 July 1941	
Harlan Fiske Stone[5] 2 July 1941	Robert H. Jackson 11 July 1941	
James Francis Byrnes 3 Oct. 1942	Wiley Blount Rutledge 15 Feb. 1943	135
Owen Josephus Roberts 31 July 1945	Harold Hitz Burton 1 Oct. 1945	62

---

[5]Note that in these instances the vacancy was created by elevation of a sitting associate justice to the position of chief justice, not as a result of the justice's departure from the Court.

Departing Justice/ Date of Vacancy	Replacement Justice/ Date of Arrival[1]	Days without Full Court[2]
Harlan Fiske Stone* 22 Apr. 1946	Fred Moore Vinson* 24 June 1946	63
Frank Murphy 19 July 1949	Thomas Campbell Clark 24 Aug. 1949	36
Wiley Blount Rutledge 10 Sep. 1949	Sherman Minton 12 Oct. 1949	32
Fred Moore Vinson* 8 Sep. 1953	Earl Warren* 2 Mar. 1953	174
Robert H. Jackson 9 Oct. 1954	John Marshall Harlan II 28 Mar. 1955	170
Sherman Minton 15 Oct. 1956	William J. Brennan, Jr. 22 Mar. 1957	161 (between Minton's departure and Whittaker's arrival)
Stanley Forman Reed 25 Feb. 1957	Charles Evans Whittaker 25 Mar. 1957	
Harold Hitz Burton 13 Oct. 1958	Potter Stewart 15 May 1959	213
Charles Evans Whittaker 1 Apr. 1963	Byron Raymond White 16 Apr. 1962	45
Felix Frankfurter 28 Aug. 1962	Arthur Joseph Goldberg 1 Oct. 1962	34
Arthur Joseph Goldberg 25 July 1965	Abe Fortas 4 Oct. 1965	71
Thomas Campbell Clark 12 June 1967	Thurgood Marshall 2 Oct. 1967	112
Abe Fortas 14 May 1969	Harry A. Blackmun 9 June 1970	391
Earl Warren* 23 June 1969	Warren Earl Burger* 23 June 1969	0
Hugo Lafayette Black 17 Sep. 1971	Lewis F. Powell, Jr. 7 Jan. 1972	112
John Marshall Harlan II 23 Sep. 1971	William H. Rehnquist 7 Jan. 1972	
William Orville Douglas 12 Nov. 1975	John Paul Stevens 19 Dec. 1975	37
Potter Stewart 3 July 1981	Sandra Day O'Connor 25 Sep. 1981	84
Warren Earl Burger* 26 Sep. 1986	William H. Rehnquist* 26 Sep. 1986	0
William H. Rehnquist[5] 26 Sep. 1986	Antonin Scalia 26 Sep. 1986	0
Lewis F. Powell, Jr. 26 June 1987	Anthony M. Kennedy 18 Feb. 1988	237

Departing Justice/ Date of Vacancy	Replacement Justice/ Date of Arrival[1]	Days without Full Court[2]
William J. Brennan, Jr. 20 July 1990	David H. Souter 9 Oct. 1990	81
Thurgood Marshall 1 Oct. 1991	Clarence Thomas 1 Nov. 1991	31
Byron R. White 1 July 1993	Ruth B. Ginsburg 10 Aug. 1993	40
Harry A. Blackmun 3 Aug. 1994	Stephen G. Breyer 3 Aug. 1994	0
William H. Rehnquist 3 Sept. 2005	John G. Roberts Jr. 29 Sept. 2005	26
Sandra Day O'Connor 31 Jan. 2006	Samuel A. Alito Jr. 31 Jan. 2006	0

Further Reading

The U. S. Supreme Court

Best, Bradley J. *Law Clerks, Support Personnel, and the Decline of Consensual Norms on the United States Supreme Court, 1935–1995*. New York: LFB Scholarly Publications, 2002.

Dickson, Del, ed. *The Supreme Court in Conference, 1940–1985*. New York: Oxford University Press, 2001.

Greenberg, Ellen. *The Supreme Court Explained*. New York: Norton, 1997.

Hall, Kermit L., James W. Ely Jr., and Joel B. Grossman, eds. *The Oxford Companion to the Supreme Court of the United States*. 2nd ed. New York: Oxford University Press, 2005.

Irons, Peter H., and Stephanie Guitton, eds. *May It Please the Court: The Most Significant Oral Arguments Made before the Supreme Court Since 1955*. New York: New Press, 1993.

Marcus, Maeva, et al., eds. *The Documentary History of the Supreme Court of the United States, 1789–1800*. 8 vols. New York: Columbia University Press, 1985–2007.

McCloskey, Robert G. *The American Supreme Court*. 4th ed. Revised by Sanford Levinson. Chicago: University of Chicago Press, 2005.

O'Connor, Sandra Day. *The Majesty of the Law: Reflections of a Supreme Court Justice*. Edited by Craig Joyce. New York: Random House, 2003.

Patrick, John J. *The Supreme Court of the United States: A Student Companion*. 3rd ed. New York: Oxford University Press, 2006.

Provine, Doris Marie. *Case Selection in the United States Supreme Court*. Chicago: University of Chicago Press, 1980.

Rehnquist, William H. *The Supreme Court*. New York: Knopf, 2001.

Roosevelt, Kermit. *The Myth of Judicial Activism: Making Sense of Supreme Court Decisions*. New Haven, CT: Yale University Press, 2006.

Starr, Kenneth W. *First among Equals: The Supreme Court in American Life*. New York: Warner, 2002.

Ward, Artemus. *Deciding to Leave: The Politics of Retirement from the United States Supreme Court*. Albany: State University of New York Press, 2003.

Supreme Court Justices

Abraham, Henry J. *Justices, Presidents, and Senators: A History of the U.S. Supreme Court Appointments from Washington to Clinton*. Rev. 4th ed. Lanham, MD: Rowman & Littlefield, 1999.

Cushman, Clare, ed. *The Supreme Court Justices: Illustrated Biographies, 1789–1995*. 2nd ed. Washington, DC: Congressional Quarterly Press, 1995.

Friedman, Leon, and Fred L. Israel, eds. *The Justices of the United States Supreme Court, 1789–1995: Their Lives and Major Opinions:* New York: Chelsea House, 1995.

Urofsky, Melvin I., ed. *Biographical Encyclopedia of the Supreme Court: The Lives and Legal Philosophies of the Justices*. Washington, DC: Congressional Quarterly Press, 2006.

White, G. Edward. *The American Judicial Tradition: Profiles of Leading American Judges*. 3rd ed. New York: Oxford University Press, 2007.

Supreme Court History

Allen, Austin. *Origins of the Dred Scott Case: Jacksonian Jurisprudence and the Supreme Court, 1837–1857*. Athens: University of Georgia Press, 2006.

Belknap, Michael R. *The Supreme Court under Earl Warren, 1953–1969*. Columbia: University of South Carolina Press, 2004.

Casto, William R. *The Supreme Court in the Early Republic: The Chief Justiceships of John Jay and Oliver Ellsworth*. Columbia: University of South Carolina Press, 1995.

Currie, David P. *The Constitution in the Supreme Court: The First Hundred Years, 1789–1888*. Chicago: University of Chicago Press, 1985.

Currie, David P. *The Constitution in the Supreme Court: The Second Century, 1888–1986*. Chicago: University of Chicago Press, 1990.

Ellis, Richard E. *Aggressive Nationalism: McCulloch v. Maryland and the Foundation of Federal Authority in the Young Republic*. New York: Oxford University Press, 2007.

Ely, James W., Jr. *The Chief Justiceship of Melville W. Fuller, 1888–1910*. Columbia: University of South Carolina Press, 1995.

Fiss, Owen M. *History of the Supreme Court of the United States*. Vol. 8, *Troubled Beginning of the Modern State, 1888–1910*. New York: Macmillan, 1993.

Gerber, Scott Douglas, ed. *Seriatim: The Supreme Court before John Marshall*. New York: New York University Press, 1998.

Gunther, Gerald, ed. *John Marshall's Defense of McCulloch v. Maryland*. Stanford, CA: Stanford University Press, 1969.

Hobson, Charles F. *The Great Chief Justice: John Marshall and the Rule of Law*. Lawrence: University Press of Kansas, 1996.

Hoffer, Peter Charles, Williamjames Hull Hoffer, and N. E. H. Hull. *The Supreme Court: An Essential History*. Lawrence: University Press of Kansas, 2007.

Johnson, Herbert A. *The Chief Justiceship of John Marshall, 1801–1835*. Columbia: University of South Carolina Press, 1997.

Killenbeck, Mark R. *M'Culloch v. Maryland: Securing a Nation*. Lawrence: University Press of Kansas, 2006.

Magrath, C. Peter. *Yazoo: Law and Politics in the New Republic: The Case of Fletcher v. Peck*. Providence, RI: Brown University Press, 1966.

Maltz, Earl M. *The Chief Justiceship of Warren Burger, 1969–1986.* Columbia: University Press of South Carolina, 2000.

Newmyer, R. Kent. *John Marshall and the Heroic Age of the Supreme Court.* Baton Rouge: Louisiana State University Press, 2001.

Pratt, Walter F., Jr. *The Supreme Court Under Edward Douglass White, 1910–1921.* Columbia: University of South Carolina Press, 1999.

Schwartz, Bernard. *A History of the Supreme Court.* New York: Oxford University Press, 1993.

Semonche, John E. *Charting the Future: The Supreme Court Responds to a Changing Society, 1890–1920.* Westport, CT: Greenwood Press, 1978.

White, G. Edward. *The Marshall Court and Cultural Change, 1815–1835.* New York: Oxford University Press, 1991.

Wiecek, William M. *History of the Supreme Court of the United States.* Vol. 12, *The Birth of the Modern Constitution, The United States Supreme Court, 1941–1953.* New York: Cambridge University Press, 2006.

Yarbrough, Tinsley E. *The Rehnquist Court and the Constitution.* New York: Oxford University Press, 2000.

The Rise of Judicial Review

Clinton, Robert Lowry. *Marbury v. Madison and Judicial Review.* Lawrence: University Press of Kansas, 1989.

Kahn, Paul W. *The Reign of Law: Marbury v. Madison and the Construction of America.* New Haven, CT: Yale University Press, 1997.

Nelson, William E. *Marbury v. Madison: The Origins and Legacy of Judicial Review.* Lawrence: University Press of Kansas, 2000.

The Constitution

Amar, Akhil Reed. *America's Constitution: A Biography.* New York: Random House, 2005.

Amar, Akhil Reed, and Alan Hirsch. *For the People: What the Constitution Really Says about Your Rights.* New York: Free Press, 1998.

Barnett, Randy E. *Restoring the Lost Constitution: The Presumption of Liberty.* Princeton, NJ: Princeton University Press, 2004.

Bernstein, Richard B., with Jerome Agel. *Amending America: If We Love the Constitution So Much, Why Do We Keep Trying to Change It?* New York: Times Books, 1993.

Biskupic, Joan, and Elder Witt. *The Supreme Court and Individual Rights.* 3rd ed. Washington, DC: Congressional Quarterly Press, 1997.

Blanchard, Margaret. *Revolutionary Sparks: Freedom of Expression in Modern America.* New York: Oxford University Press, 1992.

Burns, James McGregor, and Stewart Burns. *A People's Charter: The Pursuit of Rights in America.* New York: Knopf, 1991.

Cortner, Richard C. *The Supreme Court and the Second Bill of Rights: The Fourteenth Amendment and the Nationalization of Civil Liberties*. Madison: University of Wisconsin Press, 1981.

Dinan, John J. *Keeping the People's Liberties: Legislators, Citizens, and Judges as Guardians of Rights*. Lawrence: University Press of Kansas, 1998.

Ellis, Joseph J., ed. *What Did the Declaration Declare?* Boston: Bedford/St. Martin's, 1999.

Farber, Daniel A. *The First Amendment*. 2nd ed. New York: Foundation Press, 2003.

Farber, Daniel A., and Suzanna Sherry. *Desperately Seeking Certainty: The Misguided Quest for Constitutional Foundations*. Chicago: University of Chicago Press, 2002.

George, Robert P., ed. *Great Cases in Constitutional Law*. Princeton, NJ: Princeton University Press, 2000.

Glasser, Ira. *Visions of Liberty: The Bill of Rights for All Americans*. New York: Arcade, 1991.

Hall, Kermit L., ed. *By and For the People: Constitutional Rights in American History*. Arlington Heights, IL: Harlan Davidson, 1991.

Hall, Kermit L., and Peter Karsten. *The Magic Mirror: Law in American History*. 2nd ed. New York: Oxford University Press, 2008.

Irons, Peter. *The Courage of Their Convictions: Sixteen Americans Who Fought Their Way to the Supreme Court*. New York: Free Press, 1988.

Kersch, Ken I. *Constructing Civil Liberties: Discontinuities in the Development of American Constitutional Law*. New York: Cambridge University Press, 2004.

Kyvig, David E. *Explicit and Authentic Acts: Amending the U.S. Constitution*. Lawrence: University Press of Kansas, 1996.

Maltz, Earl M. *Rethinking Constitutional Law: Originalism, Interventionism, and the Politics of Judicial Review*. Lawrence: University Press of Kansas, 1994.

Raskin, Jamin B. *We the Students: Supreme Court Cases for and about Students*. 3rd ed. Washington, DC: Congressional Quarterly Press, 2008.

Shiffrin, Steven. *The First Amendment, Democracy, and Romance*. Cambridge, MA: Harvard University Press, 1990.

Stephens, Otis H., Jr., John M. Scheb, II, and Kara E. Stooksbury, eds. *Encyclopedia of American Civil Rights and Liberties*. Westport, CT: Greenwood Press, 2006.

Urofsky, Melvin I. *100 Americans Making Constitutional History: A Biographical History*. Washington, DC: Congressional Quarterly Press, 2004.

The U.S. Constitution Overseas

Casto, William R. *Foreign Affairs and the Constitution in the Age of Fighting Sail*. Columbia: University of South Carolina Press, 2006.

Sparrow, Bartholomew H. *The Insular Cases and the Emergence of American Empire*. Lawrence: University Press of Kansas, 2006.

Tushnet, Mark V., ed. *The Constitution in Wartime: Beyond Alarmism and Complacency.* Durham, NC: Duke University Press, 2005.

Yoo, John. *The Powers of War and Peace: The Constitution and Foreign Affairs After 9/11.* Chicago: University of Chicago Press, 2005.

The Bill of Rights

Adams, Willi Paul. *The First American Constitutions: Republican Ideology and the Making of the State Constitutions in the Revolutionary Era.* Expanded edition. Translated by Rita and Robert Kimber. Lanham, MD: Rowman & Littlefield, 2001.

Amar, Akhil Reed. *The Bill of Rights: Creation and Reconstruction.* New Haven, CT: Yale University Press, 1998.

Bodenhamer, David J., and James W. Ely, Jr., eds. *The Bill of Rights in Modern America.* 2nd ed. Bloomington: Indiana University Press, 2008.

Carnes, Jim. *Us and Them: A History of Intolerance in America.* New York: Oxford University Press, 1996.

Cogan, Neil, ed. *The Complete Bill of Rights: The Drafts, Debates, Sources, and Origins.* New York: Oxford University Press, 1997.

Conley, Patrick T., and John P. Kaminski, eds. *The Bill of Rights and the States: The Colonial and Revolutionary Origins of American Liberties.* Madison, WI: Madison House, 1992.

Estep, William. *Revolution within the Revolution: The First Amendment in Historical Context, 1612–1789.* Grand Rapids, MI: William B. Eerdmans, 1990.

Haynes, Charles, Sam Chaltain, and Susan M. Glisson. *First Freedoms: A Documentary History of First Amendment Rights in America.* New York: Oxford University Press, 2006.

Hentoff, Nat. *Living the Bill of Rights: How to Be an Authentic American.* Berkeley: University of California Press, 1999.

Howard, A. E. Dick. *The Road from Runnymede: Magna Carta and Constitutionalism in America.* Charlottesville: University Press of Virginia, 1998.

Levy, Leonard W. *Origins of the Bill of Rights.* New Haven, CT: Yale University Press, 1999.

Miller, William Lee. *The Business of May Next: James Madison and the Founding.* Charlottesville: University Press of Virginia, 1992.

Schwartz, Bernard. *The Great Rights of Mankind: A History of the American Bill of Rights.* Expanded ed. Madison, WI.: Madison House, 1992.

Capital Punishment

Banner, Stuart. *The Death Penalty: An American History.* Cambridge, MA: Harvard University Press, 2002.

Masur, Louis P. *Rites of Execution: Capital Punishment and the Transformation of American Culture, 1776–1865.* New York: Oxford University Press, 1989.

Miller, Arthur S., and Jeffrey H. Bowman. *Death by Installments: The Ordeal of Willie Francis.* New York: Greenwood Press, 1988.

Civil Rights

Banner, Stuart. *How the Indians Lost Their Land: Law and Power on the Frontier.* Cambridge, MA: Belknap Press, 2005.

Bernstein, David E. *Only One Place of Redress: African Americans, Labor Regulations, and the Courts from Reconstruction to the New Deal.* Durham, NC: Duke University Press, 2001.

Braeman, John. *Before the Civil Rights Revolution: The Old Court and Individual Rights.* Westport, CT: Greenwood Press, 1988.

Branch, Taylor. *Parting the Waters: America in the King Years, 1954–1963.* New York: Simon & Schuster, 1988.

Cottrol, Robert J., Raymond T. Diamond, and Leland B. Ware. *Brown v. Board of Education: Caste, Culture, and the Constitution.* Lawrence: University Press of Kansas, 2003.

Fehrenbacher, Don E. *The Dred Scott Case: Its Significance in American History.* New ed. New York: Oxford University Press, 2001.

Graham, Hugh Davis. *Collision Course: The Strange Convergence of Affirmative Action and Immigration Policy in America.* New York: Oxford University Press, 2002.

Hyman, Harold W., and William M. Wiecek. *Equal Justice Under Law: Constitutional Development, 1835–1875.* New York: Harper & Row, 1982.

Klarman, Michael J. *From Jim Crow to Civil Rights: The Supreme Court and the Struggle for Racial Equality.* New York: Oxford University Press, 2004.

Kluger, Richard. *Simple Justice: The History of Brown v. Board of Education and Black America's Struggle for Equality.* Rev. ed. New York: Knopf, 2004.

Kull, Andrew. *The Color-Blind Constitution.* Cambridge, MA: Harvard University Press, 1992.

Maltz, Earl M. *Dred Scott and the Politics of Slavery.* Lawrence: University Press of Kansas, 2007.

McClain, Charles J. *In Search of Equality: The Chinese Struggle Against Discrimination in Nineteenth-Century America.* Berkeley: University of California Press, 1996.

Nelson, William E. *The Fourteenth Amendment: From Political Principle to Judicial Doctrine.* Cambridge, MA: Harvard University Press, 1988.

Nieman, Donald G. *Promises to Keep: African-Americans and the Constitutional Order, 1776 to the Present.* New York: Oxford University Press, 1991.

Salyer, Lucy E. *Laws Harsh as Tigers: Chinese Immigrants and the Shaping of Modern Immigration Law.* Chapel Hill: University of North Carolina Press, 1995.

Sitkoff, Harvard. *The Struggle for Black Equality, 1954–1992.* Rev. ed. New York: Hill and Wang, 1993.

Commerce Power

Baxter, Maurice G. *Daniel Webster and the Supreme Court*. Amherst: University of Massachusetts Press, 1966.

Baxter, Maurice G. *The Steamboat Monopoly: Gibbons v. Ogden, 1824*. New York: Knopf, 1972.

Benson, Paul R., Jr. *The Supreme Court and the Commerce Clause, 1937–1970*. New York: Dunellen, 1970.

Ely, James W., Jr. *Railroads and American Law*. Lawrence: University Press of Kansas, 2001.

Criminal Justice

Bodenhamer, David. *Fair Trial: Rights of the Accused in American History*. New York: Oxford University Press, 1992.

Carter, Dan T. *Scottsboro: A Tragedy of the American South*. Rev. ed. Baton Rouge: Louisiana State University Press, 1979.

Friedman, Lawrence M. *Crime and Punishment in American History*. New York: Basic Books, 1993.

Walker, Samuel. *Popular Justice: A History of American Criminal Justice*. 2nd ed. New York: Oxford University Press, 1998.

Double Jeopardy

Garcia, Alfredo. *The Fifth Amendment: A Comprehensive Approach*. Westport, CT: Greenwood Press, 2002.

Sigler, Jay A. *Double Jeopardy: The Development of a Legal and Social Policy*. Ithaca, NY: Cornell University Press, 1968.

Thomas, George C., III. *Double Jeopardy: The History, the Law*. New York: New York University Press, 1998.

Due Process

Orth, John V. *Due Process of Law: A Brief History*. Lawrence: University Press of Kansas, 2003.

Phillips, Michael J. *The Lochner Court, Myth and Reality: Substantive Due Process from the 1890s to the 1930s*. Westport, CT: Praeger, 2001.

Eleventh Amendment

Cortner, Richard C. *The Iron Horse and the Constitution: The Railroads and the Transformation of the Fourteenth Amendment*. Westport, CT: Greenwood Press, 1993.

Orth, John V. *The Judicial Power of the United States: The Eleventh Amendment in American History*. New York: Oxford University Press, 1987.

Free Exercise of Religion and Separation of Church and State

Alley, Robert S., ed. *James Madison on Religious Liberty*. Buffalo, NY: Prometheus, 1985.

Curry, Thomas J. *The First Freedoms: Church and State in America to the Passage of the First Amendment*. New York: Oxford University Press, 1986.

Gaustad, Edwin S. *Proclaim Liberty Throughout All the Land: A History of Church and State in America*. New York: Oxford University Press, 2003.

Lambert, Frank. *The Founding Fathers and the Place of Religion in America*. Princeton, NJ: Princeton University Press, 2003.

Levy, Leonard W. *The Establishment Clause: Religion and the First Amendment*. 2nd rev. ed. Chapel Hill: University of North Carolina Press, 1994.

Long, Carolyn N. *Religious Freedom and Indian Rights: The Case of Oregon v. Smith*. Lawrence: University Press of Kansas, 2000.

Miller, William Lee. *The First Liberty: Religion and the American Republic*. Expanded ed. Washington, DC: Georgetown University Press, 2003.

Patrick, John J., and Gerald P. Long. *Constitutional Debates on Freedom of Religion: A Documentary History*. Westport, CT: Greenwood, 1999.

Williams, Peter. *America's Religions: From Their Origins to the Twenty-first Century*. 3rd ed. Urbana: University of Illinois Press, 2008.

Wilson, John F., and Donald L. Drakeman, eds. *Church and State in American History: Key Documents, Decisions, and Commentary from the Past Three Centuries*. 3rd ed. Boulder, CO.: Westview, 2003.

Witte, John, Jr. *Religion and the American Constitutional Experiment*. 2nd ed. Boulder, CO.: Westview Press, 2004.

Wuthnow, Robert. *America and the Challenges of Religious Diversity*. Princeton, NJ: Princeton University Press, 2005.

Freedom of Speech

Baker, C. Edwin. *Human Liberty and Freedom of Speech*. New York: Oxford University Press, 1989.

Bernstein, David E. *You Can't Say That!: The Growing Threat to Civil Liberties From Antidiscrimination Laws*. Washington, DC: Cato Institution, 2003.

Chafee, Zechariah. *Free Speech in the United States* Cambridge, MA: Harvard University Press, 1967.

Curtis, Michael Kent. *Free Speech, "The People's Darling Privilege": Struggles for Freedom of Expression in American History*. Durham, NC: Duke University Press, 2000.

Eastland, Terry, ed. *Freedom of Expression in the Supreme Court: The Defining Case*. Lanham, MD: Rowman & Littlefield, 2000.

Goldstein, Robert Justin. *Flag Burning and Free Speech: the Case of Texas v. Johnson*. Lawrence: University Press of Kansas, 2000.

Graber, Mark A. *Transforming Free Speech: The Ambiguous Legacy of Civil Libertarianism.* Berkeley: University of California Press, 1991.

Johnson, John W. *The Struggle for Student Rights: Tinker v. Des Moines and the 1960s.* Lawrence: University Press of Kansas, 1997.

Kalven, Harry, Jr. *A Worthy Tradition: Freedom of Speech in America.* Edited by Jamie Kalven. New York: Harper & Row, 1988.

Levy, Leonard W. *Freedom of Speech and Press in Early American History: Legacy of Suppression.* New York: Harper & Row, 1963.

Polenberg, Richard. *Fighting Faiths: The Abrams Case, the Supreme Court, and Free Speech.* New York: Viking, 1987.

Smith, James Morton. *Freedom's Fetters: The Alien and Sedition Laws and American Civil Liberties,* Ithaca, NY: Cornell University Press, 1956.

Stone, Geoffrey. *Perilous Times: Free Speech in Wartime from the Sedition Act of 1798 to the War on Terror.* New York: Norton, 2004.

Freedom of the Press

Friendly, Fred W. *Minnesota Rag: The Dramatic Story of the Landmark Case that Gave New Meaning to Freedom of the Press.* New York: Random House, 1981.

Levy, Leonard W. *Emergence of a Free Press.* New York: Oxford University Press, 1985.

Lewis, Anthony. *Make No Law: The Sullivan Case and the First Amendment.* New York: Random House, 1991.

Rudenstine, David. *The Day the Presses Stopped: A History of the Pentagon Papers Case.* Berkeley: University of California Press, 1996.

Habeas Corpus

Duker, William F. *A Constitutional History of Habeas Corpus.* Westport, CT: Greenwood Press, 1980.

Irons, Peter. *Justice at War: The Story of the Japanese American Internment Cases.* Berkeley: University of California Press, 1993.

Robinson, Greg. *By Order of the President: FDR and the Internment of Japanese Americans.* Cambridge, MA: Harvard University Press, 2001.

Illegal Search and Seizure

Long, Carolyn Nestor. *Mapp v. Ohio: Guarding against Unreasonable Searches and Seizures.* Lawrence: University Press of Kansas, 2006.

Stevens, Otis H., and Richard A. Glenn. *Unreasonable Searches and Seizures: Rights and Liberties Under the Law.* Santa Barbara, CA: ABC-CLIO, 2006.

Limiting Presidential Power

Marcus, Maeva. *Truman and the Steel Seizure Case: The Limits of Presidential Power.* 1977. Reprint, Durham, NC: Duke University Press, 1994.

Westin, Alan F. *The Anatomy of a Constitutional Law Case: Youngstown Sheet and Tube Co. v. Sawyer, the Steel Seizure Decision.* New York: Macmillan, 1958.

New Deal

Cushman, Barry. *Rethinking the New Deal Court: The Structure of a Constitutional Revolution.* New York: Oxford University Press, 1998.

Leuchtenburg, William Edward. *The Supreme Court Reborn: The Constitutional Revolution in the Age of Roosevelt.* New York: Oxford University Press, 1995.

Maidment, Richard A. *The Judicial Response to the New Deal: The US Supreme Court and Economic Regulation, 1934–1936.* Manchester, UK: Manchester University Press, 1991.

White, G. Edward. *The Constitution and the New Deal.* Cambridge, MA: Harvard University Press, 2000.

Police Power

Gillman, Howard. *The Constitution Besieged: The Rise and Demise of Lochner Era Police Powers Jurisprudence.* Durham, NC: Duke University Press, 1993.

Kens, Paul. *Judicial Power and Reform Politics: The Anatomy of Lochner v. New York.* Lawrence: University Press of Kansas, 1990.

Privilege against Self-Incrimination

Baker, Liva. *Miranda: Crime, Law, and Politics.* New York: Atheneum, 1983.

Levy, Leonard W. *Origins of the Fifth Amendment: The Right Against Self-Incrimination.* New York: Oxford University Press, 1968.

Stuart, Gary L. *Miranda: The Story of America's Right to Remain Silent.* Tucson: University of Arizona Press, 2004.

Right to Freedom

Abraham, Henry J., and Barbara A. Perry. *Freedom and the Court: Civil Rights and Liberties in the United States.* 8th ed. Lawrence: University Press of Kansas, 2003.

Richards, David A.J. *Conscience and the Constitution: History, Theory, and Law of the Reconstruction Amendments.* Princeton, NJ: Princeton University Press, 1993.

Vorenberg, Michael. *Final Freedom: The Civil War, the Abolition of Slavery, and the Thirteenth Amendment.* New York: Cambridge University Press, 2001.

Rights of Property Owners

Ely, James W., Jr. *The Guardian of Every Other Right: A Constitutional History of Property Rights.* 3rd ed. New York: Oxford University Press, 2008.

Epstein, Richard A. *Supreme Neglect: How to Revive Constitutional Protection for Private Property*. New York: Oxford University Press, 2008.

Epstein, Richard A. *Takings: Private Property and the Power of Eminent Domain,* Cambridge, MA: Harvard University Press, 1985.

Hamilton, Daniel W. *The Limits of Sovereignty: Property Confiscation in the Union and the Confederacy During the Civil War*. Chicago: University of Chicago Press, 2007.

Nedelsky, Jennifer. *Private Property and the Limits of American Constitutionalism: The Madisonian Framework and Its Legacy*. Chicago: University of Chicago Press, 1990.

Siegan, Bernard. *Economic Liberties and the Constitution*. 2nd ed. New Brunswick, NJ: Transaction Publishers, 2006.

Right to Petition

Barber, Lucy G. *Marching on Washington: The Forging of an American Political Tradition*. Berkeley: University of California Press, 2002.

Miller, William Lee. *Arguing about Slavery: The Great Battle in the United States Congress*. New York: Knopf, 1996.

Walker, Samuel. *The Rights Revolution: Rights and Community in Modern America*. New York: Oxford University Press, 1998.

Right to Counsel

Cortner, Richard C. *A "Scottsboro" Case in Mississippi: The Supreme Court and Brown v. Mississippi*. Jackson: University Press of Mississippi, 1986.

Lewis, Anthony. *Gideon's Trumpet*. New York: Random House, 1964.

Taylor, John B. *The Right to Counsel and Privilege against Self-Incrimination: Rights and Liberties under the Law*. Santa Barbara, CA: ABC-CLIO, 2004.

Right of Privacy

Alderman, Ellen, and Caroline Kennedy. *The Right to Privacy*. New York: Knopf, 1995.

Barnett, Randy E., ed. *The Rights Retained by the People: The History and Meaning of the Ninth Amendment*. Fairfax, VA: George Mason University Press, 1989.

Garrow, David J. *Liberty and Sexuality: The Right to Privacy and the Making of Roe v. Wade*. Updated ed. Berkeley: University of California Press, 1998.

Johnson, John W. *Griswold v. Connecticut: Birth Control and the Constitutional Right of Privacy*. Lawrence: University Press of Kansas, 2005.

Rosen, Jeffrey. *Unwanted Gaze: The Destruction of Privacy in America*. New York: Random House, 2000.

Right to Bear Arms

Cornell, Saul. *A Well-Regulated Militia: The Founding Fathers and the Origins of Gun Control in America*. New York: Oxford University Press, 2006.

Hallbrook, Stephen P. *A Right to Bear Arms: State and Federal Bills of Rights and Constitutional Guarantees*. New York: Greenwood Press, 1989.

Tushnet, Mark V. *Out of Range: Why the Constitution Can't End the Battle Over Guns*. New York: Oxford University Press, 2007.

Trial by Jury

Jonakait, Randolph N. *The American Jury System*. New Haven, CT: Yale University Press, 2003.

Kalven, Harry, Jr. and Hans Zeisal. *The American Jury*. Boston: Little Brown, 1966.

Levy, Leonard W. *The Palladium of Justice: Origins of Trial by Jury*. Chicago: Ivan R. Dee, 1999.

Voting Rights

Gillette, William. *The Right to Vote: Politics and the Passage of the Fifteenth Amendment*. Baltimore, MD: John Hopkins University Press, 1965.

Kousser, J. Morgan. *Colorblind Injustice: Minority Voting Rights and the Undoing of the Second Reconstruction*. Chapel Hill: University of North Carolina Press, 1999.

Case Index

Abington School District v. Schempp, 374 U.S., 203 (1963), 1, 186, 370
Abrams v. Johnson, 521 U.S. 74 (1997), 3, 298
Abrams v. United States, 250 U.S. 616 (1919), 4, 321
Adamo Wrecking Co. v. United States, 434 U.S. 275 (1978), 388
Adamson v. California, 332 U.S. 46 (1947), 5, 89, 134, 201, 266
Adarand Constructors, Inc. v. Pena, 515 U.S. 200 (1995), 112, 218, 294, 301, 362
Adkins v. Children's Hospital, 261 U.S. 525 (1923), 378
Afroyim v. Rusk, 387 U.S. 253 (1967), 355
Agostini v. Felton, 117 S.Ct. 1332 (1997), 159, 396
Aguilar v. Felton, 473 U.S. 402 (1985), 159, 396
Akron v. Akron Center for Reproductive Health, Inc., 462 U.S. 416 (1983), 305, 352
Alberts v. California, 354 U.S. 476 (1957), 311
Albertson v. Subversive Activities Control Board, 382 U.S. 70 (1965), 69
Allegheny County v. American Civil Liberties Union, Greater Pittsburgh Chapter, 492 U.S. 573 (1989), 199
Allen v. Board of Elections, 393 U.S. 544 (1969), 359
Allgeyer v. Louisiana, 165 U.S. 578 (1897), 10, 190
Ambach v. Norwick, 441 U.S. 68 (1979), 129
American Booksellers Association, Inc. v. Hudnut, 771 F.2d 323 (1985), 222
Amistad, The, United States v., 40 U.S. 518 (1841), 12
Apodaca v. Oregon, 406 U.S. 404 (1972), 24, 166, 381
Aptheker v. Secretary of State, 378 U.S. 500 (1964), 69, 136
Argersinger V. Hamlin, 407 U.S. 25 (1972), 122, 168
Arkansas v. Sanders, 442 U.S. 753 (1979), 52
Arlington Heights v. Metropolitan Housing Development Corp., 429 U.S. 252 (1977), 16, 232, 274
Ash, United States v., 413 U.S. 300 (1973), 370
Associated Press v. Walker, 388 U.S. 130 (1967), 251
Atherton v. Johnston, 259 U.S. 13 (1922), 20
Austin v. Michigan Chamber of Commerce, 494 U.S. 652 (1990), 106
Ayers, In re., 123 U.S. 443 (1887), 391

Baggett v. Bullitt, 377 U.S. 360 (1964), 94
Bailey v. Drexel Furniture Co., 259 U.S. 20 (1922), 145
Baker v. Carr, 369 U.S. 186 (1962), 20, 68, 125, 130, 281, 291, 295, 376
Ballard v. U.S., 329 U.S. 187 (1946), 154
Ballew v. Georgia, 435 U.S. 223 (1978), 14, 381
Bank of the United States v. Deveaux, 9 U.S. 61 (1809), 25, 195
Barker v. Wingo, 407 U.S. 514 (1972), 180
Barr v. Matteo, 360 U.S. 564 (1959), 50, 254
Batson v. Kentucky, 476 U.S. 79 (1986), 27, 92, 119, 164, 282
Beauharnais v. Illinois, 343 U.S. 250 (1952), 250
Bellotti v. Baird, 443 U.S. 622 (1979), 261
Belmont, United States v., 301 U.S. 324 (1937), 230
Bennis v. Michigan, 516 U.S. 442 (1996), 19
Benton v. Maryland, 395 U.S. 784 (1969), 267
Berger v. New York, 388 U.S. 41 (1967), 262
Berea College v. Kentucky, 211 U.S. (1908), 42
Bethel School District No. 403 v. Fraser, 478 U.S. 675 (1986), 236
Betts v. Brady, 316 U.S. 455 (1942), 30, 122
Black & White Taxicab Case, 276 U.S. 518 (1928), 98
Black v. Cutter Laboratories, 351 U.S. 292 (1956), 329
BMW of North America, Inc. v. Gore, 517 U.S. 559 (1996), 42, 265, 275
Board of Education v. Allen, 392 U.S. 236 (1968), 186, 276
Bolger v. Youngs Drugs Product Corp., 463 U.S. 60 (1983), 137
Bolling v. Sharpe, 347 U.S. 497 (1954), 40, 111
Bonham's Case, 8 Coke Rep. 107 (1610), 204
Boos v. Barry, 485 U.S. 312 (1988), 351
Booth v. Maryland, 182 U.S. 496 (1987), 271
Bowers v. Hardwick, 478 U.S. 186 (1986), 137, 307, 339
Bowsher v. Synar, 478 U.S. 714 (1986), 34, 159, 235
Boyd v. United States, 116 U.S. 616 (1886), 375
Bradwell v. Illinois, 83 U.S. 130 (1873), 35, 292
Brandenburg v. Ohio, 395 U.S. 444 (1969), 5, 351, 380, 392
Branti v. Finkel et al., 445 U.S. 507 (1980), 95, 314
Brecht v. Abrahamson, 507 U.S. 619 (1993), 103
Breedlove v. Suttles, 302 U.S. 277 (1937), 145
Brewer v. Williams, 430 U.S. 387 (1977), 209
Briscoe v. Bank of Kentucky, 36 U.S. 257 (1837), 74

Topical Index